# THE
# HEART
## *of the*
# BIBLE

The Old Testament
is the New Testament concealed.
The New Testament
is the Old Testament revealed.

# THE
# HEART
## *of the*
# BIBLE

## HUGH HILL

MONARCH
**BOOKS**

Oxford, UK & Grand Rapids, Michigan, USA

Published by Monarch Books
an imprint of
**Lion Hudson plc**
Wilkinson House, Jordan Hill Road,
Oxford OX2 8DR, England
Email: monarch@lionhudson.com
www.lionhudson.com/monarch

ISBN 978 0 85721 413 3
e-ISBN 978 0 85721 447 8

**Acknowledgments**
Scripture quotations taken from the Holy Bible, New International Version, copyright © 1973, 1978, 1984 International Bible Society. Used by permission of Hodder & Stoughton, a member of the Hodder Headline Group. All rights reserved. "NIV" is a trademark of International Bible Society. UK trademark number 1448790. Extracts marked "KJV" are from The Authorized (King James) Version. Rights in the Authorized Version are vested in the Crown. Reproduced by permission of the Crown's patentee, Cambridge University Press. Scripture marked "The Message" is taken from The Message. Copyright © by Eugene H. Peterson 1993, 1994, 1995, 1996, 2000, 2001, 2002. Used by permission of NavPress Publishing Group. Scripture marked "The Living Bible" is from The Holy Bible, Living Bible Edition, copyright © Tyndale House Publishers 1971. All rights reserved.
Extract on page 40 taken from the song "When I Look Into Your Holiness" by Wayne & Cathy Perrin. Copyright © 1981 Integrity's Hosanna! Music. Adm. by worshiptogether. com songs excl. UK & Europe, admin by Kingswaysongs, a division of David C Cook tym@kingsway.co.uk Used by permission.
Extract on page 526 taken from the song "Jesus is King" by Wendy Churchill. Copyright © 1982 Authentic Publishing. Adm. by Kingswaysongs, a division of David C Cook tym@kingsway.co.uk Used by permission.

A catalogue record for this book is available from the British Library

Printed and bound in the UK, December 2012, LH27

# Contents

# Acknowledgments

I would like to thank all my friends in Greenview Evangelical Church, Glasgow; Worthing Tabernacle and Maybridge Christian Fellowship, Worthing; The Slade Evangelical Church, London; and the faculty and students of London Theological Seminary. I am eternally grateful for the love and patience shown to me over the years as I grew in knowledge and understanding of the gospel, and for the many helpful conversations we enjoyed. Special thanks to the members and friends of Thomas Cooper Evangelical Church, Lincoln, who heard the original contents of this book live Sunday by Sunday over a period of three years. Your comments and encouragement helped to inspire this book.

For their advice and encouragement, a special word of thanks is due to Ian Kirkby, Elder of TCM Baptist Church; Richard Lee, lecturer at PfS North and founder of the East Midland School of Theology; Revd Gordon Campbell BA Med; and Clive Birks, owner of CRB Associates, who edited the first edition of the book.

And finally I would like to take this opportunity to thank the men and women who have written the evangelical Bible commentaries and articles I have read over the past twenty-nine years. I would also like to thank those of you who led Bible studies, spoke at the conferences I attended and preached the Word to me. Brothers and sisters, I listened to you, took copious notes, read your books and discussed them with like-minded friends and grew in knowledge – much of which has ended up in this book. To God be the glory!

# Introduction

The book I wish I'd read before going to Bible college – that's what I wanted to call this book, for it sums up much of what I felt was the foundation on which to build biblical knowledge.

The Bible can be looked at in many ways enabling the study of doctrines, themes, characters, timelines and so forth, and to some degree *The Heart of the Bible* attempts all of these. It began life as a three-year series of Sunday morning sermons at Thomas Cooper Memorial Evangelical Baptist Church in Lincoln, UK, which, for understandable reasons, is known as TCM.

God had graciously blessed the church, and the fellowship was growing in three particular people groups: new converts to Christianity who knew little or nothing about the Bible; students who arrived in Lincoln to attend the new university, many of whom had evangelical church backgrounds though a number of their friends whom they brought along to TCM were unchurched; and folks who for a variety of reasons had moved to the Lincolnshire area.

For some in the third group it was job relocation, others were taking up employment at the new university, and still others were taking advantage of the lower house prices in an attractive part of the country. Many of these men and women had a church background, and all of them expressed a desire to learn more about God and His plan and purpose for their lives. But for reasons which are unfortunately quite common today, many of them, especially the new and recent converts to Christianity, had a superficial view of the Bible.

My response to this wonderful God-given mixture of men and women of all ages and backgrounds was to embark on a three-year preaching plan to bring the message of the Bible, Sunday by Sunday, to the TCM congregation. Beginning with Genesis, each message aimed to cover the historical setting and purpose of a Bible book, as well as including its main theological message and what it means for us today.

*The Heart of the Bible* clearly has its limitations but, derived as it is from the spoken message, it is deliberately relaxed in style yet packed with information, explanation and clarification. It answers many of the questions that men and women have regarding God's Holy Word, the Bible, and is the book I wished I'd read before going to Bible college.

# How to Use this Book

You will find this book is quite unlike other books on the Bible. *The Heart of the Bible* was conceived when each chapter was originally spoken to a live audience. It is not a chapter-by-chapter commentary on the Bible, nor is it an exhaustive study of the text. It is instead a thought-provoking overview explaining the geographical, historical and socio-political background of each book of the Bible, which then brings out the main theological message of the book. In the belief that God's Word is unchanging and relevant for us in our day, the book explains what that means for our modern day society and ourselves as individuals as we strive to live the Christian life in an increasingly godless society. Furthermore, it is a book for Christians old and new.

**For the newish Christian:** You will find that the *The Heart of the Bible* answers many of the questions you have when trying to reach an understanding of the Bible. As the book provides an overview of each Bible book through straightforward explanations and contemporary illustrations, it is especially useful for providing you with a greater knowledge and understanding of God's Word, and, most importantly, its relevance for you today. It is a must-have companion book to read alongside Scripture and should be referred to each time you start to read a new book in the Bible. This means it is also helpful to use this book as a study aid on discipleship courses such as Alpha, Christianity Explored, and Emmaus.

**The mature Christian** will find the *The Heart of the Bible* to be a fascinating source of answers to many of the questions you have always wondered about – "Oh, that's what that means!" and "I've always wondered where that fits in…" You will also find the background information and explanation of what is behind current events to be extremely helpful for house groups and cell group, and for Bible studies.

**Christians of all ages and levels of experience** will gain much personal benefit from using *The Heart of the Bible* for daily reading. You know the blessings that come from a deeper relationship with God. This book will give you further insights to His Word, which will build on your existing knowledge and so broaden your understanding of His plan and purpose for your life.

# PART 1

---

## THE OLD TESTAMENT

# 1

# Genesis
## – Foundation for Life

The word *genesis* is Greek for "origin" and the original Hebrew *bereshith* means "in the beginning". Christians believe Genesis is the Bible's account of the origin of all the basic entities of life and beyond, including the beginning of the universe, life, the human race, marriage, sin, death, family, civilization, literature, culture, music, art, language, warfare, nations and religion. While none of these subjects is examined in absolute detail, Genesis tells us this is how life began and goes on to lay the foundation upon which the human race is built. It could be argued, therefore, that if you deny the traditional view of Genesis, you accept that men and women are the product of animal evolution and therefore animals themselves and nothing more. However, Genesis lifts our eyes above the animals towards a Creator God with the inescapable conclusion that, if we do not have a sense of the supremacy of God, we will never get our lives right.

Genesis tells us "God saw all that he had made, and it was very good" (Genesis 1:31). Chapter 3, however, records how humankind's representatives, Adam and Eve, gave in to the devil's temptation – resulting in all of creation falling into sin. But God had anticipated the fall and prepared the second Adam who would come in time and regain all that the first Adam lost, and more.

This means that almost every important church doctrine is found in "seed" form in the book of Genesis: creation, the fall, redemption, the doctrine of the Trinity, the promise of the Messiah, the establishment of the covenant and the hope of the resurrection are all to be found here. Other Old Testament books explain it more clearly, but a "seed" is planted in Genesis, and through the giving of the Law and the establishing of worship, that "seed" sprouts and grows throughout the rest of the Bible until it finds its fruition in the person and work of Jesus Christ. Therefore, all that the Law points towards, all the prophets proclaimed, all Jesus said and all the apostles expounded, depend absolutely for accuracy upon the teaching contained in the book of Genesis, for no other book of the Bible is quoted as frequently or referred to so often as this book.

Chapters 1 to 11 tell of four major events around which the foundation of the Bible is built, and four significant people around whom the Genesis narrative flows.

# Creation

The first major event is that of creation. Genesis 1:1 – 2:35 reveals God as the creator of matter, energy, space and time. That men and women are the pinnacle of His creation is of vital importance for it means that as He created us, He alone perfectly understands us and therefore He alone can govern us wisely. Without this message, when we look at our world through the media, when we nurse our hurts and perplexities and fears and doubts, we most often don't see anything that points to an almighty, all-loving God. Nevertheless, when God said, "Let us make man in our image, in our likeness" (Genesis 1:26) and gave us authority over the whole earth, we are brought to realize that something profoundly important has occurred. And while, like Paul, in Corinthians 13, we currently see it as if through a poor reflection in a mirror, nevertheless we know that the one who has the power to make us in His own image and likeness has the power to remake and overcome the damage we have caused to ourselves and His creation.

# The fall

The second major event was the fall (3:1 – 5:32). Adam and Eve were not created as robots. God created them sinless but, as the Heidelberg Catechism of 1563 states, "within them was the capacity to choose evil if they so desired". That free choice which we so highly value, and the wrong choices we so often make, are part and parcel of the human makeup. In fact, God was so insistent on humans having freedom of choice that He allowed us to live as though He did not exist, even to crucify Him. For only love can summon a response of love that is the response God wants from us and the reason He created us. Therefore, the secret for the fulfilment of our life is faith in God expressed in obedience to Him. That was the battleground in Eden when Satan tempted Adam and Eve's faith in God with his sly innuendo, "Did God really say, 'You must not eat from any tree in the garden?'" (Genesis 3:1).

Adam's first mistake was his failure to protect his wife from listening to the tempter; his second was to collaborate with her in rebellion when Satan called into question the goodness and truth of God by his lie, "You will not surely die" (Genesis 3:4). Adam and Eve's faith wavered through listening to a slander about God and resulted in their act of disobedience. From this we learn that faith and obedience are always linked. When Adam and Eve's faith failed, obedience ceased and sin entered creation, infecting both the human race and indeed the whole of creation. Sin's escalation is seen where the first sin resulted in men and women being separated from God, while the second, Cain's murder of his brother Abel (Genesis 4), separated man from man.

## Adam and Eve on trial

As representatives of the human race Adam and Eve were summoned to appear before God, their Creator and Judge, to answer for the crimes of rebellion and blasphemy. In the biblical context, blasphemy is an attitude of disrespect that finds expression in an act directed against the character of God.

Adam and Eve knew they were guilty and that their crime carried the death penalty. But as they stood before God, something unexpected happened: God chose to intervene on their behalf. He pronounced a curse on the serpent and instead of appearing against them as an enemy He announced His plan for their restoration. The wonder of this was that God Himself was taking their case into His own hands as if He, and only He, had the right and the power to deal with it.

Speaking to the serpent the Lord God said, "I will put enmity between you and the woman and between your offspring and hers; he will crush your head, and you will strike his heel" (Genesis 3:15). This meant that their deliverance was to be part of God's sovereign purpose. It would not come into effect immediately but through the intervention of the "seed of the woman." So, as human seed is of the man, here in Genesis chapter 3 we have the first suggestion of the virgin birth. This miraculously born person would at some future date enter into conflict with Satan, and while He would suffer, He would be victorious, crushing Satan's power and delivering humankind from the condemnation of sin and even death itself. The plan of salvation is

*Here*

decreed to be by the grace of God. No terms are imposed, no works required, no mention of any human intervention, only the suffering of the woman's seed. Everything depends upon this Mediator. He is the hope of humankind. He alone can redeem fallen men and women from the curse of the law and restore them to favour and friendship with God. So, although paradise was lost by the devastating curse of the fall God promised paradise would be regained through the seed of the woman.

The crucial importance of Adam and Eve's trial for rebellion and blasphemy would become evident thousands of years later when the Son of God, Jesus Christ, was tried before the religious and secular authorities of Jerusalem and Rome for the same crimes. He was condemned by the Jews for blasphemy for claiming He was God, and by Rome for rebellion for setting Himself up in revolt against lawful authority. And it is here that we see in the fullest sense how He stood in our place. As our Substitute, Jesus suffered, died and rose again for us, and these charges of blasphemy and rebellion that God has against us sinful human beings are the same charges laid on Christ when He took our place. This was no weak, defenceless Jesus being rushed to the cross and nailed there against His will by ruthless men. No! This was God carrying out His carefully premeditated plan of salvation conceived before the foundation of the world and foretold in Genesis chapter 3.

## The flood

Third, 6:1 – 9:29 records that the Lord saw how great man's wickedness on the earth had become, and that every inclination of the thoughts of his heart was only evil all the time. The Lord was grieved that he had made man on the earth, and his heart was filled with pain. So the Lord said, "I will wipe mankind, whom I have created, from the face of the earth" (Genesis 6:5–7). The world was under a death sentence.

A righteous man and his family in a hostile, God-hating world, awaiting the judgment of God, was a prophetic glimpse of the future of humankind, "But Noah found favour in the eyes of the Lord" (Genesis 6:8).

Noah's salvation from the judgment of the flood by the grace of God illustrates God's way of salvation through His Son. In symbolic language, Jesus can be seen as the ark: He alone is the means of safety from the coming judgment, and His offer of salvation is open to all who believe and enter His shelter by accepting Him as Saviour and Lord. From this we learn that just as the ark was closed by God and it was then too late for people to be saved

(Genesis 7:16). If we are to enjoy the blessings of God, before we die we must be in the ark.

God then confirmed that His covenant with Adam still remains in force, but now adds the provision of human government and its responsibility to enforce law and order. This is known as the Noahic covenant, and as a sign of His promise to never again destroy the earth by flood, God set His rainbow in the sky.

## Civilization

The fourth major event – that of civilization – is established after the flood (10:1 – 11:9). Civilization began upon the plain of Shinar and reminds us of the unity of the human race: we are all children of Adam through Noah. The arts flourished and the skills of craftsmen developed, but sin also flourished as the hands that made tools of iron also made weapons of war. Human pride and greed remind us that the arts and crafts are no guarantee humankind will become more humane. Then, in a shocking act of idolatry motivated by the rebellion and pride now deeply ingrained within the human make-up, the Tower of Babel was built to demonstrate humankind's own greatness and his ability to do without God. The fact that the European Parliament building in Strasbourg is deliberately modelled on a painting of the Tower of Babel should provide food for thought.

God's response was to fragment the single culture and language of the post-flood world and scatter the people over the face of the earth. And so began a new phase in Genesis with God focusing on four important individuals.

## Abraham

The first important patriarch in the Bible was Abraham, recorded in 12:1 – 25:18). Abraham's calling in Genesis chapter 12 is a pivotal point in the book. In the same way that God began creation with the one man, Adam; He began redemption with Abraham, and through His covenant with Abraham initiated a theme that continued throughout the Bible until Jesus instituted a new covenant at the Lord's Supper on the eve of His crucifixion.

The story of Abraham starts in Genesis 12 when he was called by God to leave the pagan culture of Haran and travel to the land of Canaan, which he would later inherit. This is a brilliant example of the Christian "call". Like

Abraham, Christians too are called to leave their old way of life and follow Jesus into a new life they have never seen but by faith believe in.

In His promise to Abraham God repeats His words of intention, "I will," six times. His first promise to them was to give them a place to live. His second promise was to give them descendants, and the third to make them a blessing to other nations (Genesis 12:1–3).

In return, God required every Jewish male to be circumcised as a sign they were born into the covenant He had made with Abraham. The ethos of this covenant is at the very heart of the Bible and is the basis upon which God said, "I will be your God and you will be my people" (see Exodus 6:7 and Jeremiah 7:23). This tells us that God wants to be in a relationship with us, a relationship which will be consummated at the end of the age when, as Revelation 21 explains, God Himself will move out of heaven to live with us forever on a new earth.

## Isaac

Isaac was the second patriarch in God's plan to separate a people from the surrounding nations (25:19 – 26:35). To this people would be entrusted the holy revelations of God and from their line the Saviour would be born. By allowing himself to be offered as a sacrifice under Abraham's knife on Mount Moriah (Genesis 22), Isaac offers us a glimpse of Christ's faith and submission in Gethsemane and Calvary.

## Jacob

Isaac's youngest son, Jacob (27:1 – 36:43), was the most colourful of the four men. His deception to ensure the birthright of the oldest son came to him, rather than passing to his godless older brother Esau, is a classic example of the right motive executed in the wrong way. His subsequent hard and painful lessons, including being cheated by his uncle Laban, and his wonderful conversion at the brook Jabbok where he wrestled with God, transformed Jacob from a man of selfishness to a servant of God. In recognition of the change in his life, God changed his name to Israel and he became the father of the twelve tribes of the nation of that name (Genesis 32:28).

# Joseph

With the benefit of biblical hindsight we can view Joseph's story (37:1 – 50:26) as much more than the downward route from favourite son to household slave and disgraced prisoner then all the way up again to prime minister and saviour of the Egyptian nation and beyond. For, wonderful though that was, the real beauty lies in seeing how God, who does not speak directly to Joseph but gives him dreams, works behind the scenes to arrange circumstances to advance His purposes for the Hebrew nation. This is seen in the move of Joseph's family to Egypt and his insightful reply to his brothers who were understandably worried that he might exact his revenge for what they had done to him: "You intended to harm me, but God intended it for good to accomplish what is now being done" (Genesis 50:20).

In the way God used Joseph to bring reconciliation and salvation to his brothers making them fit to be the foundation of the holy nation of Israel, we see a type of Christ and His mission to bring salvation and reconciliation to the unholy men and women of planet Earth, making them new creations fit to inhabit the new heavens and earth – the kingdom of God. The object of special love from his father, hated by his brothers, conspired against and sold for silver, imprisoned though innocent and raised from humiliation to glory. A prophet foretelling both plenty and famine, Joseph became the saviour of the nation and all the surrounding nations by filling the storehouses with life-giving grain and throwing the gates wide open that all may come to him and live. In Joseph we are given a wonderful glimpse of the "seed of the woman", the mediator, Jesus Christ Himself.

## What does all this mean for us today?

By imparting the knowledge of how everything began and the rationale for good and bad, Genesis builds a foundation for life that is based on God's truth and which teaches us there is great significance in our lives.

Jesus taught that there are two ways to go about our lives:

1. we can hear His teaching and put it into practice (which He likened to building a house on rock), or

2. we can hear His teaching and ignore it (which He likened to building a house on sand).

Sand symbolizes the ever-changing philosophies of the world: the wisdom of man. If we reject the teaching of Jesus we build on sand, and no matter how good it looks, sooner or later it will fall like a house of cards. Rock, on the other hand, is the foundation laid by God, and if we listen to Jesus and put His teaching into practice by building our lives on Him and living His way, then we build on security, stability and eternal principles. Genesis reveals God's hand in human affairs through His creative acts, His miraculous interventions and gracious judgments, His call to a life of faith and His covenant promises to us. As the apostle Paul reminds us, "in all things God works for the good of those who love him" (Romans 8:28).

But Genesis does not present these truths as abstract, intangible principles. We are given a succession of stories of real life people. Individuals, who loved and quarrelled, believed and doubted, married and had children, experienced sin and grace. And if we think it through we begin to see ourselves represented in these very accounts.

Like Adam and Eve, we too have believed, doubted, been tempted and fallen, only to find the wondrous truth that there is a way back to God through His grace.

Cain and Abel bring us face to face with sibling rivalry resulting in different religious viewpoints: Cain's humanistic lifestyle made his worship offensive to God and his refusal to submit to God led to a terrible legacy of violence and death. This teaches us that when men and women become obsessed with themselves and refuse to live according to the laws of God, all that matters to them is getting their own way. Such people die as they lived: away from God.

Noah's drunkenness and moral lapse after the flood reminds us of the danger of letting our guard down after an amazing display of faith (Genesis 9:21).

Think of Abraham's faith in emigrating to a strange land on the command of God, having the title "God's friend" and yet compromising his testimony in a very human way by pretending to be his wife's brother to protect his skin. But much more serious was his going along with Sarah's plan for him to have a child by Hagar after having God's promise of a son. In doing so he produced Ishmael who would eventually be regarded by Muslims as Abraham's first son with all the repercussions for Jews, the Middle East and the rest of the world as we have it today (Genesis 16:15; 21:8–20).

Sarah's pain of childlessness, along with God's response, encourages us to know that God understands when we cry out, "You have given me no children, no partner in life, no relief from weakness or pain...." He hears us and loves us and comforts us. Perhaps not the way we want or when we want, but He will encourage us with the glorious things He has prepared for us in the age to come.

Many can empathize with Isaac and Rebekah, a dysfunctional family suffering from mistrust, intrigue and favouritism. Their story reaches its climax in chapter 27. Think of the lessons for us in Isaac overlooking Esau's irreligious nature and through his misguided favouritism attempting to circumvent God's purpose by blessing the wrong son. And Rebekah the manipulative wife and mother who, displaying a mother's zeal for her son, disregards the personal consequences. When we see the manner in which she instigated the deception against her husband Isaac we realize that Jacob did not owe his natural deception to his father. He was truly his mother's son, and we thus learn the influence a mother has on her children for good or evil.

Jacob and Rachel exemplify a difficult marriage with dreadful in-laws. Read their story in chapters 29–33 and you can imagine Rachel holding onto Jacob's coat-tails, trying to slow him down and consider more fully his latest business scheme. Yet when you look at the elderly Jacob, who won Pharaoh's respect when he blessed him in the royal court of Egypt in chapter 47, and compare him to the impetuous, conniving schemer of earlier days, you marvel at God's ability to work within such an unlikely man like Jacob who became a "prince with God" and began to show "godlike qualities" towards the end of his life.

Jacob's brother Esau warns us of the danger of living for the present. Today, Esau would be the media celebrity contrasting Jacob the mummy's boy. Sexual immorality, the dishonest deal on the side, the desire for material things that push the married couple into debt, despair and bankruptcy. Esau is every one of them and by recording his story, Genesis warns us not to allow our passions and appetite for today to blind us to the consequences for tomorrow and the eternal realities. As Paul put it in 2 Corinthians 4:18, "what is seen is temporary, but what is unseen is eternal".

And what do we learn from Joseph and his brothers? Jealousy, treachery, rejection, betrayal, pain, loneliness and the plain unfairness of life. But also the transformation in the character of the brothers, as God uses Joseph as His instrument to lead his brothers through a life-changing experience of repentance and salvation. And most importantly in Joseph we have an example of faith: the faith that keeps us hanging on in there with nothing to see or encourage it but a love for God and a determination to stand fast when our world is collapsing around us. A faith that causes us to hold on to God's promise never to leave or forsake us, firmly believing that He has a plan and purpose for our lives and even the very trials are for our good.

So we take heart. The people we meet in Genesis are ordinary men and women, yet through them God did extraordinary things. This should teach us to believe that no matter how unimportant or insignificant we may feel we are, God loves us and has a plan and purpose for us. No matter how fearful or how world events may unfold, God is in charge. And gloriously, no matter how sinful and separated from God we feel we are, His salvation is available to us.

# 2

# Exodus
# – The Great Escape

In Genesis, the "book of beginnings", we saw how God calls men and women to Himself. This is known as the doctrine of election. And just as the Christian life begins with being called by God, the next stage is to be brought through a miraculous transformation from the old life into the new. This is known as the doctrine of redemption. It is the theme of Exodus and it is presented to us through a historical account that tells us, through a series of unusual events, how a Hebrew slave's baby boy, Moses, becomes a prince in Pharaoh's palace. Then, as a fugitive in the wilderness, after a supernatural encounter with God at the mysterious burning bush, Moses becomes God's instrument to challenge Pharaoh and lead God's people from slavery in Egypt to freedom in the Promised Land.

Time and again, through the Bible story, we see the amazing way God prepares a leader in advance for the purpose to which He calls them. When Moses received the summons from God in Exodus to be the man to bring the nation of Israel out of Egypt, his response was negative: "Who am I, that I should go to Pharaoh and bring the Israelites out of Egypt?" (Exodus 3:11). It may well be that Moses was afraid of returning to see Pharaoh, because he had murdered one of the king's soldiers. He also knew that Pharaoh, probably Ramesses II, was regarded as a god and could not simply be approached. To enter Pharaoh's presence involved an elaborate diplomatic and religious procedure which Moses alone of all the Israelites would know, having been brought up as a prince in Pharaoh's palace. This is confirmed in Stephen's speech (Acts 7:22) and by the writer to the Hebrews (11:26). So, like Joseph before him, we see how God had His hand on Moses' life and brought about the unique circumstances that led him to become God's appointed representative.

So the major theme of Exodus is God's redemptive activity:

> *In your unfailing love you will lead*
> *the people you have redeemed.*
> *In your strength you will guide them*
> *to your holy dwelling.*
>
> EXODUS 15:13

In identifying with these needy people we are invited to participate by faith in the salvation that is found through our Great Redeemer. Just as Israel was physically in bondage to Egypt, we too are in captivity to sin before being saved by God's grace. Egypt represents the secular world and Pharaoh is identified with Satan, the enemy of God's people. And as Moses was sent by God to deliver his people who were unable to effect their own escape, he foreshadows the Great Deliverer, Jesus Christ, who was sent to save His people and deliver them from the bondage of sin and the power of death (Matthew 1:21).

## Setting the scene

A total of 400 years had passed since Jacob's Hebrew family of seventy settled in Goshen, Egypt at the time of the great famine (Genesis 47:4). Several generations later the situation in Egypt changed dramatically: "Then a new king, who did not know about Joseph, came to power in Egypt" (Exodus 1:8). Joseph was dead and persecution began. Yet even under these adverse conditions the Hebrew people grew and numbered over two million. It begs the question: Why did God, who so wonderfully saved Jacob and his family by bringing them from the famine in Canaan to Egypt, now allow the Egyptians to persecute His people for so long? The answer to that question is that it was to prepare the Israelites for their inheritance. The trials they went through in Egypt would toughen them for what would lie ahead in their battles to secure the Promised Land. And of course, time was needed to multiply a family into a nation.

In keeping with the theme of redemption, the Hebrews were faced with the possibility of salvation in the same way that we are given the opportunity to be saved. Egypt, like Babylon, symbolizes the world as a system in rebellion against God, and what made Egypt particularly arrogant was its confidence in itself. The River Nile ensured a fertile land, and before the dawn of effective naval power no neighbours could seriously attack the country, situated as it was with the wilderness behind and the Mediterranean before it. Wealthy, confident, and with her strange religion of the dead, Egypt basked in her own glory.

It is noticeable that throughout the Scriptures, Egypt always appears to symbolize an evil influence upon the people of God. Here we see Israel being tempted to return to the land of bondage from which they had escaped. Later, in their journey, they were to moan about their difficulties in the desert: "There we sat round pots of meat and ate all the food we wanted, but you [Moses] have brought us out into this desert to starve this entire assembly to death" (Exodus 16:3).

Although they had been slaves with all the suffering that entailed, "distance made the heart grow fonder".

The truth is that the Israelites had compromised. Joseph was no longer there to warn them and they had settled down in Egypt, forgetting they were destined to be God's people in their own land of Canaan. Worst of all, they worshipped Egyptian gods. For proof of this, look no further than Aaron's golden calf of Exodus 32 – that's pure Egyptian style of worship.

## God's redeeming plan

It was never God's intention for the Israelites to settle in Egypt and adopt their gods. The Lord had a far better plan and purpose for the Israelites. In much the same way He has something better for us. He never intends His children to be absorbed into the world. Like the Israelites, we are meant to be travellers looking forward to a better place. For the Hebrews it was only when the taskmasters' whips cut their skin that they remembered God and fell to their knees in sorrow as they recounted His covenant promises to their forefathers Abraham, Isaac and Jacob.

In a similar way it's often when we are brought to the end of our own resources that we turn to God. And though painful and unpleasant at the time, the "whip" in its variety of forms can be the means to remind us that this world, like Egypt, is a land of burden, and so we look to the Lord and His promises. Hence the "taskmaster of the world" is allowed to chastise us, for we need to be jolted out of our compromising slumber and turn again to God. It is then that an important truth becomes apparent: we cannot deliver ourselves. There is no escape for us by our own efforts. We need help from someone outside our system, someone who can deliver us from bondage in such a way that we need never fear captivity again. We need Jesus who promises "if the Son sets you free, you will be free indeed" (John 8:36).

Chapters 1–6 of Exodus show us the need for redemption, pictured by the Hebrews' enslavement to a power greater than themselves. In chapters 7–11 we see the power of the Redeemer through the dramatic effect God's plagues had on Egypt.

Attempts have been made to show how the chain of disasters in Egypt was caused by natural events. For example it has been suggested that the polluted water drove the frogs on to the land where they died, then flies carried disease to the animals killing them and so on, but Scripture tells us God caused the disasters to happen and whether He used natural cause and effect is immaterial. God said it would happen and it did, and God's timing is always right.

The catastrophe resulting from the plagues that hit Egypt was so dramatic that we are apt to overlook the underlying meaning behind the judgments that are often seen simply as a contest between God and Pharaoh. But it was very much more than that. Pharaoh was the living symbol of a society that had developed over two thousand years. He was worshipped as a god, and supported by magicians who were the priests, and court officials who made the government effective. So Moses faced not merely the stubbornness of one man, but the whole weight of an advanced civilization that had held sway for two millennia. God's purpose in attacking Egypt with the plagues was to expose the falseness of nature worship that was universal at that time. Every one of those plagues was an attack on a particular god worshipped by the Egyptians to reveal how Egypt's premier gods the Nile (Khuum) and the Sun (Ra) were unable to protect their worshippers. The problem this presented Pharaoh and his advisers was that for them to agree to Moses' demand and set the Hebrew slaves free would effectively mean denying the whole basis of Egyptian society and admitting they were worshipping false gods.

## Moses' change of heart

In Exodus 7:10 we see a change in Moses. Now he is no longer timid and hesitant. The gauntlet has been thrown down and from now on the omnipotent power of the Lord is displayed. War is declared between almighty God and Pharaoh's gods, and as a result, Egypt as a nation and world power would never recover from the catastrophe visited upon her.

In spite of Moses' best efforts Pharaoh was determined to resist him and, in effect, fight God. Hammer blow followed hammer blow (nine in all), until, with his country devastated, his people shattered, and every house in Egypt containing a firstborn dead, Pharaoh was brought to the end of himself and his country's resources. He rose in the middle of the night, called for Moses and Aaron and told them to go! Leave Egypt (Exodus 12:31–32)!

From this we can learn that in being chosen and called to be His people God has promised that nothing will separate us from His divine authority (Romans 8:38–39). If, however, we resist and are slow to respond, He will take such time and trouble as is needed to bring us to Himself, including the use of force.

One of the reasons the church comprises so many bruised and hurting people is that God has had to shake them hard before they would leave the world. Many who embraced the Christian faith as adults can testify to having an experience of God in their youth to which they either did not respond or did respond only later to fall away. God continued to call them when they had health and strength but they wouldn't come. Then later some crisis happened to give them cause to think about eternal things – a health scare or some such experience that made them stop in their tracks. And like Pharaoh they *said* they would but when God removed the difficulty they again, like Pharaoh, broke their word. This went on until at last, through some problem or personal hardship, they finally came to their senses and recognized their need of God. Had they responded sooner to the call of God they often could have saved themselves a great deal of pain and unnecessary suffering.

# The picture of redemption

This was not a coming out party. In effect, God said, "Let my people go!" (Exodus 5:1) and Satan responded, "No! I will not let them go; they are slaves to fear, sin, and death, they are mine and I will not let them go" (Exodus 5:2). It's spiritual warfare, and the battlefield is the hearts and souls of men and women. Recognizing this truth is a key to understanding how the Hebrews" deliverance from Egyptian captivity is a picture of the Christian's deliverance from this world. In the Old Testament sacrificial system, redemption was purchased through the innocent blood of a lamb – that is the Passover (Exodus 12:1–13). Under the new covenant, redemption for the Christian is found by sheltering under the blood of the crucified Lamb of God, Jesus Christ.

The exodus story makes it clear that a lamb was to be killed, for death must be inflicted upon either the guilty wrongdoer or the innocent substitute. Then the lamb's blood was to be smeared upon the doorframes and lintels of the houses where the Israelites were sheltering (Exodus 12:7). This is known as the "Passover" and is central to the story of redemption in the Bible for both Jews and Christians. The theology of the event is described by the writer of Hebrews: "without the shedding of blood there is no forgiveness" (Hebrews 9:22).

This basic and very important truth of taking the "blood" and covering the door and lintels was the only means of escape for the Israelites (Exodus 12:7). And it's not until the blood is applied that it becomes effective. A concerned Israelite may well have selected and killed a lamb, but unless he applied the blood to the doorpost and lintel, the Angel of Death would have entered his house and slain his firstborn. Likewise today, it's not enough to know that the precious blood of Jesus, the Lamb of God, was shed for the forgiveness of our sins – that knowledge must be acted on. A Saviour provided is not sufficient, He must be received. It is not the profession of faith, but the possession of faith that counts. We have to take it, believe it and act upon it. You believe in Jesus, you believe He died on Calvary's cross and paid the price of your sin, then by faith, take His blood and apply it. By faith place it between your sins and a holy, righteous God. Shelter under it and rely upon it and see it as the sole ground and reason for your safety and acceptance. The sequence of events and the consequences are evident in the Exodus account:

> I will pass through Egypt and strike down every firstborn – both men and animals – and I will bring judgment on all the gods of Egypt. I am the Lord. The blood will be a sign for you on the houses where you are; and when I see the blood, I will pass over you. No destructive plague will touch you when I strike Egypt.
>
> Exodus 12:12–13

When the executioner of God's justice saw the blood upon the Israelite homes, he did not enter. Why? Because death had already done its work there. The innocent (lamb) had died in place of the guilty (sinner) so justice was satisfied. Those who sheltered within a blood-sprinkled house were safe.

Immediately following redemption, we learn that salvation means farewell to the old life (chapters 13–14).

How long did the Israelites remain in Egypt after they were saved? Not one day. They left immediately. On the very day that they were saved, they were delivered from Egyptian rule and left that life behind. And so it is with men and women when they become born-again Christians. They cannot remain in "spiritual Egypt" for a moment longer than necessary. Having believed in

Christ and been born again, the Holy Spirit of God takes up residence within the new believer and his or her body becomes the temple of the living God (1 Corinthians 6:19). The devil can no longer hold them in his kingdom, for they are no longer slaves to sin (Romans 6:6). In the same way that not even food delayed the Israelites, no worldly thing should delay the new Christian from forsaking the past and embracing his or her new life with Christ. Now, of course, Satan will attempt to hinder, but the Holy Spirit is in control. The Christian's new nature belongs to Him and He will not allow Satan to rule or reign over his or her life any longer (John 10:27–29).

# A promise fulfilled

In Exodus 12:32, we see that at last the promise that was made more than 400 years before by God to Abraham was fulfilled:

> *The Lord said to him, "Know for certain that your descendants*
> *will be strangers in a country not their own, and they will be*
> *enslaved and mistreated four hundred years. But I will punish*
> *the nation they serve as slaves, and afterward they will come*
> *out with great possessions."*
>
> GENESIS 15:13–14

It's another wonderful example of the way in which God keeps His promises. In Egypt, the Israelites were strangers in a country not their own and were enslaved and mistreated for 400 years. Egypt was severely punished – so much so, it never regained its leading nation status in the world and the Israelites were brought out of Egypt greatly enriched.

Looked at from the spiritual dimension, the transformation in the fortunes of the Israelites is a model of the assurance that not only will all God's people be saved, but that all the rightful possessions of God's people will be restored. Salvation lost through the sin of Adam will be restored through the cross of Jesus. Joy lost because of Adam will be restored through His Son. The guarantee of heaven, lost because of the rebellion of Adam and Eve, is promised by God to Christians through the resurrection of Jesus.

It has been truly said that, "God is no one's debtor". When men and women embrace the Christian faith they find one of the most comforting promises in all Scripture applies to them. This was put into words by the prophet Joel: "I will repay you for the years the locusts have eaten" (Joel 2:25). That is a promise from our Redeemer to those who believe. Therefore, Christians should not waste time looking back to Egypt or at what they had in Egypt. Everything they need for their new lives they have now. That being the case they should rejoice in the fact that they are what they are by the grace of God and be expectant, believing in His Word. The likelihood is that in a way beyond human understanding, they will have the greatest surprise of their lives as they discover that many of the things they thought were vitally important to their happiness pale into insignificance in the light of the new-life agenda brought about by embracing the Christian faith. This is why we often hear Christians exclaim, "Who'd have believed it?" and "If anyone had told me before I became a Christian that I would be doing this, I'd never have believed them."

The way this works is this: men and women instinctively know their lives could be better. They understand how their habits and attitudes are wrong and harmful to themselves and others. Deep down they know, as Romans 1:18–32 makes very clear. And every so often they try to do something about it. They make the effort to escape from their circumstances, to make a new start and try again. For some, it's a change of job, a change of town or a change of partner. But it doesn't work out. Why not? Because the fault lies in the human spirit, the sin nature inherent to us that always screws up and seems to have a destruct button that makes everything eventually turn sour. When you become a Christian, when you are born again you are what the Bible calls a new creation – "the old has gone, the new has come!" (2 Corinthians 5:17).

This means you are under new management and what you were unable to accomplish in your own strength, Jesus, your new Master and Friend, will accomplish for you by pouring His love, His patience and His thinking into your heart, so that the salvation He effects in your life will be seen immediately by the new way you see things, by the new things you do and many old things you no longer want to do! Often, it's not so much that your circumstances radically change, but because of the change in you due to your new Christian lifestyle and thinking, your circumstances will not influence you in the same way as before. You will no longer want the old life the world offers. Its treasures and prizes are dross by comparison to the silver and gold of Jesus Christ and all that He has become for you. You are freed from greed and insecurity; you have a self-worth beyond price. After all, God died for you. And you no longer feel driven by a godless, ignorant, hell-bent society that corrupted and exploited you. You stand on the threshold of a new beginning, freed and forgiven from your past, a new life beckons with Jesus at your side as your lover and it leads on and on into the wonderful mysteries of eternity and promises you a joy incomparable. So, without a backward glance to Egypt, looking forward in faith to the unseen, you step forward into the promise! Have faith, for our God is able.

## Nothing and no one was left behind in Egypt

Even Joseph's bones were taken with the Israelites (Exodus 13:19). Joseph had left instructions for his bones to be kept for burial in the Promised Land. By taking them in the exodus from Egypt the Israelites were publicly proclaiming their faith that Joseph's bones would be buried in the land promised to them by God. The Egyptians could not claim to have one piece of Israel's property; it had all gone. There were no prisoners or hostages to be paraded in front of the world.

Can you imagine it? A Hebrew slave exhibited in front of the Egyptian media saying, "I don't understand why the blood didn't work for me? I mean, I did everything Moses said, I killed the lamb and applied it to the door as instructed – but I guess it's unreliable!" Surely, we would have heard about that! There's no way Satan would turn down an opportunity like that to discredit the saving power and promise of almighty God. Significantly, Moses had declared to Pharaoh, "not a hoof is to be left behind" (Exodus 10:26). There is no trophy of the battle in hell. There is no helmet or shield picked up from the battlefield and held up in hell to scorn Christ. Christian, coming out of Egypt, you have lost nothing. His victory was complete! That is why you have the assurance to say: "If God is for us, who can be against us?" (Romans 8:31) and "Where, O death, is your victory? Where, O death, is your sting?" (1 Corinthians 15:55).

For God's people have so much to thank Him for, that to shout "Hallelujah" or "Praise God" is simply an echo from our hearts of the sheer wonder of the joy of our salvation. There is no question about it, He has conquered and His people are marching out with flying colours, taking their shields with them.

## God's victorious army

And so it was that they left Egypt by their divisions – an army of soldiers (Exodus 12:51). Who were they? Who comprised this victorious army marching out of Egypt? They were the children of God: no longer slaves, but soldiers. They were the very same children of Israel who but a short time ago were slaves to Pharaoh and whose babies were left in the Nile for the crocodiles. They made bricks without straw and were beaten and whipped when failing to meet their quotas. They were hopeless and degraded, slaves to an evil power stronger than themselves. These chosen people cried out to the Lord and He sent them His Word and they believed it and acted upon it. In that instant, not the next day or next week, but on that very same night, they were exalted to the greatest place among the nations. From slaves they became soldiers, and not merely soldiers, but soldiers of the living Lord, hosts of the Lord God Almighty, commissioned to fight His battles under His banner of the Lord of Hosts – King Jesus is His name.

## After salvation comes baptism

After salvation and leaving the world of slavery and bondage behind, what comes next for the Christian? It's baptism (Exodus 14:21–31).

Following their deliverance from Egypt, the crossing of the Red Sea could be seen to illustrate the Christian act of baptism as Paul makes clear in Romans chapter 6. There he teaches that becoming a Christian involves dying to the old life and leaving it behind to emerge with Jesus into the new life He offers. In John 3 a religious man called Nicodemus, asked Jesus how he might find salvation and received the reply, "You must be born again". He was mystified, but Jesus explained that just as flesh gives birth to flesh so the Spirit gives birth to spirit. In other words, being born again is something that happens inside a new believer spiritually. We are remade and become new persons in Christ. How then do you illustrate outwardly, something that has happened inwardly, signifying you are born again? The answer is baptism. By going down under the water and re-emerging, Christians are symbolically showing that they have died to their old lives and been reborn into the new – that they have new lives in Jesus.

## The absolute power of God

It is God's act of judgment against the Egyptian army that illustrates the absolute power of God. It is proof positive that, no matter how it may look to the contrary, God can and will deliver His people. As they set out in their new Christian lives with their walk through the wilderness ahead of them they can trust in God's love and ability to protect and bring them safely home. This sense of joy is recorded in the Song of Moses, by the Israelites and Miriam (Exodus 15:1–21). On the Passover night, Israel was secured from the doom of the

Egyptians; at the Red Sea they were delivered from the power of the Egyptians. Thus delivered – that is, "redeemed" – they sang. It is only a redeemed people who are conscious of their deliverance that can really praise Jesus Christ as their Deliverer. Not only is worship impossible for those without faith but real heartfelt worship cannot be rendered by professing Christians who are in doubt as to their standing before God. And rightly so, for praise and joy are essential elements of worship. How can those who question their salvation – who are not certain whether they would go to heaven or hell should they die this moment – how can such people be joyful and thankful? It's impossible! Uncertainty and doubt produce fear and distrust, not gladness and adoration.

## What comes after baptism?

After a journey of three months the Israelites reached the foot of Mount Sinai and here, near where Moses met with God at the burning bush, the relationship between God and Israel entered a new phase. Now that God's people have experienced His deliverance, guidance and protection, they are ready to be taught what God expects of them. The redeemed people of God must now be set apart to walk with God. In theological language, after justification comes sanctification. This is why the narrative changes from story form to legislation in chapters 19–40. Now Moses receives the Ten Commandments that explain how God's people are to love God (commandments 1–4) and how to love others (commandments 5–10).

The instructions Moses received from God enabled him to teach the Israelites the real purpose of their deliverance from Egypt and they began to see God in a new way. The exodus taught them that He was incomparable and unique. Their redemption from slavery revealed His grace and holiness, His pity for the oppressed and His unapproachable majesty. But at Sinai, Israel learned the further lesson that this God of grace and power was also a Being who delighted in justice and condemned cruelty and oppression.

In the course of the forty days of seclusion on the mountain, Moses received from God exact instructions for building a "tent of meeting". It was to be the focal point of ceremonial sacrifice for sin and God would dwell within it. A building of beauty in a barren land, it revealed much about the person of God and the way of redemption and it speaks powerfully of how Christians should approach God today.

The tabernacle was designed in the form of a "temple" and, with its position in the very centre of the camp, was a visible symbol of the presence of Jehovah (Yahweh) in the midst of His people (Exodus 29:42). The tabernacle was also the place where sacrifice was made. In its outer court stood the brazen altar to which the animals were brought and on which they were slain. There the blood was shed and atonement was made for sin. In chapters 9 and 10 of the New Testament book of Hebrews, we learn that Christians have no visible altar. Altars are for offering sacrifices upon and, since the death of Jesus Christ on the cross at Calvary made a once-and-for-all sacrifice for our sin, the requirement for a physical altar is made redundant. Further, any attempt to make sacrifice for sin undermines the clear biblical teaching of the sufficiency of Christ's one-time, unique sacrifice.

# 3

# Leviticus
# – God's Manual for Worship

When we began our overview of the Bible we saw how the theme of Genesis focused on election – that is God calling people to Himself seen in the examples of Noah and Abraham. Exodus followed with the theme of redemption, with men and women being saved. This was illustrated by the Israelites' escape from bondage in Egypt through a miraculous intervention by God and the shedding of innocent blood on their behalf at Passover. We then saw how the next step was baptism, symbolized by the passing through the Red Sea, followed by the Commandments and the Law, teaching what God expected of His redeemed children. So, what's next for the new believer? It's worship! That is the theme of Leviticus: how to worship, serve and obey a holy God.

## Fulfilling the priestly calling

In Leviticus the Israelites are taught how to fulfil their priestly calling.

The book opens with the Israelites still in the wilderness and camped at the foot of Mount Sinai. The Lord calls to Moses from the tent of meeting and speaks to him, giving him instructions about how offerings should be made.

Today, when people struggle with loneliness, rejection and despair because they are alienated from God, Leviticus answers the age old complaint that "God seems uncaring and remote!" Made in the image of God, we were created to have a close relationship with Him. According to the teacher in the book of

Ecclesiastes, "He [God] has… set eternity in the hearts of men" (Ecclesiastes 3:11), which speaks of the God-shaped void in our hearts that only He can fill. So when fellowship with God is broken, we sense an emptiness within us: we suffer, and desperately need our relationship with God to be restored. Leviticus answers this problem by teaching that for an unholy people to approach a holy God, sin must first be dealt with and lives lived in obedience to His commands before fellowship can be restored.

The principal message in Leviticus is found in 19:2, "I, the Lord your God, am holy." In chapters 1–17 we have detailed instructions for offering sacrifices that acted as symbols of repentance and obedience, teaching us that God must be approached through sacrificial offering. Because sin is abhorred by a holy and righteous God, the blood sacrifices remind the worshippers that the blood of an innocent sacrificial animal is a substitute for the life of the guilty offender. The key verse is Leviticus 17:11:

> For the life of a creature is in the blood, and I have given it to you to make atonement for yourselves on the altar; it is the blood that makes atonement for one's life.

It has been said that the "Old Testament is the New Testament concealed and the New Testament is the Old revealed." This truth is seen perfectly in Leviticus. Whether bulls, goats or sheep, the sacrificial offering had to be perfect with no defects or blemishes. This pictures the ultimate sacrifice: the Lamb of God, Jesus Christ, who came to offer His blood for our sins. In Leviticus, priests, ritual and the sacred Day of Atonement opened the way for the people to come to God. This repetitive pattern of sacrifice has been nullified in the New Testament by Jesus who died once for all and confirmed this by proclaiming from Calvary's cross: "It is finished" (John 19:30). Hebrews reminds us that "without the shedding of blood there is no forgiveness" (Hebrews 9:22). Then the writer to the Hebrews goes further when he says:

> … brothers, since we have confidence to enter the Most Holy Place by the blood of Jesus, by a new and living way opened for us through the curtain, that is, his body, and since we have a great priest over the house of God, let us draw near to God with a sincere heart in full assurance of faith, having our hearts sprinkled to cleanse us from a guilty conscience and having our bodies washed with pure water.
>
> HEBREWS 10:19–22

This means that when people repent, confess their sins and accept Christ as the One through whom they can approach God, the way is open to have a new and living relationship with Him.

The question of how we approach our Holy God and live as His holy people is answered in chapters 18–27, which focus on sanctification.

To be holy means to be "set apart" and it appears eighty-seven times in Leviticus. The Israelites are to be "set apart" from the other nations. The key verses are:

> *Consecrate yourselves and be holy, because I am the Lord your God. Keep my decrees and follow them. I am the Lord, who makes you holy.*
>
> LEVITICUS 20:7–8

Sometimes it refers to ceremonial holiness (ritual requirements), sometimes it's moral holiness (purity of life), or the rules for daily living concerning family responsibilities, such as sexual conduct and relationships. As we see how these guidelines involve one's daily, holy, walk with God, we learn that worship also has a horizontal aspect, in that God is honoured as we relate to others and live holy lives.

Leviticus 19:35–36 gives us an example about holy living:

> *Do not use dishonest standards when measuring length, weight or quantity. Use honest scales and honest weights, an honest ephah and an honest hin. I am the Lord your God, who brought you out of Egypt.*

This teaches the shopkeeper to give his customers fair value for their money not just because the abstract concept of justice is a good thing, but as a response of obedience to God who blesses His people. The reflection of His justice helps create a pattern of honest dealing in the world at large and so reflects upon His character.

That's why the life of God's people had to be a continual act of worship focused on their liturgy in the tabernacle and lived throughout the week. Not because it is good insurance, but because God had revealed Himself as holy and His people were to reflect His holiness. This is confirmed in the New Testament in Ephesians:

> *... among you there must not be even a hint of sexual immorality, or of any kind of impurity, or of greed, because these are improper for God's holy people. Nor should there be obscenity, foolish talk or coarse joking, which are out of place, but rather thanksgiving.*
>
> EPHESIANS 5:3–4

So from Leviticus we learn that in worship and in our lifestyle, we are expressing our love to God; showing who He is, what He's said, and what He's doing.

While God required holiness in the inner person, there is much emphasis in Leviticus on outer actions in worship. Its teaching was with visual aids: the temple, robes, sacrificial animals and blood, ceremony, ritual, clean and unclean, holy and unholy. In the New Testament Jesus inaugurated the time of the new covenant as He told His disciples in the Upper Room at the Last Supper (Luke 22:20). As believers are now the temple where the Holy Spirit dwells (1 Corinthians 6:19) and as Jesus is the altar and our blood sacrifice, the emphasis is now on the inner person, that is, our character, personality, thoughts and motives, which influence our outward actions. The apostle Paul expressed this essence of worship perfectly in Romans:

> *Therefore, I urge you, brothers, in view of God's mercy, to offer your bodies as living sacrifices, holy and pleasing to God – this is your spiritual act of worship.*
>
> ROMANS 12:1

The primary purpose of our worship is to bring pleasure, satisfaction, and delight to God with our lives.

John 4:23 tells us Jesus said:

> *... a time is coming and has now come when the true worshipers will worship the Father in spirit and truth, for they are the kind of worshippers the Father seeks.*

So worship in the Bible means to bow before God, both outwardly and inwardly, acknowledging His worthiness and submitting to His will. It means serving God in everyday obedience, reverencing Him by recognizing His holiness and responding to it by living a life of godliness. Sunday worship is just one aspect of our week-long worship; it is not confined simply to singing hymns and worship songs. There are many appropriate ways to express our love towards

God in a church service: teaching, preaching, listening and responding to His Word, financial giving, reading of Scripture, praying and giving testimony to the goodness of God are all acts of worship. When the body of Christ meets in the presence of God, all its activities should constitute acts of worship since they are intended to glorify God (1 Corinthians 12:7; 14:26; Ephesians 5:19; Colossians 3:16). God, not man, must be the focus and centre of our worship. The modern worship song expresses it well:

> *When I look into Your holiness, when I gaze into Your*
> *    loveliness,*
> *When all things that surround become shadows in the light*
> *    of You;*
> *When I've found the joy of reaching Your heart,*
> *When my will becomes enthroned in Your love,*
> *When all things that surround become shadows in the light*
> *    of You:*
> *I worship You, I worship You, the reason I live is to worship*
> *    You.*

## The challenge

Leviticus teaches us the awfulness of sin and the awesome holiness of God who hates and punishes sin. Leviticus also shows how sinners can approach a holy God through the blood of an innocent substitute killed on their behalf. Christians recognize Jesus as their innocent substitute who died on their behalf on Calvary's cross. This book goes on to teach that believers must be holy and lead lives that are honouring to God. So, in the same way that Israel was set apart from other nations to show forth God in daily and national life, Christians must set themselves apart and be seen to be different as they live as disciples of Jesus allowing Him to lead, guide, teach and train them in works of righteousness so that they may glorify and honour the Lord Jesus Christ in their lives day by day.

# 4

# Numbers
# – Walking through the Wilderness

Having been called by God in Genesis, in Exodus we read how Israel was saved and delivered through miraculous circumstances, followed by Leviticus where the Israelites were taught how to worship their holy God. Next is pilgrimage symbolized by the Israelites' walk through the wilderness towards the Promised Land. To belong to God's people is an immense privilege, and with that privilege comes responsibility, and with responsibility, costs.

Where the book of Leviticus covered only a month of the Israelites' journey, Numbers stretches over almost thirty-nine years, beginning with the nation still being located at Mount Sinai, then following them in their wanderings around Kadesh Barnea. Finally, in their fortieth year of wanderings, they arrive on the plains of Moab.

## There is no discipleship without discipline

The journey from Mount Sinai to Kadesh Barnea, the last oasis in the Negev Desert and the entrance into the Promised Land, should have taken the Israelites eleven days on foot. It took them forty years because of their disobedience, due entirely to their lack of faith in God. The painful process of teaching, training, faith building and learning to trust and work with each other as a nation of free men and women was necessary so that God could reveal more and more about Himself and His ways to His people. They had to learn what it means to be loved, to face up to the challenge of being liberated, to be constantly reminded of the necessity to be holy, and the need to have God-given vision and goals. They had to realize they were loved, liberated, holy and with a purpose – and while you have to walk through the wilderness you don't have to live there.

The book of Numbers opens by recalling the offspring of Abraham, Isaac, Jacob and Joseph. This was meant to remind the nation that they were a privileged people chosen by God. They were called into being by a miracle of His undeserved grace and were objects of His special care. One of the great lessons learned from the failed Communist experiment of the twentieth century was that people are not units or isolated numbers designed to tend the great machine of state; they are social creatures who belong to each other. Numbers brings this out in the way it relates the story of a people who have been repeatedly reassured that they are valued and loved by God.

## A concern for love

The first point to note is that Numbers is more concerned with love rather than rules.

Look closely and you see how the two are mutually inclusive. It was because God loved them that He entered into a covenant with them and recorded His eternal love for them, promising to care for them, protect them and meet all their needs. They in turn covenanted to love Him exclusively and not follow other gods.

As the story of Numbers unfolds, we see how God's love is far more than an insubstantial philosophy. It is practical and rooted in reality, demonstrating His compassion for His people. Based on the census figures in Numbers chapters 1 and 26, Israel probably comprised two-and-a-half million people and their camp would have covered an area of several square miles. Anticipating the danger of relational breakdown such as tribal rivalry, God tells the people precisely where each tribe is to pitch its tents and in what order they are to march in their long columns.

Though they had no trained army to protect them God gave them military success. He provided spiritual leaders, and in times of stress and anxiety, compassionate priests. God miraculously fed them, clothed them, protected them and supplied all their needs during their time in the wilderness, and this has an important message for us today.

Ours is an extraordinarily insular society seriously lacking the strong, dependable relationships and commitments of earlier generations, seen at its worst in the shocking statistics of marriage and family breakdown. Our modern preference for "believing but not belonging" challenges the church and Christian organizations to be models of loving and mutually supportive examples to the community. For example, in Numbers 3:17 – 4:49 we see the principles of a co-ordinated ministry. In 3:43, three clans were counted and the best years of all the men aged from thirty to fifty were given for work within the tabernacle (4:43). There was no place for jealousy or rivalries; all were to work in harmonious relationships and in dutiful submission to their colleagues, the priests. This anticipated the interdependent supportive relationships that were meant to characterize the early Christian churches, but sadly this was not always evident in either Israel or church history.

Numbers teaches that a life of obedient sacrificial love is never easy. People who have been called, led and commanded by God find themselves in the very mixed company of men and women who grumble, bicker and sin in so many ways. So we need help to get along with each other, which means God's discipline and training so that we become a valued people of God, made for community by a God who cares.

## The challenge of being liberated

The second point is that Numbers addresses the challenge of being liberated.

Western nations have found to their cost that you may win the military battle but building a nation is an altogether different and more difficult task. The Israelites were liberated but now they must learn to build a united society. Numbers teaches the Christian that freedom has its temptations, and these temptations must be faced and overcome during the wilderness walk or they will cause them to languish in that very wilderness.

The old generation that came out of Egypt was led by God to the edge of the Promised Land, and what happened there in chapters 13 and 14 becomes the pivotal point in the book. Chapter 13 tells us Moses sent twelve men, one from each tribe, to spy out the land of Canaan. After forty days they returned with a glowing report of a land flowing with milk and honey (13:27). But ten of the twelve spies had a negative report. Yes, the land was good, but… the people are too powerful – there are giants in the land! (13:31–33).

Siding with the ten objectors, the people showed they lacked faith that God was able to take them into the land He had promised to them. Chapter 14 opens with the nation grumbling against their leaders, complaining that it would be better to go back to Egypt and blaming God for bringing them out to the desert to die. They had forgotten the God of the exodus and were about to stone Moses, Joshua and Caleb who were all for trusting God and pushing on. God was so angry with the complainers because of their unbelief He vowed that, with the exception of Joshua and Caleb, the generation that came out of Egypt would not see the Promised Land (14:34). The old generation was doomed to literally kill time in the wilderness, one year for every day the spies spent in Canaan. They were punished by disinheritance and death, and their journey changed from anticipation to aimlessness.

In chapter 14 we see how the doubters despised God's generous provision.

In verses 3–4 they asked, "Why is the Lord bringing us to this land?" (14:3). The reason was that He loved them and it was the most incredibly wonderful thing He could do for them, but they threw His gift back in His face. Then they questioned His promised protection and doubted his unfailing love: "Our wives and children will be taken as plunder" (14:3). They disowned His unique redemption: "Wouldn't it be better for us to go back to Egypt?" (14:3). And in spurning His appointed leader, Moses, "We should choose a leader" (14:4), they were looking for someone to take them back to a pre-Moses lifestyle, a life of slavery with no hope, no security and no future; in fact, no God.

This anticipates the apostle Peter's warning:

> *If they have escaped the corruption of the world by knowing*
> *our Lord and Saviour Jesus Christ and are again entangled*
> *in it and are overcome, they are worse off at the end than they*
> *were at the beginning. It would have been better for them not*
> *to have known the way of righteousness, than to have known it*
> *and then to turn their backs on the sacred command that was*
> *passed on to them.*
>
> 2 PETER 2:20–21

The clue to why they made their fateful decision to rebel and disobey God and not move into the land He had promised to them can be seen in their attitude beforehand. There was an ever-increasing pattern of grumbling and defiance that led to indiscipline and death. From this we learn that the most dangerous enemies in our wilderness journey are the adversaries lurking within us such as dissatisfaction and discontent (Numbers 11:1–9); bitterness and jealousy (12:1–2); fear and unbelief (13–14); arrogance and disobedience (14:39–45) and rebelliousness and irreverence (16:1–14). Even leaders are prone to these temptations, such as Miriam and Aaron's attempted coup-d'état against Moses in chapter 12, and Moses losing his temper in chapter 20. As if that was not enough to contend with, alongside the inner temptations waiting ahead of the Israelites there were the nations who worshipped other gods who would expose them to apostasy and idolatry including their horrendous sins of spiritual and physical adultery (Numbers 25:1–16 and 33:50–56).

The very same temptations that were faced by the Israelites have to be faced by the people of God today. Like them, Christians have to learn that on their own they are no match for the foes ranged against them but, united with and holding the hand of Jesus, they are "more than conquerors through him who loved us" (Romans 8:37), and with Him we are more than a match for the temptations of the world, the flesh and the devil.

## The need to be holy

Thirdly, Numbers shows the need to be holy.

Holiness in Numbers is illustrated in the way the camp was set up. The tabernacle of God was in the centre with the camp around the tent of meeting. The priests and Levites followed ritual sacrifices, cleansing procedures, feasts and festivals. Here we have, in visual form, God's ideal community – reverent, submissive, obedient and grateful. But men and women for all their best intentions make mistakes and more than once in Numbers we read "We have sinned", "We will die", "We are all lost" (see Numbers 14:39–40; 17:12; 21:7). But despite their transgressions they belong to a loving God who made provision for His children's cleansing and pardon through atoning sacrifices for sin portraying gratitude for forgiveness. So Numbers beautifully illustrates Christ's coming and His atoning sacrifice.

An example of this is the incident concerning the bronze serpent on a stake. In Numbers 21:4–9 we read:

> the people grew impatient on the way; they spoke against God and against Moses, and said, "Why have you brought us up out of Egypt to die in the desert? There is no bread! There is no water! And we detest this miserable food!"
>
> Then the Lord sent venomous snakes among them; they bit the people and many Israelites died. The people came to Moses and said, "We sinned when we spoke against the Lord and against you. Pray that the Lord will take the snakes away from us." So Moses prayed for the people.
>
> The Lord said to Moses, "Make a snake and put it up on a

> *pole; anyone who is bitten can look at it and live." So Moses*
> *made a bronze snake and put it up on a pole. Then when anyone*
> *was bitten by a snake and looked at the bronze snake, he lived.*

Another picture of Christ is found in Numbers 16:41–48. There we read how the sons of Korah staged a rebellion against Moses' leadership but it was really against God. When God responded by striking down the rebels the Israelites were unhappy and began to complain, whereupon God decided to punish the whole nation. But following Moses' instructions Aaron ran into the midst of the assembly and made atonement for them. Verse 48 records that he stood between the living and the dead and the plague stopped. Both incidents point forward to Jesus who is a better mediator and intercessor than Moses (Hebrews 7:25) and teaches that One greater than Aaron has made atonement for us having offered Himself as our unique sacrifice on Calvary's cross. So, Numbers teaches us that with freedom comes responsibility and always there is accountability for sin, either by the sinner himself or the innocent substitute.

## The need for godly vision and purpose

Fourthly, Numbers shows the need for godly vision and purpose.

Throughout the Numbers story, mention is made of the pillar of cloud by day and fire by night. Numbers 9:17 tells us that, "Whenever the cloud lifted from above the Tent, the Israelites set out; wherever the cloud settled, the Israelites encamped." In the following verses we read that whether for a day, a week, a month or a year, if the cloud remained stationary so did the Israelites, and if the cloud moved they struck camp and followed it. The cloud was a reminder of the Lord's holiness and nearness but it also taught the Israelites to keep a dependent eye on the Lord. Their agenda was the Lord's agenda; where He went they went and He always led. Perhaps it's a lesson for Christians today in their wilderness walk to fix their eyes upon Jesus, take their guidance from Him and make their life decisions based on His Word plus counsel from spiritually mature friends.

There's something else here in Numbers to do with purpose and vision.

The land has been promised and God never breaks His Word. His ability to fulfil His promise despite the odds against is demonstrated by another of Numbers' larger-than-life characters, Balaam (chapters 22–24).

During their journey to the Promised Land, the king of the Amorites refused permission for Israel to travel through his kingdom. Mustering his entire army he went out to attack the Israelites but was defeated. News of Israel's conquests quickly spread to the next country on their route, the kingdom of Moab. Its ruler Balak was distraught at the prospect of an invasion, and rather than rely on military strength he decided to seek supernatural assistance and hired the widely acclaimed soothsayer Balaam from Mesopotamia to put a curse on the Israelite nation. Balaam was forbidden by God from going to help Balak, but persuaded by the offer of an even larger fee from the king, Balaam set off on his donkey to do the dirty deed (22:21). On three occasions an angel blocked his path and each time his donkey, aware of the divine messenger brandishing a sword, tried to turn aside but was angrily beaten by Balaam. The donkey, annoyed at this unjustified punishment, miraculously spoke to Balaam who then saw the angel for himself and was told that God was willing for him to go to Balak but he must only speak the word the Lord would give him. The upshot was that Balaam was given a series of messages from God that were completely contrary to what King Balak desired. Israel was persistently blessed, not cursed, and an angry and frustrated King Balak went home.

Now here's the point: Balak's attempt to halt the Israelite advance and Balaam's dramatic encounter with God took place on a hilltop above the plain upon which the Israelites were camped, and they knew nothing about it. When they later heard what had happened it would reassure and encourage God's people to move on in obedience and faith.

Balaam was ignorant of Israelite history and could not know that his words were encouraging Israel. First he recognizes Israel's unassailable security (23:7–8), then he emphasizes the nation's distinctive identity and heritage (23:9–10a) and yearns for its ultimate destiny (23:10b). In chapter 24 he announces a series of divine proclamations that would fill the Israelites with joy, culminating in verse 23: "who can live when God does this?" The lesson is: the conquests Israel would enjoy would not be due to their superior numbers, military skills or political diplomacy but due to the power of Israel's God. The future would confirm the truth of this prophecy. The Israelites would enter their Promised Land, and later unlikely heroes such as Gideon, Samson and David would testify to what God had done in routing out their enemies. The same could be said of the menacing Moabites (24:17b), proud Edomites (24:18), arrogant Amalekites (24:20), invincible Kenites (24:21), cruel Assyrians (24:22), boasting Babylonians, prosperous Persians, powerful Greeks and triumphant Romans. Like the taunt songs of the later prophets, the closing lines of Balaam's oracle gave voice to one of Scripture's cardinal truths: God is sovereign, He is not simply in control of Israel's destiny; the whole world is in His hands.

There is a wonderful postscript to the message of Numbers.

The twelve men sent to spy out the Promised Land would be Israel's brightest and best with proven track records and vision for the future. There's no way Moses would choose, "wannabes or has-beens" to check out the land. These men had a great start, they saw the miracles of God, yet out of the twelve we know the names of only two and today we call our sons by their names: Joshua and Caleb – that's testimony.

The time came when under Joshua's command God did lead His people across the river Jordan into the Promised Land. Cities were conquered one after the other but stubborn pockets of resistance fought on, especially in the well-fortified hill country. Forty-five years had passed since Caleb first caught sight of that country and the time came for Joshua to allocate the conquered land to the Israelites. It's a fantastic scene. The nation of Israel was gathered at Gilgal listening to General Joshua when out of the ranks walks this white-haired, 85-year-old citizen. It's Caleb from Numbers 14; and walking up to Joshua he claims his inheritance. Joshua 14:12 captures the moment perfectly: "Now give me this hill country that the Lord promised me that day." The hill country he had been promised was Hebron: the Canaanite's most powerful stronghold, guarded by their strongest giants. That was the land Caleb had been promised and that was the land he wanted. And Caleb won it and drove out the enemy and was the only person given land who succeeded in completely expelling the Canaanites.

There are great lessons for us to learn from this story.

Caleb's name was never mentioned as part of Korah's rebellion (Numbers 16). He wasn't part of Miriam's spiteful attack on Moses (Numbers 12) and he kept his testimony untarnished. Here was this 85-year-old man asking for the opportunity to conquer a mountain range guarded by the enemy's elite troops. Eighty-five is a good age to settle down in some comfortable valley but Caleb wanted the mountaintop God had promised him. Caleb is the example for Christians to look forward and not backwards. His attitude reminds us of Paul's great exhortation: "Forgetting what is behind and straining toward what is ahead, I press on towards the goal to win the prize for which God has called me heavenward in Christ Jesus" (Philippians 3:13–14).

When the nation of Israel finally entered the Promised Land, Caleb could have sat down and sulked and said, "I told you we could do it, but no you wouldn't listen to me and you've wasted forty years in the wilderness", and he would have been right. But instead of complaining and looking back, Caleb looked ahead and claimed his mountain. It's Caleb's secret, and it can be ours. He had a love that never faltered. When he saw the Promised Land for the first time something touched his heart. It wasn't the milk or honey or grapes, it was

Mount Hebron. Hebron in Hebrew means "fellowship, love and communion". That's the place Caleb longed for with all of his heart and that's the place, the place of fellowship, love and communion with our Lord and each other that we must seek and strain towards. But it is guarded by the strongest and craftiest of the enemy who will use every trick in the book to stop us pressing ahead to the mountaintop.

"Here, Christian, take some of the milk and honey, take some of the land in the valley and the plain, that's all you need and you will be happy there!"

"No it's not, Satan! I have an inheritance to claim and I will not be satisfied with second best. Nothing in life can compare to fellowship, love and communion with my Lord and Saviour Jesus Christ, I will press on!"

"For what? What's more important than your career, home or ambition?"

"I'll tell you. I have a destiny! When I stand before the Lord on the day of judgment, all my works will burn. My plans and contracts, policies and deeds, none of these things were ever to be my destiny; rather it's to be more and more like Jesus, to grow in holiness, righteousness and purity; that's my destiny, that's the best gift I can leave my family and friends."

The challenge for Christians today is to fulfil their destiny.

Are we going to be more like Jesus this year than we were last year? Do the people who know us and deal with us see Christ in us? Are we pressing on towards the goal to win the prize for which God has called us heavenwards in Christ Jesus? Because of the victory Caleb won he was able to leave that mountain inheritance to his children and grandchildren, teaching us that the decisions we make in this life affect other people. If we run from the challenges of life we lose the inheritance we could leave for others. But if, like Caleb, we face the challenges and claim them by faith, then we enrich our inheritance and this means blessings to those who follow.

# 5

# **Deuteronomy**
# – Moses' Farewell Message

The book of Deuteronomy covers a period of about one month.

The nation of Israel is camped on the plain of Moab, and across the River Jordan lies Jericho and the Promised Land. The Israelites have been through constant tests and trials in the past forty years while wandering in the wilderness: miraculous deliverance, rebellion, wars, God-given commandments, covenant conditions and sacrificial procedures for their worship and guidance. Now they are ready to cross the Jordan and possess the land of promise.

Moses, who has faithfully led God's people since their exodus from Egypt, knows he will not be accompanying them into Canaan and preaches his final sermon to the nation of Israel. The new generation listening to him were only children when they escaped from Egypt through the Red Sea and camped at Mount Sinai. Most of them would not recall having received the Law of God, so Moses read and explained the Law a second time. Hence the Ten Commandments appear twice: once in Exodus, given to the original generation from Egypt, then again in Deuteronomy to the new generation who would enter the Promised Land. God brought the Israelites out of bondage in Egypt and through the Red Sea before He made the covenant at Sinai with them. He did not tell His people how they must live until He had saved them, and this is a pattern throughout the Bible. God first saves us then explains how we should live as His people.

This new generation was going to see God take them through the river Jordan, which, at that time of the year, was in full flood and impassable. Then, having experienced that miracle, they would go on to their own equivalent of Mount Sinai when Joshua repeats the blessings and curses of the Lord at Mount Ebal and Shechem (Joshua 8:30; 23:6–24:1ff.). It was a repeat performance at the end of forty years for an entirely new generation, for Moses knew when they entered the Promised Land their lifestyle had to change from that of desert nomads to permanent citizens who will make their home and build their society in a difficult and dangerous environment. In Moses they have the authoritative message of a faithful prophet, the encouraging support of a compassionate pastor and the inspiring example of a committed believer. All three elements of preaching, pastoral care and spirituality are found in this important book.

The theological importance of Deuteronomy cannot be emphasized enough.

It stands as the source of historical, biblical revelation for both Old and New Testament theology. When the prophets speak of God and His message they speak of the God and message of Deuteronomy and of the relationship contained in its covenant treaty. The warnings of doom from the prophets, particularly Jeremiah, are the warnings or curses of Deuteronomy. Conversely, the promises of blessing for Israel when she lives in faith, love, and obedience to the Lord are the blessings of Deuteronomy. The way of life of the people of God begun in Exodus, Leviticus and Numbers is fully established in Deuteronomy and forms the basis for all subsequent revelation of the way of life acceptable to God.

These people belong wholly to the Lord; they are His treasured inheritance. He redeemed them from the bondage of Egypt and is about to fulfil His promise to Abraham, Isaac, and Jacob by giving them the Promised Land, their inheritance. So the theme for the book of Deuteronomy is the renewal of the covenant established at Mount Sinai.

On the plains of Moab the covenant is renewed and enlarged as Moses speaks to the nation of Israel in three sermons.

## Moses' first sermon

In his first sermon (1:1 – 4:43), Moses reminds the nation of how forty years previously they had been on the verge of entering the Promised Land but had failed to do so through fear of what lay ahead.

Fear is natural; it's how we handle fear that matters. The memory of their failure was etched on the Israelite psyche and embedded in their history. But Deuteronomy 1:20–21 teaches us that the future is not something to dread. The future is God's gift to us. It's His future, not simply ours. We don't face it alone but with the assurance that He knows the future and plans to bless us in it for the glory of His name. When we look into what may seem to be a dark and uncertain future we must hear the words addressed to these despondent Hebrew pilgrims, "See, the Lord your God has given you the land" (verse 21). God knows all the future; it is His gift before it is our threat.

Deuteronomy 1:34–46 reminds us there are key moments in life with crucial opportunities and it's tragic if we miss them. Shakespeare captured this perfectly in his play *Julius Caesar* when Brutus said,

> *There is a tide in the affairs of men*
> *Which, if taken at full flood, leads on to fortune;*
> *Omitted, all the voyage of life is bound in shallows and in*
> *miseries.*

Freedom of choice is a gift but it is also a serious responsibility. In God's conduct with the Israelites we learn that genuine love exposes itself to the risk of rejection. But we must also remember God's holiness and wrath as well as His mercy. A good father does not only love, feed and protect his children, he also disciplines them (8:5).

But here is something wonderful. Though the Lord may discipline His children He never abandons them. On the surface this story of the history of the Israelites appears to be about homeless nomads, tribal squabbles, fortified cities and even iron bedsteads. And though all factual, the passage from 2:1 – 3:11 conveys a far deeper message of great significance.

## God is merciful

First we learn that God is merciful; discipline does not last forever (2:3).

When we grieve God we feel guilty and may harbour these feelings for too long. As a disciple of Jesus, Peter knew what it was to feel guilt (he denied knowing his Lord three times), but by the seashore on an early morning the opportunity came for him to renew his loyalty and love (John 21:15–19). Later the apostle John was to remind us that the contrite confession of our sins guarantees their immediate cleansing (1 John 1:9). We must learn to deal with the past and move on looking not to our sins but to the One who pardons them.

## God is generous

Despite their disobedience and wickedness God had been good to them (2:7). The fact that they had sufficient funds to pay for whatever food and drink they needed as they passed through Edom (2:6) and Heshbon (2:28) is proof enough of God's generous provision during the wilderness period as was His provision of manna. God does not deal with us the way we deal with Him.

## God is just

Verses 5 and 19 of chapter 2 show how God spared the peoples of Seir, Moab and Ammon. From this we learn that Israel was not God's sole interest. They must not make the mistake of thinking that they can do anything they want: God had wider interests than Israel, and still has (John 3:16).

## God is powerful

In 2:25 we see how God could put fear in the hearts of those who oppose His people. Decades earlier it was the Israelites who were afraid to possess the land but now their enemies are terrified. That's exactly how God could have accomplished it forty years ago if the fathers of the present soldiers had done what they were told. We are apt to put ridiculous limits on the power of God. He overcame immense difficulties for these stateless refugees and has promised the same power to deal effectively with our problems too, such as in Philippians 4:12–13.

# Moses' second sermon

## The covenant developed

Moses' second sermon can be found in 4:44 – 26:19. In chapter 4, before the people enter the Promised Land, it is imperative they understand who God is, what He has said and what He can do. They need to think deeply about the uniqueness of their God before they enter a land where their enemies worshipped false gods. The failure of their fathers to enter the land forty years previously was due to defective vision: they refused to look up! Looking ahead they saw giants, looking around they saw their own slender resources, looking within they saw their fear and misgivings, and looking back they allowed the past to assume a rosy tint and distort the truth. They had to learn to look up to God and learn that He is a generous giver (verses 1–12); a sovereign Lord (verses 13–28); a merciful deliverer (verses 29–34); and an incomparable lover (verses 35–43).

The moral and legal instructions comprise the longest of Moses' sermons because Israel's future as a nation in Canaan depended on their right relationship with God. In 5:2 Moses reminds them of God's Law and the covenant they had received at Mount Sinai, and although the people he was addressing were less than twenty years of age at the time, the covenant remained in force for all generations. For unlike the treaties and agreements between the surrounding nations, this was not a contract of human design nor a covenant between equal parties, but a covenant with their majestic and glorious God.

The phrase "all Israel" used throughout Deuteronomy (see, for example, 5:1) reminds the people that the unity of their nation was a gift from God who by unique agreement has made them His own people. There was no opting out and no way the individual Israelite should act in a selfish individualistic manner. The people were bound together with strong cords of loyalty to God and to one another. To break the covenant was not only to grieve God but also to harm one's fellow men. The sin of Achan in Joshua 7:21 where the entire nation suffered from one man's sin is an example of this.

Moses knew men and women would be tempted to publicly or secretly worship false gods and he makes it very clear that this is not allowed; the punishment is death (Deuteronomy 13:1–18 and 29:18ff.). Today, the idea of God setting the standard for everyone is very unpopular and people argue for the right of the individual to behave as they choose. They plead situation ethics and hold that nothing is intrinsically good or bad, with the result the Ten Commandments become the ten suggestions. But God's covenant presents firm, irrevocable principles. David was not exempt from the serious charge of adultery simply because he wore the crown. When God sets His standards there are no favoured exceptions. Nor can there be any neutrality: if they don't love God they will hate Him as Jesus taught in John 14 and 15. There is no sitting on the fence with regard to Christ: you are either for Him or against Him. In Deuteronomy 11:26ff. Moses emphasizes the need for radical decision. He points to Mount Gerizim and Mount Ebal, the two mountains which would rise up on either side of the pilgrims when they entered the land and depicts them as two silent witnesses for Israel to chose where her allegiance lay. One typified blessing, the other cursing.

The commandments are not only to be heard, they have to be learned and taught to others, and history testifies to the grim truth that societies that reject these laws die. God's Word repeated time and again, obey that you may live, is an encouragement to the obedient and a warning to the rebel. The Ten Commandments are highly relevant for today. They explain who we are, not simply just what we should or should not do. They make clear that in our very different but no less sinful world we are people who have been made by God the Creator to live as committed worshippers, reminding us that men and women must acknowledge, exalt and consider their Creator.

## Moses' third sermon

Chapters 27–24 see Moses' life and ministry drawing to a close and four things remain to be accomplished: he will give a closing address, commission his successor, teach the people a unique song and deliver a farewell blessing.

His closing address reminds us that if we are to cope with tomorrow's problems we must remember yesterday's blessings. The God who answered your prayer yesterday will do so again tomorrow. In 29:10–15 Moses assures the Israelites of this truth, affirming that the covenant is a present reality for them in their day and New Testament Christians have the same assurance from the lips of their Saviour for our day: "surely I am with you always, to the very end of the age" (Matthew 28:20).

Moses is tired. He has been a valiant warrior and his earthly work is nearly at an end.

His realistic attitude to life teaches us to view the advancing years and old age not as a frustrating lack of ability to do what we once could do, but rather to accept that life has different stages bringing different rather than diminishing opportunities. Deuteronomy also reminds those who are older in years that, like Moses, they have a responsibility to prepare the next generation for the work of God. They may yet fulfil their most significant role in life by serving as persistent, well-informed, sympathetic intercessors.

In 31:7 Moses calls Joshua, and in the presence of the people he reminds the younger man that the Lord had chosen him for the work. For anyone wishing to serve the Lord nothing is more important than a clear and compelling sense of call. Whether we are willing volunteers like Isaiah or reluctant conscripts like Jeremiah, we must know beyond doubt that the Lord wants us to do a particular work for Him. Without the assurance of the "call" we may be easily deflected from the task and give up when things are discouraging or difficult.

Notice too that it was not sufficient for Joshua to hear these inspiring words from Moses in the presence of all Israel:

> *Be strong and courageous, for you must go with this people*
> *into the land that the Lord swore to their forefathers to give*
> *them, and you must divide it among them as their inheritance.*

> *The Lord himself goes before you and will be with you; he will*
> *never leave you nor forsake you. Do not be afraid; do not be*
> *discouraged.*

DEUTERONOMY 31:7-8

Joshua needed a fresh encounter with the Lord himself (31:23) and the Lord commissioned him by reminding him of three things here: I was with you in the past, I am with you today and I will be with you tomorrow.

- "I promised them on oath" – that's legitimacy in the past.
- "I myself will be with you" – that's shared aims in the present.
- "You will bring the Israelites into the land" – that's assurance for the future.

Moses was going home to be with the Lord while Joshua was going forward into the Promised Land, but both men rejoiced that Israel's unchanging leader was the Lord Himself. They were merely His privileged agents, appointed for a limited period of time to do His work.

And so it was time for Moses to lay down his staff.

Although God said "No" to his wish to enter the Promised Land he was encouraged by what he saw and heard. In 32:49 he is told, "Go up into the Abarim Range to Mount Nebo in Moab, across from Jericho, and view Canaan, the land I am giving the Israelites as their own possession." There are several references in Deuteronomy about seeing the land with your own eyes (3:27; 32:52; 34:4). This begs the question: Why this repeated emphasis on viewing the land? What's the point of seeing it if you're not allowed to go into it?

In Hebrew law, viewing the land had significant legal implications. We see this principle in the life of Abraham: "Lift up your eyes... and look... All the land that you see I will give to you" (Genesis 13:14–15). This helps us to understand the significance of the discourteous excuse in Jesus" parable in Luke 14:18: "I have just bought a field, and I must go and see it." Today we think it's absurd that anyone should first buy a field without seeing it, but what is being described here is the formal legal transfer of that man's newly acquired property. By looking out over the land, Moses was being given the unique privilege of legally taking possession of that entire country on behalf of its new people. That's why in Deuteronomy 3:27 he is told to look out as far as he can see in each direction; it was his, even though he wasn't personally allowed to put a foot on it.

Here we have an important spiritual principle. Not everything that is given to a believer is an immediate acquired possession. Some Christians want everything this side of heaven – health, wealth and happiness – now. But Scripture makes it plain that much of what is promised is reserved for the future. There are better things to come:

> ... *an inheritance that can never perish, spoil or fade – kept in heaven for you, who through faith are shielded by God's power until the coming of the salvation that is ready to be revealed in the last time.*
>
> 1 PETER 1:4–5

We can look now, but for the moment our feet must stay this side of the river. So be encouraged, you who are struggling with hardships of one kind or another. Look up to your God, survey the land, know what awaits you and prepare to receive it as a precious child of God.

# 6

# Joshua
## – Possessing the Land

The book of Joshua covers the life of Joshua from the age of eighty to one hundred and twenty. This forty-year span, matching exactly the length of Moses' leadership, falls into two sections: the seven-year conquest of Canaan (chapters 1–13) and the eight-year period of distribution and settlement (chapters 13–24).

## The Israelites enter the Promised Land

Joshua resumes the narrative where Deuteronomy left off, and takes the former slaves into the land promised to them by God nearly 500 years previously, when He told Abraham, "To your descendants I give this land" (Genesis 15:18). The book opens with God commanding Joshua, who had already been designated as Moses' successor, to cross the Jordan and take possession of Canaan. Then, with victory over the Canaanites secured, he was to divide the land among the people as their inheritance with the assurance that God understood his nervousness, and the reassurance that if he faithfully observed His laws, God would be with him as He had been with Moses (Joshua 1:5).

## Rahab and the spies

Chapter 2 records how Joshua first sent two spies into the land. Their experiences are described in considerable detail, not due to their hazardous exploits but because what they saw and heard confirmed the Lord's promise from Deuteronomy, "No man will be able to stand against you. The Lord your God, as he promised you, will put the terror and fear of you on the whole land, wherever you go" (Deuteronomy 11:25). This promise was reassuringly confirmed inside the city of Jericho by Rahab telling the spies, "I know that the Lord has given this land to you and that a great fear of you has fallen on us, so that all who live in this country are melting in fear because of you" (Joshua 2:9).

## Crossing the Jordan

Israel could have crossed the River Jordan and entered the land of Canaan by building rafts and constructing bridges, but God was going to bring His people through the river dry-shod for several reasons.

We need to bear in mind that nine of the plagues recorded in Exodus were directed against Egypt's gods to demonstrate the absolute superiority of Israel's God. In Canaan, Baal was the great Canaanite god who was supposed to control the elements of weather including rain, sun and water that were vital for an agricultural community. The drying up of the River Jordan proved that Baal was as powerless before God in Canaan as Pharaoh's gods had been against the plagues in Egypt. The marvels God performed in Egypt, in the Red Sea crossing and in sustaining His people in the wilderness were about to be added to in Canaan to teach the covenant people, and the surrounding nations too, that the gods of the idolatrous unbelievers were false gods who could accomplish nothing. Jehovah was the living and true God of all the earth (see Joshua 3:11, 13).

But there was another reason why the Lord intervened on their behalf in such a spectacular manner: it vividly demonstrated His love, faithfulness and power. It was as if He opened to them the door of the land that He had promised, and personally conducted them through it. This would be a wonderful assurance and give an enormous boost to the Israelites' confidence for the task of conquest that lay ahead.

By publicly blessing Joshua in his new role as leader, God gave the nation divine confirmation of his office.

Joshua 3:2–4 records:

> *After three days the officers went throughout the camp, giving orders to the people: "When you see the ark of the covenant of the Lord your God, and the priests, who are Levites, carrying*

*it, you are to move out from your positions and follow it. Then*
*you will know which way to go, since you have never been this*
*way before."*

The ark of the covenant, the symbol of the divine presence, was carried by the priests into the middle of the River Jordan. They had been told that when the soles of their feet touched the water the river would divide in two and the way ahead would be open for the people to follow. Think of the faith required. They were to march forward in front of two million onlookers towards a swiftly flowing river that would only part when their feet touched the water. It's a marvellous lesson of faithful obedience and trust in God's timing. Scripture records that the ark, that symbol of the Lord's presence, went before them to make a path through the divided river and stayed behind them to hold back the threatening waters till all the people had crossed over safely (3:17).

This has a wonderful application for Christian men and women today. They are travelling onwards but the future is hidden from their eyes. It's not as if life is some great plain and they see ahead from horizon to horizon. It's more like journeying through a deep valley where they cannot see what storms are gathering behind the mountains or what lies over the next hilltop. Their horizon is limited: what "Jordans" they will be called upon to cross they don't know but they do know they too have an "ark" which makes the one that accompanied Israel but a faint and feeble shadow. For their ark is Jesus Christ who has promised, "Never will I leave you; never will I forsake you" (Hebrews 13:5) and "surely I am with you always, to the very end of the age" (Matthew 28:20).

## The memorial of stones

After the Israelites crossed the river they built a memorial:

> *Joshua set up at Gilgal the twelve stones they had taken out*
> *of the Jordan. He said to the Israelites, "In future when your*
> *descendants ask their fathers, 'What do these stones mean?' tell*
> *them, 'Israel crossed the Jordan on dry ground.'"*
>
> JOSHUA 4:20–22

The generation entering the land on a mission of conquest needed a memorial because the road ahead would be hard and when they became discouraged they would be tempted to forget past blessings. By returning to Gilgal on a regular basis (which they did, since Gilgal was their base of operations), they would see the stones and be reminded of the power and faithfulness of their great God who was with them and would lead them on to conquest. Ahead of them lay the heavily fortified city of Jericho and it had to be captured. When the people were tempted to protest, "No way Joshua! It's impossible! Look at us, we're weak, there's no way we can do this!" Joshua could point to the monument and reply, "Look at the stones. These stones say it's not impossible. These stones say the Lord God who brought you this far will help you again. These stones say it is not only possible, it is certain!"

Christians also, have to move forward to possess the land God has given to them. And there are many trials and difficulties in their way. There will always be a Jericho. At times they will be tempted to say, "No way! I've done my bit. I've given everything I've got. I've nothing left. I can't move forward." The answer is to "Look at the stones, look at the stones!" Let the Spirit of God speak deep into your soul, reminding you of His power and His strength. "The one who calls you is faithful and he will do it" (1 Thessalonians 5:24). He knows of what we are made. He knows our weakness and understands our anxieties and concerns and loves us as a Father loves his children.

## Circumcision and the Passover celebrations

Now that the people were delivered from their enemy's power and raised up to a newness of life in God's promised land of milk and honey, they must have felt it was time to march forward and bring down the enemy strongholds. But Scripture makes it plain they were still not ready. The Holy Spirit had yet to perform one more work.

Joshua 5:2 tells us: "Make flint knives and circumcise the Israelites". Circumcision was the outward covenant sign given to Abraham. The Hebrew used was *barah berith*, which means "to cut off" or "to cut away". It was the mark of God's promise that His seed would possess the land of Canaan (Genesis 17). When finally all the Israelite men had been circumcised God said, "Today I have rolled away the reproach of Egypt from you" (Joshua 5:9).

From this we learn that all along, in spite of God's love, protection, guidance and blessings, the Israelites had been carrying something secret in their hearts. They had hidden their father's idols in their baggage. Yes, they wanted to move on, but they still clung to their idols and the past. The Lord had been patient, so very patient, but no more. To paraphrase what was happening, they received the ultimatum, "I am moving on with holy people only. There is a land of peace and joy with victory after victory ahead of you – but you cannot bring the reproach of Egypt with you, it stays here. Cut it off. Sharpen the knives. No sinful flesh is allowed from here on in. No idolatry. No clinging lusts. No secret reproach." God had them line up and submit to the cutting knife to show them outwardly what He expected of them inwardly – submit to the knife and cut off all sin. In the New Testament the apostle Paul links the spiritual meaning of circumcision to Christian baptism which is also an outward sign of an inner happening (Colossians 2:11–12).

Something else very important happened at Gilgal: Joshua had a revelation (5:13–15). He went out to reconnoitre the approach to Jericho when suddenly a man with a drawn sword in his hand appeared and challenged him. Joshua boldly approached the man, obviously wondering who he was and asked, "Are you for us or our enemies?" The reply was crystal clear: "Neither," he replied, "but as the commander of the army of the Lord I have now come." Without a moment's hesitation Joshua was on his face at the feet of this great commander. The dialogue that followed was exactly the same words that the same commander had spoken to Moses forty years previously. The appearance of God to man is known as a theophany. When Joshua worshipped before this great commander, he allied himself with the commander's power and accepted His leadership in the battle about to take place. The lesson for Christians in times of trial is to remember that, "If God is for us, who can be against us?" (Romans 8:31) and "we are more than conquerors through him who loved us" (Romans 8:37).

## Now it's time to move on

Chapters 6–8 record Joshua's military campaign, which was to place his army as a strategic wedge between the north and south preventing a Canaanite alliance forming against the Israelite forces. That was sound military thinking. But God's directions in 6:1–5 for taking the first fortified city, Jericho, made no military sense. The Lord was doing this to teach the people that Israel's success in battle will always be by His power and not by their own might or cleverness.

This truth needs to be learned by all God's people.

When people come to faith and enter the Christian life they do so knowing there is no going back to a past without God. But when an obstacle like Jericho stands in the way they, too, discover that there is no going around it. The Israelites did not even consider bypassing Jericho, for it would open up an enemy front at their rear, and the further forward they advanced the longer their supply line would stretch and the more vulnerable it would become. No, it had to be dealt with head-on, but how?

The measure of how men and women grow in their Christian walk will be determined by how their faith is strengthened and it will be strengthened by being sorely tried and tested by Jericho-like experiences. What is Jericho to Christians today? To some it is a force within their own personality: a weakness of character or temperament, something within that poses a threat and has to be tackled, defeated and dealt with. Or it may be a factor outside themselves – in the work place or the home and family. Some person or situation that constantly confronts them when they attempt to move forward. It has to be overcome, but how? The answer is by faith and obedience to God and His Word.

According to the Scriptures it was "By faith the walls of Jericho fell, after the people had marched around them for seven days" (Hebrews 11:30). We can imagine the jeers and taunts from the inhabitants on the city wall. But for all their apparent bravado they were a frightened people. The opening verses of the chapter indicate that there was something intimidating about an army walking silently around the city. Aware of what God had already accomplished for Israel, the population of Jericho were very uneasy.

But it was a testing time of faith for the Israelites. Six times they walked around the city wall and did not appear to be accomplishing anything. The wall looked the same when they returned to their tents night after night. But notice how the ark of the covenant was a central feature of the procession. This was the symbol of the Israelites' faith. They were able to walk around the city in silence because although they did not know what God was doing, He was walking around Jericho with them and that was good enough for them. "Shout!" called Joshua on the seventh walk, "For the Lord has given you the city!" (6:16). In answer to their roar and the blowing of their trumpets, the walls collapsed and the people marched victoriously into the fallen Jericho.

Christians will find their Jericho will stand strong and powerful in front of them, blocking their way forward, and they bypass it at their peril, because one day they will have to return and deal with it. But having left it so long, they will have allowed it to grow. Then, at some point in their lives, when in tears they plead with God for victory over their personal difficulty, they will finally understand Jericho for what it is – a gift from God to them in Christ. The victory over it is theirs for the taking but only when they admit that they are unable to take it themselves and so allow Him to work through them and give them the strength they need to prevail.

# The division of the land

Chapters 13–21 cover eight years during which the land was divided among the twelve tribes. Here is the fulfilment of the gift made to Abraham and his seed. It was to be their special territory where God could develop a people who, by honouring and serving Jehovah, would bless the nations.

God's promise to give Abraham and his descendants the land of Canaan does not mean the physical land of Canaan will remain in Israelite hands for eternity. The Messiah has now come, and while God still has a purpose for His people, Israel, God's people today are no longer identified with any one nation. They are truly international, in a way only foreshadowed in the book of Joshua by God's mercy on the Jericho woman Rahab, and perhaps by the Gibeonites (see chapter 9).

# Joshua's farewell

Finally after fifteen years in Canaan, Joshua convened a great assembly at Shechem, the place where on first entering the land the nation made a solemn covenant with God (chapter 23). There they listened as Joshua, speaking in language tender and impressive, recalled the great mercies and divine victories God had shown towards the people of Israel (chapter 24). We are reminded of Moses in the plains of Moab in the closing chapters of Deuteronomy, or of Paul's farewell to the Ephesian elders in Acts 20:13–38.

Joshua exhorts his listeners in the strongest terms to make up their minds to follow the Lord. For he knows that the nation's future wellbeing depends upon the preservation of true religious worship, with its virtue of truth and wholesomeness, in stark contrast to the superstitious idolatry and disgusting vices of the surrounding nations.

Mustering his failing strength he reminds the nation of Jehovah's great blessings. He appeals to them, the chosen people, to remember that their future depends upon their loyalty to almighty God. Then, his challenging call rings forth to make the decisive personal choice of Jehovah as their God: "choose for yourselves this day whom you will serve… But as for me and my household, we will serve the Lord" (24:15).

This was Joshua's last exhortation to the nation of Israel. His days on earth were rapidly coming to an end and he himself, a monument to the times, was able to speak from that unique position which at one and the same time could look back through an astounding century of change, yet with crystal clarity and quiet assurance look forward towards his approaching death and heavenly future.

He bore testimony as one who had toiled under the taskmaster's whip in the quarries of Egypt. He was with the fleeing Hebrews as they escaped through the Red Sea. He had been at Sinai and shrunk from the thunder as God spoke to His people. He had accompanied the nation in its forty-year wandering in the wilderness and with Caleb brought back a good report about the Promised Land. And as the nation's leader he had watched the Jordan waters miraculously roll back welcoming the children of God into the land of promise. This man had been there. He had a testimony. He knew there were decisions to be made in this life. Truth and lies are spread before us along with light, darkness, life and death. Decisions that only the individual can make – so choose you this day who you will serve.

This reminds us of John chapter 6 when the people who would have served an earthly King Jesus faded away when faced with the reality of a suffering servant. Jesus, turning to His disciples asked them, "You do not want to leave too, do you?" (John 6:67). Then Peter, speaking for the disciples and for the millions of men, women, boys and girls down through the centuries to come, said, "Lord, to whom shall we go? You have the words of eternal life. We believe and know that you are the Holy One of God" (John 6:68–69).

Christians are people who have confessed their poverty of spirit. They are people who know there is no one other than Jesus with the power to forgive sins and save them from the consequences of their actions. There is no one else who can offer a fresh start and a new beginning. Only God can take His people by the hand and lead them from slavery to freedom and joy inexpressible. The powers of Egypt are nothing to Him. The wilderness is nothing. The Red Sea is nothing. The Jordan is nothing. Walls, fortresses and armies are nothing. Communism was nothing, religious terrorism is nothing. The New Age and the false religious systems are nothing. The problems and perplexities of this life are as nothing. The old enemy death itself is to be faced fearlessly, secure in the knowledge that its sting is removed: nothing, but nothing "will be able to separate us from the love of God that is in Christ Jesus our Lord" (Romans 8:39).

God leads His people, and keeps them as the apple of His eye and does it day after day and year after year till He ushers them into His presence in glory. He did it then and He does it now. As their great earthly leader Joshua is about to die he brings them all together – all those children who God has for so long blessed and loved and says, "choose for yourselves this day whom you will serve" (Joshua 24:15).

Joshua's challenge to the nation of Israel still challenges us today. Great is the joy of the men and women who respond positively and want to serve God: the Promised Land is their inheritance.

# 7

# Judges
## – God's War against Humanism

The primary purpose of the book of Judges is to show how Israel's spiritual condition determined its political and material condition. In Joshua, an obedient nation – through trust in the power of God – conquered the land. But in Judges when a disobedient nation worshipped the gods of Canaan they were defeated in battle, and time and time again came under the rule of tyrants. As the book progresses through nearly 400 years, God raises up military champions to throw off the yoke of oppression and restore the nation to pure worship. However, all too soon the sin-cycle begins again as the nation's spiritual temperature grows cold and we see how Israel's plight worsens as it sets aside God's law and instead "everyone did as he saw fit" (21:25).

The message of Judges speaks to unbelief, hypocrisy and lack of faith within the covenant community – the church. It's for those who have an ear to hear God's Word.

## Setting the scene

The book of Joshua concludes with the Hebrew nation under the leadership of Joshua at Shechem as they prepared to consolidate their victories in the Promised Land. Joshua knew the nation's weak spots and before dying he called the people together to give his final word of encouragement and instruction. They responded positively to Joshua's speech and three times promised they would serve the Lord their God and obey Him. And the men and women of that generation remained faithful to their promise. We may well ask how could they not remain faithful when in sight of Abraham's altar, Jacob's well, Joseph's tomb and Joshua's memorial stones at Gilgal? But time passes, and the Israelites ask God, "Who will be the first to go up and fight for us against the Canaanites?" (Judges 1:1). This tells us that after the death of Joshua the enemy had in some measure recovered their strength and moved against Israel.

In the purposes of God there appear to be two strands in which history can be divided: on the one hand there are those who see history as linear progression – things move forward with the present building on the past; while on the other hand there are those who see history as a series of cycles where things tend to go round and round with little forward movement. This, it would appear, is the way of the Israelites in the book of Judges! This is demonstrated in the struggles of the tribal communities in the Promised Land.

In this, the earliest of their troubles, the Israelites went before the Lord not to enquire whether or not to fight, for the question was beyond debate. The man who led seventy kings captive was closing in and fight they must. The question was who would do it? The divine answer was that the royal tribe of Judah was to lead the fray. The battle was successful, King Adoni-Bezek was captured after an attempted escape, and verse 6 tells us the tribe of Judah cut off his thumbs and big toes. This form of mutilation, common in those days, was intended to render a man unfit for military service. For without thumbs you cannot wield a sword, spear or bow effectively, and the removal of the big toe adversely affects the balance (Judges 1:5–7).

Then the Israelites turned their attention to the enemy within their borders (1:17–18). City after city fell to them and did so because they were relying upon the power and promise of almighty God. If only they had maintained their faith and resisted the deceit of unbelief then nothing could have stopped them from bringing the entire country under their control and so coming into the inheritance of the land the Lord had promised to their fathers. Though they started well their progress began to falter, "The men of Judah also took Gaza, Ashkelon and Akron – each city with its territory" (Judges 1:18). That's wonderful, but there were five Philistine cities. What about Gath and Ashdod? They didn't capture them: "The Lord was with the men of Judah. They took possession of the hill country, but they were unable to drive the people from the plains, because they had iron chariots" (Judges 1:19). Excuse me! – "because they had iron chariots"? Didn't God bring them out of bondage in Egypt, part the Red Sea and annihilate the Egyptian army under its waters? Hadn't He stopped the flow of the Jordan, brought Jericho's walls tumbling down and brought them victorious into the Promised Land? And most telling of all hadn't God promised in Deuteronomy:

> *When you go to war against your enemies and see horses and chariots and an army greater than yours, do not be afraid of them, because the Lord your God, who brought you up out of Egypt, will be with you.*
>
> DEUTERONOMY 20:1

Did you notice that? He did include "chariots" didn't he? God was willing – but the Israelites lacked faith.

This is always the way in spiritual battles. Think of Paul challenging the Galatians: "You foolish Galatians! Who has bewitched you?" (Galatians 3:1) Or in the book of Revelation the Ephesian church seduced from her first love, the churches at Pergamum and Thyatira following Baal and Jezebel and the Laodecean church being led into cosy complacency (Revelation 2–3). Think of Christians today with the temptation to compromise or doubt – "Did God really say…?"

An important lesson to be learned from this episode is that the enemy remembers our failures. Five hundred years later the Syrians were encouraged to attack Israel and the argument to do so was based on this incident:

> *… the officials of the king of Aram advised him, "Their gods are gods of the hills. That is why they were too strong for us. But if we fight them on the plains, surely we will be stronger than they."*
>
> 1 KINGS 20:23

The problems are the same today when the church lacks faith to declare its belief in Scripture and the book of Judges shows us the consequences. Judah failed in the plains and now Benjamin fails to take Jerusalem (Judges 1:21). Consequently the city was not purged from idolatry, the tares and the wheat grew side by side and as it was in Jerusalem so it was throughout the land.

Manasseh fared no better. They failed to drive the enemy out, "for the Canaanites were determined to live in that land" (1:27). Of course they were. They were comfortable: it was home to them. It's the same for men and women today. It's our habits and sin, "they've grown accustomed to our ways", and it will take more than a New-Year-type resolution to defeat sin because of its insidious nature. Then again, "When Israel became strong, they pressed the Canaanites into forced labour but never drove them out completely" (1:28). It speaks for itself doesn't it? There are many reasons why unbelieving people may be actively involved in church life, for example worldly people who do not accept the authority of Scripture, yet enjoy a form of religion or church involvement and mingle with true believers. The problems become apparent when unbelievers take authority in the church. We find an example of this in this chapter: "Nor did Ephraim drive out the Canaanites living in Gezer, but the Canaanites continued to live there among them" (1:29). Gezer was commercially important. It was on the Mediterranean coast and well able to pay a large tax. See the temptation? "Leave us alone, we'll make it worth your while, think of all the good things you can do with our money." The Ephramites, tempted by worldly interests, turned a blind eye to sin in their midst and disobeyed God's command.

When it comes to Asher they were just as bad: "the people of Asher lived among the Canaanite inhabitants of the land" (1:32). The Hebrew word used here literally means "lived in the bowels of the Canaanites". This is when the people prefer low morals, lies and sleaze rather than fighting for the things of God.

In verse 34 the tribe of Dan was chased out of the cornfields back up the hillside to the very place where Joshua commanded the sun and moon to stand still and so win that incredible battle (Joshua 10:12–14). Now in that place, the detestable Canaanite tribes were the masters. So chapter 1 closes with its account of the failure of the tribes to eject the heathen from their territory. Verse 36 tells us that the Amorites had a border. This means they were so strong they had a clearly defined territory recognized as their own. They were not just hiding out in Israel's territory.

# A five-step cycle

Chapter 2 is the key chapter to the whole book of Judges. It encapsulates all that happens in Judges: the transition from godly to ungodly generations, the cycles of sin and salvation and the purpose of God in destroying the Canaanites.

Judges 3:5 – 16:31 describes seven enslavements and seven deliverances and each of the seven failings have five identical steps – rebellion, retribution, repentance, restoration and rest.

The cycle is fully described in Judges 3:7–11 when the first judge (Othniel from Judah) fights against the Arameans. Israel sins (3:7), this incurs God's anger (3:8a) and their subjection to the Arameans (3:8b), which causes them to pray for help (3:9a). God answers by sending a deliverer (3:9b) and the "Spirit of the Lord" empowers Othniel (3:10c), so the land knows peace for forty years (3:11b).

The second judge is Ehud from Benjamin who killed the overweight Moabite king Eglon and led the nation to freedom from Moabite repression (3:12–31).

Then Deborah from Ephraim turned her attention to the northern Canaanites who were oppressing the Israelites (4:1 – 5:31). The difference in this story is its focus on two women who overshadow the actual deliverer Barak. Deborah initiates the action in the name of the Lord and Barak's refusal to go into battle without her leads Deborah to prophesy that the Lord will hand over the enemy commander Siserea to a woman. The woman does not turn out to be Deborah but Jael (4:21). Deborah's song retells the story with some added details and while it praises God it also shames the tribes who did not help.

Judges 6:1 – 9:57 tells of Gideon from the tribe of Benjamin who fought against the Midianites and Amalekites. In his story there is much more detail. The narrator starts with the familiar, "Again the Israelites did evil in the eyes of the Lord". This time the oppression comes from hordes of easterners led by Midian and Amalek causing Israel to cry to God who reminds them they have broken their covenant with Him (6:7–10). Gideon is portrayed as fearful and doubting but obedient (6:11–40). He starts well by tearing down the altar of Baal (6:24–32) and leads a God-planned and orchestrated victory over Midian (chapter 7). But then attempting something of a personal vendetta over the death of his brothers he ends up siring a thoroughly degenerate son called Abimilech and falls into idolatry (8:19–27).

The downward spiral continues and Judges 10:6 – 12:14 introduces Jephthah from eastern Manasseh who fought the Ammonites and their allies. Jephthah is something of a successful outlaw when he responds to an appeal for help against the Ammonites (11:3–6). He comes across as rash and self-centred, and while he is successful in battle because the Spirit of the Lord was upon him he was also responsible for the deaths of thousands of Israelites (12:1–6).

Known as the "Minor Judges", Ibzan, Elon and Abdon now appear on the scene, and continuing the drift towards humanism, they show signs of desiring status and position. They also seem to see themselves as above certain aspects of the law, particularly the prohibitions against polygamy. As the trappings of kingship appear, the powerful were beginning to act less like the servants of the people and more like the aristocracy. Their attitude and lifestyle contrast sharply with Boaz in Ruth chapters 2 and 3.

The final chapter in the cycle story is fittingly the most tragic and confusing of them all, for Samson represented all that was wrong in Israel during the time of the judges. It's in Judges 13:1 – 16:31 where Samson is pitted against the Philistines.

Although unbeatable when the Spirit of God is with him, Samson breaks his Nazarite vows by taking honey from the carcass of a dead lion, disobeying his parents by marrying a non-Jewish girl and sleeping with a prostitute (chapters 14 and 16). All these sins mirror Israel's own story of disobedience to God's law and the nation's prostitution with the gods of Baal and Ashtoreth.

There's a lesson for us in the way Samson thinks he's in control but in fact is completely out of control. He has no idea of his calling to be judge and saviour or of the real nature of his Nazarite vow. Nor does he see how his inter-racial marriage with his Philistine wife is the complete opposite of the marriage relationship of the first judge Othniel, who married Caleb's daughter (1:13). He seems to be quite unaware that his fraternizing with the Philistines runs counter to everything his forefathers fought for. With such a man becoming leader: all action, and no understanding of anything that really matters, where can Israel expect to find the sound judgment so desperately needed? Nonetheless, the Spirit of God continues to come upon him until finally, blind and imprisoned, Samson is enabled by God to kill many Philistine leaders in a temple, though he himself dies in the process (16:23–30). This incident sets the stage for the long struggle with the Philistines that marks the reigns of Saul and David that are to come.

## The corruption of Israel

The book of Judges ends with two stories that illustrate Israel's corruption.

They are carefully crafted around the phrase, "In those days Israel had no king; everyone did as he saw fit" (17:6; 18:1; 19:1; 21:25).

The first episode, in chapter 17, reveals Israel's new age multi-faith society. Contrary to God's Law, Micah's mother donates her silver (which had been consecrated to Jehovah) for her son to make an idol. Also against God's Law, Micah then hires a non-Levite as his own priest to work in their private temple. Deluding himself, Micah is happy and believes his god is prospering his work. After all from his perspective he can't lose now, can he? He has a priest, a sanctuary, an ephod and an idol; he's got it made and hopes to live happily ever after. But his plans are built on sand and the tide is coming in with trouble on the way. Chapter 18 records how Micah's false gods prove unable to protect him and he loses his idols and his priest.

The second story, in chapter 18, gruesomely illustrates how folly, unbelief, disobedience and wickedness were the cause of the Israelites' failure to conquer the land. This leads us to understand that here in the book of Judges is a story of God's grace. Two great gospel truths from the pen of Paul might sum up the final message of Judges: "where sin increased, grace increased all the more" Romans 5:20 and "if we are faithless, he will remain faithful, for he cannot disown himself" (2 Timothy 2:13).

# 8

# Ruth
# – The Romance of Redemption

The Bible is a book for everyone and it should not be approached just as a technical, theological textbook, for then only scholars would scan its pages. Since the message of Christianity is essentially practical, the Bible presents it in living terms and the discerning reader takes in a great deal of theological truth as he or she moves from one human situation to another. The book of Ruth is a classic example of this. Here, theology is naturally and unobtrusively woven into human events as we are drawn into the experience of the three-times bereaved Naomi. We watch her part with one daughter-in-law but witness the refusal of another, Ruth, to leave her. Then, after Naomi and Ruth return to Bethlehem we are skilfully introduced to Boaz and his deepening relationship with the Moabitess Ruth.

This book, however, is more than a tale of two women or an exquisitely told love story. Against the background of increasing national anarchy that was described in the book of Judges, God is seen caring for two ordinary women. Loyalty, conversion, faith and sovereignty are defined in the narrative. Here is living theology for the housewife or househusband, the businessman or woman, the bereaved and the teenager: in short, a book for everyone.

## A new future

Emigrating to a strange country with a family is a major undertaking, and although Elimelech and Naomi would not be burdened with the contents of a modern home it nevertheless must have been a great upheaval for them to leave Bethlehem. It is not clear why Elimelech chose Moab, for it would not be the natural choice for an Israelite family. Centred on the high plateau east of the Dead Sea, Moab was populated by descendants of Lot (of Sodom and Gomorrah fame). The Moabites worshipped the god Chemosh in a ritual of human sacrifice, making it a very strange choice for a worshipper of Jehovah from Bethlehem to choose to live. In any respect, it didn't work out for this family for after a few years Elimelech died and his two boys married local girls. Sadly, both boys died leaving Naomi with her daughters-in-law Orpah and Ruth. Naomi is now a widow, with her husband, sons and inheritance all gone. What does the worship of Jehovah mean to her now?

It's a challenge to faith when a terrible accident or unexpected illness occurs. It may be a dad, a wife or child. It can be very personal and the temptation is to ask the question, "Why?" or even perhaps, "Why me?". Why has God dealt so harshly with these women? And Naomi's reaction "the Lord's hand has gone out against me!" (1:13) is an example of how, in times of trouble, we can be guilty of blaming God, which here resulted in Naomi crying, "Don't call me Naomi… Call me Mara [bitter], because the Almighty has made my life very bitter" (1:20).

Naomi, broken-hearted and poverty-stricken, decides to go back and die in her native land. She had no thought of taking her two daughters-in-law with her and as she clasps them in a farewell embrace they weep and lift up their voices to say that they will go with her back to the land of Judah.

Naomi now has the delicate task of explaining that if they go with her they will find no welcome from her people. Orpah weighs up the options: to go on to the new destination will mean great changes. It will mean a new life with challenges and struggles as she gives up her old way of life and leaves behind her people, friends and family and worshipping a God she did not know. Could she? Would she? In speaking to Ruth, Naomi records Orpah's decision: "Look… your-sister- in-law is going back to her people and her gods" (1:15).

Orpah had made her decision, she was staying in Moab. Now it's the moment of truth for Ruth. As she stood before Naomi with all these thoughts racing through her mind she weighed up the pros and cons of moving to Israel with its unsettled future and unknown trials. It seems almost foolish to choose that path. Naomi has already pointed out that to go back home to Israel with her would mean staying in the land with the people with whom she was unfamiliar. But it's more than that: it's a small still voice that speaks gently but persistently inside of Ruth, a voice that talks of compassion, faith and love. It's the voice of God, her maker, presenting her with an opportunity to respond to

His call to a new life. And with a resolution revealing a glimpse of fire, Ruth speaks to Naomi and to countless millions down the centuries with the most decisive confession of faith and love in all literature:

> *Don't urge me to leave you or to turn back from you. Where*
> *you go I will go, and where you stay I will stay. Your people*
> *will be my people and your God my God. Where you die I will*
> *die, and there I will be buried. May the Lord deal with me, be it*
> *ever so severely, if anything but death separates you and me.*
>
> RUTH 1:16–17

With her declaration of love, faith and loyalty, Ruth left behind her Moabite religion and moved into the arms of Jehovah promising a new life under His protection and love. In her statement, "Your God [will be] my God," we have a clear commitment. She grew up following other gods but now in her words, "my God," we understand her to have come into a personal relationship with God sealing it with her words, "May the Lord deal with me".

In Ruth's action we see how true conversion brings commitment to the Lord's people. "Your people will be my people" is the pattern of the New Testament. When men and women come into the Christian faith they identify, worship and get alongside their newfound brothers and sisters in Christ. When Ruth said, "Where you go I will go, where you stay I will stay," she stated another principle of conversion: to be identified with the Lord's people means being prepared to share in their joy and their sorrow. And her example of moving forward and putting the past behind her is very important. The statement, "Where you die I will die," speaks of life-long commitment.

## The stranger finds a friend

It should be borne in mind that Ruth, the main character of this story, is an ordinary woman: she is not a queen like Esther or a prophetess like Deborah but a straightforward Moabite girl, practical, honest and courageous. It has a real-world feel that's so important. It reminds us of Maria in the film *The Sound of Music* – remember how she was the girl who was definitely not an asset to the abbey? It's not Shakespeare, but it points to a real person with whom we can identify, and the same goes for Ruth.

Chapter 2 tells us that while the whole town was moved by Naomi's return it didn't seem to have touched their hearts to offer practical support.

And in need of food, Ruth made the decision to glean in the barley fields. The Law of Moses instructed landowners to leave behind what the harvesters had missed and allow the poor, the widow and the orphan to collect the leftovers. This Ruth decided to do and she providentially found work in a field belonging to Boaz, her kinsman: the man from her husband's family who was to change her life.

Does God lead and guide His children? Of course He does. Sometimes dramatically but generally through the unfolding of ordinary everyday events of life and His timing is perfect. "Just then Boaz arrived from Bethlehem and greeted the harvesters, 'The Lord be with you!' 'The Lord bless you!' they called back" (2:4). Then, obviously attracted to Ruth, "Boaz asked the foreman of his harvesters, 'Whose young woman is that?' The foreman replied, 'She is the Moabitess who came back from Moab with Naomi'" (2:5–6).

As the story develops Boaz ensures Ruth is looked after, and at the end of the day gives her a present of barley to take home with the promise that if she stays in the company of his servant girls there will be plenty (2:8–10). Ruth went away satisfied, and realizing that her good fortune didn't just happen by chance, she wanted to make Naomi happy by telling her the good news. This was the method God was using to bring Naomi back to Himself. Naomi responds with pleasure: "The Lord bless him… He has not stopped showing his kindness." Then she added: "That man is our close relative; he is one of our kinsman-redeemers" (2:20).

Naomi was a woman who had made a mistake: she had moved away from the Lord and the Lord brought her back to the place where the mistake was made, Bethlehem. This moment in the story is crucial; it's the pivotal point. The awakened hope in Naomi will renew her faith and change her life. For Ruth, the promise she made to follow the God of Israel is about to transform an already changed life into a future beyond her wildest dreams.

## The role of a kinsman-redeemer

In Israel's history, the Law in Deuteronomy 25:5–10 stated that a kinsman-redeemer was to be responsible for protecting the interests of the extended family. He would undertake to buy back land, which, due to adverse circumstances, had been sold outside the family. In addition, if someone fell into slavery due to debt then the redeemer would undertake to buy back their freedom. The story of Hosea buying his wife Gomer back from the slave auction is a case in point (Hosea 3:1–3). Finally, and most importantly for the story, if a male member of the family died and the redeemer was unmarried he was expected, if it suited his purposes, to marry the widow and ensure the inheritance stayed within the family.

## Cover me, my Kinsman-Redeemer

In chapter 3 the theme of redemption unfolds and as we follow the historical context we're being pointed towards the Great Redeemer, Jesus Christ. Through Ruth we learn that participation in the kingdom of God is not decided by birth or blood: Ruth was not a Jewess. It is decided by the conformity of one's life to the will of God through the obedience that comes from faith. As we follow through the events we find it starts by an admission of need: "I am your servant Ruth... spread the corner of your garment over me, since you are a kinsman-redeemer" (3:9). This was a delicate request for marriage. The "spreading of the garment" is referred to in Ezekiel 16:8 in the Lord's word of love to Israel:

> *Later I passed by, and when I looked at you and saw that you*
> *were old enough for love, I spread the corner of my garment*
> *over you and covered your nakedness. I gave you my solemn*
> *oath and entered into a covenant with you, declares the*
> *Sovereign Lord, and you became mine.*

Boaz certainly understood Ruth's request in terms of her desire for marriage, as we can gather from his response in Ruth 3:10. Some respected commentators are not too happy with Ruth's indiscreet actions, but we have to take into account the time that which passes between chapters 2 and 3. Both the wheat and the barley harvests have passed and there is the strong likelihood that Boaz and Naomi were in contact and Naomi was well aware of the honourable intentions of her relative towards Ruth. Certainly Naomi was correct in judging that the kindness showered on Ruth from Boaz was more than just sympathetic benevolence – he desired to marry her. We must interpret the story in the time and culture of the historical setting and not allow the crude sexuality of the twenty-first century to spoil what was a beautiful action by Ruth, demonstrating the trust and confidence she had come to have in Boaz as her kinsman-redeemer.

Here we sense Ruth's vulnerability in casting aside the protective shell that shields her from hurt and rejection. For trust and faith in God means lowering the barriers and allowing the real person to rise to the surface, making ourselves vulnerable – it is a humbling experience and is the reason the Spirit of God brings men and women to the "threshing floor". That's where God sorts out the wheat from the chaff and does what He longs to do – to remove the pride and fear and bring healing and deliverance. This is what the threshing floor is all about. At your Redeemer's feet is where you will find security, peace, happiness and satisfaction. It's the place where you open yourself up and say, "Here I am, wholly available. I need You. Spread the corner of your garment over me since You are my Kinsman-Redeemer." For Ruth to make this statement meant renouncing all else and taking Boaz for better or worse. It's that step of faith that makes it so easy to see why Jesus and the apostle Paul used marriage as His illustration of belonging to Him (Matthew 9:15; 25:1; Mark 2:19; John 3:29; Ephesians 5:23–29).

Ruth is saying in effect, what everyone who comes to Christ must say, "I, sinner, take Thee, Jesus, to be my lawful wedded Husband, to be faithful to You from this day forward, whether that is easy or difficult, whether rich or poor, in health or illness. I will love and cherish You. I make You that solemn promise." That's the spiritual route to salvation, and because it means opening up ourselves and exposing our vulnerability, many hold back and try to come to Jesus on their own terms. But God says, "No!" It has to be His way. It has to be from a broken and contrite heart, a cry for shelter and a cry of need.

The Bible teaches that until we become Christians all humankind are slaves to sin, serving our master, the devil (see Ephesians 2:1–3). We need to be redeemed from slavery, and it is the step of faith that takes us into the arms of our Kinsman-Redeemer, Jesus. He is related to us. His unique birth makes Him man, and though Mary was his human mother, God was His Father. He called God, Abba, which means "Daddy", and so will we when we come into His family. Then Jesus becomes our brother even though He is a King. Jesus our Kinsman wants to redeem us and take us out of our present lives to cleanse us, forgive us and give us a new life with a hope and a future.

But redemption has a price. To unlock the gates of heaven and move into paradise after our death carries a cost. We ask, "How much?" The answer is, "It's the blood sacrifice of a sinless man – spotless, pure, untainted blood."

"But," we reply, "we can't pay that price, our blood is contaminated by sin."

Well, that's the price demanded by God's law. That's the price your Kinsman-Redeemer will have to pay for your deliverance from the slavery of sin into the freedom of salvation.

In the action of Boaz we have a foreshadowing of the redeeming work of Jesus Christ. The redeemer must be a family member and Jesus is a member of our family, the seed of David according to the flesh. The redeemer must be able to pay the price of redemption and 1 Peter 1:18–19 assures us that Jesus can pay. It affirms: "it was not with perishable things such as silver or gold that you were redeemed… but with the precious blood of Christ, a lamb without blemish or defect."

The kinsman must be willing to redeem, and Galatians 4:4 tells us: "when the time had fully come, God sent his Son, born of a woman, born under law, to redeem those under law".

So Jesus qualifies as our Kinsman-Redeemer for as the Son of Man He is related. He wants to redeem us and can do so for that is His mission as the Son of God.

## The farmer finds a wife

Both the wheat and the barley harvests have passed and verse 3 of chapter 4 suggests Naomi was aware of the honourable intentions of Boaz towards Ruth. Boaz, heart in mouth, desperately wanted Ruth but was determined to honour God's Law. And the other fellow? (See 3:12.) Well, he wanted the field but not the responsibility of a wife, saying in effect: "You redeem her yourself, I cannot do it, I don't want her" (see 4:6). In truth, Ruth did not seem to have much going for her and in this she is a picture of our need for a redeemer.

The story unfolds in a dramatic and romantic way as Boaz cleverly negotiates with a rival kinsman. Motivated by love for Ruth and his willingness to give money for Ruth's sake and for the name of Elimelech, Boaz cleverly places this kinsman in the situation where he can do nothing but offer the right of redemption to Boaz, which means Ruth is legally able to marry him (4:6).

The story ends with Boaz and Ruth a happy couple with a future before them that they could not have dreamed of. Can you see how the church of Christ, with a dash of romance and mysticism should have seen in Ruth's husband, Boaz, a type of her own husband, Jesus Christ? For she, the church, like Naomi and Ruth, was disinherited, despised, forgotten and without a kinsman-redeemer in famine and in distress when His eye fell upon her – "and unto us a child was born". And His book, the Bible, testifies as to how well Jesus performed His Kinsman-Redeemer role. He not only redeemed us, but He brought us into His family, into His house and covered us with His mantle of love: "I, Jesus, take you, sinner, to be my lawful wedded wife, to be faithful to you from this day forward, I will love you, cherish you, and death will never set us apart. This I solemnly promise."

*So Boaz took Ruth and she became his wife. Then he went to*
*her, and the Lord enabled her to conceive, and she gave birth*
*to a son… Then Naomi took the child, laid him in her lap and*
*cared for him. The women living there said, "Naomi has a son."*
*And they named him Obed. He was the father of Jesse, the*
*father of David.*

RUTH 4:13, 16–17

Boaz the Bethlehemite and Ruth the Moabitess made a noble marriage. Their son, Obed, was the father of Jesse, the father of King David, whose son was Solomon, whose descendants led to Joseph and Mary and the child in the manger, Jesus Christ, the Son of the living God, our Kinsman-Redeemer.

# 9

# 1 Samuel
## – Samuel, Saul and David

The book of 1 Samuel describes the transition of Israel's leadership from judges to kings. The narrative centres on three prominent men: Samuel the last judge and first prophet (chapters 1–7), Saul the first king of Israel (chapters 8–31), and David the king-elect, anointed but not yet accepted (chapters 16–31).

## Samuel

Samuel's birth and call is recorded in chapters 1–3 and set during the turbulent time of the judges when Eli was the judge-priest of Israel.

The account surrounding Samuel's call in 3:1–10 seems to be a parable of the low spirituality in Israel at that time. In verse 2 we read that his (Eli's) "eyes were becoming so weak that he could barely see". This implies spiritual deterioration and is evidenced when God had to call Samuel three times before Eli recognized His call. Then we read in verse 3: "The lamp of God had not yet gone out". The light that had been lit in the triumphs of Joshua's day and which had burned fitfully during the time of the judges was now almost extinguished. When God did speak, His voice was continually mistaken for Eli's. And while verse 7 tells us that Samuel "did not yet know the Lord", we can rightly assume that God's voice was not known at that time in Israel. However, because of Samuel's responsiveness to God, he is confirmed as a prophet at a time when the word of the Lord was rarely heard (3:19–21).

The verses in 1 Samuel 3:11–19 contain the commission that was given to Samuel and God's prophetic revelation that He was about to bring great changes to the nation.

Chapter 4 then records the corruption at the temple in Shiloh by Eli's notoriously wicked sons, which led to Israel being defeated in battle. The ark was captured by the Philistines, the priesthood disrupted by the deaths of Eli and his sons and the glory of God departed from the tabernacle. This was all summed up by the name Ichabod that Eli's daughter-in-law gave to her newborn son, which literally means, "no glory" (4:21).

One of God's methods in dealing with the Israelites and the Philistines (which came to be seen as an example to the church and nations) was to prove to the people that they had underestimated Him. He did this by bringing them to the painful reality that the lives they had created for themselves apart from God and in defiance of Him were unmanageable and unbearable, and the basic cause of all their troubles. As God is unchanging, the same hard lesson has to be learned today: that our nation has to live with the consequences of the society it has created. The nation does not like this, for people are aware of being helpless in the face of the power, fears and passions they have allowed to be unleashed in their godless society. But no matter how it feels, God will allow the circumstances to get worse until, like Israel of old, the nation comes to its senses.

But God was also dealing with the pagan Philistines as well as with His own people. Perhaps the Philistines thought God was pleased with them or that He was weak or even dead! There was never a greater mistake for them to make. By a sequence of events, seemingly disastrous to Israel and culminating in the capture of the ark, God invaded the inner sanctuary of the powers of darkness and anti-Christ, and there in the temple of Dagon He demonstrated His unquestionable power and victory (5:3–5).

First, we see the idol Dagon flat on his face and his pitiable devotees having to re-erect and prop up their toppled god. Then we see nothing left of Dagon but bits and pieces; their god had disintegrated. But the ark of God, symbolizing His presence and His Law stood strong. The lesson for us is clear: set up the Word of God in the midst of the most diabolical situations, open it up and let it loose and there will be power released beyond human understanding which will confound the works of darkness.

Chapter 6 records God demonstrating that He is the almighty God outside of Israel as well as in it. His actions in demoralizing and punishing the Philistines set the stage for Samuel to assume his prophetic ministry which leads to a revival in Israel, the return of the ark, and twenty years later the defeat of the Philistines (7:3–17).

In chapter 8 we see how, when Samuel grew old and his sons proved to be corrupt judges, the people, wanting to be like the other nations, cry out for a king (8:1–3; 5–20). They had forgotten that the very reason for their existence was that they could be different from the other nations and set an example by having Jehovah as their king. The prophet Samuel was angry and annoyed by their demand and on three occasions warned them of the consequences. But in verse 7, "the Lord told him: 'Listen to all that the people are saying to you; it is not you they have rejected, but they have rejected me [the Lord] as their king.'"

The stage was now set for the introduction of Saul.

## Saul

The nation's impatience caused Israel to adopt the wrong standard by which to judge the personal attributes of their future king. This is confirmed in 1 Samuel 9:2: "Saul, [was] an impressive young man without equal among the Israelites – a head taller than any of the others" – it's all to do with outward appearance which is recognizable in our own celebratory culture today. It's a far cry from the apostle Paul's description of himself in 1 Corinthians:

> *I did not come with eloquence or superior wisdom… I came*
> *to you in weakness and fear, and with much trembling. My*
> *message and my preaching were not with wise and persuasive*
> *words, but with a demonstration of the Spirit's power, so that*
> *your faith might not rest on men's wisdom, but on God's power.*
> 1 CORINTHIANS 2:1, 3–5

Saul looked like the type of man on whom they could project their secret dreams and hopes. But underneath his handsome physique and charismatic personality he was flawed. His heart was dark with jealousy and his insecurity ran so deep that any hint of excellence in others was perceived as a personal threat to himself.

Of course this wasn't apparent on that great day at Gilgal (1 Samuel 11:14) when the nation of Israel gathered at the spot where Joshua had erected the memorial to the crossing of the Jordan. When the prophet Samuel led the people to rededicate their lives to God and crowned Saul as king, Saul's personality flaws were not apparent to the onlookers. They saw only his charm and natural ability, but Scripture records a steady downward progression in a series of incidents that give us the clue to Saul's personality problem.

## The first incident

The first occurrence appears in chapter 13. Saul's son Jonathan had attacked a Philistine outpost which was guaranteed to incur the enemy's wrath. The problem was that Israel was militarily weak. Verse 19 tells us that the Philistines prohibited the manufacture of weapons by the Jews. So here we have a critical situation with a huge Philistine army facing the poorly equipped Israelites. This presented Saul with a dilemma: in 1 Samuel 10:8 Samuel had instructed him to wait up to seven days for him to arrive and perform the religious ceremony before leading his men into battle. By the morning of the seventh day when Samuel had still not arrived the soldiers began to desert, thereby reducing Saul's 2,000 men to 600.

We can imagine what was going through Saul's mind: "Samuel, where are you? You said seven days, I can't wait much longer!"

Which begs the question: "Why, Saul? Tell us, why can't you wait?"

"If I wait any longer I'll have no army left!"

"Surely that's not your overriding concern? You're being obedient; you're waiting for Samuel just as you have been these past six days. Come on, Saul, tell us your real reason."

"I'll look a fool, I'm supposed to be king and unless I do something I'll be ridiculed, everyone will think Samuel controls me. I'll be small in their eyes!"

"What do you do then Saul? Do you wait till the seventh day is ended or do you take the matter into you own hands and exert your authority even though to do so is against the express wish of God's anointed prophet, Samuel?"

Saul's decision is to go ahead and perform the religious ceremony himself. Samuel's anger at what he did and his warning of the consequences for Saul is recorded in 1 Samuel 13:13–14.

## The second incident

Another clue to Saul's personality problem appears in chapter 14.

Again, it's Jonathan who sparks it off. This time accompanied only by his armour bearer, Jonathan attacks a garrison of Philistines. It's a bold attack and twenty of the enemy are slain. God then caused the enemy to think it was a much larger Israelite raiding party so they panicked in retreat. Saul's lookouts reported this to him and he gave the order to attack but foolishly instructed his army to fast until that evening (14:24). It was a rash decision that placed his men at a physical disadvantage at a time when extra strength and stamina were required. But as Saul had bound the people under an oath before the Lord it was not to be taken lightly.

Meanwhile, Jonathan, separated from the main Israeli force and unaware of Saul's oath, was in hot pursuit of the enemy. Noticing honey he collected it on the tip of his staff and ate to regain his strength. However, when Saul realized the Lord was not giving him victory in battle he knew sin had been committed and sought the guilty party, rashly promising that even if his own son Jonathan was the guilty man, he would die. And of course eventually he discovers Jonathan unknowingly did eat some honey, and astonishingly he really is prepared to sacrifice his innocent son (14:44). But the people, who did not agree with Saul's original foolish decision requiring a ban on eating and his subsequent rash promise to punish by death any who disobeyed, said, "No!" pointing out that it was completely inappropriate to take the life of the one God had used to deliver His people from the Philistines.

The implication in the account is clear: Saul had placed himself in a humiliating position, with his son and the people being right, and he being wrong. He refused to admit that he was mistaken in the first place, even when God's Word, the people and common sense all pointed it out to him. His reaction warns us of the length Saul will go to in order to avoid what he considers to be public humiliation.

## The third incident

Chapter 15 explains Saul's problem.

In verse 3 God, through Samuel, commands Saul to "attack the Amalekites and totally destroy everything that belongs to them." Saul attacked and won the battle but verse 9 records that "Saul and the army spared Agag and the best of the sheep and cattle, the fat calves and lambs – everything that was good. These they were unwilling to destroy completely, but everything that was despised and weak they totally destroyed."

When Samuel arrived on the scene Saul told him, "I have carried out the Lord's instructions" (verse 13). You can just imagine Samuel's raised eyebrows: "What then is this bleating of sheep in my ears? What is this lowing of cattle that I hear?" (verse 14). Saul then attempted to justify his disobedience, which led to Samuel reaching the bottom line:

> *To obey is better than sacrifice,*
> *and to heed is better than the fat of rams.*
> *For rebellion is like the sin of divination,*
> *and arrogance like the evil of idolatry.*

*Because you have rejected the word of the Lord,*
*he has rejected you as king.*

1 SAMUEL 15:22B–23

The point Samuel was making is that the Lord was not, and is never, interested in show and pretence. External form without inward obedience is an offence to God. Saul's own will was his own "god" – and he proved it in his telling reply to Samuel's rebuke in verse 24: "I have sinned. I violated the Lord's command and your instructions. I was afraid of the people so I gave in to them." Here we see the giveaway in Saul's reply. Even though he's guilty of gross disobedience and sin, and been stripped of his kingship by God, his main concern is to be honoured before the elders and the people of Israel. In other words Saul is more concerned with what his peers think of him than with what God thinks of him. His overriding regard for himself displayed in his general disobedience shows his lack of genuine faith in God.

# David

Chapter 16 begins the story of Saul and David.

Saul remained king for seven years till his death and it was to be a further three years before David sat on the throne of a united kingdom. These years were used by God to train David and advance the work of His kingdom for the ultimate blessing of His people. God would also use David as a "type" of Christ to foreshadow and point towards a better king and a more enduring kingdom not yet revealed. And, just as Christ's kingdom would be inaugurated in the least likely circumstances of a manger in Bethlehem, God ordered Samuel to go to that same town to anoint the least likely person as the nation's future king.

When Samuel arrived at Bethlehem no one involved in that family drama would have ever thought David, the least of Jesse's sons, would be God's choice of Israel's future king. The term "the youngest" (16:11) carries overtones of "the least", the "insignificant one". As far as Jesse was concerned it hadn't been worth even introducing David to Samuel and the prophet had no idea he was God's chosen one. In fact, Samuel would have chosen Eliab as God's anointed (verse 6). Here we see how strange it is that Samuel was drawn to another just like Saul. This confirms the human tendency to choose men and women by their outward appearance, their presence and substance, even when that method of selection has failed in the past. The Bible's answer to this is in one of the most powerful verses in Scripture. It's a beautiful statement from

God to us in 1 Samuel 16:7: "The Lord does not look at the things man looks at. Man looks at the outward appearance, but the Lord looks at the heart."

This raises the question: Why anoint David as king such a long time before he is appointed and crowned?

Firstly, the Spirit which came upon Saul for his kingly service can now be removed and placed upon David. It is in the Spirit that David will now grow and mature and minister to Saul as God prepares him for service. How ironic and unexpected that David will serve the king to prepare him to serve as king. How true it is that God's Word and His ways are not our ways (Isaiah 55:9).

Secondly, the anointing of David resulted in a test for all the Israelites. David's anointing, unlike Saul's, was semi-public. His father and brothers as well as the prominent men of the city who were attending the sacrificial feast knew that the new king to replace Saul was being designated and their response to him would determine their place in David's kingdom. This was illustrated in the story of the fool Nabal and his wise wife Abigail in chapter 25. Nabal knew exactly who David was and refused to have anything to do with him because he might suffer repercussions from Saul. Abigail was a wise and godly woman who also knew who David was and her response and appeal to David was based upon her submission to him as her coming king. So David's early designation as Israel's future king thus becomes a test for the population.

In chapter 17 we see how God moved the young insignificant man David, to the forefront of the nation's consciousness and so prepare the way for him to be accepted as its future king by giving him an astonishing victory over the apparent invincible enemy giant, Goliath.

While that is the main purpose of the story, biblical typology also allows us to "see" David as a "type" of Christ and the victory won by Jesus and what it means to Christian men and women.

The Philistine champion is described in 17:4–11 in terms of his towering physical stature and impressive armour. There is no doubt this man was a formidable foe. Goliath represents Satan. He is strong and frightening, standing at the forefront of an army intent on attacking the people of God. Facing him on the other side of the divide is his opponent, the Christian church. They are the great army of God's people in a covenant relationship with their Creator through the blood of the cross as a result of the atoning sacrifice of the Son of God. They are men and women who, indwelt by the Holy Spirit, belong to the Lord Jesus Christ. Yet, like the Israelites in the valley of Elah, they seem helpless against such a powerful adversary. Yes, they are a well-equipped army. Yes, by and large they are organized. Yes, they know their enemy and are all set for battle. But like the Israelites they often seem unable to cope with the powers of darkness ranged against them. And isn't it significant that the Israelites were led by a man who through his disobedience had lost his anointing of the Spirit of God and as a result the army was in fear and disarray. It's not the size of Goliath or his arrogance that should cause us to wonder but rather the unbelief and fear of God's people. The situation is neither new nor novel. The odds are no worse here than elsewhere. Israel simply lacked faith and godly leadership. The man chosen on behalf of God's people to fight the Philistine champion would decide the outcome of the war, and just as Spirit-filled David was destined to be Israel's champion, we see in his preparation and victory over Goliath a foreshadowing of the life and ministry of our Lord and Saviour Jesus Christ.

It's heart-warming and encouraging for the people of God.

David, when called by God to enter His service, was publicly anointed for his future position by Samuel (1 Samuel 16:13) and in the same way Jesus, the carpenter from Nazareth, was likewise publicly anointed and Spirit-filled (Matthew 3:16). David was sent by his father Jesse to the battleground (1 Samuel 17:17) and the apostle John tells us "we have seen and testify that the Father has sent his Son to be Saviour of the world" (1 John 4:14). The commencement of this conflict is recorded in Matthew with the account of Jesus facing Satan in the wilderness for forty days and nights (Matthew 4:1–11). When David arrived at the battlefront he was derided heartlessly by his elder brother Eliab: "I know how conceited you are and how wicked your heart is; you came down only to watch the battle" (1 Samuel 17:28). Just as David was scorned by his brothers when he arrived at the theatre of war, it was said of Jesus: "He came to that which was his own, but his own did not receive him" (John 1:11). When David walked down into the valley of Elah to face a frightening opponent he looked so vulnerable and weak. In exactly the same way didn't the Lord Jesus look vulnerable and weak when He stumbled through the cobbled streets of Jerusalem carrying His cross upon His bloodstained shoulders? And just as two great armies watched breathlessly, aware that the outcome of this encounter would decide the future fate of their country, so too the hordes from hell cheered on Satan and were confident of victory over the despised and seemingly insignificant carpenter from Nazareth who was watched over anxiously by His army of angels from glory.

It's basic Christian doctrine. It's not Satan against the Christian army; it's Satan against God, against Jesus Christ. And He, our representative, settled the battle and its outcome when He won the war on a blood-soaked cross on Calvary's hill. As Colossians 2:15 confirms: "having disarmed the powers and authorities, he made a public spectacle of them, triumphing over them by the cross". David here in 1 Samuel 17 is a forerunner of the Lord Jesus. All who follow the vanquished Satan will follow him in defeat and death and all who follow the Lord Jesus Christ will enjoy deliverance and victory. Think of this: Christian believers are "in Christ"; He is the head, we are His body. Therefore, as we are in His body, and as He has won the conflict over Satan and darkness, so have we.

The final chapters of 1 Samuel dwell on the personal vendetta that Saul waged against his renowned son-in-law.

Chapter 18 records how Saul's jealousy of David became homicidal and he tried to get rid of his young rival by violence and cunning but David emerged unscathed with the king's daughter for his wife (18:27).

Eventually Saul's relentless hostility drove David into exile (chapter 19). The narrative that follows, of David's exploits with his band of outlaws at the cave of Adullam, his acquisition of Goliath's sword, his pretence of madness in order to deceive the Philistines and his elusiveness and generosity of spirit are the stuff of legend. However, Saul's unpredictable mad fits eventually drove David to seek protection from the Philistines. For his base he was given the town of Ziklag from which, unbeknown to his apparently dull-witted Philistine patron, he and his confederates continued to attack the enemies of Israel (chapter 27).

However, larger issues are now impending as the Philistines mass for a full-scale attack against Israel. Their princes, more shrewd than David's protector, refuse to allow him to take his place in their ranks. He therefore returns to Ziklag and uses the opportunity to wipe off an old Israelite score against the Amalekites who are never heard of as a tribe again (chapter 29).

As you read these closing chapters you cannot help but notice the way in which God led David step by step from a low period in his life to the high ground of the joy of knowing and pleasing the Lord. It's an illustration of what our Father in heaven often does in the lives of His children. The way in which Jesus woos believers through His Spirit is often an uncomfortable wooing, but the low path of humbling is a sure sign of His love for us and is how the Holy Spirit brings us into a close and personal relationship of faith, obedience and devotion to the Lord. We see this in the way God let David have his own way by allowing him to enmesh himself in the silken threads of lies, then the thick cords of treachery, and finally in the chains of deceit until poor deluded David was so trapped by his life of lies that the only way out was by a mighty intervention of God's gracious providence. Rocked by the capture of his women and children at Ziklag (chapter 30), David was brought to an awareness of his helpless state without God, and then by the grace of God to a renewal of his faith. The windows of heaven then opened and the blessing that poured out was more than David could speak of.

Meanwhile, facing the Philistine invasion with the knowledge that God had deserted him, in desperation the ill-fated Saul consults the witch of Endor in the hope that the spirit of the dead Samuel might give him counsel and comfort (chapter 28). The ghostly voice had nothing to offer but death, and the sombre prophecy was fulfilled the following day when the Israelite army was massacred. Saul's sons were killed in battle and Saul took his own life. And if it were not for the grateful homage of some brave men from Jabesh Gilead who remembered their benefactor, his dishonoured body would have been left to rot on the walls of Beth Shan (chapter 31).

In this way the book of 1 Samuel ends with the death of one of Scripture's most unfathomable characters and opens the way for David to ascend to the throne of Israel.

# 10

# 2 Samuel
## – The Life of David

In 1 Samuel we saw David being trained by God in the fields as a shepherd, in the palace as a musician and courtier, and while a fugitive in the wilderness as a leader of fighting men. Each role prepared him for the position to which he had been appointed and anointed. After Saul's death, in which David had no part, he became king of Judah where he reigned in Hebron for seven-and-a-half years then in Jerusalem from where he reigned over all Israel for thirty-three years. Historically, the book is placed halfway between Abraham and the birth of Christ and can be viewed in three parts: chapters 1–10, David's victories; chapters 11–12, David's disgrace; and chapters 13–24, David's difficulties.

## David's victories

Chapters 1–4 record David's seven-year reign in Judah. Even though Saul had been his greatest enemy David did not rejoice at his death, for he recognized Saul had been divinely appointed as king. Saul's chief military officer, Abner, installed Saul's son, Ish-Bosheth, as a puppet king over the northern tribes of Israel. However, Ish-Bosheth was defeated in battle by David causing Abner to switch allegiance to David, thus bringing the northern tribes with him. But David's military commander Joab forestalled that by killing Abner in revenge for the murder of Joab's brother (3:27). Ish-Bosheth, now powerless, was killed by his own men and at thirty years of age David was made king of Israel (5:3).

David soon captured and fortified Jerusalem and made it the civil and religious centre of the now united kingdom of Israel. Under his rule the nation prospered politically, spiritually and militarily. In chapter 7 David brought the ark of God back to Jerusalem and with his enemies defeated and the nation at peace he lived in royal splendour with time to devote to other enterprises. Seeing the ark of the Lord housed in a tent, the plan to build a house – a temple for God – takes shape in David's mind. So he calls his friend and confidant, the prophet Nathan, and outlines his intentions. Believing David's plans will be pleasing to God, Nathan approves. But that night God corrects Nathan and he has to return to David with his revised prophetic evaluation that God has something incomparably more wonderful in mind than anything David can plan. David, full of what he's going to do for God, is now subjected to a comprehensive rehearsal of what God has done, is doing and will do for him. What yesterday looked like a bold initiative by David for God now looks trivial by comparison to what God is going to do for David instead.

God promised David three things: a land forever (7:10); an unending dynasty (7:11, 16) and an everlasting kingdom (7:13, 16). But he will not be allowed to build the temple, and 1 Chronicles 22:8 tells us why: "You have shed much blood and have fought many wars. You are not to build a house for my Name, because you have shed much blood on the earth in my sight."

David could be a prophet and a king but his hands were too bloodstained to be a priest. He would not be the right person to build the temple of God that was to be the symbol of peace and rest, so God said, "No!"

Here's the marvellous lesson for us today: David's acceptance of God's refusal became the opportunity for him to experience tremendous blessing. It's recorded in 2 Chronicles 6 when, years in the future, Solomon, David's son, had completed the Temple and was dedicating it to the Lord, he said:

> *My father David had it in his heart to build a temple for the*
> *Name of the Lord, the God of Israel. But the Lord said to*
> *my father David, "Because it was in your heart to build a*
> *temple for my Name, you did well to have this in your heart.*
> *Nevertheless, you are not the one to build the temple, but your*
> *son, who is your own flesh and blood – he is the one who will*
> *build the temple for my Name."*
>
> 2 CHRONICLES 6:7–9

How we react when God says, "No!" is vitally important. For the temptation is to sit down in despair and let our life and ministry go to waste. David did not do that. On the contrary, God's refusal became for him the occasion for tremendous blessing.

Think of the Lord's word to David that he did well to have the desire within his heart, and how comforting that must have been to him. It means the person rejected by God for a specific ministry is on a far higher level before the Lord than the person who has never felt the desire to be committed to serve him.

David sets the example that if you can't go you can send someone else; if you can't build you can gather the materials. The vision does not need to have been in vain even though it remains unfulfilled by you. For God's refusals are loaded with incredible opportunities. It all depends upon our response when He says, "No!" Do we sulk or seek? God never rejects an aspiring servant. He whispers into the heart a word of encouragement: It was good to have the desire. Encouraged by this word of assurance David gave himself wholeheartedly to the task of gathering the materials needed to build the temple and years later when his son, Solomon, built the Temple, it would be known as "David's Temple".

## The Davidic covenant

God's promise to David in chapter 7, known to us as the Davidic covenant, has a special significance. First, it led David to write Psalm 18, which is first recorded in 2 Samuel 22:1–51. This is a prophetic foretaste of the promised Messiah in whom the deeper meaning of David's kingdom would be fulfilled. Second, it calls us to look beyond the immediate context concerning the Israelite nation and see in the future the advent of the kingdom of God in the person and work of the Lord Jesus Christ. So important was this prophetic event in David's life that from then on his descendants always kept careful records of their family tree wondering if their son might be the son of David spoken of in the covenant (see 2 Samuel 7:14). This promise became the focus of national hope as the Jews waited expectantly for their promised Messiah.

A thousand years later the promise was fulfilled when Jesus was born in David's birthplace, Bethlehem, to a humble couple of the royal birth line. Jesus was the legal son of David through Joseph his father, but also a physical son of David through his mother Mary (Matthew 1:1–16; Luke 3:23–37). He was twice over the "Son of David" and that was a title by which He was known throughout His life. These writings proclaim that all authority in heaven and on earth is given to the Son of David. Such authority is Jesus' for all time and eternity.

# David's disgrace

Chapter 11 begins the story of King David's disgrace. His crimes of adultery and of murder were a catastrophe that plunged him from the pinnacle of success to the valley of despair and would tear his family and the nation apart in the years to come.

By committing adultery with Bathsheba, David inexorably slides towards tragedy. It warns us that if a man of David's character can fall like this we must all be on our guard. Notice, too, just after he sleeps with Bathsheba, Scripture places the words of verse 4 in brackets, "(She had purified herself from her uncleanness)", which means that David cannot deny responsibility for her pregnancy.

The news of Bathsheba's pregnancy filled David with dismay, for her husband Uriah was one of the nation's heroes. If their crime was revealed the consequences for Israel would have been disastrous for, strictly speaking, both David and Bathsheba deserved death by stoning. Something had to be done quickly. David's answer was to give Uriah leave of absence from the army to enjoy time with his wife so that the child would be assumed to be his. But Uriah was a better man than David gave him credit for, and he refused the pleasures of wife and home while his fellow soldiers were serving at the front.

To grasp the full impact of Uriah's words in verse 11 you have to go back to 1 Samuel 21:1–5. When David first fled from Saul he went to Ahimelech the priest and asked for some provisions and a sword. The priest only had sacred bread, which he would allow David and his men to eat only if they had "kept themselves from women" (1 Samuel 21:4). David's answer and especially the tone of it is significant to our current text. He confidently assured the priest that he and his men had kept themselves from women and was angry the priest would think otherwise. And the reason that David gives for this is that he and his men are on a mission for the king. The inference is that this is a military (or at least an official) mission.

Do you see the irony? David, years earlier, was adamant that those on a mission for the king should keep themselves from sexual intercourse. Now, years later, David is amazed that a man on a mission for the king is willing to abstain for the same reason. Worse, David sets out to encourage Uriah not to do so though it will cause Uriah to violate his conscience. This is not "causing a weaker brother to stumble" (see Romans 14:20); this is cutting off a stronger brother's legs at the knee. Uriah is now acting like the David we knew from earlier days. Uriah is the "David" that David should be.

Uriah's refusal to enjoy the comforts of home left David with a mounting sense of desperation at the inevitable consequences of the exposure of his guilt. So, if Uriah would not oblige by sleeping with his wife and become the public "father" of David's child, then the mother of David's child must become David's wife. David's national image as an upstanding family man must be maintained at all costs, and the cost would be the elimination of innocent, upright and unsuspecting Uriah.

The order given to Joab by David to place Uriah in the most dangerous part of the battle and then withdraw support from him was pre-meditated murder (2 Samuel 11:14–15). The Ammonites had retreated into their city and were prepared to withstand a siege, and Joab, David's skilled commander, knew where their greatest warriors were stationed and obeyed his orders, as a man in his position was expected to do. He was aware that the Hittite had fallen out of the king's favour but whether or not he knew the reason for the execution is not revealed. Maybe he was aware of David's misconduct; however, it's recorded, "Uriah the Hittite died" (2 Samuel 11:17). We could paraphrase David's response in verse 25 as, "Don't worry about it, that's the way it goes," which sounds heartless. Uriah, a great warrior and a man of godly character has just died, and David does not express a word of grief or sorrow or even a word of tribute. Uriah dies and David is unmoved. This is not the David of a few chapters earlier; this is a David hardened by his own sin.

So, here we have this man of God, nearly fifty years of age, married with adult children, king of Israel with an obligation to set a moral example to the nation, committing the foulest crimes of adultery, deception and murder.

His cover-up in place, Bathsheba moved into the palace, after a suitable time of mourning, as David's latest wife and the baby was born. As far as David was concerned his tracks were covered; dead men tell no tales. But one enormous problem remained – it's told in verse 27: "the thing David had done displeased the Lord."

About a year later, when the son of the illicit union was rocking in his cradle, it looked as though David has got away with it. But not so, a price was being paid: David was a very unhappy man. Verse 3 of Psalm 32, which he wrote at that time, records:

> *When I kept silent,*
> *my bones wasted away*
> *through my groaning all day long.*

This from the man who had walked and talked with God and known the power and authority of the Holy Spirit. But, as he resisted the pressure of the Spirit and fought against guilt and confession of sin, his soul became dry and barren.

## God sends the prophet Nathan

Then God, who always sooner or later confronts His children with their sin, sent the prophet Nathan to be His instrument in the king's humbling, and from this we must learn the importance of Proverbs 27:6 (KJV): "Faithful are the wounds of a friend; but the kisses of an enemy are deceitful." True friendship is honest.

The indirect approach Nathan took in chapter 12 is instructive. He told a story and solicited an opinion designed to prevent David from flaring up in the kind of violent defensiveness that often results from a guilty response to direct confrontation.

The story that Nathan told David was that of a rich man who stole a poor man's precious lamb to serve to a guest, and almost before Nathan had finished the story David burst out, "As surely as the Lord lives, the man who did this deserves to die!" (12:5). At David's outburst the prophet turned to him with the arrow of God and drove it home: "You are the man!" (12:7). Thunderstruck, David immediately realized he was the rich man, Bathsheba the stolen lamb and Uriah the poor man. Condemned out of his own mouth he stood guilty before the bar of heaven. Without pause, Nathan proclaimed the findings of the judge: "This is what the Lord, the God of Israel, says".

First, he reminded David, God had done great things for him (12:7–8). Second, he rebuked David for despising the word of the Lord in killing Uriah and taking Bathsheba for a wife (12:9), and thirdly (12:10–12) he pronounced a two-fold sentence in which the punishment will fit the crime: the sword will never depart from his house. And what David did in secret would be done to him in public.

It was at this time David wrote Psalm 51, which contains such moving and powerful verses as:

> *Have mercy on me, O God,*
> *according to your unfailing love;*
> *according to your great compassion*
> *blot out my transgressions.*
> *Wash away all my iniquity*
> *and cleanse me from my sin.*

*For I know my transgressions,*
*and my sin is always before me.*
*Against you, you only, have I sinned*
*and done what is evil in your sight,*
*so that you are proved right when you speak*
*and justified when you judge...*

*Cleanse me with hyssop, and I will be clean;*
*wash me, and I will be whiter than snow.*
*Let me hear joy and gladness;*
*let the bones you have crushed rejoice.*
*Hide your face from my sins*
*and blot out all my iniquity.*

*Create in me a pure heart, O God,*
*and renew a steadfast spirit within me.*
*Do not cast me from your presence*
*or take your Holy Spirit from me.*
*Restore to me the joy of your salvation*
*and grant me a willing spirit, to sustain me.*

PSALM 51:1–4, 7–12

We see that the son born through David and Bathsheba's illicit relationship died as a further indication of God's displeasure towards David (2 Samuel 12:18–19). (Later, David and Bathsheba were favoured by God as a couple because another son, Solomon, was born whom the Lord blessed (12:24).)

## David's difficulties

And so began David's difficulties recorded in chapters 13–24.

Having confessed his guilt and having been restored to the Lord, David could get on with his life, but his glory and fame fade and were never the same again as the prophecy of the sword in his house plagued him.

As you read these chapters you realize that although David received divine pardon for his sins he also began to reap that which he had sown. Something seems to have snapped somewhere, the bonds of integrity in his home life collapsed and David seemed unable to cope with it. His son Amnon sinned sexually with his half-sister, Tamar, and David had sinned sexually with

Bathsheba. Absalom, David's spoiled child, arranged the murder of his brother Amnon as David did Uriah, and as David watched his family fall apart around him, he seemed powerless to do anything about it – which of course he was.

Verse 21 of chapter 13 tells us David was furious when he heard about Amnon's rape of Tamar but he was incapable of exercising any real discipline. How could he rebuke his son for his crime against his sister when the memory of his own crime against Bathsheba was so recent in his heart? And how could he discipline Absalom for murdering Amnon when the death of Uriah was on his own conscience?

Then, motivated more by sentimentality than common sense, David allowed Absalom to return home from exile. But he did so without a deserved discipline or adequate safeguard that would have brought his son properly under his control and authority. Absalom repaid his father by fostering a rebellion against him. Says 2 Samuel 15:6, "he stole the hearts of the men of Israel." David not only lost control of his family but also of the national government of Israel. When he was forced to flee Jerusalem while Absalom set himself up as king he was never more vulnerable, and would have been ruined had not God prevented Absalom from pursuing him, thus allowing time for David to escape and rebuild his army.

Yet, in spite of all David's personal failures, his reaction to the punishing hand of God, by admitting that though his sin was forgiven he had to accept the personal consequences for it, proved he was still a man after God's own heart.

We can fight against God's discipline and harden our proud hearts against it. We can resist and refuse to accept it, we can deny it and become hard and callous and we can do all that with the outward appearance of normality. But unless and until we accept that God's discipline is justly deserved and for our own good, we will damage ourselves and others whom we love. We have to allow the potter to take the clay that has been spoiled and in His loving hands make a new vessel for His use.

How did David feel? You can read his thoughts in Psalm 3 where we see him accepting his chastening from the Lord. He goes to sleep happily and awakens in the morning brightly for the Lord is his shield and helper.

In Chapter 18, Joab disobeyed David's order to spare his son and killed Absalom. Chapter 20 records David trying to consolidate the kingdom as fighting breaks out between the ten northern tribes of Israel and the two southern tribes of Judah and Benjamin. Joab defeats the rebels in this civil war and peace ensues.

The closing chapters are not in chronological order and refer to previous incidents in David's life. They act as an appendix to the book, summarizing David's words and deeds, showing quite conclusively how intimately the affairs of the people as a whole are tied to the spiritual and moral condition of the king.

And so to chapter 23:

> *These are the last words of David:*
>
> *The oracle of David, son of Jesse,*
> *the oracle of the man exalted by the Most High,*
> *the man anointed by the God of Jacob,*
> *Israel's singer of songs:*
>
> *"The Spirit of the Lord spoke through me;*
> *his word was on my tongue."*
>
> 2 SAMUEL 23:1–2

In spite of David's sins he remains a man after God's own heart because of his repentant and responsive attitude towards God. His story, warts and all, tells how he sometimes fails in his personal life but through God's grace retains his relationship with Him. Unlike many of the kings who succeeded him, he never allowed idolatry to become a problem during his reign and his is the standard by which all future kings will be measured.

David set himself to free his country from its enemies, to secure it against invasion, and to unite the people as one nation. Making Jerusalem the national capital was the work of his hands and he strove to make it the religious and political centre of his kingdom. He was in every sense David the king, yet his life and history, written for us in his psalms, are a magnificent lesson on the human dilemma of spiritual progress and warfare lived out in his life. Who of us cannot sympathize with David as he struggles to come to terms with human weakness and strives for what is good and best? His anguished soul searching for what is right? His perplexities over the paradoxes? His never-ending struggle against the dark forces within and without leading to tears of repentance until, encouraged to rise again, he struggles back to get on with life in the sphere to which God has called him? Haven't we all faced similar challenges in life? They may, of course, not be like David's adultery and murder, but there are other areas where we may have failed the Lord, repented, received His forgiveness and been raised up by God to "live" again.

When David finally died, it was with the quiet exultant epitaph recorded in 1 Chronicles 29:28: "He died at a good old age, having enjoyed long life, wealth and honour." He went to be with the Lord and entered into the quiet rest of the redeemed in heaven.

Meanwhile the promises of God's everlasting covenant remained in the hearts, lives and experiences of God's people, awaiting their revelation in fullness with the advent of Jesus, the Son of David, to be the once-and-final Saviour of sinners, the King of kings and Lord of lords.

# 11

# 1 Kings
## – Kings and Prophets

The book of 1 Kings divides clearly into two sections: chapters 1–11, the united kingdom, and chapters 12–22, the divided kingdom.

## David's last days

The first two chapters recounting David's last days can hardly be called inspiring. We find him now a frail seventy-year-old, still susceptible to pretty women and still holding on to the throne. There were two rival claimants for the succession: Adonijah, full brother of Absalom and apparently equally spoiled, and Solomon, son of David's favourite wife Bathsheba who now reveals herself as a formidable champion of her own flesh and blood. On Adonijah's side the most notable support came from the ruthless old Joab, while Solomon's claim had backing from, among others, Nathan the prophet. Between them, Bathsheba and Nathan managed to persuade the elderly King David to nominate Solomon as his successor, and while Adonijah is holding a feast to celebrate what he thinks is his succession, back in the palace at Jerusalem Solomon is anointed king (1:5–53).

# The beginning of Solomon's reign

Solomon came to the throne in 970 BC. Recorded in 1 Kings 2:12–46 is how Solomon inaugurated his reign with a bloodbath in which he disposed of Adonijah, Joab and Shimei, the last significant survivor of the house of Saul, and finally Abiathar, the last of the priestly house of Eli, was removed from his office. Having removed all likely sources of opposition, Solomon made Benaiah commander-in-chief of the army and Zadok head of the priesthood, and lost no opportunity to make Israel a byword for economic prosperity as he brought the nation to its peak of prestige and glory. In this he was greatly helped by his legendary wisdom (3:1–15). But wisdom and greatness, although admirable and highly desirable, are in themselves insufficient to guarantee spiritual progress and stability. We must walk in daily dependence on God or we will fall and fail. And in Solomon we see how there was always a mixture of good and evil that prevented him reaching the status of an Abraham or a David. Outwardly, he looked magnificent in his power and kingdom achievements, but the weakness was there and it brought on the collapse of the empire in the next generation.

# Construction and dedication of the Temple

Solomon's construction and dedication of the Temple occupies chapters 5:1 – 8:66.

For this purpose he enlisted the aid of Hiram, king of Tyre, who provided craftsmen and timber from the renowned cedars of Lebanon in return for wheat and oil. Solomon also introduced forced labour; 30,000 Israelites quarried stones, felled trees and then transported the building material to the Temple site. When you consider that an Israelite farmer had to give up four months every year to do the king's work, it's not surprising that resentment began to build up (5:13–14).

Archaeologists have discovered that both iron and copper were extensively mined in Solomon's day. The book of Deuteronomy described the Promised Land as "a land where the rocks are iron and you can dig copper out of the hills" (Deuteronomy 8:9). In Solomon's time Israel had the largest blast furnace in the Near East, together with copper refineries and factories that produced a variety of tools and other metal articles for the home and export markets. This, then, was the main source of Solomon's legendary wealth that transformed Israel from a peasant agricultural community into a top-rank industrial and commercial nation. When the queen of Sheba visited Solomon from her fabulous "land of spice" in southern Arabia "to test him with hard questions" (10:1) and "talked with him about all that she had on her mind" (10:2), it's likely that the outward purpose of her journey was a trade mission.

When the Temple was completed, the ark containing the stone tablets of the Ten Commandments was brought from the old city in Jerusalem where David had placed it and installed with proper ceremony in the new Temple. As in ancient times the cloud of the Presence descended upon the tabernacle and the glory of the Lord was seen again in Israel (8:1–11).

We may still capture some of the elation and exaltation that found expression in the prayer of thanksgiving, supplication and blessing on the occasion of the dedication of the Temple. Solomon's prayer in 8:23–53, in which he binds the people by oath to be faithful to the Lord, is one of the most inspiring prayers in Scripture. But we have to take note, especially in light of what happens later, that he finishes his blessing to the nation with the proviso that the blessing depends on their hearts being fully committed to the Lord their God, living by His decrees and obeying His commands (8:61).

We would expect God to respond to that kind of public worship and His appearance to Solomon is described in 1 Kings 9:4–5, where He repeats a promise very similar to that made to Abraham:

> *if you walk before me in integrity of heart and uprightness, as David your father did, and do all I command and observe my decrees and laws, I will establish your royal throne over Israel forever.*

Yet God also sees the need to add a note of warning:

> *But if you or your sons turn away from me and do not observe the commands and decrees I have given you and go off to serve other gods and worship them, then I will cut off Israel from the land I have given them and will reject this temple…*
>
> 1 KINGS 9:6–7

## Solomon's love of power – and its trappings

Reading the extensive details of chapter 10, we become conscious that Solomon had acquired a taste for the perks of power. The grandeur of the Temple, the number of animals sacrificed at the dedication and the statement in verse 27 that "the king made silver as common in Jerusalem as stones, and cedar as plentiful as sycamore-fig trees in the foothills", says it all. Solomon's love for luxury was matched only by his desire for women. What probably started as a small number of wives to enhance his foreign policy clearly became an obsession as the sensuality made possible by his incredible wealth and power brought Solomon onto the slippery slope of idolatry.

1 Kings 11:1–2 records:

> King Solomon, however, loved many foreign women besides
> Pharaoh's daughter – Moabites, Ammonites, Edomites,
> Sidonians and Hittites. They were from nations about which
> the Lord had told the Israelites, "You must not intermarry
> with them, because they will surely turn your hearts after their
> gods."

Solomon proved the truth of the saying, "there is no fool like an old fool", for we read of him: "As Solomon grew old, his wives turned his heart after other gods, and his heart was not fully devoted to the Lord"(1 Kings 11:4).

What a classic understatement, for we read:

> On a hill east of Jerusalem, Solomon built a high place for
> Chemosh the detestable god of Moab, and for Molech the
> detestable god of the Ammonites. He did the same for all his
> foreign wives, who burned incense and offered sacrifices to
> their gods.
>
> 1 KINGS 11:7–8

That this was a hard lesson Israel would need to learn again is highlighted when Nehemiah refers to Solomon's sin of idolatry, which brought God's judgment upon the nation (Nehemiah 13:26).

Predictably, God became angry with Solomon and pronounced a double judgment that fell onto the very achievement for which Solomon had sold his soul (1 Kings 11:9–11). Above all, Solomon wanted a united empire to bring together the glory and power of the kingdom and eliminate internal factions and external enemies. But in His judgment God effectually said, "You wanted unity but I will give you disunity: you wanted a kingdom, but I will tear it away from your son." Showing His mercy, God did not bring this judgment into force during Solomon's lifetime, "for the sake of David my servant and for the sake of Jerusalem, which I have chosen" (1 Kings 11:13). Yet Solomon did not get off scot-free. God's second judgment came during his last years as king in the form of harassment by old enemies (verses 14, 23). These adversaries were a judgment on Solomon's unwillingness to repent of his sin.

The message is clear: whatever we value as being more important than God, He will stop us from enjoying. God will see to it that the axe will fall precisely on the idol that caused our disobedience. He loves us too much to allow us to go our own selfish way and must discipline those He loves (Hebrews 12:6).

# The kingdom splits

Before Solomon passes from the scene in 11:26–43 we are introduced to Jeroboam I, Solomon's successor over ten of the tribes.

This man, one of Solomon's overseers, led an unsuccessful rebellion and had to flee to Egypt. We are now, however, forewarned that on Solomon's death the kingdom will split and ten of the tribes will follow Jeroboam I while the tribes of Judah and Benjamin will remain faithful to Solomon's son, Rehoboam. The reason for the collapse that followed Solomon's death, leaving his son with the rump of the kingdom, was the result of Solomon's heavy-handed policies. Heavy taxation might have been endured had it not been obvious that the wealth was for Solomon's own pleasure and not for the good of his people. There was still too much of the nomadic spirit in Israel to tolerate Solomon's kind of autocratic monarchy that was so unlike his father, David, whose early struggles and hardships kept him humble and a "man of the people".

After Solomon's death the resentment and disaffection that had been brewing in his kingdom boiled over when his son Rehoboam presented himself at Shechem for confirmation of his accession. The result was that Shechem, the place where the twelve tribes first found unity under Joshua, now became the scene of the split between north and south that brought that unity to an end. Saul had failed, David had failed and Solomon had failed. The kings and the kingdom had been weighed in the balance and found wanting.

From the death of Solomon and the end of the undivided kingdom of Israel the story is a sad and sordid one of disruption, intrigue, war and corruption, until finally the remnant of Israel collapsed less than 500 years after Saul became its first king. Israel had paid the price for playing power politics, becoming almost indistinguishable from any of the other city principalities that staggered from one crisis to another in the ancient Mediterranean world.

But the Israelites were the people of God, a people with a call and a mission. They could not be allowed to disintegrate or become identical to their neighbours. Saul's madness might make him unfit to govern his people; David's heart might be stronger than his head; Solomon's vanity might induce him to strive to bring his people into the mainstream of progress. But even the emergence of godly kings like Hezekiah or Josiah could not prevent headstrong, spiritually blinded people seeking the pursuit of wealth, power, prestige and the false security these things bring, rather than the path that the people of God must follow.

The lesson had to be learned and it could only be learned in the bitterness of painful experience with the collapse of disappointed hopes. Israel had to be convinced – as we have to be convinced – that the people of God must look to godly people like Samuel (not Saul); Nathan (not David); Ahijah (not Solomon) while listening to the word God is speaking.

## Step forward, Elijah

In the remaining chapters of 1 Kings, Elijah stands out from the intricate pattern of Israel's social and economic development.

Elijah was a prophet of the calibre of Moses who was ready to challenge kings and commoners if they deviated from the faith and practise of the covenant to ensure that the values for which Moses, Samuel and Nathan stood were not forgotten. It was Elijah and people like him who during the sad years of Israel's decline and fall made certain that out of the disaster would come a new beginning and ensure that a wiser and chastened Israel would arise out of the ashes of military defeat and captivity.

In 1 Kings 16:24 we are told how evil King Omri was responsible for transferring the capital of the northern kingdom to a virgin site at Samaria, which became a city worthy to stand comparison with Jerusalem. The story, however, turns to deal at length with Omri's son, Ahab, and his wife, Jezebel, because it was through them the greatest threat to the supremacy of Jehovah worship arose since Israel became a kingdom.

Ahab became king about 870 BC and no doubt his father reckoned he had made a prudent match for him with a princess of Tyre named Jezebel. However, this lady possessed much stronger religious convictions than her husband and set out to eliminate Jehovah worship from Israel by removing any trace of its heritage. The issue here was nothing less than an attempt of a domineering and fanatically religious foreign queen, with the connivance of an easy-going

Israelite king, to substitute her own god, Baal, for Israel's God, Jehovah. To meet this challenge God called forth His man, Elijah.

Elijah was something special. On the one hand, he was the holy man who was fed by the birds and who miraculously provided grain and oil for a poor widow whose son he brought back to life (17:1–24). On the other hand, he was the courageous hero who single-handedly confronted and defeated Jezebel's prophets, selected a successor for Ahab and the throne of Syria, and denounced the king in the same way that Nathan had denounced David for the murder of a humble Israelite (18:1 – 21:29).

When Elijah appeared on the scene Israel was in the grip of one of its periodic droughts with consequent famine. Worse than that from the point of view of the faithful supporter of the Lord, Jezebel, in her fanatical determination to substitute Baal worship, had a large number of the prophets of Jehovah murdered. Elijah appeared and disappeared with dramatic suddenness and always his presence denoted trouble for the king's household. His appearance was like that of John the Baptist, wearing a cloak of camel hair and with his head unshorn. His iron constitution and nervous energy enabled him to out-pace a horse and fast for days on end. The air of mystery that surrounded this impressive character throughout the narrative is sustained to the end when he does not die in the usual way but is taken up to glory in a chariot of fire.

The breathtaking account of the encounter between Elijah and Jezebel's 400 prophets of Baal begins in 1 Kings 18:16. In a highly dramatic scene on Mount Carmel, Elijah challenged them to prove the supremacy of their god, Baal, over the Lord God. The mad cries of the ecstatics, their self-mutilation, Elijah's ribald taunting of their slumbering god and the conclusion when the fire of the Lord falls and consumes Elijah's sacrifice, is one of the most vivid and exciting episodes in the Old Testament. Baal worship suffered a mortal blow. Many of its prophets were massacred and the Lord was reinstated as Israel's God (18:1–46).

Elijah had proved conclusively that the Lord God could bring or withhold rain better than any Canaanite fertility god and this, together with Baal's inability to save his prophets from slaughter, was an argument that the ordinary person could understand. Elijah on Mount Carmel made Israel face up to the choice: "If the Lord is God, follow him; but if Baal is God, follow him" (18:21). Israel chose the Lord.

In chapter 19, with his life in danger from Jezebel's fury, we next see an emotionally drained Elijah seeking inspiration and courage at the holy mountain where God had spoken to Moses. There, Elijah learned that it is not in storm or fire that God speaks, but in the silence and stillness of a receptive heart, a whisper (the Authorized Version's "still small voice") (verse 12). He learns, too, that he is not as he thinks the sole defender of the Lord's cause, but that 7,000, although unrevealed, witnesses for God stand with him in spirit.

After an interlude in which, once more, the influence of the prophets in political and military affairs is emphasized (chapter 20), we next encounter Elijah making one of his dramatic appearances in Naboth's vineyard to defend the moral principles of Jehovah against godless selfishness. Ahab and Jezebel had conspired to steal Naboth's vineyard by arranging false charges to be brought against him, which led to Naboth's execution as a criminal and allowed Ahab to steal his land. In Ahab's greeting, "So you have found me, my enemy!" (21:20), we can detect the guilty conscience of a king who was still himself an Israelite, bound by the Law of Sinai, and who accepted the prophet's curse on the royal house as just and warranted (21:27).

## The prophet Michaiah

The last chapter of 1 Kings contains the revealing story of the prophet Micaiah.

King Ahab and his reluctant ally King Jehoshaphat of Judah planned to rescue the town of Ramoth Gilead from the hands of the Syrians. The court prophets, who comprised 400 "yes-men", were supposed to declare the will of the Lord but they went along with their king and gave the enterprise their blessing. However, even King Ahab recognized them as sycophants and sent for Micaiah because although he hated him for it, he knew that from this one man he would get the truth as the Lord disclosed it to him.

At first, Micaiah mockingly supports the representatives of the state religion. But Ahab will have none of it: "How many times must I make you swear to tell me nothing but the truth in the name of the Lord?" (22:16). In the king's reaction we see the power of the true prophet in Israel as opposed to the false prophets of the establishment. The prophet might, like Elijah, be a wild outspoken man from the desert and walk with death as his companion, or be hated like Micaiah and rot his life away in some royal dungeon, but even the worst backslider from the faith acknowledged that from such men alone came the word of God.

Micaiah foretold Israel's defeat and Ahab's death. So, in an attempt to prevent this happening Ahab cunningly disguised himself in order that he would not be recognized by the enemy, "But someone drew his bow at random and hit the king of Israel between the sections of his armour" (22:34), and Ahab's body was brought back to Samaria to be buried in the shadow of his splendid palace (22:37). Jezebel outlived her husband and saw two reigns before the prophecy of Elijah was terribly fulfilled that "dogs will devour Jezebel by the wall of Jezreel" (1 Kings 21:23; 2 Kings 9:30–37).

So we have seen that 1 Kings records the history of a nation passing from affluence and influence to poverty and paralysis.

It opens with the death of David and ends with the death of Ahab. Again and again we are reminded of two thrones: that on earth with its succession of kings and that in heaven with its one king. In looking at the former we see the failing government of men with disruption, disintegration and disaster. In looking at the latter we see the unfailing government of God through His prophets declaring His grace, His guidance, His judgment and His mercy.

# A final word of warning

The conclusion we are to draw is that humankind cannot govern itself, whether by material magnificence, the assumption of autocratic power or even by democracy, unless we first submit to the government of God over our lives. If men and women rule their countries or their lives as though God does not exist – whether that be with a dictatorship, communist, socialist or democratic governments – then it will ultimately fail disastrously. The consequence will be prisons, hospitals, mental institutions filled to capacity. And alcoholism, drug addiction, social disease, and broken homes and families will all give rise to the evidence of a failed society no matter how much time, expense and effort goes in to papering over the cracks. The heart-rending truth is that the lesson of the book of 1 Kings is seen outworking in our sick, sad, society today, where individual and national refusal to pay heed to God's guiding principles for life contained in His book, the Bible, have produced the worst social statistics in living memory.

So the lesson of 1 Kings is that in the midst of man's pathetic failures to build his version of heaven on earth, God builds His kingdom in heaven and calls out men, women, boys and girls who, with Him, will rule the new heaven and new Earth for evermore. This is the biblical promise that helps sustain and encourage sorely tried Christian men and women who are placed here to show the way to that better kingdom.

# 12

# 2 Kings
## – Kingdom Decline and Captivity

The drama of the kings of Israel and Judah continue in 2 Kings, and with the advantage of historical perspective, provides an analysis that shows these two nations to be on a collision course with captivity.

## A divided kingdom

The book opens with the kingdom of Israel torn in two. Ten tribes made up the northern state that retained the title Israel with its capital in Shecham, which later moved to Samaria. This left two tribes, Judah and Benjamin, which comprised the southern state. This became Judah with its capital in Jerusalem. The united kingdom had lasted 112 years, from 1043–931 BC. The northern kingdom would survive a further 209 years till 722 BC, when it was taken into captivity by the Assyrians, while the southern kingdom of Judah continued for a further 136 years until 586 BC, before it was taken into captivity by Babylon. During the 457-year period covering 2 Kings there were great movements in world power as Egyptian and Assyrian control over Israel fluctuated, with Assyria coming out on top only to decline and ultimately be conquered by Babylon.

The author of 2 Kings hints that the reign of Jeroboam II was a time of expansion and prosperity for Israel (14:23–29). The reason for this is thought to have been a temporary "decline" in Assyrian power. But, no matter how things may appear, the prophet Amos, who ministered at the end of Jeroboam's long reign, indicates with a wealth of detail that this was Israel's Indian summer. The prophet paints a picture of a land lulled into a false sense of security by an economic boom, yet rife with flagrant social inequality and injustice, completely blind to the signs of impending disaster.

In chapter 15, king follows king in rapid succession and the Assyrian monster comes clawing at the door. Tiglath Pileser, also called Pul in verse 19, has to be bought off and the book of the prophet Hosea, who followed Amos, emphasizes concern for the future that is now shared by all. Despite the fact that it led to the Assyrians cutting off more than the fringes of the northern kingdom, Israel's King Pekah, in alliance with the Syrians, thought fit at this time to attack Judah (2 Kings 15:29, 37).

The fall of Damascus in 732 BC meant the end of Syria as an independent state and is mentioned as an aside in 16:9. However, the author of 2 Kings is more interested in the impoverishment of the Temple furnishings made necessary when King Ahaz of Judah had to ask for help from Assyria against five northern neighbours (16:7).

Verses 10–18 of chapter 16 catalogue Ahaz's religious innovations, all of which speak clearly of his deepening apostasy. According to 2 Chronicles 28:24–25, Ahaz went as far as to mutilate the Temple furniture and close the Temple itself so that the services within the Holy Place were discontinued. "Worship services" would henceforth be held only in connection with the new altar or at one of the several altars erected throughout Jerusalem or at the high places dedicated to the various gods that were established throughout Judah by royal edict. All this not only speaks of Ahaz's depraved spiritual condition but was probably carried out as an expression of his goodwill towards Tiglath-Pileser. Officially, nothing offensive to the Assyrian king would henceforth be practised.

The prophet Isaiah, unlike the majority of the prophets, belonged to the aristocracy, and from his vantage point as a counsellor to the king, was able to influence state policy from the inside. On this occasion he failed to dissuade King Ahaz from having any dealings with the Assyrians and Tiglath-Pileser was not slow to take advantage of the invitation to intervene in Palestinian affairs. Samaria's turn came ten years later and in 722 BC the northern kingdom of Israel met the same fate as Damascus. According to Assyrian records, 30,000 people were carried off to captivity in Assyria and settled in its dominions, while foreign captives were brought in to replace them in Samaria. Not only, therefore, were the people of the northern kingdom no longer pure Israelites but their religion was no longer solely the religion of Jehovah. Thus the Samaritans became a mixed and alien people with whom in later days pure Jews would have no dealings. This is the explanation for the hostility encountered by Ezra and Nehemiah when they returned to rebuild Jerusalem and their refusal to allow the Samaritans to be involved in the reconstruction. It also explains the background to Jesus' encounter with the Samaritan woman in John 4.

# The fall of Judah

With the northern kingdom gone, the fall of Judah is covered in chapters 18–25.

After the fall of Israel, Judah lingered on for 136 years and considerable attention is given to the reign of King Hezekiah, one of two rulers after the division of Solomon's kingdom who received high commendation from the author of 2 Kings. The reason for this was that in his reign a real attempt was made to purify the worship of Jehovah of its pagan associations (18:1–6). However, more space is devoted to one of the best-known incidents in Judah's history, and is recounted at length. A punitive force under Sennacherib, having dealt with the rebels in Mesopotamia, descended on Palestine. Sennacherib's own account of this campaign is described in detail on a hexagonal prism now in the British Museum in London and confirms the biblical record.

In 701 BC detachments of his great army under an official called Rabshakeh approached Jerusalem. Lord Byron's pen recorded what it was like when the Assyrian army took the field:

> *The Assyrians came down like a wolf on the fold,*
> *And his cohorts were gleaming in purple and gold;*
> *And the sheen of their spears was like stars on the sea*
> *When the blue wave rolls nightly on deep Galilee.*
> "THE DESTRUCTION OF SENNACHERIB", LORD BYRON (1788–1824)

This is the calamity Hezekiah faced. An overwhelming implacable foe stood opposed to him and defeat was staring him in the face. Psalm 44 is regarded as a commentary on this incident describing Israel's helplessness.

Talks were held between Rabshakeh and the Jerusalem defenders but Isaiah encouraged the king to stand firm. Events proved him right. 2 Kings 19:35 records how a plague broke out among the Assyrian army and the siege was lifted. Jerusalem, for the time being, was spared the fate of Sennacherib's other victims. But Hezekiah had to pay a heavy tribute.

The reigns of Manasseh and his son Amon recorded in chapters 21–25 marked a new level of depravity in Judah's religious life.

Nothing that any of the kings of Israel or Judah before them had done could compare with the infamous record of this ill-starred pair. The author of 2 Kings regards them as worse than heathens and says that they were so bad it was as if Hezekiah's reformation might never have occurred. Shrines were multiplied, worship of foreign deities encouraged, astrology and spiritualism practised and human sacrifice once again made its appearance.

By contrast, their successor Josiah (chapters 22–23) is given the highest praise accorded to any king in Israel or Judah. For it was in his reign that the most thoroughgoing reformation of the state took place. To read 23:1–25 is to realize why the prophets Hosea and Isaiah thundered against the travesty the worship of Jehovah had become because every imaginable variety of superstition and black magic were included in Jewish worship.

Josiah died at the battle of Megiddo in 609 BC fighting for Judah's political and religious freedom against the Egyptians. Assyria had been defeated in 612 BC by the new empire of Babylon, and the prophet Nahum voiced the exultation of all the victims of Assyrian brutality at the liberating news of the fall of her capital Nineveh. Egypt, her ally, met the same fate a few years later and the way was left open for King Nebuchadnezzar of Babylon to become master of the world.

In the process, the Babylonian war machine disposed of the tiny state of Judah. The book of 2 Kings gives us the bare bones, while the book of Jeremiah, who lived through these days and saw Jerusalem crushed, gives us the flesh and blood of the story. In 598 BC Nebuchadnezzar ravaged Israel and took Jerusalem captive. King Jehoiachin, the leading citizens and the craftsmen were deported to Babylon and Zedekiah, a "puppet king", was put on the throne (24:17).

Ten years later, however, Zedekiah rebelled against his masters in Babylon and in 587 BC Nebuchadnezzar laid siege to Jerusalem. The city was taken and burnt, the walls broken down, the Temple treasury pillaged and the king captured and blinded before being carried in chains to Babylon. A second and greater deportation of the population took place and none was left but "some of the poorest people of the land" (25:12). Jerusalem's plight was vividly portrayed by Jeremiah in the book of Lamentations.

Babylon then appointed a governor, Gedaliah, who was soon assassinated, and disregarding Jeremiah's earlier advice to the exiles in Babylon to settle in the land (see Jeremiah 29:4–9), the remaining "remnant" fled to Egypt (2 Kings 25:26). Thus, to all intents and purposes, Israel was finished and the promises made to Abraham and Moses seemed doomed. The land of milk and honey now flowed with blood and tears.

## 2 Kings in tandem with writings of the prophets

The key to understanding the history and background of this period lies in the writing of the prophets, for this was their hour.

Reading 2 Kings apart from the prophecies is disappointing, but, reading the book as the background to the prophecies, we see not only man's failure, but also, in the foreground, God's overwhelming victory. What we learn is that the cause of human failure was the lost sense of Jehovah resulting in the lost ideal of national identity, the loss of conscience and finally the loss of purpose and direction.

The proof of the people's lost sense of Jehovah was seen in their kings. There were exceptions who served the Lord, but even in their reigns it was written, "the high places, however, were not removed" (2 Kings 12:3). They either compromised or fell away. The only two kings who stand out as men who followed the Lord were Hezekiah and Josiah, yet even they failed to some degree. Those two apart, the history of the kings is one of men who had no vision of God, who persisted in doing evil and turning their backs on the principles of righteousness, and who thus multiplied their wickedness throughout their kingdom.

Furthermore, the lost awareness of Jehovah meant that the people turned to idolatry, for men and women will always worship something. The presence of the "high places" of Baal and Ashtoreth and the "passing" of their children through the fires of Molech proved their inability to detect the hand of God as it fell in punishment. This was a truth Isaiah declared in Isaiah 1:5: "Why should you be beaten anymore? Why do you persist in rebellion?"

Because of their spiritual blindness, sin was lightly thought of and the false pride of nationality was fostered. We see this in the writings of the prophet Jonah quoted in 2 Kings 14:25. Remember, the book of Jonah was written for Israel at a time when she was pursuing two contradictory attitudes. They thought they were exclusive and did not believe there could be any pity or mercy in the heart of God for other peoples except themselves. But while thinking that, they failed to be exclusive in the way God wanted them to be and, contrary to divine command, they were forming alliances with other nations looking to them for protection. When the people lost their clear vision of God they lost their calling and purpose as the people of God and so lost all meaning for their national life.

It's worth remembering that as you read through this book covering 457 years, the following prophets were ministering to the nations of Israel and Judah.

In the northern kingdom:

Elijah

Elisha

the Schools of the Prophets

Amos

Jonah

Hosea

Joel

And in the southern kingdom of Judah:

Obadiah

Isaiah

Micah

Nahum

Zephaniah

Jeremiah

Habakkuk

Daniel (in exile)

Ezekiel (in exile).

It's food for thought that the result of the ministry of these people appeared to be insignificant. Isaiah, speaking of his own ministry and that of all the prophets, enquired, "Who has believed our message and to whom has [the arm of] the Lord been revealed?" (Isaiah 53:1). We can sense the hopelessness they must have felt trying to reach a gospel-hardened people who could listen to such godly men as these and yet stubbornly turn their back on God and continue in their wicked sinful ways.

And there's something else to think about: when reformations did occur they were relatively shallow. Hezekiah was a godly king who saw spiritual revival throughout Judah, but as soon as he passed away the people returned to their old ways of evil. King Josiah conducted a remarkable reformation and yet the prophet Zephaniah who was ministering at that time never referred to it. Zephaniah's silence over Josiah's reformation was followed by Jeremiah, who criticized the reformation because it was all external and no real heart change took place and no alteration to conduct (Jeremiah 5:24; 7:1ff.). For further proof we have the prophetess Huldah's prophecy in 2 Kings 22. When the revival was under way and the book of the law was discovered, they sent it to Huldah and she, inspired of God to deliver her message, said in effect that there was no real value in the reformation; that the king meant well and would be rewarded, but that the people were not following God.

This will become more apparent when we come to the books of Chronicles for they deal with the life of the people from the standpoint of the Temple. Verse 16 of 2 Chronicles 29 tells us that when Hezekiah began his reformation he started with the Temple and for sixteen days all the priests and Levites cleaned out the rubbish, which tells us that the Temple had become a rubbish tip. When King Josiah carried out his reformation the book of the law was found, which means it had been lost. The Holy Scriptures lost! And so astonishing was the teaching in them that Josiah halted in the middle of his work to enquire from the prophetess Huldah. The people had so forgotten the law of their God that when it was found it was completely unfamiliar to them. Now you can see how their failure to live as children of God led to their downfall.

This should sound alarm bells to our nation with its children who no longer know what Easter means and see Christmas only as a winter festival when Santa brings presents.

But don't lose sight of the promises of God.

When God promised Abraham in Genesis 22:15 that He would bless him and through his seed the whole world would be blessed, He swore by His own name. Hebrews 6:13 tells us God could swear by nothing greater than Himself, and we must remember it is impossible for God to lie. God entered into a covenant with Abraham and He will fulfil it. He will be true to Himself. He will allow nothing to thwart the purpose of His love and throughout all this awful 457-year period God remembered His promise.

We have a wonderful illustration of this in 2 Kings 11. As Satan's instrument to thwart God's promise to bring forth the Messiah from the line of David, Queen Athaliah, the wicked daughter of wicked parents, devised a scheme to destroy all the royal family.

This evil queen with her blood-soaked hands seems to have succeeded in her diabolical plan, for if the royal family is destroyed then the Christ-child cannot be born as the legal son and heir of David, and if that happens God's plan will have failed and His promise to Abraham and David broken.

Then we read in 2 Kings 11:2:

> *But Jehosheba, the daughter of King Jehoram and sister of Ahaziah, took Joash son of Ahaziah and stole him away from among the royal princes, who were about to be murdered. She put him and his nurse in a bedroom to hide him from Athaliah; so he was not killed.*

How wonderful are the ways of God. For when we see Joash again, a crown is on his head and the people are shouting, "Long live the king!" (11:12). Queen Athaliah is executed and the promise is saved; the Christ will be born of David's birth line and be a blessing to all nations.

Jehovah remained faithful to His Davidic promise through the remnant in Babylonian captivity as evil Evil-Merodach frees Jehoiachin, ex-king of Judah, from prison and treats him kindly (25:27–30), so ensuring David's succession continues down through history to Mary and Joseph in Bethlehem. The significance of this incident should be a source of great encouragement for Christian men and women, for it reminds us that God will allow nothing to thwart His promised plan and purpose for His people.

So, what's the message of this book for the people of today?

There are two very pertinent quotations that come right out of this period. The first is Proverbs 29:18: "Where there is no revelation, the people cast off restraint", or as the KJV has it: "Where there is no vision, the people perish".

The second is Isaiah 46:10:

*I make known the end from the beginning,*
*from ancient times, what is still to come.*
*I say: My purpose will stand,*
*and I will do all that I please.*

It's not difficult to see the pattern. At the beginning of the period, 1 Samuel 3:1 tells us, "In those days the word of the Lord was rare; there were not many visions." That's how it all began. Now come to the end – the last period recorded by Jeremiah in Lamentations 2:9: "the law is no more, and her prophets no longer find visions from the Lord." Between these two, lies the problem. If the vision of God is lost, ideals will be degraded, consciences dulled and the nation will lose its way laying itself open to the judgment of God.

But hold on to that other message and thank God for His loving patience and the realization that He will not be discouraged. Remember that was said by Isaiah and he could only make that declaration because in the midst of all the apostasy and decadence of his age, to use his own words, "In the year that King Uzziah died, I saw the Lord seated on a throne, high and exalted" (Isaiah 6:1). That vision ultimately enabled him to say:

*Why do you say, O Jacob,*
*and complain, O Israel,*
*"My way is hidden from the Lord;*

*my cause is disregarded by my God?"*
*Do you not know?*
*Have you not heard?*
*The Lord is the everlasting God,*
*the Creator of the ends of the earth.*
*He will not grow tired or weary [that's power],*
*and his understanding no one can fathom [that's knowledge].*
*He gives strength to the weary*
*and increases the power of the weak.*
*Even youths grow tired and weary,*
*and young men stumble and fall;*
*but those who hope in the Lord*
*will renew their strength.*
*They will soar on wings like eagles;*
*they will run and not grow weary,*
*they will walk and not be faint.*

Isaiah 40:27–31

That's assurance and encouragement.

Remember, these wonderful words were penned in that awful period of human failure by the man who saw the eternal throne and the almighty God who sat upon it. And that's the message for us in this dark and desperate time – He will not grow tired or weary; He will not fail or be discouraged. If we are to serve our age we must see God, and seeing Him we shall be inspired by the certainty of ultimate victory.

# 13

# 1 Chronicles – "Roots"

According to Jewish tradition and other biblical clues, the priest Ezra, who wrote the book that bears his name, was also the author of 1 and 2 Chronicles.

Ezra brought the first Jewish settlers back from Babylonian captivity to Jerusalem. As these people were restored to their homeland but still subjects of the Persian empire they felt rootless and forsaken, and Ezra's purpose in writing this book was to remind them where they had come from, and, yes, though things are bad, they must look at how good they were and can be again! So, for those Israelites back in their land but suffering from an identity crisis, Ezra's long list of genealogies serves the purpose of reminding them of their history. In effect saying "This is how the history of you Israelites, who know and love God, can be traced back from our day through every generation of ancestors to the beginning of time."

Ezra was not writing another version of the books of Kings or Samuel, which the people would have read; he was explaining to them things they already knew in a new and helpful way. And in order to make his spiritual point he either emphasized or ignored historical material as suited his message. For example, though his narrative focuses on the kingship and priesthood, that is, the throne of David and the Temple of Solomon, and though he nowhere departs from the truth, he is unashamedly selective in what he writes such as while he focuses on King David he does not mention his sin with Bathsheba.

The reason Ezra did this was that from the books of Samuel and Kings everyone knew what David was really like. But for all his faults he was unquestionably Israel's greatest king. And though by the time of Chronicles David's world was long gone and the glory departed, neither his nation nor his ideals were extinct. Ezra's message was that the religious understanding laid down by God and lived out by the nation in David's reign was still the only one by which the life of God's people could be structured if it was to have any meaning and purpose. That's why he begins chapter 9 with Saul as a foil to set off the character of David. Saul was unfaithful, disobedient, did not seek the Lord and so failed disastrously. David was faithful, obedient, did seek the Lord and founded the greatest kingdom in Israel's history.

## Ezra speaks to a new generation

Chapter 11 focuses on David's capture of Jerusalem, which had been thought to be impregnable. It would become forevermore the earthly centre of Jewish national life and aspiration. Ezra's point is that at the heart of the kingdom is a city, both eternal and historical, the repository of spiritual truth and the seat of strong government, and it is this that holds the people together.

At face value this must have been quite difficult for the first readers of Chronicles to come to terms with. It's all very well to say that with a king like David reigning over a city such as Jerusalem, God's people would find their true identity, but no such king existed in their day and Jerusalem was a pile of rubble. So they had to figure out how to apply Ezra's message in their own lives.

New Testament believers do not have such a problem. They do have a king enthroned amongst His subjects and can see something of the inner meaning of these chapters which teach us that God's people can only be what they should be when their king is at the centre of their lives. And when God is proclaimed and obeyed as in 11:1–3 His people will be gathered to Him. Just as in Israel of old, Christian men and women must acknowledge their king is among them, that He is at one with them, has delivered them from their enemy offering a new covenant, asking only that they accept His rule.

The king, then, is the centre around which the people are bound in unity – "one church, one faith, one Lord". But this common identity does not mean they lose their individuality. God is concerned for individuals, a point that Ezra is at pains to demonstrate in chapters 11 and 12, where he describes a diversity of loyal individuals illustrating that in the King's service there is room for each and every one.

Ezra is highlighting the contrast between his present age and what had gone before in the time of the Judges. Then, Israel was a politically loose confederation of tribes that went their individual ways with mutual suspicion and recrimination, arguing among themselves and unable to unite and work together. In other words, the very individuality that should have been appreciated in a united nation was the very problem that tore them apart. This selfish and destructive attitude was summed up as "everyone did as he saw fit" (Judges 17:6).

David's example was to take the distressed and discontented individuals and make them into the people they should be: individuals united and serving their king in their many different ways. This is the heart of Paul's teaching in 1 Corinthians 12–14 concerning the "various spiritual gifts" that Christians are expected to use "for the common good", the "building up of the church" in "loyalty to the same Lord".

For Christians, as for ancient Israel, the enormous diversity to be found among the king's people is drawn together in unity around our King.

> *How good and pleasant it is*
> *when brothers live together in unity!...*
> *For there the Lord bestows his blessing,*
> *even life forevermore.*
>
> PSALM 133:1, 3B

This unity was expressed by our Lord Jesus himself when he said:

> *I have given them the glory that you gave me, that they may*
> *be one as we are one: I in them and you in me. May they be*
> *brought to complete unity to let the world know that you sent*
> *me and have loved them even as you have loved me.*
>
> JOHN 17:22–23

## The ark of God

In chapters 13–16 Ezra reminds his readers of the importance of the ark of God.

Ezra does not describe the ark, even though none of his readers would have seen it – they would all have been familiar with the descriptions of it from Exodus 25 and 37. Nor does he need to explain why it is located at the beginning of David's reign in the town of Kiriath-Jearim, for they knew from the Samuel/Kings story of how it was taken into battle as a "national mascot" by the Israelites, captured by the Philistines and passed from one Philistine city to another like a hot potato, leaving burnt fingers wherever it went before eventually returning to its homeland in a southern Israelite town (1 Samuel 4:1 – 7:2).

In recounting the incident of David's seventeen-mile round trip from Jerusalem to Kiriath-Jearim and back with the ark, and Uzzah being struck dead for reaching out his hand to steady the cart carrying the ark when it jolted, Ezra is reminding the Israelites of the overriding importance of compliance with God's Word. David knew that the Law commanded that permanent poles were to be used to carry the ark, since no one was allowed to touch it and only priestly (levitical) personnel were allowed to carry it (Numbers 3:31), but in his joy and zeal he thought God wouldn't mind if the ark was carried a different way.

His confidence shaken and his faith under trial, David reflects and prays over the incident and comes to the conclusion that he is to blame. The ark belongs to God and must not be approached in a casual manner, it must be treated with respect; it is holy. Having learned this important lesson about God, David instructed the Levites to bring back the ark according to the law and three months later it was restored to its rightful place in Jerusalem.

So what were the lessons for Ezra's readers of 1 Chronicles in their day when there was no ark, no Temple and no standing city of Jerusalem?

Ezra's point is that you folks today who don't have an ark don't need an ark, God's grace is not bound to its symbol, grace is free! God is pouring His grace on us here and now without the ark, and will be doing so when the entire system of Old Testament Israel, priests, kings and all of it is ancient history. As Philip Yancey so memorably said in his book *Amazing Grace*, "There's nothing we can do to make God love us more, there's nothing we can do to make God love us less." God's grace is not dependent on what we do or where we go and so forth, His grace is bound to nothing at all except His own love and goodness.

This reminds us of what Jesus told the Samaritan woman at Jacob's well and was to prove to be revolutionary in religious thinking:

> *Believe me, woman, a time is coming when you will worship the Father neither on this mountain nor in Jerusalem... a time is coming and has now come when the true worshippers will worship the Father in spirit and truth, for they are the kind of worshippers the Father seeks. God is spirit, and his worshippers must worship in spirit and in truth.*
>
> JOHN 4:21, 23–24

It's not where we worship that's important, but who, when and how we worship. The fundamental question is: "Is our spiritual worship real?" For

123

the value of our devotion to God does not depend upon the place where it is expressed. True worship has its temple in the inmost soul in the spirit and heart of men (1 Corinthians 6:19).

## Lessons for Christians today

In chapter 17 Ezra focuses on David's desire to build God a Temple to contain the ark.

Though God denied David the opportunity to build a Temple to contain the ark of the covenant due to the blood shed in his past, God nevertheless recognized that David's intention was honourable and He was pleased with it. Although denied the fulfilment of his vision, instead of sulking about it, David gave himself completely to the work of preparing for that which he himself would never be able to complete. The important lesson for Christians today is worth repeating: if we cannot build we can gather, if we cannot go we can send. Our vision need never have been in vain even though it is not to be carried out by us, and may even remain unfulfilled in our lifetime. The materials we gather, the effort we put into it, the time, money and prayers we expend will be used by God to bring it to pass in His timing. From this we learn that God's refusals in our lives are loaded with immeasurable possibilities of blessing. It all depends on whether we react to God's "No" by sulking or seeking. Sulk, and we lose out; seek, and we will discover God is right in there alongside us with more blessing than we can imagine.

Ezra's theme becomes clear in chapters 28 and 29. For all the greatness of David, God is immeasurably greater still, as David exclaims:

> *You hem me in – behind and before;*
> *you have laid your hand upon me.*
> *Such knowledge is too wonderful for me,*
> *too lofty for me to attain.*
>
> PSALM 139:5–6

When David has become dust and when the twenty kings in succession after him have come and gone, and the day of the kingdom has given way to the "day of small things", the Lord is here to be acknowledged with His plan unfolding down through the centuries. These verses stress that truth again.

Ezra was writing in an age when for Israel the power of David and Solomon and the political kingdom itself were things of the past. And yet, through all the discouraging days for which the book was written, even when God's people seem of small account, their God reigns. Even when there is no throne in Jerusalem, there is a throne, and it is the Lord's. Even when the kingdom of David and Solomon is no more than a tale in a book of old chronicles, still the king will be enthroned among His people.

And for a Christian community marginalized by a godless society and increasingly witnessing the dismantling of their Christian heritage, where believers may be tempted to look back to the glories that once were, wondering apprehensively what the future may hold, the Chronicler's message holds good for today: no matter how it may look, our God reigns!

This is why it is so important that our nation should recognize God. Not merely because of the fact of His government, but because of the effect of the recognition of God upon national life. Take God out of the national life and national thinking, and you will have no moral standard at all. When a nation has lost its moral standard it has lost the strength of individual character and lost the concept of social relationships. It is useless to talk of a new social order unless at its very basis there is the conviction and the consciousness of the throne of God and the government of God. That is the supreme message of this book.

# 14

# 2 Chronicles
# – Spiritual Lessons for a Lost Generation

The main theme of 2 Chronicles is Ezra's intention to use true worship of God as the vehicle to reunite the nation after the Babylonian captivity.

With the glory of King David's reign long gone and Solomon's magnificent Temple in ruins for over a hundred years, the remnant of the nation of Israel, now a helpless vassal state in a political backwater, began to ponder the lessons learned through the captivity and re-think its vocation and mission. There was still a strong race-consciousness and hopes of a revival of past glories were never far from the people's heart, even to the time of the disciples who asked Jesus before His ascension, "Lord, are you at this time going to restore the kingdom to Israel?" (Acts 1:6). But stimulated by the ministries of Jeremiah, Ezekiel and Isaiah, there was a growing awareness that Israel's destiny was to be found in its religious calling and not as a super-power. As they reflected on their past they realized that what mattered most was the historical line of faith and obedience that linked them back through David, Moses and Abraham. In this, rather than in political intrigue, military campaigns or material success their true destiny lay. All these other things were inevitably part of the big picture but were not the essence of a people of God.

When the Jews accepted the exile as God's just punishment for their idolatry and acknowledged their need for repentance, it became a fruitful time of reflection for it marked a new beginning for the nation. It was here the seed was sown of Israel as a kingdom of priests, a special people, and all the distinctive marks of later Judaism as typified by the Pharisees and Sadducees, the authority of the professional priesthood, the supremacy of the Torah, rigid legalism and ceremonial scrupulousness. It's to the exile that we must look for the beginning of the synagogue and the initial stages of the process that turned circumcision, sabbath observance and dietary laws into legalistic obsessions. On all counts, therefore, the period of the exile was one of supreme significance.

Ezra appreciated that the Temple was the heart of all that was distinctively Jewish, therefore the rebuilding of Solomon's Temple amidst the ruins of Jerusalem could be the unifying force among the Jews. And even though Temple worship had ultimately failed, the fault lay not with the Temple but with the idolatry in the hearts of the people. So in rebuilding the Temple, Ezra was uniting the nation and attempting to do properly what Israel had failed to do in the past. In this he was helped by the rise of the local synagogues and priesthood that had emerged from the captivity, and, let it be said, after their return from captivity the nation never again entertained idolatry.

That's the reason much of the material found in Samuel and Kings is omitted from Chronicles; it does not develop Ezra's Temple-driven theme. The new Temple, being built as it was by a remnant of refugees from Babylon, could not possibly be as grand as Solomon's, and this was confirmed by the older people's reaction in Ezra 3:12 and Haggai 2:3. But Ezra knew that the Temple symbolized God's presence among His people, reminded them of their high calling and provided the spiritual link between their past, present and future. His bottom line was that despite their awful present circumstances the Davidic line, Temple and priesthood were still theirs.

While 1 Chronicles mirrored the life of David, 2 Chronicles focuses on David's son, Solomon, and the kings of Judah. Ezra, concerned to draw the spiritual lessons for a nation suffering an identity crisis, knew that in his latter years Solomon, with his pagan wives and their false gods, made a complete mess of his kingdom and proved his heart was not wholly devoted to the Lord, causing him to criticize Solomon's conduct in Nehemiah 13:26. But Ezra's point is that there was a genuine whole-hearted devotion to the Lord in the young Solomon and God blessed the young man's kingdom accordingly. That's the timeless message Ezra wants to teach the nation of Israel, that whenever God's people forsake Him, He withdraws His blessing, whereas trust and obedience to the Lord brings victory. This is seen in the way the book begins with Solomon's glory (chapters 1–9) and moves on to the nation's decline and captivity (chapters 10–36). And perhaps not surprisingly, in keeping with the theme of the book, it finishes with the promise of Cyrus, king of the Media-Persian empire, to rebuild the Temple in Jerusalem.

# Solomon's plans for the Temple

There's no doubt Solomon started well.

The first public act of his reign was to gather Israel at the tabernacle at Gibeon and before the altar sacrifice a thousand burnt offerings in worship to the Lord (1:2–6). God's response is recorded in verse 7, "Ask for whatever you want me to give you."

There's a lesson here for us: some Christians mistakenly pray for vague generalities, but the more we know of the character of God the more specific our prayers will be. Yes, of course, there are perplexing times when we are not sure what to pray for, then, "Thy will be done" is the proper prayer, but generally God expects us to engage in dialogue with Him. Jesus promised that the "Ask and it will be given to you" in Matthew 7:7 will be answered with good things. Our passage from 2 Chronicles illustrates this truth. The very thing Solomon asks for is the subject of an unequivocal New Testament promise from James 1:5: "If any of you lacks wisdom, he should ask God, who gives generously to all without finding fault, and it will be given to him."

Solomon, directing his prayer to the heart of the matter, not motivated by selfish desire and being prepared to ask "him who is able to do immeasurably more than all we ask or imagine" (Ephesians 3:20), is the essence of prayer – it is a prayer God will answer.

Solomon's plans for the building of the Temple are outlined in 2 Chronicles 2:3–18, and we can see how, though the building was radically new, he planned for traditional yet spiritual worship (2:4; 6:21). This reminds us that the danger of building a temple is that it can encourage an unspiritual religion. The Samaritan woman at Jacob's well gave voice to this naive but deadly theology in John's Gospel, "Our fathers worshipped on this mountain, but you Jews claim that the place we must worship is Jerusalem" (John 4:20), to which Jesus replied, "neither on this mountain nor in Jerusalem, [but]… in spirit and in truth" (John 4:21, 24). It's the danger of endowing a building with a spiritual importance Scripture does not confer upon it.

However, Solomon saw the Temple for what it was and for what it was not. Because God is so great the building and its worship must be as grand as possible (2:5); because He is so great they cannot make it grand enough (2:6) and Solomon wants his people to approach God in spirit and in truth. The

Temple is a convenience, a place to meet and do that which is appropriate for worship. For there is much truth in the saying "out of sight, out of mind", and in the nature of things if left to his own devices man is more likely than not to neglect worship. But God is still to be thought of as being infinitely too great to be constricted to any building. So worshippers are to view the building as an expression, however inadequate, of the greatness they ascribe to God and that means nothing but the best is good enough for him.

## Solomon's Temple is completed

Chapter 3 records the task for which Solomon will be remembered: the building of the Temple in Jerusalem.

Its completion and dedication are recorded in chapters 5–7. Solomon's superb prayer in chapter 6 shows that God intended the Temple to be a place where the people could be restored from the effects of sin. When Solomon finished his prayer, fire came down from heaven, consumed the sacrifice on the altar and the Temple was filled with the cloud of the glory of God, the sign that God had entered the Temple.

And so to the celebrated verse 7:14:

> *if my people, who are called by my name, will humble*
> *themselves and pray and seek my face and turn from their*
> *wicked ways, then will I hear from heaven and will forgive their*
> *sin and will heal their land.*

Herein lay the reason why it all went wrong for Solomon and for Israel. It is also Ezra's answer to those who lamented that the Temple, built by Zerubbabel (who was appointed by King Cyrus as governor of the province of Judah) was nothing by comparison to Solomon's. The truth was Solomon's Temple, which was magnificent, ultimately proved on its own to be absolutely useless because Temple worship insisted on a formal unchanging outward form of ritual. And when men and women are satisfied with the outward expression of worship only, they will inevitably begin to question the meaninglessness of their actions, which will lead them to the conclusion that they can manage without God. For when religious life is devoid of power and becomes mere formalism then men and women will turn away from it and it must sooner or later die.

Given in 1 Chronicles is an account of King David's desire to build the Temple, knowing as he did the importance to the nation of the centrality of God.

In 2 Chronicles the aspiration of David becomes the achievement of Solomon and we look in wonder at the splendour and beauty of the Temple building and listen to the songs of the singers and worship of the people. Yet how quickly we see the nation beginning to fall as step by step they sink lower and lower until finally there came the ultimate disaster in 586 BC when the Babylonians completely destroyed Solomon's beautiful Temple. Formal worship thus ended and the people were carried off into captivity.

If 1 Chronicles teaches the necessity to recognize God, 2 Chronicles teaches that if recognition is only form and ceremony it's worse than useless.

This lesson reverberates throughout history and in all the pages of Scripture. Mere formal religion is impotent in the life of a nation.

The application of this is found in 2 Chronicles 5:13:

> *The trumpeters and singers joined in unison, as with one voice, to give praise and thanks to the Lord. Accompanied by trumpets, cymbals and other instruments, they raised their voices in praise to the Lord and sang:*
>
> *"He is good;*
> *his love endures forever."*

Then the temple of the Lord was filled with a cloud.

It was a great moment: the Temple was completed the song of worship perfected and all the notes of the instruments and voices merged into one great proclamation of praise, then the glory of God filled the temple. Now read Acts 2:1–3:

> *When the day of Pentecost came, they were all together in one place. Suddenly a sound like the blowing of a violent wind came from heaven and filled the whole house where they were sitting. They saw what seemed to be tongues of fire that separated and came to rest on each of them.*

Do you see the similarity between the two temples? The first was natural, the last spiritual. The Old Testament picture of the Temple is the symbol of the presence and government of God in the centre of the nation. The New Testament picture is again the temple, no longer of material things, but of living stones (men and women) merged into the presence of God by the indwelling power of the Holy Spirit (1 Corinthians 6:19).

The lesson of 1 Chronicles to the nation was: if you think you will maintain your power and strength through politics, diplomacy and military might without God you are doomed to disaster. Israel had to learn, as we have to learn, that it is to such people of God, as Samuel and not Saul; Nathan and not David; Ahijah and not Solomon that the people of God must look and listen for the word God is speaking. In other words it is not to the politicians, captains of industry or media moguls the nation must turn to hear God, but to His living eternal Word via those who proclaim and adhere to it.

## Warning to the church

Now in 2 Chronicles the message is to the church, warning it against mere formalism and thereby failing to fulfil her mission to the nation.

The Bible knows nothing about the establishment of the church by the state but teaches that the church must establish the nation. If religious leaders wish to sit in secular government and presume to speak to the nation on behalf of God, then let them speak God's Word. For a formal, dead, ritualistic religion is worse than no religion at all. On the one hand it deludes millions into believing they are right with God, while on the other hand millions who see through the dead formality are turned off by it, rejecting the church when in fact they've never heard the truth about Christ.

If the church of God is not what it is supposed to be, the nation will be without salt and light and will rush headlong towards disaster, and the blame lies with the church. For if we were displaying the life of Christ and allowing His life to flow through and out of us, the nation would be transformed.

Think again of God's new temple at Pentecost and look at what happened in Jerusalem – the people were amazed, confounded and convicted. The tragedy today is that the church does not amaze, confound or convict because of its failure to believe and speak the Word of God. Because of its liberalism and/or formalism it is often spiritually dead and ineffective, and as a consequence the nation turns to human rationalism and says to the church, "We don't need you!"

It's not that our nation is unaware of spiritual things, the popularity of the New Age movement and occult in its many manifestations point to the latent spiritual emptiness of our people. But the church fails to respond properly and point people to God. An example of this was the funeral service held for Princess Diana on 6 September 1997. The pop star Elton John sang "Candle in the Wind" and received a knighthood for his participation. Prime

Minister Tony Blair read a well known, but sadly inappropriate, passage of Scripture. And Earl Spencer's speech, seen by many as the high point of the service, castigated the paparazzi, the media, and the House of Windsor, encapsulating all of his pent-up feelings crying out for expression. When the Earl finished, people outside Westminster Abbey began applauding and the applause swept inside in a manner quite unprecedented in a state funeral. Sentimental pop culture and liberal religion, with Jesus Christ kept well outside the proceedings.

## The remedy

The answer is for the church to be the church, and that means to be filled with the awesome presence of God, burning with His glory, glowing with His light and communicating His fire. We must learn that worship is motivated from the inside, from the heart and not by buildings and outward appearances. When Christians realize this truth they will see how their hard unyielding attitudes, filled with pride in their knowledge and their insistence on doing things their way, is the major stumbling block to new life in the church. When, in line with 2 Chronicles 7:14, they are prepared to face up to the poverty of their spirit, the selfishness of their worship and lack of blessings upon their ministry, then in tears of repentance the Spirit of God will lead them through the humbling experience of revival. For revival means Christian men and women on their knees in tears of confession and prayer. Then the church will go through a time of glorious growth.

Meanwhile the ministry and method available to achieve this humbling work and so reach the lost is to preach Christ, His crucifixion, His victory over death, sin and Satan, and to let the Spirit of God move in wonder-working power within His church and out to the community. This is vital – we have to let the church be the church. This is the secret of bringing about spiritual revival and growth for herein lies conviction, conversion and new life.

This is the church that Jesus Christ will bless because men and women will tell out of their souls the greatness of the Lord. They will raise Jesus Christ in sermon, prayer and praise, rejoicing in His birth, life, death and resurrection. And our heavenly Father will smile in pleasure as His children worship His wonderful Son. That smile, that pleasure, will warm our hearts and ensure we are in His good will and purpose. Christians will grow, and so the church will grow to the glory of God. The early church was but a handful of people but, because of the life that was in it and the power of the Spirit upon it, it was mighty. It shook the ancient world. It did indeed turn the world upside down, demolishing arguments and every pretension that set itself up against the knowledge of God and obedience to Christ. That is the calling and challenge the church of God must accept today if it is to reach a lost generation.

# 15

## Ezra
## – Return from Exile

Ezra continues where 2 Chronicles left off and shows how God fulfilled His promise through Jeremiah to bring His people back to the land of promise after seventy years' captivity in Babylon.

Ezra relates the account of two returns from Babylon: the first led by Zerubbabel to rebuild the Temple (chapters 1–6) and the second led by Ezra to rebuild the spiritual condition of the people (chapters 7–10). Between these two accounts is a period of fifty-eight years during which Esther lived and ruled as queen in Persia.

In 539 BC Cyrus, king of Persia, defeated Babylon and became master of the ancient world, thus making Judah a part of the Persian empire. Unlike his predecessors, Cyrus preferred to leave his subject peoples in their own lands and immediately set about restoring displaced minorities to their native countries (Ezra 1:2–4). The Jews, forewarned of this event by Isaiah's prophecy (Isaiah 44:28), saw Cyrus's rise to power as the direct intervention of God to set His people free. They took this as tangible proof that the deprivations of exile had been accepted as penance for their guilt and the return to their homeland was the token of God's forgiveness.

### The rebuilding of the Temple

So one year later, Zerubbabel led approximately 45,000 Jews back from Babylon to Jerusalem and immediately rebuilt the altar on the ruined site of Solomon's Temple and began worship services (Ezra 3:2–6).

Two years after that the foundation of the new Temple was laid. Older priests and family heads wept aloud when they unfavourably compared the new, much less grand Temple, with the old which had been built by King Solomon, but others, younger men and women who did not know the old Temple, rejoiced at the progress being made and the sign of the Lord's hand upon His people (Ezra 3:7–13).

There is a lesson here for us today: no matter what the older believers thought, God had the situation under control. They were the people selected by God and called out of captivity to live and worship in Jerusalem for that particular time. They were no longer in Babylon among those who preferred the comfort of the status quo to the unsettling experience of change. And they wanted to please God. They had many personal needs to attend to but their priority was to rebuild the Temple, which they proved by ensuring that the first thing they did when they arrived in Jerusalem was to take a freewill offering towards the cost of rebuilding the house of the Lord. They clearly put God's work above their own interests. They were also working for the right reasons for there was nothing to attract them to the desolate land and ruined city of Jerusalem except the fact it was God's holy land and the city in which He had chosen to site His Temple.

So, they were the right people living in the right place wanting to do the right work for the right reasons. Yet among them were mature believers who were in danger of missing the will of God for the times in which they lived by looking backwards in a manner dangerously similar to that of the Israelites in the wilderness, who looked back with longing to Egypt (Numbers 11:4–6). They missed out on the fact that God was doing a new thing His way. There is a world of difference between looking back with grateful thanks for past experiences, learning from them and moving on, and being so enamoured with the past that we despise the present, missing out on today's opportunities. And tellingly, as we have already seen in previous studies, Solomon's Temple, for all its magnificence, could not prevent the nation of Israel from falling into idolatry.

However, despite the good intentions of the men and women back from Babylon, the work came to a halt in 534 BC, and it was not until fourteen years later that any serious attempt was made to rebuild the Temple. The reason given was the opposition from outside forces (chapter 4), and while this was true it was not the full story. We gather from the prophets Haggai and Zechariah in Ezra 5:1–2 and the evidence from their own books that a further reason for failure to undertake the rebuilding of the Temple was not so much opposition from outside but apathy from within. Poverty, taxation, drought and famine had robbed the rump of Israel of their drive to do more than eke out a living on the few square miles that were left to them. Nevertheless, both Ezra and the books of Haggai and Zechariah agree that by 520 BC, once the necessary leadership was given, the work of rebuilding the Temple was taken in hand and completed in five years. Ezra accounts for this turnaround of circumstances in 5:3 – 6:19 by a change of heart of the king.

## God faithfully protects His people

This affords us a wonderful lesson of how God sovereignly protects His people. Though they were held captive in a hostile environment, He raised up pagan kings who were sympathetic to the Israelites' cause, allowing them to return and rebuild their homeland no matter what resistance they faced. Because this was God's promised plan and purpose for His people as expressed in Jeremiah 29:11, nothing could stop it.

Now, having stated that truth, our experience is that the path of faithfulness seldom appears to be a straight line to glory and this is illustrated in Ezra 4:4–5:

> *Then the peoples around them set out to discourage the people*
> *of Judah and make them afraid to go on building. They hired*
> *counsellors to work against them and frustrate their plans*
> *during the entire reign of Cyrus king of Persia and down to the*
> *reign of Darius king of Persia.*

Imagine the frustration and impatience of the Israelites. God had seemingly opened the door for them to rebuild the Temple, yet there was this powerful opposition determined to stop the building project. To add to their problems, offers to help with the work were made by the neighbouring Samaritans. They were the descendants of the remnant of the northern kingdom now assimilated into the mixed racial group that had been resettled in that area by the Assyrians when Samaria was destroyed in 722 BC. The Jews rejected their offer on the grounds that the Samaritans, being a mixed racial group, could not trace their lineage back to Abraham and were no longer part of the covenant people (Ezra 4:1–3; Nehemiah 2:20). On hearing this, the Samaritans angrily appealed to the Persian rulers to veto any further building in Jerusalem, using the history of Israelite troublemaking as their excuse (Ezra 4:4–24). Then, claiming that they were the rightful inheritors of the Mosaic tradition, the Samaritans broke off all relations with the Jerusalem Jews and built a rival temple on Mount Gerizim.

This led to them becoming the sworn enemies of the Jews as the Gospels testify.

Ezra 5:1 records how God sent the two prophets Haggai and Zechariah to encourage the people to get on with the rebuilding of the Temple. The Samaritans responded by once again attempting to halt the construction by writing to Darius the new emperor. However, their plan backfired. Instead of agreeing with them and calling a halt to the Temple re-build, Darius searched the archives and found the original decree from Cyrus authorising the building of the Temple. He then replied to the Samaritans with instructions which were way beyond what the Israelites could dare hope for or ask. It's recorded in Ezra 6:7–8:

> Do not interfere with the work on this temple of God. Let the governor of the Jews and the Jewish elders rebuild this house of God on its site.
>
> Moreover, I hereby decree what you are to do for these elders of the Jews in the construction of this house of God:
>
> The expenses of these men are to be fully paid out of the royal treasury, from the revenues of Trans-Euphrates, so that the work will not stop.

From this we discover that God allowed the setback in building so that the new Temple would not only be built but also paid for by Darius. This fantastic truth is confirmed by 6:22:

> For seven days they celebrated with joy the Feast of Unleavened Bread, because the Lord had filled them with joy by changing the attitude of the king of Assyria, so that he assisted them in the work on the house of God, the God of Israel.

This incident reminds us that living by faith means believing that in the words of Proverbs 21:1: "The king's heart is in the hand of the Lord; he directs it like a watercourse wherever he pleases."

God did it to Cyrus (Ezra 1:1), He did it to Darius (Ezra 6:22) and He did it later to Artaxerxes (Ezra 7:27). God rules the world and He rules history and all for the good of His people and the glory of His name. This should fill Christians with confidence when facing opposition to our work of building the kingdom of God.

There is a fifty-eight-year gap between chapters 6 and 7.

A total of eighty-one years have passed since the first return to Jerusalem under Zerubbabel. Then, in 457 BC, bringing an extremely generous offering for the Temple, Ezra comes to Jerusalem from Babylon with less than 2,000 men bearing special authority from the king of Persia to rebuild the ruined temple and commence temple worship (Ezra 7:11–26).

But Ezra had a problem: "I was ashamed to ask the king for soldiers and horsemen to protect us from enemies on the road" (8:22). Grave dangers faced travellers between Persia and Israel, as proved when some thirteen years later on Nehemiah undertook the same journey and was accompanied by an armed escort (Nehemiah 2:9). But Ezra had gone out on a limb by publicly proclaiming his faith in God's ability to protect His people, and records how he told the king the principles of faith he lived by: "The gracious hand of our God is on everyone who looks to him, but his great anger is against all who forsake him" (Ezra 8:22).

Ezra was saying that those who seek God even in their darkest hours are safe under the shadow of His wings, but those who forsake Him are continually exposed even when they seem secure. God's servants are promised His power whereas His enemies have it promised against them. Ezra believed this with all his heart, and with his mouth made confession of it before the king. Therefore, he was ashamed to ask the king for protection in case he caused the king and those about him to scorn either God's power to help His people or Ezra's faith in that power.

The application for us today is: after making sure that God's call to do something is authentic, without being presumptuous or reckless, we should not over-worry about our circumstances or count our five loaves and two fishes wondering if they will be enough, or look at the waves questioning if they will support us. We must keep our eyes fixed on Jesus, our spirit open to His voice through His Word and the advice of godly advisers, and when we are sure of His leading, put our faith into action and move forward. Remember, "If God is for us, who can be against us?" (Romans 8:31).

Aware of the potential danger Ezra proclaimed a fast (Ezra 8:21) and a prayer meeting (verse 23). Matthew Henry, the Puritan commentator, states:

> *They were strangers on the road, and were to march through their enemies' territory without a pillar of cloud and fire to lead them as their fathers had; but they believed the power and favour of God was theirs, and the ministration of his angels would be with them, and by faith expected to obtain divine assistance. God answered their prayers, the journey was uneventful and the party arrived safely.*

# Israel's sins

In chapter 9, Ezra records how the leaders come in broken-hearted contrition to confess the wrongdoing of the people:

> *After these things had been done, the leaders came to me*
> *and said, "The people of Israel, including the priests and*
> *the Levites, have not kept themselves separate from the*
> *neighbouring peoples with their detestable practices, like those*
> *of the Canaanites, Hittites, Perizzites, Jebusites, Ammonites,*
> *Moabites, Egyptians and Amorites. They have taken some*
> *of their daughters as wives for themselves and their sons,*
> *and have mingled the holy race with the peoples around*
> *them. And the leaders and officials have led the way in this*
> *unfaithfulness."*
>
> *When I heard this, I tore my tunic and cloak, pulled hair*
> *from my head and beard and sat down appalled. Then everyone*
> *who trembled at the words of the God of Israel gathered around*
> *me because of the unfaithfulness of the exiles. And I sat there*
> *appalled until the evening sacrifice.*
>
> EZRA 9:1–4

Considering that the nation had just suffered seventy years' captivity for sins just like this, the situation was fraught with the strong likelihood of God again expressing His anger at the nation's sin. Ezra's prays to God and confesses the sin of his people (9:5), and in chapter 10 God's gracious response is seen in the hearts of the people. A proclamation is issued and the nation assembles. It happens to be a day when it is raining (verse 9), but despite the rain the people stand, thousands of them, in front of the Temple and confess their guilt: the fact that they had disobeyed God. They agreed to put away the wives and children they had acquired outside the will of God and to live in accordance with God's law. This action would ultimately lead to changed lives and the great revival recorded in Nehemiah chapter 8.

# 16

# Nehemiah
## – Kingdom Builders

The book of Nehemiah has two themes: the reconstruction of the wall of Jerusalem (chapters 1–7) and the restoration of the people (chapters 8–13).

A total of 140 years had passed since the final destruction of Jerusalem by the forces of Babylon, and despite attempts to rebuild the wall it still lay in ruins, leaving the city open and vulnerable to its enemies (Ezra 4:6–23). Discouraged by opposition from those who had settled in the country during their captivity and disheartened by the sheer size of the task, the Jews grew weary, abandoned the work, and amidst the rubble, the people of God lived in misery and shame. They needed inspired leadership, and fourteen years after Ezra's return in the year 445 BC God raised up a man for the hour, prepared him for the task and called him to serve the Lord in the rebuilding of the wall of Jerusalem – that man was Nehemiah.

## Nehemiah's concern for the exiles

Chapter 1 records how after hearing from his brother Hanani of the desperate conditions the returned exiles were living in, Nehemiah underwent the life transformation of a man inspired of God: "I sat down and wept. For some days I mourned and fasted and prayed before the God of heaven" (Nehemiah 1:4).

This is the way to soul-building and Christian ministry. When God places the burden on our hearts we begin to weep for the state of the people and His church. This is a basic principle. Nehemiah was called to rebuild the wall but first he had to weep over the ruins. Then, having been brought to the point where he knows what God wants him to do, he asks the Lord for His help, recognizing that it will be a lot harder for him to leave the Persian court than it was to enter it. Although he has no idea how God will work things out, his trust in the Lord is such that he confidently expects Him to take care of the details and the answers to his prayers will "come to pass".

## God's call to ministry

Four months later the king presents Nehemiah with an opportunity to unburden himself and explain his concern for his people (2:3). By referring to the desecration of the graves of his ancestors, Nehemiah knows this will arouse the sympathies of the king who, in effect, asks "How can I help?" We then see how Nehemiah has thought out his plan of campaign and with answers prepared is ready to be questioned. In the outworking of his encounter with the king, Nehemiah will discover three vital truths for anyone who believes they may be receiving God's call to a ministry. Alan Redapth in his commentary on Nehemiah, *Victorious Christian Service*, states them clearly:

- He wanted to know he was sent – "If it pleases the king… let him send me" (verse 5).
- He wanted to know he would be safe – "may I have letters to the governors of Trans-Euphrates" (verse 7).
- He wanted to know he would be supplied – "timber… for the gates… wall and… residence" (verse 8).

What four months earlier appeared as "mission impossible" was now taking on form and structure and looking distinctly positive. The key was the priority Nehemiah placed on prayer, then, knowing he was called by God for this task, he had the assurance of being sent, safe and supplied.

Nehemiah was going to need this assurance, because more often than not when a believer undertakes a task for God of this magnitude opposition arises to hinder and stop the work. We see this in verse 10 with the warning of the impending battle he would fight: "When Sanballat the Honorite and Tobiah the Ammonite official heard about this, they were very much disturbed that someone had come to promote the welfare of the Israelites."

# The challenge before Nehemiah

As Nehemiah approached Jerusalem he would appreciate why the message he received concerning the city of God was so depressing. It was an incredible challenge; a modest estimate puts the damaged wall at 21 miles in length. Remember, also, that the destruction was enormous; the stones that had been hurled down into the valley were of massive size and weight and had to be located, exposed, hauled back up the hill and then reassembled into the wall. In addition, working against him was the psychological factor that this had been tried before and failed, which meant Nehemiah was taking on a history of defeat. So recent failure and apathy stared him in the face. This was apparent in his third problem – the workers themselves were discouraged and disheartened.

Nehemiah and his trusted friends, inspecting the ruined wall by moonlight, conjure up a dramatic scene (2:12). No doubt he did this secretly to avoid opposition from Sanballat and Tobiah and the negative comments that are all too often heard from God's people. Then, after getting the measure of the work involved, Nehemiah gathered the people together and sought their aid in rebuilding the wall.

Here we learn the secret of releasing the power within God's church: it's working in unity. However, unity does not just happen, we have to work at it. Instead of concentrating on what divides we must remember what unites:

> *There is* one *body and* one *Spirit… one hope… one Lord,* one *faith,* one *baptism;* one *God and Father of all.*
>
> EPHESIANS 4:4–6, EMPHASIS ADDED

# Nehemiah leads the team's rebuilding efforts

Co-workers with Christ means there are no superstars, only team members carrying out their God-given tasks for which they have been gifted. Men and women become useful members of God's family by setting aside their desires for personal recognition, praise and glory, rolling up their sleeves and pressing on with the task that confronts them. "They replied, 'Let us start rebuilding.' So they began this good work" (Nehemiah 2:18).

Under Nehemiah's inspiring leadership, work on the wall got off to an excellent start, and in chapter 3 we see his gift of administration as he apportions responsibility for sections of the wall to various individuals. Note how the phrases "next to them" or "next to him" occur throughout the chapter.

People from a wide variety of skills and backgrounds, trades and localities worked together to repair the ruined wall. Note, too, that many of the people made repairs to the wall near their own homes (verses 10, 23, 28, 30). People working like this would ensure the work was done well for their own personal safety, and in future years they would look at the wall as they came in and out of their homes and be reminded of their workmanship. They would not want present work to bring future embarrassment.

The workers on the wall all knew that the success of the enterprise was dependent upon God who had inspired its beginning. In addition, throughout the account in chapter 4, the recurrent problems and imminent dangers are deliberately interspersed with affirmations of faith and confidence in God. Consequently, the story of adversity becomes a testimony to the abundant sufficiency of the Lord. In addition, to make sure the glory is not misplaced, Nehemiah continually points the people God-wards. With faith in God's ability to see the work accomplished in the face of criticism, verbal assault, psychological pressure, physical danger, natural discouragement and fear, the people were able to continue the work, not because they relied on a strong faith but because they relied upon a strong God.

## Opposing forces

Of course, hand-in-hand with a good work goes the devil's work of opposition.

The leading opponents have increased to three: Sanballat the Horonite, Tobiah the Ammonite and now Geshem the Arab warlord. In Nehemiah 4:1–9 and 13:1–9 we see how Sanballat represents "secular force" and Tobiah "hatred", masked under the cloak of religion. What is fascinating is how Sanballat's political objections, Tobiah's religious sensibilities and Geshem's materialistic interests meant the tormenting trio, although motivated by different desires, were united in their opposition to Nehemiah. It reminds us of the friendship forged by Pilate and Herod over their opposition to Christ (Luke 23:12) and is symptomatic of the unlikely opposition united against the proclamation of the gospel today.

In chapter 6, with the wall rebuilt and only the gates remaining to be rehung, the opposing forces redoubled their efforts and in doing so revealed the modus operandi that Satan uses against the church of Jesus Christ.

First, intrigue. This is the personal invitation from the world to leave the work and, as friends, enter into dialogue (6:1–4). When that didn't work, Sanballat mounted his second method of attack by publicly slandering

Nehemiah's character with defamatory comments insinuating that Nehemiah was building his own kingdom in Jerusalem (6:5–7). The third phase of the opposition via Shemaiah becomes sinister as he tries to deceive Nehemiah by delivering a fake message, seemingly attempting to save Nehemiah's life but in reality tempting him to sin (6:10–14). This reminds us that Satan shows his true and most dangerous colours when he comes as an angel of light.

Nehemiah had every reason to be unsuspecting of Shemaiah's invitation to meet. After all, he was one of Jerusalem's prophets and as far as Nehemiah was concerned, he probably wanted to share his problems and assure Nehemiah of his support during intense personal opposition. However, the old friend became a new enemy and, using "the Lord told me" language in a fresh attempt to destroy Nehemiah's character, he tried to persuade him to take refuge in the temple (6:10). Shemaiah knew that if he could persuade Nehemiah, who was not a priest, to hide in the temple he would have broken the law of God. His suggestion that they close the doors means he was either going to lure Nehemiah into the area reserved exclusively for priests or, with the doors closed, say that Nehemiah had violated any of a number of holiness rules. Without witnesses, Nehemiah's denial of the prophet's word would count for nothing and his testimony, no matter what the excuse, would be compromised. They had failed to brand him a political rebel so now they attempt to make him a religious transgressor. Nehemiah's reply demonstrates his courage and faith in his mission for God: "Should a man like me run away? Or should one like me go into the temple to save his life? I will not go!" (6:11).

However, because of its intensely personal nature the most hurtful intrigue was yet to come (6:17–19). Among Nehemiah's own followers were those who were writing sympathetic letters and exchanging similar views in alliance with the adversary. It is the fifth column undermining the building work from the inside.

Today, Christians face the same trials and temptations Nehemiah faced and his response should encourage us.

To the enticement to leave the work and meet to talk, he replied that he was doing a great work and would not leave it for them (6:3). When faced with rumour and slander he openly denied their accusations, replying, "Nothing like what you are saying is happening; you are just making it up out of your head" (6:8). And he faced up to the religious opposition with utter defiance: "Should a man like me run away?" (6:11). The Sanballats, Tobiahs, Geshems and their kind will come with their sly invitations for the born-again Christian to leave the work and join in their "agenda". Should we leave God's work to join a world that is under judgment? The answer is a resounding, "No!" In spite of Sanballat, Tobiah, Geshem the Arab, the nobles, false prophets, temptations, misrepresentations, threats and fear, the wall was completed in fifty-two days and the gates hung.

# Revival in Jerusalem

When the building work ended, instead of a sense of anticlimax, an unusual event took place that was to influence the spiritual life of God's people dramatically – revival broke out at the Water Gate. In every genuine revival two major factors always appear: there is always a hunger for God's Word and there is always an enthusiastic response from God's people. Nehemiah 8:1–3 records that the people were so single-minded in wanting to hear the Word of God that they listened to Ezra read for five hours from daybreak to noon. All the people listened attentively and responded enthusiastically. "Ezra praised the Lord, the great God; and all the people lifted their hands and responded, "Amen! Amen!" (8:6).

Then comes conviction! Before happiness there are tears (8:9–10). The people wept because what they heard in the reading of Scripture condemned their lifestyle and convicted them of personal sin and guilt. Yet despite the seriousness of their sin the people were urged to dry their tears. For Scripture not only condemns sin, it proclaims the remedy, and within ten days, the holiday of Tabernacles, which had not been celebrated since the days of Joshua, would be followed by the Day of Atonement. Then, in accordance with the procedure laid down in Leviticus, all the uncleanliness and rebellion of the Israelites would be fully dealt with and pardoned through the atoning sacrifice of a scapegoat carrying the sins to a solitary place. This action anticipated a greater atonement by looking forward to that first Good Friday when God's Son carried our sins to the cross in His sinless body. By that unique sacrifice, those who repent and believe are eternally forgiven and they, too, hear the reassuring words, "Do not grieve, for the joy of the Lord is your strength" (8:10).

Out of the revival that began at the Water Gate the most significant gesture of response to God's grace and visitation was still to come. It is recorded in chapter 9 when, on the twenty-fourth of that month, three-and-a-half weeks later, they met again for a national day of repentance and recommitment during which another public assembly shared in confession (verse 2), worship (verses 3–5), reflection (verses 6–37) and promise (verse 38).

It is a life dialogue with God and it works like this. When we read Scripture, it will produce a response, for God's Word drives us into the presence of the

One of whom it so eloquently and relevantly speaks. We then come from that encounter, challenged, convicted, forgiven, taught and inspired, for every encounter with God through the pages of Scripture reveals some new facet of His nature, deeds, purpose, promise and resources. These discoveries need to be channelled through our hearts and minds into a responsive conversation with the God who has spoken to us from His Word, the Bible. This is demonstrated in this great chapter 9 where we see how, when the Israelites responded to the Levites' call to prayer, they were led into the presence of an active and responsive God. After their confession, worship and honest reflection, it was time to publicly affirm their promise of loyalty and love, and verse 38 brings it all together. They have recognized that God is the God of the covenant that He has sustained down through the years, the covenant He first made with Abraham. Now it is time for them to renew that covenant.

How do Christians do this today? Paul explains in 1 Corinthians 10:17: "Because there is one loaf, we, who are many, are one body, for we all partake of the one loaf."

Paul is referring to believers coming together around the Lord's table. When they do that, they are re-enacting the covenant. They say, "this bread symbolizes the body of Jesus – this cup symbolizes the blood of Jesus and reminds us of the new covenant through His blood." They see themselves as members of the redeemed community through the covenant that God has enacted at Calvary, and they reaffirm it every time they participate in the Communion service. They pledge their allegiance to the fact that they are members of the household of God.

When we look back over the promises made by the citizens of Jerusalem recorded in chapter 10, we see how they were confessing God's sovereign control over every aspect of their lives, whether at home or at worship, on their farms, in trading and commerce, in their social contacts and spiritual obligations. And learning from their experience we see how Christian believers wholeheartedly confess that Jesus is Lord of their relationships (verse 30), their time (verse 31) and their possessions (verses 31b–39), and prove their statement of belief by their faith in action. As the apostle James was to later to say: "faith by itself, if it is not accompanied by action, is dead" (James 2:17).

Christians must put their faith into action by showing how Jesus is Lord of their relationships, their time and their possessions.

Prior to the rebuilding of the wall, Jerusalem had been an open city, economically depressed, dangerous, low in morale, under-populated and in no way glorious for God. The new wall was vital if Jerusalem was to experience a renewal of its economic, social and spiritual life. For with its broken fortifications and missing gates, the city was neither an attractive nor a safe place to live and most of the returned exiles from Babylon felt happier and more secure in the surrounding farms and villages. Now that the walls were up, the human factors in this sad situation had to be addressed, and by now it is obvious that Nehemiah's task was much more than a works manager rebuilding the wall of Jerusalem. He now realized that his fuller task was to bring into being, with God's help, a truly godly, mature Jewish community in "the holy city" (Nehemiah 11:1, 18).

He would recall how, when he heard of the sad state of Jerusalem, he sat down and mourned, fasted and prayed. Why? Well, not only for the human needs in Jerusalem, but primarily because God was being dishonoured as long as the city by which He identified himself was laid waste. In Deuteronomy 12:4–28, Moses foretold there would be such a place where the reality of God's presence would be experienced in love and mercy by all who sought Him, and Jerusalem was that appointed place as God proclaimed through Solomon at the dedication of Jerusalem's Temple (2 Chronicles 7:12–16). The psalmists understood this; that is why they expressed such excitement at the prospect of going to the Temple: "Better is one day in your courts than a thousand elsewhere" (Psalm 84:10).

However, none of this could be real while Jerusalem lay in ruins with the Temple services unmanned and disrupted. Therefore, in chapter 11, Nehemiah outlines his plans to repopulate Jerusalem with sufficient citizens to ensure its developing economy and safety. Verse 1 tells us they cast lots to determine who was among the one in ten to make the sacrifice and move to the city. As a result, 5,000 men and women were selected and placed themselves and their futures into the unfolding of God's sovereign will for their lives. What they preferred was secondary to what God desired, and for them discovering God's mind about their futures took priority over every other consideration. You just cannot help but be impressed by the faith, courage and sacrifice of these people who were prepared to uproot themselves and their families from the comparative safety of their familiar surroundings and move to Jerusalem with all the uncertainty it held for them. In addition, they did this purely because they believed it was God's will for them. Their uncomplaining, sacrificial response to God's will sets an exemplary example for us today.

# Spiritual leadership

Some final lessons from Nehemiah on spiritual leadership.

First: Nehemiah faced up to a wrong head-on. A wrong will never be solved until it is admitted to be just that – a wrong. Problems in life whether in church, home or business have to be faced head-on. Detection always precedes solution; for you can never solve a problem you cannot define you have to identify it in order to deal with it.

Second: when Nehemiah identified a problem he stood firm against it. His example teaches that an honest acknowledgment of a wrong must be matched by courageous conviction to deal with it. It is hard not to be influenced by popularity, applause or the fear of man, but Nehemiah stood firm and dealt with the sin that needed to be dealt with. As Jesus taught, "let your 'Yes' be 'Yes', and your 'No', 'No'" (Matthew 5:37).

Third: he worked towards a permanent solution as opposed to the temporary quick fix. Nehemiah knew that God always balances a negative with a positive: "Don't do that" – "Do this".

Fourth: it all has to be tempered with deep devotion. This is where many well-meaning Christians go wrong. They can become "spiritual head-hunters" – negative, angry, suspicious and often fighting one another. We have to maintain the balance between contending for the truth and keeping our heart warm before the Lord.

Fifth: when he had done all he could, Nehemiah always followed it up with prayer, going before the Lord and asking for His blessing upon his efforts.

Nehemiah's closing prayer, that he might be remembered "with favour" (Nehemiah 13:31), was abundantly answered, for Nehemiah handed down to God's people an example of enthusiastic, determined clarity of faith to which evangelical men and women have aspired ever since. In addition, with his administrative skills, enthusiastic reforms and exemplary lifestyle, Nehemiah has enriched the believing church as the Holy Spirit, who inspired his writings, encourages and empowers the believers to be the kind of people Nehemiah was – a man of integrity, conviction and devotion.

That is the type of men and women the world desperately needs; people with conviction and enthusiasm, who bring a word of assurance from the Lord and present a cause to believe in, while being seen to be an authentic model to follow. People with God-given devotion that calms fears, solves confusion and channels energies – wall builders – who are prepared to build the wall of their lives and the church, and to do it for the glory of God.

# 17

# Esther
## – The Providence of God

As we approach the book of Esther, let us first deal with the historical setting. Following that, we will remind ourselves of the story, examine the problems with popular explanations and finally, look at the lessons for us today.

Esther is the only biblical account we have of the majority of Jews who chose to remain in Persia rather than return to Jerusalem. The story is set between chapters 6 and 7 of Ezra, that is, between the first return of the Jews from captivity in Babylon led by Zerubbabel and the second by Ezra.

## Miss Persia

The narrative opens with King Xerxes, the son of Darius (the king who put Daniel in the lion's den), hosting a lavish banquet at which his beautiful wife, Vashti, refuses to wear her crown and tread the catwalk before the assembled heads of state from India to Ethiopia. Though the motive for her refusal is not stated, she probably chose not to degrade herself before the king's drunken guests. A woman saying "No!" to the ruler whose kingdom stretched halfway around the world infuriated his male ego and caused him to suffer public insult. Fearing Vashti's example could influence other women, she was immediately removed and another queen sought for the king.

## Esther's rise to position and power

Among the girls taken to the palace as virtual prisoners was a beautiful young Jewess called Esther who captured the king's heart, causing him to proclaim her his chosen queen. Following her older cousin Mordecai's advice, she kept the fact of her Jewish background secret (2:20) and seven years pass during which Esther reigns as queen.

## A foiled plot and its aftermath

Mordecai then learns of a plot by two of the king's officials to assassinate the king and he tells Esther who, giving the credit to Mordecai, informs the king. Lest we think this was an idle threat, history records that some time later the king was in fact assassinated.

Now yet another strange twist in the story takes place. We would expect Mordecai's "loyalty" to be rewarded, but although the incident was recorded in the chronicles of the king, it was also promptly forgotten, and instead of reading of Mordecai's promotion the story runs on to chapter 3, where we learn that Haman the Agagite becomes the second most powerful figure in the Persian empire. Haman was of the evil line of Amalek, who were the first to attack Israel after the exodus (Numbers 24:20). Because of their atrocities, God commanded Saul to exterminate the Amalekites (1 Samuel 15:2–3). Saul disobeyed and the Amalekites were not defeated completely until late in the eighth century BC (1 Chronicles 4:43).

Initially, the conflict was simply between Mordecai and the king's servants at the gate when they rebuked him for refusing to abide by the king's orders: "Mordecai would not kneel down or pay him [Haman] honour" (3:2). Mordecai defended his behaviour by telling them he was a Jew and was thus exempted or prohibited from such acts. Irritated, the king's servants informed Haman, who reacted furiously. How dare this man defy him and the king? If Mordecai refused to bow down to him because he was a Jew, then this must mean all Jews would behave this way and therefore they all must be dealt with severely. Haman then waited for the opportune time and, by cleverly avoiding mentioning the Jews by name, through bribery and half-truths, he secured the king's permission to cleanse the Persian empire of all Jews. The law was written, translated into the languages of the kingdom and distributed by couriers to all the provinces.

*Dispatches were sent by couriers to all the king's provinces
with the order to destroy, kill and annihilate all the Jews –
young and old, women and little children – on a single day, the
thirteenth day of the twelfth month, the month of Adar, and to
plunder their goods.*

ESTHER 3:13

It was a dream come true for the enemies of Israel.

## Esther's dilemma and decision

A despairing Mordecai managed to get word of the desperate situation to Esther telling her she must intercede with the king for the Jews. Esther initially said, "No way," and defended her decision by explaining that it was against the law to go into the king's presence without being summoned by him. The penalty for doing so was death, with only a small chance that the king might show mercy by extending his golden sceptre and granting that the intruder might live. Since she could not go to the king uninvited, her only hope was to be summoned by the king, but she warned Mordecai not to hold out too much hope as thirty days had passed since Esther had last been in his presence.

Esther's reluctance forced Mordecai to apply considerable pressure to persuade her to intercede for the Jews. He told her not to think that she alone would escape Haman's edict because she was in the king's house. And, if she remained silent, deliverance for the Jews would come from another source, but because of her cowardice she and her father's family would perish. Wanting Esther to realize that the most dangerous thing she could do was to do nothing and hope it would all go away, Mordecai suggests that her exaltation from peasant to queen was God's way of obtaining a saviour for His people. He then posed the question that has become the classic statement of support for the doctrine of providence, and is the key to understanding of the book of Esther: "who knows but that you have come to royal position for such a time as this?"(Esther 4:14).

Under intense pressure, Esther submits and sends word to Mordecai that she will intercede with the king for her people. She instructs him to assemble all the Jews who live in Susa and have them fast for her. She and her maids will do likewise and then she will attempt to see the king. She will break the law of the land and take her life into her own hands, "And if I perish, I perish" (4:16b).

151

# The fly in the ointment

So to Esther 5:1–4.

What a tense moment this must have been for Esther. Can you imagine her state of mind as she chooses her dress, shoes, perfume and hairstyle for this occasion? The king, though surprised to see her, recognizes her distress and extends his sceptre, so sparing her life, and asks what she requires of him. Evading his question concerning the reason for her visit, Esther requests that the king and his prime minister, Haman, attend a banquet she has already prepared for them. Why she didn't take that opportunity to speak to King Xerxes about the Jews we do not know, but perhaps she was using female intuition to arouse the king's curiosity. For she continued to tantalize the king by answering this question as to what she wanted from him by saying that she would make her petition known at the next banquet.

Attending this first banquet boosted Haman's ego. He has not only won the confidence of the king, he has also managed (or so he thinks) to win over the queen. Filled with wine and swollen with pride Haman leaves the banquet for home. However, by the King's Gate, as always, is Mordecai who does not stand nor even acknowledge his position, and Haman, though furious, hides his anger. Once home, he cannot wait to boast of the way the king has exalted him above all his peers and of the banquet he has just attended and the one he will attend the following day. But as his wife and friends stroke his ego his countenance suddenly darkens, for the day has not been a total success. There is a fly in the ointment of Haman's happiness – Mordecai. In spite of all the glory which is his, Mordecai casts a large shadow by refusing to acknowledge his power and authority. The satisfaction of all his success is outweighed somehow by the stubborn rebellion of this one man.

The solution seems so simple to his family and friends – do away with Mordecai. Don't wait for the appointed day when all the Jews are to be killed, let Mordecai be a kind of "first fruits". Let Haman build an impressive gallows that very night and let him speak to the king first thing in the morning and have Mordecai hung on the gallows before the banquet. Then he can truly savour the moment of glory he shares in the presence of the king and queen. This suggestion appeals to Haman, who immediately sets out to have the gallows constructed for use in the morning.

## Sleepless in Susa

Esther 6:1–14 records how the king has a poor night's sleep, possibly kept awake by the sounds of sawing, hammering and so on from Haman's construction of a gallows. Finally, in frustration, he calls for his servants to read to him from his chronicles. What should the servant read but the account of the two traitors who plotted to assassinate the king and of the Jew, Mordecai, the hero who reported this plot. Xerxes realizes he might well owe his life to Mordecai and yet nothing was recorded about any reward given to him, so he determines to put the matter right – Mordecai will be rewarded.

At that very moment Haman arrives at the palace and is summoned to the king's presence. He cannot wait to repeat the lines he has probably rehearsed all night, the lines which will convince the king that Mordecai is a menace to society and a threat to his kingdom. But before Haman can get his words out the king asks him, "What should be done for the man the king delights to honour?" (6:6). Blinded by pride, it never occurred to Haman that the king was thinking of honouring anyone but himself, and he describes in detail the kind of honour he thinks appropriate. What a shock when Haman suddenly realizes that the honoured servant the king is referring to is his most hated enemy, Mordecai. Worst of all he, Haman is to dress Mordecai in a royal robe, lead him around the city and proclaim to all that the king is honouring this man, a man he had planned to execute that very morning.

## How the tables have turned

When he returns home with his head covered and in stunned silence, it is easy to see that Haman's day has not gone well. If he had expected to be consoled by family and friends, that was not to be either. They had no words of encouragement for him but instead they interpret the day's events as a prophecy of things to come – this is just the beginning. Not only will he not defeat Mordecai, but Haman will fall before him. Friends and family have barely spoken the words of doom when there is a knock at the door. The king's servants have come to escort Haman to the banquet. He is trapped, his doom is imminent. Even his closest friends and family see it coming.

In Esther 7:1–10 the King Xerxes and Haman arrive at Esther's banquet and the king once again brings up the subject of Esther's request. Haman's pride blinds him in yet another way. Not realizing Esther is a Jew, and therefore condemned to death by the law he passed, he fails to recognize that she is also his enemy and rather than feel threatened, he feels safe in her presence. Esther then informs the king that she has been sold, along with her people, not into slavery but unto death. This bombshell angers the king and he immediately offers to rectify the situation. "Who is he? Where is the man who has dared to do such a thing?" he asks the queen (7:5). This presumptuous person will be dealt with; all he needs is a name and where this evil person can be found. After keeping the king in suspense, Esther, to Haman's shock and horror, tells the king the villain's name, identifying Haman as both the enemy and a wicked man.

Stunned and angered by what Esther has told him, and coming to terms with the implications, Xerxes walks out to the garden, probably to clear his head, grasp what has happened and decide what he must do. Had nothing more occurred, Haman would still have been in deep trouble with the king but he may have survived. However, God's providential intervention in this matter is not yet complete. Haman, terrified, and sensing the anger in the king's demeanour, not to mention Esther's, makes one last effort to save himself, and while the king is out of the room approaches the couch where Esther is still reclining to plead with her for mercy. But in his panic, and perhaps as a consequence of too much wine, he stumbles and falls on top of Esther's couch. At that very moment the king re-enters the room and assumes the worst – Haman is now sexually assaulting his wife, the queen. There is no hope for Haman after this and one of the king's servants tells the king there is a gallows ready for use, adding another devastating blow against Haman by revealing that he had it made for Mordecai who spoke up to save the king. So Haman is led away to be executed on his own gallows (7:10). Mordecai is promoted in Haman's place, the Jews are saved and chapter 9 records the revenge taken against their enemies.

## Misinterpretation of the book of Esther

Over the years, the book of Esther has been written off as unspiritual because the name of God does not appear in the book. But this is not strictly true; God's name is in fact used four or five times – albeit as an acrostic, as in Psalm 119. This only comes across in Hebrew and sees the letters JHWH and YHWH appear in the story. JHWH is translated as Jehovah in English and Yahweh is the Hebrew.

Another criticism is that the actions of Esther and Mordecai are dishonest, for example they should have been back in Jerusalem with Ezra and Nehemiah rebuilding the land of Israel, and furthermore Esther hid her Jewish identity and kept her Babylonian name (which had been given to her in honour of one of their gods) instead of her Jewish one in the way Daniel did. In addition, she married a Gentile and ordered the slaughter of their enemies after the tables were turned.

The point could also be made that Mordecai brought all the trouble upon the Jews by refusing to bow to Haman, and his excuse for not doing so because he was a Jew was in direct contradiction to God's command that the exiles were to serve those in authority over them (Jeremiah 27:6–15). In Daniel 3, it is very clear that bowing down to Nebuchadnezzar's golden image was false worship, but this is not the case here – Mordecai's refusal to stand up or acknowledge Haman's presence is not a refusal to worship. We stand when the judge enters the court; it is that sort of thing. What's more, Mordecai accepts what he is unwilling to give. He will not honour the man whom the king has commanded all the citizens of his kingdom to honour, but in chapter 6, when the king orders Haman to see to it that Mordecai is honoured, Haman (reluctantly) obeys, and Mordecai willingly receives this honour (6:10–11). If it is wrong for Mordecai to honour Haman on the grounds that it is an act of worship, why is it suddenly right for Haman to do so to Mordecai and for him to receive it? Daniel had no problem saying to Darius the Mede, "O king, live for ever!" (Daniel 6:21). It seems that Mordecai's behaviour is an expression of Jewish national pride rather than adherence to Exodus 20:5: "You shall not bow down to them or worship them [false gods]".

What is clear is that neither Mordecai nor Esther are model saints. They are much more like Jonah and Samson than Daniel or Joseph. It is wrong to idolize Esther or Mordecai above scriptural warrant and overlook any character problems because they are "in the Bible". There are numerous examples in the Bible of great men and women of God committing immoral acts, such as Abraham passing his wife off as his sister (Genesis 12:10–20); Lot living among the wicked people of Sodom (Genesis 19) and David committing adultery with Bathsheba (2 Samuel 11). Apart from the telling fact that neither Mordecai nor Esther are mentioned in the New Testament, the Bible makes no moral judgment on them but it expects us to use our Christian sense. They were raised up by God, but were not necessarily godly. If immoral practices among the Israelites are found before the exile, why should anyone be surprised to find other expressions of ungodly conduct during and after the exile?

Could the main lesson from this book be the way in which we Christians are inclined to see Esther and Mordecai as model saints and examples of faith and godliness when there is no biblical proof that they were? In other words we are never to assume that because the right methods are present, the right meaning is present as well, for example we assume there was repentance because the Jews mourned. We also assume that because there was fasting there must also have been prayer. Since Mordecai spoke of the possibility that Esther's position as queen might prove to be the means of the Jews' deliverance, we automatically assume Mordecai had faith in God and in His providential care of His people, yet there is nothing in Scripture to prove this assumption is correct. Could it be that the author wants us to understand that we may go through the right motions and yet never really know God?

The Old Testament prophets rebuked the Jews for precisely this. They fasted, but it was mere ritual with no reality (Isaiah 58:1–12). And the same can be said for their sacrifices (Amos 5:21–24; Micah 6:6–8). Going through the right motions and yet never really knowing God was not just a problem of the Jews in Old Testament days, it was also the problem of Judaism in the days of our Lord, and later in the early days of the New Testament church as described in the book of Acts and the epistles. The scribes and Pharisees were caught up in external things, while God has always been concerned with the heart (Luke 16:15).

Perhaps it's only when we strip away the glamour and hero worship of Esther and Mordecai and instead see two gifted but flawed individuals, that we begin to discern the main purpose of this book, which is to teach us about God's providential care of His people in spite of their failings, and that we get into trouble when we deliberately hide our faith. Who of us, like Esther, have not kept quiet when we know we should speak out for God? Who of us have not hesitated and delayed doing the right thing because it might place us in danger or embarrassment? Who of us, like Mordecai, have been motivated for the right reasons into doing the wrong thing and acting in a way contrary to our Christian testimony?

Yet, throughout this story you sense God standing behind the scenes working for good, just as He does in our lives, even though we cannot see or sometimes do not want to see Him. Vashti's deposition, Esther's selection as her successor, Mordecai's discovery of the plot against the king and his subsequent reward are only a few of the many "chance" happenings that are better explained by God effecting the deliverance of His people from their persecutors. The fast-moving events that seem to be under the control of men such as Xerxes and Haman prove in the end to have been directed by God for the benefit of His people. Even the law of the Medes and Persians, which should have brought about the slaughter of the Jews, was overruled. This should not surprise us, after all, Psalm 138:2 tells us: "you have exalted above all things your name and your word."

God had promised He would bring His people back from exile to rebuild the land and nothing nor no one could stop Him (Daniel 9:17; Ezekiel 32:22–23, 32, 36; Jeremiah 29:10ff.).

Above all, the story of Esther is a magnificent display of the sovereignty of God in preserving, not only Judah, but the entire messianic line. Here is another incident when the purposes of God seemed to be on the verge of collapsing. If Haman had succeeded, then the Davidic line would have been broken – there would have been no stable in Bethlehem, no Calvary, etc. In other words, our entire salvation rested on this one woman – Esther. Esther 4:4 is the key. God putting His man (or woman in this case) in the right place at the right time.

Which brings us to the final assurance of God's providence – we win!

It is a strange truth that both the name of Jesus and the followers of Jesus can bring out the worst in some people. He in whom no one has ever found any fault, He who bled and died for the sins of humankind, He who is the source of all goodness, compassion and joy can become the excuse for almost unimaginable acts of cruelty and evil against those who bear His name as Christians. Today in many parts of the world Christians suffer terribly for their faith, and we are being marginalized and legislated against by media and hostile governments in the West. The book of Esther reminds us of the glorious fact of God's providential love for His people and proclaims the clear message of assurance that you cannot eliminate God's people. No matter how many of them you persecute or kill or even marginalize or legislate against, you cannot get rid of God-honouring, God-serving, God-worshipping men, women, boys and girls scattered all over the earth who believe what we read in Philippians 2:10–11:

> that at the name of Jesus every knee should bow,
> in heaven and on earth and under the earth,
> and every tongue confess that Jesus Christ is Lord,
> to the glory of God the Father.

If you believe that, Christian, then trust Him, and in trusting live the Christian life to the full. And through your problems and your difficulties, fears, opposition and attacks upon your faith, demonstrate the truth of the supreme promise of providence given in the New Testament in Romans 8:28: "that in all things God works for the good of those who love him, who have been called according to his purpose."

# 18

## Job
## – Suffering Saints

The book of Job is part of the Wisdom literature of the Old Testament, and being set in the period of the Patriarchs around the time of Abraham makes it one of the oldest books of the Bible.

It answers the question, "Why do good people suffer?", through the story of a righteous, God-fearing man who lost everything, and wrestles with the question, "Why?". Job passionately and persistently puts his question to God, refuses to accept silence as an answer, and gives the lie to the superficial assumption that on entering the Christian life our storms and trials will be over.

Job wrestled to the point of mental, emotional and spiritual exhaustion before he found peace in his experience of suffering. That peace came, not as you would expect when he understood the reason for his trials, but when not understanding he bowed in faith to the sovereign majesty and grace of God and accepted the outworking of God's hand on his life. Job's experience should teach us that the gospel is God's way of addressing the problems of life, yet there will be times when we do not necessarily understand the way in which the answer is being worked out in our lives and circumstances.

The book begins with us being taken behind the scenes of heaven.

### God and Satan strike a deal

In the first chapters of the story we eavesdrop on a debate between God and Satan about Job, a man who was consistently faithful to God. God challenges

Satan to consider His servant of whom He is proud. Satan replies, "Does Job fear God for nothing?" (1:9), cynically expressing contempt for Job's faith, and insinuating that he only loves God because of the divine blessing he receives. This exchange reveals that Satan knows nothing of how grace can transform a life and that he always belittles the good we do by sneering at and devaluing our efforts.

God's reply to Satan emphasizes the truth about God's ways being beyond our understanding, for within certain limits He gave Satan permission to do as he pleased with Job (1:12). We, the readers, know that Job was suffering not at the hands of God, but at the hands of Satan, and not because he was sinful as his friends alleged, but rather because he was righteous. Nor did Job realize that, in a very real sense, it was God as much as Job himself who was on trial here. But the outcome was never in doubt. God always knows what He is doing and it was His name and honour that were at stake. God was not dependent upon Job's faithfulness, real though that was, but on His own grace and power that made Job what he was. In 2 Corinthians 12:7–10 Paul explains how he found God's grace to be sufficient for him in his weaknesses: "My grace is sufficient for you, for my power is made perfect in weakness" (2 Corinthians 12:9).

When Christians recall their times of crisis, when that inflowing sense of peace and assurance strengthened them – that's the gift of grace that God ministered to them as He did to Job and Paul.

## Underserved suffering

Without the slightest warning, Satan launched a series of successive and sustained attacks against Job's wealth, family and health. We must remember this was happening to an upright man of faith living in a state of grace while undergirding his life and that of his children by prayer. And this was Job's dilemma. It just doesn't seem to be fair! Job's basic creed was to live a godly life to biblical standards and all will be well, in the belief that if you deliberately live a sinful lifestyle you will suffer. His philosophy of belief was shattered by his own experience. He had been righteous but he was suffering and he did not know why.

Job's dilemma is often ours. It's not so much suffering that troubles us, it's the fact of undeserved suffering that we struggle with. One of life's great lessons for all of us in our childhood and teens is if we disobey our parents we are disciplined, and we accept that there is a certain justice in this cause and effect – if we do wrong we are punished. But as we grow older we begin to learn that we can suffer for doing what is right, and this is the suffering that angers us – and it's the suffering that angered Job, for he was doing right when everything went wrong. To suffer and know we are to blame is bearable, but to suffer for no apparent purpose, and doubly so if those around us believe we deserve the trial, that's another story.

It is important to note how Job reacted to the awful news concerning the loss of his wealth and family by not immediately blaming God for being unfair. He responded by admitting that he started life with nothing and that all he ever had came from God as an unmerited gift of grace, and while he had been allowed to keep these gifts and enjoy them over the years, God had every right to withdraw them if He wished to do so (Job 1:20–21). In the face of such faith, Satan is confounded.

Nor did Job try to get rid of the problem by getting rid of God as his wife suggested (2:9). Her suggestion that Job "curse God and die" was singularly unhelpful. But Job's answer was surprisingly gentle in tone though radical in content. He expressed disappointment with his wife for he expected her to know better, and he continued to express his trust in God who is in control of his life and who orders all things righteously. While praiseworthy, Job does not enlighten us on the mystery of suffering, yet in his reply to his wife, asking her, "Shall we accept the good from God, and not trouble?" (2:10), he touches upon a challenging truth that confronts us all.

## Job's friends

Job is not the only character in this book.

Job 2:11–13 introduces his three friends Eliphaz, Bildad and Zophar. Full credit to them for turning up when Job needs his friends around and for sitting silently with him for seven days. But when the long debate between Job and his friends gets underway they are unable to help due to their insensitive use of wrongly applied theology.

Eliphaz insists that though the righteous suffer a little and the unrighteous prosper a little, the righteous never come to an untimely end (4:7; 5:16–19), and the wicked, even when they prosper, are in dread of calamity (15:20–26). Bildad is convinced that Job's children died because of their sins and warns Job that he will receive the same fate unless he gets right with God (8:4–6). Zophar is bent on denouncing Job as a mocker of God, pointing to his suffering as proof of his sinfulness; therefore repentance is Job's only hope (11:13–15).

Now, while some of what they say is true, much of what they say did not apply to Job for we know from chapter 1 that he was suffering for his righteousness, not because of his sin. It is not so much what Job's friends said but what was unsaid that makes their counsel so shallow. They all ultimately reached the conclusion that Job was obstinate and that his refusal to humble himself and repent proved he had committed sins of great enormity. However, Old Testament accounts of innocent sufferers, such as Abel, Uriah, Naboth and so on, all question this simplistic approach. And Jesus, of course, taught His disciples that the innocent do suffer to accomplish God's higher purpose:

> *"Neither this man nor his parents sinned," said Jesus [of a man born blind], "but this happened so that the work of God might be displayed in his life."*
>
> JOHN 9:3

So, while the book of Job is a witness to the dignity of suffering and God's presence in our suffering. It is also the Bible's primary protest against religion reduced to simplistic explanations. It also warns how the insensitive and inappropriate application of biblical facts mixed with human wisdom can be crushing and unhelpful to a tender and bewildered spirit.

Frustrated and angry with the badly chosen counsel from his three friends, Job rages against this secularized wisdom that has lost touch with the living realities of God. This warns us against the religious people who have all the answers to life's problems reduced to a system of living to rules – their dos and don'ts. It is the theology from that sort of legalistic person Job rejects, because the reasons for suffering in someone's life are not necessarily connected to personal righteousness or unrighteousness, but can be within the scope of God's good and powerful providence, resulting in the defeat of evil and the giving of glory to Himself. Later, the apostle Paul would explain this in Romans where he teaches that as God is the creator. He has the right to use men and women of his choice for noble or common purposes (Romans 9:15, 21).

In chapter 32, the young friend Elihu joins in on the debate and preaches to Job, but makes the mistake of thinking Job is pleading sinlessness, when in fact he is pleading integrity. Job is saying, "I lived a righteous life and never did anything to deserve this." So, Elihu preaches the gospel with remarkable faithfulness but he has brought Job the wrong sermon, for what he says has no application to Job's suffering and does nothing to address his situation.

# Job's complaint against God and His response

By chapter 38 Job has made his complaint against God.

The God who had blessed him so richly in wealth, family, place and honour in society had turned against him, or so he thought. Worse than that, to Job, God seems to be neutral to good or evil. It makes no difference: if you sin, you suffer; if you don't sin, you also suffer. He is inscrutable and you cannot approach Him to reason or question.

Then God steps in. His answer to Job's perplexity was not to give an explanation of all that had been happening to him, but rather to give Job a picture of His might and majesty in the wisdom and power of His creation. God declares that He is omnipotent (has infinite power), omniscient (has infinite knowledge) and omnipresent (is universally present).

He speaks of the earth and sea (38:4–11):

> *Where were you when I laid the earth's foundation?*
> *Tell me, if you understand.*
>
> JOB 38:4

He speaks of the dawn (38:12–15):

> *Have you ever given orders to the morning,*
> *or shown the dawn its place?*
>
> JOB 38:12

Of the secret things (38:16–21):

> *Have you journeyed to the springs of the sea*
> *or walked in the recesses of the deep?*
> *Have the gates of death been shown to you?*
> *Have you seen the gates of the shadow of death?*
>
> JOB 38:16–17

Of the weather (38:22–30):

> *Have you entered the storehouses of the snow*
> *or seen the storehouses of the hail…?*
> *What is the way to the place where the lightning is dispersed,*
> *or the place where the east winds are scattered over the earth?*
>
> JOB 38:22, 24

Of the universe (38:31–38):

> *Can you bind the beautiful Pleiades?*
> *Can you loose the cords of Orion?*
> *Can you bring forth the constellations in their seasons*
> *or lead out the Bear with its cubs?*
>
> JOB 38:31–32

It is almighty God who rules the created order, who also rules the animal kingdom, and we have here a picture of God present and active in every sphere of life, with everything and every person safely controlled by the government of His almighty power (38:38 – 39:30). The lesson of all this is simply that we must learn to let God be God. We are so besotted with pride, we constantly make ourselves and others the centre of the ordered universe. But Job 36:26 tells us to remember the vast stretches of God's activity hidden from us in their purpose because we are too limited to understand them. It is almost as if God were inviting Job to take over the administration of the world and order it with the same competent power as He has done.

In chapter 40, now that God has spoken of His matchless power and inscrutable wisdom, Job falls silent. Having heard the voice of God, Job will no longer vex himself about the methods of God but will yield to the person of God. And this is wise, for as we have seen, the explanation of Job's life and experience is not found on the human level at all, but in the heavenly realm, which at present we know only in part and see only as a poor reflection in a mirror. The time for us to know the secret things is not yet, and much of our lives will never be explained until we take our place in glory within the completed plan of God's redemption.

God's words to Job are painfully direct but already they are leading Job towards peace, the kind of peace that transcends all understanding and will be a strong tower of safety. Job is humble but not humiliated; his words in 40:4 might be paraphrased as "I am insignificant" – that is not a confession of sin but the realization of his "smallness" within the eternal perspective. But praise God, despite Job's "smallness", God has called him out from all humankind and used him to champion the Almighty and humiliate Satan. The wonder of that incredible truth compels Job to bow down in adoring worship.

God does not question Job's integrity; it was God who emphasized it in Job 1:8 and 2:3. But He challenges him for questioning the wisdom and rightness of His ways. In 40:8 Job is asked if he has been trying to make God appear in the wrong, and in verses 9–14 God says, in effect: "Now then, in the realm of moral issues, can you by the majesty of your person subdue evil? If you can do that, I will praise you and admit that your own right hand can save you."

Why is God speaking in such terms to His exhausted suffering servant? It's because through his religious friends Job has been targeted by Satan. Oh yes, Satan uses spiritual language and quotes the Bible – remember his temptation of Christ in Matthew 4. Through his insensitive religious friends, Job has been bludgeoned by Satan into being absorbed and overwrought by the facts of his own circumstances, and the only thing God can do to get his mind off of himself and deliver him is to tell aloud the glories of His being and works. In effect, He says, "Lift up your eyes Job, there is a God in heaven, a living God, who works His perfect design on earth by using every power, whether good or evil to do His will and advance His kingdom."

The Lord has spoken to His servant in words that declare His majesty and power, and now in Job 42:1–6 the servant opens his mouth to speak to his God. That such conversations are possible is one of the wonders of God's grace. All His dealings with us are designed to bring us to Himself that we may open our hearts and speak to Him, and this is something we can do even when we are conscious of our faults and failures, as Job is here. For when we give evidence of true repentance God is not concerned to hold things against us for ever. It is a work of Satan to shackle the mind and emotions to the past, when in the present God draws near to us in blessing.

## Job is enlightened

Job's first word is an expression of confidence in his God and a confession that his struggle with his situation was in fact a lack of faith: "I know that you can do all things; no plan of yours can be thwarted" (42:2). This does not mean we shouldn't wrestle with adverse circumstances and seek to understand them more fully in the light of God's will for our lives and service, but we must not allow such wrestlings to hurt us to the extent they exhaust body, mind and spirit. We must learn to rest, even to relax, in God. He is the mighty Worker, and when we waste our precious energies in futile mental and emotional torture asking the question, "Why?", we are left in a condition of weariness, so that when God calls us to action we are impotent and even incompetent. We need to remember that.

Job is starting to realize the awful things he has been saying about God, and Christians, too, are often ashamed at the irritable, ill-considered words they address to the Lord. It is good that they should acknowledge it. God likes honesty.

Verses 5 and 6 of chapter 42 are quite inspiring. There is a new spiritual awareness about Job's life of faith. He says he had heard of God but now he has seen Him face to face, and as a result he speaks the words of verse 6, "I despise myself and repent." Job is probably not saying, "I'm a dreadful sinner." It's more likely that the humiliating accusations of his friends have left Job feeling vulnerable – but God leaves him standing like a man and worshipping like the saint that he is.

So to the long-awaited vindication of Job's spiritual integrity. Four times over God refers to Job as "My servant", and Eliphaz and his friends are shown to have been hindrances rather than helps. Young Elihu, a man of many words, is still ignored; for all his fine theology he seems to have had no real part in the exchange of ideas. God had opposed their harsh attacks on His servant; a man who was already paying a deep price of suffering in the spiritual work committed to him by God. Though they repented, there was no easy way back to favour with God, and they had to go humbly to the man they had wronged so spitefully before they could be restored.

Job did not give in to pride nor lord it over his former detractors. Self had been cancelled out and he prayed for the men who had spoken so spitefully against him. The excruciating suffering he had endured had wrought in him a truly Christ-like spirit, and that is the final answer not merely to men, but to Satan, whose contemptuous mockery of God's grace started this whole mighty epic of the triumph of grace in a human life when everything was against it.

God restored Job, and except for his seven sons and three daughters, all his material wealth was returned twofold. Why did he receive only the same number of children that he had started with when everything else was doubled? The answer is because he never lost his first seven sons and three daughters; they were in paradise and would be reunited with Job after his death. Job lived a long time after all this and died a mature man with a full harvest that would be his crown to cast at his great Redeemer's feet.

We close with a final thought from Job's own words recorded in 19:25: "I know that my Redeemer lives, and that in the end he will stand upon the earth."

Christian men and women today know much more than Job. They know their Redeemer's name, they know it is Jesus. And the knowledge they have of Him, and the relationship they have with Him, should enable them to stand fast when the trials and troubles of life come against them. And like Job, the time will come when they are called home and hear, "You upheld the name and integrity of God in the face of satanic attack. Well done, my good and faithful servant."

# 19

# The Psalms
## – The Bible's Book of Worship

It is surely no accident that the book of Psalms is placed in the centre of the Bible, for this wonderful collection of songs and prayers expresses the heart and soul of humanity. There are no clichés in the Psalms. In them the writers pour out their souls expressing the whole range of human experience, their inmost feelings, desires, fears, concerns, perplexities and uncertainties. There are probably no circumstances in our lives not expressed in the Psalms. They contain celebrations of happiness and dirges of difficulty. They include major songs which honour moments of holiness when men and women are led to the heights, and play minor songs lamenting wilful and persistent sin that carries them to the very depths of darkness and despair. There are songs of hope in circumstances of difficulty when the glimmer of a new dawn is glimpsed on the distant horizon, and songs of despair when, in the lonely hours of darkness, there seems to be no glimmer of light at all. They cover the whole range of human passions including the negative emotions of anger, frustration, jealousy, despair, fear and envy as the psalmist expresses exactly how he thinks and feels, even cursing men and complaining about God. They also contain the more positive emotions of joy, thankfulness, hope, peace and love.

The Psalms cover 1,000 years from the time of Moses to the period after the Babylonian captivity under Ezra and Nehemiah.

This means they include the patriarchs, the exodus and wilderness experiences, the building of the nation in the Promised Land, the times of the kings to the exile, and afterwards to the homecoming and the rebuilding of

Jerusalem, the temple and the nation of Israel. More than half of the psalms were composed by the singer-songwriter King David. His God-given gift enabled him to capture the emotions of his varied life's experience and write them in beautiful lyrical terms. These became the songbook of Israel and many of the psalms were written to be sung in public, which is why you will often find at the head of psalms, "To the chief choirmaster" or "To the choirmaster". In some of our Bibles is the word *maskil*, which is simply the Hebrew word for "psalm". Psalm 90 was written by Moses, and two were composed by King Solomon. Others were written by a group called "The sons of Korah" who were especially charged with leading the singing of Israel. A man named Asaph wrote many, and King Hezekiah wrote ten of them. As you look into the book of Psalms you can see that in many cases the titles refer to the author.

The 150 Psalms comprise five books, as follows:

**Book 1 (Psalms 1–41):** written and compiled by David around 1,000 BC.

**Book 2 (Psalms 42–72):** written by David and the Sons of Korah, who were descendants from those who led the rebellion against Moses and Aaron while Israel was camped in the wilderness of Paran (Numbers 16). It was compiled around 970 BC to 610 BC.

**Book 3 (Psalms 73–89):** written mainly by Asaph who served David as one of his choirmasters. Composed around 970 BC to 610 BC, it was probably compiled by Hezekiah or Josiah.

**Book 4 (Psalms 90–106):** composed by a series of unknown authors and possibly compiled by Ezra or Nehemiah about 970 BC to 610 BC.

**Book 5 (Psalms 107–150):** again written by David and others and compiled up to about 430 BC.

It has been supposed that the five books of the Pentateuch mirror the five books of the Psalms as follows.

# Book 1 (Psalms 1– 41)

The parallel with Genesis is immediately seen in Psalm 1, which presents the picture of the perfect man who is blessed because he is in a right relationship with his Creator God, in the same way that Genesis begins with man before the fall. Then, in Psalm 2, we see man in his rebellion against God, just as Genesis 3 pictures him in Eden. In Psalm 3 we see man in his rejection and in Psalm 5 his cry for help. This theme of man's sin, cry for help and the promise of redemption continues through this first book of Psalms until God's grace is introduced. Then the scene changes as God seeks man out in the darkness just as He did in the shadows of Eden crying out, "Adam, where are you?" and moving to restore man to his lost estate (Psalm 32:1). The first book ends with the doxology, "Praise be to the Lord, the God of Israel, from everlasting to everlasting. Amen and Amen" (Psalm 41:13).

## Book 2 (Psalms 42–72)

These psalms parallel the book of Exodus and the experience of coming into a new relationship with God. Just as Exodus tells us the story of Israel in captivity in Egypt suffering the sorrow and slavery of sin and then learning something of the grace and power of God to bring them out of Egypt and deliver them, the second book of Psalms traces the same theme. In this book the psalmist often questions God, such as in Psalms 42 and 43 where the psalmist's enemies arrogantly ask, "Where is your God?" However, the psalmist's response also reveals his faith, hope and trust in God and inspires us to respond in a similar manner in our own trials. Recording the dreaded Assyrian army's advance on Jerusalem under King Hezekiah, Psalm 46 promises that "God is our refuge and strength, an ever-present help in trouble" (46:1). In the last psalm of this book, Psalm 72, God is pictured in His mighty, conquering power, setting man free from the bondage in which sin has enslaved him and bringing perfect peace. The book ends with a doxology (verses 18–19) and "This concludes the prayers of David son of Jesse" (verse 20).

## Book 3 (Psalms 73–89)

This collection of psalms corresponds to the book of Leviticus, the book of worship. Here is the revelation of what God is like when man comes into His presence and what man is like in the presence of God. Just as Leviticus reveals the inner workings of man's heart and reveals his deep consciousness of his own sin and the discovery of what God offers to do about it, Psalms 73 through 89, reveal the same pattern.

Psalm 73 is a thought-provoking admission of one man's envy of the lifestyle of his sinful fellow men. However, after thinking through their ultimate end compared to his, he thankfully acknowledges that his salvation is more important than anything the world has to offer, and resolves to trust God for his future rewards. Although God loves men and women, he will not "wink" at sin. Psalm 78 is a record of God's unfailing yet unbending love. God never compromises nor indulges our plea for leniency, but is absolutely relentless in cutting away sin. Then, when man is ready to acknowledge his sin and agree with God's judgment concerning it, God deals with him in love. The psalmist's realization that God's presence is our greatest joy and the continuous provision that God offers us is wonderfully portrayed in Psalm 84. The doxology that brings the book to a fitting end is "Praise be to the Lord forever! Amen and Amen" (Psalm 89:52).

## Book 4 (Psalms 90–106)

Paralleling the book of Numbers, which records Israel's "wilderness wanderings" and their dealings with other nations, Book 4 comprises the pilgrimage psalms which record human victory alternating with devastating defeat. In Numbers the nation experiences God's grace as He steps in and delivers the Israelites in the desert by working mighty miracles and ministering to their needs, feeding them with manna from heaven, opening the rock so that water would flow forth, and so on. Then, however, Israel murmurs and complains and falls into defeat. This pattern is pictured in the fourth book of Psalms.

Psalm 91 is a call for God's protection in the midst of danger, while Psalm 105 reminds us of God's mighty deeds in leading Israel into the Promised Land, thus encouraging us to stay close to Him by remembering His miracles.

## Book 5 (Psalms 107–150)

Just as the book of Deuteronomy was concerned with God and His Word, these psalms continue the theme of praise and thanksgiving for God and His Word.

Psalm 121 reminds us that Christian pilgrims must travel through lonely and dangerous territory to their ultimate destination, but they have the assurance of being protected, not by anything created, but by the Creator Himself. This final book sounds a triumphant note all the way through, and the closing chapter, Psalm 150, is a constant Hallelujah, praise the Lord! The doxology in verse 6, "Let everything that has breath praise the Lord" brings Book 5 and the whole book of Psalms to a close.

So, we find that the book of Psalms parallels our spiritual journey through life.

It begins in Psalm 1 with the man who is blessed because he delights in the law of God (Psalm 1:2) and contrasts him with the wicked man who will perish (Psalm 1:6). In doing so it presents us with the two roads through life – the way to life and the way to death. If we choose God's way to life, we encounter blessings and troubles, joy and grief, success and obstacles, but throughout all these experiences, God is at our side, guiding, encouraging, comforting and caring. As the wise and careful person's life draws to an end, he or she realizes that God's road is the right road. Knowing this will cause them to praise God for His leading, and for assuring their place in the perfect world He has in store for those who have faithfully followed Him.

This being the case it is helpful to note the three basic themes of the Psalms:

- they speak to us;
- they speak for us; and
- they teach us to worship.

## The Psalms speak *to* us

*Be still, and know that I am God.*

PSALM 46:10

You won't read far into the psalms before feeling that the psalmist has been reading our mail. How is it that this man who lived in such a different time and culture can express our innermost feelings and receive the reply we so desperately need? The reason of course is that we are reading Scripture that is divinely inspired, infallible and inerrant, and as such constitutes a word from God to us (1 Timothy 3:16–17; 2 Peter 1:20–21). Recognizing this, the Reformer Martin Luther said:

> *The Psalter is the favourite book of all the saints… Each person, whatever his circumstances may be, finds in the book Psalms and words which are appropriate to the circumstances in which he finds himself and they meet his needs as adequately as if they were composed exclusively for his sake, and in such a way that he himself could not improve on them nor find or desire any better Psalms or words.*

Today, Christians can agree with Luther's sentiments because there is a sense in which we look forward just like the believers in the Old Testament. They looked forward to their eagerly awaited Messiah, while we await the second coming and the final consummation of God's kingdom. It is this contrast with the reality of life today – while anticipating the glories of the future – that enables Christians to identify with the struggles of the saints of old and find the Psalms striking a familiar chord in our own hearts and lives.

There is much in the psalms about what God can do for those who trust Him. He gives them refuge, victory, vindication, guidance, joy, life, strength and forgiveness (Psalms 11:5; 19:1; 30:1). Speaking of an ideal king who never reigned in Israel's history the messianic psalms point to Jesus Christ, God's Son, who rose from the dead and is now seated at God's right hand, as the One who will reign forever and whose kingdom is over all. There are the prophetic psalms of the cross, for example Psalm 22. There are psalms that point to the resurrection (see Psalm 16:10), and psalms that foretell Christ's enthronement and the consummation of His kingdom, such as Psalms 96–99. As we obey God we will begin to discover His power in our lives and learn to run to Him in times of trouble and danger, for we find He alone answers our prayers and meets our needs.

## The Psalms speak *for* us

Secondly, the Psalms speak for us:

> Out of the depths I cry to you, O Lord....
>
> PSALM 130:1

It's one thing to be able to praise God when we have, in our modern idiom, "had a nice day", but it's quite another to do so when the bottom appears to have fallen out of our world. If there is any time when men and women have turned to the book of Psalms it is in their hour of deep despair and adversity. There they find comfort, consolation and the words to praise God even in their darkest hours.

Christians are not exempt from difficulty, and trusting in God is no guarantee of a trouble-free life. In fact, in this fallen world the innocent often suffer and the godless seem to come out on top (Psalm 73). But we can be honest and open with God, for when we share our disappointments and sorrows with Him, He hears and cares even when no one else does. God is committed to helping His own, and is both loving to us and faithful to His covenant. Although, as the psalmists sometime complained, it may seem as though God is not listening or answering our prayers, the day will come when the accounts will be squared and the wicked judged. So, times of trouble become times of trusting and proving God, and growing in our relationship with Him. It's then we see how we can praise God through the difficult times, for we know He is in control of the events which appear to be dominating our lives and, as Scripture promises, He will work out His plan and purpose for our good (Romans 8:28).

The psalms also have a unique place in the Bible because, while most of Scripture speaks to us, the psalms also speak for us. Our Lord expressed His grief at being separated from His Father on the cross by repeating the words of Psalm 22, and through the ages Christians know of times when they have prayed the words of a Psalm finding in them the best expression of their souls" desires.

One concern that keeps cropping up in the psalms is that of unanswered prayer.

God does not always seem to hear or answer our prayers as we would wish, and at such times we are temped to doubt His power or His love. For example:

> How long, O Lord? Will you forget me forever?
> How long will you hide your face from me?
>
> PSALM 13:1

Yet note how the psalmist responds:

> But I trust in your unfailing love;
> my heart rejoices in your salvation.
> I will sing to the Lord,
> for he has been good to me.
>
> PSALM 13:5–6

In a changing world with questionable relationships, the psalms remind us that "God is always the same yesterday, today and forever" and we can run to Him and hide in Him when we feel threatened or lonely or in despair (Psalms 73:21–25; 91:1–2; 88:1). Who of us has not felt such feelings and found empathy with the psalmist?

Another concern comes from what is sometimes called the imprecatory Psalms.

Imprecate means, "to invoke a curse"; imprecation means "a prayer for evil to fall on anyone". Examples of this appear in Psalms 35:1–8; 59:11–15; 69:22–28; 109:6–29; 139:19–21. Taken at face value, these psalms, apparently speaking with anger and bitterness against enemies, seem to be distinctly at odds with Christian teaching of mercy and forgiveness and about loving our enemies. But we must bear in mind that we have here the thinking of the people in the age to which they belong. They did not think in the vague abstract but rather in concrete terms; such as the sinner was identified with the sin, the man with his family and the only way to purge a city from iniquity was to destroy the wicked. So, they are praying that God will vindicate His cause in a manner appropriate to His holy nature, but they know that this is likely to mean in practice the judgment of war, which will bring suffering to people

In these petitions, therefore, the writers are not seeking personal revenge; rather, these "harsh" statements reflect the psalmist's (David's) awareness of God's justice and His intolerance of sin. They express some of the most honest and sincere thoughts of people of God in the face of distinct opposition from their enemies, who are bent on the destruction of the psalmists themselves. Fundamentally, the imprecations are expression of trust in God, rather than of hatred to man. The motive lying behind these words is a passionate longing that God will vindicate His own Name. Their deepest desire is that God, and the servants of God, should triumph over the mighty powers of darkness. The enemies of God are seen to be implacable. It is necessary for the vindication of God's authority and God's goodness that just retribution should not be long delayed. The psalmist prays for it, not shutting his eyes to the horrors that it involves. There is no sadistic pleasure in seeing his enemy suffer, no sense of getting his own back, but simply a deep desire that the world might see that God is just. This being the case, the imprecatory psalms are not essentially personal, but are the words and expressions of God Himself against evil and all that stands against Him. We must also recognize the principle of divine inspiration, which means that although the words are written by the psalmists, they must be considered to be the words of God Himself.

Christians today have a much better appreciation today of how everything "will come out in the wash" in the end times, because we have a completed Bible. For the Old Testament believer, however, seeing the ungodly and wicked judged in this life was extremely important because God and His righteous standards were vindicated. This was especially true for David (who wrote most of the imprecatory Psalms) because of his office as king of Israel. As the anointed ruler over God's chosen people, David knew that his government reflected God's standards of righteousness. We see from his last words in 2 Samuel 23:1–7 that David realized he had the responsibility as king to be God's spokesman and to uphold righteousness.

## The Psalms teach us to worship God

A major theme of the Psalms is worship. We worship God because He is the almighty, all-powerful King who commands the heavens and the earth. Nothing can withstand His purposes, and before Him all other "gods" are nothing (Psalm 145:10–13). Yet, wonder of wonders, our almighty powerful God loves and cares for us, and is especially concerned for the weak and helpless:

> The Lord is gracious and compassionate,
> slow to anger and rich in love.
> The Lord is good to all;
> he has compassion on all he has made.
>
> PSALM 145:8–9

The Psalms also encourage us to worship God because of what He has made (Psalms 24:1–2; 33:10–19; 46:10). And our praise leads on to confidence: because God is so great and powerful and has demonstrably helped His people in the past, we know He can and will save them in the present and look after them in the future (Psalm 33:18–22).

Praise also leads to prayer. By turning their needs into prayer, God's people express their trust in Him (Psalm 106:4–5). It also leads to commitment. Praising God with words is not enough; we must praise Him with lives given over to His service and fulfil the promises we made to Him:

> Make vows to the Lord your God and fulfil them.
>
> PSALM 76:11

Again and again in the Psalms we are invited to join in worshipping God by giving Him the praise and adoration He deserves:

> Ascribe to the Lord the glory due his name;
> worship the Lord in the splendour of his holiness
>
> PSALM 29:2

And in answer to the question, "Who can do this worshipping?", Psalm 24 replies:

174

*Who may ascend the hill of the Lord?*
*Who may stand in his holy place?*
*He who has clean hands and a pure heart,*
*who does not lift up his soul to an idol*
*or swear by what is false.*
*He will receive blessing from the Lord*
*and vindication from God his Saviour.*

PSALM 24:3–5

It's God's people, the men, women, boys and girls who through the cross of Jesus have placed their trust and faith in Him for the forgiveness of their sins and the promise of life eternal through His atoning blood. They are the ones God has chosen to be His own and has promised to protect:

*For this God is our God for ever and ever;*
*he will be our guide even to the end.*

PSALM 48:14

So, in the fullest way, the supreme message of the psalms is, "worship God". Make all your circumstances opportunities for worship. Are you in sorrow? Worship! Are you in joy? Worship! Are you in darkness? Worship! Are you in light? Worship! Turning to the New Testament we find the message of the psalms in Philippians:

*Rejoice in the Lord always. I will say it again: Rejoice!… Do*
*not be anxious about anything, but in everything, by prayer*
*and petition, with thanksgiving, present your requests to God.*
*And the peace of God, which transcends all understanding, will*
*guard your hearts and your minds in Christ Jesus.*

PHILIPPIANS 4:4, 6–7

# 20

## Proverbs
## – Practical Instructions for Living a Happy, Productive Life

The book of Proverbs is a marvellous collection of wise sayings and instructions for living a useful and effective life.

It deals with the relationship between heaven and earth on a practical level that covers the broad swathe of human activity. At the time of Solomon, Israel was at its spiritual, political and economic height, and the likelihood is that Solomon wrote his proverbs with the benefit of God's gift of wisdom before he succumbed to materialism and idolatry.

As the Bible's main purpose is to introduce men and women to their Creator and Saviour Jesus Christ, and subsequently guide them in this life as they are prepared for the next one, there is much instruction and advice given on how to conduct our lives here and now. Jesus expressed the same in His Lord's Prayer for this on-earth-as-it-is-in-heaven everyday living (Matthew 6:10). It's the art of living skilfully in whatever circumstances we find ourselves and it is not to be confused with information or knowledge. Knowledge is good, but there is a big difference between having the facts and applying them to our lives. This is what biblical wisdom does: it gives us the ability to apply God-given knowledge to life and skilfully avoid many of the pitfalls that are strewn ahead of us. For the Christian, making the right decisions and living a godly life in an ungodly world is no easy task. To help us, God, through Solomon, the principal author of Proverbs, in a series of parables, poems, short stories, pithy statements and wise advice, has given detailed instructions on how His people can deal successfully with the practical details of daily life. The subject matter covers a huge number of topics: raising our children, honouring our parents, handling our money, conducting our sex lives, our attitude to work, exercising leadership, using words well, treating friends kindly, eating and drinking healthily, handling our emotions, our attitude towards others, and more. Moreover, threaded through all of this is the fundamental truth that everything depends on our relationship with God and the person who follows Proverbs" advice will walk closely with God.

## "The fear of the Lord"

Therefore, Proverbs is not a secular book; its teachings are solidly based on the biblical truth that a person is wise in the measure in which they understand and fear God (1:7). This "fear" is not that of craven fright, as a child before a drunken father, but a genuine "trembling" as in Isaiah 64:1; 66:5. There appears to be an element of being overwhelmed by God, which caused Moses to remove his sandals (see also Exodus 3:5 and Hebrews 12:21); Isaiah to cry out (Isaiah 6:5); Ezekiel to fall on his face (Ezekiel 1:28) and John to prostrate himself (Revelation 1:17). We have to be very careful that our emphasis on the Fatherhood of God does not eclipse this fear and trembling and so replace the awesome God with a kind of "fuzzy warm huggable grandfather" type of God. The apostle Peter combines the fatherhood of God with this "fear" of Him as Judge in 1 Peter 1:17. There is a tendency within us to pick up the Old Testament view of God as a "judgmental figure" who is demanding and frightening – that is not intended by Peter. In fact, in the Gospels, Jesus was at pains to refer to God as "Abba", which signifies a close and intimate relationship. In addition, we are no longer "slaves" but "friends" (see John 15:14–15). *Abba* was the common word used by a child to his earthly father, and that is the main picture of God in the New Testament – so you want to be holy because of the love relationship between the believer and his Lord. That is because "perfect love drives out fear" (1 John 4:18).

"The fear of the Lord" is ultimately expressed in reverential submission to the Lord's will, and thus characterizes a true worshipper who, because of their love for God, fears offending God.

It works like this: on the one hand I fear that God might hurt me; on the other hand fear that I might hurt Him. The first is selfish fear and produces no fruit of righteousness. The other, which is the fear created by love, is my concern to avoid hurting God, which produces holiness of character and righteousness of conduct, for my desire is to please God. How do I do that? Jesus told us: by obeying His commands – "If you love me, you will obey what I command" (John 14:15).

It's living a life of worship, a life where we say that to know Christ, to follow Christ and to love Christ is more gain than life itself. It's savouring Christ, treasuring Christ, being satisfied with Christ. Paul put it perfectly in Philippians 3:8:

> *What is more, I consider everything a loss compared to the*
> *surpassing greatness of knowing Christ Jesus my Lord, for*
> *whose sake I have lost all things. I consider them rubbish, that I*
> *may gain Christ.*

Therefore, when Proverbs tells us "The fear of the Lord is the beginning of wisdom, and knowledge of the Holy One is understanding" (9:10), we learn that no one can live wisely until their life is in a proper relationship with the ultimate wisdom, who is God Himself. The book of Proverbs teaches us that this fear of the Lord is the evidence of our faith, for the wise teacher encourages people to trust in the Lord whose counsel will not fail (19:21) and not in their own understanding (3:5–7). So the purpose of proverbial teaching, then, is to inspire faith in the Lord (22:19) by the reverential loving fear that requires a personal knowledge of the Lord (9:10). To find this fear is to find knowledge (2:5), a knowledge that comes by revelation (2:6). Ultimately, however, the fear of the Lord is seen in a life of obedience, confession and forsaking of sin (28:18) and doing what is right (21:3), which is the believer's task before God (21:3). Since the motivation for faith and obedience comes from Scripture, Proverbs relates the way of wisdom to God's law (28:4; 29:18).

## The order of Proverbs

It's often thought that Proverbs is merely a collection of wise sayings lacking any systematic order, but nothing could be further from the truth. The book of Proverbs can be subdivided as follows:

**Introduction and purpose of Proverbs (1:1–7):** The prologue in verse 1 states that the author is King Solomon and the purpose is to show the value of wisdom.

**Proverbs for young people (1–18):** Ten exhortations each beginning with "My son" introduce the concept of wisdom from a father's experience to persuade his son to pursue the path of wisdom in order to achieve godly success in life.

**The proverbs of Solomon (10–24):** This collection of wisdom poems by Solomon consists of 375 proverbs that were written about 931 BC.

**Further proverbs of Solomon (25–29):** These were collected by King Hezekiah about 230 years later and concentrate on the principles of godly wisdom for healthy relationships.

**Proverbs of Agur (30):** The last two chapters form an appendix of sayings by two unknown sages, Agur and Lemuel.

**The words of King Lemuel (31):** This chapter includes an acrostic of twenty-two verses (the first letter of each verse consecutively follows the Hebrew alphabet) portraying a virtuous wife.

Verse 1 of chapter 1 informs us that these Proverbs originate from Solomon who was the wisest man who ever lived, and verses 2–6 outline its mission statement:

> *for attaining wisdom and discipline;*
> *for understanding words of insight;*
> *for acquiring a disciplined and prudent life,*
> *doing what is right, just, and fair;*
> *for giving prudence to the simple,*
> *knowledge and discretion to the young –*
> *let the wise listen and add to their learning,*
> *and let the discerning get guidance –*
> *for understanding proverbs and parables,*
> *the sayings and riddles of the wise.*

Then the truth of verse 7 undergirds everything:

> *The fear of the Lord is the beginning of knowledge,*
> *but fools despise wisdom and discipline.*

That God's wisdom is not dated and is eminently suitable for our day is seen in the way that Proverbs has much to say about the family, and its teaching that stability in society stems from a healthy family life, for example 19:13:

> *A foolish son is his father's ruin,*
> *and a quarrelsome wife is like a constant dripping.*

It's in the home that wisdom must first be learned (1:8–9):

> *Listen, my son, to your father's instruction*
> *and do not forsake your mother's teaching.*
> *They will be a garland to grace your head*
> *and a chain to adorn your neck.*

That's a wonderful description of wisdom for the family. Children are to obey this command so that they live in the fear of God in order that they can learn to love and follow the Lord Jesus. By themselves, very young children find it difficult to grasp the concept of the Infinite, so for them God is personified by the teaching and example of their father and mother. It helps to understand this when we remember that God created man and woman in His own image – "male and female he created them" (Genesis 1:27) – and both are used to reveal God. Jesus expressed the motherhood of God when He said, "how often I have longed to gather your children together, as a hen gathers her chicks under her wings, but you were not willing" (Matthew 23:37).

Instructions for rearing children are found in Proverbs.

> *Train a child in the way he should go,*
> *and when he is old he will not turn from it.*

PROVERBS 22:6

> *Do not withhold discipline from a child;*
> *if you punish him with the rod, he will not die.*

PROVERBS 23:13

> *Punish him with the rod*
> *and save his soul from death.*

PROVERBS 23:14

God does not condone cruel or harsh treatment, but rather caring, loving discipline hand in hand with the responsibility to nurture and develop our children in a way that will lead them to Jesus. Proper training will produce fruit that will endure throughout a child's life and so the training should be done with this purpose in mind.

Then comes the day when the child, as a youth, moves out into the wider circle of experience of the world. When the child enters this stage, wisdom is particularly careful to give instruction as in Proverbs 1:10, "My son, if sinners entice you, do not give in to them", and wise advice in the choice of friends, teaching the youth not to give in to the enticement of moral misfits or be persuaded by their enticements (1:11–19). Note especially verses 15–16:

> *my son, do not go along with them,*
> *do not set foot on their paths;*
> *for their feet rush into sin,*
> *they are swift to shed blood.*

The lesson is clear: the choice of right friends is vital for young people.

Chapters 1–9, while primarily aimed at young people, contain much that is helpful to men and women of all ages, while chapters 10–24 contain wisdom for everyone regardless of age, sex or position in society. It's practical wisdom for everyday living. One of the key themes is work: the slacker exaggerates his difficulties and becomes ineffective (6:6–11), whereas the industrious man acquires wealth as he takes advantage of the opportunities presented to him (10:4–5). He is given responsibility and so prospers (12:27), in line with the parable of the talents of Matthew 25:14–28.

How we use our tongues features prominently in Proverbs. The key passages are Proverbs 10:11, 13, 18–21, 31–32. How we speak reveals what we are, and what we say shows our real attitude to others. Wise men and women are careful in the words they use, whereas the foolish lack discretion and cause harm and hurt.

Chapter 18 focuses on friends and makes the point that a few close friends are better than many acquaintances. A good friend is loyal and faithful but he is also candid (27:6), and true friends are to be highly prized:

> *A man of many companions may come to ruin,*
> *but there is a friend who sticks closer than a brother.*
>
> PROVERBS 18:24

And while true friendship calls for both wisdom and sensitivity (25:17; 27:14), it is nevertheless always at risk and needs to be guarded:

> *A perverse man stirs up dissension,*
> *and a gossip separates close friends.*

> PROVERBS 16:28

and

> *He who covers over an offence promotes love,*
> *but whoever repeats the matter separates close friends.*
> PROVERBS 17:9

Words are no substitute for deeds and Proverbs has much to say about the use of speech:

> *Without wood a fire goes out;*
> *without gossip a quarrel dies down.*

> *As charcoal to embers and as wood to fire,*
> *so is a quarrelsome man for kindling strife.*

> *The words of a gossip are like choice morsels;*
> *they go down to a man's inmost parts.*

> *Like a coating of glaze over earthenware*
> *are fervent lips with an evil heart.*
> PROVERBS 26:20–23

And as you would expect when teaching about practical living, wealth and poverty are key themes.

Wealth brings a sense of security but it can be false security and Proverbs warns of the danger:

> *The wealth of the rich is their fortified city;*
> *they imagine it an unscalable wall.*
> PROVERBS 18:11

Wealth opens many doors (18:16) and attracts many friends (14:20), but there is the danger that it can harden the heart (18:23), give unwarranted power (22:7), and encourage undue self-confidence (30:8–9). However, worldly wealth is temporary and riches will be of no avail on Judgment Day (11:4). An empty purse helps a man to trust in God and walk straight (15:16), and a poor man may have great wealth (13:7). This teaching is summed up in the Lord's Sermon on the Mount:

> *Do not store up for yourselves treasures on earth, where moth*
> *and rust destroy, and where thieves break in and steal. But store*
> *up for yourselves treasures in heaven, where moth and rust do*
> *not destroy, and where thieves do not break in and steal. For*
> *where your treasure is, there your heart will be also.*
>
> MATTHEW 6:19–21

So, if we are to live wisely, skilfully, cleverly and at peace with God and the world, wisdom is the ultimate goal we should seek. This means living by God's standards, whereas the way of the fool, the man who ignores God's will, is the way of disaster.

Laziness inevitably leads to shame:

> *I went past the field of the sluggard,*
> *past the vineyard of the man who lacks judgment;*
> *thorns had come up everywhere,*
> *the ground was covered with weeds,*
> *and the stone wall was in ruins.*
> *I applied my heart to what I observed*
> *and learned a lesson from what I saw:*
> *A little sleep, a little slumber,*
> *a little folding of the hands to rest –*
> *and poverty will come on you like a bandit*
> *and scarcity like an armed man.*
>
> PROVERBS 24:30–34

In contrast 14:23 promises, "All hard work brings a profit, but mere talk leads only to poverty." The bottom line is that hard work helps us lead a godly life that is blessed by God, whereas laziness engenders an evil life that results in shame and death.

# Wise living

For the Christian the way to live wisely is summed up in Proverbs 3:5–12:

> *Trust in the Lord with all your heart*
> *and lean not on your own understanding;*
> *in all your ways acknowledge him,*
> *and he will make your paths straight.*
>
> *Do not be wise in your own eyes;*
> *fear the Lord and shun evil.*
> *This will bring health to your body*
> *and nourishment to your bones.*
>
> *Honour the Lord with your wealth,*
> *with the firstfruits of all your crops;*
> *then your barns will be filled to overflowing,*
> *and your vats will brim over with new wine.*
>
> *My son, do not despise the Lord's discipline*
> *and do not resent his rebuke,*
> *because the Lord disciplines those he loves,*
> *as a father the son he delights in.*

Several specific instructions compose this general admonition to be faithful, and the first is to trust in the Lord and not in oneself because He grants success. Our confidence is to be in the Lord and not in human understanding. We should bear in mind the teaching from Jeremiah 17:9, "The heart is deceitful above all things". This does not belittle our God-given power to reason, but we must keep in mind the deceitfulness of our hearts which will not necessarily be motivated by love for the Lord.

"With all your heart" and "in all your ways" calls for a trust characterized by total commitment – an absolute obedience and surrender in every realm of life. And when obedient faith is present, the Lord will guide the believer along life's paths in spite of difficulties and hindrances. One is reminded here of Paul's voyage to Rome in Acts 27 where, despite everything seemingly being against him, because God had promised he would speak to Caesar he arrived safely in Rome.

The second instruction in Proverbs 3:7–8 is to worship the Lord and avoid evil. Here, too, there is a difference between human wisdom and the new wisdom from above.

> *Woe to those who are wise in their own eyes*
> *and clever in their own sight.*
>
> Isaiah 5:21

There must be a higher source, and Proverbs 3:7b clarifies it: "fear the Lord and shun evil." Compliance with this is therapeutic: it will bring health and nourishment to the body and mind. However, the healing that the fear of the Lord and avoidance of evil brings, is first and foremost spiritual (Scripture often uses the physical body to describe spiritual feelings), but get the spiritual right and all else falls into place.

The third piece of advice, in Proverbs 3:9–10, is to give back to God some of one's wealth as a sacrifice in recognition of His ownership of everything. This caution reminds the faithful of their religious duties to God. Then follows the promise of blessing in the "barns" and the "vats." As the New Testament confirms in Matthew 6:33: "Seek first his kingdom and his righteousness, and all these things will be given to you as well."

The final specific instruction in Proverbs 3:11–12 warns the disciple not to rebel against the Lord's discipline because it is an evidence of His love. Wisdom literature knows that the righteous do not enjoy uninterrupted blessing, as we saw clearly with Job; suffering remains a problem even for the wise and this text records one of the answers to it. These very verses are quoted in Hebrews 12:5–6 to show that suffering is often a sign of Sonship and love.

The book of Proverbs comes to a close in chapter 31 with a poem about the woman of noble character.

As you read of her it becomes apparent that her value is derived from her godly wisdom, which is beneficial to her family and to the community as a whole. The example of the wife of noble character captures the ideals of wisdom that have been the theme of the book, and it is most likely that's the intention of the poem rather than a portrayal of the ideal wife. If so, it cannot be read as a kind of blueprint of the ideal Israelite housewife, nor for men to measure their wives against, nor for their wives to try to live up to. And, as it says nothing about the woman's personal relationship with her husband, her intellectual or emotional strengths or religious activities, it would appear that the woman of Proverbs 31 is a symbol of wisdom. This personification of wisdom would be quite in keeping with Proverbs, for example, the "woman Folly" of 9:13, who is to be avoided, contrasts with Lady Wisdom of Proverbs 4, who is to be embraced. The poem certainly presents a pattern for women who want to develop a godly family, marriage and home, but since it is essentially about wisdom, its lessons are for both men and women. The passage teaches that the fear of the Lord will inspire people to be faithful stewards of the time and talents God has given them; that wisdom is productive and beneficial for others, requiring great industry in life's endeavours. It also teaches that wisdom is best taught and lived in the home. Indeed, the success of the home demands wisdom, and wisdom is balanced living which gives attention to domestic responsibilities as well as business enterprises and charitable service.

## A final thought

We began with the ancient teaching that "the fear of the Lord is the beginning of wisdom," but the Light we now have is much greater than that of ancient times. God has come among us in the flesh and through His life and teaching we have a revelation of God's wisdom. Thus, now and for all time, at home, in the workplace, in our friendships and amidst the hurly burly of life, we can listen to the still small voice of God and, holding His hand, walk in His footsteps in the presence of the all-wise, all sufficient, perfectly patient One who loves us. Knowledge and discipline are admirable and highly desirable qualities, yet they are insufficient in themselves to guarantee spiritual progress and stability. The wise man and woman must walk in daily dependence on the Lord or else, like Solomon, they will fail and fall. In this we see the wisdom of Proverbs 3:5–6:

> *Trust in the Lord with all your heart*
> *and lean not on your own understanding;*
> *in all your ways acknowledge him,*
> *and he will make your paths straight.*

# 21

# Ecclesiastes
## – The Riddle of Life

The Old Testament speaks to us in many different ways.

There is the impassioned preaching of the prophets, the reflective voice of wisdom, the beauty of poetry, the music of love, the gravity of law, the thrill of adventure, and the awe of visions and supernatural experiences, but there is no one quite like the "Speaker" of Ecclesiastes.

The wisdom of this book is very profound and we are led to believe that the author is King Solomon as Ecclesiastes 1:1 claims. It's a record of the most thoughtful search for meaning and satisfaction of our lives here on earth, especially when viewed against the perplexities, inequalities and apparent absurdities that make up daily life. Its purpose is to provide guidance and counsel for God's people in evil days and in times of despair, and it warns us against the sin of discontentment as a result of trying to solve the problems and paradoxes of life which, in truth, are beyond our understanding.

At the end of the book the Teacher concludes with the fact that the fear of the Lord is the beginning of wisdom, but throughout the book he plays "devil's advocate". He leads us in from the opposite viewpoint as he sets himself in the position of the secular humanist – not the atheist, for they were few in number in the days when men and women toiled close to nature for their livelihood, but the person who approaches life from a worldly perspective keeping God at a distance. If you like, he's speaking as one of the many who say they believe in God but have no personal knowledge of Him and so cannot make sense out of life's unanswerable riddles. People who, deep down in their hearts, know there must be more to life than this but are not sure what is missing. Once we grasp that the Teacher is speaking from this perspective and looking at both sides of the argument, it's much easier to understand this book. It can help to imagine the speaker as a theological teacher debating life and directing his words to a secular society, in effect saying, "I have been watching the way you live, listening to the things you say, and I want to discuss your philosophy of life with you!" So, writing as a wise observer, the Teacher lays out his stall. He lived in a society where life seemed to be filled with futility and frustration – he called it meaningless, and in fact predated what Paul would later say in Romans 8:20 that the whole created order has been subjected to futility, and, consequently, human beings struggling to live meet frustration at every turn.

Now of course the Bible believer knows the reason why life is filled with futility and frustration – we only have to look back to the beginning of sin's entry into creation in Genesis 3. There we learn that when man chose to be self-centred and self-directed rather than remain God-centred and God-directed, the result was that man became earthbound and frustrated. And the book of Ecclesiastes explains that there is no firm foundation under the sun that earthbound men and women can build on to find meaning, satisfaction and the key to their existence. The more you look into it the more you find no meaning in it. To use one of the Teacher's examples:

> *The sun rises and the sun sets,*
> *and hurries back to where it rises.*
> *The wind blows to the south*
> *and turns to the north;*
> *round and round it goes,*
> *ever returning on its course.*
> *All streams flow into the sea,*
> *yet the sea is never full.*
> *To the place the streams come from,*
> *there they return again.*

ECCLESIASTES 1:5–7

In other words, the sun rises and sets yet never goes anywhere, the rain falls onto the land and runs down into rivers and flows back out to sea where it evaporates into moisture and is carried by the wind back over the mountains to condense and fall as rain and so it goes on endlessly. As the Teacher puts it, life goes on in a continuous circuit and, unable to do anything about it, we are lost in the vast machinery of an endless universe, it's "Meaningless! Meaningless!…

Utterly meaningless! Everything is meaningless" (1:2).

The fog of Ecclesiastes clears when you realize that it is really a major work of apologetics. "Apologetics" comes from the Greek word *apologia*, which means a reasoned defence of a system or idea. In ancient Athens, apologetic discussions often took place in the agora, or marketplace, where sceptics and believers came together to present, discuss and defend their points of view. When you view Ecclesiastes in this light you can see how its apparent worldliness is deliberately aimed at the men and women who are bound by the horizons of this world to convince them of life's inherent meaningless and to exhort them not to forget the world beyond this one which is infinitely more important. So, in line with the warning from Hebrews 9:27, that "man is destined to die once, and after that to face judgment," the book of Ecclesiastes seeks to press home to society its lostness by emphasizing the message of the emptiness and futility of power, popularity, prestige and pleasure apart from God, and then pointing not to religion but to Jesus Christ who said, "I have come that they may have life, and have it to the full" (John 10:10).

## The search for contentment

From 1:12 to 6:12 the Teacher describes the many ways he has used his vast personal resources to explore the riddle of meaning and satisfaction.

He begins with wisdom (1:13) but finds that ignorance is a kind of bliss: "with much wisdom comes much sorrow; the more knowledge, the more grief" (1:18). Wisdom is concerned with truth, and truth compels us to admit that success can turn to failure, dreams to nightmares and the distance between mountaintop delight and valley-depth despair can be as little as a phone call, a text, a letter or an email, and more often than not it's outside of our control. Therefore, the more you think about it and the more you try to rationalize it, explain and define it, the more hazardous it becomes; the thought that this is all there is leads people to think only of today, since when they think of tomorrow there is only the unknown, leaving them feeling that tomorrow is a great gaping void. If there is one thing the human heart is anxious about, it's emptiness; the philosophy of nothingness. And when people become aware of the meaningless merry-go-round of their lives, deep in their heart of hearts they don't like it and will try to escape reality through work, sex, fun, alcohol, drug addiction and, for some, even suicide. This is known as existentialism, in which people have reached the place where they live only for the moment because they have no certainty about the future.

## Creative expression

So if knowledge fails to provide the answer to life's deep questions, perhaps the world of creativity, of art and works may help.

In Ecclesiastes 2:4–6 the Teacher turns his attention to this aspect of life. Herein lies a danger for Christians to think dualistically and separate life into two compartments: the secular and the sacred in relation to the arts – a view not supported by Scripture. When we look through the Old Testament we see creative artists recognized by God as skilful artisans who with their God-given gifts and talents are able to be inventive and be used by God even given a spiritual anointing. This leads us to believe that creative works of art, even allowing for the fall, are fashioned using God-given gifts and we should appreciate the skills and gifts, despite at times seeing those with them as "fallen".

But of course there is contrast. On the one hand art can cause us to marvel at God's masterpiece, His creation, with the assurance of an all-powerful, wonderful God being in control and working out a grand and glorious plan for our future. On the other hand there is a negative art that points to desolation and despair; offering no hope and no answers, it leads to emptiness. Think of John Lennon. His biography paints a very different picture from that he projected in his music. He was an insecure man, addicted to drugs and drink, desperately trying to find meaning and purpose for his life through his New Age beliefs. His song, "Imagine", sums this up, painting a picture of a world in which there is nothing to believe in, nothing worth living or dying for. His life ended when he was murdered by another as hopelessly lost as himself.

So, while there is genuine pleasure for everyone in works of creative expression – art galleries, museums, ruined castles, magnificent palaces, great literature, well-tended gardens and the whole vast mosaic of human cultural achievement – which enhances the quality and enjoyment of life, the ultimate question, "Do these activities, admirable in themselves, constitute meaning in any ultimate sense?" can only be answered "Yes!" by those who believe in the creator. To non-believers, they are just another avenue of otherwise admirable human accomplishment. In truth, for those unable or unwilling to "see" the creator, even the most sophisticated of pleasures offer only an illusory escape from the prison of secularism, for they all end within themselves. Notwithstanding the ill-informed opinion to the contrary, what you see is what you get.

## Critique of modern life

The next section, 2:13–23, is a sad critique of modern life.

Granted, wisdom is more worthwhile than folly and gives light in the darkness of life, yet both wise and foolish have to face the ultimate fate of dying. The wise man, the fool, the sensual man, the ascetic, all come to the same end: "dust you are and to dust you will return" (Genesis 3:19). That's why death seems so pointless. With an insight of realism, verse 21 pictures secular man and woman thinking that perhaps after all they are fools, in effect saying, "Here I am, slaving away year in and year out amassing wealth and when I die the likelihood is it will end up with someone who will take the fruit of what I have done and in a matter of a few years squander it!" So, running through this whole chapter is the question from deep in man's heart of hearts, "What's the use?" He has searched, strived, struggled, indulged himself, denied himself and done everything he knows possible to do, and yet he knows that he has missed out on what he has searched for – the meaning and purpose of life. It's all meaningless.

## The tyranny of time

In chapter 3 the Teacher becomes philosophical and considers the unchanging laws of God.

With its variety of mood and action and its hints of different rhythms in the affairs of our life, the ebb and flow described in verses 2–8 is pleasing. But, looked at again from the two viewpoints, that is, with or without faith and knowledge of God, the message conveyed is either sinister or comforting. Without an understanding of God's plan and purpose for the human race, the disturbing implication is that we dance to a tune not of our own making, and that nothing we do has any permanence. Today's love is tomorrow's hate. Today's joy is tomorrow's boredom. That which seemed so important today is unimportant tomorrow. Looked at in this way, the repetition of "a time… and a time…" begins to be oppressive, for whatever our skills and initiatives, our real masters seem to be these inexorable seasons; not only of the calendar but the tide of events which seems to move us into an action today which can be reversed tomorrow. And while some of life's events which cause us to weep or laugh or mourn or dance, are outside our control, there is a lingering suspicion that our deliberate decisions are more influenced by the divine hand controlling times and seasons than we care to suppose.

Ecclesiastes 3:11 explains the spiritual hunger in the hearts of men and women.

When we are told that God has "set eternity in the hearts of men", it means that, as a result of being made in God's image, we have an awareness of spiritual things and cannot find complete or lasting satisfaction with earthly pleasures and pursuits.

This human dilemma is explained by Jesus in John 3:3 when he explains our need to be "born again". We have an inbuilt spiritual thirst, a sense of eternal values and an emptiness that nothing but the eternal God can satisfy, for He has built within us a restless yearning for the kind of perfect world that can only be found under His perfect rule. If you like, He has given us a glimpse of the perfection of His creation, but it is only a glimpse. We catch these brilliant moments of light and lucidity, of meaning and purpose, of faith and assurance, but lacking total clarity they leave us unsatisfied with a longing to see them in their full context. For we know something of eternity; enough at least to distinguish the temporal from the eternal. We are like the near-sighted with a magnifying glass held near their eye, inching their way along some great tapestry or fresco in the attempt to take it all in. We see enough to recognize something of its incredible quality, but the grand design escapes us, for we can never stand back far enough to view it as the creator does, whole and complete, from the beginning to the end. What the Teacher is bringing out, and what we all instinctively know, is that because eternity is in our hearts, we are never satisfied with the things of this world. Having reasoning power, we ask about the meaning and purpose of life, but without help from God we will never come up with the right answer. This explains why our inner recognition of a controlling force greater than ourselves and outside this world of men leads many to believe in the New-Age religions and even aliens and superior life forms.

## The futility of social relationships

Chapters 4 and 5 explore the futility of social relationships.

Through a collection of themes – oppression, envy, obsession, individualism and the cult of the celebrity – we are led to the conclusion that when all is said and done it is again all meaningless and produces disappointment, not satisfaction (4:8). The subject of religion is raised in 5:1, but it is an empty religion, which, as the Teacher points out, has no practical value to it. As there is no power in religious formalism to stop wrongdoing or change injustice it simply doesn't work and comes to the same thing – it's meaningless. This forces us back to 3:13: "That everyone may eat and drink, and find satisfaction in all his toil – this is the gift of God."

But to receive the gift, we must receive the Giver, and that's the rub for secular men and women.

## Practical wisdom

Chapters 7–10 explore practical wisdom.

Solomon approaches life from the standpoint of stoicism (a cultivated indifference to events) and his conclusion is that, in order to view life this way, we should aim for a happy medium. Yet while it's better to be sober and sensible than superficial and foolish, because of the uncertainties of life and the certainty of death we should grasp our opportunities while they present themselves, remembering that good fortune can suddenly change to bad (10:14b). The problem with this way of thinking, which is very common today, is that a spiritual and ethical free-for-all produces a society that ultimately becomes meaningless, for where there is no God, absolutes cannot exist. Instead, relativism rules, and that means people will do what they can get away with and justify their actions by their own standards. Yet because that thinking is the ethics of shifting sand, injustice and frustration are its most prominent fruits.

## Invest in life

As we go into chapter 11 the mood changes and the pace quickens.

The first ten chapters have shown us the meaningless of living exclusively for a life under the sun; the final two chapters, 11 and 12, tell us that there is an answer to man's sinful dilemma. Here the Teacher appeals to his readers to make the conscious decision to become a disciple of God and to live life now in the belief of a "beyond the sun" future life. As this life involves faith, it also gives rise to risk and opportunity. So, "Cast your bread upon the waters, for after many days you will find it again" (11:1). The principle being taught here is that of committing one's resources through faith in the sure expectation of future productivity and blessings. Modern proverbs in sympathy with verse 1 are "Nothing ventured, nothing gained!" and "Speculate to accumulate!" But of course the motivation behind Ecclesiastes is not selfish accumulation of worldly possessions, for when done in the right spirit the Lord's blessing will come in a variety of ways, but it definitely pays to be generous. The passage is summed up in 11:6, which encourages us to get on with it!

*Sow your seed in the morning,*
*and at evening let not your hands be idle,*
*for you do not know which will succeed,*
*whether this or that,*
*or whether both will do equally well.*

Here again you sense the atmosphere of the New Testament. The true response to uncertainty is a redoubling of effort and a determination to make the most of your time, for what you sow you will reap. Think of this, Christian: if the times seem meaningless, our call is to bring meaning into them; if the world seems to be going mad, then we are to bring sanity into the madhouse. If men and women have no answers to the problems that plague them, then it's up to Christians to supply the answers from the Bible and let them know there is a God in heaven who loves them and has a much, much better plan for them if only they will stop and listen to what He has to say.

# Decide and commit

Ecclesiastes 12:1 exhorts us to "Remember your Creator in the days of your youth".

The title "Creator" is well chosen, for it reminds us that He alone sees the beginning from the end. He alone knows the times and seasons, and that it is His workmanship that we have spoiled by our rebellious stubbornness. The Teacher gives three reasons for remembering the Lord.

## 1. You owe it to your Creator

In verse 1, God is entitled to be remembered by those whom He has made and has the exclusive rights to our worship, service and discipleship. As Romans 9:20–21 makes clear, the Potter has power over the clay, and we cannot rightly talk back to God. On the contrary, we are under an unbreakable obligation to confess him as Lord.

## 2. You owe it to yourself

"Remember your Creator, *in the days of your youth*" (verse 1b, emphasis added). Conventional wisdom says that young people will "sow their wild oats". The only trouble with that is the crop failure that follows, for we reap as we sow, and a wasted youth may well be no more than a fun-filled foretaste

194

of a miserable middle-age. If you want a fruitful life then start young. Take a long hard look at the quality of the seed you are sowing and the potential crop you can reasonably expect from your middle-age, and ask yourself if what you are building now will produce a harvest for you when you reap what you have sown.

### 3. You owe it to your future

"Remember your Creator... before the days of trouble come and the years approach when you will say, 'I find no pleasure in them'". Death has two outriders called "Infirmity" and "Old Age" and their appearance is a foretaste of what's to come. The Teacher is not being morbid, nor is he trying to make us gloomy, but rather he's encouraging us to realistically anticipate the future and its trials and to be in the spiritual condition to face them head on and win.

In verses 2–7 the Teacher tells us why he says "I find no pleasure in them", by leading us through the successive phases of advancing years: sorrow, ageing and death. He takes us to the threshold of decision – the urgency of rejecting the meaninglessness of a death-wish society by remembering the Lord of life. The wistful flow of his poetic style masks the harshness of the truth which he unmistakably presents as he lifts the bad news onto an entirely different plane: from the cold slab of the mortuary to the quietness of the personal place of meditation, prayer, and worship of God, and brings us to understand that what is lost through physical decline is not some mere phase in the under-the-sun existence that grinds on till death.

The Teacher's basic point is that the inevitable need not be the ultimate. Now, in youth, and later in old age, God will produce in all His worshipping people nothing less than the beauty of His holiness; new life redeemed from death and decay by His free grace in His own dear Son, Jesus Christ.

Verse 2 reminds us of the rainy days. The point being made is that to be encouraged in your old age, spiritual uplift will have to come from outside your personal resources. There will be many rainy days and joy will vanish if it is not grounded in the Lord through a living faith, so remember your Creator!

Verses 3–5 demonstrate that the clock cannot be turned back.

The "keepers of the house" (12:3a) are the hands and arms that shake and lose their strength. The "strong men" (12:3b) are the legs that are now bent and the "grinders" (12:3c) are the teeth long given up to dentures. "Looking through the windows" (12:3d) are the eyes, now dim in spite of glasses. "Doors to the street" (12:4a) are the ears that have lost the clarity of former days. The "sound of grinding" (12:4b) is the voice, once strong, now faded to a whisper. To "rise up at the sound of the birds" (12:4c) alludes to the way older people sleep less and wake early without the consolation of being able to enjoy the dawn chorus of the singing birds. Being "afraid of heights" (12:5a) is unsteady balance and the loss of a sure foot, and the "dangers in the streets" (12:5b) can range from the hustle and bustle of crowds to fast cars and muggers who prey on the aged. The outside world suddenly holds dangers that once would never have crossed a man's mind. The "blossoming of the almond tree" (12:5c) is hair turning grey and then white – beautiful in itself, but only for a moment, for, just as the petals drop within a few days, so the greying hair marks the passage of the fleeting passage of our life. The "grasshopper dragging himself along" (12:5d) conjures up the image of a late autumn day, with a tired old grasshopper, a survivor of the summer, slowly crawling across the ground, his joints too stiff and his muscles too cold to speed him on his weary way. Then, "desire is no longer stirred" (12:5e) means that appetite for food and past pleasures of life recede as the former fires of youthful vigour grow dim. Ultimately, this leads to death! "Then man goes to his eternal home and mourners go about the streets" (12:5f).

Plain speaking about the end of man's journey interrupts the flow of metaphors. The point is that this life is a one-way ticket to eternity: it's for once only, and once over is gone forever; there's no return, no reincarnation (Hebrews 9:27). And with the mention of mourning we are reminded of the sadness of bereavement and loss, and the way death uninvited, violently interrupts life and happiness. So we are called to reflect by remembering God. And to do it now:

> ... *before the silver cord is severed,*
> *or the golden bowl is broken;*
> *before the pitcher is shattered at the spring,*
> *or the wheel broken at the well,*
> *and the dust returns to the ground it came from,*
> *and the spirit returns to God who gave it.*
>
> ECCLESIASTES 12:6–7

In memorable language verse 6 captures the beauty and fragility of the human frame: the silver cord is the spine and the skull is the golden bowel, a masterpiece as delicate as any work of art, yet as breakable as a piece of earthenware and then as useless as a broken wheel.

Verse 8 brings us to the finale.

With the experience of the whole book behind us and this chapter's haunting pictures of mortality to reinforce the point, we come back to the initial cry that everything is meaningless and find it justified. Nothing in our search has led us home; nothing that we are offered under the sun is ours to keep. But we must not forget the context that speaks of a creator and a life beyond the sun and the invitation to discover Him and respond to what we find. It also points to the present as a time of opportunity, reminding us that death has not yet reached out to us: so when we hear its chains being rattled let them stir us into action.

So to verses 13–14: "here is the conclusion of the matter".

Outside of a loving relationship with God, life can only be meaningless. He is the goal for which we were made; that is, the Eternal One. We were meant to gravitate towards Him who put "eternity in our hearts". As we grow older it gets harder and harder to change; choices have been made that cannot easily be withdrawn, decisions and relationships entered into and even more basically, a philosophy of life will have been established that, whether we like it or not, will carry us along that road for years to come. Now we can see why the appeal is urgent; why our Creator wants us to remember Him in our early years. To remember while our ears are still open, our eyes capable of seeing, our hearts able to feel, and our wills able to respond. Because, with the passing of the years our character becomes more and more inflexible and less capable of melting and moulding.

That's how the book ends: it leaves a challenge and holds out a promise. If, for you, this life under the sun is everything, then make the most of it, for judgment will mean what pleasure you have now is all the pleasure you will ever know. If, however, you believe that man is meant for more than this life, that he has a destiny beyond the sun in the presence of "the Son", then the judgment took place on Calvary's cross: for you everything matters and you have everything to live for. You are a child of the living God with a life here and now planned by Him to work for your good and not to harm you. But more, death is not your destiny; like Christ you will rise again to enjoy a future eternity.

# 22

## Song of Songs
## – The Bible's Love Song

Song of Songs (or Song of Solomon) is the last of the five Wisdom books of the Old Testament. In order, the previous books are Job, Psalms, Proverbs and Ecclesiastes. The books of Psalms, Proverbs, and Ecclesiastes form a trilogy that major on mind, emotion and will, and in these books we find these elements in man's character. The book of Ecclesiastes is a penetrating inquiry into life, searching after answers, and in which all the philosophies that man has ever discovered find their expression. The book of Proverbs is the expression of the will in man. The mind and the heart together must apply knowledge for the will to choose the right way. All through Proverbs we find the emphasis is on the appeal to the will. Now if the book of Job is the cry of the spirit, and Psalms, Proverbs and Ecclesiastes the cry of the soul, the Song of Songs is pre-eminently the cry of the body in its essential yearning for love. Therefore, the theme of this book is love. It is a revelation of all that was intended in the divinely given function that we call sex. It is sex as God intended sex to be, involving not just a physical activity, but the whole nature of man.

Sex permeates our lives, because sexual impulse and response touches us more than just physically. It also touches us emotionally and even spiritually; God made us that way. In the Bible, sex, like every other subject, is handled frankly and dealt with forthrightly. So, first and foremost, the Song of Songs is a love song describing with frankness, and yet with purity, the delight of a man and his wife in one another's bodies. There is nothing pornographic or obscene about it, nothing licentious. As you read though it, you can see how beautifully and purely it approaches this subject.

It is important to see that the book describes married love as God intended it to be. For the full abandonment to one another in mutual satisfaction that is described in this book is possible only because it is experienced within that total oneness which only marriage permits.

In a sense, the Song of Songs is an expansion of a declaration recorded early in Genesis. After God had created the first man He said, "It is not good for the man to be alone. I will make a helper suitable for him" (Genesis 2:18). God then made woman. Then, it is stated, "For this reason a man will leave his father and mother and be united to his wife, and they will become one flesh" (Genesis 2:24), which is a euphemism for emotional and physical relationship between the two sexes, and finds its ultimate fulfilment in love and sexual intercourse within the bond of marriage.

The book's graphic description of human sexuality means that it's the one book the Sunday school generally avoids. But the Song of Songs is a celebration of physical beauty and sexual expression that the Creator Himself announced was "very good". We realize that God is not explicitly mentioned anywhere in this book, yet He is assumed everywhere.

When read by Israel at the time of Solomon, the Song of Songs, with its standards of physical and emotional love that God requires of His people, could be found to be in stark contrast to the debased moral standards that prevailed around and within the nation of Israel. But the message of the Song of Songs was also much needed in the days of the New Testament which in many ways were similar to Israel in the tenth century BC. Greek society was riddled with perverted sexual practices and had its temple prostitutes. It is for this reason that Paul exhorts his readers to renounce all conduct associated with this type of lifestyle (1 Corinthians 6:15ff.; Galatians 5:19–20; Ephesians 4:17–20ff.). Sadly, our modern-day culture is strikingly similar to Old Testament Israel and New Testament Corinth. Hence the importance that Christians learn the lessons found in the Song of Songs and also the significance of 1 Corinthians 13 which is its New Testament counterpart.

## The purpose and message of Song of Songs for us today

Since the fall of man, God's gift of sex has been perverted, with the result that male and female relationships have been warped. The misunderstanding of sex and marriage was reinforced by the Greeks' Gnostic influence that taught everything having to do with the flesh was evil and that good can only be found in the immaterial and invisible. So, virginity became the way of special piety for women, and men aiming for the heights of spirituality were encouraged to remain celibate. This led to the negative view where marriage was seen as a concession to human weakness and the need to continue the human race, which could be done by weaker folk and more worldly believers. The celibate and the virgin were the more noble.

However, the Old Testament never supported this view. First of all, human sexuality was of divine design (Genesis 1–2). Marriage was instituted by God (Genesis 2) and was pronounced good. That evaluation never changes (Proverbs 5:15–20; Ecclesiastes 9:9; Proverbs 31) and matrimonial joy is encouraged. No premium is ever placed on virginity or celibacy. Virginity and barrenness were seen rather as curses (Judges 11:34–40).

As for celibacy, the Old Testament Hebrew has no word for a bachelor. There were not supposed to be any. Every patriarch was married. The priests were all married. Every prophet was married except for Jeremiah, whose lonely life was to be seen as a parable of Yahweh's tragic divorce from Israel. Even the high priest in Israel was to be married, since the office was to be hereditary. Instead of marriage being a hindrance to communion with God, it was a prerequisite for the person who was to enter the Most Holy Place on the Day of Atonement. Only a married man could experience the most intimate communion with Yahweh. Perhaps the most symbolic fact of all is that from Abraham to Paul, circumcision, the mark that a man was in covenant with Yahweh, was at the point of intimate contact of his body with his wife.

Nor does the New Testament change that picture. Jesus reaffirms the sanctity of marriage in Matthew 19:3–9. Hebrews 13:4 tells us that the marriage bed is pure and that marriage itself should be honoured by all. Paul insists that it is desirable for elders and bishops to be married and to be model family men (1 Timothy 3:4; Titus 1:6–7). History began with a wedding (Genesis 2:18–25) and will climax with the Marriage Supper of the Lamb (Revelation 19:6–10). It would seem no accident, then, that the Lord began His earthly ministry blessing a wedding. John the Baptist, when quizzed about Jesus' ministry, described it in nuptial terms (John 3:29–30). Jesus Himself, when interrogated as to why His disciples did not fast, pictured His stay among us in terms of a wedding announcement party. A case can easily be made that the biblical philosophy of history is to be described in nuptial terms. We see this in the way that idolatry and adultery are used synonymously throughout Scripture.

Christianity is never to be portrayed as opposed to sex, just as the Song of Songs itself does not exclude sex. But what Christianity seeks to teach is a form of love that, coupled with physical love-making, within and only within marriage, is highlighted with expressions of deep affection, admiration and emotion. It refuses to allow love to sink to the depths of mere physical pleasure and gratification whether in the tenth century BC of Solomon's generation or in our own twenty-first century.

The theme of the Song of Songs can be found summarized in one statement:

> *Many waters cannot quench love;*
> *rivers cannot wash it away.*
> *If one were to give*
> *all the wealth of his house for love,*
> *it would be utterly scorned.*
>
> SONG OF SONGS 8:7

In an age when people were "buying love" through the temple and religious prostitution, the Song of Songs reminds Israel that true love cannot be bought! Similarly, true love cannot be smothered or extinguished in the floods of life's storms or troubles. No, it has to be found in the heart or not at all. The writer is seeking to point out that true love is not found merely in sexual gratification at whatever cost; it is something that grows and blossoms in the soul of a man and woman. All this is expressed in lively and vivid detail throughout the contents of this book.

The fact that Song of Songs is included in the canon of Scripture allows us to view it as pointing to the immeasurable love that God has for his people.

The heart of Christianity is a personal love relationship with the Lord Jesus, and the Song of Songs expresses this relationship, adding a wider dimension to the portrayal of the relationship between God and His people. Sometimes in the Bible God is spoken of as a husband and Israel as a wife. He courts her and marries her at Sinai where the covenant is established, and when Israel goes after other gods she is described as an adulteress. In fact, the whole relationship in the Old Testament between God and Israel is that of a husband whose wife behaves appallingly. He woos her, wins her, loses her, yet still loves her and waits for her to come back.

When we move to the New Testament, this same theme continues. Jesus is depicted as the bridegroom looking for His bride, and in Ephesians chapter 5 Paul uses very emotional and moving language to show the love between Christ and the church. On the last page of the Bible the bride is eager for the wedding and says, "Come!" She has made herself ready with white linen, which signifies righteousness. So the whole Bible is a love story from beginning to end and at the heart of the Bible is the very intimate loving relationship between Solomon and a country girl.

The cry of love from the Song of Songs, "My lover is mine and I am his" (2:16) and "He has taken me to the banquet hall, and his banner over me is love" (2:4), teaches us that the vows of love exchanged in the marriage ceremony affords the perfect illustration for what happens when men and women become Christians and find their lives dramatically changed forever. Jesus effectively says:

> *I, Jesus, from this day forward, take you, sinner, as my bride;*
> *I will love and cherish you, give you my righteousness and*
> *forgive your sins. I promise I will never leave you but will*
> *guide, protect and strengthen you through all the days of this*
> *life, and I will take your hand through the day of judgment to*
> *be with me for evermore.*

And, painfully aware of their weakness and inability, knowing their total dependence on the indwelling Spirit of God, the newly awakened Christian gratefully pledges,

> *I, sinner, take you, Jesus, as my Lord, and promise to be faithful*
> *to you, whether this is easy or difficult, whether I am rich or*
> *poor, in sickness or in health, I will love, honour and obey you*
> *in this life, and in the one to come.*

And would you believe it? The theme of the start of our new life in heaven is the celebration of a wedding! It's in Revelation 19:

> *Then I heard what sounded like a great multitude, like the roar*
> *of rushing waters and like loud peals of thunder, shouting:*
>
> *Hallelujah!*
> *For our Lord God Almighty reigns.*
> *Let us rejoice and be glad*
> *and give him glory!*
> *For the wedding of the Lamb has come,*
> *and his bride has made herself ready...*

*Then the angel said to me, "Write: 'Blessed are those who are invited to the wedding supper of the Lamb!' " And he added, 'These are the true words of God.' "*

REVELATION 19:6–7, 9

So in this book we have a picture of what God will fulfil in the heart and life of one who loves Him. Read again these beautiful words of the bridegroom to the bride:

*See! The winter is past;*
*the rains are over and gone.*
*Flowers appear on the earth;*
*the season of singing has come,*
*the cooing of doves*
*is heard in our land.*
*The fig tree forms its early fruit;*
*the blossoming vines spread their fragrance.*
*Arise, come, my darling;*
*my beautiful one, come with me.*

SONG OF SONGS 2:11–13

Springtime of life does not lie in the past. It lies in the future. One day this world will experience a springtime like that. The Lord Jesus Christ, returning at last to claim His waiting bride will greet her in words very much like those. The springtime will come, the time of singing, the time when earth shall blossom again and the curse will be lifted, and the flowers will appear on the new heaven and earth. This is a picture of what can take place in the heart of one who, being born again and entering into a close relationship with Jesus Christ, enters into springtime. The cold winter of loneliness, misery and selfishness is past and the time of singing has come.

# 23

# Isaiah
# – Salvation is of the Lord

Isaiah is one of the most attested books of the Old Testament thanks to the discovery of the Dead Sea Scrolls in Qumran in 1947. They include two scrolls of Isaiah dating from about a century before the time of Jesus and are identical to the text that forms the basis of most modern English-language versions of the book.

The book of Isaiah has sixty-six chapters – the same number as the books in the Bible, and is divided into two distinct parts with thirty-nine and twenty-seven chapters respectively, just as the Old and New Testaments. Also, the first part summarizes the message of the Old Testament, while the second part, beginning at chapter 40, summarizes the New Testament, and starts with a voice crying in the wilderness, "Prepare the way for the Lord" (40:3) – the same words used by John the Baptist in Matthew 3:3. It then moves on to the Suffering Servant of the Lord who is anointed by the Holy Spirit, dies for the sins of His people and is raised and exalted after His death. This leads to the "Great Commission's" declaration, "You shall be my witnesses… to the ends of the earth" (see Isaiah 52:10 and Acts 1:8), and ends like Revelation with God saying, "Behold, I will create new heavens and a new earth" (Isaiah 65:17). In a sense the whole Bible could be condensed into this one book, the prophecy of Isaiah.

Isaiah's personal encounter with the thrice-holy God deeply influenced his theology and mission (chapter 6).

When called by the Trinity, Isaiah was given the astonishing news that, although he was being commissioned to preach to the nation, the people would not listen to him, for God would make them gospel-hardened. In fact, God warned, the more Isaiah preached, the more resistant the people would become. This underlines a truth repeated in the New Testament that the Word of God not only opens people's hearts but can also close them. It's no wonder Isaiah asked, in effect, "How long do I go on preaching and hardening them with no response?" (6:11). The Lord's reply was, "Until… the land is utterly forsaken" (6:11–12).

Isaiah lived in momentous days of upheaval, and in the year King Uzziah died the international scene was full of threat.

Five years previously, in 745 BC, the ambitious Tiglath-Pileser came to power in Assyria and quickly conquered the surrounding kingdoms opening up the way for him to attack Judah and its capital city, Jerusalem. At the same time, there were problems on the home front; the rich were getting richer and the poor poorer, leading to great social division as corrupt injustice encouraged exploitation and repression. God was still acknowledged but only in outward form and no longer with heart conviction. So, one of Isaiah's major themes is the discipline God brings to bear on His rebellious people.

We meet the Israelites in Isaiah 1:1b–6 where they are so alienated from God that they hardly know Him anymore. Given over to corruption, they have spurned the Lord, turned their backs on Him and resisted every attempt He has made to bring them back to Himself. But He will not leave them. So, He first takes up Assyria as a rod to chastise their land (10:5–6), then uses Babylon to take them into captivity (39:5–7), and finally, when they are broken, He summons Cyrus of Persia to set them free and allow them to return home to start again (44:24–28). From all of this there emerges a group of people who being truly repentant are called "servants of God and humble and contrite of spirit" who tremble at the Lord's word (see 61:2–3; 65:13–15; 66:2). They compose a chosen remnant from which a new people of God will grow.

## The majesty of God

Isaiah understood the awesome majesty of God.

Kings Jotham, Ahaz and Hezekiah succeeded Uzziah, and the nation lurched from drama to crisis as the army of Sennacherib, the new ruler of Assyria, advanced relentlessly towards Jerusalem laying waste the Judean countryside and would have certainly destroyed Jerusalem had the Lord not intervened. Through all this upheaval Isaiah held fast to the truth engraved on his heart by his call to the prophetic ministry in the year King Uzziah died. Through this experience, he had learned much about God – His holiness, His transcendent separateness, His incomparable majesty and righteous character. He knew God as King, enthroned above all, and that He was, unlike Uzziah and other earthly monarchs, eternal. Being the Lord Almighty His authority was linked to an omnipotence enabling Him to carry out His every purpose, meaning that, as the Almighty King, He could use Assyria and Babylon as instruments of His disciplinary purpose (chapters 13–23).

That Isaiah clearly understood this awesome truth is demonstrated in chapter 36. When Sennacherib's field commander stood at the gates of Jerusalem and proclaimed in the name of the "great king of Assyria" that the city was at his mercy, Isaiah knew it was a lie, for the Lord Almighty was the supreme ruler. He and He alone would determine the fate of Assyria and Jerusalem, even going as far as having Isaiah name the Persian King Cyrus as God's chosen instrument to bring future judgment on Babylon, Jerusalem and the Jews, and all this 150 years in advance of Babylon rising to world domination (44:28; 45:1). It was that deep-seated understanding of God, borne out of personal experience, which the kings Uzziah, Ahaz and Hezekiah found so difficult to translate into practical politics. A belief which the common people paid lip service to and which Sennacherib mocked as mindless. But this was the unshakeable personal faith by which Isaiah charted his entire life and ministry. And it was his knowledge of God's character that allowed Isaiah to stand still while the world around him was consumed with madness. For ultimately Isaiah knew that no matter what the world believed, "Our God reigns!"

## A vision of renewal on a cosmic scale

Isaiah's vision begins with the historic Jerusalem of his own day, corrupt and under judgment (1:8), and ends with the end-time city of God, the New Jerusalem, the joy and delight of the whole earth (65:17–19). Much that is declared in these prophetic visions is profoundly similar to those used by the apostle John in Revelation 21.

Isaiah's vision covers God dealing with His own people, from the eighth century BC right down to our own time, and beyond to the things that will end history and usher in eternity (66:22–24). And while the vision transcends history it arises from a particular time and place and takes historical facts seriously. Isaiah saw it in the days of Uzziah and the kings of Judah – turbulent days in which battles were won and lost and the world was a dangerous and unstable place in which men and women struggled to survive and make sense of their lives – and that is how it would have remained if God had not spoken in to it.

The announcement that "the Lord has spoken" (1:2) breaks in on the scene like the "Let there be light" of Genesis 1:3, piercing the chaos of history with divine revelation and drawing back the curtain to reveal that history, with all its confusing and perplexing particulars, is the stage on which the great drama scripted and directed by God Himself is being played out. Assyria is the rod of His anger; the sufferings that lie ahead, including the Babylonian exile, are a furnace in which God will purge His people and the outcome will not just be a new people, but a new city and a renewed universe (65:17–19). History has meaning because God is taking us somewhere, and what the vision does is to set the end firmly before us and call us to live every moment in the light of it.

Significantly, and this is crucially important, the end is guaranteed only because of something else – it is the pivot on which all history turns and it lies at the very centre of Isaiah's vision. It is about a unique Person who is given the royal titles of God Himself,

> *For to us a child is born,*
> *to us a son is given,*
> *and the government will be on his shoulders.*
> *And he will be called*
> *Wonderful Counsellor, Mighty God,*
> *Everlasting Father, Prince of Peace.*
>
> ISAIAH 9:6

As the vision unfolds this male child is revealed in a different guise: He is the humble and gentle Servant of 42:1–3. Meeting opposition (49:4) He is cruelly persecuted and killed (53:8–9) but is also raised and glorified and all God's purposes prosper in His hand (53:10) – and we realize that the royal child and the Suffering Servant is one and the same person, for the Servant, too, is a royal person. He brings forth justice to the nations (42:1) and through Him the blessing promised to David is at last fully realized. The shock in all this is the realization that at the heart of Isaiah's vision is the startling revelation that the Messiah must suffer.

The rationale lies in the answer to the question, "How can a Holy God forgive guilty sinners without compromising His holiness?" The solution is revealed in the incident recorded in chapter 6. When Isaiah is summoned into the presence of God, he knows he is in deep trouble, as he confesses in verse 5: "Woe to me!" I cried. "I am ruined! For I am a man of unclean lips, and I live among a people of unclean lips, and my eyes have seen the King, the Lord Almighty."

But no sooner is the confession made than a live coal is taken from the altar and applied to his lips and he is told that his guilt is taken away and his sin atoned for (6:6–7). The lesson we are meant to learn is that forgiveness is possible only when atonement is made, and atonement is provided only by God Himself as a gift from His altar. This is the key to understanding the ministry of the Suffering Servant of the Lord in the second part of the book, for He is the final answer to the mystery of how God can forgive and remain just. He does it through a perfect sacrifice which He Himself provides, and this is what Isaiah 53:5 reveals:

> But he was pierced for our transgressions,
> he was crushed for our iniquities;
> the punishment that brought us peace was upon him,
> and by his wounds we are healed.

In this we see how the themes of judgment and salvation are focused on the substitutionary suffering and exaltation of the Suffering Servant, Jesus Christ.

This brings together the new people of God and the Servant from which springs the great missionary vision of the book. And again, the key is the work of the Servant: He is a covenant for the people and a light for the Gentiles (42:6). His sacrifice is sufficient for all and provides the rich food of pardon and forgiveness of which all who are hungry and thirsty may partake if only they will come (55:1–7). It's Jesus who called Himself the Bread of Life, the Light of the World, and offered His Living Water to all who are thirsty.

## The missionary thrust of the gospel is revealed

From the inward flow to share in the gospel banquet to the outward flow of missionary proclamation and invitation. From "I will say to the north, "Give them up!" and to the south, "Do not hold them back." Bring my sons from afar and my daughters from the ends of the earth" (43:6) and, "Turn to me and be saved, all you ends of the earth; for I am God, and there is no other" (45:22), the direction changes to an outward movement, "'You are my witnesses,' declares the Lord" (43:10, 12; 44:8), which is given further impetus by the final appearance of the Servant as a Spirit-anointed preacher:

*The Spirit of the Sovereign Lord is on me,*
*because the Lord has anointed me*
*to preach good news to the poor.*
*He has sent me to bind up the broken hearted,*
*to proclaim freedom for the captives*
*and release from darkness for the prisoners,*
*to proclaim the year of the Lord's favour…*

ISAIAH 61:1–2

The missionary thrust reaches its pinnacle in the sending out of messengers far and wide to proclaim God's glory among the nations (66:19). As servants of the Servant, their message has the same two-edged nature as His, "the year of the Lord's favour and the day of vengeance of our God" (61:2), which divides the world into the saved and the lost. In the end, salvation and judgment become synonymous with eternal life and eternal death, as both salvation and judgment express the truth of who God really is – the Holy One of Israel (see 66:22–24).

## Isaiah's witness to Jesus

The book's importance can be seen from the fact that it is directly quoted no less than sixty-six times in the New Testament and there are many further allusions made to it. But the greatest importance of Isaiah lies in the witness it bears to Jesus. At the outset of His public ministry, Luke 4:16–21 records how the book of Isaiah was placed into Jesus' hand and He read from the passage we know as Isaiah 61:1–2 already quoted. By reading from it we sense that Jesus assumed the role of the Servant with all that would mean for Him in terms of willing submission to His Father's will. In handing the scroll back to the attendant it was as though this was the start of His journey to the cross. This suggests that if we, His followers, want to know who He is and what He came to do, we must read the book.

The apostle John made clear that he understood this when he twice used sections from the book of Isaiah at the midpoint of his Gospel. First, from Isaiah 53, "Who has believed our message and to whom has the arm of the Lord been revealed?" (verse 1) and then from Isaiah 6, "He has blinded their eyes and deadened their hearts, so they can neither see with their eyes, nor understand with their hearts, nor turn – and I would heal them." And then John links them together with his own comment, "Isaiah said this because he saw Jesus' glory and spoke about him" (see John 12:37–41).

Later in the book of Acts (see Acts 8:26–35) we are given an example of how understanding Isaiah's vision would inspire the great missionary drive of the gospel from Jerusalem to the ends of the earth when, in the middle of his remarkable evangelistic ministry, Philip is told to go southward to the desert road that leads from Jerusalem to Gaza. There, in one of those amazing evangelistic moments made by God, Philip met an Ethiopian official returning home from Jerusalem and reading Isaiah chapter 53 and its story of the Servant being led like a lamb to the slaughter. Fascinated and puzzled by what he is reading the eunuch asked Philip, "Tell me, please, who is the prophet talking about, himself or someone else?" (Acts 8:34), and Luke gives Philip's response in words of immortal simplicity, "Then Philip began with that very passage of Scripture and told him the good news about Jesus" (Acts 8:35). The eunuch was then baptized and became the means of the gospel being taken into Africa.

Thus it was given to Isaiah to see the hand of God in the affairs of his day and to watch Him working out His purpose in history. Through judgment upon judgment, as wave follows wave, the prophet was able to see an emerging remnant of faithful, purified saints through whom Jehovah would bring forth His righteous King, Immanuel ("God with us"), the Servant-King, and His indestructible kingdom which would fill the earth from sea to sea.

Throughout his book, Isaiah presents us with alternatives: trust in the Lord and live, or rebel against the Lord and die. He has explained the grace and mercy of God and offered His forgiveness. He has also explained the holiness and wrath of God and warned of His judgment. He has promised glory for those who believe and judgment for those who scoff and has explained the foolishness of trusting in the wisdom of man and living to the world's agenda. He calls the spiritual people of God back to reality warning against hypocrisy and empty worship, pleading for faith and obedience shown in a heart that delights in God and a life that glorifies God.

The last verse of Isaiah's prophecy challenges us never to take our salvation lightly for the sobering suggestion in 66:24 is that we will have an eternity to ponder the alternative in sober reflection and heartfelt thanks for the greatness of our redemption and the terrible fate from which we have been saved. The only response we can offer is to worship the Servant King who loved us.

# 24

# Jeremiah
# – The Life and Times of the
# Weeping Prophet

As the book of Jeremiah is not presented in chronological order, the way to understand the progression of the narrative is to recognize that Jeremiah ministered under four kings: Josiah, Jehoiakim, Zedekiah and Jeconiah. If we follow the text corresponding to each king we have the timeline, and can read the account in the time frame in which the events took place.

Jeremiah's ministry began in 627 BC, in the thirteenth year of King Josiah, when the king was twenty-one years of age, and Jeremiah probably a year or two younger (1:6). He recorded the last forty years of Judah before and up until the Babylonians under King Nebuchadnezzar invaded, destroyed Jerusalem and took the population, including Ezekiel and Daniel, into captivity in 586 BC.

The Northern Kingdom, which retained the name Israel, had some time previously rebelled against her Assyrian masters and in 722 BC, as foretold by the prophets, was invaded. The population was deported, leaving the tiny kingdom of Judah, little more than a colony, paying tribute to the Assyrians for protection. But supported by the prophet Isaiah, the new King Hezekiah, in a daring demonstration of faith, removed the Assyrian religious symbols imposed upon Judah as part of the treaty terms forced on all vassal states and focused his nation's attention on the worship of Jehovah, which led to a spiritual revival in Jerusalem. This act of defiance placed Hezekiah in open rebellion at a terrible cost to Judah. As a reprisal, in 701 BC Sennacherib of Assyria reduced the Judean countryside to waste (Isaiah 1:7–8). Although God responded to Hezekiah and Isaiah's faith by miraculously sparing the city of Jerusalem, King Manasseh, Hezekiah's son, repudiated every religious value his father stood for and deliberately led the nation into utter corruption. His eventual repentance (2 Chronicles 33:10–17) came too late to undo the damage he had done, and the early chapters of Jeremiah, recording national life some fifteen years after Manasseh's death, reveal a people still steeped in pagan worship and immorality – yet help was on the way.

At the age of eight, King Josiah came to the throne, and in his teens he began to seek the Lord (2 Chronicles 34:3). Meanwhile, the Assyrian empire was coming under increasing pressure from surrounding tribes and nations, and in the year of Jeremiah's call by God to the prophetic ministry (627 BC), the city of Babylon broke free from the Assyrian yoke and laid the foundation for the Babylonian empire which would emerge with Nebuchadnezzar as its king in 605 BC This gave Josiah, now twenty-one years of age, more freedom to throw off the imposed Assyrian idolatry and his reforms began in 629 BC (2 Chronicles 24:36).

## The reluctant prophet

In the thirteenth year of Josiah's reign, Jeremiah was called by God to his long ministry as a prophet. But he was not at all confident in his ability, as his hesitation makes clear (1:6). Note that this response came after an extraordinary word from the Lord:

> *The word of the Lord came to me, saying,*
> *"Before I formed you in the womb I knew you,*
> *before you were born I set you apart;*
> *I appointed you as a prophet to the nations."*
>
> JEREMIAH 1:4–5

Then Jeremiah's reply in verse 6: "Ah, Sovereign Lord," I said, "I do not know how to speak; I am only a child."

That's a cry of weakness, not unwillingness. It's "I don't know what to say", not "I will not go!" It's the recognition of a destiny from which there is no escape and the fear of not being up to the challenge. When Moses behaved like this God got annoyed with him, probably because, as the son of Pharaoh's daughter he was very suited for his leadership role. However, with Jeremiah the divine response was full of grace and tenderness answering his feeling of inadequacy and assuring him of sufficient strength for the task to which he was being called. Who of us, when called into a new responsibility, has not felt that inadequacy? Yet relying on the strength of the Lord we go forth as obedient soldiers to fulfil the task to which we have been called.

God's job description for Jeremiah set the pattern for his future ministry and speaks of demolition and rebuilding (1:10). He was being commissioned to live and minister as a prophet through the destruction of Jerusalem and call the nation to accept the Babylonian yoke (chapters 27–29). But in God's name he was also to announce that the coming exile would only last seventy years (25:11–12).

Then something happened that was to have a momentous effect on Jeremiah's life and ministry.

## A rediscovery and recriminations

As the Temple was being cleaned and restored under King Josiah's command, it's recorded in 2 Chronicles 34 that the long forgotten book of the Law, with its covenant between God and the people of Israel, was rediscovered. This heralded a national renewal movement led by Josiah which encouraged Jeremiah to embark on a preaching tour of the cities of Judah and the streets of Jerusalem to bring the challenge of the covenant home to the nation (Jeremiah 11:1–8). This brought the first threats against his life and his first taste of rejection as a traitor to his upbringing as a son of a priestly family. It's a measure of how bad things were, when idolatry was considered the norm and Jehovah-worship considered pagan.

Jeremiah escaped the murder plot against his life but not the social ostracism, and became a man of contention and strife to the whole land (15:10). Yet paradoxically he could not escape the divine compulsion that drove him on and his book is famous for his tearful wrestling with God as he agonizes and pleads with Him regarding the pressures of his ministry, the awful state of the country and the hatred his enemies have for him:

> O Lord, you deceived me, and I was deceived;
> you overpowered me and prevailed.
> I am ridiculed all day long;
> everyone mocks me.
> Whenever I speak, I cry out

*proclaiming violence and destruction.*
*So the word of the Lord has brought me*
*insult and reproach all day long.*
*But if I say, "I will not mention him*
*or speak any more in his name,"*
*his word is in my heart like a fire,*
*a fire shut up in my bones.*
*I am weary of holding it in;*
*indeed, I cannot.*
*I hear many whispering,*
*"Terror on every side!*
*Report him! Let's report him!"*
*All my friends*
*are waiting for me to slip, saying*
*"Perhaps he will be deceived;*
*then we will prevail over him*
*and take our revenge on him."*

*But the Lord is with me like a mighty warrior;*
*so my persecutors will stumble and not prevail.*
*They will fail and be thoroughly disgraced;*
*their dishonour will never be forgotten.*
*O Lord Almighty, you who examine the righteous*
*and probe the heart and mind,*
*let me see your vengeance upon them,*
*for to you I have committed my cause.*

JEREMIAH 20:7–12

However, in this first real crisis the Lord had spoken to Jeremiah in words that encouraged and assured him of his personal survival:

This is what the Lord says:

*"… you will be my spokesman.*
*Let this people turn to you,*
*but you must not turn to them.*
*I will make you a wall to this people,*
*a fortified wall of bronze;*
*they will fight against you*
*but will not overcome you,*

*for I am with you*
*to rescue and save you,"*
*declares the Lord.*

JEREMIAH 15:19–20

This first encounter with opposition and the self-examination it generated set Jeremiah's pattern for the future. It was this early baptism by fire that drove him to a desperate dialogue with God, out of which he emerged strengthened and able to stand fast for the Lord's truth throughout the more difficult years ahead.

There is no doubt that the patronage of King Josiah was a great source of help and protection for Jeremiah during this time of political upheaval.

For Josiah there was increasing freedom to further his reforms and advance the spirituality of his people without hindrance from Assyria, his nominal overlord. Assyria's attention was engaged elsewhere as her own enemies closed in upon her, capturing Nineveh, her capital city, in 612 BC. The Assyrian army then retreated westwards and made a stand at Haran on the Euphrates River only to be pursued and defeated by the Babylonians in 610 BC. Egypt, hoping to receive Syria and Israel as a reward for her support, saw this as her opportunity to come to the aid of the Assyrians. But this was the last thing Josiah wanted and in 609 BC, throwing caution to the wind, he marched against the Egyptians, intercepting them at Megiddo, only to be defeated and killed in battle. This event marked the end of an era for Jeremiah and Judah as God's clock began to count down twenty-five years to 586 BC and the final destruction of Jerusalem and exile in Babylon.

Although Pharaoh failed to relieve the Assyrians, his army remained in control of Syria and Israel for the next four years. He replaced Josiah's successor with another son, the heavy-handed Jehoiakim, until Nebuchadnezzar, crown prince of Babylon, routed the Egyptian army and had the whole Near East at his feet. One year later Jeremiah prepared a prophetic scroll from the Lord warning the nation of its impending doom (chapter 36). Incredibly, God was still prepared to forgive:

> *Take a scroll and write on it all the words I have spoken to you*
> *concerning Israel, Judah and all the other nations from the time*
> *I began speaking to you in the reign of Josiah till now. Perhaps*
> *when the people of Judah hear about every disaster I plan to*
> *inflict on them, each of them will turn from his wicked way;*
> *then I will forgive their wickedness and their sin.*

JEREMIAH 36:2–3

But it was not to be; instead of repentance King Jehoiakim contemptuously cut up the scroll, burned it, and ordered Jeremiah's arrest – but the Lord had hidden him (36:22–26). Jeremiah 26:10ff. describes Jeremiah's close brush with death as factions close to the king sought to kill him.

It was as if Judah had pressed the self-destruct button.

Paganism was again the order of the day, and the Lord's servants were severely persecuted. Then, in an act of utter folly, Jehoiakim rebelled against Nebuchadnezzar (2 Kings 24:1) with the inevitable result that he was removed from office and deported in chains to Babylon. He died at the beginning of the journey and his successor, Jeconiah, barricaded Jerusalem against the Babylonian army, but he surrendered after three months and was taken into exile along with the Temple treasures and the cream of the population on 16 March 597 BC.

Considering all that had happened to Judah and Jerusalem, Nebuchadnezzar thought it safe to appoint Zedekiah, a royal nonentity, as puppet king. But Zedekiah was everybody's puppet and was soon entertaining a delegation from nearby states to plot rebellion. There were now just over ten years left before the captivity, and it was to be Jeremiah's most testing decade as God's will was now quite clear to him but hotly disputed by his fellow citizens.

Chapter 27 records how early in the reign of Zedekiah, God told Jeremiah to make a yoke out of straps and crossbars and wear it around his neck and then, through the envoys who had come to Jerusalem, send word to the surrounding kings of Edom, Moab, Ammon, Tyre and Sidon telling them to submit to Nebuchadnezzar and remain safe or be destroyed. They were also warned not to listen to their prophets, mediums and interpreters of dreams who prophesy lies. Jeremiah then gave the same message to King Zedekiah adding that all the sacred and valuable objects from the Temple would be taken to Babylon until God came to bring them back and restore them to their rightful place (verse 22).

Chapter 28 records the response to Jeremiah's warning from the prophet Hananiah who confidently prophesied that within two years God would break the yoke of Nebuchadnezzar and bring back to Jerusalem the Temple treasures and all the exiled people. Jeremiah replied to this false prophet in a most gracious way. He said, "Amen! May the Lord do so!" but went on to reject Hananiah's claim, predicting that he, Hananiah himself, would die the following year as God's punishment upon his false prophecy (28:6–9). Verse 17 tells us what happened to Hananiah.

This led Jeremiah to write his well-known chapter 29, where once again he strongly warns of God's impending judgment upon Jerusalem and tells the people that when they are in Babylonian captivity they are to settle down, marry, have children and seek the peace of the city to which they have been taken. They were not to listen to false prophets but be encouraged by God's promise to bring His people back from captivity after seventy years. Then the magnificent verses 11–14:

> *"For I know the plans I have for you," declares the Lord, "plans*
> *to prosper you and not to harm you, plans to give you hope and*
> *a future. Then you will call upon me and come and pray to me,*
> *and I will listen to you. You will seek me and find me when you*
> *seek me with all your heart. I will be found by you," declares*
> *the Lord, "and will bring you back from captivity. I will gather*
> *you from all the nations and places where I have banished you,"*
> *declares the Lord, "and will bring you back to the place from*
> *which I carried you into exile."*

Viewed as unpatriotic, this was a deeply unpopular line to take, and all the more so when Nebuchadnezzar brought an avenging army to the gates of Jerusalem in response to King Zedekiah's broken oath of loyalty to Babylon. This, said Jeremiah, was from God, and as it was His judgment there was nothing for it but acceptance, and if the king would not save the city by surrender there was no reason why the population should stay and perish (38:17–22).

By any human reckoning this was treason, and Jeremiah was given over to his enemies who vowed to put him to death. Chapter 38 records him being lowered down a dry well and sinking into the mud, but fortunately the king relented and had him rescued and kept under arrest.

Throughout the siege, Jeremiah was tantalized by Zedekiah's tentative enquiries and secret interviews, all of which came to nothing due to the king's indecisiveness (37:3, 16). And while others placed their hopes on a last minute miraculous deliverance like that of Hezekiah's day, Jeremiah held fast to what God had revealed to him concerning judgment, captivity and return – even to committing himself at the height of the siege to redeem some family property currently in enemy occupied territory (32:6–14). And proving he was no Babylonian sympathizer, when the city eventually fell he turned down the victor's offer of comfortable accommodation in Babylon to stay in his homeland with the poorest of the people and their new governor, Gedaliah.

Towards the end of the book there is an incident that reveals much about the human condition.

It shows how men and women can fail to learn the lessons that history and life teach. It also shows how God's Law, wonderful though it is, cannot by itself reach the heart to bring about the life change necessary to make people of God.

Back in Jeremiah 7:17ff. God, through Jeremiah, made clear His extreme displeasure at the public, idolatrous worship of the "Queen of Heaven". Then came Josiah's reformation and Jeremiah's prophetic warning of what was to come if the people did not repent of their idolatry and turn back to God. And now, after the destruction of Jerusalem and all the unspeakable horror that went with it, we find that Josiah's reforms still rankled. The hearts of men and women were not changed (44:15–19).

Jeremiah 42:5–6 records how, after the destruction of Jerusalem and the deportation of the majority of her citizens to Babylon, the Jewish survivors decide to leave the land and emigrate to Egypt. However, before committing themselves they ask Jeremiah to find out what the Lord wants them to do, and "whether it is favourable or unfavourable, we will obey" (42:6). Ten days later Jeremiah tells the assembled people that the Lord wants them to stay in Judah, that He will build and plant them in the land and they are not to be afraid, He will protect them. On the other hand, if they disobeyed and went to Egypt they would die from the sword, famine and disease (42:7–22).

Amazingly, considering all that gone before and Jeremiah's prophetic record of being correct, the proud men said to Jeremiah, "You are lying! The Lord our God has not sent you to say 'You must not go to Egypt to settle there'" (43:2). So men, women and children went to Egypt, taking with them the king's daughters and Jeremiah. When there, almost beyond comprehension, they build their idols and worship false gods, and yet again God speaks to them through Jeremiah. You can sense God shaking His head in exasperated disbelief and saying, "Why? Why do you commit this great evil against yourselves? Why are you destroying yourselves?" (see 44:7ff.).

God's anguish can be heard in that plea. His heart crying out for His people who He brought out of slavery and into the Promised Land and then made into a great nation. Why? Why?

The answer the people gave Jeremiah in 44:16–17 speaks powerfully and reveals the desperate situation the nation was in back then. In effect they said, "We will not do what the Bible says, we will do what we think is right!" It also tellingly speaks to our nation today.

**Excuse 1:** In verse 17 they plead that history is on their side: "Our fathers did it." They still didn't understand. They still acted with the same obstinacy that brought their troubles upon them and this is prevalent in our society today.

**Excuse 2:** They said authority was with them, it wasn't against the law. In fact, to quote them, "Our kings and officials did it." In other words, royalty does it, prime ministers and members of the government do it, and this makes it acceptable.

**Excuse 3:** "We all did it." In other words, if enough of us do it that we don't feel embarrassed, then it's all right.

**Excuses 4 and 5:** "It was done in the towns and the streets." In other words, it wasn't just practised in the quiet country villages or behind closed doors. Oh no, it was done in the cities, it was the sophisticated smart thing to do.

**Excuse 6:** "It was the practice of the mother church – it was done in Jerusalem." Jeremiah must have had outstanding patience. Here was this little frightened remnant of the Jewish nation amidst the smouldering ruins of their city with its Temple destroyed exactly as he had foretold, and they still don't see it.

**Excuse 7:** They plead prosperity – "We were well off." Today you will hear the same excuses: "I was brought up that way"; "It's not my fault, it's the system"; "It's legal"; "We all did it"; "It's my freedom of choice".

The refugees sealed their fate by ignoring the warnings and signs of the times. They demanded the rebellious independence that motivates men and women to say we will not have Jesus to rule over us – the same blind wilfulness that drives men and women deeper into sin while moving them further and further away from safety, warmth and love, into darkness and loneliness.

The only answer to this is given by Jeremiah himself:

> *"This is the covenant I will make with the house of Israel*
> *after that time," declares the Lord.*
> *"I will put my law in their minds*
> *and write it on their hearts.*
> *I will be their God,*
> *and they will be my people."*

JEREMIAH 31:33

219

The truth is that head knowledge alone will never effect the change in men and women: the heart must be changed, you must be born again.

It's significant that the last recorded words of Jeremiah should contain the challenge God gives to all the voices that refuse His prophets: they "will know whose word will stand – mine or theirs" (44:28b). All the conflicts in our country today, indeed in our world, can be summed up in this one critical conflict – the word of men versus the word of God. The day will come when every man and woman will know who speaks truth – man or God.

# 25

# Lamentations
# – Death of Jerusalem

There were two momentous events in Israelite history that were forever etched on the people's hearts and minds: the exodus from Egypt and the exile into Babylon.

Exodus is the classic account of deliverance and salvation when God led His people through the Passover, out of captivity and into the freedom of the Promised Land, while the exile is the definitive account of judgment and intense suffering when Jerusalem was laid to waste and God allowed His people to be led into Babylonian captivity. The exodus and the exile are the two bookends holding together the wide-ranging experiences of God's people that fall between the joy that accompanies salvation and the suffering associated with judgment.

It's impossible for us to overstate the intensity or complexity of the suffering that came to a head in the two-year siege and ultimate devastation of Jerusalem and continued on into the seventy years of exile in Babylon. The loss was total: famine, thirst, rape, slaughter and even cannibalism of a type unimaginable were the horrors that stalked the ruined streets of Jerusalem (4:10). The worst that can happen to body and spirit, to person and nation, happened in Jerusalem in 586 BC.

The Septuagint (the Greek translation of the Hebrew Bible) translates Lamentations as the "book of tears", and in Lamentations Jeremiah lays bare his emotions and describes the funeral of a city in five tear-stained poems or "laments" as he reviews the devastation of the city of Jerusalem. And even while acknowledging that the exile was the result of the nation's sin, there is still some surprise by the prophet at the devastating effects the exile has had on the people as well as on the Holy City of Zion.

## The first poem – the tragedy

On 11 September 2001, when terrorists flew two hijacked planes into the twin towers of the World Trade Centre, their action changed the flow of history. A catastrophe of that magnitude, especially to the people in New York, Washington and the USA as a whole brought a sense of loss and change and with it the question, "What was life going to be like from now on?" Think also of the death of a princess in September 1997, and the unprecedented national outpouring of grief, with the realization that in Diana, Princess of Wales's death something changed and the British royal family was never going to be the same again. Now try to envisage the physical and mental horror of the twin towers and the emotional/spiritual distress of Diana's death rolled into one and you can imagine God's people wondering what life was going to be like without Jerusalem, the Temple and the nation of Judah, as set out in chapter 1.

## The second poem – the cause

In his second lament, in chapter 2, Jeremiah moves from Jerusalem's desolation to the cause of her destruction by focusing on the fact that the disaster would not have happened had the people of Jerusalem listened to God. And to add to Jeremiah's sorrow, he has the torment of wondering if perhaps he could have done more to avoid it. But he also knew God had to allow the exile because He had warned that was the way He would deal with His people if they continued in their rebellion against Him (Deuteronomy 28:15–45). This becomes apparent in this second chapter where God's anger is mentioned five times.

There are two types of anger in the Bible: slow anger that simmers and the quick temper that blazes and is over with. Both cause problems at the human level. At the divine level, God is both slow and quick in His anger, though of course without the sinful element that causes problems at the human level. The Bible teaches that if we don't watch God carefully, and fail to see His anger simmering, we probably will not notice it until it boils over. Romans chapter 1 tells us that God's anger is already simmering and gives us signs to look for in our society that are likely to produce God's anger, they include exchanging natural relationships for unnatural ones, anti-social behaviour and family breakdown.

But it also raises the question of whether the evil and appalling events in the world are also part of God's sovereign design. Jeremiah looks over the carnage of Jerusalem and cries,

> *My eyes fail from weeping,*
> *I am in torment within,*
> *my heart is poured out on the ground*
> *because my people are destroyed,*
> *because children and infants faint*
> *in the streets of the city.*

LAMENTATIONS 2:11

But Jeremiah could not deny the truth that the nation had been warned of the terrible consequences of falling away from God, and in verse 17 Jeremiah refers to God's clear warning to His people recorded in Deuteronomy 28:15–45.

## The third poem – the cure

Jeremiah recognized that God was not absent from the travail and tragedy that accompanied the fall of Jerusalem. He was present as Judge, using the circumstances of the day to refine his people, and in chapter 3, Jeremiah asked a remarkably honest question: "Why should any living man complain when punished for his sins?" (verse 39), which leads to repentance:

> *Let us examine our ways and test them,*
> *and let us return to the Lord.*
> *Let us lift up our hearts and our hands*
> *to God in heaven, and say:*
> *"We have sinned and rebelled*
> *and you have not forgiven."*

LAMENTATIONS 3:40–42

Then, in a sublime statement of hope and promise Jeremiah admits that it was only because of God's great mercy the nation has not been wiped off the face of the earth but sent to Babylon instead, which means that although they were in captivity they were still alive and the nation was still a nation. This leads

Jeremiah to express one of the great texts of the Bible in Lamentations 3:22–23:

> *Because of the Lord's great love we are not consumed,*
> *for his compassions never fail.*
> *They are new every morning;*
> *great is your faithfulness.*

However there is something else here and Jeremiah expresses it in 3:37–38:

> *Who can speak and have it happen*
> *if the Lord has not decreed it?*
> *Is it not from the mouth of the Most High*
> *that both calamities and good things come?*

The clearest example that even moral evil fits into the grand design of God is the crucifixion of Christ. Who would deny that the betrayal by Judas was a morally evil act? Yet Peter says, "This man [Jesus] was handed over to you by God's set purpose and foreknowledge; and you, with the help of wicked men, put him to death by nailing him to the cross" (Acts 2:23). The betrayal was sin, but it was used by God as part of His ordained plan, and sin did not thwart His purposes.

Or who would say that Herod's contempt, Pilate's expediency, the Jews cry to "Crucify him" or the Gentile soldier's mockery was not sin? Yet Luke records the prayer of the believers saying,

> *'Herod and Pontius Pilate met together with the Gentiles and*
> *the people of Israel in this city to conspire against your holy*
> *servant Jesus, whom you anointed. They did what your power*
> *and will had decided beforehand should happen."*
>
> ACTS 4:27–28

People lift their hands to rebel against God only to find that their sinful rebellion is unwittingly serving the purpose and plan of God. He himself does not sin, nor does He encourage sin, but He will permit certain sinful acts to occur which He will use to advance His purposes. Perhaps it's best summed up by Joseph when he told his brothers, "You intended to harm me, but God intended it for good to accomplish what is now being done, the saving of many lives" (Genesis 50:20).

## The fourth poem – the consequences

In chapter 4, Jeremiah laments the loss of Jerusalem while acknowledging communal responsibility for the tragedy. The Bible teaches that God's people are called to maintain a testimony by exercising a moral and spiritual lifestyle that is likened to being salt and light in a decaying and dark world (Matthew 5:13–16), and there have been and will be consequences for our moral choices (Galatians 6:7–9). Sin will be exposed and dealt with – it was true then and is true today. So the Christian must keep a short account with God and live each day as if we could be called into His presence tomorrow.

## The fifth poem – the prayer

Lamentations reveals how the godly Jeremiah remained committed to his ministry right to the end. When the Jews were taken into captivity a lesser man might have been tempted to say, "I told you so!" But not Jeremiah: he continued to weep for the souls of his people, and only God knows how many Jews who had scorned his prophetic preaching before captivity, were now gathered into the fold of a believing remnant by praying the prayer of verse 21 of chapter 5: "Restore us to yourself, O Lord, that we may return; renew our days as of old."

Six hundred years later, the Saviour Himself came to this world and shared a similar burden as Jeremiah. Looking out from the brow of Mount Olivet, He cried:

> "O Jerusalem, Jerusalem, you who kill the prophets and stone those sent to you, how often I have longed to gather your children together, as a hen gathers her chicks under her wings, but you were not willing. Look, your house is left to you desolate. For I tell you, you will not see me again until you say, 'Blessed is he who comes in the name of the Lord.' "
>
> MATTHEW 23:37–39

In these last days, before the Lord returns, God is still calling His people, like Jeremiah, to witness to the lost multitudes.

# The conclusion

John Calvin's introduction to the book of Lamentations is an appropriate conclusion:

> *Though nothing in the land appeared but desolation, and the*
> *temple being destroyed, the covenant of God as made void,*
> *and thus all hope of salvation had been cut off, yet hope still*
> *remained, provided the people sought God in true repentance*
> *and faith.*

And so the book of Lamentations preaches the cross of Jesus, for example 1:12, for within the despair of the book is the indication that God has spoken a renewing and redeeming Word which in the fullness of time was made flesh, crucified and resurrected, bringing deliverance, healing and immortality.

Two destinies are held before men and women. On the one hand, for those who reject Christ and His offer of salvation there is destruction and captivity, an eternity of painful tears of regret. On the other hand, for those who believe and accept Christ as their Saviour is the God who will wipe away the tears from their eyes and welcome them into glory with the promise of an eternity in His presence. Two destinies involving tears: either we are weeping forever or having God wipe away our tears.

# 26

# Ezekiel
# – The Watchman Reports

The book of Ezekiel contains four main themes:

Ezekiel's personal call and commission (chapters 1–3);

God's judgment on Judah (chapters 4–24);

God's judgment on the Gentile nations (chapters 25–32);

the restoration of Israel (chapters 33–48).

King Nebuchadnezzar destroyed Jerusalem in three stages.

First, in 605 BC, he carried off prominent hostages including Daniel and his three friends, then in 597 BC he carried off 10,000 Israelites including Ezekiel, and finally in 586 BC he completely destroyed the city and took the remaining population back to Babylon leaving behind only the poorest of the poor in a devastated wasteland.

## Ezekiel's call and commission

The call and commission of Ezekiel is recorded in chapters 1–3.

Chapter 1 records how, while a captive in Babylon, God gave Ezekiel an overwhelming and unforgettable vision of His glory and power to enable him to perform his ministry. It was this phenomenal experience of God that turned Ezekiel into one of the most uncompromising and passionate spokesmen for

God in the whole of the Bible. It also enabled him to minister into a particularly difficult situation. In Ezekiel 2:3–4 God told him, "I am sending you to the Israelites, to a rebellious nation that has rebelled against me; they and their fathers have been in revolt against me to this very day. The people to whom I am sending you are obstinate and stubborn." Now, of course, Ezekiel was not being sent in the geographical sense since he already had come from Jerusalem to Babylon with the exiles. In truth, though, it would have been easier for him, as God ironically acknowledges in 3:5–7, if he had been sent to foreigners, for they would have at least listened to him even though they did not understand him, whereas his own people would understand him but refuse to listen to him.

We need to bear in mind the background to Ezekiel's ministry and how it affected the mindset of the people in Babylonian captivity. The response to Jeremiah's prophetic warning of the coming destruction of Jerusalem was one of disbelief that God would ever allow the Temple in Jerusalem to be destroyed. And as in the early days of his ministry, the city of Jerusalem was still standing, denial was what Ezekiel had to deal with, and the exiles would be encouraged to think this way by the false prophets (13:10–16). Ezekiel had to explain to the disbelieving Jewish exiles that they had no hope of returning from captivity in the near future. Later when word came of the fall of Jerusalem and the destruction of the Temple, Ezekiel then had to speak to a people in despair and explain why the nation was in such a terrible state and answer their questions: why would God do this to them, and what use was a God who couldn't protect His own people?

## God's judgment on Judah

We then come to chapters 4–24. Ezekiel captured the people's imagination by telling them a parable recorded in chapter 16 about the rags-to-riches story of an abandoned baby girl, discovered by a prince who not only cared for her but also married her. If the story had ended there it would have been happy ever after. But it didn't, because the prince ends up alone in splendid isolation while his wife solicited on the streets giving her body to any who were interested.

Ezekiel's point was that God's chosen people of Israel, like the girl in the story, had forgotten their first love, becoming prostitutes and committing spiritual adultery: "In all your detestable practices and your prostitution you did not remember the days of your youth" (Ezekiel 16:22).

Further, as Ezekiel makes clear, the sin of God's people had permeated all of society, affecting kings, church and state, men, women and children. In short, every layer of society had been corrupted and defiled by sin (chapter 22). In order to jolt his listeners into hearing what he is saying, Ezekiel resorted to shock tactics in his use of language and illustrations, for example calling the Israelites prostitutes and adulterers (chapters 16 and 23). He spared no sensitivities in his use of the metaphor and allegory, such as comparing Israel's sin to menstrual bloodstains and the ritual uncleanliness that caused (36:17).

There comes a time in some societies when God has become so remote that His reality is totally discounted, and such is most Western society today. The problem is not that men and women do not believe in God, the great majority do, but rather that they treat it as an opinion and nothing more. They do not for a moment imagine that there is a God who really exists and who will call them to account. And faced with similar thinking, in chapters 4 and 5, Ezekiel resorts to acting out visually what God was doing to the nations of Judah and Israel.

Chapter 7 has a modern ring to it: Ezekiel's message was, "the end has come!" (verses 2–3).Today he would be called a "doom and gloom merchant" but Ezekiel knew God's final judgment against Jerusalem was about to fall and he had no option but to tell the population whether they wanted to hear it or not.

As Christians who evangelize know all too well, the problem about sounding the spiritual alarm is that until disaster strikes people want to continue in the comfortable illusion that the status quo will last for ever; anyone who injects a slice of reality is certain to sound a jarring note and is likely to be told, "It's not happened yet", with the unspoken assumption that it never will.

Chapter 8 explains how the decline of any society begins with the erosion of its basis for existence. In Western societies Christianity has been the common belief for centuries, yet over recent years real commitment to gospel truth has declined. But man is fundamentally spiritual and cannot live in an ideological vacuum, and if men and women do not have a belief system of their own they will be drawn to one of the new ideas being marketed. Few will stop to ask whether the new is in fact better than the old, they simply want something in which to believe, and the new beliefs have an inviting freshness about them.

That's exactly what happened in Ezekiel's day, and in chapter 8 the Spirit of God took Ezekiel to the Temple in Jerusalem where the symbol of a rival belief was established (8:5–6). What made this idol particularly offensive was that it was set up in the very centre of the Temple itself and not in some rival church across the road. This tells us that the people had become so familiar with idolatry that it no longer drew any comment – familiarity not only breeds contempt, but toleration as well. It's most likely that many saw this as a symbol of their broad-mindedness, a welcome expression of their desire to embrace other nations and their belief systems. If you like, they allowed their true belief to be compromised to accommodate their multicultural, multifaith society, and so ended up with false belief.

But worse was to come. Verses 7–10 of chapter 8 describe how God's Spirit revealed to Ezekiel that, hidden from sight in the recess of the Temple courts, seventy elders of Israel stood in front of drawings of animals and reptiles with censers in their hands as each offered worship to his own idol. Verse 12 says it all:

> He [God] said to me [Ezekiel], "Son of man, have you seen what the elders of the house of Israel are doing in the darkness, each at the shrine of his own idol? They say, 'The Lord does not see us; the Lord has forsaken the land.'"

The tragedy was that these men who were supposed to be the guardians of faith and advocates of truth lacked the integrity to resign their leadership position and openly align themselves with the ungodly with whom they had more in common. We see the same symptoms today where men and women, who have long abandoned any belief in Jesus, His virgin birth, bodily resurrection and ascension and the reality of heaven and hell, continue to hold office in Christian churches and seminaries. However, unlike Ezekiel's day, they do not hide their lack of belief away, but openly parade and publicly advocate it in the name of progress and diversity. The one subject they are united in is opposition to the teaching of the Bible as the Word of God and the proclaiming of Jesus Christ as humankind's one and only Saviour. Ezekiel chapter 8 warns us that the living God is fully aware of such activities and, far from seeing them as "up-to-date Christianity", regards them as a cause for judgment. The rot that was destroying Israel's society in those days began at this very point and it is equally evident in ours today. It is no wonder that the final scene in Ezekiel 8:16 shows twenty-five elders of Jerusalem "with their backs towards the temple of the Lord... bowing down to the sun in the east".

What begins in tolerance ends up in takeover, for truth reduced to opinion carries no more weight than any other view, and that is what we are seeing in Western societies. This process of religious decay that loosens the anchors of society from its moral moorings has dreadful consequences.

## God's judgment on the Gentile nations

God's judgment is proclaimed in chapters 25–32.

The Lord told Ezekiel that it was detestable for people who had once known and acknowledged Him to turn away like this, and asked,

> *Is it a trivial matter for the house of Judah to do the detestable things they are doing here? Must they also fill the land with violence and continually provoke me to anger? Look at them putting the branch to their nose! Therefore I will deal with them in anger; I will not look on them with pity or spare them. Although they shout in my ears, I will not listen to them.*
>
> EZEKIEL 8:17–18

To a modern generation brought up on a religion of sentiment and humanism this sounds harsh; "God would never do that" is today's response. But God did do that to Israel – for in a few short years after this prophecy in 586 BC Jerusalem was reduced to a heap of rubble and Ezekiel's diagnosis was confirmed. We make a terrible mistake to think God would not act like this today.

For five long and difficult years the nation refused to listen to Ezekiel.

Encouraged by the false prophets, the nation in captivity was still in denial and Ezekiel continued to preach the message that there was no hope of escape, and until the Israelites acknowledged the rightness of God's actions they could not receive forgiveness. Then in 586 BC when Jerusalem fell (assumed in chapter 24) and the remaining population of Judah joined the captives in Babylon, Ezekiel's prophetic message was vindicated. Now Ezekiel had to deal with people who – no longer in denial – responded to their circumstances in utter despair. By the rivers of Babylon they sat and wept. God had forsaken them: "How can we sing the songs of the Lord while in a foreign land?" (Psalm 137:4). The normal human response to bad news of this magnitude is sooner or later to ask, "Why me? Why us?" and that leads to, "What is God thinking of? What use is a God who allows this to happen to His people; I thought He was supposed to protect us?" A biblical example of this attitude when things are going badly wrong is with Gideon's response to the angel of the Lord: 'But sir," Gideon replied, "if the Lord is with us, why has all this happened to us? Where are all his wonders that our fathers told us about… ?" (Judges 6:13).

Ezekiel knew it was essential that Israel should accept the reality of their situation, because until they understood the full scale of the judgment they faced there was no likelihood of true repentance. His task was to show these despairing people that, yes, there has indeed been a catastrophe, the people have lost their country, Temple, homes and freedom, but the great and awesome God who chose the Temple in Jerusalem as His dwelling place has amazingly revealed His glory to Ezekiel by the banks of the River Kebar (1:3), which means that the glorious, sovereign Creator God was with His people in exile (11:16). So, Ezekiel's task was to show the despairing nation that God was with them and would be at work among the wreckage and rubble of their country and their lives, sovereignly using the catastrophe to create a new people of God whom He would bring back into the land He had promised to them – so he changed the thrust of his ministry from judgment to hope.

## The restoration of Israel

But sin is not an abstract force in society: it pervades the hearts of men and women and what the people need is nothing less than a new heart and a new spirit – a heart that will be willing and a spirit that will be obedient, and that is what God promises to give them:

> *I will take you out of the nations; I will gather you from all*
> *the countries and bring you back into your own land. I will*
> *sprinkle clean water on you, and you will be clean; I will*
> *cleanse you from all your impurities and from all your idols.*
> *I will give you a new heart and put a new spirit in you; I will*
> *remove from you your heart of stone and give you a heart of*
> *flesh. And I will put my Spirit in you and move you to follow*
> *my decrees and be careful to keep my laws… Then you will*
> *remember your evil ways and wicked deeds, and you will loathe*
> *yourselves for your sins and detestable practices.*
>
> EZEKIEL 36:24–27, 31

With the benefit of the New Testament, Christians can recognize how there is much more here than Israel's return to the land of Israel which came about under the leadership of Ezra and Nehemiah in 536 BC. Some would argue that Ezekiel's prophecy was fulfilled when Israel became a nation in 1948, but that completely misses the spiritual significance of the prophecy as given in Ezekiel 34:24–38. What we have here is much more than political autonomy for Abraham's descendants – it is the fulfilment of all Old Testament prophecies concerning the Messiah, all of which are fulfilled in Jesus Christ.

If men and women are spiritually dead, which according to the Bible they are, then it takes God to do something about it. And in chapter 37 Ezekiel is given a vision of a valley of dry bones, illustrating how God will indeed raise a vanquished nation and humankind from death to life. He is commanded to preach to the bones, saying, "Dry bones, hear the word of the Lord" (37:4). So Ezekiel preached, and "there was a noise, a rattling sound, and the bones came together, bone to bone" (37:7). Now the bones are clothed with flesh and skin – but not yet living! God tells Ezekiel to pray for the Spirit of God to enter them and bring life – and Ezekiel prays: "and breath entered them; they came to life and stood up on their feet – a vast army" (37:10). Praise God for the miracle of new life. For Israel, it was the promise that God would undertake the impossible and bring the nation back from captivity to the Promised Land, which was accomplished in 536 BC. For humankind it is the promise that new life can be created in dry, dead hearts – we call it being "born again!" And it was fulfilled through faith in the death and resurrection of Jesus Christ on Calvary's Cross.

This leads us into the theology of the final chapters 40–48.

They do not make easy reading but do carry the message of hope to its climax: the return of the glory of the Lord to dwell among His people through the indwelling presence of the Holy Spirit.

There has long been disagreement between commentators who say these chapters will be literally fulfilled and those who say they are spiritual illustrations pointing towards the Lord Jesus Christ and the ministry of the Holy Spirit. Some say the picture in chapter 47 of streams of living water flowing from the altar will literally happen when Christ comes to reign in the flesh in Jerusalem, and there are others who tell us the thing is geographically impossible; that water could not rise from beneath the altar on the Temple Mount. In the absence of any tributaries, how could the river deepen so rapidly that within a mile and a half it was, as verse 5 describes, deep enough to swim in? And of course there is the matter of the limestone ridge that separates Jerusalem from the Dead Sea, the contours of which the river would have to defy as though the great mountain barriers don't exist?

However, this "earth-bound" thinking misses the point – for what we have here is theology in the form of geography just as previously, in chapters 40–46, we see theology in the form of architecture. The river of life in chapter 47 is the flow of the Spirit of God sweeping across the barren scene of human misery, corruption, sin and death, to give healing, hope, renewal and life. This is confirmed in the New Testament where John develops the theme from Ezekiel 47 when Jesus tells the Samaritan woman that the water He gives will become a spring of water welling up to eternal life (John 4:14). And of course, more explicitly, Jesus, at the Feast of Tabernacles, promises to anyone who believes in Him that "streams of living water will flow from within him" (John 7:38). John then, to avoid any misinterpretation, adds the interpretive note, "by this he meant the Spirit" (verse 39). With the background of Ezekiel 47, the indwelling Spirit within believers as accomplished at Pentecost turns each believer into a miniature temple and as such they become a source of blessing to all around them by transmitting the life-giving message of the gospel – healing the spiritually dead and making them alive in Christ and fruitful in their service for God through the river of life that flows from His altar and throne.

In exactly the same way Ezekiel's vision in chapters 40–46 was not to provide guidance on how to build the temple – for nowhere is there any command to build what Ezekiel had seen in contrast to the very particular divine instructions concerning the tabernacle in the wilderness. In Ezekiel's account there is no word at all of any human participation in the planning or building of the whole complex, it is simply presented to him as a divine fait accompli. So, even though the Israelites did rebuild a greatly simplified version of the Temple, with the benefit of the New Testament we can see that Ezekiel's temple vision pointed to a more complete fulfilment than simply the rebuilding of the Temple by people whose human failing continued to defile it. What we have here in these chapters is the gospel according to Ezekiel presented by architecture. It's messianic, and it points toward the One who Himself would be the Temple, the Altar and the Sacrifice.

The New Testament goes even further in using temple imagery, not merely of Jesus Himself, but also of the people who are "in" Him. Peter calls us both the "living stones" of the new temple in Christ, and also the "holy priesthood, offering spiritual sacrifices acceptable to God through Jesus Christ" (1 Peter 2:5, 9). And since the Temple was above all the place where the glory of God should dwell and be visible, Paul can appropriately say,

> *Do you not know that your body is a temple of the Holy Spirit,*
> *who is in you, whom you have received from God? Therefore*
> *honour God with your body.*
>
> 1 CORINTHIANS 6:19–20

Above all, the temple in Ezekiel's visions is the place to which the glory of God can and does return. Grieved by the awful apostasy of His people, the Lord was seen in chapters 10 and 11 gradually withdrawing from His Temple, leaving the city to its fate. In chapter 43 the glory returns to the new temple that has been purged of its evil: "This is where I will live among the Israelites forever" (Ezekiel 43:7). Likewise, the climax of the book of Revelation is the holy city of chapter 21, where a loud voice from the throne says,

> *Now the dwelling of God is with men, and he will live with*
> *them. They will be his people, and God himself will be with*
> *them and be their God. He will wipe every tear from their eyes.*
> *There will be no more death or mourning or crying or pain, for*
> *the old order of things has passed away.*
>
> REVELATION 21:3–4

Christians know that our godless and apostate society, like Ezekiel's, is under judgment unless something like revival happens to turn it around. But we must not allow the dark cloud to dominate our thinking, for there is a silver lining. In the gospel we have the message of a new ruler, a new heart, a new people and a new hope. God has promised to shine through the clouds and ultimately accomplish all His purposes of grace. The malignant forces that oppose us will one day be destroyed and God will bring in His king and His kingdom. That hope can hardly be better expressed than by the simple words with which Ezekiel finishes his account of the new Temple and his book: "the Lord is there" (Ezekiel 48:35).

# 27

# Daniel
# – How to Sing the Lord's Song in a Strange Land

The book of Daniel encourages believers to stand fast in the present and be assured that the future belongs to God.

At the time of Daniel's writing there was little or no evidence to encourage men and women of faith. In fact the opposite was true: the present was bleak and the future looked dark. King Nebuchadnezzar was on the throne of the mighty Babylonian empire, Jerusalem and the Temple were destroyed, and Daniel, a young Jewish man of noble birth, was captive in Babylon.

## Daniel in Babylon – cooperation without compromise

The main problem for the Israelites was that from being in charge of their country where their religion was supreme, they now had to fit in as a marginalized minority within an environment that was sometimes friendly but largely alien to their culture and faith. This presented them with the challenge of how to remain faithful to their beliefs and be distinctively different without being assimilated into Babylonian culture. In chapter 1, Daniel answers the lament of Psalm 137:4, "How can we sing the songs of the Lord while in a foreign land?" by demonstrating what Ezekiel had told the exiled Jews: that God is with them in exile and He is still God even in Babylon.

The obvious question facing the exiled Israelites was, "Do they cooperate with their captors or refuse to assimilate?" For the answer they only had to look to the prophet Jeremiah who had told them that during their seventy-year stay in Babylon they were to:

> *Build houses and settle down; plant gardens and eat what they produce. Marry and have sons and daughters… increase in number… seek the peace and prosperity of the city to which I have carried you into exile.*
>
> JEREMIAH 29:5–7

This meant that they were to say "Yes" to the opportunities offered to them and outwardly be fully involved and cooperative, but always with an inward spirit that would enable them, no matter the cost, to say "No!" for there had to be a line over which they would not cross – they should never sacrifice their inward conviction that they belonged body and soul to another kingdom greater than Babylon.

Aware of the dangers, they disciplined themselves to ensure their minds were open to hear the Word of God in the midst of the literal babel of other voices around them. Yes, they would be able to stand before the king, not as Babylonians but as dedicated Israelites, and given the choice to bow or burn, they would choose to burn. Daniel decided to draw the line over the matter of his dietary laws. He realized that relaxing on this issue could be the first step to other religious compromises, and he knew the distinctiveness of his nation depended on these very differences and the separation he was being encouraged to forego. Daniel's example reminds us that our characters are formed by the many small decisions we make over little issues, which ultimately enable us to stand for truth when faced with the big issues.

## Nebuchadnezzar's dream of a great statue

The writing of chapter 2 is puzzling. It's called apocalyptic, and is the type used in the book of Revelation. Nebuchadnezzar had a dream, and on the pain of death asked his wise men to tell him not only the meaning of the dream but the dream itself, which was beyond their capabilities. But in answer to prayer, God enabled Daniel not only to interpret the dream but to recount it as well (2:18–19).

The dream was of a large statue made from head to foot of different materials comprising a head of gold, chest and arms of silver, belly and thighs of bronze and legs of iron. And while this gives the impression of strength and solidity, the feet comprise a weak mixture of iron and clay. But it was not the weakness of the feet that caused the statue to fall, it was a rock, not cut by human hands, that smashed into the statue, pulverizing it to dust (verse 34).

Daniel's prophetic explanation of the dream revealed that the golden head represented Nebuchadnezzar and the rest of the body was an unveiling of future empires that would follow the Babylonian empire. Commentators interpret Daniel's dream in the following way: the Medo-Persian empire would replace the Babylonian empire but not with the same grandeur or glory. It would be followed by the Greek empire, which in turn would be replaced by the Roman empire, symbolized by the legs of iron – a fitting picture of what Rome became. The Roman empire would be followed by one symbolized by feet of mixed iron and clay – a brittle unstable mixture of weakness and strength. And the stone that breaks into and alters history is Jesus Christ, irresistibly overcoming everything that stands in His path. This is the Christ we have to proclaim to this unstable world today – a world that appears to be powerful and self-confident but in reality, against the "Stone" Jesus Christ, is weak and trembling.

## The well known account of the fiery furnace

Then we turn to chapter 3. Probably as a result of his dream, Nebuchadnezzar ordered a gigantic gold statue 90 feet high and 9 feet wide to be erected in the plain of Dura and decreed that whenever the state band played everyone had to bow down to this idol. It was a relatively quick and easy attempt to amalgamate the multicultural, multifaith empire by introducing a type of established state religion and uniting the empire around one belief. But Daniel's compatriots from Jerusalem – Shadrach, Meshach and Abednego – refused to obey and, when brought before the king, made it clear that there was no possibility of argument or compromise: they would burn rather than bow (verses 16–18).

There is an important lesson here for Christian men and women living in an unsympathetic secular age. These three young men refused to compromise their faith even if it meant death: "the God we serve is able to save us… but even if he does not…" (verses 17–18). Here we see how testimony to God is kept alive in a pagan world and Christians today must be prepared to face their "fiery furnace" of testing in the belief that it is our duty to do right and leave the consequences to God as confirmed by James 1:12.

As punishment the three young men were thrown into a fiery furnace that was heated to seven times the usual temperature. However, the appearance of a heavenly being standing alongside and sustaining the three men he was persecuting was the final straw that broke Nebuchadnezzar and brought him to place his faith in the God of Daniel and his three friends. Nebuchadnezzar had challenged God, and in face of such an awesome display of God's power he could only admit his defeat. There is a great lesson here about the sovereignty of God among the nations and His ability to bring a Gentile king, who was the most powerful man in the world, into the kingdom.

## The danger of "Me"

Greek historians such as Strabo and Diodorus Siculus provide the background to this chapter 4: Nebuchadnezzar married a princess named Amytis of Media who came from the mountains of Persia, where Tehran, the capital of Iran, is located today. She lived in Nebuchadnezzar's palace but, missing the fragrant plants of home, she was soon homesick. When Nebuchadnezzar heard the source of her complaint he constructed a huge mountain of brick and stone covered with trees, shrubs and plants. It was so outstanding that it became one of the seven wonders of the ancient world and tourists flocked to see the "Hanging Gardens of Babylon" also known as the Hanging Gardens of Semiramis.

Nebuchadnezzar then dreamed of a huge tree that reached the sky. Animals found shelter under it and there were birds in its branches. Then the tree was cut down with only the stump bound in iron remaining, and it began to grow again. Once again he asked Daniel for an interpretation, and was told that he, Nebuchadnezzar, was the tree who would be driven out from among men for seven years until he acknowledged that the Most High ruled the kingdoms of men and gave them to anyone He wished. A year later, God told Nebuchadnezzar that the prediction would be fulfilled. Sure enough, shortly afterwards, while walking on the roof terrace of his magnificent palace and filled with pride by what he had achieved, he boasted, "Is not this the great Babylon I have built as the royal residence, by my mighty power and for the glory of my majesty?" (4:30). God's response was to afflict Nebuchadnezzar with a madness that lasted for seven years so that his own people had to lock him up in his zoo where he ate grass. His hair grew like the feathers of an eagle and his nails became like the claws of a bird. At the end of seven years, his sanity restored, he lifted his eyes to heaven and "praised the Most High; I honoured and glorified him who lives for ever. His dominion is an eternal dominion; his kingdom endures from generation to generation" (4:34). God then restored him to his throne and made him greater than before.

From this, believers are warned that an especially dangerous time is when their hard work has brought them some measure of success. For then, a sense of accomplishment may tempt them to think that the impressive "world" they have built is due to their own cleverness, even to suppose that they are being justly rewarded for their righteousness of life. The danger then is that they will be satisfied with the level of spirituality they have attained and the people they have become. This will lead them into a sense of self-satisfaction, which in turn feeds their pride making them unable to go through the humbling process of allowing the Spirit of God to break, melt, mould and build them into the men or women Jesus wants them to be. Jesus warned that men and women can easily gain the world and lose their lives if they become engrossed with solving all the questions surrounding them, neglecting the ultimate one: how do they have a personal relationship with Jesus Christ that will take them through the Valley of the Shadow of Death into the world beyond?

As if to underline the importance of personal issues raised in this chapter, the same theme is taken up in the next two chapters and is presented as a matter of life and death. In chapter 4 one king is saved because he faces the subject and answers it with repentance and faith; in chapter 5 his successor is condemned because he refuses to repent. Even the king cannot escape this challenge.

## Belshazzar's Feast – the downfall of Babylon

Note, in chapter 5, how quickly the nation had degenerated under an ungodly king. Whereas Nebuchadnezzar treated the sacred vessels of God with respect (1:2), Belshazzar used them sacrilegiously to add a little novelty to his last drunken orgy. Permissiveness has replaced discipline.

Verse 5 presents an unforgettable picture conjuring up the sense of impending doom when, in the middle of Belshazzar's party, a human finger appears and begins to write a message on the wall and which verse 25 records: *"mene, mene, tekel, parsin"*. Once again, Daniel was the interpreter and explained to the frightened Belshazzar the meaning of the message from God, "Your reign is over, you don't measure up, and your kingdom is divided and given to the Medes and Persians" (see verses 26–27). Here, incidentally, is the origin of the phrase "the writing is on the wall".

When Belshazzar used the Temple vessels in his drunken profanity it was a sign that he believed the God of the Jews, whose vessels he was abusing and whose name he was insulting, had no reality or power in Babylon. It was a challenge to God, and Belshazzar was smashed against "The Rock". He had to learn that the living God watches over His own concerns as well as those of His people and never lightly discards what He had called to belong to Himself.

The question for society today is: "Who is in charge of our world"? Pagan men and women say "they are!" but Scripture teaches and the example of Belshazzar serves to warn the secular kings of this world that the Sovereign Lord moves them on the chessboard of the political scene. The way we have witnessed world leaders falling from grace should teach our current rulers that they would do well to remember the power of God in our own land to establish or remove leaders who reject Him and lead immoral lives.

# Daniel in the lions' den

The story of chapter 6 is well known, but what's not so well known is that there was now a different king and a different empire, and that Daniel was around ninety years of age.

As foretold by Daniel, the Medo-Persian empire had replaced the Babylonian empire, and Darius was king. Once again the Jews were being persecuted and the population was ordered, on the pain of death, to worship the king and forbidden to pray to any other God for a month. Daniel had served his king and country faithfully for many years and there was no human reason why he should be hated and conspired against by his contemporaries, other than the fact that he stood for the truth, loved the Lord God and lived out his faith in the culture of the time.

Christians believe, and history proves, that there is an irrational hostility against Jesus, the Bible and the Lord's people. For example in the crucifixion of the innocent Jesus, in whom no sin was ever found, we see that hatred is essentially directed towards God. The reason for this is that deep in every human heart there lies a love for sin and resentment against biblical moral truth that teaches that there is a right and wrong way to live our lives. Hating the thought of being judged by a higher authority explains the popularly held belief in full secular evolution. For it teaches that as we are part of the animal kingdom, and as there is no God, there is no accountability for our behaviour, therefore no judgment for our actions. This means, as truth is relative, we can sin as much as we wish with no fear of the consequences. The humanists' advertising slogan, "There's probably no God. Now stop worrying and enjoy your life", plays into that sentiment exactly.

When Daniel continued in his prayer habit his enemies had the ammunition to denounce him to the king and force Darius to apply the penalty for disobedience.

The story is well known: Daniel was thrown into the lions' den, but an angel shut the lions' mouths and he was delivered from death. For believers this is a wonderful assurance that our God is in control, and gives us confidence to face trials and difficulties to honour our King, Jesus. History records that later in Jewish history, at the time of the Maccabean revolt, the inspirational courage of these three Hebrews and their faith in God greatly encouraged the Jewish patriots and their leaders in their own struggle against Antiochus Epiphanes.

Jesus warned His disciples that when Christians make the same stand for their faith as Daniel, they will experience the same problems Daniel faced (John 15:20). When they serve Him loyally and tell the world clearly and faithfully that He alone is "the way and the truth and the life" (John 14:6), that He alone is Saviour and that there is "no other name under heaven given to men by which we must be saved" (Acts 4:12), they cannot help but present the same kind of offence.

# The End Times

The book now turns to chapter 7; from episodes in Daniel's life to a series of unique predictions that are so detailed and so dated in sequence that it's simply history written down in advance. It begs the question, "Does God know the future?" The Bible's answer is not only does God know the future but also He shapes it. However, this does not mean everything is predetermined and pre-planned; there is a delicate balance in Scripture between divine sovereignty and human responsibility. Although God does shape events we are not robots.

Any illustration we try to make concerning God is bound to be inadequate. The best we can do is think of examples like this: consider passengers aboard a cruise ship – they are free to make decisions and do all kinds of things but the ship is sailing with a purpose and a plan and will reach dock according to the schedule set in advance.

God has unlimited power over time, space, people, circumstances and events, and is more than able to allow us to make our moves yet still bring to pass His will upon our lives. For though we are not robots and responsible for our actions, God is nevertheless totally in control. But we must hold on to that flexibility in God's sovereignty, which is very precious, lest we begin to think that every little thing in our lives is predetermined and the decisions we make do not matter.

The visions of the future in chapters 7–12 cover two periods of time: one leading up to the first coming of the Messiah and one leading to the second coming. Daniel, like most Old Testament prophets, did not realize how much time there would be between these peaks and saw it all as one future period, which he called "kingdom". He did not realize that the kingdom would come in two stages because the King would come twice. So, these chapters predict the events leading up to the first coming of Jesus and also the events leading up to His second coming. The astonishing thing is that these two series of events are almost identical. In the first period there is a man called Antiochus Epiphanes and in the second there is a person called the Antichrist, and the descriptions of these two figures are remarkably similar. Thus, as we study the events that lead up to the first coming of Christ we have an insight into the events leading up to the second coming.

Many predictions from chapter 7 have already been fulfilled. Nebuchadnezzar's first dream in chapter 2 revealed a series of human kingdoms of decreasing quality from the golden king at the head, through the silver, down through the iron, to the feet of clay. This series of human kingdoms will lead to the inauguration of the divine kingdom. So we have had the Babylonian, Medo-Persian and Greek kingdoms, followed by the Roman empire during which Jesus, the divine King, came into the world. Daniel expected that the divine kingdom would completely take over from the human kingdoms, not realising that the divine kingdom would go through a period in which it was on earth alongside the human kingdoms. He was seeing this second peak as almost part of the first and didn't realize there would be a gap of at least 2,000 years.

The second coming of Jesus is also clearly in view but we must bear in mind the very real hazard in attempting to be dogmatic about the fulfilment of future prophecies. For example, many commentators (in the West) believe that the lion with wings is the USA and the UK, the bear is Russia and the leopard the Arab world. But there is no basis in Scripture for these predictions, and in truth throughout church history each generation of believers has tried to interpret these "kingdoms". Examples include a whole series of man-made interpretations from Calvin and the Reformers that have no basis, since these periods are now past and the predictions were not fulfilled. The same is true of modern predictions about these "kingdoms" of Daniel, which could be a combination of "kingdoms" that have not yet appeared in the history of the world. Obviously, each generation of Christians has to live with the view that Christ could well come in their time – but we have had 2,000 years of Christians believing that, and Christ's final coming is still a mystery locked in the sovereign plan of God and could be hundreds of years away. Further food for thought is the fact that the USA and the UK could hardly be considered to be leading "Christian nations" anymore, for much has changed in the last 100 years. The church of the West has to accept that the growing church of the future appears to be in Africa and China, south-east Asia and parts of South America. Moreover, the idea that the Arab world is somehow a "dangerous kingdom" is also suspect – that was said of the Soviet Union and China because of Communism. Who would have thought in the 1950s that the Chinese church would not only survive but become one of the strongest churches in the world some fifty years on? The fact that the commentators who suggest the view concerning the USA, UK, Russia and the Arab world are all western Bible interpreters says it all!

## Another prophecy fulfilled

So far Daniel has been writing in Aramaic, but now, from chapter 8 to the end, he writes in Hebrew, indicating that we are moving to a section that is primarily for God's people.

The focus is on a ram and a goat with two horns. The ram signifies the Persian empire, which stretched from India to Turkey and down to Egypt, and everything that chapter 8 says about the Persian empire came true. The goat in verse 5 stands for Alexander the Great who was given the nickname "The Goat" because he was always charging ahead. His Greek empire followed the Medo-Persian empire and though he was only thirty-one when he died, he had conquered the entire civilized world and is revered as one of history's great conquerors. However, he was a self-indulgent man and his sinful lifestyle contributed to his downfall. When he died his empire was divided between his four generals.

## Chapter 9: "Daniel's seventy weeks'

Verse 2 of chapter 9 records how Daniel was given to understand Jeremiah's prophecy that after seventy years in captivity the Jews would go back to Jerusalem. This motivated Daniel to intercede with God for the Israelite nation, and while he was praying, confessing his sin and the sin of his people, the angel Gabriel appeared to Daniel and imparted a vision of how long it would be before the divine King arrived. Bible scholars call this passage "Daniel's seventy weeks" (9:20–27). The word "seven" means not a week but seven years. So it isn't seventy "weeks" at all; seventy sevens is 490 years. Verse 25 says the period of time from the Israelites returning from Babylon to Jerusalem until the coming of the King would be 483 years (that is, sixty-nine sevens). And in fulfilment of this prophecy, just under 500 years from this time of Daniel, Jesus was born in Bethlehem. There is much disagreement about the final week but whatever view you hold about the exact dates there is enough fulfilled prophecy to encourage believers to look forward to the second coming.

## Daniel's vision of a man

Daniel is given the understanding that earthly conflicts are matched by a heavenly conflict between angelic and demonic forces. However, chapter 10 should not be used as a model for our prayer and evangelism. Proactive spiritual warfare should be left to the angels. Unless we are presented with a clear God-given specific set of circumstances we should not go looking for demons to bind but get on with the task of making disciples for the kingdom. See Paul's lesson on spiritual warfare in Ephesians 6.

## The revelation of the sixty-nine weeks

Chapter 11 contains the most astonishing predictions of the future in the whole Bible. In 35 verses 135 major events are predicted, covering a total of 366 years. Liberal commentators cannot handle this chapter and say Daniel could not have known about these events and it must have been written 400 years later, but Bible-believing Christians believe that God knows the beginning and the end and He enabled Daniel to write it down.

Historical proof of Daniel's identity and the authenticity of the book is to be found in the Septuagint (sometimes abbreviated LXX), the name given to the Greek translation of the Jewish Scriptures. The Septuagint has its origin in Alexandria, Egypt, and was translated between 300 and 200 BC. Verses 21–35 mention Antiochus Epiphanes (175–164 BC), who was to be the greatest scourge of the Jewish people before the Messiah came. He became the regent in the Greek empire north of Israel and was the guardian of a young boy who was in fact the king. But he killed the boy, took the throne for himself and was determined to wipe out the Jewish religion. He desecrated the Temple by sacrificing a pig on the altar, filled the Temple rooms with prostitutes and even erected an image of Jupiter in the Temple. He also massacred 40,000 Jews and sold an equal number into slavery. The result was the Maccabean Rebellion in 168 BC.

From Daniel 11:36 to 12:4 a strange thing happens. The passage appears to be describing Antiochus Epiphanes, and yet it says things that cannot be attributed to him. Up until Daniel 11:35 the chapter has been historically perfect, as detail after detail has been fulfilled with breath-taking accuracy. It's when we move into chapter 12 we realize that it is the end of the world that is being spoken about, and we realize Daniel is speaking about the anti-Christ.

## The end

There is no doubt that the church will face trials and tribulations, but it will go hand-in-hand with great blessings. What we must appreciate is that even Daniel comes to no clear understanding of when the end will come. Only time will reveal the times, for it is when these events are being re-enacted in history that we will recognize them. That's why these apocalyptic passages are in the Bible; not to help us calculate exact future dates, but to help us recognize the signs of the times. For example, today we can better understand Isaiah 53, which talks about the Suffering Servant who was "pierced for our transgressions" and "crushed for our iniquities", than the human author who penned the words centuries ago. And the day will dawn when we will be able to better understand the prophetic aspect of the book of Daniel.

Finally, Daniel was told: "Go your way till the end. You will rest, and then at the end of the days you will rise to receive your allotted inheritance" (Daniel 12:13).

After his death Daniel will rest, to be raised later to share in the glory of Christ's kingdom. Thus the book that reveals so much about God's plans for the nations of the world closes with the comforting revelation that He also has a plan for individuals, and that plan includes eternal life in the presence of King Jesus for those who believe.

# 28

# Hosea
# – A Marriage Made in Heaven

Hosea's ministry covered the period from around 755–710 BC and is set in the northern kingdom of Israel.

When Hosea's ministry began, Israel was experiencing a time of economic and political prosperity. However, coinciding with the rise of the Assyrian empire was the failure of successive kings to govern properly. This led to the confusion and decline that characterized the last years of the northern kingdom and resulted in their conquest and deportation into Assyrian captivity in 722 BC. Through all his forty years of ministry, the nation refused to listen to Hosea's warning of God's judgment and sank into spiritual decline marked by sin and idolatry.

The question is often asked, "Why, if God is an all-powerful and loving God, does He not rid the world of evil?" Hosea answers that question with extraordinary frankness. He does so by introducing us to a dysfunctional family that represents our world in, which God compares His situation to a loving father whose wife has left him and whose children are fast destroying themselves. We see how there is no quick fix for such subtle and sensitive relationship problems. And if you think all God has to do is wave His wand and solve problems painlessly, you only have to think of the cross, that hideous instrument of torture, and His Son's prayer in the Garden of Gethsemane, for your answer! Jesus obviously did not relish the thought of going to the cross, yet when Peter preached the first sermon of the New Testament church, he said that the whole hideous business had been part of "God's set purpose and foreknowledge" (Acts 2:23). With hindsight we realize that on the cross Jesus won a glorious victory over sin, death and hell, but it did not appear that way in Gethsemane. The lesson for us is that we have to trust God even in dire circumstances. To quote Habakkuk:

> *Though the fig-tree does not bud*
> *and there are no grapes on the vines,*
> *though the olive crop fails*
> *and the fields produce no food,*
> *though there are no sheep in the pen*
> *and no cattle in the stalls,*
> *yet I will rejoice in the Lord,*
> *I will be joyful in God my Saviour.*

Habakkuk 3:17–18

## Love hurts

To vividly illustrate His painful relationship with His people God ordered Hosea to do the last thing a prophet would contemplate. He was told to marry a prostitute, because, to paraphrase, "this is exactly what I, the Lord, have married in pledging myself to my chosen people" (Hosea 1:2). Hosea's marriage was to be a public spectacle, illustrating God's marriage to His chosen people.

And let it be understood, God did not make it easy for Hosea and find him a prostitute with a heart of gold, but instead presented him with a mercenary, untrustworthy woman who would be unfaithful and would leave him as and when it suited her. Hosea's marriage would then become a picture of God's love to His people even though they are unfaithful to Him by committing spiritual adultery with the world and being obsessed with its values. Hosea was to play the part of God, his wife Gomer would play the part of unfaithful Israel, and through Hosea's response to his soiled, unfaithful, adulteress of a wife the nation would see God's love for His people.

Gomer bore Hosea a son and then had a further two children out of wedlock before walking out on him.

In Hosea 2:2 we read, "Rebuke your mother, rebuke her, for she is not my wife, and I am not her husband." Hosea is not talking to his children about Gomer who has left home and is living with another man. No, this is the language of God to the people of Israel who have rejected Him as their

God and are worshipping idols. But the pain of Hosea's own heart due to the rejection and sorrow he was suffering mirrored God's feeling of rejection and hurt caused by the people of Israel who were playing the harlot with false gods.

To help us appreciate what was happening to Hosea represents how God feels, and what was happening to Gomer is what happens to us who reject Him, consider the following examples:

> *She [Gomer/Israel] said, "I will go after my lovers,*
> *who give me my food and my water,*
> *my wool and my linen, my oil and my drink."*
>
> HOSEA 2:5

> *She has not acknowledged that I [Gomer/God] was the one*
> *who gave her the grain, the new wine and oil,*
> *who lavished on her the silver and gold.*
>
> HOSEA 2:8

> *Therefore… I will take back my wool and my linen,*
> *intended to cover her nakedness.*
> *So now I will expose her lewdness*
> *before the eyes of her lovers;*
> *no one will take her out of my hands.*
>
> HOSEA 2:9–10

A modern account of these events in chapter 2 could go something like this:

> *The attractive and sophisticated Gomer leaves her husband,*
> *Hosea, for a successful entrepreneur and moves in to his luxury*
> *apartment overlooking his motor yacht in the marina. It's the*
> *high life, it's glamorous and exciting, and Gomer is enthralled*
> *by all the novel experiences her new circumstances offer her. But*
> *time passes and her lover takes a younger mistress and Gomer*
> *is discarded. Oh, she finds another man, she's a good-looking*
> *woman, but age and lifestyle are leaving their marks, and now*
> *she's in the suburbs living in a three-up two-down semi-detached*
> *house. She's drinking heavily, increasingly addicted to pills, and*
> *her new relationship doesn't work out either. After a few years*
> *pass she's living in a dingy flat in a run-down inner-city estate.*
> *She's made a fool of Hosea and a fool of herself. Her new lover*

*turns out to be as useless and heartless as herself, and she's his unpaid housekeeper trapped in poverty and degradation.*

*God tells Hosea where Gomer is living and the state she's in, and suggests he take round some provisions for her. So Hosea buys a few bags of groceries and, because he knows Gomer's liking for certain creams and oils, he includes some toiletries especially for her. He takes them round to the flat, knocks at the door and her live-in lover answers. Eyeing Hosea warily, he asks, "What do you want?" "I've brought some groceries and toiletries for Gomer," Hosea replies. The fellow says, "OK, I'll see she gets them," takes the bags and closes the door in his face. As Hosea hesitates, through the open window he hears Gomer ask, "Who was at the door?" and her lover answer, "It's the delivery boy, bringing some stuff I bought for you!" The knife turns in Hosea's heart as he hears Gomer's cry of joy as she throws her arms around the scoundrel's neck and thanks him.*

*Now deep down Hosea realized that Gomer knew that her selfish, thoughtless partner would never dream of doing such a thing for her. He was emotionally incapable of showing love in such a considerate way, but she deluded herself because she wanted to believe he loved her and was thinking of her.*

Israel, deep down, knew there was no way Egypt or Assyria could guarantee their safety. They knew the good things and good times they experienced came from Jehovah God. His hand alone controlled the rain and sun that produced such an abundance of crops, yet they pretended otherwise and turned the knife in the God who truly loved them.

And today, especially for those who believe and trust in Christ, in all areas of our lives – our health, employment, finances and relationships – we know it wasn't luck or chance or our cleverness or charm. It was God who loved us, and wanted us to respond gratefully and thankfully towards Him, recognizing who He is and what He has done for us. As James reminds us, "Every good and perfect gift is from above, coming down from the Father" (James 1:17).

When men and women begin to take the gifts of God as a right, believing they either deserve or have earned them, the gifts will be perverted, and motivated by pride, people will turn their backs on God (after all they don't need Him, they're the clever gifted ones) and will justify their sin and become selfish.

# Amazing grace

Chapter 3 reveals the answer to the question: How will God, whose sorrow is deeper than Hosea's, respond to Israel's unfaithfulness?

God brought Hosea into a new and incredible revelation of the heart and love of God, which the New Testament expresses in Romans 5:20: "where sin increased, grace increased all the more".

Here was something new, something Hosea had never experienced before. Somehow through the pain, hope was created. Gomer was still away, still degenerate and suffering. What was God saying to Hosea – and by inference, to Israel? The answer is incredible – we hear God saying to Hosea: "Go, show your love to your wife again, though she is loved by another and is an adulteress. Love her as the Lord loves the Israelites" (Hosea 3:1).

Suddenly Hosea realizes a new and glorious truth: he knew God could not tolerate or condone sin, and he had learned that God suffers when His people are unfaithful, but nevertheless still loves the sinner in spite of his sin. And most wondrously of all, that being so, God seeks out the sinner in order to restore him. So after many years' separation from his adulterous wife, Hosea, in obedience to God's instructions, seeks her out and walks into the market place where, presumably through debt, Gomer was being auctioned off as a slave, and he proceeds to buy her back.

As was the custom, Gomer would be naked and the men of the city would be there to see her nakedness as they bid for her. She apparently had been a beautiful woman, and even in her fallen state some of her former beauty could be seen. So when the bidding started the offers were high as the men bid for the body of the female slave.

One man started the bidding. "Twelve shekels of silver!"

"Thirteen!" said Hosea.

"Fourteen shekels of silver!"

"Fifteen!" said Hosea.

The lower bidders dropped out, but someone added, "Fifteen shekels of silver and 200 litres of barley."

"Fifteen shekels of silver and 330 litres of barley!" said Hosea.

The auctioneer looked around for a higher bid, but seeing none, said, "Sold to Hosea for fifteen shekels of silver and 330 litres of barley!" (see Hosea 3:2).

Hosea now owned his wife, but this is not the language of repossession, for God had told to him to "Go, show your love to your wife again, though she is loved by another and is an adulteress. Love her as the Lord loves the Israelites, though they turn to other gods" (3:1). Nor is this the language of overbearing authority, for power alone would solve nothing in this tale of the "eternal triangle". Instead there is rejection, hurt, humiliation, patience, personal approach and appeal, then, at last, mutual commitment and cost – mostly the cost of risking rebuff, reopening wounds, working at a difficult relationship determined it shall last and grow. God says, "I am now going to allure her... and speak tenderly to her" (2:14), and "I will betroth you to me for ever" (2:19). Hosea, for his part, says to his wife, Gomer, that he was not for sharing and neither was she – she was to work at loving him while he promised that he would love her (3:3).

## Our bridegroom and lover

However, as the remaining chapters make clear, when God draws out the large-scale meaning it turns out that in seeking the affection of the people, the pattern of relationships between Him, His people and His rivals is not so much a triangle as a veritable polygamy of relationships. The people have been unfaithful in religion, with other gods and cults; in politics, with sleaze and corruption; and in morals with unbridled and unnatural sex, violence and selfishness. God's reaction might well have been to write them off and waste no more affection on them but He is not so easily dismissed.

Aware of this, we must not make the mistake of thinking that because, so far, the role of forceful intervention has been played down, that in the face of our sinful intransigence God is reduced to standing in the wings wringing His hands in despair. God shows His anger and His judgment in this book; it's not all pleading. But think of what was said at the beginning: God is showing us how it is from His perspective. In the book of Hosea we see that God responds in a number of ways:

He is cool: "he has withdrawn himself from them [Israel]" (5:6), and "leave him [Ephraim/Israel] alone!" (4:17).

He is tough: "I will be like a lion to Ephraim... I will tear them to pieces" (5:14) and "God will remember their wickedness and punish them for their sins" (9:9).

But above all, God is tender: "How can I give you up, Ephraim? How can I hand you over, Israel?... My heart is changed within me; all my compassion is aroused" (11:8).

So we see that God's response to us is to give us space to learn, but, within the framework of His non-negotiable law, backed up by punishment if necessary, and encompassed by His overriding love for us.

And what was Israel's response to all this?

She got it wrong as usual and mistakenly assumed God wanted more religion. "They offer sacrifices," says God (8:13), "they go with their flocks and herds to seek the Lord" (5:6). But that was not the way to find Him. These were religious things and He wanted people, converted people, changed people, people who would be forever and wholly His. And this is what the book's scathing illustrations, dire predictions, warnings, threats and tender appeals add up to – looking forward to the fruit of all the agony when this unequal marriage, like Hosea's, will no longer be full of tensions and betrayals, but secure and blissful; its long winter over and its spring at last arrived and in full flower.

## Some lessons for us today

God is not the remote magician of our childish imaginings, but One who works within the very limits and freedoms that can make or break a marriage, a family, a person or a people. He loves the loveless and values the otherwise worthless enough to let the ransom for them cost Him everything. But equally, He will never be content to form one side of any relationship triangle with another god; still less be a party to polygamy or to be the bridegroom for a day or two. He will settle for nothing less than love, nothing shorter than forever.

Out of the terrible experience of his failed marriage and its subsequent restoration by him swallowing his pride and not allowing his hurt and rejection to overcome his obedience to God, Hosea came to see more clearly than any prophet before him the depths of God's divine love for Israel. He saw, irrespective of God's love, that the nation had shown ingratitude and gone whoring after idols and other nations. Falling deeper and deeper into sin, she must learn the utter folly of her ways and be made to drink the dregs of the judgment cup. God cast her off, but never ceased to love her. Though she must for a time go into Babylonian captivity; be without a place of worship; experience separation from her rightful husband and lover, He would buy her back to Himself, redeem her, and make her His own once more. This, Hosea saw clearly and so learned that the essence of the divine nature was not judgment but love.

This was anticipating the gospel of love which would be demonstrated to its fullest upon Calvary's hill when the Prince of Glory was to die for humankind, redeeming them from God's righteous justice and wrath against their sin. And it is Hosea we have to thank for bringing the gospel of love so clearly out of the Old Testament to its rightful place before man, and magnifying the great and infinite love of God.

# 29

# Joel
## – Sign of the Times

The background to the book of Joel was a catastrophic locust invasion that threatened to devastate the nation of Judah. When disaster strikes, men and women who haven't given God a thought in years become authorities in theology, asking, "How could a good God allow such a disaster?" and reasoning, "If God is good He must lack the power to prevent a disaster, and if He has power to stop it and doesn't, He can't be good!" Then it is the task of the man or woman of faith to explain who God is and how He acts. If people are truthful when disaster happens, the disaster becomes an instrument for addressing their sin in this life and opens their minds to the reality of God and the life to come. Joel was truthful and used the drought, locust plague and famine to illustrate a coming, unstoppable and even worse disaster that would be far more terrible than the invasion of the locusts. He pointed the people to the day of the Lord.

Jesus did exactly the same thing in Matthew 24 where He warned the day of the Lord was coming and likened it to Noah's flood. In Luke 13, Jesus also used local tragedy that touched on everyday lives. He pointed beyond the obvious, immediate problem and said that it served to illustrate an even greater tragedy that will occur ultimately and permanently to everyone who is careless about the spiritual condition in which they leave this world at the point of death. This is the bottom line, which is the point of Joel's prophecy. The delays in God's judgment and the judgments in such catastrophic events as locust plagues and earthquakes are both for our good, that we might be aware of the fragility of life and what awaits us after death, and repent.

## The promise of spiritual blessing

Scripture does not leave us without hope.

In Joel 2:28–29 the prophet also predicts that God would reveal Himself in a new way by making Himself available to every man, women and child, and on the day of Pentecost, Joel's prophecy was fulfilled. If Isaiah 53 is the key Old Testament scripture for our appreciation of Christ's experience on the cross, then Joel 2 is essential for our understanding of the coming Holy Spirit. This is confirmed in Acts 2:16–21 when, on the day of Pentecost, in the first sermon of the New Testament church the apostle Peter quoted Joel 2:28–32.

The root of the promise in Joel's prophecy lies in an incident concerning Moses recorded in Numbers 11:29.

The Israelites were complaining of the repeated diet of manna in the wilderness and Moses was overcome with the burden of leading them while coping with their complaints. God sympathized and told him to select seventy elders of Israel and bring them to the tent of meeting where He promised to take the Spirit that was on Moses and put it on them as well (Numbers 11:17). And that's what happened. These men received the Holy Spirit and began to prophesy as a sign to the people that they had received the gift and were therefore chosen by God to minister alongside Moses. Two elders were not present but nevertheless the Spirit came upon them as well and this bothered some who were close to Moses. In Numbers 11:27–29 we read:

> A young man ran and told Moses, "Eldad and Medad are prophesying in the camp."
>
> Joshua son of Nun, who had been Moses' aide since youth, spoke up and said, "Moses, my lord, stop them!"
>
> But Moses replied, "Are you jealous for my sake? I wish that all the Lord's people were prophets and that the Lord would put his Spirit on them!"

This incident shows that in this early period God's Spirit was not given to all His people in the same way that He is now. At that time, God was with His people but His Spirit did not come on them or dwell in them; He came upon individuals for a specific purpose. For example, Joseph's interpretation of

255

Pharaoh's dream is the first reference in the Bible in which a person possessed the Spirit's enabling to do this (Genesis 41:38). And sometimes the Spirit departed; for example from King Saul (1 Samuel 16:14). So when Moses said, "I wish that all the Lord's people were prophets and that the Lord would put his Spirit on them," he was expressing a very real need and longing, and it was not until God spoke through Joel that there was even a promise of such blessing.

What makes this particularly striking is that it's a promise of spiritual rather than material blessing. We can readily understand the need of material blessings when we remember the disaster caused by the locust plague, but we must never underestimate the importance of spiritual blessings. Jesus, teaching of the folly of relying upon the material, said, "What good is it for a man to gain the whole world, yet forfeit his soul?" (Mark 8:36).

What made Joel's prophecy significant was the way it was to be for "all the people", rather than only for some as previously.

And just in case we miss the point, he spells it out in detail:

> *Your sons and daughters will prophesy,*
> *your old men will dream dreams,*
> *your young men will see visions.*
> *Even on my servants, both men and women*
> *I will pour out my Spirit in those days.*

JOEL 2:28–29

This is truly momentous, for it's saying that in the coming church age, in the time of the New Testament, the Holy Spirit would come and inaugurate all believers as ministers of God, not merely a special group from the one selected tribe of Levi. And in Jerusalem at Pentecost, Joel's prophecy was fulfilled when the Holy Spirit came upon all believers and inaugurated a new era for the church (Acts 2:44–47).

## The age of grace

But something else Joel brings out in his prophecy is the age of grace.

The promise of the Spirit is uncompromisingly placed in the context of the "great and dreadful day of the Lord" (2:31). This comes as a bit of a shock after the promise of so much blessing in the previous paragraphs. Now to be confronted with the dramatic imagery of apocalyptic language must have taken the people's breath away:

*I will show wonders in the heavens*
*and on the earth,*
*blood and fire and billows of smoke.*
*The sun will be turned to darkness*
*and the moon to blood*
*before the coming of the great and dreadful day of the Lord.*

JOEL 2:30–31

Think of this: the blood of the Passover lamb secured safety for the Israelites from the angel of death and guaranteed their exodus from Egypt. A pillar of fire led the people through the darkness of the wilderness night for forty years, and Mount Sinai was wreathed in smoke as the Lord descended to speak with Moses and his people. All three, blood, fire and smoke, speak of the overwhelming reality of a Holy God present with His people, protecting, preserving, providing, proclaiming and thereby calling them to Him and through them bringing the watching world to account.

Before the great and dreadful day of the Lord comes there will be another such demonstration of God's all-consuming holiness. Jesus Himself said the same thing in Matthew 24:27–31:

*For as lightning that comes from the east is visible even in the*
*west, so will be the coming of the Son of Man… Immediately*
*after the distress of those days,*
*"the sun will be darkened,*
*and the moon will not give its light;*
*the stars will fall from the sky,*
*and the heavenly bodies will be shaken."*
*At that time the sign of the Son of Man will appear in the*
*sky, and all the nations of the earth will mourn. They will see*
*the Son of Man coming on the clouds of the sky, with power*
*and great glory. And he will send his angels with a loud*
*trumpet call, and they will gather his elect from the four winds,*
*from one end of the heavens to the other.*

And in Revelation the apostle John picks up the prophecy of Joel and the words of Jesus and speaks of the same event:

*I watched as he opened the sixth seal. There was a great*
*earthquake. The sun turned black like sackcloth made of goat*
*hair, the whole moon turned blood red, and the stars in the sky*

> *fell to earth, as late figs drop from a fig tree when shaken by a*
> *strong wind. The sky receded like a scroll, rolling up, and every*
> *mountain and island was removed from its place.*
>
> REVELATION 6:12–14

While Joel used the drought, locust and famine to make people think beyond their present circumstances, he was hinting that the locusts were forerunners of an even greater disaster to come. So restoration from the locusts, followed by the people's experience of the Spirit of God being poured out upon them in a new and special way, will signify divine intervention in readiness for the great day of judgment. Therefore, the gift of the Spirit was not for personal satisfaction or even for national recovery and stability, it was to strengthen the people of God to take their rightful position of prophetic leadership among the nations in a world heading for an apocalyptic day of final reckoning. If the individual prophets had the task of taking God's word to a nation at risk of God's judgment, a prophetically inspired people would have the task of taking God's word to a world on the brink of ultimate judgment.

Incredibly, Joel makes it clear that to live in Mount Zion and in Jerusalem will not guarantee surviving that day of judgment. It will be terrible for Israel and all the nations, and the only issue of any consequence will be, "is salvation possible?" And through Joel, the Lord says "yes!": "everyone who calls on the name of the Lord will be saved…" (Joel 2:32)

Note the double-sided phrase, "everyone who calls on the name of the Lord" and, all "whom the Lord calls" (see verse 32). This reflects the initiative of God in making His call clear, and the responsibility of the hearers to respond by calling on the name of the Lord.

This answers the questions as to why Peter chose this passage from Joel in the first New Testament sermon, and why Luke recorded it in Acts 2 to explain what happened to the followers of Jesus on the day of Pentecost several centuries later.

Firstly, there is no recorded happening of anything which could have been taken as fulfilment of Joel's prophecy during the period of 800 years from the prophet Joel to the apostle Peter. Which, incidentally, teaches us that God is not in the hurry that we are in, nor does He share our opinion that we must be the generation in which it must all happen. But Peter was quite clear, that at nine o'clock in the morning on that particular Pentecost day what he witnessed both personally and publicly convinced him that, in the words of Acts 2:16, "this is what was spoken by the prophet Joel."

God's choice of Pentecost was crucial. Back in Egypt, Passover for the

Israelites was a glorious gift from God, which brought about their deliverance from slavery. Fifty days later, with the enemy destroyed and cut off by the Red Sea, and with no possibility of pursuit, Israel was free from the power of Egypt. And what do we find? They gathered as a nation at Mount Sinai and celebrated the "feast of weeks". Now move forward in time, and we find that the Jews in the New Testament still observed this feast, but have changed the name from the "feast of weeks" to "Pentekostos", which in Greek means "fiftieth". It was still the feast of weeks, still held fifty days after Passover but now known by its Greek name Pentekostos.

Consider it like this: Passover in Egypt resulted in salvation for a nation through the blood of a lamb; Passover in Jerusalem is salvation for humankind through the blood of Jesus. Pentecost at Sinai yielded the Law and the Ten Commandments: Pentecost in Jerusalem, Christ the first fruit of the Father bringing with Him not only the saved of Israel but the harvest of 3,000 souls: the first-fruits of the Christian mission.

When Peter changed the words from "afterwards" (Joel 2:28) to "in the last days" (Acts 2:17), one senses that the promise to pour out the Spirit is bound up with the winding down of history and the fulfilment of God's eternal purposes. And at Pentecost Peter made clear that the pouring out of God's Spirit indicated that the final chapter of God's history of the world had begun with the birth, life, death, burial, resurrection and ascension of Jesus of Nazareth. At first glance it appears strange that Peter did not mention the last section of Joel 2:32 – "everyone who calls on the name of the Lord will be saved" – but a few minutes later he does in fact quote the sentiments expressed when his listeners, convicted of sin and cut to the heart, ask him, "what shall we do?" (Acts 2:37). Peter replies,

> *Repent and be baptised, every one of you, in the name of Jesus*
> *Christ for the forgiveness of your sins. And you will receive*
> *the gift of the Holy Spirit. The promise is for you and your*
> *children and for all who are far off – for all whom the Lord our*
> *God will call.*

ACTS 2:38–39

## Biblical prophecy

Two facts about Joel help us to see how God speaks not only to Joel's contemporaries but also through him to us.

Like all prophets, when Joel predicts the future he can see only from where he is in history. He doesn't have the knowledge or hindsight that we have – or the overview God has. Think of it as though he is describing a distant mountain range. Some peaks are obviously more remote than others, but he can't tell how great the in-between distance is. With hindsight, we know his prediction about the Spirit and salvation in Joel 2:28–32 came true on the day of Pentecost and is still being fulfilled today. But the judgment of all the nations (3:2) has still to be fulfilled, although twenty centuries have gone by since Pentecost. On the other hand, the judgment of Tyre, Sidon and Philistia had already taken place more than three centuries before Christ. Joel nevertheless saw all these events as part of the same "mountain range" yet to come, as Joel 3:1 puts it, "In those days and at that time".

In other words, Bible prophecy gives us a view of what God will do and we are not meant to use it as a map that will tell us in advance how it will all come together. Joel is limited in what he knows he takes it that God's people are the Israelites, God's land is Judah, God's city is Jerusalem and God's house is a building on Mount Zion. He may sense that one day God will give all these terms a far deeper, broader meaning, but he does not know how he will do it: the detail escapes him.

In exactly the same way, God gave Ezekiel a prophecy concerning the rebuilding of the Temple, and Amos one of a "repaired tent of David" (see Amos 9:11) because these are terms that they and their readers could understand. Only in New Testament days will it become clear that it represents the worldwide spread of the gospel of the kingdom of Christ. The prophets may have sensed something of that, but the people to whom they were speaking could not remotely comprehend the worldwide church of the New Testament – the full extent of the world had not yet been discovered.

So we have to ask whether things foretold in the Old Testament are to come true literally (like the ones concerning the first coming of Christ), or if they are picture language used to convey the meaning to people down the centuries, including us. If the latter is the case, how it unfolds may not be so clear. But Scripture does assure us that God will leave no unfinished business and however long it takes He will see to it that the nations are punished for their lawless violence, especially to His people. This important factor in God's judgment of the world should strongly dissuade us either from taking things into our own hands, or from ever doubting our faithful and just God.

The day will come – the Day of the Lord – when, from His complete records, "He will bring to light what is hidden in darkness and will expose the motives of men's hearts" (1 Corinthians 4:5). His verdict will then be made public and will make clear the radical and eternal difference that God makes between those who are His people and those who are not. No doubt there will be many surprises, but the time for discussion, argument and decision will be over.

# 30

# Amos
## – God's Message for Today

The message of Amos is a message for today, from a man of God who was addressing an affluent society that would not accept the warning of divine judgment.

Two centuries of growth had produced a golden age for the nation of Israel. But prosperity had generated the twin evils of selfish, pleasure-seeking materialism and conscience-dulling, meaningless religion. To make matters worse, when concerns were voiced the nation's leaders reassured the people by telling them what they wanted to hear, and were angry when Amos spoiled the party. Their annoyance with Amos was all the greater because he was not a religious professional with a theological training, nor even a priest; the Hebrew suggests he was an animal breeder from Tekoa (1:1) a village south of Jerusalem and twelve miles south of the border with Israel.

In his journeys to Jerusalem and the cities of the Northern Kingdom, the contrast with Amos's simple life in the Judean wilderness would allow him to observe the evils practised and condoned in Israel's materialistic societies. Their godlessness would disturb him, and we can imagine Amos lying at night beside his sheep under the magnificent star-filled eastern sky, sensing within him that prompting from the Lord to be one of the first recorded missionaries in the Bible: to go and warn the nation of Israel of the danger it faced by offending God.

That this was not an easy calling is obvious when we consider the disadvantages he laboured under. There was his lack of formal religious training, coupled with the deep suspicion Israelites held for anyone from Judah. But perhaps most telling of all, Amos had a message no one wanted to hear. At a time of peace and plenty no one wanted to listen to a shepherd who rocked the boat with a message that judgment was coming.

Amos begins his prophetic warning with eight sermons preached on the steps of the Temple in Bethel about 755 BC.

## Ripe for judgment

The first six oracles (1:3 – 2:3) portray God judging the six nations that formed a ring around Israel and each was, according to Amos, ripe for judgment. When we see nations involved in murder, oppression, tyranny and racism, and feel unable to assist and helpless to bring change, it is comforting to know that God cares and will judge accordingly.

We should also note that none of these nations had the Bible, nor had they been favoured with a special revelation from God, but their ignorance was no excuse. They were to be judged, for every one of us has a conscience and that alone is enough to make us accountable to our Creator, as the apostle Paul made clear (Romans 1:18–20; 2:14–15). As far as Amos was concerned, their crimes against humanity had provoked God beyond His patience. They did not need the Bible to tell them that their brutality, exploitation, treachery and needless aggression was wrong; their conscience should have accomplished that.

The message for us today is clear: God judges societies.

In the same way that God reminded Israel that He destroyed the Amorite (all the inhabitants of Canaan) who stood before them, "though he was tall as the cedars and strong as the oaks" (Amos 2:9), He can say that he delivered us from a pagan past, from Islam in the Middle Ages, from Roman Catholic legalism in the sixteenth century and from Fascist and Marxist dictatorships in the twentieth century. Moreover, just as God raised up prophets and righteous men to preach to the nation of Israel (2:11), God has blessed the Western nations with extraordinary preachers who were used by Him to bring the nations under His authority. The result is that we see chapels and churches in every city, town and village throughout the land. Yes, it's true there may be nations worse than us, and Israel could make that excuse too, but God still judged her, for she, with her spiritual heritage, should have been so much better. The lesson of Amos is that a nation's future does not depend on its political or economic treaties. What finally decides a nation's fate is whether it is a godless society where anything goes or where truth and justice, right and wrong are recognized, respected and upheld. And we should remember, in a world with a history littered with the wrecks of civilizations and empires there is nothing immortal about the Western nations.

Amos certainly wasn't afraid to speak his mind, and in chapter 4 of his prophecy he concentrates on four specific areas:

## Morally corrupt religion

First, girl power:

> *Hear this word, you cows of Bashan on Mount Samaria,*
> *you women who oppress the poor and crush the needy*
> *and say to your husbands, "Bring us some drinks!"*
>
> Amos 4:1

The cows of Bashan were renowned for their high quality, and if Amos had followed up his opening remark in the right tone of voice and with a compliment he would have had the sophisticated ladies of Samaria eating out of his hand. But instead, in a voice heavy with sarcasm, he compared the noble ladies to pampered pets who were absorbed with their own luxurious lifestyle concerned only with satisfying their appetite and like brute beasts completely lacking in spiritual understanding. The revulsion felt by Amos was shared by God (4:2). These women behaved like cows and so they would be butchered like cows. You do not get language more brutal than this. Amos is saying their expensively pampered, sleek carcasses will be dragged outside the ruins of their luxury homes like so much offal unfit for human consumption.

## No sense of sin

Second, Amos spoke against religiosity.
In 4:4–5 you can again hear his derision:

> *Go to Bethel and sin;*
> *go to Gilgal and sin yet more.*
> *Bring your sacrifices every morning,*
> *your tithes every three years.*
> *Burn leavened bread as a thank offering*

*and brag about your freewill offerings –*
*boast about them, you Israelites,*
*for this is what you love to do.*

Bethel and Gilgal were the sites of Israel's worship of golden calves set up by King Jeroboam (1 Kings 12:26–33). "Go to Bethel and sin; go to Gilgal and sin yet more," speaks of empty, meaningless religion where the focus is on man rather than God. In other words, the Israelites worshipped God on their own terms. God said, "Jerusalem," they said "No, Bethel and Gilgal." God said, "No idols," they made golden calves. You wonder what could possibly motivate people to go to so much time and trouble to attend meaningless, formalistic religious services week after week, and Amos tell us it was their spiritual conceit (verse 5): they "brag and boast". They enjoyed being known as religious. God had nothing to do with it – it was self-satisfaction, an ego trip, pure and simple.

## No sense of God

Third, Amos turns to an issue which is not so well understood by Christians and is completely lost on our society: the ability to understand the times.

In 1 Chronicles 12:32 we meet the men of Issachar, "who understood the times and knew what Israel should do", but these days had gone. There had been famine, drought, blight of mildew and plagues of locust, disease and war, earthquake and what we call "natural disasters" (Amos 4:6–11), and Amos is claiming that there is nothing natural about any of them. As far as he is concerned these catastrophes were warnings sent by God to shake the people out of their dangerous complacency and point them in the direction of the spiritual priorities they should be concerned with. Yet, unable to discern the times, the people did not see God's warning hand and ignored what was happening to them.

Many Christians are not too happy with the concept of disasters being sent by God, and usually blame them on the devil or the permissive will of God, which means He is the passive onlooker of disasters. But Amos doesn't see it that way. Notice the first person singular introducing every disaster: "I gave... I withheld... I sent... I struck... I killed... I overthrew... ." Christians must not squirm or shrink from the truth: God is the sovereign ruler of the universe who works things according to His own will and purpose, and hard as it may be to accept, God says, "I did it!"

It's not "cruel", because behind all natural disaster God has a loving purpose that is demonstrated in His words, "yet you have not returned to me", which follow every catastrophe. And neither is it "predestined fatalism", because God has left room in His universe for voluntary human response. In fact, says Amos, the whole purpose of what's been happening to Israel is that they might respond to God. God's cry, "yet you have not returned to me", is not that of an angry tyrant, it is the appeal from the lips of a heartbroken and perplexed lover, towards people who have freedom of choice to follow or turn away from Him, and have chosen to turn away.

## Religious complacency

Fourth, Amos sarcastically and accurately responds to the manner in which his warning of coming judgment has been received: "Woe to you who are complacent in Zion, and to you who feel secure on Mount Samaria" (Amos 6:1a).

The people demonstrated their spiritual complacency by responding in the way used by the propagandist for centuries; that is: divert, exaggerate and reassure.

Diverting attention from problems by pointing to places worse off is classic deception.

> *Go to Calneh and look at it;*
> *go from there to great Hamath,*
> *and then go down to Gath in Philistia.*
> *Are they better off than your two kingdoms?*
> *Is their land larger than yours?*
>
> AMOS 6:2

Firstly, we can imagine Amos sarcastically parodying a government spokesman from Jeroboam's palace as he replies to someone who is making a complaint. "Get real Amos! What's the matter with you? You think we're bad – go and have a look at social conditions in Hamath; the inflation rate in Gath is through the roof, and if it's corruption you want, get on your camel and have a look at Calneh, then you'll see what corruption really is. But please stop complaining, you've never had it so good, we're the top nation, be glad you are an Israelite!"

Secondly, Amos shows how the guilty take the heat off themselves by exaggerating their minor successes so as to obscure major failure: "you who rejoice in the conquest of Lo Debar and say, 'Did we not take Karnaim by our own strength?' " (Amos 6:13).

Lo Debar and Karnaim were battles that Jeroboam's armed forces had recently won and thereby became ideal propaganda material by which to boost the military pride of the nation and the reputation and success of the government. But Lo Debar and Karnaim were insignificant when compared to the real threat posed by the awakening menace of Assyria. By pointing to the minor success, the administration hoped to beguile the people from discerning where the real danger lay. Only Amos seemed to spot the irony, for in Hebrew Lo Debar literally means "nothing".

The third response Amos encountered was the authorities" attempt to reassure the people by making optimistic claims: "You put off the evil day" (Amos 6:3).

In other words their attitude was, "Don't worry, it will never happen." Jesus warned in His parables about the necessity to prepare for trouble that lies ahead. The wise and foolish builders in Matthew 7, building foundations on either rock or sand demonstrated the danger of short-term complacency. And His parables of invitation tell us that the foolish are preoccupied people who ignore His invitations, or in the words of Matthew 22:5, who "pay no attention", will find that their complacency will take them to hell.

In chapters 7 to 9 Amos has five visions that illustrate the danger Israel was in.

## Amos is threatened

After delivering the first three visions, Amos provokes an angry response from Amaziah, a priest from Bethel, who, as a spokesman for the established state church, attempted to silence the prophet. With no hint of spirituality he talked like a senior civil servant concerned that Amos represented a threat to the stability of the nation, and cleverly applied pressure on the prophet.

Firstly, he caused the maximum embarrassment to Amos by going public in writing a letter, so drawing the king on to his side (7:10). This tactic of attempting to embarrass and frighten an innocent party by writing a letter was also used by Sanballat in his attempt to stop Nehemiah from rebuilding the wall of Jerusalem (Nehemiah 6:5).

Secondly, Amaziah put a spin on what Amos said to construct his words in the worst possible way (Amos 7:10b–11). Yes, Amos did say the things he is accused of saying, but they are presented falsely. Amaziah knows full well that governments take political sedition far more seriously than religious fundamentalism, so he portrayed Amos as the ringleader of a plot to overthrow the government. Then, having blackened his character, Amaziah told lies and talked of conspiracy, implying that Amos was a menace to the social and spiritual health of the nation and a danger to the king himself (verse 10).

Amaziah has cleverly shifted the ground from principles to personalities. Amos said his words came directly from the Lord; Amaziah, by removing the theological context of Amos's message, reduces it to the level of a terrorist movement.

Thirdly, Amaziah plays the nationalistic card: "Get out, you seer! Go back to the land of Judah" (7:12). This is a powerful card to play when the person comes from a different background. "He's not really one of us!"; "He never quite fitted in"; "To be perfectly honest he would be better going back to his own type!"; "Amos, this is Bethel Cathedral, not some tin chapel out in the sticks of Judah. You're out of your class, brother!"

Fourthly, he accused God's servant of mere professionalism (7:12d). Amos was not to be the last minister who would be falsely accused of being "in it for the money" by people who themselves are financially motivated.

Fifthly, he implied that Amos had no right to be there: "because this is the king's sanctuary and the temple of the kingdom" (7:13). When all else fails, produce the rulebook and use procedure so that God can be silenced on a technicality.

Amos responded by defending his commission from God and getting on with the task he was called to do. You have here the contrast between the establishment person and the called person. The establishment person has political influence; the called person has spiritual authority. The establishment person threatens court action; the called person threatens divine judgment. For in the final analysis, Amos's conviction that God has called him gives him purpose and inner resilience producing courage that a hundred Amaziahs could never browbeat.

In verses 16–17 we can imagine Amos resolutely looking his detractor straight in the eye and saying in effect, "You say do not prophesy. Well Amaziah, listen to this:

> *This is what the Lord says:*
> *"Your wife will become a prostitute in the city,*
> *and your sons and daughters will fall by the sword.*
> *Your land will be measured and divided up,*
> *and you yourself will die in a pagan country.*

*And Israel will certainly go into exile,*
*away from their native land."*

AMOS 7:17

The incredible courage shown by Amos reminds us of the inherent dangers of being controlled by political religion and that it is better to be an Amos on the bishop's carpet than an Amaziah on the bishop's throne.

In chapter 8, Amos makes it clear that social ethics and passion for justice are obligatory and disobedience would be punished by God.

After a catalogue of outrageous social injustices, many of which they would call standard business practice (7:4–7), Amos warns the nation that the Lord will never forget anything that they've done and will punish their sin.

We can be sure that evil perpetrated in this world does not merely vanish into history. Our moral indignation is not wasted breath; it corresponds to God's own feelings. The deeds of the exploiters and oppressors are recorded in the memory of the One who is far more concerned with social justice than we are, and who assures us that one day the books will be opened and the deeds of the rich and poor, small and great will be told. At that time no one will defiantly cry, "Who says so?" They will know, "The Lord has sworn… 'I will never forget anything they have done" (8:7).

## Restoration is promised

But then, from Amos 9:11, like a silver cloud from a dark and angry sky, in the closing verses of his book the prophet strikes a new and very significant note.

Israel was not to be sent to the rubbish tip but to the reclamation bin. In the midst of all the harrowing experiences about to befall her, in the midst of judgment, God had a plan of salvation – for according to Amos, judgment will be but the prelude to a new society: "In that day I will restore David's fallen tent" (9:11). A new day will dawn on the other side of this judgment upon Israel. A new day with a new kingdom, not the pathetic shambles of a nation divided and a monarchy weakened as it was in the day of Amos. And when God's refining judgment had done its work a new King in the promised line of David would appear to rule a new kingdom:

> *"I will bring back my exiled people Israel;*
> *they will rebuild the ruined cities and live in them.*
> *They will plant vineyards and drink their wine;*

269

*they will make gardens and eat their fruit.*
*I will plant Israel in their own land,*
*never again to be uprooted from the land I have given them,"*
*says the Lord your God.*

AMOS 9:14–15

That the early New Testament church believed this prophecy of Amos had been fulfilled in their day is seen in the book of Acts when James the brother of Jesus, now leader of the Christian church at Jerusalem, summarized its proceedings:

*James spoke up: "Brothers, listen to me. Simon has described*
*to us how God at first showed his concern by taking from the*
*Gentiles a people for himself. The words of the prophets are in*
*agreement with this, as it is written:*

*'After this I will return*
*and rebuild David's fallen tent.*
*Its ruins I will rebuild,*
*and I will restore it,*
*that the remnant of men may seek the Lord,*
*and all the Gentiles who bear my name,'*
*says the Lord, who does these things."*

ACTS 15:13–17

In quoting Amos 9, and in the context of his statement, James was expressing his belief that Gentile believers now belonged to the true Israel, called and chosen by God to belong to his one and only people and to glorify his name. For James, it is in the birth, resurrection and ascension of Jesus Christ that the tent of David has been rebuilt. In the twilight of theocratic Israel, the fallen tent of David will be Joseph and Mary. The new King will be born in the stench and dirt of a stable in Bethlehem. The true royal family of Israel and Judah was not that of Herod but that of the Nazareth carpenter and his expectant wife. This new age of which the prophet Amos speaks has begun in the new Israel of the Christian church. Amos is anticipating the conversion of the Gentiles and their incorporation into the church when he speaks of "all the nations that bear my name" (Amos 9:12). So, wonderfully, these closing verses of Amos present the New Testament age culminating in the future glory of the new heavens and new earth which will be ushered in by the return of the Lord Jesus Christ.

# 31

## Obadiah
## – A Major Message from a Minor Prophet

Obadiah, the shortest book in the Old Testament, conveys a major message for our times.

Written after the grim prophecy of Amos had come to pass, the book of Obadiah has two interrelated themes:

- the destruction of "Edom" (also referred to as Esau and Teman) because of its pride and cruelty against Israel when Jerusalem was invaded and the inhabitants were carried off as captives by the invaders;
- the ultimate vindication and exaltation of "Judah" (verse 12) referred to by the names "Jacob", "Jerusalem" and "Mount Zion".

As Obadiah's theme is a denunciation of Edom, it helps if we know something about this ancient kingdom.

Edom today lies within the land of Jordan, and historically was neighbour to Israel with long memories and rival interests. Both nations had a strong sense of being different from other people, but while in Israel this pride was due to being conscious of a peculiar destiny not yet realized, in Edom it was a self-satisfied pride that took little heed for the future and felt no need for the divine, relying instead upon their remarkable isolation, vast store of wealth and a reputation for worldly wisdom.

The deep valley of Arabah runs from the southern extremity of the Dead

Sea to the Gulf of Aqaba. Rising steeply on the eastern side of the valley is the range of red sandstone hills called Mount Seir. The real importance of Edom, also known as Seir, lay in the fact that it straddled the great trade route between Syria and Egypt. The landscape consisted of narrow gorges and high cliffs which made it ideal territory for the Edomites to extract a toll from passing traders and to wage war from their almost impregnable fortresses. It was here that Esau, the warrior brother of Jacob settled (Genesis 32:3), and this gives us a clue as to the character of the Edomites. Esau was spiritually dead with no respect of birthright, no faith in the future and no vision, caring only to satisfy his carnal appetite.

The Edomites were widely regarded as being wise. A proverb of the time speaks of the "cleverness of the men of Edom", but you can be sure that the wisdom they were renowned for was worldly wisdom. This was exemplified by their most famous son, King Herod, whom historians describe as ruthless, cunning, scheming and clever. Herod bought the throne of Israel from Caesar in 37 BC. That's why, when the Wise Men came asking where they could find the newborn king of the Jews, Herod was angry. He didn't want a Jew on his throne, for Edom had conquered Israel. This is what's behind the slaughter of every boy-child less than two years of age in Bethlehem (Matthew 2:16).

Israel had bitter memories of the insults that Edom had inflicted upon their nation, and Jeremiah, Ezekiel and Obadiah all called out in anger for revenge on the Edomites. The history between the two nations went back a long way. After the exodus, when Israel came out of Egypt on route to the Promised Land, the Edomites refused them passage through their territory, even though Moses promised to harm nothing and pay for whatever water the people drank (Numbers 20:14–21). But worst of all by far was the way the Edomites reacted when their nearest kin, the Israelites, were attacked by the Babylonians. Psalm 137 records:

> *By the rivers of Babylon we sat and wept*
> *when we remembered Zion…*
> *Remember, O Lord, what the Edomites did*
> *on the day Jerusalem fell.*
> *"Tear it down," they cried,*
> *"tear it down to its foundations!"*

PSALM 137:1, 7

It's said that the Edomite chiefs danced with delight at each massive push against the Jerusalem walls, shouting encouragement to the Babylonian soldiers. Then they stood guard in the passes to intercept Israelites who tried to escape by way of the Jordan valley and handed the fugitives over to the Babylonians. And finally, when the city of Jerusalem was left a smoking ruin, they swarmed in to loot and indulge their idolatrous and disgusting practices on the Temple hill. For this God judged Edom, and the nation lost its independence around the fifth century AD. Since then the area has been an uninhabited wilderness with only the ruins of the Edomite cities as a grim reminder that God's judgments will come to pass.

The sin of Edom was the sin of pride that says, "we can do without God", individually, as a family or as a nation. This was the sin of Satan, father of all sin. It was pride that caused him to say, "I will ascend above the tops of the clouds; I will make myself like the Most High" (Isaiah 14:14).

Nothing lies so much at the heart of the problems of the human race as this prideful desire to take over God's place or, which amounts nearly to the same thing, to have our own way rather than obey God.

So what was it about Edom that made her so proud?

## Israel's defences

To reach the city you had to pass through a one-mile long, 15-foot wide canyon that allowed a handful of defenders to hold off an army. From the human perspective it's hard to imagine a safer place, yet God said He would bring Edom down. And He would do it not just by sending an invading army that would allow Edom to rebuild, but He would do it in a way that would leave the nation desolate for evermore. The grape pickers leave a few grapes; thieves leave some belongings, but not so with God's judgment, everything would be taken forever (1:4–6).

From this we can discern a pattern for the nations. As God exalts a people, those in power mistakenly see it as a cause for personal pride and boast of what they have achieved. They consider how they are better off than others, how their armed forces are superior to everyone else's and how they don't need God – then God brings that nation down. This has been the case with all the great kingdoms of the world. Historians tell us that the world has seen twenty-one great civilizations, but each has passed away in time to make room for the next. Think of Egypt, Babylon, Greece, Rome, England and Soviet Russia. And tomorrow, perhaps, the United States.

This should be a warning to us in our day when we are so proud of our strength. Yet financial, political and social insecurity carry a solemn reminder to each and every one of us concerning the foolishness of trusting in wealth that can vanish overnight. In the words of Jesus:

> *Do not store up for yourselves treasures on earth, where moth and rust destroy, and where thieves break in and steal. But store up for yourselves treasures in heaven, where moth and rust do not destroy, and where thieves do not break in and steal. For where your treasure is, there your heart will be also.*
>
> MATTHEW 6:19–21

## Israel's allies

Secular and church history are filled with stories of nations in trouble turning to their allies for help, only to be disappointed. As we consider verse 7, think of Britain in World War II struggling alongside the Allies against the might of the German onslaught until America was compelled to join the War and in so doing strengthen the Allied war effort. We should be very careful. Yes, make alliances with other nations, but do so in the knowledge that they are only human and we should not rely upon them. We are to place our trust only in God and show it by attempting to establish righteousness and justice in our land.

## The Edomites' wisdom

According to verse 8, people were more or less saying, "No matter what comes, we can handle it!" From the human perspective this was not just empty arrogance; the Edomites really were noted for their wisdom. For example, Eliphaz, the foremost of Job's friends and the chief character in that book of human wisdom, was from Edom. Another of Job's friends was a Shunite, a name given to a mountain in Edom, and there are other Scripture references regarding the wisdom of the people of Edom, for example 1 Kings 4:30.

Today we are proud of our scientific and technological abilities, medical knowledge and great learning. Our politicians and leaders constantly assure us of their ability to solve our problems and lead us on into Utopia. But the same science and technology that has undoubtedly helped in so many ways is also killing people today through mistakes, ignorance or deliberate misuse. Pride in our achievements and arrogant confidence in our ability to succeed without God will lead to our downfall. History and common sense tell us that we cannot solve the world's problems and it would be much wiser if we developed a national humility that encouraged us to look to God for guidance and strength.

Look at how the sin of Edom's pride worked out in the life of their nation. First there was the sin of standing aloof when a brother stumbles:

> *On the day you stood aloof*
> *while strangers carried off his wealth*
> *and foreigners entered his gates*
> *and cast lots for Jerusalem,*
> *you were like one of them.*

OBADIAH 11

Christians have a responsibility to other men and women, especially their natural families and the family of God, which is the church. God holds them accountable. Where they can help, they must help. Where they can encourage, they must encourage. Where they can support and defend, they must do so.

## One thing leads to another

Committing the first offence of being stand-offish leads to the second: "You should not look down on your brother in the day of his misfortune" (Obadiah 12a).

The Hebrew suggests being inquisitive and taking a delight in bad news. Our obligation as a Christian is to restore the fallen and not rejoice over their downfall – which is the third offence: "nor rejoice over the people of Judah in the day of their destruction" (Obadiah 12b).

The warning is the downward progression of unchecked sin.

For example, whenever there is bad feeling between brothers, nations or even churches, and one sees misfortune happening to the other, the immediate natural response is to be pleased about it. Often Christians are not immune, and will talk about other Christians and even be pleased at their misfortune because somehow it makes them appear better.

At this stage the fourth offence is reached – it's boasting: "nor boast so much in the day of their trouble" (Obadiah 12c).

It grows out of pride and is closely related to rejoicing over another's misfortunes. If we saw ourselves on the same level as others we would mourn with them and thank God that we have been spared: "there, but for the grace of God, go I."

So far all the steps in unbrotherliness have been negative sinful attitudes, but the next progression moves to positive action.

The fifth offence was that in the day of their disaster, the Edomites "marched through the gates of Jerusalem" (see verse 13). This refers to the fall of Jerusalem in 586 BC when Edom was implicated with the Babylonians in the destruction of the city and the Temple.

The sixth was that they seized the Israelites' wealth, and finally their seventh offence: they waited "at the crossroads to cut down their fugitives, and hand over their survivors in the day of their trouble" (see verse 13–14).

The biblical principle at work here is that Edom would reap what she had sown: "As you have done, it will be done to you" (verse 15). God will punish all who harm His people. Believers are in a covenant relationship with Jesus Christ. He is our champion and we can trust Him to bring true justice. As children of God we are secure and chosen in Christ. No matter what we may have to go through now, we are on the winning side and ultimate victory is guaranteed.

A further confirmation that underlines the age-old conflict between Isaac's twin sons Jacob and Esau was seen when Jesus the Jew met King Herod the Edomite. Herod, like Esau, the founder of his race, devalued his birthright and showed contempt for the spiritual realm by wanting Jesus to perform tricks like a court entertainer (Luke 23:8). But King Jesus who was bringing to a climax the age-old rift, and by not speaking a word in reply, went on to achieve what Scripture had foretold by the prophets, namely union between Gentiles and Jews through salvation obtained by His work on the cross (Ephesians 2:11ff.).

# The house of Jacob

Verse 17 of Obadiah speaks of Mount Zion and the house of Jacob.

The "house of Jacob" is not limited to the physical descendants of the Jews, who indeed saw the prophecy wonderfully and partially fulfilled at the return from Babylonian captivity and again in 1948 with the recognition of the state of Israel. It was said of Jesus by the angel speaking to Mary concerning her virgin child that, "he will reign over the house of Jacob forever; his kingdom will never end" (Luke 1:33). Today God's holy nation is His church – that is, all who have trusted in Christ for their salvation and given their lives to Him. These are the people who are God's born-again and adopted children. In this world, the ungodly often seem to flourish while the godly suffer, but God says that in the ultimate working out of His plan and purpose the ungodly are in for a shock and will be punished. The day of the Lord will come upon them – while those who are His people will be lifted up and blessed in Jesus Christ. God has promised and He will do it – and Obadiah is the proof we need to encourage us while we wait.

## Learning from history

Look at the lesson from history. Edom seemed impregnable, a godless nation with wealth, power and wisdom. By contrast, Israel, chosen of God, was punished for her sin and her city, Temple and nation were overthrown, and her people scattered. A quick glance would be sufficient to conclude, "That's the end of Israel. Off they go to Babylon. They're never coming back from there. Who ever heard of a captive nation rising and repossessing their land? It's unheard of and it's not going to happen now." Yet God brought Edom down, and exalted His people.

There are many lessons to draw from Obadiah's prophecy. Not least is the fact that the ruins of the Edomite nation are a reminder of the truth that God's Word always comes to pass. By New Testament times a people of Arabic origin known as the Nabateans had established a commercial empire with its centre in the formerly Edomite territory east of the Arabah. Their chief city was Petra.

Notice too how the nations of Israel and Edom each identified with the personal quarrel between Jacob and Esau, and how, as the centuries roll on, their hostilities remain as severe as ever. But as time passes we see how Jacob and those descended from him are seen passing through suffering, which is of the nature of discipline, to ultimate restoration, whereas Esau is seen as proud, rebellious, defiant and moving towards destruction.

The living message of this book is to present the challenge: "What sort of person am I? Am I as profane as Esau or am I like Jacob?"

Esau sold his birthright and, yes, afterwards full of regret and remorse, he wept – but he did not repent. The lesson from Obadiah is, a person may be wonderfully successful materially, they may build their nest among the stars and act independently of God, but God is already working towards their downfall and their life will ultimately end in ruin.

Instead we must be like Jacob and allow God to wrestle with us until we are submissive. Even those of us who believe in God, who have a deep desire to love and serve Him, must allow Him to take us to the Ford Jabbok and cripple us in order to crown us. For God who chastens us and leads us through trouble is set upon doing good to us at the end, and all the discipline and pain and punishment are in order that we at last may realize our own deepest divine purpose and satisfy the heart of God.

Esau, Jacob! History has spoken and we do well to learn from it. There is no nation of Edom, there are no Edomites in the world – but Jacob, whose name was changed to Israel, has a vibrant nation named after him today and is on the map of the world after 2,000 years.

# 32

# Jonah
## – The Reluctant Prophet

The book of Jonah is set in the Northern Kingdom of Israel after Amos and before Hosea.

The warlike superpower Assyria, whose capital city was Nineveh, was building up as Israel's most obvious military threat and of course we know that later God would in fact use her to destroy Israel. However, that lay in the future. At this period, under the leadership of King Jeroboam, Israel was experiencing unparalleled prosperity.

Verse 25 of 2 Kings 14 suggests that Jonah was already a well-established prophet in Israel before God called him to go and preach to the Assyrians at Nineveh. This should change the perception many have about Jonah and the lesson this book has for us. He was not an amateur called as it were from the plough, he was an experienced prophet of God whose role in the expansion of Israel would be well known at home and would not have been missed by the Assyrians.

Jonah's refusal to obey God and go as an evangelist to Nineveh was not because he was afraid for his life or that it would be too difficult a task, although there is truth in that. He refused to go because he feared success. He had been brought up in the belief that God's sympathy was limited to His chosen people, Israel, and Jewish prophets preached to Jews and only to Jews. Jonah was in an unheard of situation when called by God to bear his testimony in a foreign land among Gentiles, and it was extremely difficult for him to believe that God's mercy was being extended to the heathen of Nineveh. Also, it did not take much imagination for a prophet to realize that Nineveh was destined to be the instrument God would use to punish the Israelite nation. After all, three times in their past history Nineveh had warred against Israel. So, rather than wanting to see Nineveh repent and be saved, Jonah would prefer to see them judged and destroyed, and instead of travelling 500 miles north east to Nineveh he attempted to travel 2,000 miles west to Spain.

But God will not be thwarted.

> *Then the Lord sent a great wind on the sea, and such a violent storm arose that the ship threatened to break up. All the sailors were afraid and each cried out to his own god. And they threw the cargo into the sea to lighten the ship.*
>
> *But Jonah had gone below deck, where he lay down and fell into a deep sleep.*
>
> JONAH 1:4–5

Where is the prophet? What's God's man doing when the ship is in grave danger? He's asleep. And we ask, "How could Jonah possibly sleep through that storm?" That poses questions for today: How can men and women within the church act as if they do not see the work that has to be done? Are they like Jonah, asleep when others are awake?

The battle is intense, the war is raging, casualties are mounting, victories are being won, progress is being made, land reclaimed for God, souls saved and the army is on the move – and where are the Jonahs? Asleep! If ever there was an age of need for the believer, it's today. From every side of the ship the cry for help can be heard. Be forewarned, there can be no blessing for the believer who slumbers and ignores the cry for help.

But though Jonah tried to forget God, God did not forget Jonah.

The frightened sailors cast lots to find out who was responsible for what was happening to them. They rolled the dice, but it is God who makes the spots come up, and they came up pointing to Jonah. "So they asked him, 'Tell us, who is responsible for making all this trouble for us? What do you do? Where do you come from? What is your country? From what people are you?'" (Jonah 1:8).

Note the irony. Jonah had run away to avoid preaching to the heathen, and here he is, in spite of himself, about to do just that. Interestingly, in spite of the rupture in his relationship with the Lord, Jonah does a brilliant job of giving testimony: he is very relevant and most wonderfully becomes the instrument used to bring these pagan men to a saving faith (see verse 16).

# The reaction to Jonah's sermon

*He answered, "I am a Hebrew and I worship the Lord, the God
of heaven, who made the sea and the land."*

*This terrified them and they asked, "What have you done?"
(They knew he was running away from the Lord, because he
had already told them so.)*

JONAH 1:9–10

The reason these seafarers were afraid by what Jonah told them is they knew about Jonah's God. These men sailed the Mediterranean visiting the ports and meeting travellers from all the adjoining lands. Do you think for one moment that they had never heard of the Hebrews or their God, Jehovah? Of course they had heard of Him. He was the God who struck Egypt with plagues and destroyed that mighty empire so His people could be led out to freedom. He was the God who parted the Red Sea to allow the Israelites to escape into the desert and then closed the waters over the Egyptian army. He was the God who led the Hebrews for forty years in the barren wilderness guiding and protecting them by a pillar of cloud by day and a pillar of fire by night. He provided manna to eat and water to drink and brought them supernaturally through the Jordan River into the land He had promised. He caused the sun to stand still at Gibeon to allow Joshua victory over the Amorites. He was the God of Abraham, Isaac, Jacob, David and Solomon and now this great God of the Hebrews was pursuing them for the sake of this man Jonah – no wonder they were terrified!

Their next questions were entirely predictable.

"They asked, 'What have you done?... What should we do to you to make the sea calm down for us?'" (verses 10, 11). Here is Jonah's opportunity to make amends. He has answered their questions properly. By confessing his sin and accepting his responsibility the stage is being set for him to get right with God and bring salvation to the mariners. And Jonah did what only a believer with faith could do, he instructed the sailors to "Pick me up and throw me into the sea... and it will become calm. I know that it is my fault that this great storm has come upon you" (verse 12).

To all intents and purposes this was a sentence of death.

However, in verse 17 we read that "the Lord provided a great fish to swallow Jonah, and Jonah was inside the fish three days and three nights." Finding himself alive inside the fish, in his distress Jonah prays to the Lord his God (see Jonah 2:1–9). His example causes us to marvel at God's love towards us as He condescends to deliver us out of the self-inflicted troubles we get ourselves into. And just as the sailors celebrated their deliverance with sacrifices and vows, Jonah likewise promises to do the same and after calling upon the Lord he makes the profound statement, "Salvation comes from the Lord" (verse 9), and is then vomited out of the fish onto dry land (verse 10).

When Jesus was asked by his doubters to give a sign that would authenticate His mission He verified the miracle of Jonah:

> *A wicked and adulterous generation asks for a miraculous sign!*
> *But none will be given it except the sign of the prophet Jonah.*
> *For as Jonah was three days and three nights in the belly of a*
> *huge fish, so the Son of Man will be three days and three nights*
> *in the heart of the earth.*
>
> MATTHEW 12:39–40

It should be noted that, although Jesus was only in the tomb for thirty-six hours, according to Jewish tradition "three days and three nights" can mean "no more than three days" or "the combination of any part of three days", since they included parts of three separate days.

Saved in order to serve, Jonah is restored to God's service and gets a second chance: "Then the word of the Lord came to Jonah a second time: 'Go to the great city of Nineveh and proclaim to it the message I give you'" (Jonah 3:1–2).

Jonah was to learn that when God says "Go," He means it. Notice, too, that not only are God's orders the same, "Go to Nineveh", but so is the method – preaching! "Go to the great city of Nineveh and preach against it…" (Jonah 1:2).

## God's message to Nineveh

God went to great lengths in order that Jonah could deliver his message to Nineveh. So what message do we expect him to give? Will it be a powerful sermon from the likes of Whitefield or Spurgeon? No, the message is summarized in eight words: "Forty more days and Nineveh will be overturned" (3:4). That's it! We do well to remember that God is jealous for His word however brief and simple it may appear to us, as Paul confirms to the Corinthian Christians (1 Corinthians 1:18 and 22).

Jonah probably felt self-conscious walking through Nineveh with a message like that, but we take comfort from Paul's words in 1 Corinthians 4:10: "We are fools for Christ". Sure, Christian men and women may feel irrelevant to modern concerns as the world laughs at them and tramples underfoot all they consider so precious, but, as servants of the living God, success or failure is not ultimately their responsibility. They must get on and do what they are called to do: show forth Christ in their lives, preach the Word, and as a result of hearing it some will be saved and others condemned. Either way God is glorified (2 Corinthians 2:15–16).

So, Jonah goes marching into Nineveh proclaiming, "Forty more days and Nineveh will be overturned." That his message was clearly from God and not from himself is proved in Jonah 3:5: "The Ninevites believed God." They didn't believe this was Jonah's idea, this was an authentic message from God to them; they believed it and acted upon it.

This raises the interesting question: Where do you find God's love and mercy in "Forty more days and Nineveh will be overturned?"

## An opportunity to repent

The answer is that when God gives a warning of His intentions it is good news. There was no warning to Sodom and Gomorrah, fire just rained down from heaven and destroyed them. The very fact that God sent His prophet to Nineveh holds out hope, for the greatest thing that can happen to an individual or a nation is that God speaks directly to them warning them of their sin and giving them the opportunity to repent and turn to Him, and so be saved.

The people believed Jonah's message from God and repented of their sin. Why? What is it that makes men and women suddenly and dramatically believe what they previously thought of as a foolish message? The reason is that implanted in every heart is the knowledge of God. Ecclesiastes 3:11 confirms this: "He has... set eternity in the hearts of men; yet they cannot fathom what God has done from beginning to end."

This God-shaped wedge in the human heart has stamped on man's conscience knowledge of a holy and just God. And when confronted with it, it brings men and women to an awareness of that which they already know. They may well attempt to suppress it and do all in their power to ignore it, but in spite of all their arguments they know there is a holy Creator God. This fundamental truth is confirmed by Paul in his letter to the Romans where he teaches that:

*The wrath of God is being revealed from heaven against all the*
*godlessness and wickedness of men who suppress the truth*
*by their wickedness, since what may be known about God is*
*plain to them, because God has made it plain to them. For*
*since the creation of the world God's invisible qualities – his*
*eternal power and divine nature – have been clearly seen, being*
*understood from what has been made, so that men are without*
*excuse.*

ROMANS 1:18–20

That's why the people of Nineveh could react the way they did. They knew
they were living wickedly, and when they heard the divine message it struck a
chord deep in their spirits, convicted them of sin and convinced them of their
need of God's mercy.

## Jonah's response

Humanly speaking, Jonah had experienced God's grace in such a marvellous
way that you would never think it possible he would put a foot wrong again,
and would desire nothing more than to please his Saviour. But no, we read,
"Jonah was greatly displeased and became angry" (4:1). His reaction was
completely irrational. Why? What's wrong with this man? Jonah was angry
with God, for he had done what God wanted him to do, but God had not done
what Jonah wanted God to do. He had told the Ninevites that judgment was
coming in forty days but it had not come and he felt betrayed. He felt God had
let him down by not destroying the city as he had predicted. He hadn't the
slightest concern for the people of Nineveh. As far as he was concerned, instead
of rejoicing at their deliverance, he would have been happy to see God wipe
them off the face of the earth and the fact He didn't do so made Jonah angry.

Jonah tried to justify himself by rationalizing his original disobedience.

He says, "This is why I refused to go to Nineveh in the first place when
You wanted me to; what's more, I was right in refusing" (see 4:2).

When Jonah used Scripture to justify his sinful attitude he was attempting
to use God's word against Him in a twisted desire to show that he, Jonah, was
right, and God was wrong. He quoted Exodus 34:6–7; which says:

*The Lord, the Lord, the compassionate and gracious God, slow*
*to anger, abounding in love and faithfulness, maintaining love*
*to thousands, and forgiving wickedness, rebellion and sin.*

"Now," says Jonah, "if that's true, why send me to Nineveh with a message of destruction that You never intended to fulfil?"

Jonah's anger caused him to ask God that he might die: "Now, O Lord, take away my life, for it is better for me to die than to live" (Jonah 4:3). He should have been happy; he's been instrumental in the gift of spiritual life to many thousands, yet he wants to die. He claimed to know God's grace and mercy, which he himself dramatically experienced, yet he resents God for it and says he would rather have had Nineveh destroyed. Jonah is still not reconciled to the will of God. Deep down, Jonah's attitude had not changed: he was still unwilling to see the people of Nineveh saved and he resented the God of mercy for saving them.

What also made Jonah angry was that while he knew much about God, he did not know Him or His ways well enough to grieve over sin as God grieves over it or to rejoice at repentance the way heaven rejoices. In fact, he was like the prodigal son's older brother who sulked and felt cheated while his father and the rest of the household celebrated (Luke 15). We have to remember that God is a God of judgment, but also a God of mercy. This Jonah had to learn, so God began to teach him by asking three questions.

## The first question

With the question in 4:4 ("Have you any right to be angry?", it's as if God was saying, "Jonah, we are looking at this situation from opposite viewpoints. I am pleased with it, you are angry, so which of us has the proper perspective?" Now we know whatever our thoughts or feelings God is always right. But Jonah refused to see it that way, so he just left the city and built a shelter to watch and see if God might not destroy Nineveh after all: "Jonah went out and sat down at a place east of the city. There he made himself a shelter, sat in its shade and waited to see what would happen to the city" (Jonah 4:5).

In doing this he made three basic mistakes:

1. He abandoned Nineveh without having permission from God to do so. He should have stayed and taught the population about this wonderful God who had saved them.

2. He built a shelter for himself – a private retreat just for poor Jonah. Were there no shelters in Nineveh – no places there where the prophet of Israel who had brought such great blessing to the city could not stay? Of course there were. But Jonah wasn't interested in their shelters, he secretly despised the people and still hoped God would zap them.

3. He became a spectator.

Then God prepared Jonah's heart for His second question (see 4:6–9).

He did so by causing a plant to spring up next to Jonah's shelter to give him shade from the hot sun. Now, at last, for the first time in this story Jonah is happy about something. In fact, he was very happy (verse 6). Throughout this whole saga nothing had pleased Jonah, despite all the wonderful things that had happened to him. But here at last Jonah was very happy. Why? The answer is obvious: God was finally doing something specifically for Jonah. Selfish? Of course it was, and petty! For the vine was a trifle compared to saving Jonah's life and the population of Nineveh.

## The second question

Then God caused a worm to attack the vine so the plant withered and He brought the scorching wind to blow in from the desert, which brought Jonah to the point of fainting. At this point God asked His second question, which exposed Jonah's pettiness: "Do you have a right to be angry about the vine?" (4:9). To be angry against God was something, he at least is a worthwhile opponent but to be angry at a vine and a worm – it's just pathetic.

Often anger works in a similar way in our lives. We begin by being angry at big things but progress to anger against petty things. First it's anger against God, then it's anger against life's circumstances, and finally we blow up over something as petty as the cap left off the toothpaste. God was showing this truth to Jonah saying, in effect, "Jonah, is this what you want? Is this the kind of angry petty life you want to live? Annoyed and bitter against everyone and everything?"

# The third question

Then God asked His third question.

> *You have been concerned about this vine, though you did*
> *not tend it or make it grow. It sprang up overnight and died*
> *overnight. But Nineveh has more than a hundred and twenty*
> *thousand people who cannot tell their right hand from their left,*
> *and many cattle as well. Should I not be concerned about that*
> *great city?*
>
> JONAH 4:10–11

With this, the book ends.

Jonah had been sorry for the vine, so God talks about the innocent cattle and little children, was God not right to show mercy for their sake? Does not even Jonah's concern for the vine exonerate God's judgment? So the book ends with a question in order that we may ask ourselves the same question: Is God not right – is He not great for showing mercy?

In Jonah we see a type of all believers.

Don't we all run from God at some time in our lives and need to be disciplined? Don't we all have the tendency to want to do our own thing? Don't we all at times believe in our spiritual superiority and, like the first disciples of Jesus, even become quite happy to see fire and brimstone rain down on those we think deserve it?

But the greatest lesson of all from this book is that we discover how great is the mercy of God. God cares for the sinners in Nineveh as well as the saints in Jerusalem. While Jonah is wrapped up in himself and holding a pity party, God is concerned for the men, women, children and animals in Nineveh, and yet He still takes quality time to deal positively with His servant Jonah.

Jonah is the religious bigot of all ages: he believed the Jewish nation held the franchise for salvation. The paradox was that he was a good man. His prayer in chapter 2 cannot be improved; no ungodly man could pray like that. Jonah was a good man, but blinkered, trapped in his own belief system, unwilling to let God be God, and, if he could, he would limit God's love and mercy to his own nation. God sought to enlarge his vision by piercing his pomposity and wounding his self-love to teach him to look beyond his "holy huddle", to become the envoy of Jehovah, whose purpose fulfils itself in many peoples, and whose love embraces all humankind.

Religious exclusiveness and bigotry are rebuked, and we are taken to the cross with its fullest expression of love and mercy when we see the Lord Jesus Christ dying for our salvation. That is the wideness of God's mercy and the length to which His love goes. Furthermore, it begs the question: How can men and women, who having had their sins forgiven and forgotten and so benefited from that love and mercy, be less than merciful to others? How can we, as ambassadors of Jesus, do less than to love them and take the gospel to them using all the strength and ability we have at our disposal?

# 33

# Micah
## – God's "Socialist"

The book of Micah is set in the latter half of the eighth century BC.

The kingdoms of Judah and Israel were experiencing the most affluent period of their history since their break up after the death of Solomon. Both capitals, Samaria in the north and Jerusalem in the south, had begun to enjoy immense material prosperity. However, as sadly as is too often the case, hand-in-hand with prosperity came increasing godlessness. In response, the prophets spoke boldly the "word of the Lord" to both parts of the divided nation: Amos and Hosea in the north, Isaiah and Micah in the south. Micah, a workman from the obscure village of Moresheth, was an evangelist who dealt with social morality and personal religion and his book, which was not a single speech delivered on one occasion but rather a collection of messages that moves from one topic to another.

Micah, whose name means "God's man/prophet" made clear that he was not a false prophet but a prophet from God with His timely message to the nation:

> The word of the Lord... came... to Micah...
>
> I am filled with power,
> with the Spirit of the Lord,
> and with justice and might,
> to declare to Jacob his transgression,
> to Israel his sin.

MICAH 1:1, 3:8

289

Micah was a man of the people with an instinctive empathy for the farmers, shepherds and smallholders – if you like, a Christian "socialist" who was not lured away by the glittering façade of the new consumer culture of fine houses, up-to-date fashions and get-rich-quick business schemes. Called the "conscience of Israel", Micah was charged with the difficult task of combating the subtle combination of social injustice and the corrupt religion that supported it. His overriding message was justice between men and a right attitude towards God. He took the principal teachings of Amos, Hosea and Isaiah and bound them into one embracing statement in his striking declaration:

> *He has showed you, O man, what is good.*
> *And what does the Lord require of you?*
> *To act justly and to love mercy*
> *and to walk humbly with your God.*

MICAH 6:8

## Selfish wealth

The wickedness Micah was homing in on was being practised by the wealthy landowners and men of property. Their victims were ordinary people with small fields and homes that they were losing to the corporate raiders from the city under the guise of cost-effectiveness and profitability.

One's perspective depends upon where you live and work. In the city of Jerusalem it may have simply seemed to be the operation of big business as wealthy men increased their property holdings. But in Moresheth and the country towns it was seen as cruel, hard-hearted oppression. The philosophy that "greed is good" was the motivating principle, and as the rich became richer a population of "new poor" was emerging. For Micah this was not a matter of politics or economics but one of justice.

Micah recognized that the time-honoured system of the "jubilee and inheritance" given to the nation by God in Leviticus 25, specifically to keep Israel from suffering the extremes of poverty and wealth, was being ignored. He knew that if the unrestrained greed and corruption driving the affluent society was not brought to an end the national fabric and social cohesion of the nation would perish. To put it bluntly, their history, tradition, custom and God-centredness was being replaced by a greedy, irreligious, "me first" mentality, and as a result the nation was in big trouble.

Micah warned that this downward moral slide would not be halted by political change, economic reform or new business ethics, for none of them had the answer or the solution. Ultimately, nothing less than the intervention of God Himself can tackle the human sin which lies at the root of fraud, greed, corruption, pride and the unrestrained selfishness which motivates so many in our world today. The bottom line is that when restraints are removed, greed becomes the central driving force, the kind of greed that, because it becomes a way of life, is never satisfied, scarcely recognized, rarely admitted and generally rationalized.

It's a principle of Scripture that the Lord is on the side of vulnerable people (Deuteronomy 10:17–18).

Widows and orphans had few legal rights and for that reason the king was personally held responsible for their protection. Judah was a theocracy: God ruled the people through the prophet, priest and king, and it was to express His compassion that the rulers were under such social obligations. However, in Micah's time, far from fulfilling their charge, they were in league with the landowners to defraud and exploit the vulnerable, and heartlessly drove them from the land with no regard for all the social consequences that followed.

Later, in exile, the danger to a nation that acts this way was spelled out by Ezekiel, who said that the sins of the citizens of Sodom were not simply that they did "detestable things", but that they were "arrogant, overfed and unconcerned; they did not help the poor and needy" (see Ezekiel 16:49–50). Aiding and abetting those who exploited the people were the false prophets, and Micah renounced them as well (Micah 2:6–11). He said truth was being distorted and those whose job it was to comment fearlessly and truthfully on the current events were soft-pedalling the less welcome truths, even going as far as to deny that God wanted them to speak about them. The fact was that the religious people of the day were hand-in-glove with the corrupt people Micah had been talking about. Sadly, the people didn't mind listening to a preacher but they wanted a preacher who would endorse their lifestyle.

Those in power are seldom averse to the legitimization provided by the patronage of religious people, and the reverse is also true. Religious people enjoy the patronage of the rich and powerful as Micah's word indicates. And as you would expect, the powerful, both secular and religious, attempted to have Micah silenced because he was not prepared to go along with such collusion. They reckoned that preaching should not tackle issues of daily behaviour and business ethics: preachers should concentrate on spiritual matters and not interfere in marketplace issues. They should talk about worship and prayer and personal relationships with God, not fraud, corruption, pride, greed and selfishness.

To make matters worse, Micah insisted in talking about God's judgment bringing imminent disaster, which provoked the false prophets to argue against him, "Disgrace will not overtake us! Who's this man Micah to talk to us this way? It's arrogant, harsh and insensitive to talk about divine judgment because of our lifestyles! The way we choose to live and work is our business not his, what does he know about it anyway!" (see Micah 2:6).

In reply, through Micah, God poses a rhetorical question: "Do not my words do good to him whose ways are upright?" (2:7). It's a masterclass question and not one person in the land would dare deny the truth of it. So, clearly a lot more uprightness was called for along with far less corrupt and sinful behaviour.

The problem from Micah's perspective was that the nation had reached the point of no return, and any further preaching would not achieve anything positive for Micah's audience had so thoroughly rejected his message that it was useless to say anything more about God. No, they say, speak sweet nothings and empty clichés to the people. Tell them the things they want to hear, not what they need to hear. Talk to them about the things they enjoy – like wine and beer (2:11). If you do that, you will be just the sort of preacher for this people – but whatever you do, don't talk about God. They're so caught up in their fantasy world of the lottery, pop music, materialism and fun, that they have no time or inclination for the serious things of God.

An example of how the insidious influence of sin captures people by pandering to their sinful nature without them even realizing it is the way John Lennon's song "Imagine", was voted the nation's favourite song and was also featured in the London 2012 Olympics closing ceremony. To imagine that heaven does not exist means no creator, no Bethlehem, no Jesus, no Bible, no cross, no atoning blood, no victory over evil, no resurrection, no Holy Spirit, no second coming and no life after death – imagine!

Who do you think these sentiments would appeal to? Why, surprise, surprise, the very people who don't want to be reminded of sin and selfishness, or greed, pride, lust, jealousy, hatred, anger, social disease or addiction. The people who want to imagine existence without heaven do not want to be reminded of personal accountability, responsibility, judgment or punishment – so for them, not having hell below either is the comforting message they want to hear because it allows them to continue in their chosen lifestyle answerable to no one but themselves. If ever there was a message from the pit it's that there's no heaven and no hell.

But Lennon's lyrics also pose the question: "If there's no heaven and no hell, what's the meaning and purpose of life?"

John Lennon, a false prophet of the sixties, has the answer to that one too, suggesting that living for today is the better option. Forget the naughty, bad things you did yesterday, forget the sin and the guilt, forget the lies and stealing and cheating, forget the adultery and deception, the hurt and pain you've caused, forget the anger and jealousies, and – here it comes, the big lie, packaged to appeal to the sin darkened souls of the men and women of Western society – "don't worry about tomorrow – just think of everyone living for today!" To quote Micah 2:11:

> *If a liar and deceiver comes and says,*
> *"I will prophesy for you plenty of wine and beer,"*
> *he would be just the prophet for this people!*

A nation thinking and behaving this way is destined for judgment. Ignorance and lack of understanding will be no excuse, for their conscience has told them, in their heart of hearts, that they know the truth, as Romans 1 makes clear.

## A nation on trial

In chapter 6 God summons the nation of Israel to the law court and puts them in the dock.

God's insistence that this trial should be heard, not just in public, but before all creation, underlines His intention that His dealings with His covenant people will be scrupulous and above board for all to see.

But something wonderful becomes apparent: The Lord is not intent on reading out a long list of charges to which the people are guilty; instead, like a brokenhearted parent pleading with a wayward child, this is the plea from a loving God, hurt by His people's rejection of Him. We are reminded of 1 Corinthians 13:5: "[love] keeps no record of wrongs." Here God is not interested in the record; He is working on the relationship. In fact, His opening question disarms the people and turns the situation on its head. He says, "What have I done to you? Give me your evidence. How have I burdened you? What have I done – or failed to do – that's made you grow tired of Me?" (see Micah 6:3).

You can almost imagine Israel tossing her head, turning away and saying nothing – and God almost blurting out, "Answer me!"

Israel's silence can be taken as an admission of guilt. The truth was that they were bored stiff with the mechanics and routine of worship. They had reached the point where they found it a burden, and having found other more stimulating and interesting things to do with their time, had opted out of worshipping God. They had lost the plot and the passion, and if the truth be told, they wearied the Lord.

## Recalling days of blessing

God then highlights three or four key events from Israel's history.

He recalls times when the people walked close to Him, and just the mention of a place or person was enough to evoke memories from the past: Egypt; Moses, Aaron and Miriam; Balak and Balaam, Shittim and Gilgal – names of people and places that carried a special significance for the children of God.

Egypt recalled the exodus and freedom, brought home to the nation by the feast of the Passover, but like any memorable celebration it could become a meaningless routine if they failed to identify it with the saving acts of the Lord. How on earth could they find the memory of how God miraculously rescued them from slavery and bondage boring?

By mentioning Moses, Aaron and Miriam, God was comparing the leaders of Micah's day with those of her history, and they didn't stand comparison. By the time of Micah the political, commercial and religious leadership was utterly corrupt and the Lord is saying, "Remember Moses and Aaron and Miriam, where do you think they came from? Do you think they just happened? No, says the Lord, I sent them to you to be your leaders, and if you read Scripture you will see that it was no easy task persuading Moses to take on such a leadership role: he thought of every excuse in the book to get out of it!" (see Micah 6:4). Leadership doesn't just appear out of thin air: it comes from the people God has chosen, called and commissioned with His authority.

In Balak and Balaam we have the incident where God intervened and spoke through a donkey to save the nation of Israel:

> *When Balak son of Zippor, the king of Moab, prepared to fight against Israel, he sent for Balaam son of Beor to put a curse on you. But I would not listen to Balaam, so he blessed you again and again, and I delivered you out of his hand.*
>
> JOSHUA 24:9–10

It's quite likely God was reminding the nation of this particular incident because they too were being threatened by a powerful Assyrian enemy and there was a notable lack of God's man for the moment coming forward to lead the people in their approaching hour of need. You can almost hear God saying through Micah, "Don't you believe I can still deliver you? You have the Assyrians as an enemy instead of the Moabites, and you have no one to lead you in your time of crisis – but I am still the unchanging God. And think of Shittim where you camped before crossing the Jordan, the Promised Land was impossibly near across the raging Jordan, yet Gilgal was the place on the other side where you erected a memorial of stones to remind you of the miraculous crossing I effected for you. So, Israel, if you exercise your memory you must know my saving acts from first-hand experience, and that will radically transform your worship of me now."

## Bring it up to date

Christian, your testimony – that time you will never forget when God was so real to you and did such a wonderful thing in your life that the thought of it will remain with you all your life – mustn't be allowed to become an intellectual experience only: you must allow God's acts of salvation to become a living possession of your being. And as you remember the warmth of the memory, so you will renew your commitment to Him as your personal relationship with Him matures and your love, faith and hope in Him flourishes. Yes, of course, God may confront us with language coloured by the law court, but He deals with us from His heart of love. He may enter a plea against us, but He constantly pleads with us to deepen our relationship with Him.

And so to chapter 6, verse 6.

Moved and humbled by such an emotive plea and wanting to see the relationship between God and the nation restored, Micah, as national spokesman asks, "With what shall I come before the Lord and bow down before the exalted God?" God's plea has had its effect. In recognition of the truth of God's words there is a new awareness of personal sin and the people's representative wants to come before Him and make atonement.

As is usually the case, when people with a religious background resolve to take God seriously again, they often begin by wanting to step up their acts of devotion:

*Shall I come before him with burnt offerings,*
*with calves a year old?*
*Will the Lord be pleased with thousands of rams,*
*with ten thousand rivers of oil?*

MICAH 6:6–7

The notion of atonement by expensive gifts, the thought that you can buy off God, dies hard in the human heart. In Micah's time, just like today, money talked, and you could get anything for a price – God was just a bit more expensive than other things. "Shall I offer my firstborn for my transgression, the fruit of my body for the sin of my soul?" (verse 7b). But as soon as the words are out of their mouths, they know God does not and cannot work that way. God never asks for what is not ours to give. So, we come to Micah's best known and fundamental teaching:

*He has showed you, O man, what is good.*
*And what does the Lord require of you?*
*To act justly and to love mercy*
*and to walk humbly with your God.*

MICAH 6:8

God quietly replies that He is not asking for anything new. He is not laying down further religious ordinances, all He asks is what He has asked from the beginning. It's not ritual or routine; it's the reality of a devoted life, not the outward form of prayer and worship. It is to act justly, to love mercy and to walk humbly with God. In other words, God wants us, our lives and our love. That is the costliest sacrifice we can bring: a living sacrifice of our body and soul. What God desires is the penitent heart of the individual turned towards Him and one's neighbour. The "good" that He requires is the doing of His will, and to "act justly" is to act towards God and man according to the divine standard of righteousness as revealed in God's law. To "love mercy" is to show a compassionate warm-heartedness towards your fellow men and women. And "to walk humbly with your God" is to recognize the absolute holiness and righteousness of God, and to walk in humble and submissive obedience to His desire and will.

In teaching that it's only by walking humbly with God that we are able to act justly and love mercy, we see the Old Testament's version of our Lord's teaching from Mark 12:30–31, to "love the Lord your God with all your heart and with all your soul and with all your mind and with all your strength" and 'Love your neighbour as yourself.' There is no commandment greater than these."

'To walk humbly with your God" does not mean "your god as you know him": it's not an excuse for multifaith services. In the context of Micah's prophecy and of the Scriptures it means God as He has revealed Himself as Creator, Redeemer, Father and Judge. In New Testament terms this is the only God, fully incarnate as Emmanuel, God with us in Jesus Christ of Nazareth, who invites each person to join in a personal and loving relationship and walk with Him ensuring there is never a day when we are without Him.

As Micah lifts his prophetic eye above the present, through the coming disaster and on to the far future, the picture changes from one of despair to sublime hope.

He sees the mountain of Jehovah's house as above all powers and kingdoms, and beholds Jehovah in His righteousness, ruling and judging the nations through a ruler who would be born in Bethlehem, a ruler who is co-eternal with Jehovah (Micah 5:2). Thus Micah was anticipating a period of transformation sometime in the future, not in wild dreams of a Utopian era immediately after the Babylonian exile – an era that never materialized – but rather in the messianic promise that finds its fulfilment in the saving work of Christ and the eventual fruition of God's eternal purposes in history.

We can praise God that Micah's message didn't go unheeded, for we learn from Jeremiah 26:18ff that Hezekiah, upon hearing Micah's prophecy, feared the Lord and sought His favour which heralded in a great revival. It started, as always, with spiritual reform, for behind social injustice is spiritual decline. However, spiritual reform must be allowed to run its full course and not fall short of social reform. Thankfully, Hezekiah's reform did not fall short and it's recorded that following the great revival acts of worship,

> ... the Israelites who were there went out to the towns of
> Judah, smashed the sacred stones and cut down the Asherah
> poles. They destroyed the high places and the altars throughout
> Judah and Benjamin and in Ephraim and Manasseh. After they
> had destroyed all of them, the Israelites returned to their own
> towns and to their own property.
>
> 2 CHRONICLES 31:1

God's response was to stay His hand of judgment on Judah, shown in Micah 7:18:

> Who is a God like you,
> who pardons sin and forgives the transgression
> of the remnant of his inheritance?
> You do not stay angry forever
> but delight to show mercy.

May each of us delight in the pardon of God and may we take to heart the lesson from Micah 6:8:

> He has showed you, O man, what is good.
> And what does the Lord require of you?
> To act justly and to love mercy
> and to walk humbly with your God.

# 34

# Nahum
# – God's Anger and the Nation's Applause

There are two prophetic books in the Old Testament that have no direct reference to the Lord's people – those of Jonah and Nahum, and both of them are concerned with the fate of Nineveh, capital city of the Assyrian empire which has been so frequently mentioned by Amos, Hosea, Isaiah and Micah.

One hundred years had passed since the great city of Nineveh responded in repentance to Jonah's preaching, but their great revival was now a dim memory and the city had returned to its old habits of violence and idolatry. And as Assyria became the most powerful and hated empire in the world, their humility changed to arrogance.

As we learned from Micah, at the beginning of the previous century both Israel and Judah had been strong and prosperous. However, due to their persistent idolatry and unfaithfulness to God the people of the northern kingdom, Israel, were conquered and enslaved by the Assyrian empire and sent into exile in 722 BC (2 Kings 17). One could be forgiven for thinking that following God's punishment upon their sister nation, exactly as foretold by the prophets, the people of Judah would have learned their lesson and wholeheartedly returned to the Lord, but sadly this was not the case. So God allowed His people to be oppressed and, led by Sennacherib, the Assyrians came close to capturing Jerusalem in the reign of King Hezekiah in 701 BC. However, in the face of the overwhelming threat from Assyria, Nahum was sent by God to proclaim that Judah's punishment was soon to be ended for He would overthrow Nineveh and liberate His people.

Nineveh was founded by the mighty hunter Nimrod (Genesis 10:8–12). It wasn't animals Nimrod hunted, it was men. Not surprisingly, therefore, Nineveh had a long blood-soaked history and became the byword of human violence and conquest, typifying man's inhumanity to man. It was the metropolis of the ancient world and was located on the east bank of the River Tigris. The Assyrians had diverted the river around the city by a system of canals, thus it was in effect an island and with its 100-foot high walls it was militarily impregnable. It was also large. When, 150 years earlier, Jonah referred to a three-day walk across Nineveh, it was no exaggeration.

Nineveh was destroyed by the Babylonians in 612 BC when, after two years of siege, an unprecedented flood breached a large part of the city wall and the enemy poured in. This fulfilled part of Nahum's prophecies in 1:8, 2:6 and 3:13 – and so effectively did God dig Nineveh's grave that every trace of its existence disappeared for over 2,000 years. The city was never rebuilt, confirming Nahum's prediction that "trouble will not come a second time" (1:9). It wasn't until 1850 that Nineveh was discovered by archaeologists, and it's interesting to read liberal commentaries from before 1850, for the archaeologists had problems believing the books of Jonah and Nahum as there was no visible record of Nineveh. This also was a fulfilment of Nahum's prophecy that the city would be "hidden" (3:11).

Historians give various reasons for Nineveh's fall, ranging from internal corruption to the rise of Babylon, but Nahum, at the beginning of his prophecy, gives the true answer: it was destroyed by the avenging wrath of God.

Many people do not like to think of God this way. They prefer the sentimental, politically correct God, not the almighty Creator God who reveals himself in His Bible. This is where Nahum begins his prophecy. God's vengeance, which in biblical terms means justice, is stressed by the complete devastation that is coming. Tornadoes, hurricanes and earthquakes demonstrate His power. He can dry up the sea, wither the vegetation and destroy everything on the earth. God has the power to do whatever He desires. No one can stand in His way.

But His wrath and power are tempered by His mercy. God is also aware of those who trust in Him and will preserve them. For example: "The Lord is good, a refuge in times of trouble. He cares for those who trust in him" (Nahum 1:7).

This should be a comfort to Christian men and women when they see society disintegrating around them and terrible trouble coming upon their land. The biblical example is the Hebrews in Egypt during the ten plagues. Even though the Egyptian people and animals suffered and died horribly, not one Israelite or any of their livestock came to any harm (Exodus 9:6). Even though our nation is in turmoil, if we remain faithful, God will watch over us and reward us – either by protecting us here on earth as He did the Hebrews or by taking us to heaven. We often feel like it has to be now but eternal rewards really are far greater, and we should not expect deliverance from every difficulty in this life.

## Focus on Nineveh

Having started with God, everything else falls into perspective and Nahum now focuses on Nineveh (1:9–15).

Nineveh made war on God's people and therefore made war against God (verses 9–11). Assyria was God's instrument for destroying the northern kingdom of Israel, but the honour went to their heads and they attributed success to their own power. The one on top will be brought down. The one at the bottom will be restored. God always operates this way: "the last will be first, and the first will be last" (Matthew 20:16). God humbles those who exalt themselves and exalts those who humble themselves: "Although I have afflicted you, O Judah, I will afflict you no more" (Nahum 1:12).

God was going to remove the oppression that Assyria had placed on His people.

In 2:1–13, Nineveh's doom is described: first – how?

Nahum assumes the role of watchman and prophetically announces the coming of Nineveh's enemies to restore the splendour of Jacob. Then he describes the battle, beginning with the attack on Nineveh's defences, and goes on to describe the enemy army approaching with their copper-red shields and scarlet uniforms depicting the bloodshed that was coming. The reference to the torches and lightning flashes probably refers to the light reflecting off enemy chariots, armour and swords. The "streets" they are "storming through" are most likely those approaching the main city's walls, and the "stumbling" is falling over the dead bodies of the people in the suburbs.

So, everyone is poised for battle, but to no avail. The Babylonians are God's instrument. He opens the way for them and Nineveh can't stand before His wrath. In 2:6 we see that the river floods, the walls cave in, and as the enemy enters the city the defeated Assyrian army flees.

In verses 8–10 Nahum sees the city being plundered and her wealth captured. According to the historians, there was so much loot that the

Babylonian soldiers didn't bother to pursue the fleeing army but helped themselves to the treasure.

In verses 11–13 Nahum brings out the Assyrian fascination with lions. Archaeologists have excavated several reliefs depicting Assyrian kings hunting lions. In their society it was important that a king demonstrate his prowess as a hunter, the reasoning being that if he could rule the animal kingdom he would be a better ruler over the people. We might express amusement but we too elect successful military leaders and athletes to important leadership roles. Assyria is compared to a lion because of her lion fetish and her fierce conquests, and as Nineveh was the capital of Assyria it is called the lions' den, which makes sense of Nahum's question: "Where now is the lions' den?" (verse 11).

In 3:1–7 "how" now gives way to "why?"

Nahum tells us it's because of her cruel conquests and slave trade. History records that Assyria's conquests were bloody and brutal. Her monuments abound with graphic descriptions of her atrocities and destruction of life. Her philosophy was to get rich by plundering others, and they exacted tribute from other nations for "protection". Verse 1 sums it up pretty well:

> *Woe to the city of blood,*
> *full of lies,*
> *full of plunder*
> *never without victims!*

Verses 2–3 describe one of the most moving descriptions of the fierceness of battle to be found in any literature. The verses need little comment as they speak for themselves. All that's required is a bit of imagination and the ability to see the nightmare the prophet is foretelling:

> *The crack of whips,*
> *the clatter of wheels,*
> *galloping horses*
> *and jolting chariots!*
> *Charging cavalry,*
> *flashing swords*
> *and glittering spears!*
> *Many casualties,*
> *piles of dead,*
> *bodies without number,*
> *people stumbling over the corpses...*

With this breathless description the prophet pauses and places the blame of this entire carnage fairly and squarely on Nineveh, whom he likens to a "lust motivated harlot and mistress of sorceries" (see verse 4). Nineveh had faked lovemaking to entice nations into her trap, and through her use of witchcraft she had seduced and led many to destruction.

But it wasn't a nation she was up against this time: it was almighty God, and He said that the time of her judgment had come, she was finished. His use of the description in verse 5 – "I will lift your skirts over your face" – would be to expose her nakedness to shame and contempt before the nations and kingdoms of the earth. "I will pelt you with filth" (verse 6) means she would be like a vile and dirty woman exposed for all to see what she is, and the world would turn up their noses in disgust.

With her grandeur gone and her shame exposed, her fall will be total: "Nineveh is in ruins – who will mourn for her?" (verse 7). No one would bemoan her passing, no one would bring a word of comfort to her. The message of her fall would be good news to people of the world who had suffered so severely from her cruelty.

And just in case Nineveh's pride deluded them into thinking they were strong enough to withstand the destruction that was heading towards them, God, through Nahum, reminds them of their own conquest and the destruction of the Egyptian city of Thebes. Just as Thebes was unable to repel the Assyrians, Nineveh would be unable to repel the Babylonians (verses 8–10). Thebes was supposedly impregnable because of the River Nile and a series of canals that surrounded it. Thebes had great defences; so did Nineveh. Egypt had vassal nations as allies; so did Assyria. And more to the point, Nineveh would have known all this because Assyria was the one who defeated Thebes.

## Nineveh destroyed

And so to the inevitable destruction (3:11–18).

God says the city would be hidden, and Nineveh was lost for nigh on 2,000 years. Verse 12 says that after a winter with no fresh fruit, the first ripe figs are eagerly sought after as a delicacy, and fall readily into the mouth of the eater. So Nineveh's fortresses would easily capitulate to the enemy as they advanced. Verse 13 is not politically correct, but it's true to say that an army of women would be defeated by an army of men and the Assyrians would be like women to the Babylonian warriors. Verse 14 refers to the frantic preparations for the coming siege, filling the moats, repairing the walls and building fortifications, but to no avail. As locusts flee so the Assyrians fled when the attackers came through the walls (verse 17). And not only were they unable to defend themselves, they could not depend on other nations for help because every other nation hated them for their cruelty and would rejoice and clap their hands at Nineveh's destruction (verse 19).

What a way to go! But worse, to have lived in such a manner that when the end came there was universal rejoicing. And not the rejoicing of selfish glee, but rather the rejoicing at the vindication of righteousness over evil: "for, who has not felt your endless cruelty?" (verse 19).

The message of Nahum portrays the patience, power, holiness and justice of the living God: He is slow to anger, but He settles His accounts in full.

For over 400 years of Middle Eastern history Assyria and her gods were in control. Nineveh with her idols stood as the capital of the most powerful kingdom the world had ever seen. "Where, then, is your God?" the sceptic might rightly ask the Jewish believer. "And if He exists, what kind of God is He?" And into this situation came the word of the Lord:

The Lord is a jealous and avenging God; "slow to anger and great in power; the Lord will not leave the guilty unpunished" (Nahum 1:2–3).

But it is not merely divine retribution that emerges from the picture. There is also good news to proclaim: "Look, there on the mountains, the feet of one who brings good news, who proclaims peace!" (Nahum 1:15).

Judah is called to celebration as God's people inevitably are when the day of Jehovah's wrath is fully understood and the remnant are prepared in righteousness.

To the Christian longing for the day of good tidings, the message is clearly set forth in the new covenant. Paul, in Romans 10:15 extolled the preaching of the gospel of salvation with a quotation from this ancient book of judgment: "As it is written, 'How beautiful are the feet of those who bring good news!'"

In this age it is the preaching of the gospel that will ensure the ultimate triumph of God even as verse 18 of the same chapter of Romans points out: "Their voice has gone out into all the earth, their words to the ends of the world."

This promises that not the Assyrian or even the Roman dominion will be the final word on history.

However, when the forces opposing God are so firmly ensconced and the flickering lamp of God's people appears to be at the point of extinction, it is easy for the remnant to forget. Nahum reminds us, as do the ruins of ancient Nineveh, that God Himself is the ultimate ruler. He will have the final word and that is good news for the people of God. Just as the waiting believer in

Nahum's day could look ahead to such a day, so can believers in our day. It was then – and continues today – to be the hope of the people of God: our eyes shall see the salvation of the Lord.

# 35

# Habakkuk
# – The Perplexed Prophet

In Habakkuk we have a new style of prophet who, instead of speaking to the nation on behalf of God, spoke to God on behalf of the nation. The other prophets concentrated on Israel's sin, the proclamation of God's judgment and His grace, but Habakkuk focused on God Himself, asking what He means by allowing tyranny and evil to flourish. In a sense, Habakkuk was the Old Testament's "Thomas", the questioning disciple: a free thinker who voiced what others were thinking, even daring to lift his eyes to heaven and ask God. As Judah and its capital, Jerusalem, sank deeper into godlessness, society was shaken by lawlessness and violence with the fabric of national life beginning to come apart at the seams. Habakkuk, a righteous man dismayed by the moral collapse, asked God why He allowed such immorality and corruption to flourish with impunity in a once God-fearing land.

## The first complaint against God

Chapter 1 records Habakkuk's complaints against God, the first of which is that God seems inactive:

> How long, O Lord, must I call for help,
> but you do not listen?
> Or cry out to you, "Violence!"
> but you do not save?

HABAKKUK 1:2

Habakkuk's asking "Are you there, God? And if so, why don't you do something?" It's the dilemma of unrestrained wickedness along with the silence of God and it raises the question, "Why?" God replies that He is doing something. He is raising up the Chaldeans (Babylon) as His instrument of justice to destroy Jerusalem and punish the nation for its crimes (see verses 5–11). And Habakkuk, understandably, is horrified. This is not the answer he expected, which leads to Habakkuk's second complaint that God seems inconsistent. How could a holy God use such wicked people as the Babylonians to punish the chosen people of Israel? So in chapter 1 we see Habakkuk in the depths of despair complaining that God was indifferent, inactive and inconsistent.

Now before you criticize him, ask yourself how many times you have made the same accusations against God: "God, You don't seem to be listening to me, are You indifferent to my prayers? Why are You inactive? Why are these things happening? Why are the righteous suffering while the ungodly seem to be prospering? God, it seems so unfair!"

There are valuable lessons for Christians in this passage, and to learn them they must remind themselves that God's ways are often misunderstood. What the world may regard as terrible may well be the very thing God is using to chastise and discipline His people for their good or the good of others. Psalm 73 demonstrates the danger of speaking hastily. The psalmist, on seeing how evil men appear to succeed and good men suffer, begins by complaining to God that there doesn't seem to be any point in being godly: "Surely in vain have I kept my heart pure; in vain have I washed my hands in innocence" (Psalm 73:13).

But then, he pulls himself up, thinks things through, and sees that all is not what it seems, concluding: "till I entered the sanctuary of God; then I understood their final destiny" (Psalm 73:17).

The psalmist is admitting, "When I saw the big picture with its eternal consequences I realized the present situation is not at all what it seems." And if still uncertain, take it to God in prayer and leave it with Him. That's what you see Habakkuk doing as he teases out his two problems: the apparent reluctance of God to act, and the reconciling of God's use of the evil Chaldeans with His holy character (Habakkuk 1:12–13).

So Habakkuk's first complaint is that God seems to be inactive.

The big questions perplexing Judah were: "Why does God allow the Chaldeans to get away with behaving in such a cruel and evil way? Was God helpless in the face of their power?" People still ask the same questions today: "Why does God allow evil to hold sway in our land? Why are deviant sexual practices encouraged throughout our nation? Why doesn't God do something about the violence, lust, greed and family breakdown that is rampant in our society? Is He reluctant to act?"

Habakkuk has thought through the problem, and after making his point the prophet declares, "O Lord, are you not from everlasting?" (verse 12). He is, for the moment, putting the immediate problem on the back burner and restating basic principles concerning God. In verse 11 God said the Chaldeans attributed their success to their god. But what is their god other than something they fashioned with their own hands? Yet, the God of Israel is from everlasting to everlasting. He is not the God of the Chaldeans, He is God from eternity to eternity, He is the Creator of history and His throne is outside this world. This basic truth about God would reassure Habakkuk.

Then Habakkuk reminds himself of another great truth: "My God, my Holy One" (verse 12). He knows that God is absolutely righteous and holy and incapable of acting in any way that would contradict His holiness. So, "that being the case," Habakkuk reasons, "we will not die" (verse 12). The God of Abraham, Isaac and Jacob is the God of the covenant who repeatedly said, "I will be their God and they will be my people." So no matter how powerful the Chaldeans might be they could never exterminate Israel because God had given certain promises to Israel, which He could never break.

Therefore, having thought through the problem, voiced it and reaffirmed basic principles, Habakkuk comes to the only possible conclusion: as God is in complete control of history and will not destroy Israel under any circumstances He must be allowing this to happen to Israel for Israel's benefit. He verbalizes this in verse 12: "O Lord, you have appointed them to execute judgment; O Rock, you have ordained them to punish."

## The second complaint

The second complaint is: How can a holy God use wicked people for His purposes?

Habakkuk's argument is, if God is all-powerful and in control of events, how can His method of using the ungodly Chaldeans as an instrument to punish God's people be reconciled to God's holy character? Isn't it wrong to exalt such wicked people? Is this not an endorsement of evil?

Again, Habakkuk goes through the ritual of restating first principles: "Your eyes are too pure to look on evil" (verse 13). He is saying, "Whatever else I am uncertain of, I know God hates evil and cannot look upon it." "Why then do you tolerate the treacherous? Why are you silent while the wicked swallow up those more righteous than themselves?" (verse 13).

What is Habakkuk to do now in his perplexity? He moves to the next stage and in faith commits the problem to God. When Habakkuk says he will go to the watchtower and station himself on the ramparts, he is in fact stating, "I will leave the problem with God" (2:1).

In his commentary on Habakkuk (*From Fear to Faith*), Dr Martyn Lloyd-Jones said this is one of the most important principles in the psychology of the Christian life, and the one where we so often go astray.

We have a problem, we are perplexed. We have applied the proper method of looking at the situation in the light of God's character and in the context of our situation, yet still we find no satisfactory answer. Perhaps the problem is guidance. Perhaps relationships within the church. Whatever; we can find no answer to the situation which confronts us and, having failed to find an answer despite seeking the guidance of the Holy Spirit, we take it to God in prayer and leave it there. But what often happens is that, having told God what it is that's worrying us and asking him to solve the problem for us, we rise from our knees and immediately begin to worry about it all over again. Then to compound our error we tell others about it as well. If you do this, you might as well not have prayed.

If you have a problem like this, pray properly about it and leave it with God. Do what Habakkuk did and go to the watchtower. But, expect an answer. Just because we have left something with God and ceased to worry about it doesn't mean we should forget about it entirely. Here again Habakkuk's image of the watchtower is helpful. The tower is detached from the crowd, but the person who enters it does so to keep an eye on the landscape: he's on duty, he has work to do.

## Watching and waiting

In chapter 2 Habakkuk received two instructions from God: "Write" and "Wait".

In verse 2 the Lord effectively tells Habakkuk, "Write this vision down. I want it to be a permanent reminder for future generations will need to read it. And write it in such a way that those who read it will run to tell others what they have heard." In other words, the message is worth the telling. It's a bit like the resurrection message in Matthew 28:6–7, "Come and see – go and tell."

Second, he was commanded to wait:

> *For the revelation awaits an appointed time...*
> *Though it linger, wait for it;*
> *it will certainly come and will not delay.*
>
> HABAKKUK 2:3

Our problem today is that we do not like to wait, and we have to learn that waiting in faith is a biblical principle (Hebrews 10:35–38).

Chapter 2 also records the Lord's reply to Habakkuk.

It took the form of a vision that contains five universal principles that incur God's wrath and judgment:

1. The problem of greed (verse 6). It's the destructive characteristic of the unbeliever. As our society becomes more godless, the problem of personal greed increases.

2. Injustice (verse 9).

3. The problem of violence (verse 12).

4. Alcohol misuse and sexual perversion (verse 15). In our society today adultery, sodomy, sex before marriage and even before puberty. TV soaps, the media and films are all obsessed with the subject, and constantly miss the true biblical meaning of "love".

5. Idolatry (verse 19). It's hard to understand why educated, scientifically minded modern people should be so caught up in spiritism and the occult in its many forms, but this chapter explains it perfectly. It's simply the end condition of a people who will not walk by faith in God. They place their trust in themselves but find they are inadequate, so, finding no help in people, and having rejected God, they turn to superstition and idolatry.

Consequently, greed, injustice, violence, alcohol misuse, sexual perversion and idolatry were the sins for which Babylon was to be judged. Interestingly, these were the very same sins taking place in the nation of Judah. It reminds us that there lurks within all of us a desire for God to judge the sins of others. We read the newspapers and say, "God should do something about that!" but we don't want Him to do anything about those same things in our own lives. It's easy to be convicted about other people's sins.

Against this dark background of wrath and judgment, God gives Habakkuk three glorious assurances that shine like stars in a storm (2: 4, 14, 20).

# 1. The assurance of God's grace

*See, he is puffed up;*
*his desires are not upright –*
*but the righteous will live by his faith.*

HABAKKUK 2:4

The first half of the verse describes the proud, puffed up Babylonians; the second half is talking about the believer – "the righteous will live by his faith". This is the assurance of the grace of God, and so important is this verse it is quoted in three New Testament books: Romans 1:17, where the theme is how a sinner can be justified before God; Galatians 3:11, where the theme is how to be justified before God's law; and Hebrews 10:38, where the theme of the book is faith. So, in Habakkuk 2:4 we have the assurance of God's grace to believers who being declared righteous in Jesus Christ, live by faith.

# 2. The assurance of God's glory

*For the earth will be filled with the knowledge of the glory of*
*    the Lord,*
*as the waters cover the sea.*

HABAKKUK 2:14

Glory is not just one attribute of God; it is the characteristic of all His glories. He is glorious in power, glorious in wisdom, glorious in grace, glorious in mercy – there is no one who has glory like God: He is unique and one day that glory is going to cover the earth, "as the waters cover the sea".

# 3. The wonderful assurance of God's government

*But the Lord is in his holy temple;*
*let all the earth be silent before him.*

HABAKKUK 2:20

God is in control, the King is on the throne. He is caring for His own and knows what He is doing.

This must have been a great comfort to Habakkuk. Yes, the Babylonians were coming, and, yes, they might destroy Jerusalem and its Temple, but the temple in heaven was being kept pure and holy, no one could invade that temple, so be submissive, "let all the earth be silent before him".

## Worshipping and witnessing

Chapter 3 reflects the enormous change that's taken place in Habakkuk's thinking about God.

He has moved from watching and waiting to worshipping and witnessing. When Habakkuk says "in our day" and "in our time" (verse 2), he is asking God to do today what He has done in the past, and this confirms that he has reached the stage where he believes that the present hopelessness can be transformed by God's fresh intervention in the life of the nation.

Many believers can identify with this thinking when their Christian walk can be something of a trudge through the lowlands of routine and duty with little expectancy of anything new or different from the hand of God. But, Habakkuk knew that if God had worked in the past, not just once, but in many occasions, there was good reason to expect that He would work again, so he prays, "Renew your work O God, in our day, in our time, and make it known that it is You who have done it!" (see 3:2).

God may repeat His actions of the past, but He can be expected to do in a new way what He is in the habit of doing – bringing life! The temptation for us when we read of God's exploits and interventions in previous times and places is to want Him to repeat it here and now for us in the same way, when in fact He is committed to doing something altogether new that's appropriate for our time and circumstances. The challenge for us is that if we are to recognize and rejoice in God's work in and around us today, we, like Habakkuk, need to have our eyes opened to see Him at work in new ways, while praying that He will make Himself and His work known. For unless God opens blind eyes through divine revelation, His work remains unseen, unrecognized and unappreciated and people will put it down to chance, coincidence – anything but God. Hence Habakkuk's double plea to "renew Your work and reveal Your work": both are necessary today.

But Habakkuk is not naïve.

In his final plea, "in wrath remember mercy" (3:2), he realizes God's righteous anger is directed to all human pride: Israelite and Babylonian. Although he knows his people deserve God's wrath he has the faith to pray that mercy will prevail. In this Habakkuk is on firm theological ground. He knows the love of God is so strong that even when He is flagrantly ignored, deserted or rejected, He is drawn as a mother to her child, to love in spite of their actions. The wrongs are real, but so too is the compassion and desire to forgive if the desire for forgiveness and for restoration is present.

Habakkuk brings his prayer to a close with two responses.

# 1. "I will wait patiently"

He began in Habakkuk 1:2 with "How long, O Lord, must I call for help?" Now, after his agonizing and prayer he is transformed from an impatient prophet to a calm and expectant servant of God: "I will wait patiently" (3:16). God had spoken His word into his situation and Habakkuk had listened, learned and placed his trust in God. He now knows that whatever judgment God has promised will come to pass and he can base his life upon it. This teaches us to wait quietly for something for which we have God's promise but no date. This is not outward tranquillity masking inner turmoil, but a resting in the Lord, a refusing to be turned aside by what the eye sees or the ear hears – it's trusting in the invisible qualities, in the very promise of God.

Here, Christian, is your answer to the turmoil within you as you look at the state of the country. Yes, weep for godless men, women and children. Yes, pray God will intervene and pluck brands from the fire. Yes, get involved in reaching and rescuing the lost – but do not despair, do not give up hope, do not lose faith. God is in control and He will allow all kinds of things to happen as part of His long-term plan and purpose. This is what Habakkuk had to learn in his day, and we do well to learn it today. The King is on the throne and all will be well!

# 2. In the light of this, "No matter what, I will rejoice!"

For Habakkuk, in an agricultural community, it is loss of food and water, not just a devastated economy but the end of everything that keeps body and soul together:

> *Though the fig tree does not bud*
> *and there are no grapes on the vines,*
> *though the olive crop fails*
> *and the fields produce no food,*
> *though there are no sheep in the pen*
> *and no cattle in the stalls.*

HABAKKUK 3:17

Yet in the face of such conditions Habakkuk is saying, "yet I will rejoice in the Lord, I will be joyful in God my Saviour" (3:18). This quiet rejoicing in God, no matter what circumstances we find ourselves in, is only made possible from an inner peace in God.

As Habakkuk faces up to the worst possible scenario, we have here one of the most important verses in the Bible. It's one thing to thank and praise God for all the good things in our lives, it's quite another to rejoice in the midst of suffering when all the material blessings have been removed. Habakkuk has learned to rejoice, not in the particular quality or quantity of blessing, but in God Himself.

If we learn this fundamental truth, we are liberated to find joy in the Lord irrespective of outward appearances. Regardless of the good things we may or may not receive at His hand, He remains a continuous source and cause of rejoicing. This is because God is the Lord, the creator of the universe. A covenant-keeping God who can be known and appreciated for His unchanging characteristics of compassion and holiness. Never changing in these qualities, He remains a cause for great joy because of who He is. This type of rejoicing in adverse circumstances cannot be an academic exercise, but comes from the fruit of a personal relationship in which we "taste and see the Lord is good" (Psalm 34:8) and the growing realization that true blessedness comes not from receiving good things from God but rather by having a close personal relationship of love and trust in Him. It's declaring your faith and allowing that belief to move your heart and change your life. It's saying, "I believe Jesus died for me and dealt with my sins on Calvary's cross. I believe He has taken up residence within my heart. I believe that I belong to Him and He belongs to me, and as a consequence we belong together and have a close relationship of love and trust. Whether in good times or bad, whether rich or poor, whether in sickness or in health – everything I have I give to Him, everything I am I owe to Him. It's all or nothing – He is my God and I am His child and in Him I will rejoice."

# 36

# Zephaniah
## – The Day of the Lord

Zephaniah's ministry was set in the turbulent period in the days of King Josiah (640–609 BC).

This places the prophet between two important dates: the fall of Samaria in the northern kingdom of Israel to the Assyrians in 722 BC and the fall of Jerusalem in the southern kingdom of Judah to the Babylonians in 586 BC.

During Manasseh's reign of fifty-five years he practised the black arts of the occult, reinstated phallic symbols and asherah poles, and child sacrifice to Molech. The result was that the spiritual, social and moral life of the nation of Judah was, to all intents and purposes, much worse than it had been in the northern kingdom of Israel which, as a direct result of God's judgment, was taken captive by Assyria in 722 BC. It appears that there were four things that dominated the minds of the people of Judah – and it is worth noting how contemporary these elements of evil were:

- They focused on money and possessions – and abused the poor.
- They deified sex – through the worship of Baal.
- They worshipped the stars – by using astrologers.
- They were superstitious – and used charts for guidance.

Following Manasseh's death Amon reigned for two years and was followed by Josiah who came to the throne as a young boy. Following the "discovery" of the long neglected "Law" (Torah) of God, Josiah led the nation in spiritual reformation in 621 BC. As a result the nation turned to God, but the people had been prepared for that "revival" through the prophetic announcements of Zephaniah and other prophets.

As a contemporary of Jeremiah and Habakkuk, Zephaniah was the last of the prophets who would warn the nation of Judah of the coming judgment. The remaining three prophets, Haggai, Zechariah and Malachi all dealt with the Jews returning to their homeland after the Babylonian captivity. Zephaniah's prophecy was probably meant to act as a summary of the previous prophets" teaching that God is holy and must vindicate His righteousness by calling all the nations of the world to account before Him, in what Zephaniah called the "day of the Lord". However, there is salvation too, but not as a result of "easy faith"; it would only be obtained at the price of genuine repentance and a complete change of lifestyle. Therefore while the message Zephaniah was commissioned to give was primarily one of judgment, it was not entirely without hope.

It has to be remembered that this was a message the people did not want to hear, nor when they heard it did they want to believe it. They were in denial, having deluded themselves by reasoning that, as they were the chosen people of God, He would never harm His children. They were being selective in their theology by only recognizing the blessings God had promised to the faithful and obedient, while ignoring the equally valid conditional promises to judge the faithless and disobedient (Deuteronomy 28).

Zephaniah's prophecy contains twenty-three references to the "day of the Lord", referring to a future day when God would intervene, call a halt to the everyday business of life, wrongs would be righted and wickedness punished. It's generally believed that Zephaniah's prophecy was fulfilled when the Babylonian army invaded Jerusalem and carried off the able-bodied population in 586 BC. But even then, not everything was consumed as Jeremiah and a remnant of Jews remained in the land. His extreme language, "utterly sweeping away everything from the face of the earth and cutting off mankind from the face of the earth" (see 1:2–3), would lead us to believe that while Zephaniah is thinking of historical judgments upon specific cities and countries, including Jerusalem (and that is indeed what did happen), at the same time he is warning us that as God is still the righteous Judge of the universe, He will no more tolerate sin in us than He would with His chosen people in the Old Testament.

Supporting this view is the fact that there are many passages in the New Testament that also refer to the day of the Lord, and they all agree that in the time when men are proclaiming peace, but preparing for war, when they are holding to a form of godliness but denying the power thereof, in a time when they are declaring that the problems of life are being solved, but when actually they are in greater danger than they have ever been before, then the day of the Lord will come suddenly and without warning. Jesus Himself warned about this future day in Matthew 24, and in 1 Thessalonians 5 Paul speaks on the same subject using the very term "the day of the Lord".

## The coming judgment on the nations

In chapter 1 there are several points to notice about the coming judgment.

God Himself announces it. God Himself will perform it and it will affect the whole world. Everything in all creation will come under the judgment of God. Nothing will be spared.

In chapter 2, God's judgment is proclaimed upon the nations.

Several references are made to the way in which God has historically intervened, crippled and eliminated national and international powers in centuries past. For example, the Philistines no longer exist (verses 4–7). This advanced and warlike people with their marvellously fortified seaport towns and once flourishing commercial centres have gone! Ashod was emptied and Ekron uprooted as prophesied.

From the Philistines in the east, attention swings to Moab and Amon in the west (verses 8–11). These people had been relentless in their opposition to God's people. Where the apostle Paul could say to the Romans, "If God is for us, who can be against us?" (Romans 8:31), for these nations these words are turned upside down to say, "If God is against us, who can save us?" The answer is, no one.

And as if to underline this truth, Zephaniah's prophecy continues with the words, "surely Moab will become like Sodom, the Ammonites like Gomorrah" (2:9). Considering that they were located in the same region as these ancient cities this warning could not have been more graphic.

Having foretold God's judgment on nations east and west of Judah, Zephaniah next directed attention to nations south and north: Cush and Assyria (1:12–15). In ancient times the power of Assyria seemed unstoppable. In just the same way as the downfall of the Soviet Communist empire seemed improbable in the twentieth century, no one could have foreseen the destruction of Nineveh. But just as Zephaniah predicted, it happened. The citizens of Nineveh who boasted of their indestructibility, "This... carefree city... said to herself, 'I am, and there is none beside me'" (see verse 15), were wiped from the face of the earth.

Jesus Christ issued the solemn warning: "Heaven and earth will pass away, but my words will never pass away" (Matthew 24:35).

Those with a cynical attitude towards biblical prophecies concerning the end times, the return of Christ and the day of judgment, would do well to consider the incredibly accurate way in which the prophecies of the little known Zephaniah were fulfilled with such uncanny detail.

# The judgment on Jerusalem

The main thrust of chapter 3 is: "There's none so blind as those who will not see."

Having dealt with the surrounding nations, Zephaniah turns his attention to Jerusalem and in the first eight verses focuses almost exclusively on its sins and God's judgment upon them. Verse 2 of chapter 3 sums up the charge against God's people:

> *She obeys no one,*
> *she accepts no correction.*
> *She does not trust in the Lord,*
> *she does not draw near to her God.*

As God's people they should have done the opposite, but they were as vain as the godless nations of Moab and Amon and as arrogant as Nineveh. Verses 3 and 4 carry the indictment further, by implicating the leaders and condemning the officials as "roaring lions", her rulers are described as "wolves", the prophets as "arrogant and treacherous", and the priests as those who "profane the sanctuary and do violence to the law".

It should give us cause to reflect that despite the fact that Jerusalem was the home of the Temple, and supposed to be the city of light in a sin-darkened world, no amount of light and privilege can keep a people right before God if their hearts are not given over to Him. Nineveh, Babylon, Tyre or Sidon could not equal the gravity of the crime against God by this once chosen city – that they should have known better.

What was God to do?

The nation had been amply warned: Judah had even seen the prophets' warning come true when God's judgment fell on her sister nation, Israel, to the north, yet it still made no impression. There was nothing left for God to do, so we read in verse 8:

*Therefore wait for me," declares the Lord,*
*'for the day I will stand up to testify.*
*I have decided to assemble the nations,*
*to gather the kingdoms*
*and to pour out my wrath on them –*
*all my fierce anger.*
*The whole world will be consumed*
*by the fire of my jealous anger.*

## But there is a glimmer of hope

But mercifully verse 9 reveals that another distinct part of the day of the Lord is restoration, and, as verses 14–17 tell us, the day of the Lord holds no fear for the people of God. They are at one with Him:

*The Lord your God is with you,*
*he is mighty to save.*
*He will take great delight in you,*
*he will quiet you with his love,*
*he will rejoice over you with singing.*
Zephaniah 3:17 (Note that this is the only reference in Scripture to God singing!)

The prophet has leapt to the end of time, and all is not doom and gloom. Carefully consider verses 9, 12 and 14, and compare them with Romans 10:13. Future salvation is envisaged which will gladden the heart of man and God. Zephaniah is on tiptoe and straining his eyes into the distant future. By implication he is in the messianic era. A new Israel of God has emerged, and Paul's teaching about the restoration of Israel in Romans 9–11 inclines us to the view that parts of this chapter refer to the church and, ultimately, to the Jews who will be gathered into the body of Christ, the Israel of God, on confession of faith in the Saviour, prior to His second advent.

# 37

# Haggai
## – Get Your Priorities Right

When the Babylonian army completed its divinely appointed task of destroying Jerusalem with its sacred Temple in 586 BC, the Jewish people faced seventy years in captivity.

No Temple meant no sacrifice, so the heart of their religion had been removed and this threatened to wipe out their national identity. Thus it was with heartfelt joy that the Jews heard the decree of Cyrus, king of Persia, allowing exiles from various countries to return to their own lands. As a result, in 536 BC, about 50,000 Jewish exiles in Babylon returned to Jerusalem and settled in or around the ruined city where they began the restoration of the Temple (Ezra 1:2–4). They cleared the Temple courts of rubble and replaced the altar of burnt offerings at its base, making it possible for the daily sacrifice to be offered again. By the following spring they had laid the new foundations for the Temple. Then their troubles began.

The neighbouring tribes were hostile to the Jews, especially the Samaritans whose offer to help with the work of restoration was declined in exactly the same way their offer to help rebuild the wall would be refused by Nehemiah. Their response was predictably aggressive. To make matters worse King Cyrus was killed in battle and his successor was urged to stop the Jews rebuilding their Temple, so the work came to a halt and the people turned to their own private affairs. As time passed, they became more concerned with the building of their own houses than with the building of the Temple of God and gradually they became used to worshipping among the ruins of the once great Temple. That was until September 520 BC, sixteen years after their return to the land, when God sent his prophet Haggai to challenge the people to get on with rebuilding the Temple. Haggai's book records four sermons preached in that year.

# First sermon: A plea for priority

The first sermon can be found in Haggai 1:1–15. Four times in this book God says, "Give careful thought to your ways. Think about what you are doing – or not doing – to build the kingdom" (see 1:5, 7; 2:15, 18).

The people were desperately disappointed. They came back from Babylon with great expectations but were now disillusioned, for despite all their efforts they cannot find happiness and prosperity, and God tells them why: "Because of my house!" (see verse 4). God was drawing a direct comparison of cause and effect between the misery of their lives and the neglect of their spiritual responsibilities. Not only had the people stopped work on the Temple, they had done what Christians who become lazy in the Lord's work always do, they had begun to make excuses. And here is a clue to the underlying guilt. If there's no wrongdoing there's no need to make excuses but there was guilt and excuses were being made: "These people say, 'The time has not yet come for the Lord's house to be built'" (Haggai 1:2).

We have all heard that one before: "We would like to do more evangelism but we can't spare the time!"; "I know I should tithe, but I have too many obligations this year!"; "Thanks for asking me to help out with church work, but I can't serve just now. Perhaps later!"

## God challenges this excuse for inactivity with two arguments

The first is in verse 4: "Is it a time for you yourselves to be living in your panelled houses, while this house remains a ruin?"

That's a biting argument. God is accusing the people of having plenty of time for themselves while pleading lack of time for God.

The second argument God uses is an observation of what is actually happening in their everyday lives. They had put other things before God and God, who will have no other gods before Him, sent leanness. We read this in verses 5–6:

> Give careful thought to your ways. You have planted much, but
> have harvested little. You eat, but never have enough. You drink,
> but never have your fill. You put on clothes, but are not warm.
> You earn wages, only to put them in a purse with holes in it.

Saying "you have planted much", to an agricultural community means "you're always working!" They were working overtime, working through lunch, and going into work at the weekends: always pushing to get ahead but in truth not really going anywhere. They were on the treadmill, wearing themselves out in pursuit of all the wrong priorities.

But there is a deeper truth here, and it speaks volumes for men and women of today: Not only were the Israelites falling behind in their effort to get ahead, but in what looks like a picture of frustration they were also dissatisfied with what they had achieved. Isn't that the message from, "You have planted much, but have harvested little. You eat, but never have enough. You drink, but never have your fill" (verse 6)? They had to wake up and realize God had sent emptiness to alert them to their wrong priorities, and turn them from their spiritual indifference back to Him.

'Get your priorities right!" is the timeless truth proclaimed by Haggai. Man's number one priority must be God – for to trust, love, revere, worship, obey and serve Him is the chief end of man. It's a message taken up by the Lord Jesus who taught: 'seek first his kingdom and his righteousness, and all these things will be given to you as well" (Matthew 6:33).

For Haggai, the rebuilding of the Temple was the outward visible sign of the desire and determination to put God first.

The people's response to Haggai's message is positive, and off to work they go (see Haggai 1:14–15). Buoyant in spirit, keen to pick up where they left off sixteen years earlier, and with renewed vision, they settle down to the task in hand. What a day! It may be the end of a chapter in our Bible but it marked the beginning of a whole new era for the Jewish nation. It's not easy to start again, to pick up where you left off some time ago. It can feel lonely: the memories can play havoc, and pride must be swallowed, but thank God there is a way back as we submit once again to His plan and purpose and obey Him as He opens up a new and fresh chapter in our lives.

## Second sermon: A message about prosperity

We see in Haggai 2:1–9 that after a promising start, the people began to compare the former King Solomon's Temple to the one they were currently building, and their enthusiasm soured into discouragement (verse 3 and Ezra 3:12). We see here the danger of making comparisons. Some look to the past, to the Reformation or the Great Awakening, and compare the present unfavourably with what they perceive to be a former golden age.

And something else that added to their discouragement was that their expectations were not being met. The day Haggai spoke to them was the day of the Feast of Tabernacles when they would have read Ezekiel's vision of the future Temple recorded in chapter 47 of his book, and which he prophesied when he was with them in the Babylonian captivity. It presents a magnificent picture of the future Temple. And we can easily imagine how the people without New Testament understanding, and missing the messianic message of the future kingdom of God that Ezekiel was referring to, would read about the magnificent structure they thought Ezekiel was saying would be built and compare it with the disappointing structure they were building and conclude that they were wasting their time.

Pondering these unfavourable comparisons led to another reason for their discouragement: the realization that their problems would not be solved overnight – there was no quick fix. They recognized that the only way the Temple was going to be rebuilt was through their blood, sweat, toil and tears. Which means, when you add up all the negatives, you have the dynamics of discouragement. One's view may become like those of whom it has been said, "Blessed are those who expect nothing, for they shall not be disappointed."

There is a real lesson for us in the way God addressed His people when they were discouraged. He begins by acknowledging that things are really bad, and says He knows how they feel and that it is true the work they are doing now does not compare with what was done previously. "Does it not seem to you like nothing?" (verse 3).

Then building upon this realism, the Lord speaks a word of encouragement through Haggai: "Be strong"! (verse 4). It's a command from God. It brooks no argument. It's not a suggestion; it's a command from God that must be obeyed. But God does not tell His people to do something without giving them the resources to do it. He is not an Egyptian taskmaster ordering us to make bricks without straw. And we also know that if God tells us to be strong then He will supply the dynamic required to bring that about, for that's the kind of God He is.

Then God further encouraged them with the command, "Be strong... and work!" This means that every one of them, from the governor down, was to set his hand to the work and get on with it. This principle was taught by Jesus in His parable of the talents (Matthew 25:14–30).

Then the third motivating factor: "'For I am with you,' declares the Lord Almighty" (Haggai 2:4). This was so important for them to hear. For with the tabernacle gone, the Temple in ruins and the glory departed, they needed to hear that even though the tabernacle had decayed into dust, the Temple had been destroyed and the glory of the visible presence was no longer seen, the Lord's assurance to His people was unchanged: "I am with you!"

This is what makes God's people strong: His presence with us and within us. We ourselves are not equal to the spiritual tasks that need to be done to build the kingdom of God. But we can be strong and equal to the task because God is with us and in His strength we are more than conquerors, so we can be courageous. He has promised, "I am with you" (Matthew 28:20; Acts 18:9–10).

Then God gives encouragement to His discouraged people: "This is what I covenanted with you when you came out of Egypt. And my Spirit remains among you. Do not fear" (Haggai 2:5).

In the first part of this verse, God encourages His people by reminding them that the covenant in Exodus 19:4 is the foundational statement of their faith. They are to remember their history and recognize that they were part of something great and grand and glorious that transcends anything they could imagine! The message for Christians today is to look at what they are involved in now and recognize that, even though in the grand scale of things it may appear to be relatively unimportant, it is part and parcel of the building of God's kingdom and they should therefore be encouraged.

In the second part of verse 5, God gives them another wonderful word of encouragement: "And my Spirit remains among you." There can be no greater encouragement than that. The Spirit of God remains with us to strengthen and help us in the ministries He has given us, and to motivate and encourage the whole church to put their spiritual gifts to use and exercise their ministries. Isn't this New Testament Christianity in action – a church where every member recognizes they are ordained for service (Romans 12:4–8)?

## Third sermon: A message about purity

In His third message (2:10–19), God is concerned that sometimes it's possible to be involved in the work of the Lord to such an extent that the work of the Lord is more important than the Lord of the work.

God instructed Haggai to consult the priests, and enquire, "If a person carries consecrated meat in the fold of his garment, and that fold touches some bread or stew, some wine, oil or other food, does it become consecrated?" The priests answered, "No" Haggai then asked, "If a person defiled by contact with a dead body touches one of these things, does it become defiled?" The priests said, "Yes" (see Haggai 2:12–13). Immediately, the Lord makes the application: 'So it is with this people and this nation in my sight... Whatever they do and whatever they offer there is defiled" (Haggai 2:14).

The point is this: they are building the Temple and involved in the work of the Lord, but the tragic thing is that they are ceremonially unclean. Because of this, even though they are doing the work of the Lord, what they are doing in the name of the Lord is defiled. And that's serious. Look at it this way: you could construct a magnificent building for your church but it doesn't mean you will necessarily produce a holy congregation. You can engage in tremendous Bible studies and participate in the most spirited worship, but that doesn't mean you're going to produce holy people. For it is possible to be engaged in the work of the Lord but have hearts that are not right with the Lord.

The problem with the people rebuilding the Temple was that there were things fundamentally wrong in their lives that were defiling the work in which they were engaged. Christian men and women must always be aware of the danger that in losing sight of the reality of their own condition it's just possible that they are bringing into the work of the Lord that which is defiling. The danger then is when people look at them, instead of seeing God, they see people just like themselves and assume Christianity is irrelevant. This is why holiness is so important, for by being holy, Christians become ambassadors of God. This is their greatest privilege, their immediate responsibility, and their ultimate destiny.

## Fourth sermon: A prophecy of assurance

In 2:20–23, we learn that through His servant Haggai, God gave David's ancestor, Zerubbabel, governor of the land of Judah, an insight into events at the end-time.

The day is coming when the Lord will shake the heavens and the earth. Thrones are going to be overthrown, principalities and powers are going to be removed, there will be all kinds of conflict and all kinds of upheaval – politically, militarily and internationally. No one knows exactly what's going to happen but the word of the Lord keeps coming through with this message: kingdoms and nations will continually be overthrown one after the other – the Lord will have His day.

> *"On that day," declares the Lord Almighty, "I will take you,*
> *my servant Zerubbabel son of Sheatiel… and I will make you*
> *like my signet ring, for I have chosen you."*
>
> HAGGAI 2:23

So just what's the meaning of the signet ring?

We all know the heart warming story of Joseph, sold as a slave to Egypt, imprisoned on false charges but raised to political leadership and so able to save the Middle East from famine. Well, in Genesis 41:41–42 we read:

> *Pharaoh said to Joseph, "I hereby put you in charge of the whole*
> *land of Egypt." Then Pharaoh took his signet ring from his*
> *finger and put it on Joseph's finger.*

The signet ring symbolized Pharaoh's authority by which Joseph could now act. God was reassuring Zerubbabel, "Zerubbabel, I will make you like my signet ring. You, Zerubbabel, are actually a member of the royal birth line. You wouldn't think you were, because right now you are overseeing a messy building project in a disaster area, but you're doing much more here than working on a building project: you are building for the glory of God and the future of my kingdom."

When Jerusalem was overthrown Jeremiah spoke the word of the Lord to the compromised King Jehoiakin. It's recorded in Jeremiah 22:24, where he says God removed his signet ring. This means that God's glorious, kingly dynasty from King David, that's supposed to be an eternal kingdom, was disrupted with Jehoiakin and it looked as if the plans of the Lord had come to a screeching halt. But now, back in the land starting to rebuild the Temple in Jerusalem with the past behind them and an uncertain future opening before them, God says to Zerubbabel, "I will make you like my signet ring. The kingdom will be restored." God had kept track of David's birth line that was so violently interrupted, and was able to continue it through Zerubbabel, who was in the line – for the Lord God Almighty had promised that the kingdom would be restored. Five hundred years later the King was born in a stable in Bethlehem and inaugurated His kingdom.

# 38

# Zechariah
## – Prophet of Hope

The work of Temple rebuilding had been going on for five months. During this time the people had been discouraged when they compared their handiwork to the former splendour of Solomon's Temple.

At that time Haggai had brought his message from the Lord encouraging them to press on with the work by reminding them that they were part of something much bigger than themselves, but the people were still unhappy. Everything seemed to conspire against them. They had suffered much in Babylon, and now returning from exile with comparative freedom, things still seemed to be going wrong: the harvest had failed and they felt insignificant in comparison to their powerful enemies. Were they ever to be a great nation again? Would God bless them as He had done in the glorious days of David? It was at this time, five months into the rebuilding project, when God again spoke to the Israelites through His prophet Zechariah, and He did so through a series of eight visions and two oracles.

It has to be admitted that Zechariah is one of the most difficult books of the Old Testament. Having become used to God speaking through His prophets in sermons, symbols, revelation and prophecy, God now uses apocalyptic visions to drive home His truth. This means that though the visions are hard to interpret and the meaning of some details uncertain, they are still as exciting and encouraging to us today as they no doubt were in the time of Zerubbabel, Joshua, Haggai and Zechariah.

## The first vision: The watcher and the myrtle tree

The first vision (in 1:7–17), a man, who is riding a red horse with an assortment of riders on other horses behind him, is standing among myrtle trees looking out over the people in the valley. The picture seems to be that Israel are the people down in the valley, symbolized by the lowly myrtle shrub, and they could see that they were in a shadowed place. It was a time of despair and difficult days. The prophet was revealing to them what they could not see: that this unseen one who was watching the whole procedure, and saw what was going on, had with him the great resources to meet their need in the hour of despair. In other words, God had departed from the nation and allowed them to be taken into Babylonian captivity, but now He was in the midst of His people and would rebuild the nation.

## The second vision: Four horns and four craftsmen

The horns of the second vision in 1:18–21 symbolize the nations that persecuted and scattered Israel, and Zechariah sees that these craftsmen are the divine hammers who are to demolish the enemy's stronghold. This vision teaches us that Jehovah is the judge of all and that every nation meets its match in Him. God will not be put to shame. Those who once terrified His people will themselves be terrified and His people will triumph over all their enemies. Not only enemies past, but present and future, as Paul was to teach in 1 Corinthians 15:25: "For [Christ] must reign until he has put all his enemies under his feet."

## The third vision: The man with a measuring line

Zechariah's vision of a man with a measuring line in his hand who went out to measure the city of Jerusalem (2:1–13) builds on the previous visions, and now God shows Zechariah what His intention is for the city of Jerusalem. This raises an interesting question: Jerusalem was in ruins, and had been for seventy years, there was no way it could be measured, and as it would be another seventy-five years before Nehemiah would rebuild the city walls, what was this man doing?

The vision has two parts: part one is the expansion and prosperity of Jerusalem, which indeed came about. But the final section of chapter 2 makes it clear that the fulfilment of the vision was to be more than temporal and material. It was also to be timeless and spiritual and include many nations and peoples other than the Jews – the Gentiles – which happened in the establishment and growth of the Christian church. We see here the New Jerusalem, which Paul refers to in Galatians 4:26–27, that is, the people of God, the church, with the Lord dwelling in their midst. And just as the "wall of hostility" resembling the wall in the Temple area that separated the Jews from the Gentiles was to come down (Ephesians 2:14), so in Christ every barrier and wall will be removed and all true believers from every tribe and nation can come into the presence of the Lord Almighty.

There are practical lessons to be learned from Zechariah's first three visions.

Firstly, although the final size of Zion is not complete, the measuring line has indicated that its scope encompasses the whole earth, and, if this future extension of the kingdom was to motivate the Jew in his work of rebuilding the Temple of wood and stone, how much more should it motivate Christian people today in their work of building a great spiritual temple on the foundation of Jesus Christ.

Secondly, in these visions we learn that the true glory of the church is not in external pomp and circumstance, rites or ceremonies (however traditional), nor in splendid cathedrals or gorgeous music and wonderful choirs, but in the indwelling glory of the invisible God.

Thirdly, God's glory is displayed in the punishment of the wicked just as much as in the salvation of the righteous.

This is a subject that is not understood by many Christians. When the gospel is preached there will be results, and God will be glorified. His saving love and mercy will be glorified in the salvation of some; His justice, holiness and righteousness will be glorified in the damnation of those who do not believe.

Fourthly, the wicked will ultimately be given up to the "lusts" of their hearts (see Romans 1:24) and be tormented by that which they should have controlled.

Fifthly, the church of God shall become in fact what it is in right: the greatest organization in human history. Though now feeble and despised her day will come, and every knee shall bow and every tongue confess that Jesus Christ is Lord to the glory of the Father.

But Zechariah must have wondered how God could possibly bless His people after all they had done. Bearing in mind that their sin had led them into Babylonian exile, could it be that it also removed God's blessing forever? The next and most dramatic vision answers that very question in chapter 3.

## The fourth vision: Joshua, the high priest

The scene of the fourth vision (3:1–10) is the heavenly courtroom. Joshua, the high priest, is being accused before the Lord by Satan. His filthy clothes symbolize Joshua's shame (verse 3). Satan is pointing to Joshua's filthy garments, accusing him of sin and inappropriate appearance for entry into God's presence. Then, the filthy garments are removed and appropriate ones made available. And so it is with us; at best till we arrive in glory we are but burning sticks plucked out of the fire. We are painfully aware of our shortcomings and understand that God expects us to deal with our sin, and is not pleased with any disobedience. But the gospel message promises us that through confession of sin and acceptance of Jesus as Saviour and Lord we are accepted in Christ, and God shuts the devil's mouth by telling him, "You say this man, this woman, this boy or girl is dirty. Of course they are. What did you expect? I plucked them out of the fire. I have chosen them, I will cleanse them, so the Lord rebuke you, Satan." Not a word from Joshua, not a word is necessary: the Lord's rebuke completely silences Satan – he is speechless.

Then the order was given for Joshua to be clothed in clean garments (Zechariah 3:4). The symbolism is wonderful. Just as God, and only God, can remove the filthy garments symbolizing sin, so only He can reclothe us with rich garments symbolizing righteousness and acceptance.

## The fifth vision: The lampstand and the olive trees

In 4:1–14 we learn that following God's cleansing comes the Spirit-filled life, pictured in the vision of the lampstand and the two olive trees. Here, burning brightly, were olive trees continually dripping oil out of their branches into the bowl of a lampstand. The golden lampstand therefore symbolizes God's people, both individually and collectively, bearing witness to Christ's gospel of salvation to a sin-darkened world. Just as the Jews in Zechariah's time were to be witnesses to God by rebuilding the Temple (the place of light), so today God's people, the Christian church, are to be His witnesses by reaching out to others with the gospel of good news. Christian people are light-bearers in this dark world. They accomplish this not just by missionary endeavour, but also by their lives and witness within society. And the astonishing revelation from this vision is that God would do a new thing. He's saying that the day is coming when the individual will no longer have to go and fetch oil for the Temple lamps by their own efforts; God Himself will supply the power to light them as His oil flows directly into the lampstand. How will this be done? By God's Spirit (verse 6).

## The sixth vision: The flying scroll

So far, Zechariah's visions have been encouraging, pointing towards blessings for the people of God. But now, in 5:1–4, comes a warning as Zechariah turns his listeners' attention to the darker theme, namely, that the Lord God is holy and cannot tolerate evil.

Zechariah sees a flying scroll the size of a modern advertising poster, 30 feet long and 15 feet wide. From its contents of curses against thieves and blasphemers it's obvious that what we have here symbolizes the law of God.

The Ten Commandments were inscribed on two tablets of stone that Moses brought down from Mount Sinai. The middle commandment on each stone, the third and the eighth, warn against blasphemy and stealing. And this is what is noted on either side of the scroll in verse 3. Blasphemy is a crime against God, stealing is a crime against man, and loving the Lord and one's neighbour is the essence of the Law as Jesus taught in Luke 10:27. So the scroll speaks of the guilt and condemnation of those who are guilty of a double breach of the commandments against God and man. Flying throughout the whole land means it can't be missed; everyone would see it and read the message on both sides and in this we see how the law has a universal application.

## The seventh vision: The woman in a basket

The next vision comes in 5:5–11. Apparently bewildered, Zechariah asks the question, "What is it?" (verse 6), and the angel who has been acting as an interpreter again helps him.

The basket that came into view was the kind used during the time of harvest for measuring amounts of seed and grain. As it draws near, its lid, which was made of lead, was being raised and a woman inside was trying to escape but an angel pushed her back in and slammed the lid shut. Two women then appear with wings like a stork, a bird that we know from Leviticus 11:19 was ceremonially unclean. With outstretched wings the bird seized the basket and its occupant, and flew off between heaven and earth. When asked their direction, the answer was given that the basket and its contents were being taken to Babylon where it would be set down in its place, encased on a base, which speaks of permanent banishment. Here, then, is the picture of the judgment of the false church, very much as we find in the book of Revelation, where a woman who is the false church is called "BABYLON THE GREAT" (Revelation 17:5). Zechariah sees the same thing: God's judgment upon false religion.

## The eighth vision: The four chariots

In 6:1–8, the prophet sees four chariots which ride out upon the earth, very much like the vision in Revelation 6 of the four horsemen who ride out and bring judgment upon the world. The curtain comes down, then, on this great drama of redemption in the future. It is God's great symbolic picture of the way back to Him: first by cleansing, then by the filling of the Holy Spirit, then the putting away of evil in its various forms, and finally the judgment of the entire earth as God brings the evil of men to the seat of judgment and He reigns supreme.

## Two years later

By chapter 7, almost two years have passed since Zechariah received the eight visions God had given to him to encourage the Jews to press on with the work of rebuilding the Temple and instituting regular worship. Now the work was going well, and we learn from Ezra 6 that it was completed two years later.

We now find God speaking in a different way. Instead of using visions, He speaks to the prophet in a direct address that begins with His plea to the people to be honest and open before Him. It is again a rehearsal of their failures in His sight and a reminder that while He is unfailing in His mercy and grace, He is unchanging in His standards. He always supplies what is necessary but He never lowers the standards. And the people react as people often do, in three ways:

1. they pretend not to hear (verse 11);

2. they deliberately disobey (verse 12); and

3. they play the hypocrite (verses 6–7).

We hear the same excuses today as people rebel against God's moral law. Men and women pretend not to hear by not studying the Bible teaching on this subject; then they rebel against God's teaching with the excuse, "it feels good", and finally the play the hypocrite, "we love one another". All of this against the social tragedy of increasing marriage and family breakdown. This captures perfectly the deceitfulness of the human heart.

# The coming of the Messiah

In chapter 9, as if to prove that the result of living like this will be blindness to truth, we have the first of several amazingly accurate glimpses of the coming of the Messiah.

Zechariah's visions were literally fulfilled when Jesus mounted an ass and rode in triumph through the streets of Jerusalem with the people going before and shouting, "Hosanna to the Son of David! Blessed is he who comes in the name of the Lord!" (Matthew 21:9). This exactly fulfilled the prophecy of Zechariah 9:9:

> *See, your king comes to you,*
> *righteous and having salvation,*
> *gentle and riding on a donkey.*

With historical hindsight, the lesson for us is that for all their awareness of the Lord Jesus, they did not know Him as their Messiah and did not recognize the nature of this king when He came, even in such a remarkable way, and subsequently crucified Him. The ironic sign nailed to this cross said it all, "THIS IS JESUS, THE KING OF THE JEWS" (Matthew 27:37). Further proof of spiritual blindness is seen when Jesus drew near to Jerusalem. Looking out over the impenitent city He wept and spoke these remarkable words: "If you, even you, had only known on this day what would bring you peace – but now it is hidden from your eyes" (Luke 19:42).

That's what happens when God moves in the lives of people who do not listen: they lose their ability to hear, and the things of God are hidden from their eyes. They become inoculated against Christianity.

But that was not the end of the story, just as chapter 9 is not the end of the book of Zechariah.

For this tragedy, dark and terrible though it was, was within the plan and purpose of God to bring salvation not just to Israel, but also to the whole world. Not everyone rejected Jesus: around that crucified King gathered a new people of God who were destined to herald the good news of His kingdom to the ends of the earth. God's kingdom had drawn near: the end of the world had been put in motion.

## The second result of an unrepentant heart

In chapter 11, after many rebuffs, the sheep, weary of the Good Shepherd, pay him off with thirty shekels of silver (verse 12), the very amount Judas received for the betrayal of God's Son (Matthew 26:14–16). In Zechariah 11:15–17 we see the second result of an unrepentant heart. If you refuse the true shepherd, God will allow you to have a false shepherd. Again it was the Lord Jesus who said to the spiritual blind Pharisees of his day: "I have come in my Father's name, and you do not accept me; if someone else comes in his own name, you will accept him" (John 5:43).

This is the character Paul tells us about in 2 Thessalonians 2:3ff., called the "man of lawlessness", who comes to Israel as their deliverer and is received as the Messiah but turns out to be the anti-Messiah (what we know as the anti-Christ), the false shepherd who comes when the people reject and refuse the truth.

## Jerusalem surrounded by her enemies

In Zechariah's day Jerusalem appeared to be weak: the city was half built and the broken walls would not deter a determined attack. But Jerusalem had a secret weapon: the Lord has His watchful eye on the house of Judah (12:4). As Romans 8:31 puts it, "If God is for us, who can be against us?" These verses in chapter 12 reinforce the truth that the church of Jesus Christ is like a strong city whose outward appearance looks weak and insignificant. Satan, with his hosts, regards her as a cup which can be easily drained and thrown away. However, this cup will prove to be a cup of trembling to them and they shall tremble with disappointment and helpless rage at their failure to destroy the church, and will find their evil initiatives thwarted as their fiery arrows are extinguished against the shield of faith (Ephesians 6:16). God's people will not only be able to defend themselves, they will be able to take the initiative and go out to the people of the world with the gospel message where it will spread like wildfire. But it will be only those who look on Him and recognize who He is and what He has accomplished through His pain and suffering and repent who will be a redeemed people (12:10).

# "On that day..."

What follows in chapter 13 is identified with what precedes it: the prophet's favourite phrase, "on that day". In this context, three great inter-related events are brought together to produce and effect salvation:

1. the piercing of the Lord (12:10),

2. the opening of the fountain to wash away sin (13:1), and

3. the smiting of the shepherd (13:7).

In the piercing of him on whom they looked, a fountain, which suggests an abundant provision was opened for all people for the cleansing of sin. In Zechariah 13:8 it's apparent that this will be a time of great trouble, but verse 9 tells us that God is refining His people.

We are often perplexed when trouble and difficulties hit us and the tendency is to question, "Why?" and wonder if we have done something wrong. And, yes, it may be our sin is the reason for our problems, but often God sends trouble upon His people not to punish them but to sanctify them, to make them holy. He takes away all the things they lean upon until they learn to trust Him. This godly remnant, who have been refined and purged through the fires of affliction will then call upon the name of the Lord because they know Him, they belong to Him and are in a covenant relationship with Him. And when they call, He will graciously answer them and confirm His covenant with them. He will say, "They are my people" and the resounding affirmation will resound back to heaven, "The Lord is our God" (verse 9).

Chapter 14 focuses on the final coming of God Himself to judge the world and reign in glory.

The church thus cleansed and sanctified is going to be presented to Him as "radiant, without stain or wrinkle or any other blemish, but holy and blameless" (see Ephesians 5:26–27).

The promise is true and it's for today. While Christians live in the gospel age the going will be tough: the enemy is constantly attacking us and all we do for the Lord's glory. Yet there is a blessed day ahead when the Lord Jesus will return again. A new age will be established with a new heaven and a new earth when God will dwell with His people.

The Lord's people must remember the promises of Zechariah. There may well be many mountains of difficulty ranged against the progress of God's kingdom, but we can take comfort from the promise: "'Not by might nor by power, but by my Spirit,' says the Lord Almighty" (Zechariah 4:6)

So, however we view these chapters, one point from this book of Zechariah stands supreme: this world is still in the control of a sovereign, omnipotent God. Though we dimly perceive His timetable, it is evident that the coming of the Lord draws nigh, and though malignant forces of evil attempt to strike the Lord's people, we are promised that the powers of righteousness are more than a match. Therefore, with despair behind us, strengthened and encouraged by God's own Word, let the redeemed of the Lord proclaim that glorious truth – as by gospel proclamation in face of great difficulties they extend the kingdom and await the coming of the King!

# 39

# Malachi
# – How Have We Robbed God?

As a result of the prophetic activity of Haggai and Zechariah, the Temple was rebuilt by 515 BC and full-scale worship of the Lord was resumed. The new Temple was dedicated with great rejoicing, and once again the festivals of the Lord were faithfully kept. In 458 BC Ezra led another group of exiles back from Babylonian captivity to Jerusalem, and in 445 BC a high-ranking Jewish official in the Persian government, Nehemiah, received permission to journey to Judah to lead his people in rebuilding the walls of Jerusalem. Nehemiah completed this important task in fifty-two days (Nehemiah 6:15), and under his vigorous oversight a new governor was installed, financial reforms effected to help the poor, an agreement signed with the other leaders promising to avoid mixed marriages, to keep the sabbath and to contribute annually to the costs of the Temple and the upkeep of the Levite priests. After completing his twelve-year stint in Jerusalem, Nehemiah returned to the Persian king, and it was during his absence the prophet Malachi ministered to the Jewish people. With Nehemiah gone, the people violated all the terms of their agreement. Tithes were withheld, the sabbath profaned, intermarriage was rampant and the priests became corrupt.

It is always difficult to minister to a people who feel they have a right to be discouraged, and if their depression is the result of feeling that "God has forgotten about them' the task is that much harder. Malachi faced such a predicament: the early leaders from the exile are dead, the Temple is completed – but where is God? Where are the blessings that Haggai and

Zechariah had promised? Isn't the temptation always at hand to believe that living a life governed by spiritual disciplines is unrewarding and a waste of time? After all, the spiritually indifferent seem to get on all right and do well (2:17; 3:13–15). Don't think this was only an Old Testament predicament, the apostle Peter faced it when he was challenged about the seeming inactivity of the Lord (2 Peter 3:3–4).

This then is the background to Malachi. You can imagine him walking the streets of Jerusalem being heckled as he delivers his message. The "But you ask...?" question and answer dialogue of the book reads in the form of argument and Malachi addresses several issues.

# 1. How have you loved us?

"How have you loved us?" is the theme of Malachi 1:1–5. The book begins with the statement, ""I have loved you," says the Lord" (verse 2), and the people respond with the appalling question: "How have you loved us?" God replies by telling them He loved Jacob over Esau. The Hebrew word translated here as "love", has more of an emphasis on choice or election than on emotion, although emotion is involved. Therefore God "loved" Jacob can be translated as God "chose" Jacob.

Many of us mistakenly think of love as a warm, touchy-feely emotion towards someone, but that is not the basis of true love and is unlikely to withstand the test of time. Yes, of course, feelings and emotions are involved, but it is the conscious decision of commitment to make the relationship work generated by emotion that is the foundation upon which love is built. In the same way, God had chosen Jacob and was committed to building a relationship with him. God didn't have some warm fuzzy feeling for Jacob. He decided He would use Jacob and would do whatever it took to bring Jacob around to Him. It's also important to remember that God chose Jacob while he was in his mother's womb (Psalms 22:10; 139:13–16), so he certainly couldn't have done anything to have deserved this commitment and love. In fact, Jacob's life illustrates the independent man trying to control his own destiny and live life without God.

In precisely the same way as the Hebrew word for love emphasizes choice, the word for "hate" brings more the suggestion of not being chosen rather than an emotional response like anger. Esau's descendants (the nation of Edom) exemplified those who despised God's grace. Edom's downfall resulted in God's glorification (verse 5) because it was a testimony to what happens to those who despise and reject God and mistreat God's chosen people. And, as we saw from the book of Obadiah, history has spoken and there is now no nation of Edom for there are no Edomites in the world. However, Jacob, whose name was changed to Israel, has a vibrant nation named after him today, and is on the map of the world after 2,000 years.

The significance of this is: if God's choice of Israel made Israel God's people, then God's choice of us makes us His people. And we need to remember that God's choice of us is not related to our personality or character – and not understanding this truth can lead to emotional problems such as legalism, guilt, identity crisis, etc. God's love for Jacob and hatred for Esau is directly related to the doctrine of predestination, and is quoted by Paul in Romans 9:13 where he teaches that God alone chooses individual men and women for salvation.

## 2. Unacceptable sacrifices

We now turn to 1:6–14. When Temple worship was first reinstated, no slovenly approach was permitted in the selection of animals for sacrifice, but now, by the time of Malachi anything goes (verses 8, 13). If sons respect their fathers and slaves their masters, should not the Jews show their reverence for God by thoughtful consideration in their acts of worship? It would have been better had the Temple doors remained locked; the whole business was both offensive to God and useless for the worshippers (verses 6, 10).

There are key phrases in this book that reveal the spirit of the age and the sad condition of God's people: they are introduced by "but", "how" and "yet", and used seven times:

"But… 'How have you loved us?' " (1:2);

"But… 'How have we shown contempt for your name?' " (1:6);

"But… 'How have we defiled you?' " (1:7);

"How have we wearied him?" (2:17);

"But… 'How are we to return?' " (3:7);

"But… 'How do we rob you?' " (3:8);

"Yet… 'What have we said against you?' " (3:13).

These obstinate self-righteous argumentative replies from the people to God's just complaints against them reveal their unspiritual condition.

Consider this: the Temple is rebuilt, the altar set up, sacrifices are being offered, the feasts and fasts are observed, yet it is to these people, whose outward form and ritual is perfect to the last minute detail, that the divine complaint is made. And their response is to look at the prophet with astonishment and incredulity and say, "But... how? What do you mean? You charge us with having despised God and polluted His altar but look at our sacrifices and offerings. You tell us we've wearied Him but we don't see how or when. We're not conscious of having done anything to displease Him. You tell us to return but we don't see where we should return from or where we are to return to. You tell us we have robbed God, we want to know when. You say we have spoken against God, we don't recall having done that, when was it?"

This is not a people in rebellion against God, nor do they deny His right to their offerings, but they are labouring under the delusion that because they have brought their offerings they are being faithful to Him. Their hearts, lives and inward nature are a contradiction to the faith they profess and the name they worship. If you like, in the language of Paul to Timothy (2 Timothy 3:5), "having a form of godliness but denying its power". They have moved into the dangerous condition of imagining that what God asks for is the outward letter of the law and fail to appreciate that the letter is at best but an awkward representation of what God demands from the inner spirit. This is precisely what Jesus accused the Pharisees of in Matthew 23: an outward show of religiosity while neglecting the more important matters of the law – justice, mercy and faithfulness.

## 3. A deficient priesthood

Malachi goes on to unsparingly discuss the clergy's sins in 2:1–9, calling for repentance and threatening a curse on the priests if they do not heed his warning. The priests were offering defiled sacrifices to God, harming the people by their selfish regard for their own betterment, disparaging the priestly office by their ungodly conduct and brazenly defying God by their refusal to acknowledge their sin and do something about it. They, of course, were unwilling to admit it but the text tells us they were offering diseased and crippled animals that no one else would want. The Lord says ironically, "Try offering them to your governor!" (1:8).

We don't have literal altars today, but many ministers nevertheless do offer God defiled sacrifices in the way they do their work. In 1996 Billy Graham addressed more than 1,200 evangelicals from 100 countries on the theme "Stains on the Altar". He suggested that many, even outstanding evangelical leaders, had been offering God defiled sacrifices in the areas of their devotional lives. A number had absolutely no devotional life of their own. For some it was in the area of their call to service, double standards; the "don't do as I do, do as I say" theology. Others demonstrated a lack of social concern. Many delivered a watered down man-pleasing message, and others did not see the need for evangelism, talking as if all are saved and denying the reality of judgment and punishment. And for many in their relationship with each other they had allowed minor doctrinal matters and petty jealousies to divide and weaken their ministries and thereby defile the sacrifice of their lives given to God.

In light of the priests' perversion of justice and overall negligence, God had to make them "despised and humiliated before all the people" (verse 9). The same priests who despised the name of the Lord (1:6) and who considered the sacrificial system contemptible (1:7, 12) are now themselves held in contempt. Their actions brought on themselves the judgment they deserved.

In verses 5–7 we find an excellent description of a true minister of God:

- Reverence – it's the fear of the Lord that brings wisdom and it is vital.
- Commitment to the truth of God's word – when they speak God's word they proclaim what is eternally truthful, and that carries a huge responsibility.
- Walking in peace and uprightness – it's the essential requirement of godliness.

"True instruction was in his mouth and nothing false was found on his lips" (verse 6).

## 4. Mixed marriage and divorce

The section 2:10–16 shows that God did not accept their offerings because they were marrying foreign women in direct violation of the covenant against marrying foreigners. One reason for the command against mixed marriages was to avoid introducing the worship of foreign gods into Israel, as did Solomon's wives. That this is God's concern is confirmed in verse 11, where it describes the women as "daughter[s] of a foreign God". The main reason this was forbidden was because God had chosen Abraham and his offspring as the means of saving the world. In the Abrahamic covenant God said the nations would be blessed through the seed of Abraham and if everyone intermarried there would be no distinct ethnic race left though whom God could fulfil His promise. The fact that most Jews are distinctly Jewish and know their lineage is a testimony to how God has set them apart as a distinct people.

Basic to all the sins Malachi exposes is a breach of covenant, and here we see the double reference to "broken faith" (verses 14, 16). In verses 10–12 we see how promiscuity in the area of matrimony is reproduced as the Israelites take on pagan gods and become idolatrous. This was the downfall of Solomon, the most gifted of men, who married many wives and adopted their religions, eventually becoming an idolater. Such a crime brings with it the forfeiture of blessings as promised to Jacob's descendants and for Israel (verse 11). Solomon's sin led to the break-up of the kingdom.

Marriage, of course, is basic to the Old Testament. Polygamy never received divine approval and marriage is considered to be the most solemn official commitment a person can make. In this context divorce receives explicit censure. God says He hates it, and it's not hard to see why. It breaks faith, it harms the couple and their children and it brings instability to a society where the institution of marriage is neglected. We are all too well aware in these days the awful damage divorce inflicts upon our society.

# 5. Embezzlement

The notion that a creature can rob God is astonishing. But the point is clearly made in 3:8–12. Malachi is speaking of the tithe. Ten per cent of earnings were to be given to the service of the Lord. This was not a voluntary love offering, this was a due, and failure to pay what was owed was in effect to commit theft.

Robbing God is costly for it forfeits blessings. It indicates an attitude of mind with mixed priorities, and it betrays at best a careless and at worst a grasping spirit – and such is alien to God. We have to take note that Jesus Christ sanctioned the tithe in Matthew 23:23, and disregarding it risks the consequence of not entering into the fullness of blessing.

Malachi 3:11 mentions a "devourer". In that culture it was any pest that came along and ate the plants the people were growing. In our day we might relate it to motor-car problems, central heating boiler or washing machine breakdowns. God allows things to come along and use up our money to force us to return to Him. If our priorities are right and we are seeking happiness in God, then we give to Him faithfully and gratefully, and find satisfaction in life through relationship with Him who always provides enough for our needs.

The issue of giving is established in Scripture, particularly in 2 Corinthians 8–9, where we learn, among other things, that giving is proof of one's love and glorifies God before others as tangible testimony to the gospel.

# 6. The day of the Lord

The day of the Lord is the theme of the next section (4:1–6). Malachi is given a foreknowledge of the coming of the Lord, and he uniquely couples this with the advent of a forerunner. In other words, the ministry of John the Baptist and that of the Lord Jesus is anticipated. The voice of one crying in the wilderness is heard, and the surprising appearance of the Lord as He preached His revolutionary message in the Temple area is foreseen (3:1–2).

The prediction of the return of Elijah in 4:5 is intriguing, and it raises the question once again whether subjects like this are to be taken literally. The Jewish fathers believed in a literal return of Elijah, and that's what they asked of John the Baptist, "Are you Elijah?" (John 1:21). John denied that he was Elijah, yet the Lord Jesus indicates that he was. Matthew 17:10–13 tells us:

> The disciples asked him, "Why then do the teachers of the law say that Elijah must come first?"
>
> Jesus replied, "To be sure, Elijah comes and will restore all things. But I tell you, Elijah has already come, and they did not recognize him, but have done to him everything they wished. In the same way the Son of Man is going to suffer at their hands." Then the disciples understood that he was talking to them about John the Baptist.

This is a perfect example of the confusion that occurs when wooden literalism is applied to the interpretation of comments in Old Testament prophecy. Surely what John the Baptist is denying is the idea that he is literally, in the flesh, the reincarnation of Elijah. But all that Elijah stood for, all that in spirit he represented, John most clearly was. Hence the accuracy of the comment of the angel speaking about the future birth and life of baby John to his father Zechariah in Luke 1:17:

> He will go on before the Lord, in the spirit and power of Elijah, to turn the hearts of the fathers to their children and the disobedient to the wisdom of the righteous – to make ready a people prepared for the Lord.

The famous commentator T. V. Moore put it perfectly when he said that God sent a succession of Elijah's to forewarn of judgment to come in the light of possible rejection of the salvation message of the Messiah.

The day of the Lord in the final chapter is perhaps best interpreted as the gospel day: the long day of grace that climaxes in the final judgment – the end of the day. It is a sober thought that the last verse of the Old Testament is one that pronounces a curse on the disobedience of men and women because of their breach of the covenant. By contrast, the final word of Revelation in the New Testament is one of grace, with an acknowledgment of the soon return of our Lord Jesus.

# PART 2

## "The Silent Years" – The 400 Years between the Old and New Testaments

At the close of the book of Malachi in the Old Testament the nation of Israel is back again in the land of Israel after the Babylonian captivity. However, now they are under the dominance of the Medo-Persian empire, the great world power of that day. In Jerusalem the Temple had been restored, although it was a much smaller building than the one that Solomon had constructed in such marvellous glory. Serving within the Temple was a direct line in the priesthood that could be traced back to Aaron, and the priests were still worshipping, carrying on the sacred rites as they had been ordered to do by the Law of Moses. But the royal line of David had fallen into evil ways. The people knew who the rightful successor to David was: the books of Haggai, Zechariah and Malachi tell us it was Zerubbabel, the royal prince. Yet there was no king on the throne of Israel: it was a puppet nation under the domination of Persia. Nevertheless, although they were beset with weakness and formalism, as the prophets have shown us, the people were united. There were no political schisms or factions, nor were they divided into groups or parties, and having learned the lesson from the captivity they kept well away from idolatry.

Four hundred years later, at the dawn of the New Testament, we are presented with an entirely different world. The centre of power has shifted from the east to the west, and Rome is now the dominant influence with her legions spread throughout the length and breadth of the civilized world.

Israel is still a puppet state, the Jews never did regain their own sovereignty, but now there is a king on the throne. However, this king is an Edomite, a descendant of Esau instead of Jacob, and his name is Herod the Great. Furthermore, the high priests who now sit in the seat of religious authority in the nation cannot trace their ancestry back to Aaron: they are hired priests to whom the office is sold as political patronage. The Temple is still the centre of Jewish worship, although the building has been partially destroyed and rebuilt about half a dozen times since the close of the Old Testament. However, the synagogues, which began in the captivity and have sprung up in every Jewish city, seem to be the centre of Jewish life, even more so than the Temple.

So, what happened during these 400 so-called "silent years" after the last of the inspired prophets spoke and the first of the New Testament authors began to write? In Paul's letter to the Galatians he says, "When the time had fully come, God sent his Son" (4:4).

This tells us that the time of our Lord's birth was God's appointed hour; the moment for which God had been long preparing, and many of the preparations for His birth took place during those 400 "silent years". Furthermore, we will understand our New Testament much better if we appreciate something of the historic events that took place during the time between the Testaments.

After Malachi had ceased prophesying and the canon of the Old Testament closed (that is, the number of the books in the Old Testament was fulfilled and the inspired prophets ceased to speak), God allowed a period for the teachings of the Old Testament to penetrate throughout the world. During this time He rearranged the scenes of history in much the same way as a stage crew will rearrange the stage sets after the curtain has fallen in preparation for a new scene when the curtain rises.

In 330 BC a tremendous battle between the Persians and the Greeks entirely altered the course of history as Alexander, a young man only twenty years old, led his army to victory and destroyed the power of Persia, thus shifting the centre of world power further west to Greece.

In 323 BC Alexander died in Babylon when he was only about thirty-three years old. With no one to inherit his empire, the generals who had led his armies divided it between themselves. One was Ptolemy, who gained Egypt and the northern African countries; another was Seleucus, who gained Syria. This resulted in Israel being caught in the meat-grinder of the unending conflicts between Syria in the north and Egypt in the south, exactly as foretold by the prophet Daniel in chapter 11 of his book.

During this time, Grecian influence was becoming strong in Israel, and a group emerged among the Jews called the Hellenists. They were eager to bring Grecian culture and thought into the nation, and to liberalize some of the Jewish laws. This forced a split into two major parties, one of which comprised the strong Hebrew nationalists who resisted all the foreign influences that were coming in to disrupt the long-established Jewish ways. This party of traditionalists became known as the Pharisees. They were courageous and devout, demonstrating Jewishness at its best, and represented thousands of followers who were determined to resist the attempts of the Greek evangelists to persuade them to denounce Moses and turn to Greece. Because Greek pressure was so strong, the Pharisee response was equally strong. It had to be, for if they gave an inch all that they stood for would begin to unravel with disastrous consequences. Unfortunately, as time passed, the rules accumulated and to keep the separation intact they became increasingly legalistic and rigid in their requirements. By the time of the New Testament and the appearance of Jesus the Pharisees had become religious hypocrites, keeping the outward form of the law but completely violating its spirit, and so became the target for some of the most scathing words our Lord ever spoke.

The second party was the Hellenists, the Greek lovers who became more and more influential in the politics of the land. They were affluent and aristocratic, interested in gaining power and influence by associating with the important people in government and culture, and formed the party that was known in New Testament days as the Sadducees. They turned away from the strict interpretation of the law and became the rationalists of their day, ceasing to believe in the supernatural. We are told in the New Testament that they came again and again to the Lord Jesus with questions about the supernatural like: "What will happen to a woman who has been married to seven different men? In the resurrection, whose wife will she be?" (see Matthew 22:23–33). They did not believe in a resurrection, and by asking these questions were trying to put Jesus on the spot.

Also at this time a young rebel Jewish priest married a Samaritan. In rebellion against the Jewish laws, he built a temple on Mount Gerizim in Samaria that became a rival of the Temple in Jerusalem. This caused intense, fanatical rivalry between the Jews and the Samaritans, and this rivalry is also reflected in the New Testament.

Then, a little later on, around 200 BC, a king named Antiochus the Great came to power in Syria. He captured Jerusalem from the Egyptians and began the reign of Syrian power over Palestine. He had two sons, one of whom, Seleucus, succeeded him and reigned only a few years. When he died, his brother took the throne. This man, Antiochus Epiphanes, became one of the most vicious and violent persecutors of the Jews ever known. In fact, he is often called the Antichrist of the Old Testament, since he fulfils some of the predictions of Daniel 11 concerning the coming of one who would be "a contemptible person" and "a vile king". Under his reign, the city of Jerusalem and all the religious rites of the Jews began to deteriorate as they came fully under the power of this Syrian king.

In 171 BC, Antiochus invaded Egypt and once again Israel was caught in the middle. Israel is the most fought-over country in the world, and Jerusalem is the most captured city in all history. It has been pillaged, ravished, burned and destroyed more than twenty-seven times to date, and of course it is still the focal point of Middle East tension today.

While Antiochus was in Egypt it was reported that he had been killed in battle and Jerusalem rejoiced. The people organized a revolt and overthrew the pseudo-priest in charge of the Temple. However, when the news reached Antiochus, who was very much alive in Egypt, that Jerusalem was delighted at the report of his death, he organized his armies and swept back in fury, falling upon Jerusalem with terrible vengeance. It's recorded that 40,000 people were slain in three days of fighting during this awful time. Forcing his way into the Temple's Holy of Holies, he destroyed the scrolls of the law and to the absolute horror of the Jews sacrificed a pig on the sacred altar. Then, with a broth made from the flesh of this unclean animal, he sprinkled everything in the Temple, thus completely defiling and violating the sanctuary. It is impossible for us to grasp how horrifying this was to the Jews: they were simply appalled that anything like this could ever happen to their sacred Temple.

That act of defiling the Temple was referred to by the Lord Jesus in Matthew 24:15 as the "abomination that causes desolation" which Daniel had predicted (Daniel 9:27; 11:31; 12:11). Daniel had said in his book that the sanctuary would be polluted for 2,300 days (Daniel 8:14). In precise accordance with that prophecy it was exactly 2,300 days (six and a half years) before the Temple was cleansed under the leadership of Judas Maccabaeus. He was one of the priestly line who, with his father and four brothers, rose up in revolt against the Syrian king. They captured the attention of the Israelites, summoned them to follow the call to war and, in a series of pitched battles in which they were always an overwhelming minority, overthrew the power of the Syrians, captured Jerusalem and cleansed the Temple. The day they cleansed the Temple was named the Day of Dedication, and it occurred on the twenty-fifth day of December. To this day, Jews celebrate the Feast of Dedication on that date.

The Maccabees ruled as priests in Jerusalem for about the next three or four generations, all the time having to defend themselves against the constant assaults of the Syrian army who tried to recapture the city and the Temple. So, during the days of the Maccabees there was a temporary overthrow of foreign domination, which is why the Jews look back to this time and regard it with such tremendous veneration.

During this period, one of the priests made a pact with the rising power in the west, Rome. He signed a treaty with the Senate, which provided for help in the event of a Syrian attack. Though the treaty was made in all sincerity, it was this pact that introduced Rome into the history of Israel.

As the conflict between the two opposing forces grew in intensity, Rome was watchful. Finally, the governor of Edom, a man named Antipater who was a descendant of Esau, made a pact with two other neighbouring kings and attacked Jerusalem with the intention of overthrowing the authority of the high priest. This battle raged so fiercely that Pompey, the Roman general who happened to have an army in Damascus at the time, was besought by both parties to come and intervene. One side had a little more money than the other and persuaded by that factor, Pompey came down from Damascus, entered the city of Jerusalem, again with terrible slaughter, overthrew the city and captured it for Rome. That was in 63 BC, and from that time on Israel was under the authority and power of Rome. Pompey and the Roman senate then appointed

Antipater as the Procurator of Judea, and he in turn made his two sons kings of Galilee and Judea. The son who became king of Judea is known to us as Herod the Great (Matthew 2:1–2).

By now the Jews, having failed in all their efforts to re-establish themselves, had given up hope of freedom and were brought to the point where they realized that no human means could ever resolve the conflict and discord in which they found themselves. But, and this is vital, gradually they came to understand not only the depth of conflict and discord sin wrought in the world, but also its power and capacity within the human heart, and the only hope they had left was the coming, at last, of the promised Messiah.

This explains the hope that becomes increasingly evident down the generations of the Old Testament – the hope of the arrival of the mediator promised by God in Genesis 3 – the long-awaited Messiah. The people had Temple worship, but the Temple worship was symbolic at every point. It pointed forward by teaching how men and women ultimately approach God through the Lord Jesus Christ. The altar, the sacrifice and the mercy seat of the ark were all symbols of His sacrificial atonement for sin. In addition, scattered throughout the civilized world were Jews who had fled persecutions and genocide (with their synagogues), some of whom were ready to receive Paul and the other apostles when they arrived with the good news. When God got His people to that point in the fullness of the time, the strategic moment had arrived. The Jews were ready to be the launch pad of Christianity into a pagan world.

But it was also God's fullness of time in relation to preparing the secular world for the gospel by arranging the political, religious, and moral conditions here on earth.

In order to facilitate the spread of a new idea or creed two instruments are particularly helpful, especially in the early stages. The first is a common language capable of conveying new thoughts and ideas without risk of misunderstanding by having to translate, and the second is a common social system of law and government.

The Romans who spoke Latin were in control, but Greek influence remained so strong throughout the civilized world that when Greece was conquered by Rome, educated Romans learned Greek. By the time of our Lord the language of commerce and culture was Greek and the Roman empire had become just like the Greek civilization. Greek influence is seen everywhere in Israel, only the small towns and villages in Galilee and Judah retained their Jewish style of architecture. Most importantly of all, Greek, the language in which the New Testament was to be written, was the common language of the civilized world. Therefore, when Paul and the missionaries travelled from place to place in the Roman empire they did not have to learn the hundred and one local dialects; all they needed was Greek. The criterion for language was in place.

Secondly, there was a common social system of law and government. During the fifty years prior to the birth of Christ, the Roman empire was consolidated politically with Israel, Spain, North Africa and South Germany, and administered by a single government in Rome. Politically, "the Peace of Rome" brought stability. Fences and borders were removed, and routes through countries opened up. With roads built, sea-lanes and regular shipping established, unhindered travel throughout the Mediterranean became possible and for the first time in the history of humankind people could travel the length and breadth of the civilized world peacefully with a common language throughout. The highway was open for the coming of the King.

Another requirement of preparation for Christ's arrival was the awakening of a spiritual awareness and readiness in men and women.

The ancient world worshipped many gods, and by the time of the Caesars, religion had become debased and superstitious. The stage had been reached where the highest minds of the most gifted races had done their best with heathenism and the result was a loathing of the present and a longing for something better for the future. The old religions of myths and capricious gods had sickened and disgusted many people. Intellectually, morally and spiritually, the world was bankrupt, and into this world of despair and frustration, where the hearts of men and women were hungry, the gospel of Jesus Christ was about to bring light and hope.

There was also a preparation in the moral values of humankind. From Greece the Epicureans and Stoics came to the fore and practically divided the ancient religious world; one motivated by pleasure and the other by pride. However, within the human soul enough of the conscience and moral law written by God on the hearts of men and women remained for them to condemn pagan practices. People wanted a better way.

The Romans fared no better. While not in decline like the Greeks, underneath their magnificent empire a cancer of rottenness was slowly and steadily eating away the heart and soul of Rome. Family life was unspeakably horrible. Cruelty and tyranny were rampant and the people degraded and brutalized, their favourite pastime being human slaughter in the arenas. Two people out of three who walked the streets of Rome were slaves and subject to every whim of their masters. The best of them embraced Christianity when it came; the worst debauched and corrupted Rome.

Fifty years later the Apostle Paul exposed the awfulness of their position in chapter 1 of his letter to the Romans: a world without God, none to pray to for either comfort or inspiration except the goddess Rome or the half-mad Caesar.

But people were thinking and thinking hard. With their heaven like that of the Greeks, empty of gods worthy of worship, they began to investigate the mystery of conscience, slowly beginning to recognize its authority, which was a big step forward for pagan men. As they became aware of their moral lack and spiritual vacuum they began to yearn for a deliverer. Although vague and ill-defined, this dissatisfaction with corruption and longing for better things marked the close of the period and announced that the time had fully come.

In a remote corner of the Roman empire a young Jewish couple make their way towards Jerusalem. The girl is heavily pregnant, it's evening and she needs to rest. In another time and another place it would be recognized that she was a princess betrothed to a prince in the royal line of David. But although the Jews had long forgotten about kings and royal births, God had not forgotten, and as the couple pass through Bethlehem they stop for the night and there, in the city of David, the Christ child is born.

> *Glory to God in the highest,*
> *and on earth peace to men on whom his favour rests.*
>
> LUKE 2:14

> *The Word became flesh and made his dwelling among us.*
>
> JOHN 1:14

What happened next is another story!

# PART 3

## THE NEW TESTAMENT

# 40

# Matthew
# – Behold Your King

Matthew's purpose in writing his Gospel was to win Jews for Christ.

Hence he is at pains to prove that Jesus is the fulfilment of all the shadows, types and prophecies the Old Testament pointed forward to, and that the Messiah had come in the flesh to proclaim the kingdom of God had arrived.

In order to prove to his Jewish readers that Jesus is indeed their king, Matthew opens with a genealogy that traces Jesus" ancestral line from Abraham to Joseph who was called "the husband of Mary" (1:16). From this we learn that as Joseph was in the royal line of David, it is from Joseph that Jesus gets His royal right to the throne of Israel because He was the heir of Joseph, and it is through Mary, who was also of the royal line of David, that He gets His genealogical right to the throne. His legal right comes through Joseph; His hereditary right through Mary.

But Matthew's account of the genealogy of Jesus is telling his readers something else of great importance, for surprisingly it includes the names of four women: Tamar, Rahab, Ruth and Bathsheba. Normally the names of men are sufficient in biblical genealogies and women's names are added only if they will ensure the purity of the line or enhance its dignity. These four women do not qualify on these grounds: all four are non-Jews. Tamar was a Canaanite, Ruth a Moabite, Rahab a Jerichoite, and Bathsheba, through her husband Uriah, a Hittite. Matthew wants the church to know that God's work has always been interracial; God is no narrow nationalist or racist! Therefore, the people of God should also be interracial, intercultural and international.

But more, all four women departed from the normal accepted ethical standard of the Hebrews. Few parents would consider stories of Tamar, Rahab or Bathsheba as positive moral instruction for their sons and daughters but rather as examples of behaviour to be avoided at all costs! Their inclusion here, at the commencement of the Gospel, is to demonstrate that God can overcome and forgive sin, and use sinful but repentant people for His great and noble purposes in history. These four names each, in their own way, preach the gospel of divine mercy and remind us that Jesus came not for the righteous but for sinners. But also Jesus came not only for sinners, but through sinners.

There is another line of teaching that Matthew places at the start of his Gospel that also arouses comment.

The prophet Isaiah famously foretold that the Messiah would be born as the male child of a virgin (Isaiah 7:14). But what this meant in practical terms had not really been thought through. Consequently, when, in fulfilment of Isaiah's prophecy, the Holy Spirit brings Jesus into history, much that good people think proper is contradicted. In Galilee, the province of the story, an engaged couple were not to come together as husband and wife until their marriage. Thus, Mary's pregnancy before marriage was humiliating for Joseph who, being a righteous man, found what was happening to his fiancée offensive (Matthew 1:19). But overcome by divine intervention, he made the positive decision to proceed with his marriage to Mary. Joseph now dared to believe the angel's word that Mary's child was God-given and so, trusting God, decided to go on the initially embarrassing and lonely route of marrying a pregnant fiancée.

It begs the question, "Why should the gospel story begin on such a scandalous note?" It could have hugely reduced the embarrassment, especially with the devoutly religious Jews, if Mary alone had been involved rather than with Joseph. But seen in the context of the entire gospel story the initially embarrassing account of Mary may serve the purpose of showing at the very beginning of his Gospel that God's ways are not our ways, and that God's righteousness is not necessarily our righteousness. And, if you add the inclusion of the four ladies with questionable backgrounds in Jesus' genealogy, God is making it perfectly clear right at the beginning of the New Testament that there is room in His family for all who will repent and believe. For us today this means that no matter what your past, no matter what you have done to offend God, He can and will forgive, forget and accept you if you genuinely repent and accept Jesus as your Saviour.

As the Olivet Discourse (chapters 24 and 25) anticipates the destruction of Jerusalem and the book has a strong Jewish flavour, the likelihood is that at the time of writing, the early church, comprised converted Jews and some converted Gentiles, did not at this time call themselves Christians nor fully understand the full significance of the cross.

But they had accepted Jesus as Messiah and Lord, been baptized into His name and now wanted to know how to live for Him among countrymen who accused them of being enemies of the law, the religion of Moses and the nation of Israel.

Here were little gatherings of men and women who believed that Jesus was the long-awaited Messiah promised in the Old Testament. They believed the law and the prophets had been fulfilled in this carpenter from Nazareth, which meant this new sect was questioning Jewish behaviour that had been accepted for centuries as essential to Jewish life and religion. These upstart Jesus followers were giving this carpenter from Nazareth the status of Son of God, Son of Man and Messiah, and thus claiming for Him an authority greater than the law and greater than the Temple. In the eyes of the other Jews this was blasphemy. No wonder this Gospel so loudly echoes the bitter hostility that must have arisen between the Christians and the Jews.

Matthew's Gospel can be outlined as follows:

The appearance of the King (1:1–4:11).

The proclamation of the King (4:12–7:29).

The authority of the King (8:1–11:1).

The increasing opposition to the King (11:2–16:12).

The preparation of the King's disciples (16:13–20:28).

The reception and rejection of the King (20:29–27:66).

The proof of the King (28:1–20).

# 1. The appearance of the King

The first section can be found in 1:1 – 4:11. God's promise to Abraham back in Genesis 12:3 was that "all peoples on earth will be blessed through you". Matthew 1:1 tells us that Jesus Christ, the Saviour of the world, is the "son of Abraham" and "the son of David". As David's direct descendant He is qualified to be Israel's King. His virgin birth fulfils prophecy and emphasizes His divine origin as "God with us". Following His birth the Wise Men came to Jerusalem and asked, "Where is the one who has been born king of the Jews?" (Matthew 2:2). And in His baptism and forty-day testing in the wilderness, Jesus assumes the role of the nation of Israel (through the Red Sea, followed by forty years in the wilderness) and foils Satan with passages from Scripture, precisely where Israel failed the test. Thus the King wins the first round against the enemy.

## 2. The proclamation of the King

Fresh from His baptism and temptations, Jesus launched His public ministry. Starting in Galilee, He gathered disciples, proclaimed the good news of the kingdom and healed the sick. Then, set on a mountain, which is reminiscent of Moses on Mount Sinai, He delivers the Sermon on the Mount – the Christian manifesto of the kingdom (see 4:12 – 7:29). In this He explained the essence of His teaching and what it demanded of men and women who were enlisting as His disciples. Right at the beginning of His ministry the King makes it abundantly clear that the new kingdom age has dawned and that to follow Him demands a totally different way of life with radically distinctive values and ambitions that are at variance with life outside the kingdom.

## 3. The authority of the King

The next section is 8:1 – 11:1. The King's power is revealed in a series of ten miracles that display His authority over every area of Satan's realm – disease, demons, death and nature. In this way He was establishing His identity as King, proving that He was who He said He was – God in the flesh on earth.

He proves that He is Lord over all creation by transforming water into wine, multiplying loaves and fishes, stilling the storm and so forth. The earth obeys Jesus!

He shows that as God He is Lord over the demonic, and that the prince of this world has no hold over Him by resisting the temptations and destroying the power of the evil one at the cross.

He demonstrates that as Lord, He is God, the creator of men and women, and that health and sickness are under His power, by performing miraculous healings – the blind see, the lame walk and so on.

He proves that He is God over death. As Lord of life and death, He raised the ruler's daughter and others from death to life, and supremely demonstrates His wonder-working authority and power by His own resurrection from the grave.

## 4. The increasing opposition to the King

As the first half of the book draws to a close the kingdom of God is seen to be embodied in Jesus, and the challenge of what people will do with Jesus comes through again and again in this section.

Now we move on to 11:2 – 16:12. As the claims of Jesus to be Satan's victor, the ultimate judge, and greater than Solomon, Jonah and the Temple, become more insistent, chapter 12 reveals that on the whole the Pharisees were unwilling to accept Him. As their response becomes more harsh the mood becomes more dangerous, and the chapter that begins with the Pharisees' rejection of Jesus ends with the disciples being welcomed into the most intimate relationship with Him as He publicly recognizes them as His "mother and brothers" (see 12:49). The contrast is plain, and the issue of whether people are for or against Him is brought to a climax in chapter 13's parables. These enable the men and women to see themselves as they truly are, and answer the question of whether or not they are going to receive Him for who He truly is.

## 5. The preparation of the King's disciples

In the fifth section (16:13 – 20:28), Jesus' teaching is primarily directed to those who accept Him. It is upon Peter's glorious breakthrough declaration that Jesus is "the Christ, the Son of living God" (16:16), that Jesus immediately begins to teach the doctrine and nature of His church. In chapter 17 He speaks of the power and authority of the church, in chapter 18 of the church community, in chapter 19 of the church at home in marriage and divorce, money, sexual ethics, promise keeping and truthfulness, and in chapter 20 of church leadership and service.

## 6. The reception and rejection of the King

Most of Christ's message in this section is aimed at those who reject Him as King. In the sixth section of the Gospel (20:29 – 27:66) He predicts the terrible judgment that will fall on Israel resulting in the dispersion of the Jewish people, which was fulfilled in AD 70 when Rome destroyed the city of Jerusalem. He reveals what is going to happen in the intervening years till His return: how the forces of darkness will shake, test and try God's own people and then, looking beyond these events, He describes His second coming as Judge and Lord of all the earth.

Finally in chapters 26 through 27 we see the betrayal, trial, agony and crucifixion of King Jesus. When cross-examined by Governor Pilate, Jesus was asked, "Are you the king of the Jews?" He replied, "Yes, it is as you say" (Matthew 27:11).

Willingly, Jesus steps into the darkness of the valley of the shadow of death and there, alone and forsaken by His friends, He enters into battle with the powers of darkness. In the mystery of the cross, He lays hold of the forces that have mastered the human spirit and He shatters them, winning victory over them and publicly humiliating them. Astonishingly, though the Gospel of Matthew presents Jesus as King, the only crown He ever wears in His earthly life is a crown of thorns; the only throne He ever mounts is a bloody cross, and the only sceptre He ever wields is a broken reed.

# 7. The proof of the King

The final section is to be found in 28:1–20. On the cross above Jesus' head, Governor Pilate placed the written charge against Him: "this is Jesus, the king of the Jews" (Matthew 27:37). And then, seeming defeat is turned to victory by the bodily resurrection and the proclamation that the king of the Jews is alive.

The message that flashed across the ancient world, that set hearts on fire, changed lives and turned the world upside down, was not, "love your neighbour" – every morally sane person already knew that – but the incredible news that a man who claimed to be the Son of God and the Saviour of the world had been crucified on a cross and had risen from the dead.

When the Christian missionaries went out from Jerusalem to face the world they did so with the startling declaration recorded in Matthew 3:2, saying in effect that, "The time we have been waiting for has arrived." The new age, long expected by wise men and prophets, had broken in from beyond. A man with a mission to save humankind had projected Himself from the remote future into the immediate present. The time was fulfilled and God was fashioning His new creation. That was the tremendous truth that conditioned the thinking of the early church; it gave not just a flavour to their preaching, it was their preaching, and the message of the resurrection throbbed through every word they said. How could it be otherwise? Christ, risen and alive, was for them the one dominating reality of life and the very centre of the universe.

The great message of Matthew's Gospel, then, is that God is not away up yonder on some throne, nor is He waiting in some judgment hall for us to arrive so He can pass His condemnation on us. He is ready and waiting to move right into the centre of a hungry, thirsting person's heart to minister the blessing of His own life, His own character, His own being. When the King is enthroned in a human life the kingdom of heaven is present. That's the message of Matthew: "Repent, for the kingdom of heaven is near" (Matthew 3:2).

Matthew's "heaven" does not mean some place out in space; it means the realm of the invisible where God reigns in the Spirit. Where the King is, the kingdom is! If Jesus is enthroned in the heart, the kingdom of God has come.

Therefore, the great question to which Matthew demands an answer is the most crucial and personal question facing humankind today: "Is Jesus Christ king of your life?" Is He the single most important person in the entire universe to you? And only when you respond in obedience to the message of Matthew can you truly behold the King and surrender to the King. Then you cast out the throne of your own ego, self-will and pride, and replace it with the blood-soaked, glorious throne of Jesus – the cross of Calvary. Then His rule in your life will be complete – body, soul, and spirit.

# 41

# **Mark** – The Servant King

Mark's Gospel is very different from Matthew's.

Whereas Matthew wrote primarily for the Jews and liberally quotes from the Old Testament, Mark writes for the Romans. And whereas Matthew is written to present Christ as the king, the Gospel of Mark presents Him as a servant. This is why, for example, in Matthew the Wise Men are recorded as coming to offer their gifts for a king but, as there are no gifts for a servant, the incident is not recorded by Mark. Similarly, there is no genealogy of our Lord in Mark, for kings require genealogies; you have to know their descent in the royal family line, but no one cares about the ancestry of a servant. And, of course, a Jewish genealogy would mean nothing to the Gentiles in Rome to whom the letter was addressed.

The message of Mark's Gospel is summed up for us in a key phrase about the Lord Jesus in Mark 10:45: "For even the Son of Man did not come to be served, but to serve, and to give his life as a ransom for many."

Chapter by chapter, the Gospel of Mark reveals the dual focus of Christ's life, service and sacrifice, and does so with a sense of urgency: the word "immediately" appears dozens of times.

Mark begins his Gospel in 1:2–3 by quoting Malachi 3:1 and Isaiah 40:3, which leads to Isaiah's glorious chapter 53 in which the "suffering servant of God" is seen to be pierced for our transgressions, crushed for our iniquities and with the punishment that brought us peace laid on Him by His wounds (that is, His suffering and His death), we are healed, meaning saved. Thus at the heart of the prophetic vision of the Servant of God is the picture of the Passion through which, in the fulfilment of His mission, He accomplishes the plan and purpose of God for humankind. As the Second person of the Trinity, Jesus remained God in a man's body living as the Servant of God – the form alone changed; the essential being remained the same. That's why in the first half of the Gospel chapters 1 through 8 place the emphasis on Jesus" ministry to serve and His authority and effect on people.

## His unique authority

First, His personal authority:

> *The people were amazed at his teaching, because he taught them*
> *as one who had authority, not as the teachers of the law…*
> *The people were all so amazed that they asked each other,*
> *"What is this? A new teaching – and with authority! He even*
> *gives orders to evil spirits and they obey him."*
>
> MARK 1:22, 27

Jesus always speaks with the final word of authority. He never apologizes, never ventures a mere opinion, never hesitates or equivocates. He speaks with the same authority that once said, " 'Let there be light,' and there was light" (Genesis 1:3). That's why the words of Jesus have power in themselves to convict men. The scribes and Pharisees constantly needed to bolster themselves with references to authorities and quotations from others, but not our Lord. He never quotes anything but Scripture.

Jesus' authority over the mysterious forces of darkness is revealed again and again in the Gospel of Mark, where we see the power the demonic have to influence people for harm; such as to isolate them in the wilderness, to behave in lawless ways, to torment themselves and others and generally threaten society. There is a reality here that is all the more dangerous for being invisible, which is why the Bible warns us to keep away from the occult in any shape or form. Not because there's nothing in it, but because there is!

Mark also reveals the power of the Servant over disease. The first account is given in Mark 1:30–34 where Jesus heals Peter's mother-in-law. Next was the healing of a leper (1:40–45). Not just healing, but done in a way that was unheard of – Jesus touched him. In those days no one touched a leper. The Law of Moses, which in many ways was the law of health and hygiene as much as the law of morality, forbade that lepers be touched. Lepers had to call out, "Unclean, unclean," and no one would remotely think of touching one of them.

But Jesus did, and in doing so revealed the compassion of the Servant's heart. This is the first recording in all of Scripture of a leper being healed in a way which according to the Law of Moses brought defilement, and then sent to a priest as the Law demanded.

The ease with which Jesus crossed social and religious boundaries is breathtaking. You only have to think of someone suffering from AIDS and the way they were feared and shunned when the disease appeared in the 1980s, to appreciate what touching a person with leprosy meant to orthodox bystanders in Jesus' day. Yet this was fundamental to Jesus – not to His strategy but to His being. It wasn't media spin to be accepted as someone special. For if our life is motivated by divine love we do not have to be concerned about the prospective success or failure of a particular word or deed. For love says what is necessary and does what has to be done. Yes, people are attracted by the crossing of the boundaries to reach the outcast and needy, but what they are meant to discover is the love at the heart of it. Sadly, all too often they stay with the sign and miss the reality.

## For or against, love or hate, delight or despise

The second emphasis in this first section of Mark's Gospel (chapters 1–8) is the powerful effect Jesus had on the people with whom He came into contact.

As Jesus the Servant goes about His ministry He affects people, so that they become either for or against Him. He warned in Matthew 12:30, "He who is not with me is against me". There is no neutral ground with Jesus; He either inspires devotion or hatred.

In chapter 6 we see the effect on His disciples after He feeds the five thousand and then miraculously walks on water and calms the storm. In verses 51–52 we read:

> *Then he climbed into the boat with them, and the wind*
> *died down. They were completely amazed, for they had not*
> *understood about the loaves; their hearts were hardened.*

This hardening of the heart is a characteristic of the attitude of many toward our Lord in His servant ministry.

In chapter 7 we see the hypocrisy and criticism of the religious leaders revealed for all to see in Jesus' scathing remarks, but we also see the positive response from the astonished onlookers who were deeply affected after seeing

His miraculous healings. In verse 37 we read: "People were overwhelmed with amazement. 'He has done everything well,' they said. 'He even makes the deaf hear and the mute speak.'"

That's the mark of a believing heart – someone who can say of Jesus, "He has done everything well."

Then, there is a very significant act of our Lord recorded in Mark 8:22–26, where we read: "They came to Bethsaida, and some people brought a blind man and begged Jesus to touch him. He took the blind man by the hand and led him outside the village" (Mark 8:22–23).

It begs the question, "Why did Jesus lead him out of the village?"

Bethsaida was one of ten cities Jesus had pronounced judgment upon, saying:

> *Woe to you, Bethsaida! If the miracles that were performed in*
> *you had been performed in Tyre and Sidon, they would have*
> *repented long ago in sackcloth and ashes.*
>
> MATTHEW 11:21

So, having rejected Jesus and His ministry, He would not allow any further miracles to be worked there and led the blind man out before He healed him. This is the only case where our Lord did not have an instantaneous, complete healing the first time He spoke. When the healing was complete, He would not even allow the formerly blind man to go back into Bethsaida, for having rejected the ministry of the Servant of God, the village was marked for judgment.

That incident ends the first division of Mark's Gospel – the Son of Man did not come to be served, but to serve. From this point on it focuses on Jesus' sacrificial ministry as our Lord sets His face towards Jerusalem and the cross – to give His life as a ransom for many.

## The road to Calvary

The shadow of the cross has been hanging over the story since the beginning. It was suggested by the baptism of Jesus in Mark 1:9, where at the very outset of His ministry, Jesus, though having no sins of His own to confess, nevertheless submitted Himself to a baptism of repentance for the forgiveness of sins. By doing this, Jesus, the divine substitute, was proclaiming His identity with human nature, weakness and sin (2 Corinthians 5:21). And in Mark 2:20 Jesus says, "the time will come when the bridegroom will be taken from them".

But notice in Mark 8:32 who stood up to thwart His plan. It was not Judas Iscariot, not Pontius Pilate, not some demonic spirit. No! It was Jesus' close and trusted follower, Peter – the one who had just confessed that Jesus was the Christ. His response to Jesus was, "Don't do it Lord, spare yourself!"

This is the way of fallen men and women, for it is the philosophy of the world: "Look after yourself and don't do anything you don't have to do!" But Jesus rebuked him, saying in effect, "Peter, I know where that comes from. That's the wisdom of Satan, not God. Get that kind of talk out of my way!" Then Jesus called His disciples and the crowd to him and said: "If anyone would come after me, he must deny himself and take up his cross and follow me" (Mark 8:34).

From this we learn that the "cross" is not something God puts upon us, neither is it an accident or some set of circumstances beyond our control. There is a widespread but wrong belief that "bearing one's cross" is bravely putting up with an illness or whatever misfortune befalls us. Those who think this way say things like: "Oh well, that's my cross and I'll just have to bear it!" That's bad theology. The cross is something we deliberately choose, Jesus said, "If anyone…" Taking up our cross and following Jesus could be defined as a decision with costly consequences. It's severing our connections with the old way of life, for anything that would interfere with our loyalty to Jesus must be crucified.

Strange isn't it? For Jesus to say to those who are already His disciples, "If anyone would come after me", for surely the disciples were doing just that! However, the truth is that not all disciples continue on the road as followers, as Peter had just verbalized. To accept the invitation to take up our cross also means two things: first, to disown the lordship of our own thinking by removing self from the throne, and second, coming under new management by accepting the authority and rule of King Jesus, which means going public. The reason for this is that self-renunciation could remain a private affair but cross-bearing was a public and outward act – "Live a life following me" (8:34). It is the decision to follow Jesus that enables us to turn our backs on ourselves and be prepared to die to self for Him.

And be assured, "whoever loses his life for [Jesus] and for the gospel will save it" (8:35). Doesn't the self-confidence of Jesus thrill you? It's the challenge to be completely Christ-centred. The destruction of self-advancement in this world is the most constructive step towards the kingdom of God. We do not find ourselves by looking out for number one; we find ourselves by risking honest discipleship. Real life, Jesus is claiming, is the gift on the last day to His humble follower. It is the wonderful surprise that will come when, having obeyed Jesus in a thousand small self-renunciations and seeing oneself no great success in this life, one finds at the last judgment that someone was noticing all along.

Mark 9 contains two major stories: the transfiguration and the disciple's inability and restoration.

The lesson is perfectly clear: the church both individually and corporately finds her authoritative power when she obeys the transfiguration's voice to "Listen to him!" (see 9:7), and she finds her helpful power when she obeys her Master's counsel to "talk to him" in believing prayer (see 9:29). This is exactly what Christians have at the heart of their worship service, where they listen to God in the sermon and where they talk to God through His Son in their prayers. These same two instructions (listen to Him, talk to Him) are at the heart of the disciple's devotional life – listening to God through reading His word and talking to God through personal prayer. And it's these two up-and-down movements that form the divine pump that keeps Christians alive and causes churches to grow and reach out in mission.

The remainder of chapter 9 shows quite graphically what happens to disciples who lack power because they neglect faithful prayer: The disciples' defeat: they are unable to deliver the demonized boy due to their lack of prayer (verses 14–29).

Lack of prayer means they didn't understand Jesus' mission (verses 30–32). Again the lesson is obvious; if we do not listen to Jesus and do not talk to Him, we will be out of step with Him and will not understand much that happens to us. In turn, this produces:

- Disunity and division, seen in the disciples' dispute as they strive for position and prestige (verses 33–37).
- The disciples' dilemma: they refuse to recognize competition (verses 38–41).

The possibility is that their argument concerning their own greatness may have arisen from the failure the nine disciples experienced with the demonized boy. You can imagine how, after the event when the twelve were all together, the three who had experienced their own glorious encounter on the Mount of Transfiguration could deride the nine for their inability to exorcize the demon from the boy. Jesus' response was to teach His disciples a very important lesson. He took a child and said that anyone who ministered to that child in His name was actually ministering to Him. In other words, we are not to make the mistake of thinking that if we minister to significant people our ministry is significant. It does not matter to whom we minister because all ministries should be ministry to Christ and for Christ. To welcome a child is to welcome

Him. To serve a child is to serve Him.

In chapter 14 two acts show the gracious character of the servant.

Mary offered her sacrifice of expensive perfume which she poured out on the feet of Jesus, then, Judas went out and betrayed Him for money: one an act of utter selflessness, the other an act of complete selfishness.

## The final chapter

Beginning with chapter 15, we have the account of the cross.

In Mark's description, this is an act of almost incredible brutality done in the name of "justice". The Lord outwardly seems to be a defeated man, a tragic failure, His cause hopelessly lost. He is hounded, bludgeoned and spat upon; as He Himself said, "The Son of Man must suffer many things" (8:31). Finally, He is crucified.

Notice when you read this account there are three things they could not make our Lord do.

Firstly, they could not make our Lord speak:

> So again Pilate asked him, "Aren't you going to answer? See how many things they are accusing you of."
> But Jesus still made no reply, and Pilate was amazed.
>
> MARK 15:4–5

Secondly, they could not make him drink:

> Then they offered him wine mixed with myrrh, but he did not take it.
>
> MARK 15:23

The reason for His silence and abstinence was that if He had answered Pilate He could have saved Himself, and had He drunk the anaesthetic He would have dulled some of the agony of the cross and the weight of the world's sin and the divine punishment for it coming upon His shoulders, but He would not. He would not spare Himself.

Thirdly, they could not even make Him die:

> With a loud cry, Jesus breathed his last.
>
> MARK 15:37

This is really an interpretation: what the Greek says is, "He unspirited himself". He dismissed His spirit. John 19:30 says, "With that, he bowed his head and gave up his spirit." He did not die at the hands of the murderers; He let His spirit go, dismissed it. For He Himself said, "No one takes [my life] from me, but I lay it down of my own accord" (John 10:18). He could have refused to die, and they could not have taken His life from Him; He said so. He could have hung on the cross and taunted them with their inability to put Him to death, but He did not; He died, He unspirited Himself.

When we come to the last chapter, the resurrection of Jesus, we learn of His reason. He was silent and refused to appeal to Pilate or to the crowd because He had assumed our guilt, and a guilty man has nothing to say before his accuser (see Romans 3:19). However, as a victorious Saviour He was laying the basis for a coming day when, in resurrection power, He would appeal to a far greater crowd, when every knee will bow and every tongue confess that Jesus Christ is Lord. He would not drink to dull His senses because He was laying a basis by which even those who stood around the cross might enter into a life so wonderful, so vigorous and so abundant, that the most zestful moments of earth would pale by comparison. He would not let men take His life, but voluntarily laid it down in order that He might overcome man's greatest enemy, death, and forever deliver all who would believe in Him from its dreadful power.

As we look at the life of the greatest Servant who ever lived, as we seek to pattern our lives after His, may we always bear upon our lives the selfless sacrificial imprint of the One who, by refusing to save Himself saved others.

# 42

# Luke
# – The Son of Man

As a physician, Luke writes with the warmth and compassion of a family doctor as he carefully documents the perfect humanity of the Son of Man, Jesus Christ.

The key to Luke's Gospel, which forms a brief outline of the book, is found in Luke 19:10: "For the Son of Man came to seek and to save what was lost."

## The miraculous birth

This is why Luke's genealogy of Jesus in chapter 3 traces His lineage back to Adam (the start of the human race), while Matthew's stops at Abraham. Whereas Matthew was writing to the Jews and presenting Jesus as their King, Luke is writing to the world and presenting Jesus as the new, perfect man. Hence, Dr Luke puts his physician's seal of approval on Jesus' virgin birth.

For 2,000 years the virgin birth had been a major obstacle to faith. It was deemed a physical impossibility, and men and women argued vehemently that the thing was ridiculous. Then, in the latter half of the twentieth century, science discovered artificial insemination, and lo and behold a woman could be made pregnant without "knowing a man" and can have what to all intents and purposes is "a virgin birth". The unspoken assumption is that if science can do it, so can God.

It's vitally important that we realize the huge significance of the virgin birth. It stands guarding the entrance of the New Testament, heralding the supernatural nature of Jesus and warning that if we find it offensive or irrational there is no point in going any further, for all that follows is of the same order. If we fail to accept the virgin birth as fact, what will we make of the feeding of the five thousand, stilling the storm, raising Lazarus from the dead, the transfiguration and the resurrection? The virgin birth is also a sign of God's verdict on human nature. The human race needs a Redeemer, but by itself cannot produce one; the Redeemer must come from outside. This is why Jesus was not a created being like other men and women. If He were, He would have inherited the sin of Adam and would have been unable to present Himself on our behalf as faultless before God and the only acceptable sacrifice for human sin. A good-living, hard-working kind and considerate man with a social conscience and an insight to philosophy and physiology sacrificially dying for us would have achieved precisely nothing. This is why Luke pays so much attention to the temptation in the wilderness in chapter 4. He is going right back to the beginning. In Eden, the first Adam, the head of the human race and our representative, disobeyed God by succumbing to the devil's temptation, and so plunged the human race into sin that we inherit through our natural mothers and fathers. However, the "second Adam", Jesus, was obedient to God and did not give in to Satan but was victorious over him and so proved His claim to be the New Man able to be the Saviour of the world. From that moment, the writing is on the wall for Satan and the possibility of a new start for humankind suddenly appears.

This is why, just after the victory over Satan, Jesus announced His mission statement.

## The good news

> The Spirit of the Lord is on me,
> because he has anointed me
> to preach good news to the poor.
> He has sent me to proclaim freedom for the prisoners
> and recovery of sight for the blind,
> to release the oppressed,
> to proclaim the year of the Lord's favour.

LUKE 4:18–19

But failing to understand Jesus and His mission, yet amazed at the wisdom of His teaching, His listeners praise Him as the local boy made good: "Isn't this Joseph's son?" (4:22). However, they were wrong. He is not Joseph's birth-son, as the voice at His baptism declared, as His family tree revealed, as the centurion at the crucifixion recognized, and as the devil's followers admitted, "You are the Son of God!" (Mark 3:11). What it means to be the Son of God, the new Adam, Jesus, goes on to make clear in Luke 4:25–27, where a paraphrase of Jesus" words could read, "I have come with the good news of salvation not just for Nazareth, but for all Galilee, and indeed for all Israel. Furthermore, although this will scandalize you – if Israel turns out to be as blinkered and narrow-minded as you are – then she will forfeit it, while the rest of the world receives it." Salvation is, in other words, not restricted to the sons of Abraham: it is for every son of Adam, for Jesus has come to save not just Jewry, but humanity – He is to be the Saviour of the world.

This does not mean that God will save even those who wilfully reject Him; such thinking runs contrary to the basic teaching of the New Testament. Rather, Jesus' claim to be the saviour of the world means there is no type of person the gospel cannot reach and no boundary it cannot cross. Luke is not saying that everyone will be saved but that anyone can be saved. The gospel is not only for Jews but also for Greeks and Romans, and for Samaritans too. It is not only for males but also for females – and not simply important women but widows and the infirm and prostitutes as well. It is not only for freemen, it's also for slaves – and indeed for all whom society despises: for the poor, the weak and the outcast, for the thief and the prisoner. It is also for children and young people. And all of these Luke delights in parading across the pages of his Gospel as he reveals the all-too-human stories that are the hallmark of men and women of this world.

## Seeking the lost

The second part of the Son of Man's mission given in the key verse 19:10 – to seek and to save what was lost – is clearly seen in chapters 15 and 16.

Beginning with tax collectors and sinners eating inside a house with Jesus, while Pharisees and scribes murmur outside, what follows flows out of this setting and explains it. Jesus tells the story of a sheep that is lost (15:4–7); it is far away from where it should be and knows it. Then he speaks of a coin that is lost at home (15:8–10). One story is for the men, one is for the women, but both concern "lost" items. Then comes the major story of two lost sons (15:11–31), with the emphasis not on the younger, but the elder. He is more "lost" than the younger one but he does not know it. The younger son is therefore like the lost sheep, lost far away and knowing it. The older son is like the lost coin, lost at home but not knowing it.

The parallels do not end there, however, for when we move on to chapter 16, we again see two characters corresponding to the two sons in chapter 15. The first is a puzzling story about a rogue whom Jesus commends for dishonesty (16:1). Interestingly, exactly the same word is used to describe the younger son wasting his substance in the far country as for the rogue wasting his master's substance. So, we have the same word and the same characteristic. Likewise, just as the elder son claimed he did everything right – "[I] never disobeyed your orders" (15:29) – so the rich man in the second story (16:19–31) is not described as guilty of any sin, vice or crime, yet he finishes up in hell because of his indifference to others, his indulgence of himself and his independence from God.

The message through all this is: "How can a man or a woman be saved?" The answer is by repentance! Some understand their need – the prodigal son was lost and he knew it ("I have sinned against heaven and against you", 15:18). Some, like the older son, think they are all right ("[I] never disobeyed your orders", 15:29), and so, by relying on their own goodness like the Pharisees, they are not safe: they are in deadly danger.

Just as the steward prepared for his future, and used the means at hand to ensure he would be all right when the time came, in exactly the same way we all face dismissal from this sphere of life into the unknown realms of eternity. So, "use worldly wealth to gain friends for yourselves, so that when it is gone, you will be welcomed into eternal dwellings" (16:9).

We must not read too much into the financial theme. That's not the point of the parable, for money itself is neither good nor bad. The point is that although property, ability and time belong to us in this life, what will happen to us when we pass on to the next life, according to Jesus, will be influenced by what we are doing with what is ours now.

The Pharisees sneered at this teaching of Jesus (16:14). They, like so many today, lived a double life. For them the sacred and secular were separate, watertight compartments. In the religious compartment they were "Pharisees" with certain beliefs and practices by which they were assured of a good standing before God. However, the secular compartment was quite separate: in that side of their lives they could afford to be greedy and selfish, for as far as they were concerned their attitude in these matters had no bearing on their religious status. That was why they ridiculed the idea that getting to heaven might be in some way connected with ordinary life. Thus, from verse 19 in His parable of the rich man, Jesus highlights the consequences of misusing the opportunities of secular life and avoiding the real demands of religious law. If you must compartmentalize your life in this way, says Jesus, I must warn you that in neither area – neither your secular life nor your spiritual life – are you going the right way to escape hell and reach heaven.

Again, we must not fixate on the use of wealth: it's just a convenient peg on which Jesus can hang His teaching. The story could just as well have featured a politician with his power, or an academic with his brains – indeed anyone with any kind of resource or skill. To every one of us is given a "Lazarus at the door", and the challenge is how we will use our possessions, gifts and skills – rightly or wrongly, with love or self-indulgence, bringing God's will into the matter or leaving it out. These parables are an exhortation to men and women who are willing to hear, and a warning to men and women who are not, that our destiny in the world to come depends on how we respond to the teachings of Jesus here and now. It is a challenge to the born-again Christian for the far-sighted use of the things of this world, the things we shall not be able to take with us, but which nevertheless constitute the raw material out of which our inner character is built.

## The entry of the King

In Luke 19:28 Jesus prepares to enter Jerusalem.

However, the welcoming crowd sees the event as political rather than spiritual. They expect the kingdom of God to be a Jewish kingdom in which the Gentiles would be excluded rather than be equal candidates for admission.

The explanation as to why so many got it so wrong can be found in chapter 18. Jesus has just explained that His coming death is the fulfilment of Old Testament prophecy, and though He will die He will rise again. Luke 18:34 reveals the disciple's response: "The disciples did not understand any of this. Its meaning was hidden from them, and they did not know what he was talking about."

Now it's logical to assume that if those closest to Jesus didn't understand what He was talking about, there was no way the crowds would either. This inability to understand Christ's mission and message is very significant and contains an important truth for us today. People in Jesus' day thought they knew what the kingdom of God meant: people in our day think they know what Christianity, the church and the gospel means – but more often than not their understanding is wrong and needs to be clarified.

The kingdom of God centres on the cross and must first come to the human heart, for only when the soul is transformed will society be transformed. This is not understood today. Governments pass laws meant to improve our society at an unprecedented rate. The result by any measurement when compared with society fifty years ago is that morally we are worse. How can this be? The reason is that, back then the secular and the sacred (Christianity) were recognized as the framework of society. Today the sacred, Christianity, has been marginalized, and the secular, with its god of the bottom line and political correctness, reigns supreme. Unfortunately, for the many who suffer from an increasingly dysfunctional society, this social experiment can never work because no government, no matter how good its intentions, can legislate that its population show love, joy, peace, patience, kindness, goodness, faithfulness, gentleness and self-control, for they constitute the fruit of the Holy Spirit. This fruit is evidenced only in the lives of Christians who strive with the Spirit's help to follow Christian teaching, and so, importantly, allow the sacred to balance the secular.

## From the garden to the cross

Luke records the Lord Jesus moving from Mount Olivet down into the city, cleansing the Temple, teaching and preaching in it and returning to the Mount to deliver the Olivet Discourse. Then He goes on to the Upper Room for the Passover feast, and from there to the Garden of Gethsemane, Pilate's judgment seat and thence outside the city gates to the cross.

By accepting His sinless Son's sacrificial death on our behalf, God's righteous law against sin was satisfied. At the cross justice and mercy kissed ("righteousness and peace", see Psalm 85:10). The old covenant was abolished and the new covenant, to be written in the hearts of men and women, was unveiled and established. Having disarmed the powers and authorities and accomplished the work His Father had sent Him to do, Jesus called out with a loud voice, "Father, into your hands I commit my spirit" (Luke 23:46). The price was paid; sin was defeated and in Christ's resurrection death lost its sting – and Satan knew he was beaten.

Luke recounts the wonder of the resurrection morning in 24:13–35.

He does so very differently from Matthew and Mark by adding an account of Cleopas and his companion (probably his wife).

The picture is of Cleopas and his companion, after the crucifixion, with tears in their eyes, shaking their heads in shocked disbelief as they retrace their steps along the seven miles from Jerusalem to Emmaus as if in retreat from some awful campaign defeat. Hearts heavy with unexpected loss and grief, they comfort each other as they talk about everything that happened. "I just don't understand how could it end this way? Do you remember when He asked Peter who we thought He was? And Peter answered for all of us by telling Him, 'You are the Christ, the Son of the living God!' And do you remember His answer? 'On this rock, I will build my church, and the gates of Hades will not overcome it!' Well, it looks as if they have, doesn't it? Things couldn't be worse! It's finished all right, and we are all in trouble!"

Then verse 15: "Jesus himself came up and walked along with them". And so began the life-transforming encounter brought about by a new understanding of Scripture: "He explained to them what was said in all the Scriptures concerning himself" (Luke 24:27).

Cleopas and his companion began their walk to Emmaus in disillusionment and despair. Their words in 24:21, "we had hoped that he was the one who was going to redeem Israel", are deeply moving. We sense their sorrow, their disappointed hopes, faded vision and loss of faith. But now their hearts are burning within them – and this is the point of the encounter. Knowledge of Jesus, who He is and what He has accomplished, comes through a new understanding of Scripture – and faith in Jesus and His message transforms lives, giving new meaning, purpose and hope. In verse 27 we see how it all comes together when the pieces begin to fall into place: "beginning with Moses and all the Prophets, he [Jesus] explained".

He explained the meaning of the great events of the Old Testament and showed how they all pointed to Him: the seed of the woman, the paschal Lamb, the scapegoat, the bronze snake, the blood on the lintel and the manna in the wilderness, the Temple, the Holy of Holies and the mercy seat, thirty pieces of silver, being despised and rejected, a man of sorrows acquainted with grief – and from Isaiah 53 and Psalm 22:

> *He was oppressed and afflicted,*
> *yet he did not open his mouth;*
> *he was led like a lamb to the slaughter,*
> *and as a sheep before her shearers is silent,*
> *so he did not open his mouth.*

ISAIAH 53:7

*I am poured out like water,*
*and all my bones are out of joint.*
*My heart has turned to wax;*
*it has melted away within me.*
*My strength is dried up like a potsherd,*
*and my tongue sticks to the roof of my mouth...*
*Dogs have surrounded me;*
*a band of evil men has encircled me,*
*they have pierced my hands and my feet.*
*I can count all my bones;*
*people stare and gloat over me.*
*They divide my garments among them*
*and cast lots for my clothing.*

PSALM 22:14B–18

*My God, my God, why have you forsaken me?*

PSALM 22:1

*He was pierced for our transgressions,*
*he was crushed for our iniquities;*
*the punishment that brought us peace was upon him,*
*and by his wounds we are healed.*

ISAIAH 53:5

*For he bore the sin of many,*
*and made intercession for the transgressors.*

ISAIAH 53:12

And Cleopas, heart burning and pounding within him, realized that these prophetic Scriptures from the Old Testament were what he had witnessed that very week in Jerusalem. What he thought was blackness and despair, the end of the story, was in truth victory and joy, and the beginning of something wonderful for the future of the human race. And this is the difference, a new realization that there is purpose and hope, that all is not lost. What looked like defeat was victory: it was God reconciling the men and women of planet Earth back to Him through the cross of His Glorious Son the Lord Jesus Christ.

That supper was never eaten, the stranger broke bread and handed it to them, and looking down at His offering they would have seen hands that were nail-pierced. "Then their eyes were opened and they recognized him" (Luke 24:31).

Luke brings his Gospel to a close with Jesus encouraging and motivating His transformed disciples into outward-looking apostles. In 24:46 they are given the biblical theology that underpins their Christian life. In verse 47 their future evangelistic programme is explained, and verse 48 confirms their apostolic authority. Finally, in verse 49, they are promised the resource of spiritual power from the indwelling presence of the Holy Spirit and in this way the new people of God are commissioned. For as the Son came into the world bringing His message of salvation, so His people are now to go out into the world bearing the same message.

# 43

# John
# – Jesus Son of God

In Matthew Jesus was the King, in Mark the Servant, in Luke the Son of Man, and now in the Gospel of John He is the Son of God. The focus of Jesus' origins is now not from Abraham through the royal line of David; or from Nazareth without genealogy; or from Adam without a father; instead Jesus is from eternity and from God. John's purpose is clear – to bring people to spiritual life through belief in Christ's person and work as the Son of God.

"In the beginning" (1:1) is deliberately used by John to invoke Genesis 1:1: "In the beginning". He is drawing a comparison by saying, "When the world was first called into being, the Lord Jesus Christ was existing; He had no beginning, He is eternal. He did not begin when born in Bethlehem's stable, nor even with His miraculous conception in Mary's womb, but before then the eternal Christ shared with God the Father and God the Holy Spirit in the work of creation." Colossians 1:16 tells us: "By [Jesus] all things were created: things in heaven and on earth, visible and invisible".

So, John's opening verses tell us of the life of Christ in eternity before the world was created: a life of purpose, rich and glorious, filled with unspeakable blessedness in the company of His Father and the Holy Spirit.

When we grasp this truth, the voluntary nature of His sacrifice in leaving His Father in heaven to become a man of flesh among sinful men and women on polluted planet Earth becomes truly wonderful. If you then think of Him going obediently to the cross and submissively allowing evil, ignorant men to nail His body there, then you join with John's statement in his old age: "How great is the love the Father has lavished on us, that we should be called children of God!" (1 John 3:1).

There were times of wonder and of reservation when, like us, the disciples asked, "Who is this man?" But so overwhelming and convincing was the evidence they saw and heard that when they reached the end of the story and John started to write down the recollections of those amazing days, he began by declaring the deity of Jesus: "In the beginning was the Word, and the Word was with God, and the Word was God" (John 1:1).

Many sects and false religions try to make out that the phrase "Son of God" means there was a distinctive difference between Jesus and God. But the Hebrews would never see it that way. To call someone "son" of something or someone was to say that they were identified with that thing or person. In Acts 4:36 Barnabas is called "Son of Encouragement", because he was that type of man – an encouraging kind of fellow. His nickname meant he was the very embodiment of encouragement. To the Hebrews the use of this term, "Son of God", meant "this One is God". That's why when our Lord used the term of Himself He was challenged by the unbelieving scribes and Pharisees who scathingly asked Him, "Who are you? What do you make yourself out to be? Why do you make yourself to be equal with God" (see John 5:18). Of course He did. That is what the title means.

By the time John was writing his Gospel, Matthew, Mark and Luke had written theirs, so in a sense John is writing to bring them all to a conclusion in the key verses 20:30–31:

> *Jesus did many other miraculous signs in the presence of his disciples, which are not recorded in this book. But these [that is these signs] are written that you may believe that Jesus is the Christ, the Son of God, and that by believing you may have life in his name.*

That is the two-fold purpose of the book: First, to present evidence that anyone in any age or in any place can fully believe that Jesus is the Christ (or, to use the Hebrew title, the Messiah, the Promised One), and second to show that He is the Son of God

# Jesus is the Christ

When people questioned the ministry of John the Baptist they asked him, "Are you the Christ?" He replied, "No, but He is coming after me." And when Jesus began to preach throughout Judea and Galilee people everywhere asked, "Is this the One? Is this the Messiah?" Jesus declared again and again that He was the Messiah, for example, John 10:1: 'I tell you the truth, the man who does not enter the sheep pen by the gate, but climbs in by some other way, is a thief and a robber."

The sheep pen was the nation of Israel. Jesus means there is one (Himself) who was to come by an approved way, by the door. If anyone comes in any other way he is a thief and a liar, but He who enters by the door, the approved opening, will be recognized as the Great Shepherd. He goes on in verse 3: "The watchman opens the gate for him". He is referring to the ministry of John the Baptist, who came as the opener of the door, the forerunner of the Messiah. Thus Jesus came as the One who was authorized, with the proper credentials.

If we look at these credentials of the Messiah alongside the seven miracle signs that John chose from the Lord's ministry, we see that they are chosen because they are the signs that prove Jesus is the Christ. This is seen in the order they appear in John's Gospel.

## 1. Jesus changes water into wine

The first miracle of our Lord was the changing of water into wine and signified the law being replaced by grace (2:1–11).

Each earthenware jar placed at the doorway of a house and used for washing and ceremonial cleansing held approximately 20–30 gallons of water. John was using what they represented in a broader context as an illustration of the old order of Jewish law and custom that Jesus was to replace with something much better. Without Jesus life is tasteless and flat but the miracle of new birth brings with it a joy indescribable. We are also meant to notice how the people did not have to do anything but believe: "Now draw some out" (2:8). That's all! Believe in faith! Grace is free! If there's anything Jesus wants everyone to understand it's this: God loves people simply because they are the people they are. Not for what they do for Him, but for what they are. That's why He treated people as He did. He forgave the girl caught in adultery, healed the untouchable leper who asked for cleansing, honoured the blind beggar who lay by the roadside, and healed the worn out exasperating man filled with self-pity by the pool of Siloam. It's an illustration of the great theme of the New Testament: grace replacing law.

## 2. The healing of the nobleman's son

The second sign is spiritual restoration (4:46–54). This is illustrated by the healing of a nobleman's son. The central figure in the story is not the son who lies sick at death's door, but the grief-struck official who came to the Lord "and begged [Jesus] to come and heal his son" (4:47). Jesus not only healed the son at a distance with a word, but healed the broken heart of a father. As he said, He was anointed to heal the broken-hearted.

## 3. The healing at the pool of Bethesda

The third sign of healing the invalid at the pool of Bethesda demonstrated His ability to set at liberty those who are oppressed (5:1–9).

The waters of the pool were popularly believed to possess curative powers. The traditional location of the pool is beneath the present site of the Church of Saint Anne on the northwest corner of Jerusalem and near the gate by the sheep market. Excavations have shown that it was surrounded by a colonnade on all four sides and down the middle of the pool making five "porches" in all.

Unable to get into the pool himself, this man had lain captive to a debilitating disease for thirty-eight years. He had been brought to that pool hoping to be healed, hoping to be set free, and our Lord singled him out of the great crowd of impotent folk and healed him: "Get up! Pick up your mat and walk" (5:8). Here Jesus demonstrated His ability to set at liberty those who are oppressed.

## 4. The feeding of the five thousand

In the fourth miracle Christ satisfied spiritual hunger (6:1–14).

The account of the feeding of the five thousand is a marvellous demonstration of the desire of the Lord to meet the deepest need of the human heart: man's hunger for God. He Himself had said, "Man does not live on bread alone, but on every word that comes from the mouth of God" (Matthew 4:4). Then He demonstrated what kind of bread He meant, "Then Jesus declared, 'I am the bread of life. He who comes to me will never go hungry, and he who believes in me will never be thirsty.' " (John 6:35).

## 5. Jesus walks on water

The fifth sign is the transformation of fear to faith (6:16–21).

A gale was blowing; the sea was rough and the disciples were terrified at the sight of Jesus walking towards them on the water. He calmed them by saying, "It is I; don't be afraid" (6:20). In the double miracle of the feeding of the five thousand and the walking on water there is a symbolic representation of our Lord's ability to satisfy the need of the human heart and deliver it from its greatest enemy, fear. This is wonderful news and a blessed assurance.

### 6. Jesus heals the man born blind

In the sixth miracle, bringing sight to the man born blind, Jesus demonstrated His ability to overcome darkness and bring light (9:1–12).

In Luke 4:18 our Lord said he came "to proclaim… recovery of sight for the blind". By physically healing a man who was blind from birth, Jesus demonstrated that though men and women are spiritually blind from birth, they can be healed.

### 7. The raising of Lazarus

The seventh and last miracle was the raising of Lazarus from the dead. It shows that the gospel brings people from death to life and that sickness and death do not have the last word (11:1–44).

By this miracle Jesus proved His claim and confirmed that the life He gives is nothing less than the indestructible life of the resurrection; the very life of the deathless God Himself.

Thus, by these seven signs John proves beyond question the first part of the key verses 20:30–31: Jesus is the Messiah, He is the expected One.

## Jesus is the Son of God

Jesus is not only the Christ, the Promised One: in the second part of the proclamation He is the Son of God. To prove that statement, John picks up seven great declarations of our Lord. He bases them all on the great name of God that was revealed when God spoke to Moses at the burning bush and said, "I AM WHO I AM" (Exodus 3:14). That is God's nature. That is, "I am exactly what I am. I am nothing more. I am nothing less. I am the eternal I am." Jesus' miracles proved He was the Messiah, the Promised One; His words attest to His divinity – He is God.

### 1. "I am the bread of life"

In 6:35, Jesus claimed to be the only permanent satisfaction for the yearning in the human spirit. To a society that has experimented to the point of saturation with every form of material, physical and spiritual palliative to fill the inner emptiness of the human heart, Jesus" invitation comes with wonderful relevance: "He who comes to me will never go hungry".

## 2. "I am the light of the world"

To follow Christ is to give one's body, soul and spirit in obedience to the Master – and as a result to walk in His light, hence "I am the light of the world" in 8:12. When we walk alone we are bound to stumble and fall, for so many of life's problems are beyond our solution. When we walk alone we are bound to take the wrong way because we have no secure chart for our lives. We need heavenly wisdom to walk the earthly way. The man or woman who has a sure guide and an accurate map is the person who is bound to arrive safely at their journey's end.

## 3. "I am the gate"

Through Him, and through Him alone, men and women find access to God. Until Jesus came we could think of God, at best, as a stranger and, at worst, an enemy. But Jesus came to show us what God is like and to open the way to Him. As Jesus said in 10:7: "I am the gate." He is the sole gate through whom entrance to God becomes possible for humankind.

## 4. "I am the good shepherd"

Verse 11 of chapter 10 emphasizes that in His self-sacrifice for His sheep, Jesus presents the true model for leadership. The aim of many leaders today is their own glory. Not properly loving those they lead, they use them as a means of obtaining their own satisfaction and self-advancement. It is the leadership of the hireling, not of the shepherd. Leadership, whether in political life, industry, commerce or community, follows one of two routes: either it is directed to the self-life of the leader, or it is directed selflessly for the good of those who are led. The former is the way of the world, which leads to death; the latter is the way of Jesus that leads to life.

## 5. "I am the resurrection and the life"

Jesus pronounces this in 11:25. He has revealed Himself as the giver of life in a number of ways. He offers the new spiritual life of the born-again to Nicodemus and the new life that springs up within a person, satisfying all spiritual thirst, to the Samaritan woman. Physically, He imparts life to a dying boy, a long-standing paralytic, a man born blind and, most tellingly of all, by raising Lazarus from the dead. Thus Jesus is the good shepherd who brings life to the full, a life which is nothing less than the indestructible life of the resurrection; the very life of the deathless God Himself.

## 6. "I am the way and the truth and the life"

John records Jesus as saying "I am the way and the truth and the life" in 14:6. If we asked for directions in a strange town and in reply were given an incomprehensible set of street turnings, the chances are we would soon be lost. But suppose the person asked said, "Come, I'll take you there." In that case the person is to us "the way", and we can't miss reaching our destination. That's what Jesus does for us. He not only gives advice and directions, He takes us by the hand and leads us; He strengthens us and guides us personally every day. He does not tell us about the way; He is the way.

Moral truth cannot be conveyed solely in words; it must be conveyed by example. An adulterer teaching the necessity of purity just doesn't ring true and will be found out for what he is because a person's character makes all the difference. And no one has ever fully embodied the truth they taught except Jesus. People can say, "I have taught you the truth", only Jesus could say, "I am the truth." The exceptional thing about Jesus is that not only does the statement of moral perfection find its ultimate in Him; it is that moral perfection finds its example in Him. In the final analysis men and women are always searching for life. Their search is not for knowledge for its own sake, but for what would make life worth living. A novelist makes one of his characters who has fallen in love say, "I never knew what life was until I saw it in your eyes." Love brought life. That's what Jesus does – life with Jesus is life indeed.

## 7. "I am the vine"

Finally, in pronouncing "I am the vine" (15:5), Jesus is saying that He alone is the producer of fruitfulness and the source of fellowship and communion.

In this way Jesus takes the identity of God and connecting it with these simple "I am" statements, enables us to understand God. John says:

> The Word became flesh and made his dwelling among us. We have seen his glory, the glory of the One and Only, who came from the Father, full of grace and truth.
>
> JOHN 1:14

That is the tremendous theme of this book. There is not a greater theme in the entire universe than the fact that this one who heals, loves, serves, waits, blesses, dies and rises again – this Jesus is God. That is what John reveals.

The one truth that John leaves with us, then, is that in believing that Jesus is the Messiah and that He is God, we may have life in His name. Jesus is the key to life.

This answers the age-old quest of the human race: to see fulfilled all the possibilities and potential that men and women sense lie deep within them. They want those deep yearnings satisfied: they want to be what they were designed and intended to be. That being the case, says John:

> These are written that you may believe that Jesus is the Christ, the Son of God, and that by believing you may have life in his name.
>
> JOHN 20:31

# 44

# Acts
## – Witnesses in Action

Christ's last words before His ascension, recorded in Acts 1:8, were so perfectly realized in the book of Acts that they effectively and concisely outline its contents:

> ... *you will be my witnesses in Jerusalem [chapters 1–7], and in all Judea and Samaria [chapters 8–12], and to the ends of the earth [chapters 13–28].*

The only Gentile writer in the New Testament, Luke, was a doctor by profession (Colossians 4:14). This means that Luke was an educated man well able to document and record the events of his day. We read in Acts that he travelled extensively with Paul, and being in Paul's company during the three stages of his journey from Jerusalem to Rome (recorded in Acts 27–28), would give Luke plenty of opportunities to hear and absorb Paul's teaching and write about his experiences.

Luke also impresses us as a historian. Covering a period of around thirty years, he takes us to and around the Middle East, while introducing us to a variety of cultures with all kinds of people. Court scenes in Caesarea, the Areopagus in Athens, kings and government officials – and his account of the shipwreck is still considered to be the classic and best historical account of a voyage of its kind ever recorded. Each archaeological discovery only serves to confirm that Luke uses the proper terms for the time and places being described.

But more importantly, to bring these vivid accounts to us, he interviewed eyewitnesses, some of whom would have known Jesus. It's most probable that he interviewed Mary the mother of Jesus, who, by Luke's time, would be an elderly woman. His account of the pregnancy, birth and growth of her firstborn son includes intimate details of the conception and is told from her viewpoint. Thus he must have gone back to her for the source of this information. Peter and John, Philip and the Lord's brother, James, all go back to the beginning of the ministry of Jesus. They, along with others, would have given Luke a first-hand account of the ascension, the day of Pentecost, the first sermon and the opposition from the Jewish authorities leading to the martyrdom of Stephen and resulting in the church breaking out from its Jewish background and growing into its Gentile future. This man, Luke, was there; he witnessed it for himself and spoke to others who were involved.

He begins his second volume, the book of Acts, where his first book, the Gospel of Luke left off. In Luke 24:46–49 we read:

> *This is what is written: The Christ will suffer and rise from the dead on the third day, and repentance and forgiveness of sins will be preached in his name to all nations, beginning at Jerusalem. You are witnesses of these things. I am going to send you what my Father has promised; but stay in the city until you have been clothed with power from on high.*

Moving forward to Acts 1:8, we then read: "you will receive power when the Holy Spirit comes on you; and you will be my witnesses in Jerusalem, and in all Judea and Samaria, and to the ends of the earth."

There we have the theme and purpose of the book of Acts – the story of the men and women who took the Great Commission seriously and began to spread the news of a risen Saviour to immediate friends and family, then further out to their neighbours and ultimately to the uttermost parts of the earth.

The book of Acts has four sections:

The coming of the Holy Spirit (chapters 1–2).

Evangelism and church growth in Jerusalem (chapters 3–7).

Witnesses in all Judea and Samaria (chapters 8–12).

To the ends of the earth (chapters 13–28).

# The coming of the Holy Spirit (Acts 2)

*All of them were filled with the Holy Spirit and began to speak*
*in other tongues as the Spirit enabled them.*

ACTS 2:4

As is told in Acts 2, on the day of Pentecost there was a new unity in the Spirit with the gift of communication. And this unity and the message to be communicated would not be stopped by race or language. That's why in verse 5 Luke emphasizes the cosmopolitan nature of the crowd: "Now there were staying in Jerusalem God-fearing Jews from every nation under heaven." This does not mean that every nation in the world was literally present, but that they were represented. Luke painstakingly records a list of who was there and it includes descendants from Noah's sons, Shem, Ham and Japheth. When we look at the various nations represented, we come to the conclusion that Luke in his own subtle way is telling us that on the day of Pentecost the United Nations were present. The message is that the kingdom of God is multiracial, multilingual and multinational.

To help us understand the miracle of Pentecost, it's best seen as a dramatic reversal of the curse of Babel. At Babel, as recorded in Genesis 11, God confused human communication by introducing different languages and scattering the nations into people groups. Now at Pentecost in Jerusalem the language barrier was supernaturally overcome and all present could hear in a language they could understand:

> *When they heard this sound, a crowd came together in*
> *bewilderment, because each one heard them speaking in his*
> *own language. Utterly amazed, they asked: "Are not all these*
> *men who are speaking Galileans? Then how is it that each of us*
> *hears them in his own native language?"*

ACTS 2:6–8

The symbolic significance is that now the nations would be gathered together in Christ, prefiguring that day the apostle John saw and recorded in Revelation 7:9:

> *After this I looked and there before me was a great multitude*
> *that no one could count, from every nation, tribe, people and*
> *language, standing before the throne and in front of the Lamb.*

At Babel, humankind, in their pride, attempted to reach heaven, whereas in Jerusalem on the day of Pentecost heaven humbly descended to earth.

With the disciples transformed and empowered by the Holy Spirit it was given to Peter to preach the first sermon of the New Testament church, and what a sermon it was! About 3,000 were added to the Christian church that day, and immediately we are led into the second section.

## Evangelism and church growth in Jerusalem

The next section spans chapters 3–7. Chapter 3 records how, after dramatically healing a man who was lame from birth, Peter delivers a second powerful message to the people of Israel resulting in thousands more converting to Christ. This upset the religious authorities; they had Peter and John arrested, giving Peter the opportunity to preach a special sermon to them in which he states the fundamental truth of Christianity: "Salvation is found in no one else, for there is no other name under heaven given to men by which we must be saved" (Acts 4:12).

Told to keep quiet about their faith, and under threat of their lives, the apostle's response is wonderful:

> *Now, Lord, consider their threats and enable your servants to speak your word with great boldness. Stretch out your hand to heal and perform miraculous signs and wonders through the name of your holy servant Jesus.*
>
> ACTS 4:29–30

It is significant that they did not pray for protection! On the contrary, what in essence they pray is, "Here we are in trouble and in danger of our lives, but this is great, Lord. Do it again." They are asking for more. And in response, God answered their prayer: "After they prayed, the place where they were meeting was shaken. And they were all filled with the Holy Spirit and spoke the word of God boldly" (Acts 4:31).

By shaking the place where they were praying, God is saying to them that He would shake Jerusalem and the world by the message the disciples were proclaiming. Less than forty years after this event the city of Jerusalem was surrounded by Roman armies and the authority of the priests was shaken: the religious theocracy of Israel was shaken and the people were dispersed throughout the nations of the world. Within two hundred years the Roman empire was shaken to its core as Christianity penetrated and permeated all strata of Roman society, transforming it and becoming the state religion of the empire in the fourth century AD.

However, it probably didn't look quite so wonderful when we see how in Acts 4:32 – 7:60 the early church discovered that the enthusiasm and joy brought by their phenomenal growth were also marred by internal and external problems. Internally, chapter 5 records how Ananias and Sapphira received the ultimate punishment due to their treachery, and in chapter 6 we see seven men being incorporated as deacons to assist the apostles. Externally, in chapter 7 we read how Stephen was brought before the Jewish Sanhedrin, and in his defence quoted from Old Testament Scriptures to prove that the man they tried and crucified was the Messiah Himself. Their angry reaction was to drag Stephen out of the city and stone him to death making him the first Christian martyr. So began the persecution of the Christians, which was to be the impetus to fulfil the second part of the Great Commission.

## Witnesses in Judea and Samaria

*On that day a great persecution broke out against the church at Jerusalem, and all except the apostles were scattered throughout Judea and Samaria.*

ACTS 8:1

The next section (chapters 8–12) regards the witnesses in Judea and Samaria. The persecution led to Philip going to Samaria and successfully preaching the gospel to a people hated by the Jews, and then to a high-ranking official of the Ethiopian government. What is truly remarkable is that despite their difference in racial origin, social class and religious belief, Philip presented them both with the same good news of Jesus.

Acts 9 then records the Damascus Road conversion of Saul of Tarsus transforming him into the apostle Paul. In Acts 10 Peter has a very special and personal vision leading him to the realization that God has broken down the barrier between Jew and Gentile, and after Cornelius and other Gentiles accepted Christ through his preaching, Peter convinces the Jewish believers in Jerusalem, "that the Gentiles also had received the word of God" (11:1).

Chapter 12 records an event that had particular significance: Peter's miraculous escape from prison. Here was the tiny emerging New Testament church facing persecution and extinction from powerful enemies of the gospel. The situation looked particularly bleak, even hopeless. What could a little community of Christians do in their powerlessness against the armed might of Rome and the religious power of Judaism? Yet, Luke wonderfully records the complete reversal of the church's situation. At the beginning of the chapter, Herod is on the rampage arresting and persecuting church leaders. In the end, he himself is struck down and dies. The chapter opens with James dead, Peter in prison and Herod triumphing. It closes with Herod dead, Peter free, and the word of God triumphing. Such is the power of God to overthrow hostile human plans and to establish His own in their place. Tormenters and persecutors may be permitted for a time to boast and bluster, to oppress the church and hinder the spread of the gospel, but they will not last. In the end, their power will be broken and their pride humiliated.

This should be an encouragement to all Christians who see their faith scorned and their church marginalized in an ungodly society.

# Section 4: To the ends of the earth

Here, in chapters 13–28, Luke has reached a decisive stage in the advance of the gospel. So far, in fulfilment of the prophecy in 1:8, the witnesses have preached Jesus in Jerusalem, Judea and Samaria. Now, as they accept the commission to take the gospel to the ends of the earth, Luke's focus switches from Peter to Paul and Antioch begins to replace Jerusalem as the headquarters of the Christian church. It is from there that all three of Paul's great missionary journeys begin. Now the world is to hear the good news.

## Paul's first missionary journey

Paul's first missionary journey is recorded in Acts 13:1 – 14:28. The journey concentrated on the Galatian cities of Pisidian Antioch, Iconium, Lystra and Derbe and covers the years c. AD 48–49. The staggering success of the mission in which so many Gentiles came to Christ raised eyebrows back in Jerusalem. Chapter 15 records how Paul and Barnabas were selected to return to Jerusalem to attend a council of apostles and elders, the outcome of which was the agreement that Gentile converts need not submit to the Law of Moses. With the burden of Jewish legalism lifted, the newly planted churches were encouraged and the Holy Spirit continued to bless the preaching of the Word with power, so that many more people were saved by grace alone.

## Paul's second missionary journey

The second journey (in 15:36 – 18:22) covers the years AD 50–52, when Paul again visited the Galatian churches. For the first time, he went on to Europe, visiting Macedonia and Greece and spending much of his time in the cities of Philippi, Thessalonica and Corinth before returning to Jerusalem and Antioch.

## Paul's third missionary journey

This journey covers the years AD 53–57 (see Acts 18:23 – 21:16). During this period Paul spent nearly three years in the Asian city of Ephesus before visiting Macedonia and Greece for the second time. Chapter 21 records the prophet Agabus warning Paul not to return to Jerusalem as his life was in grave danger. Verse 13 records Paul's reply: "Why are you weeping and breaking my heart? I am ready not only to be bound, but also to die in Jerusalem for the name of the Lord Jesus."

When you read the biblical account of these missionary journeys you hear of men and women living and dying for the Christian gospel. You read of bravery and courage, of suffering and despair, of prisons and beatings, stoning and lashing. During this period of his life Paul experienced hardships such as danger, cold, hunger, thirst and lack of sleep. Later he was shipwrecked, imprisoned and endured much more. We read in 2 Corinthians 4:8–9 that he is "hard pressed on every side, but not crushed; perplexed but not in despair; persecuted but not abandoned, struck down but not destroyed." However, astonishingly, he goes on to say in verses 16–17: "we do not lose heart... For our light and momentary troubles are achieving an eternal glory that far outweighs them all."

# Jerusalem, and on to Rome

Back in Jerusalem it is not long before Paul is falsely accused of bringing Gentiles into the Temple and only the intervention of the Roman commander saves Paul from being killed by the mob. His defence before the crowd and the Jewish Sanhedrin ended in uproar (chapters 21–23). A Roman commander, afraid the mob would tear Paul to pieces, removed him by force and held him in safety within the soldiers' barracks. Acts 23:11 records the Lord speaking to Paul, strengthening him and assuring him that he would testify about Jesus in Rome. Then the commander, learning of a conspiracy to assassinate Paul, sent him as a prisoner to Governor Felix in Caesarea. During his two-year period there, AD 57–59, Paul defended the Christian faith before the governors of Judea – Felix and his successor Festus – and King Agrippa and his companion Bernice. Agrippa decided that as Paul was a Roman citizen he should be sent to Rome and stand trial before the emperor.

So the scene is set for Paul's epic voyage to Rome.

By any account Acts 27 is a remarkable chapter. Naval architects and nautical historians regard Luke's account of the events leading up to the shipwreck as the classic description of a ship going through a severe storm, being driven onto the rocks and breaking apart, with the crew and passengers having to abandon ship and head for the shore and safety through the pounding waves. But the amount of space given to this incident raises the question, "Why did Luke spend so much time recording Paul's journey to Rome?" The answer is, to underline the importance of the providence of God.

In Ephesians 1:11 we are told that "In him we were also chosen, having been predestined according to the plan of him who works out everything in conformity with the purpose of his will".

And God who calls us to His plan and purpose for us says: "There is no wisdom, no insight, no plan that can succeed against the Lord" (Proverbs 21:30).

But even more, much more, God can, and will even work through evil and transform it for the good of those who love Him (Romans 8:28).

Paul knew the going would be difficult and that danger lay ahead. God's men and women have always known that. But they have a burning desire and an inner assurance. The big truth in this account is not that Paul said, "I must visit Rome" (Acts 19:21) but that Jesus had said to him, "you must also testify in Rome" (23:11). Paul experienced what he had long known to be true both from the doctrine of God's Word and from his experience of God's dealings with him: namely, that whatever happens to us in life falls within the purpose of God. No storm, no shipwreck, no snake bite, no Sanhedrin, no riotous mobs, no murderous threats – nothing, but nothing, could separate him from the love of God, nor thwart God's plan and purpose for him (see Romans 8:37–39). And this is as true today for believing Christian men and women as it was in the days of Acts.

After the shipwreck, Paul spent three months introducing Christianity to the people on the island of Malta before setting sail once more. On arriving in Italy, the final lap of the journey was on foot, and Paul's heart must have been bursting with emotion as he walked the famous Appian Way that led straight to Rome. Christians from there, on hearing of his coming, set out the thirty-three miles to meet him and were waiting at the Three Taverns Inn, while others pressed on a further ten miles to the market town called the Forum of Appius.

It must have been emotional for Paul to meet personally the first Christians from the city he had so longed to visit and to whom he had addressed his first great theological paper – his letter to the Romans. It's not surprising at the sight of them he was encouraged and thankful to God (28:15). They escorted him along the Appian Way and Paul finally arrived in Rome (AD 60–61), where he settled in his own lodgings, though remaining under house arrest until his trial and execution. Speaking of his time in prison Paul refers to the spread of the gospel to the Roman guards and maintains that this was part of the purposes of God in sending him to Rome (Philippians 1:12–13). And significantly, even though he was a prisoner, Paul never failed to recognize all things worked in the purposes of God even when they appeared unfavourable – he still saw the help that comes from God (see Acts 26:22).

The Acts of the Apostles finished long ago, but the acts of the followers of Jesus will continue until the end of the world, and their words will spread to the ends of the earth.

# 45

# Romans
## – The Way of Salvation

Paul's letter to the Romans is a type of Christian manifesto and is commonly thought to be the greatest of Paul's epistles.

Although the Roman church was destined to become one of the major centres of Christendom, next to nothing is known about the circumstances surrounding its planting and early history. Paul does not write about these things because he had not founded or even visited the church at Rome. However, from his writings we can determine two main points.

First, Paul's future plans.

It's spring, AD 58, and Paul, resting in Corinth after his third missionary journey, is turning his attention to the remote regions of the West where the gospel had never been preached (see Romans 15:24). For this campaign he would need the backing and support of the large, influential church in Rome and, while they would have heard about Paul, they did not know him personally. His letter would introduce the man and his message.

Second, the constant criticism and personal attacks Paul received resulted in some of the most meaningful revelations found in the New Testament.

Paul received constant criticism and personal attacks from the Judaizers who followed him around the Roman empire attempting to subvert the churches he founded by teaching new converts that the Law of Moses must be included in the gospel. They also maligned Paul's character, so knowing they would rush to Rome as soon as they heard about his plans, his letter to the Roman Christians offers a statement of his true teaching. The fact that hostility and criticism caused Paul to write some of the most meaningful revelations found in the New Testament must not be lost on us. God's method has not changed: some of our clearest and deepest insights into the plan and purpose of God for our lives will often come to us out of the heartaches life's circumstances force upon us.

This all means that this letter is not a tract to be put into the hands of someone in order that they might be saved, rather it is to be put into the hands of Christian men and woman in order that they may know how they have been saved.

The letter breaks down into three main sections:

The revelation of God's righteousness (chapters 1–8).

God's great plan of salvation (chapters 9–11).

Living the Christian life (chapters 12–15).

# 1. The revelation of God's righteousness

The revelation of God's righteousness appears in chapters 1–8. It is important to remember that when Paul uses the word "righteousness" he means a right relationship with God. So the person who is righteous is the person who is in a right relationship with God and whose life shows it.

In Romans 1:17 Paul states:

> *For in the gospel a righteousness from God is revealed, a righteousness that is by faith from first to last, just as it is written: "The righteous will live by faith."*

That's Paul's theme – the righteousness of God that is revealed in the gospel. To establish the need for this, Paul looks at the world around him and from verse 18 of chapter 1 through chapter 2 and most of chapter 3, he brings before us the human race which he divides into three groups: immoral pagan society (1:18–32); critical moralizers whether Jews or Gentiles (2:1–16); and well-taught, self-assured Jews (2:17 – 3:8). He then concludes by accusing the whole human race (3:9–20).

He starts with the unrighteous and reveals an astounding truth: "The wrath of God is being revealed from heaven against all the godlessness and wickedness of men who suppress the truth by their wickedness" (Romans 1:18).

"Suppressing the truth" tells us that the trouble with men and women is not that they do not know God exists and don't know the difference between right and wrong, they do know, but they don't want to know, and so they suppress the truth.

In 1:19–20 Paul says that creation bears clear witness to its maker and the evidence of a Creator is "plain to them". This is termed "natural revelation" as opposed to "special revelation" which comes through the Scriptures. Natural revelation happens "naturally", when men and women look at the awesome display of the stars in the sky, at the beauty of a flower or the wonder of a newborn baby, and instinctively they know that there is a Creator. Their reaction should be to ask questions that would ultimately lead them to their Creator, Jesus Christ. But, and this is Paul's point, men and women have deliberately refused to accept the truth before them and are therefore left without excuse.

This has enormous consequences for the human race, and the reason is, because of their suppression of God's truth, the wrath of God is continuously pouring itself out upon humankind. That wrath is described for us as this chapter develops, and it turns out not to be lightning bolts from heaven flung at wicked people who step out of line, but rather God, in effect saying to humankind, "Look, I don't want you to do a certain thing because it will damage and destroy you, but if you insist upon doing it, you may, but you will have to accept the consequences. You can't make a choice to live wrongly and still avoid the consequences that come from that choice."

Three times in chapter 1 the wrath of God is indicated in the repeated phrase "God gave them up". This raises the question: "How does God give men over to the sinful desires of their hearts?" The answer is that He does so by simply removing His restraining hand from them. This allows men and women to respond to temptation and desire by doing whatever the natural inclination of their hearts leads them to do. And as all humankind is sinful and biased towards sin as a result of the fall, they will make selfish, sin-motivated choices.

If men and women cry out against spiritual light, God judges them by removing it and leaving them in spiritual darkness. The result is that instead of reaching the heights, they plumb the depths. Instead of securing liberty and freedom, they chain and bind themselves to bad habits, lust and base emotions as they remove themselves from the divine protection which is the only force that can guard them from corruption and degradation. The progression and ever-increasing intensity in these verses reveals how sin is not an unsubstantial entity, but a certain, malignant reality. The progression is from emptiness and futility of thinking, to pride and foolishness, which leads to idolatry and sensuality, and on to harmful behaviour with its unnatural vices and complete depravity (verses 26–27). And verses 29–31 tell us the result:

> They have become filled with every kind of wickedness, evil, greed and depravity. They are full of envy, murder, strife, deceit and malice. They are gossips, slanderers, God-haters, insolent, arrogant and boastful; they invent ways of doing evil; they disobey their parents; they are senseless, faithless, heartless, ruthless.

That is the condition of the defiant people who display their enmity towards God and their suppression of the truth of God by flagrantly disobeying Him. They observe no standard, live as they please and do what they like. The result is moral decay and perversion. Even the sexual drive becomes perverted so that men give themselves to men and women to women, as this chapter describes. This is exactly what is taking place in society today where men and women live in open rebellion against God.

However, that's not the full story for not all of society lives like that.

In chapter 2 Paul turns the spotlight onto the so-called "moral" Jews who by this time are happily pointing the finger at those living in open and vile wickedness. Paul says to them:

> You, therefore, have no excuse, you who pass judgment on someone else, for at whatever point you judge the other, you are condemning yourself, because you who pass judgment do the same things.

> ROMANS 2:1

Then he shows how this is true by revealing that the people who say, "We don't do these things", are equally as guilty of breaking God's Law as the others.

True, they may not indulge in sexual immorality or drunkenness or the like, but they, too, are guilty of some of the things on the list above as fully as those who do the more open things. They indulge in malice, strife and deceit, they gossip and slander and so forth. They, too, are insolent, arrogant and boastful; they are senseless, faithless, heartless and ruthless. They may cover these things by an external appearance of being good, but inside their hearts are as filled with malignity, envy, jealousy, strife and evil against one another as are the others.

By way of response, the religious self-confident Jew enters the argument and says, "What about me? After all, I am a Jew; I live by the law and have certain advantages before God." Paul examines this claim and shows that the religious Jew is in exactly the same boat as everybody else. Despite his advantages, he is filled with the same kind of heart-enmity as the others, for despite their self-righteous protestations they do not obey the Law nor believe the oracles of God (3:1–8).

The divine verdict is universal (3:9–20), "for all have sinned and fall short of the glory of God" (3:23). It is God's picture of the human race: "You are all guilty! There is no difference." So Paul's conclusion is that all of humankind stands, without exception, in need of a Redeemer.

How we are saved.

The progressive stages in salvation are regeneration, faith, repentance, justification, sanctification and glorification.

The route leading to a person's salvation begins with regeneration, that is, a God-given awareness of personal sin and guilt. Then we are given the gift of faith to believe that on the cross Jesus Christ died for our sins and paid the price we should have paid, by dying the death that we deserve to die. This stage in the salvation process is followed by personal repentance of our sin and evidenced by a deep desire to turn away from the old lifestyle associated with it, and embrace the new life being offered by Christ. Next comes justification, for at this point God then "justifies" us. That is, He declares us innocent before Him and removes the barrier that exists between human beings in their natural state and God. Justification is far more than forgiveness of sin, although it includes that: it is to be in a position before God as though we never had sinned at all. It is Christ's righteousness imputed to us, reckoned to our account. When this takes place we are delivered from the penalty for sin and born again. We could never do this for ourselves for we are totally incapable of pleasing God apart from this change that occurs in the heart. It makes no difference whether we live moral, respectable lives or kick over the traces and live sin-filled lives. Both lives are to some extent or another guilty of sin. Therefore, the only way righteousness can come to us is by accepting the gift of God in Jesus Christ, and everything else in the Christian life flows from this. Paul illustrates this in chapter 4 with Abraham and David, who were both justified on this basis and not by circumcision, by obeying the law or by any of the things that men do in their attempts to please God. Abraham looked forward and saw the coming of Christ, believed God and he was justified by faith. David, although he was guilty of the twin sins of adultery and murder, believed God and was justified. Thus these men are examples from the Old Testament of how God justifies.

Unfortunately, many Christians stop right there. They think that this is all salvation is about – a way to escape hell and get to heaven. But there is more to the human life than the spirit; there is also the soul and the body, and, beginning in chapter 5, Paul sets forth for us the way God works to deliver the soul – our mind, our emotions and our will.

Even though we are regenerated and justified in God's sight, and although perfect in terms of our standing before God, we are far from perfect in our actual thoughts and conduct. Sanctification aims to close this gap and does so through the indwelling presence of the Holy Spirit leading, guiding and changing us into a likeness of Jesus. Though we are free from the penalty of sin, over time increasingly we can be free from the power of sin and ultimately prepared to be free from the presence of sin and receive our glorification.

In chapter 5 Paul outlines the whole programme.

He takes these two basic categories of humankind: man in Adam and man in Christ, puts them side-by-side and says, "Look, when you were a man in Adam (that is, before you became a Christian) you acted on the basis of the life that you had inherited from Adam: you did things naturally, and what you did naturally was wrong – it was self-centred. But when you become a Christian, God does something to that old life: He cuts you off from it. You are no longer joined to fallen Adam but are now joined to a risen Christ, and your life is now linked with Him. He plans now to express His life through you in the same natural way as Adam once expressed his life through you. What you experienced of defeat, misery, heartache, bondage and blindness in Adam will be exceeded much more by what you will experience of victory, glory, blessing, peace and joy in Christ. When, with God's help, you learn to think biblically, it starts to become as natural to be good in Christ as it was to be bad in Adam. It may take you quite a while to really see what Paul is talking about, but when you do, you will discover that where once sin reigned over you unto death, Christ is now reigning over you unto life. Now, in this life, you can begin to experience victory in Christ where once you experienced only defeat in Adam. Yes, of course, some battles are more easily won than others, and some may never be put to rest this side of glory, but as the Christian matures in his relationship and understanding of Christ, so more and more victory over the world, the flesh and the devil is assured.

Chapter 6 begins to show us how.

In verses 1–14 Paul, sixteen times, in various ways, explains deliverance from the overwhelming power and dominion of sin through the process of sanctification by which the Christian believer grows into spiritual maturity in Christ. This is wonderful news for Christians. In justification God breaks the power of sin to condemn us, and then in sanctification He breaks the power of sin to control us! This is what many Christians have not experienced – freedom from the past and victory over personal sin. They have to learn that what is potential in the initial experience of salvation must be appropriated to their needs in order to meet the power of sin and defeat it in actual daily experience. It is this secret of victory, the practice of actually experiencing death to the power of the old nature, that Paul is referring to in these verses. The key, in fact and symbol, is baptism! The baptism God does seals us as a believer and the baptism that we do identifies us as one.

In chapter 7 Paul speaks of our inner struggle.

This is the warfare between our old Adamic nature and our new Christian nature, between the flesh and the spirit: "I do not understand what I do. For what I want to do I do not do, but what I hate I do. And if I do what I do not want to do, I agree that the law is good" (Romans 7:15–16).

This leads to verse 24: "What a wretched man I am! Who will rescue me from this body of death?"

We can hear the anguish of Paul's soul as he wrestles with himself, and we can identify with him. How do we solve this? The answer is in 7:25 – 8:3. We have to learn that the victory over temptation, the urge to sin and breaking addictive habits, cannot be won by our strength alone – we need God's help. Then, our resolve and faith put into action, plus God's underpinning power, is the way we win the battles.

A real-life example of this power in action is given in my testimony book, *I Did It His Way*, under the heading "Battling the Last Addiction":

> *I was still a heavy cigarette smoker. I knew intellectually that I should stop for my health's sake and I disliked the thought of being dependent on anything other than Jesus. But having failed to stop smoking many times in the past I was reluctant to make another attempt. We were planning a holiday at the Keswick Christian Convention in the company of other church families. I knew I would be expected to climb the surrounding Lakeland hills and would not be able to do so unless I stopped smoking. So, bearing in mind my many, many failed attempts, I spoke directly to God. "Lord," I said, "I sense You want me to stop smoking and I want to, but I know I lack the strength to make it happen, but You don't. You have already proved this by removing my addiction to alcohol and radically changing my lifestyle. So here's what I'll do Lord: tomorrow morning I will not buy cigarettes as I usually do. And providing I have*

*no craving I will never buy cigarettes. But if I have that awful*
*nerve-end craving I will not fight it, for I know I will be unable*
*to resist buying cigarettes." I said, "Lord, I am not being*
*presumptuous, but if I have to fight the craving in my own*
*strength it's foolish, for I know you have the power to do it for*
*me!" The following morning I went to work, didn't stop to buy*
*cigarettes, and have never experienced a craving for tobacco*
*since that day.*

One victory over one part of our fallen nature does not automatically mean
victory over every other part, but it does point the way and gives wonderful
confirmation that we can, by God's help, increasingly become free from the sin
that entangles us.

In chapter 8 Paul deals with the body. He explains that while we are still
in this life the body remains unredeemed, but the fact that the spirit (that part
of us that connects us to God) has been justified and the soul (that part of us
that makes our character and personality) is being sanctified is a guarantee that
God will one day redeem, that is, glorify, the body (our recognizable physical
being) as well. When we enter at last into the presence of Christ, we shall stand
– body, soul and spirit – perfect before Him: "those he predestined, he also
called; those he called, he also justified; those he justified, he also glorified"
(Romans 8:30).

That line of thought erupts into a tremendous climax of praise at the close
of chapter 8, which promises that nothing – but nothing – can separate us from
the love of God:

*Who dares accuse us whom God has chosen for His own? Will*
*God? No! He is the one who has forgiven us and given us a*
*right standing with Himself. Who then will condemn us? Will*
*God? For He is the one who died for us and came back to life*
*again for us and is sitting at the place of highest honour next*
*to God, pleading for us there in heaven. Who then can ever*
*keep Christ's love from us? When we have trouble or calamity,*
*when we are hunted down or destroyed, is it because He doesn't*
*love us any more? And if we are hungry, or penniless, or in*
*danger, or threatened with death, has God deserted us? No,*
*for the Scriptures tell us that for His sake we must be ready to*
*face death at every moment of the day, we are to be like sheep*
*awaiting slaughter. But despite all this, overwhelming victory*

*is ours through Christ who loved us enough to die for us. For
I am convinced that nothing can ever separate us from His
love. Death can't, and life can't. The angels won't, and all the
powers of hell itself cannot keep God's love away. Our fears
for today, our worries about tomorrow, or where we are, high
above the sky, or in the deepest ocean, nothing will ever be able
to separate us from the love of God demonstrated by our Lord
Jesus Christ when He died for us.*

ROMANS 8:33–39, THE LIVING BIBLE

## 2. God's great plan of salvation

This theme can be found in chapters 9–11. In chapter 9 Paul answers many of
the questions that naturally arise from his teaching in the first eight chapters,
including the paradoxical fact that while human beings seem to have free will,
God in His sovereignty chooses whom He wishes to save. We tend to think of
ourselves as being in a neutral condition before God and depending upon how
we live or act, or what choices we make, we will either fall off and be lost or
go on to be saved. But this is not the case. This chapter explains that the entire
human race is already lost, lost in Adam; we were born into a lost race. We lost
our right to be saved in Adam when he sinned, and we have no rights before
God at all. Therefore, it is only God's grace that saves any of us. No one has
any right to complain to God if some are saved when none have any right to be
saved. Thus Paul sets before us in a most powerful way the sovereign power
and choice of God.

He gets into his argument at verse 13, where he quotes the prophet
Malachi: "I loved Jacob, but Esau I hated." We need to remember that the word
"hate" means "not prefer" as used by Jesus in Luke 14:26 when He talks of us
needing to hate our families, that is, make the conscious decision to prefer Jesus
over our families, and in the context of family life in the time of Jesus it will
seem that we hate them.

First, we should note that the Bible and human history show us that it is
a fact that God preferred Jacob to Esau. The Bible takes us through the story of
these two men from Genesis 28, and it is painfully obvious that God's mercy
followed Jacob all the days of his life right up to the very end, but it is equally
obvious that His mercy did not follow Esau. He allowed Esau to continue in his
chosen path of sin and so prove this dreadful text, "Esau I hated".

So, why did God love Jacob? The answer lies in scriptures like Ezekiel 36:32

which tell us that the way God dealt with the nation of Israel and with selected individuals like Jacob was not because of some good thing in them or because they deserved it. No, it is sovereign grace. There was nothing in Jacob that made God love him. In fact, there was much that deserved the "hate" that Esau received, and we are forced to the only conclusion that God chose Jacob as an object of His love. Jacob confirms this on his deathbed where he testifies God has been his Shepherd all his life, and the angel who delivered him from all harm (see Genesis 48:15–16). When you look at his life, and the continuing love of God upon it, you are forced to confess that there is no reason other than that God so chose it to be. He will have mercy on whom He chooses to have mercy (see Exodus 33:19; Romans 9:15) and the same truth applies to each individual today. There is no reason for God to save any of us except the mercy of God's own heart.

This begs the question: "Why did God hate Esau?" The only satisfactory answer to the question, "Why does God 'hate' someone", is because the person deserves it. We cannot imagine that God creates some men and women for the sole intention of damning them; that's monstrous and does not reflect on the character of Jesus. However, we can say the reason that God loves a man is because God chooses to do so. There is no reason within the man, that's what we have proved in the life of Jacob. But we cannot give the same answer as to why God hates a man. If God hates a man, then the man deserves it. In hell there will not be one soul who can say that God has been unfair to him and he has received more punishment than he deserves. Everyone in hell will understand his damnation is his responsibility, and God has nothing to do with his condemnation except as a judge rightly condemning a criminal. He himself by his actions and the decisions he has made when alive has brought himself into guilt and sentence after his death.

The key to all of this lies in the character of Esau.

If we ask the question, "Did he deserve that God should hate him?" the answer is, "Yes!" Hebrews 12:16 tells us that Esau was godless. In Genesis 25:27 we are told "Esau became a skilful hunter", and a glance at a concordance quickly shows that the word "hunter" is generally found within an evil context. In Scripture, only Nimrod and Esau are specifically termed hunters, and the fact that Esau's name is linked with Nimrod's reveals his true character. Link this with the next part of verse 27, which tells us, he was "a man of the open country" (other versions more accurately say, "a man of the field"), and when you remember that Jesus in Matthew 13:38 compared the field to the world, you have a picture of Esau as a "man of the world". Genesis 25:29 supplies the confirmation, when Esau comes in from it (the world) unsatisfied. The world couldn't satisfy him then, any more than it can satisfy the men and women of the world today. The insatiable desire for more, for new, for better, possessions, husbands or wives is still present. And in verse 32 Esau is the spokesman for the men and women throughout history when he says to his brother Jacob, "Don't talk to me about the future: about life after death!" That's what he's saying to Jacob, He couldn't care less about the blessings of Abraham. He's saying, "Look Jacob, the time's coming when I am going to be dead. And what good to me then are the promises of God to Abraham and his seed? I'm not living on promises, I'm going to eat and drink and make merry, I couldn't care less about life after death."

Who do we blame for Esau's decision?

Did God make him do it or influence him to do it? No way! God is not the author of sin. Esau voluntarily gave up his own birthright, and the Bible's doctrine is that every man and woman who loses heaven and everlasting life in the company of King Jesus does so because they have given it up and rejected Him who loved them. God does not deny it to them; they will not come to Jesus that they might have life in all its fullness. And they cannot use the argument that if they're meant to be saved they will be saved, so there's not much point in doing anything about it. The teaching of the New Testament rejects that sophisticated reasoning by reminding us that the onus is on us to seek and we will find and knock and it will be opened to us (Matthew 7:7–8) – inactivity will not be blessed and accepted as an excuse. Chapter 10 of Romans reminds us that the reason people will go to hell is because they have refused to believe in Christ as their Saviour, for no one has or will ever come to Him for forgiveness of sins and eternal life and be turned away. Our Lord Jesus said: "All that the Father gives me will come to me, and whoever comes to me I will never drive away" (John 6:37).

Chapter 10 also shows that no one could ever accuse Paul of not caring about the conversion of his own people.

So just what was the obstacle for the Jew in Paul's day? It was religious zeal without knowledge and legalistic law without life. Paul's argument is that where the Gentiles had exchanged the truth about God for a lie (Romans 1:25), the Jews had exchanged the righteousness of God for a system of works that they added on to the Ten Commandments. The result, as Jesus observed in Matthew 23:1–4, was that the nation was swamped with religious dos and don'ts. And far from the religious leaders viewing the Lord as the fulfilment and thereby the end of the Law, they didn't perceive the Law as ever coming to an end (Romans 10:4). The concept of Christ crucified heralding the fulfilment of the Law baffled the Jews. Terms hallowed in Christian thought, such as

"Suffering Servant", "Crucified Messiah" and the "Lamb of God slain before the foundation of the world", were, and are, an offence to them, and that means they cannot enter into the righteousness which Christ alone offers.

In verses 9–10 Paul explains what we have to do to be saved.

Jesus said in Luke 12:8–9: "whoever acknowledges me before men, the Son of Man will also acknowledge him before the angels of God. But he who disowns me before men will be disowned before the angels of God."

This is of vital importance. Luke 23:39–43 gives the biblical example of a man becoming a Christian in the closing moments of his life: the thief on the cross. His public confession that he deserved to be there is his recognition of sin. And when he asked Jesus to remember him when He comes into His kingdom, he is displaying saving faith in line with Romans 10:9. Inward belief and outward confession belong together. This is not salvation by slogan but a declaration of belief that Jesus died for our sins, was raised from the grave and exalted, and now reigns as Lord, bestowing salvation upon all who believe in Him.

## Israel's future

Romans 9 and 10 explain why many Jews have failed to accept Jesus Christ as their Messiah: God has not chosen them and they have not chosen Him. God never promised to save every individual offspring of Abraham though He has made promises concerning the nation Israel as a whole. What of these promises? Were they not to be honoured? Were God's dealings with the nation of Israel throughout its history an exercise in futility? Are we to conclude, as some theologians teach, that God has no programme for Israel as a nation, distinct from the church? Here in Romans 11, Paul argues that the rejection of God in Christ by the Jews was neither total nor final – that there is still an Israelite Christian in the present, and there is going to be an Israelite Christian recovery in the future which will lead to blessings for the whole world.

It is important that we understand that when we talk about Israelite or Jewish restoration we do not mean a Jewish religious state such as present-day Israel becoming a Jewish superpower. We are talking here of Jews converting to Christianity in Israel. Christians are not interested in the restoration of Solomon's Temple, animal sacrifice and all the rest of the Old Testament ritual. The writer of the book of Hebrews makes it crystal clear that all of that is finished: the one full and final sacrifice has been made by Jesus Christ at Calvary (see Hebrews 9). Thus we are looking forward to Jews converting to Christianity, and that's what Paul is talking about here.

In Romans 11:1 Paul goes straight to the heart of the matter, and in verse 2 he emphatically states, "God did not reject his people". He then brings in his evidence to prove his belief. The first is personal: if a fanatical Jew like Paul could be made to do a spiritual about face and become a Christian, surely there is hope for Israel. His second point in verse 2a is theological: Israel has hope for a bright future because God foreordained in eternity past to create a nation on which He would bestow special privileges and blessings and this cannot be revoked. Thirdly, in verses 2b–6, Paul presents biblical evidence. He makes the point that Israel's present situation can be likened to that in Elijah's day, meaning that God has always kindled the fires of Israel's hope by maintaining a faithful remnant through whom He can fulfil His promises. Paul's fourth piece of evidence in verse 5 was contemporary. Just as in Elijah's day there was a believing remnant of 7,000, so too in Paul's day there was a remnant – and it was probably quite sizeable, for James was to tell Paul that there were many thousands of Jews who had converted to Christianity (Acts 21:20).

Well then, what about the rest of the Jewish people? Summing up the matter in Romans 10:7–10, Paul says that Israel as a Jewish nation failed to arrive at that for which they sought, but those who were chosen by grace obtained salvation and the rest, the Israelite majority, were hardened by God. This is the only explanation of why Israel failed, and still fails, to see what is so patently obvious – God has spiritually blinded them.

The big question about the future of the Jewish nation begins to be answered by Paul in verse 11a, where he asks and answers his second question: "Again I ask: Did they stumble so as to fall beyond recovery? Not at all!" Paul is saying that the Jewish nation's fall, which in the first paragraph he has proved was not total, is not final either. On the contrary, they haven't fallen beyond recovery but rather to rise, and in rising they would cause the Gentiles to experience greater blessings than would have been the case if they had not fallen in the first place. So, astonishingly, behind Israel's rejection of Jesus, we see God's grand plan for the human race, and Paul, elaborating in verse 12 says that just as the world was greatly blessed by the Jews" rejection of the gospel, so the world will be even more blessed when the Jews are converted in great numbers to Christianity.

## 3. Living the Christian life

A discussion of the Christian life appears in chapters 12–15. As behaviour must be built upon belief, Paul's practical exhortations appear after his teaching on the believer's position in Christ.

In chapter 12 Paul lays down the ethical character of the Christian faith, and verses 1–2 encapsulate the gospel imperative that Christian men and women must honour God at all times through lives that are lived in keeping with His will. In other words, worship is the way Christians live, not just what they do on Sundays: "Therefore, I urge you, brothers, in view of God's mercy, to offer your bodies as living sacrifices, holy and pleasing to God – this is your spiritual act of worship" (Romans 12:1).

One of the greatest dangers facing Christians is the temptation to compartmentalize their lives and show their spirituality only on certain occasions, for example Sunday worship. This is dangerously wrong. We should give God thanks for what we eat: our conversation at the dinner table should be honouring to Him. Our attitude in the work place should bring honour to Him whose name we bear. Our leisure activities should be Christ-honouring. In other words, every aspect of our public and private lives should bring honour to the name of Christ. And as a result, as the reminder of this chapter and chapter 13 make clear, we will find our lives being changed in all of our relationships, both Christian and secular.

Chapters 14 and 15 deal with an ever-recurring problem.

In the church there was a narrow-minded group who believed that they must abstain from certain food and drink, and who regarded special days and ceremonies as of great importance. Paul thinks of them as the weaker brethren because they believed that their faith was dependent on these external things; what we might call the dos and the don'ts. There was another group who had liberated themselves from these external rules and observances, and Paul thinks of them as the brethren stronger in the faith. He makes it quite clear that his sympathies are with the more "broad-minded" group, but lays down the principle that even so, no one must ever do anything to hurt the conscience of the weaker brother or sister or cause them to stumble in their faith. Paul's point is that Christians must not do anything that makes it harder for someone to be a Christian, and that might mean the giving up of something that is right and safe for us theologically, for the sake of the weaker brother or sister. Christian liberty must never be used in such a way that injures another believer's conscience. An obvious example would be abstaining from alcohol in the presence of a reformed alcoholic. There is no scriptural reason for us not to drink, but if enjoying our liberty causes our weaker brother to stumble, then we should refrain.

Chapter 16 brings Paul's letter to a close.

The letter concludes with a series of personal greetings, a final admonition (verses 1–24), and a doxology (verses 25–27), which is a fitting way to bring this overview to an end:

> *Now to him who is able to establish you by my gospel and the proclamation of Jesus Christ, according to the revelation of the mystery hidden for long ages past, but now revealed and made known through the prophetic writings by the command of the eternal God, so that all nations might believe and obey him – to the only wise God be glory forever through Jesus Christ! Amen.*

# 46

# 1 Corinthians
# – A Church Letter for Today

On his second missionary journey, the apostle Paul founded the church in Corinth (see Acts 18).

Situated on a narrow strip of land, Corinth was a strategic centre for commerce by land and sea, and had become the most important city in Greece. As is often the case, thriving commerce led to thriving immorality, and Corinth took depravity to new depths. If you want to know what Corinth was like, read Romans 1:18–32 which Paul wrote to the Romans from Corinth. Dated AD 57, 1 Corinthians was written five years after his first visit, and its purpose was to correct serious doctrinal and moral sins of Christian living in and out of church life. These errors included incest, adultery and other acts of sexual immorality (1 Corinthians 5); un-Christian actions in taking fellow Christians to court (1 Corinthians 6); misuse of Christian liberty (1 Corinthians 8 and 10); disorders in observing the Lord's Supper (1 Corinthians 11:17–34); disorders in the worship service (1 Corinthians 14); and false views of the resurrection of Christ and the resurrection of the body (1 Corinthians 15). This means the content of his letter covers a wide range of subjects that we will find to be helpful in the age in which we live. Our age is very similar to that of Corinth, where the church had been contaminated by a sick society. Instead of the church influencing Corinth for Christ, Corinth had influenced the church, and the sins of society were apparent within it.

# A divided church

In chapters 1–4, Paul begins by answering Chloe's report of divisions within the church at Corinth (1:11).

Groups of followers within the church were gathering in factions around certain individuals who claimed to possess particular gifts. Paul mentions a few names to indicate what he means. Some were following Peter, some Apollos, and some were gathering around Paul's name. And then there was an exclusive little group who said they were the purest of all; they said they were following only Christ, and they were the worst troublemakers. The problem was, by thinking that their leader's special insight represented a superior view, they were doing exactly what the non-Christians out in the city were doing – causing division over the views of men.

In his response to this lamentable state of affairs, Paul says, "I'm not going to waste any time at all arguing with you about Socrates, Plato, Aristotle or any other wisdom of men. They have their place, but when it comes to solving the deep-seated problems of human nature there is only one answer." And he goes on to explain that human insights are always incomplete and to a great degree untrustworthy, and the Corinthians will never learn anything until they give themselves to the wisdom of God. Paul says it wasn't through the world's wisdom that it came to know God (see 1:21), and they will never get to the heart of their problems by trying to pursue the insights of current popularity or secular philosophers.

So the apostle's answer to the divisions in the church is to confront his readers with the word of God that presents the cross of Christ as the instrument by which God cuts across all human wisdom. Not that human wisdom is worthless in its own narrow realm; God never attempts to set aside or call the pursuit of knowledge worthless. He intends us to learn things – He designed us that way – but it must be knowledge based upon a right beginning. That being the case, Paul says he had come to the Corinthians, not with the self-confidence of the philosopher, but with a simple witness to bear testimony to the fact that the Son of God had died for our redemption. And aware of his own weakness, Paul spoke to them in trembling and fear, relying for success not on his own powers of persuasion or the self-important language philosophers enjoyed, but that which the Holy Spirit dictated. The devastating conclusion is that if anyone dismisses Paul's message, the fault was neither in the doctrine he taught nor in the manner they were presented, but in the objector himself.

In chapter 3 Paul explains that God's servants can only build the church of Christ by building on the foundation laid down by preaching the cross of Christ (1:18).

This is very important, and needs to be understood by Christian men and women. Paul is saying that after the second coming of Christ, the labour and spiritual materials put in to building up the church of Jesus Christ will be judged. Then, the right kind of work, that is, that which has been accomplished through the worker by God's Spirit (Paul calls it gold and silver) will be rewarded. By contrast, the wrong kind of work – that which has been done in the flesh for human pride and glory (Paul calls it wood, hay and stubble) – will be burned up, judged by God to have been completely worthless. Except for the fact that they have received Jesus Christ as Lord and Saviour, this type of work results in the Christian's life being a wasted enterprise (3:12–15).

The stark lesson for us is that within the church environment it is quite possible to hold a leadership position, enjoy the favour of others and the prestige that comes from position, yet at the end still discover that the absolutely relentless judgment of God has not been impressed at all by that which originates from anything else but the work of the Spirit of God in us. It has to be the Spirit and not the flesh.

## The church response to immorality

In 1 Corinthians 5:6–13, having dealt with the sin of divisions within the church at Corinth, Paul now takes up the subject of another major problem which underlines the immaturity of their discipleship: sexual immorality and the necessity for church discipline.

First, there was a case of sexual immorality that was not only being tolerated but in which they had allowed the man who had married his father's wife to remain in church membership. Paul, using his apostolic authority, excommunicated the incestuous person, and by doing so Paul says he was handed over to Satan (see 5:5). Christian doctrine teaches us that, as God can forgive all sin, the goal of church discipline must be restoration. But this can only apply when the guilty individual proves he wants to be restored by repenting of his sin and restoring relationships towards those sinned against. If, after due warning, a member of the church family refuses to repent and insists on continuing in their sinful actions, then church discipline comes into effect and the individual is barred from communion, stripped of ministry roles and finally removed from membership. This "last resort" is meant to bring the offender to his senses, to preserve the honour of Jesus' name, and to protect the local church from misrepresentation. Handing them over to Satan is saying that all the protection offered by their position within God's family has been removed and the unrepentant offender is now in the world, whose master is Satan. The church's prayer would be that the ensuing experience endured would cause the person to reflect, repent and be restored to Christ and His family.

Paul then directs the church as a general duty to exclude immoral members from their communion. He scolds the leaders for not judging the conduct of church members and dealing with the iniquity that was eating away at their ranks. There is a lesson here for today's Christians: we are not the charity called the "Samaritans", we are the church of God. When people get themselves into difficulty they can speak to the Samaritans who listen but do not judge. That is a worthwhile secular vocation. But Christians are to judge those inside the church, which means that we do not just offer a listening ear; we correct, advise and where necessary rebuke and discipline in a positive manner (5:12–13).

## Litigation between believers

In 1 Corinthians 6:1–11 Paul, in no uncertain terms, condemns the Corinthian practice of suing other believers in the law court in front of heathen magistrates.

Christians should not attempt to settle their differences with other Christians in the law court. We should be clear that this teaching concerns our dealings within the Christian church. While Paul makes clear his ban on Christians taking each other to court, it is equally clear from the book of Acts that he believed it to be important for those in secular authority to administer justice with integrity and consistency. Paul did not hesitate to appeal to Roman justice, but he never did this in matters between Christians. He believed in the God-given rights and responsibilities of those in authority, and he also believed that as a citizen he was under a divine obligation to insist that the authorities acted within the limits of their office and that justice was seen to be done. When wrongly imprisoned at Philippi, he insisted that the letter of the law was publicly administered, and had the local authorities apologize and escort both Silas and himself from prison. Further, when his liberty was threatened he appealed under Roman law to Caesar (Acts 25:10–11).

The reason Christians must not sue one another is given in 1 Corinthians 6:1: they would be washing their dirty linen in public. Non-believers are very quick to pounce on the slightest inconsistency in a Christian or a church. That's why church sexual and financial scandals are given such prominence in the media. The answer is not to turn a blind eye or sweep it under the carpet, pretending Christians are all wonderfully holy. No! Matters have to be dealt with. But there is a very proper place for godly discretion and a due sense of shame when it comes to our failures as brothers and sisters in Christ – hence Paul's use of the word "dare" in verse 1.

# Paul's answer to difficult church problems

From 1 Corinthians 7:1 Paul turns to the four major problems the church had written to him about.

## Guidelines for marriage

The first concerned marriage. Marriage involves commitment, a mutual pledge of openness and trust, a promise that neither will walk away in difficult times and so forth. It is from within this covenant of loyalty and love that new life should be brought into the world. In view of the sexually obsessed society surrounding them, the Corinthian Christians asked Paul if they should give themselves to the service of God in an abstemious life and not marry. Although Paul himself was not married, he nevertheless told them it is good for men and women to be married, that marriage is a perfectly proper way of life and because of the temptation to immorality each man should have his own wife and each woman her own husband. Then in verse 8 he said that remaining single is a perfectly honourable way of life if God grants this as a special calling to any individual. Marriage is not a necessity, though it often is an advantage, and yet it also can be a problem. In chapter 7 Paul deals very thoughtfully, helpfully and carefully with the whole question of marriage and divorce.

## The law of liberty

Next, chapter 8 concerns their ongoing tensions regarding leftover food that had been offered to idols as part of heathen worship.

This was a great problem to the Corinthian Christians as they were constantly having such meat placed before them, and not wanting to commit idolatry they asked Paul for clear guidelines for them to follow.

The general principle Paul lays down is that participation in the religious service of a people brings us into communion with those people as worshippers, and therefore with the object of their worship. Consequently, to eat heathen sacrifices under circumstances that gave a religious character to the act of eating was idolatry. To prove his point, Paul appeals to their own convictions. They knew that all who came to the Lord's Table were joining in the worship of Christ, and all who attended the Jewish altars and ate of the sacrifices joined in the worship of Jehovah. Well, in the same way, by taking part in a pagan religious festival they were joining in the worship of idols. On the other hand, if meat used in a heathen service was later sold for public consumption with no religious connotations, there was no problem in purchasing it for their own use. However, to save believers with weak faith from acting against their own convictions it would be helpful if the Corinthian believers abstained from the use of such meat (8:1–13).

Though we today are no longer troubled by the problem of whether we ought to eat meat offered to idols, the principle also covers those areas in which some Christians have reservations, such as smoking and drinking. What do we do about these?

It is thought provoking that Paul, with all the authority of an apostle, absolutely refused to make up any rules about such issues. This is because the Christian with the weaker faith always wants somebody to put them under law – "Thou shall, and thou shall not!" But if you put a Christian under law, then they are no longer under grace. And Paul knows that Christians must learn to deal with what he calls "the law of liberty". The fact is that all things are right and nothing is wrong in itself: the devil never made any of the capabilities and capacities that are in the human being – God made them all. And no urge or desire, or tendency is wrong in itself – we are at liberty in these things.

But, and it is an important "but", Paul links two other laws with this principle. One he calls the "law of love". This is the law that says, "I may be free to do it, but if I am putting a stumbling block in somebody else's path, I won't do it." The limitation is imposed not by my conscience but by another's conscience. The second is the "law of expediency". That is, everything is legal and lawful but not everything is helpful. There are a lot of things I could do and many directions I could go in as a Christian, but if I spend all my time doing all the things I am free to do, I no longer have any time to do the things that I am called to do, and therefore it is not always helpful. These are the things that can be a waste of time and drag us back, even though they are not wrong in themselves.

## Principles for public worship

In chapter 11 Paul answers their problems concerning the serious abuses that had been introduced into public worship.

The women's dress was distracting, the Lord's Supper was degraded, and the misuse of spiritual gifts gave rise to enormous confusion.

With regard to the first of these abuses, women's hats were the issue. If a woman was seen bareheaded in Corinth she was immediately identified as a prostitute from the temple of Aphrodite that had made Corinth infamous. That's why Paul, in effect says, "Ladies, when you come to church put a hat on; it is a sign that you are a Christian woman in a right relationship with your husband." The same principle would apply today. Prostitutes are characterized by a certain style of dress, and if one of these ladies joined our service dressed in her "working clothes" it would have a disrupting effect on our worship, just as it did back in the Corinthian church. The lady of course would be made welcome but as she learns to put the interests of the church community first, her style of dress will alter to spare us the distraction.

As for the Lord's Supper, it seems probable that it was incorporated into an ordinary meal in which all the Christians met at a common table. However, instead of being a feast of brotherly love, the rich ate by themselves and left the poorer brethren no part in the feast. This of course was the complete opposite of what is intended, and Paul reminds them again of what he had originally communicated to them concerning our Lord's Last Supper as He himself had received it from the risen Christ. It was designed not to satisfy hunger, but to commemorate the death and resurrection of Christ. It was therefore a religious service of a particularly solemn character. The bread and wine were symbolic of His flesh and blood; to eat and drink in a careless manner was to be guilty of sinning against the body and blood of the Lord (11:17–34).

## The use and misuse of spiritual gifts

In chapter 12 Paul begins to deal with the church's confusion concerning spiritual gifts.

He explains that spiritual gifts are given by the Holy Spirit and were distributed according to the good pleasure of God. They were not for the exaltation of those who received them but for the edification of the church. Paul illustrates this important fact by a reference to the human body. As the body is one, being animated by one soul, so the church is one, being animated by the Spirit. There should therefore be no discontent or envy on the part of those who have lesser gifts, and no pride or ostentation by those who exercise the more highly preferred gifts, especially as the more "showy" gifts were not the most helpful. Therefore, as gifts were objects of desire they should seek those that were the most useful. There was, however, one thing more important than any of these gifts, and without which all others, whether faith, knowledge or the power to work miracles would be no use, and that is love: the love that makes one meek, kind, humble and enduring. This, the highest grace, will endure when all the other extraordinary endowments have passed away.

In 1 Corinthians 13:1–13 Paul is saying that all the most dramatic and wonderful gifts are useless without love.

"If I speak in the tongues of men and of angels" – that is spiritual exultation. "If I have the gift of prophecy and can fathom all mysteries" – that is knowledge. "If I have a faith that can move mountains" – that is accomplishment. "If I give all I possess to the poor" – that is humanitarianism, and if I "surrender my body to the flames" – that is self-denial. Paul says that all these patently one-sided inadequate representations of Christianity are to be repudiated, not because there is anything inherently wrong with spiritual exultation, intellect, achieving goals, humanitarianism or self-denial, but when they become the driving force then they are wrong. Not only wrong, but also, because they squash love and replace it with something else which is deceitful and empty, they are negated and become worthless.

In chapter 14 Paul takes up another problem that was causing confusion.

The two gifts most conspicuous in the church of Corinth were those of prophecy and tongues. The latter excited more admiration than the former, and so it was unduly desired and self-importantly performed. Paul explains that it was very much subordinate to the gift of prophecy, because the prophets were inspired to communicate divine truth in an intelligible manner for the edification of the church. Speaking in tongues, on the other hand, where the language used was not understood by others, could only edify the user (14:2).

We do well to remember that believers in Christ have all they will ever need to meet any trial or any difficulty they may encounter in this life. Other than Jesus there is no mysterious transcendental secret, no ecstatic experience, no super-spiritual wisdom that takes us up onto some higher plane of spiritual life. The apostle Peter says that, "[Jesus'] divine power has given us everything we need for life and godliness through our knowledge of him who called us by his own glory and goodness" (2 Peter 1:3).

In this age of confusion, and in the face of spiritual phenomena of various kinds, we must not be childishly gullible on the one hand, nor dismissively sceptical on the other. It does our Lord no service to be constantly spotlighting what some regard as exceptional and extraordinary, but equally it is not honouring to him to preclude any manifestation of power that we find hard to explain or control. The Corinthian Christians wrongly concentrated on what they reckoned to be the more dramatic gifts, and Paul found them in disorder, heresy, immorality and division. While heeding this warning we should not in reaction adopt an understanding of the spiritual gifts that effectively excludes a God who transcends our finite minds and who in His love reveals Himself unexpectedly in our human existence.

## Teaching on the resurrection

In chapter 15 Paul focuses upon those in the Corinthian church who did not believe in the resurrection, and maintains that denial of Christ's physical resurrection from the grave destroys the gospel.

If the dead cannot rise, Christ is not risen, and if Christ is not risen, we have no Saviour, and if we have no Saviour we are lost. He therefore proves the fact of the resurrection of Christ and then shows how Christ's resurrection secures the resurrection of His people. Finally, he goes on to show that the objection that the material bodies we now have are unsuitable to the future state is founded on the false assumption that matter cannot be refined so as to furnish material for bodies adapted to the soul in its highest state of existence after resurrection (15:35–58).

Before we leave this notoriously confused church at Corinth it is worth noting that Paul is much more hopeful with regards to the future of the Corinthian church than we would be led to believe. If we removed the first nine verses of this letter then it's pretty certain we would arrive at a pessimistic view of this church, for the positive statements of faith, hope and love that so often appear in those early verses would have no context. But Paul first looks at the church as it is in Christ before homing in on the defects and blemishes. The danger of not doing this is that we major on the negative faults and miss the positive things God is doing in the church. Paul's points in the early verses of chapter 1: "[God's] grace given you in Christ Jesus" (verse 4); "in him you have been enriched in every way" (verse 5); "you do not lack any spiritual gift" (verse 7), all speak of the lavish generosity of God towards these redeemed sinners at Corinth. We should bear in mind that these statements are about the church of God at Corinth, not about individual believers. If we are to know the fullness of God's blessing, if we are to experience the gifts of grace that are ours in Christ, it has to be together in fellowship. Potentially, the local church has every spiritual gift within its corporate life, and under the guidance of good leadership and from the individual Christian's own desire to serve the church, believers should prayerfully expect God to bring them into mature expression. This means that spiritual church growth is quite possible for every church if they, like Paul, base their expectations on God's generosity and faithfulness.

# 47

## 2 Corinthians
## – When I Am Weak I Am Strong

Acts 18 records how Paul planted the church in Corinth during his missionary travels and how from the beginning he suffered much opposition from the influential Jewish community who lived there.

After eighteen months he moved on to Asia, settling in Ephesus where he stayed for a number of years. But the troubles in Corinth did not cease with his departure: false teaching, sexual immorality and divisiveness crept into the fellowship, and the relationship between Paul and the church deteriorated (1 Corinthians 4:18). In order to deal with these matters, Paul wrote the letter we know as 1 Corinthians. Unfortunately, not only did his letter fail to solve the problems, but the church leadership composed of an anti-Pauline group organized opposition to the apostle's teachings. In response Paul revisited Corinth for the second time (2 Corinthians 13:2) but was rebuffed. Paul described this visit to the Corinthian church as immensely painful (2:1). The leadership challenged his apostolic authority, ministerial credentials and personal spirituality. Yet Paul knew that it was he and not they who represented real spiritual leadership. They took their inspiration for leadership from the spirit of the age; he took his from the Spirit of God. They drew their examples from the spiritual gurus of the day; he took his from the Lord Jesus Himself. So Paul returned to Ephesus from where he wrote a short, sharp letter, which was hand delivered by Titus, rebuking and reproving the Corinthian church for their attitudes. Unfortunately, this letter has been lost to us. However, while Titus took the letter to the church at Corinth, Paul remained in Ephesus, anxiously waiting to hear what the results would be.

While awaiting Titus's homecoming, serious opposition against Paul's ministry arose in Ephesus (Acts 19). When the uproar against Paul ended, he left the city and as his anxiety concerning the Corinthian church was so great he decided to travel to Macedonia and meet Titus on his return journey. Titus told Paul that the sharp, scathing letter he had written had accomplished its work and that the majority of the Corinthian Christians had repented of their rejection of his ministry and had begun to live again the life of Jesus Christ (2 Corinthians 7:6–7). A minority, however, were still unyielding and rebelling against the authority of the apostle. So, from the city of Philippi, Paul wrote the letter we know as 2 Corinthians. With that background we can understand something of the passion of the apostle as he writes, and from the trouble, tears and heartache that is reflected in this letter come the three great themes that it embodies.

## Paul's explanation of his ministry

The emphasis Paul placed on his visit provides the clue to the heart of a number of problems he was having with the church. He was being viewed as an absentee pastor who was trying to sustain a relationship with a congregation through the occasional visit, the use of on-site men like Timothy and Titus, and the occasional letter that was intended as a substitute for his apostolic and pastoral presence. Some in the leadership at Corinth were quick to spot the failings of this approach and exploited its weakness by accusing Paul of making travel plans he never intended to keep and writing threatening letters that he never intended to enforce. In his reply, Paul's main purpose in writing 2 Corinthians was to bind the majority of the congregation closer to himself by gaining their complete confidence and distance the majority of the church from the minority of self-acclaimed apostolic leaders whose aim was not to help the church but to subjugate it (11:20).

The first seven chapters record Paul's endeavour to gain the Corinthians' trust by demonstrating the validity of his ministry. His strategy is twofold. First, to present the Corinthian Christians with credentials that inspire confidence in him as a minister of the gospel and serve as ammunition against the criticisms of the intruders who were seeking to displace him at Corinth (5:12). Second, he longs to show how closely intertwined their lives are, implying that to reject him would in effect be to reject themselves. After his greeting and thanksgiving for God's comfort in his trials and dangers, Paul unfolds his theology of suffering in which he makes it very clear that Christians are not spared all the pains of this life.

The trouble in the church at Corinth was that the "spiritually superior" people believed, just as many in the church today believe, that great Christian leaders should be strong personalities who never make mistakes of judgment and have CVs which show an unblemished track record, proving how they moved with distinction through their careers. The reason the Corinthian church thought like that is the same reason we think like that today: it was the secular model of leadership. The ancient Greeks admired success. In their society, the important thing, whether you were an actor, an athlete, a soldier or a politician, was that you should be successful. The cult of hero worship was at the centre of their philosophy and religion, and in Paul's day a group of teachers called sophists made their living by giving ambitious young people lectures on the skills and virtues they would need to make it to the top of their career. However, spiritual discernment and ability is not measured by secular attainments, but that's what the self-styled "apostles" offered to the Christians at Corinth: the kind of strong leadership that the secular world of that day admired. But in doing so they brought the worst of the world into the church and clashed with Paul.

Paul explained that his delay in visiting them in Corinth was not due to indecisiveness; it was because he wanted to give them time to repent (1:12 – 2:4). He then graciously asks them to restore the repentant offender who was rude to Paul into fellowship (2:5–11).

From 2:14 to 6:10 Paul embarks upon an extended defence of his ministry and declares what true Christian ministry ought to be. In chapter 3 he states that it is not the ministry of the old covenant, but of the new. In other words, the gospel message is not the demand of the law upon people compelling them to follow certain rules and regulations. When Christianity becomes like that it becomes a deadly, stultifying, dangerous thing. As Paul says, the old covenant exemplified by the Ten Commandments, makes its demand upon us without an accompanying dynamic to fulfil it: it is always a ministry of death. He says, "the letter kills, but the Spirit gives life" (3:6b). He then goes on to set forth the liberating ministry of the new covenant and espouses the new way to live: not the old, grim determination to clench your teeth and try to do what God wants you to do – that is never Christianity – but the realization that God has provided the Holy Spirit to minister to all believers the life of a risen Lord in whose strength and grace we can do all that He asks of us. That is the new way to live, and in this section Paul sets forth the two key resources of a Christian.

First: the Word of God, which every Christian is to declare.

Notice how Paul puts it in 4:1–2a:

> *Therefore, since through God's mercy we have this ministry,*
> *we do not lose heart. Rather, we have renounced secret and*
> *shameful ways; we do not use deception, nor do we distort the*
> *word of God.*

There is a great lesson here for today's church. Much of the failure of the church today is due to tampering with the Word of God, undermining its authority, changing its message, ignoring its declarations or refusing to act upon the facts that are declared. Like Paul, we too should renounce all this (2b).

Second: the treasure of the indwelling Spirit of God (4:7).

Paul's point, which would not be lost on the Corinthian congregation suffering from egotistical leaders, is that it is not personality or cleverness that enables us to live the Christian life victoriously, for what is involved is something far beyond what we can naturally do.

To illustrate his point Paul likens the Holy Spirit residing within us to treasure in an earthen vessel, in order to show that the power is not ours but that it belongs to God. With this Paul links the principle of the cross as the secret by which the power is released (4:10). Paul is saying, "I am always carrying about with me that sentence of judgment upon the natural life in order that the life of Jesus with all its glorious possibilities might be apparent in me." Furthermore, while we live we "are always being given over to death for Jesus" sake" (4:11), that is, that we are always being put into places of difficulty, pressure, hardship and trouble. Why? In order that the life of Jesus may be evident in our lives. That is the secret of the new way to live, and that is what Paul says is the glory of the Christian ministry and the Christian life. Paul goes on to declare the great hope of the believer: "we fix our eyes not on what is seen, but on what is unseen. For what is seen is temporary, but what is unseen is eternal" (2 Corinthians 4:18).

God has a great future ahead for us. The life we now live is the preparation for that life which is to come. Therefore, says Paul, "our light and momentary troubles are achieving for us an eternal glory that far outweighs them all" (2 Corinthians 4:17).

Paul's point is that the present is but a prologue to the future. Then he declares his motives: "Since, then, we know what it is to fear the Lord, we try to persuade men… For Christ's love compels us" (2 Corinthians 5:11, 14). This means it constrains us and drives us to move forward.

In 5:16–21 Paul gathers up his argument with a great declaration of the transforming character of the gospel of Jesus Christ. This good news does what nothing else in the world can ever accomplish, be it philosophy, a line of argument or an education process. It is a transformation on the inside by the implantation of a new life. Moreover, says Paul, God has entrusted to us his message of reconciliation and we are therefore Christ's ambassadors, charged with relaying His message to all men to "be reconciled to God" (5:20).

## Paul's collection for the saints in Jerusalem

At first glance, one might think Paul's teaching on money (chapters 8–9) is introduced abruptly and out of place in the context of his previous subject, but nothing could be farther from the truth. Paul's teaching on giving is directly related to the problems in the Corinthian church he has been addressing.

When Paul first arrived in Corinth on his second missionary journey, he preached the gospel and a number of Corinthians came to faith in Jesus Christ. As a result of their newfound joy and gratitude they determined to contribute towards the relief of the poor Christians in Jerusalem. Titus apparently had already visited Corinth and helped instigate a plan by which a contribution for the poor would be collected over a period of time (8:6). However, it appears from Paul's writing here that the Corinthians lost heart for this relief operation and neglected their regular contributions. Paul had written a painful letter to the church at Corinth which caused both Paul and the Corinthians great sorrow (7:8) but now the Corinthians have truly repented (7:9). They longed to see Paul and are looking forward to his coming. But Paul is concerned that when he does come to Corinth, accompanied by others, to collect the gift the Corinthians promised for the poor in Jerusalem it would be highly embarrassing for everyone if there should be no generous offering to collect from the Corinthian church. That would not be the kind of reunion for which Paul or the Corinthians hoped. Consequently, he writes these two chapters encouraging the Corinthians to complete the project they have begun, thereby paving the way for a joyful reunion.

But Paul had another important reason for the collection from the churches. It helps here to consider the background.

It was difficult enough for the Jews that the Messiah came as a suffering servant rather than an all-conquering king like David, but then, for Him to die on the hated cross was an even greater stumbling block. To add to their discomfort, the despised Samaritans were turning to Christ, and, even worse, thanks to Paul, the despicable Gentiles were now becoming Christians. Due entirely to the historical prejudice against the Samaritans and Gentiles, the negative reaction to this astonishing turn of events from the Jews in Jerusalem, even though they had become Christians, was becoming a major obstacle to the growth of the church outside Jerusalem, and threatened to halt the advance of the gospel. The "outsiders" were trying to become "insiders", and you can imagine all the tensions this brought to the "insiders" in Jerusalem. Paul, the apostle to the Gentiles, then based in Antioch, realizing the seriousness of the developing situation gets involved and decides to take up an even bigger collection than previous ones. As a result, whenever he went on his missionary journeys among the Gentile churches, he would gather together as much money as he could so that he could make a really significant contribution for God's people in Jerusalem, and this is what's referred to in our passage from 2 Corinthians 8. It surfaces again in 1 Corinthians 16 and Romans 15, where Paul says that if the Gentiles have shared the spiritual blessings of the Jews then they owe it to the Jews to share their material blessings. The importance of this offering is the impact that such a large gift from all the Gentile Christian churches would have on the Jewish converts. It would be a huge sign of how the Gentile converts wanted to stand together as one with their brothers and sisters in Jerusalem.

We can use a modern-day analogy to understand Paul's thinking. Many Bible-believing churches of Britain do not apply to the National Lottery for financial help. The reason being that if they do, they validate the lottery – if they accept money from the lottery they are saying it's all right, it's acceptable. That's the thinking behind Paul's collection for the poor Christians in Jerusalem. The same principle was at work: if the Jewish Christians took the financial gift from the Gentile Christians they were validating their Christianity – they were saying these brothers and sisters are genuine believers like us: we are all together in the one church.

We pick up the story in Acts 19:2. After about three years in Ephesus the time had come for Paul to deliver the collection for Jerusalem. Then as Acts 20:16 records: "Paul had decided to sail past Ephesus to avoid spending time in the province of Asia, for he was in a hurry to reach Jerusalem, if possible, by the day of Pentecost."

Now we ask, why the hurry? Why would Paul want to be in Jerusalem for the day of Pentecost? Scripture does not tell us, but the likely answer is to be found in the symbolism. Paul wants to arrive with the gift from the Gentile churches on the very day the Jerusalem church is celebrating the gift of the Holy Spirit. He knows that if the Jerusalem church accepts him and the gift from him and his converts, there is one church. If they don't, it would not be one Lord, one faith one gospel one church: it would be one Lord, two faiths, two gospels and two churches and Paul knows that's an anathema to God. That's why Paul says in Acts 20:22 that he was compelled by the Spirit to go to Jerusalem – he was in no doubt that the future of the united Christian church proclaiming one faith was at stake. Yes, it sounds dramatic but that is what it was all about: the future of the united Christian church proclaiming the one message of good news was at stake. Paul knew there was something greater than just a collection; he knew that the money he was carrying was part of his life's goal of making sure that the Gentile churches and believers were accepted as part of the international church of God.

## Paul's defence

Paul concludes his letter with a defence of his apostolic authority and credentials directed to the hostile minority in the Corinthian church (chapters 10–13).

In chapters 10–11 Paul distinguishes himself and the other authentic apostles by contrasting the characteristics of false apostles with the doctrine, attitudes and practice of the true apostles. He is making the point that his meekness and gentleness not only identifies him with Christ and his fellow-apostles, but also clearly distinguishes him from the false apostles who are anything but meek and gentle. Paul rebukes the Corinthians for allowing fools to take charge of their church and push them around. Further, the church seemingly enjoys the situation while Paul dramatically and decisively distances himself from such leaders (11:19–21a).

To demonstrate his apostolic credentials, Paul is forced to boast about his background, accomplishments, sufferings, visions and miracles (11:1 – 12:13). It's obvious he did not enjoy talking this way; in fact, he tells us that boasting makes him feel foolish (11:16). Then, after a series of admissions about all the appalling things that befell him during his missionary travels, Paul admits to his weakness in verse 29 but dramatically points to the Lord Jesus as the source of his strength. Paul was reversing the glamorous image of Christian spirituality with which the Corinthians were being fed by the false teachers. These false teachers saw a church leader as a dynamic superman who exudes success in everything he does. This is very wrong and terribly misleading, for genuine spiritual leaders are not always noticeable by success in their secular or church lives, and are definitely not characterized by a dictatorial leadership style. Do we doubt for a moment that the humiliating way the successful Pharisee, Saul of Tarsus, was brought into the Christian faith by lying blinded on the dust of the Damascus Road and accepting as his Lord the Jesus he was persecuting made him all the better a man to be the apostle Paul? If we need any help in answering this question, let us ask ourselves who we would rather have deal with our disciplinary problems: Saul of Tarsus or the apostle Paul?

Chapter 12 records Paul's account of his vision and his thorn. Again, he confesses that he is not happy about such disclosures but felt forced by circumstances to match his rivals boast by boast. His answer to those who accused him of being unspiritual is not to try to compete with them but to use a blend of irony and paradox to demonstrate that their ideas of spirituality were poles apart from his. It simply is not true to say that to be spiritual is to project an image of superior supernaturalism and power. On the contrary, real spirituality looks ordinary; it looks weak even as Christ looked weak and ordinary as He lay in the manger, wept in the garden and hung on the cross. Reticence about one's supernatural experience and lack of boasting about what one does is a mark of real spirituality.

It should also be borne in mind that extraordinary religious experiences often carry a personal cost. When Jacob wrestled with God he hobbled away lame (Genesis 32:25) and when Paul entered paradise he came away with a thorn in his flesh (2 Corinthians 12:7). What this was is difficult to determine. Some think it was a person; as we would put it, "a pain in the neck", and the biblical reference for this is Numbers 33:55. But it is unlikely Paul would pray for the removal of opposition. Much more likely is the suggestion that he suffered from some physical ailment, possibly an eye problem which he hints at in Galatians 4:14–15, "my illness was a trial to you… you would have torn out your eyes and given them to me", and hinted at again as he closes his letter to the Galatians with, "See what large letters I use as I write to you with my own hand!" (6:11). Whatever the thorn in his flesh was, it tormented Paul and he called it "a messenger of Satan" (2 Corintians 12:7).

Paul then reveals his plans to visit them for the third time and urges them to repent so that he will not have to use severity when he comes (12:14 – 13:10), and the letter ends with an exhortation, greetings and a benediction (13:11–14). It is wonderful that this last word is a word of peace. The apostle sees beyond all the fragmentation in Corinth to the basic unity of the church. God created that unity. It exists even though there is divisiveness, quarrelling, jealousy and division among them. Christians belong to each other. They are part of the family of God and they ought to act that way, he says. Beyond the rebellion Paul sees the grace and the power of God, which is able to heal these breaches and restore men and women of faith, and he encourages them to openly demonstrate to one another their love, affection and unity in Christ.

What better way to end the letter than by pointing to the perfect model of "congregational" unity – the unity of Father, Son and Holy Spirit. So Paul's concluding benediction is more than a theological flourish. The order "Christ's grace", "God's love" and "the Holy Spirit's fellowship" is eminently practical. Through Christ's gift of Himself we experience, in the most concrete terms, God's love for us and the Spirit's power to fashion us into a oneness that serves as a beacon of hope in a fragmented and broken world.

> *May the grace of the Lord Jesus Christ, and the love of God, and the fellowship of the Holy Spirit be with you all.*
>
> 2 CORINTHIANS 13:14

# 48

# Galatians
# – Liberated for Life

When Martin Luther wrote his commentary on Galatians he introduced the concept of grace and faith as opposed to law and works, and his commentary became the manifesto of the Protestant Reformation, leading the book of Galatians to be rightly called the "Magna Carta of Christian liberty". It maintains that only through the grace of God in Jesus Christ is a person enabled to escape the curse of their sin and God's law, and be enabled to live a new life in genuine freedom of mind and spirit through the power of God.

## Paul's motive for writing this magnificent letter

At the time of the early church, the first converts to Christianity were mainly from Judaism and they had to come to terms with the dilemma of a dual identity. By recognizing Jesus as the Messiah they had moved away from their heritage, which was an especially difficult action for them to take when you remember that Judaism was constituted by God. While there was nothing wrong with the old covenant of Law it has been fulfilled and then superseded with the life, death and resurrection of Jesus Christ and the introduction of His new covenant of grace through His atoning blood. The early converts from Judaism to Christianity found that their Jewish upbringing constrained them to follow the Law, while their newfound faith in Christ invited them to celebrate a holy liberty. This tension intensified when non-Jews, called Gentiles, began to embrace the Christian faith following the evangelistic efforts of Paul and his associates. The new converts knew nothing of Judaism or the Law, which raised the following questions:

- Was the Christian church to open wide her doors to all comers regardless of their relationship to the traditions of Judaism?
- Were her boundaries to be as wide as the human race or was she to be only an extension of Judaism to the Gentiles?
- If so, was it necessary for a Gentile believer to observe the Law of Moses and thus be circumcised in order to become a Christian?

Questions like these must have been raised with increasing force throughout the Roman empire wherever the church of Jesus Christ camped on Gentile soil.

Around AD 48–49, Paul's first missionary journey, in the company of Barnabas, took him west of Antioch in Syria to the area of Galatia – today's Turkey. Together, they evangelized and planted churches in the four principal cities of Derbe, Lystra, Iconium and Antioch of Pisidia. After establishing these churches they turned around and travelled back through the area, strengthening the saints, before returning to the church at Antioch of Syria. As the apostle to the Gentiles, Paul had deliberately not brought up questions of conformity to Jewish Law when presenting the gospel in non-Jewish communities. He had followed this practice in Galatia and taught that salvation is never to be achieved by any amount of conformity to rules and regulations, even God-given regulations. The reasonfor this is that the Law condemns, as Paul points out in 3:10–14. Consequently, if there is to be salvation for sinful men and women it must come in another way, and God has offered this other way through Jesus Christ. Jesus, as our substitute, died for our sin to satisfy the Law's demands upon us so that now God can justly offer salvation to all who put their trust in Him. This is the gospel Paul taught to the Galatians, and it had been well received as Galatians 4:13–15 makes clear.

Due to a serious illness, Paul had been unexpectedly detained in Galatia, but instead of rebuffing him, as they might have done, the Galatians actually embraced both him and the gospel willingly. So much so that these former pagans (4:8) were now baptized (3:27) and received the Holy Spirit, who began to work miracles among them (3:5). Following his usual custom, Paul established churches in Galatia and then moved on.

The wonderful news of the conversion of so many Gentiles to Christianity spread far and wide, even back to Jerusalem itself where the church rejoiced. But the joy was not universal – not everyone was pleased with Paul's evangelistic results. Acts 15:5 records that some believers who belonged to the Pharisee sect were unhappy. They were men who believed in the resurrection of the dead and, probably impressed with the evidence of Christ's resurrection and the power of His miracles, chose to identify with Jesus and His church. But at heart they remained Jewish legalists, and they were convinced it took more than simple faith in Jesus to be saved; strict observance of Jewish ceremony, particularly circumcision, was also necessary for salvation. So, when the news of the conversions of the Gentiles in Galatia reached these men and they heard that it had been accomplished by faith in Jesus and not by works of law or circumcision, off to Antioch they went with a protest in their hearts and a warning on their lips which they proceeded to preach to the startled converts of Galatia. It's recorded in Acts 15:1, "Unless you are circumcised, according to the custom taught by Moses, you cannot be saved." One can imagine the consternation among the mainly Gentile congregations on being told that, contrary to them believing their salvation was by faith in the cross and the resurrection of Christ, by not adopting Jewish practices they were lost and heading to hell. When Paul heard that the Galatian believers were being influenced by the Judaizers and were on the point of departing from the faith they had previously received so openly, he was filled with righteous indignation. He realized that if the views of the Judaizers prevailed, grace and the cross of Jesus Christ would be emptied of all value (Galatians 5:2; Romans 4:14). Moreover, if the Galatian Christians were to let themselves be circumcised and thus have to live their lives according to Old Testament Law, Christianity would lose its distinctive character and soon become little more than a minor sect of Judaism. So, in righteous anger, Paul wrote this letter to reprove legalism and regain the Galatian churches for Jesus.

It appears that Paul had heard of three distinct charges made against him by his Jewish opponents.

## The first charge

The first charge against Paul was directed against him personally.

It alleged that he was not a true apostle and that the gospel he preached had not been revealed by God. "After all," his enemies argued, "Paul had not lived with Jesus when He was here on earth, as had the 'true' apostles: he was not one of the Twelve. Actually," they asserted, "he was merely an evangelist who, after he had received some knowledge of Christianity, turned to his own devices and, in order to please the Gentiles, taught an easy gospel that was opposed to that of the apostolic model" (see 1:10). They said that Paul must teach as the Judaizers taught or be rejected.

Paul answered their accusation by retelling his life story, particularly as it related to the other apostles (chapters 1 and 2). Then he made three other points:

- his teaching is not something he made up, nor is it dependent on other human authorities, and this is what makes him an apostle, for the teaching of an apostle must come directly from God (1:11–12).
- his authority had been acknowledged by the other apostles on each occasion they had come in contact (1:18–24; 2:8–10).
- he had proved his worth by remaining firm at Antioch when others, including even Peter and Barnabas, had wavered (2:11–16).

## The second charge

The second charge directed against Paul is found in chapters 3 and 4. It was that his gospel was not the true gospel and that one needed more than faith in Christ to be saved. Their argument was that when Paul taught that the Law could be set aside, he was wrong. "God's Law," they said, "is eternal and it can never be set aside. All who have ever been saved have been saved by keeping the Law. Moreover, it is perfectly evident from all that is known of the life of Jesus that Jesus Himself kept the Law. The Judaizers did likewise. Who, then, was Paul to dismiss the requirements of the Law for salvation?"

Paul answered this serious charge by arguing that the concern is not one of who does or does not keep the Law, but rather of the true basis on which God reckons a sinful man righteous. In other words, just how is a man or woman saved? And in chapter 3 he appeals first to the personal experience of the Galatians themselves, and then to the plain teaching of Scripture. He asks pointedly, "I would like to learn just one thing from you: Did you receive the Spirit by observing the law, or by believing what you heard?" (3:2). His point being, "You did not receive forgiveness of sin and the assurance of salvation through the indwelling presence of the Holy Spirit by obeying the law: you received it by faith."

Then, secondly, Paul points them to Abraham in Genesis 15:6 as an example, where Scripture says, "Abram believed the Lord, and he credited it to him as righteousness." Paul's point is, as God had declared Abraham righteous on the basis of his faith 430 years before either circumcision or the Law were given (Galatians 3:17–18), imputed righteousness obviously does not come either from the Law or circumcision. Then, in verse 19, Paul asks the obvious rhetorical question: "What, then, was the purpose of the law?" His answer is that the Law was given to convince the world of the reality of sin, and through their consciences men and women are made aware of sin in their lives. Paul confirms this in Romans 7:7 when he says, "I would not have known what sin was except through the law."

But the second function of the Law is to bring us to recognize our need of a Saviour. The Law was never given that by keeping it men and women might be saved. No, it's the opposite; that by the demands of the Law and our abject failure to live up to its standard, we see that we cannot do what God wants us to do even when He has written it down on tablets of stone. We cannot keep the Ten Commandments, and our inability to keep the Law is intended to drive us to confess our helplessness and hopelessness and admit that we need help with ourselves. We need a mediator between us and God. And God so loved the world that He sent His own Son, Jesus, as the mediator for humankind, not to destroy the Law, but by His life, death and resurrection, to fulfil it.

## The third charge

The next charge was that the gospel Paul preached led to loose living. Their point was that by stressing the Law, Judaism stressed morality, and they argued that if the Law should be removed, lawlessness and immorality would increase. In Galatians 5 and 6 Paul argues in a most telling manner that this is just not true, because Christianity does not lead the believer away from the Law into nothingness, it leads them into a greater understanding of God's will for men and women and gives them a deeper desire to please God by obeying His will. Believers are enabled to do this by the Holy Spirit who at conversion comes to dwell within them, furnishing them with the new nature that alone is capable of doing what God desires, and producing the fruit of the Spirit: "love, joy, peace, patience, kindness, goodness, faithfulness, gentleness and self-control" (5:22–23). Life in the Spirit is both free from, and above, the kind of religion that would result in either legalism or license. It is true freedom; freedom to serve God fully, unencumbered by the shackles of sin or regulations.

In 6:12–13 Paul tells the Galatian Christians that the Judaizers are Christians in name only.

Paul's accusation is that the Judaizers were insincere and inconsistent, and their real aim was to escape persecution from the Jews and obtain personal glory by gaining followers to their cause. By way of contrast, Paul, aware that "religious" men and women make much of their outward profession (the position they have and the things they do while ignoring the message of the cross), speaks the words of 6:14, which eloquently sums up the Christian position in relation to the world: "May I never boast except in the cross of our Lord Jesus Christ, through which the world has been crucified to me, and I to the world."

We today cannot appreciate the shock these words would have had on his listeners. Refined minds and Gentile sensibilities would recoil and shudder in disgust. The cross was a hideous thing, but Paul will not gloss over it; he glories in the cross. He says, "It's the object upon which the Prince of Glory died. His blood running down that wooden cross planted on Calvary's hill satisfied the righteous wrath of almighty God against lawbreakers. On that cross our Lord Jesus Christ, our Saviour and Redeemer bled and died for me. And I thank God for it. Hallelujah! I glory in it. Not, of course, the piece of wood itself but the glorious doctrine it represents. Our Saviour, Immanuel, God with us, dying a criminal's death on a bloodstained tree. In this I boast."

The truth is that we cannot boast in ourselves and in the cross simultaneously. If we boast in ourselves and our ability to find our own salvation because of our good works, then we shall never boast in the cross and the ability of Christ to save us. We have to choose. Only when we humble ourselves and admit our sin, confessing that we are hell-deserving sinners and unable to save ourselves, then, and only then, shall we stop boasting of ourselves, and kneeling in tears before the Lord Jesus with arms outstretched, we will cling to the cross trusting in His blood for our salvation. Then for evermore we will glory and boast in the cross.

And the outcome is that we part company from the world.

Paul speaks of three crucifixions. First, that of Jesus on the cross. Then as a result two other crucifixions take place: the world is crucified to the Christian, and the world regards the Christian as crucified. It's in verse 14b, where Paul says in effect, "I judge the world damned, and the world judges me damned, thus we crucify and condemn one another."

> *Neither circumcision nor uncircumcision mean anything;*
> what counts is a new creation.
>
> GALATIANS 6:15, EMPHASIS ADDED

As Isaac Watts' (1674–1748) hymn, "When I Survey the Wondrous Cross", says:

> *Forbid it, Lord, that I should boast,*
> *Save in the cross of Christ my God:*
> *All the vain things that charm me most,*
> *I sacrifice them to His blood.*

*Were the whole realm of nature mine,*
*That were an offering far too small;*
*Love so amazing, so divine,*
*Demands my soul, my life, my all.*

There is a postscript:

The Galatian Christians decided to do something about the tensions, and rightly suspecting that their problems were coming from troublemakers who had no authority from the church in Jerusalem (Acts 15:24), they agreed to refer the whole matter to a general conference in Jerusalem where the matter could be openly discussed by the apostles, disciples and the whole church (Acts 15:2). They delegated Paul, Barnabas and other selected men to go to Jerusalem to represent the church at Antioch and every uncircumcised Gentile convert everywhere. In all probability there was a private meeting of leaders before the Council described in Acts 15 met. Paul alludes to this in Galatians 2:2. Complete agreement was evident: Titus was not to be circumcised and the basic doctrine of salvation of faith without works or ceremony was to be preached fearlessly. James gave his judgment recorded in Acts 15:20–21 which shows complete exoneration and agreement with the position Paul adopted. Paul had won the day, and the decision was sent back to the churches and received with great joy.

# 49

# Ephesians
## – New Life in Christ

Ephesus was the most important city of the Roman province of Asia and along with Alexandria in Egypt and Antioch in Syria it formed a triangle that dominated international trade.

As a major port and trade route Ephesus was a cosmopolitan community famous for the arts and a renowned haven for philosophers, poets, artists and orators of all descriptions. Only Corinth, just across the Aegean Sea, could rival Ephesus in this respect. But what really made Ephesus distinctively famous was the immense temple dedicated to the goddess Diana. It was also a centre of worship to the Emperor Augustus, as well as other "deities", and drew all who were interested in spiritism and magic.

Paul came to Ephesus around AD 52–53, where he found twelve followers of John the Baptist who professed to be Christian "disciples" but in whom Paul discerned something amiss. They had only received John's baptism of repentance, and were not aware of the Holy Spirit and church-age mysteries (Acts 19). Paul spoke to them about Jesus, after which they were baptized with water and the Spirit almost simultaneously. Paul then spent three months teaching in the synagogue, and finally, in the face of Jewish opposition, he moved his classes to the lecture hall of Tyrannus where he taught daily for two years. During this time exorcists were converted and a number of new converts burned their books of magic. At this stage Paul visited Corinth before returning to Ephesus and writing his first letter to the Corinthians. However, this time his ministry in Ephesus was cut short by a riot instigated by the silversmiths and craftsmen who made articles for the worship of Diana. Their angry response to the loss of business due to the many conversions to Christianity put Paul's life in danger (Acts 19).

Unlike Paul's other letters, his letter to the Ephesians was not intended to combat error and expose the inconsistencies of false teaching. Rather, his aim was more detached and therefore more exalted. Rising above the smoke of battle, he focused on what God did through the life and ministry of Jesus Christ, and is doing through His Spirit today, in order to build His new society in the midst of the old. Yet Paul's objective was not purely inspirational. He sought to relate his vision to the practical demands of Christian living in a hostile society and prevent problems in the church by encouraging believers towards spiritual maturity. So, where his previous letters (Romans, 1 and 2 Corinthians and Galatians) develop the phrase "Christ in you", teaching us what the indwelling life of Christ is intended to do within us, the letter to the Ephesians is intended to make believers more aware of their position "in Christ", because this is the basis for their conduct in their everyday lives.

## Blessed in the heavenly realms

> *Praise be to the God and Father of our Lord Jesus Christ, who has blessed us in the heavenly realms with every spiritual blessing in Christ.*
>
> EPHESIANS 1:3

Some have taken the phrase, "blessed us in the heavenly realms" to refer to heaven after we die, but that misses the whole thrust of Paul's letter which is primarily concerned with the life Christians lead right now. The heavenly realms in which we are blessed is not a far-off heavenly place, it's simply the realm of invisible reality in which the Christian now lives in contact with God and Christ's power, and in conflict with the devil. We see this from Ephesians 2:6: "God raised us up with Christ and seated us with him in the heavenly realms in Christ Jesus."

But also in 3:10 and 6:10–12 we learn that here also is the headquarters of the principalities and powers of evil:

> *For our struggle is not against flesh and blood, but against the rulers, against the authorities, against the powers of*

*this dark world and against the spiritual forces of evil in the heavenly realms.*

GALATIANS 6:12

So, "blessed us in the heavenly realms" is not referring to heaven but to the invisible realm on earth – that spiritual kingdom which surrounds believers – constantly influencing and affecting them for good or evil, depending upon their wilful choice and their relationship to these invisible powers.

Unconverted people think mainly of earthly blessings, and generally do not care to remember where they come from. Their thoughts are taken up with money, health, friends, family, travel and ambition. These are the things that matter to them, and generally they consider wealth to be of particular importance because it makes other earthly blessings easier to acquire. But Christians know that this world is passing away and that they already belong to another world. An invisible world, yes, but that doesn't make it unreal. They are in fellowship with God, they are aware of Him, they know Him and they love Him. They have come to know Him through the Lord Jesus Christ, who is a reality to them. Their lives are lived in a different dimension, which is distinct from, but not distant from, the one in which all men and women live.

This dimension is the world of the invisible, of Christ, the angels and demons. As members of this invisible world, being blessed in the heavenly realms means that God has already blessed them with every spiritual blessing. That is, He has given them all that it takes to live in their present circumstances and relationships. That means that when we receive Jesus Christ as our Lord, even the weakest believer has access to all that is ever possessed by the mightiest saint of God. We have everything because we have Christ, and in Him is every spiritual blessing and all that pertains to life and godliness.

Thus we have what it takes to live life as God intended. Any failure therefore is not because we are lacking anything but because we have not learned to appropriate what is already ours.

Paul uses six images to explain the nature of the church and of the Christian in relationship to Jesus Christ.

## 1. The church as a body

*God placed all things under his feet and appointed him to be head over everything for the church, which is his body, the fullness of him who fills everything in every way.*

EPHESIANS 1:22–23

Ephesians 1 is entirely devoted to the wonder and amazement that we ordinary sin-polluted human beings should be called by God before the foundation of the earth to become members of His body. It is a tremendous declaration. You sense that Paul never got over his amazement that he, with his health problems and lack of eloquence, who came to the Corinthian church "in weakness and fear, and with much trembling", preaching "not with wise and persuasive words", and who was despised and regarded with contempt in many religious circles, was nevertheless a member of the body of Jesus Christ. He was called of God before the foundation of the earth and given such tremendous blessings that he was equipped for everything that life could demand of him. That is what it means to belong to the body of Christ, and it begs the question: "What is the purpose of the body?" The answer is that it is to be "the fullness of him who fills everything in every way" (1:23b). In other words, it is the expression of the head. That is what our body is for. It is intended to express and perform the desires of the head. The body acting on its own without direction from the head is uncoordinated.

## 2. The church is God's temple; Jesus Christ is the foundation

*In him the whole building is joined together and rises to become a holy temple in the Lord.*

EPHESIANS 2:21

As Paul was dictating his letter in Ephesus, within his view stood one of the seven wonders of the ancient world: the fabulous marble temple of Artemis with its inner shrine to the goddess Diana. At the same time, in Jerusalem there stood the magnificent Jewish temple built by Herod the Great barricading itself against the Gentiles. It now stood against God, whose Shechinah glory it had housed in its inner sanctuary for centuries but whose glory as now revealed in its Messiah it had extinguished. Two temples, one pagan and the other Jewish, each designed as a divine residence, yet both empty of the living God. Now, however, there is a new temple. The old temple in Jerusalem was God's dwelling place on earth; the new temple is the dwelling place of God in the Spirit within His people. It's His new society; His redeemed people throughout the earth, no longer a physical structure but His spiritual temple where His glory can be seen in the world. No church, building, cathedral or basilica is graced with the special presence of God; He lives in His people by His Spirit. There are no holy places on this planet; no believer needs them, for all Christians "are being built together to become a dwelling in which God lives by his Spirit" (2:22). When all the products of human endeavour have crumbled into dust, when all the institutions and organizations have long been forgotten, the temple which God is erecting will be the central focus of attention through all eternity. That is what the passage implies. Furthermore, He is building it now using human building blocks. He is shaping them, edging them, sandpapering them, preparing them just as He desires and placing human beings into this temple where He wants them to be.

## 3. The church is a mystery: a sacred secret now revealed

> *Although I am less than the least of all God's people, this grace was given me: to preach to the Gentiles the unsearchable riches of Christ, and to make plain to everyone the administration of this mystery, which for ages past was kept hidden in God, who created all things. His intent was that now, through the church, the manifold wisdom of God should be made known to the rulers and authorities in the heavenly realms....*
>
> EPHESIANS 3:8–10

Paul uses the term "mystery" three times in 3:1–6. Mystery in the New Testament means an open secret or revealed truth, and the "mystery of Christ" is the union of Jews and Gentiles with each other through their union in Christ.

God has had His secret plans working through the centuries; they had never been fully revealed to anyone. He has had a goal and a purpose in mind that He intends to fulfil, and the instrument by which He is doing it is the church. This is something we can never fully grasp, but it involves the redemption of the whole universe. Think of it this way: as the gospel spreads throughout the world this new and wonderfully varied Christian community develops. It is multiracial and multicultural, and no other community on earth resembles it. Its diversity and harmony are unique. It's as if a great drama is being enacted. History is the theatre, the world is the stage, and the Christians in every land are the actors. God Himself has written the play, and He directs and produces it. Act by act, scene by scene, the story continues to unfold. But who is the audience? The audience comprises the cosmic intelligences, the principalities and powers in heavenly places who we are to think of as spectators of the drama of salvation. Thus the history of the Christian church becomes a graduate school for the angels.

## 4. The church is a new man because every Christian in it is a new man

> ... *put on the new self, created to be like God in true* *righteousness and holiness.*
>
> EPHESIANS 4:24

This is linked with Paul's word in 2 Corinthians 5:17: "if anyone is in Christ, he is a new creation; the old has gone, the new has come!" The present creation that God made in the beginning has long since grown old and is passing away. The world with all its wealth and wisdom belongs to that which is passing. But, gradually through the centuries, God has been building up a new creation, a new race of beings, a new kind of person that the world has never seen before and these people, the born-again ones, will inherit the universe with Jesus Christ when this world as we know it is long gone.

So, God's new creation is being made right now and believers are invited to put on this new man, moment by moment, day by day, in order that they might meet the pressures and problems of life in the world today. That is why the church is here. It consists of new men and women whose purpose is to exercise a new ministry. In this same chapter of Ephesians we read in 4:7 that "to each one of us grace has been given as Christ apportioned it". This new character within each Christian has been given as a spiritual gift that we never had before we were born again. Here is one important reason why the church has flagged and faltered, and why so many Christians act as if it were an arm of the welfare system or a casualty hospital. It is because too many Christians have lost the great truth that the risen Lord has given a spiritual gift to each to be used for the building up of His church, and in doing so to discover and love, more and more the giver of that gift.

# 5. The church is a bride

*Husbands, love your wives, just as Christ loved the church*
*and gave himself up for her to make her holy, cleansing her by*
*the washing with water through the word, and to present her*
*to himself as a radiant church, without stain or wrinkle or any*
*other blemish, but holy and blameless.*

EPHESIANS 5:25–27

And then in verse 31 Paul quotes the words of God from Genesis 2:24: "For this reason a man will leave his father and mother and be united to his wife, and they will become one flesh."

In Ephesians 5:32 Paul adds, "This is a profound mystery – but I am talking about Christ and the church."

The church is a bride, and it is to be a bride for the pleasure of the bridegroom. Paul says Christ's intention in preparing the church as a bride is that He might present it to Himself. Isn't that what every bridegroom desires – that his bride shall be his? During their early days of courtship she may go out with some other fellows, but when they are engaged she is promised to be his, and they are both waiting for the day when that can be realized. Then at last the day comes when they stand before the marriage altar and promise to love, honour and cherish one another until death parts them. They then become each other's – she is his and he is hers – for the enjoyment of each other throughout their lifetime together. That is a picture of both the church and the Christian. If we think about this and see ourselves this way it can revolutionize our relationship with Jesus. We realize that the Lord Jesus is looking forward to our time together, and if we miss it He is disappointed.

# 6. The church as a soldier

*Therefore put on the full armour of God, so that when the day of*
*evil comes, you may be able to stand your ground, and after you*
*have done everything, to stand.*

EPHESIANS 6:13

The purpose of a soldier is to engage in both offensive and defensive warfare, and that is what God is doing in the Christian now. He has given the Christian the great privilege of being on the battlefield upon which His great victories are won. This is the privilege to which God is calling Christians in this day of world unrest and distress, to be soldiers equipped with every spiritual blessing so that they might be a body, a temple, a mystery, a new man, a bride and a soldier for Jesus Christ. That is quite a calling.

The exhortation, then, of this letter is contained in just one verse in which Paul says,

> *As a prisoner for the Lord, then, I urge you to live a life worthy of the calling you have received.*
>
> EPHESIANS 4:1

Do not lose sight of what God is doing. The world cannot see it; it has no idea what is taking place. But Christian, you know and you can see it, so do not lose heart.

# 50

## Philippians
## – Contentment, Confidence and Joy

The account of Paul's first visit to Philippi is recorded in Acts 16, in which the Apostle, while he and his companions worked in the region of Phrygia and Galatia, had a vision of a man begging him to "Come over to Macedonia and help us" (Acts 16:9). Responding to the "call", upon arrival at Philippi they did not find a specific man but, rather, a handful of women who, on the sabbath day outside the city by the riverbank, had gathered for prayer. One of them was a Gentile businesswoman named Lydia and Acts 16:14 records how "the Lord opened her heart to respond to Paul's message." The next converts to Christianity were a clairvoyant slave-girl and a prison gaoler. There is a wonderful lesson here for us concerning the nature of the Christian church.

Lydia, who had made her money in the "rag trade", was probably a wealthy woman. She certainly had a house large enough to accommodate the missionaries as well as her household (Acts 16:15). But the slave-girl came from the opposite end of the social spectrum; you did not come much lower in public estimation than in being a female slave. She owned nothing, not even herself. She had no possessions, rights, liberty or life of her own. Even the money she earned by fortune-telling went straight into her masters' pockets. The gaoler was socially halfway between the two women. By holding a position in local government he would be described today as respectable middle class; the slave-girl working class and Lydia upper class. Yet all three were admitted into the New Testament church on the same terms and conditions: the shed blood of Jesus.

There's a possibility that here we have an example of God's humour: each day the male head of a Jewish household would say the same morning prayer in which he would thank God that he was not a Gentile, a woman or a slave. And here in Philippi, the first three converts marking the foundation of the Christian church in Europe were the three despised categories redeemed and united in Christ – the living example of what Paul had recently taught in his letters to the Galatians: "There is neither Jew nor Greek, slave nor free, male nor female, for you are all one in Christ Jesus" (Galatians 3:28).

Paul was writing to the Philippians from captivity in Rome and although allowed to stay in his own rented house while awaiting trial before the Emperor Nero he was chained day and night to a Roman soldier. He knew he faced the death penalty when he appeared before Nero, yet his letter radiates joy, contentment and peace. The four chapters in his letter each present Christ in a different way and combine to present Paul's theme of how the Christian may know victory and joy amidst the normal and even exceptional trials and difficulties of life.

Each chapter has a key verse.

## Gain in life, gain in death

In chapter 1 Christ is presented as "our life, our everything": "For me, to live is Christ and to die is gain" (Philippians 1:21).

Many people are miles from the heart of Christianity and often their knowledge of it stops at contact with those who claim to be Christians. But since many who profess faith in Christ are far from what God intends them to be, this contact can present a false idea of real biblical Christianity. Others get closer, and conclude that Christianity is the visible congregation or ceremonies and ritual, and they fall short of discovering that the real thing about Christianity is a person – the Lord Jesus Christ. Nothing about Christianity will be rightly understood until there is faith in Christ and a personal relationship with Him that recognizes Him as the centre and purpose of our lives. Some Christians misunderstand this verse and place the emphasis on its ending of "to die is gain". They see it as referring to the attitude of someone who has had enough of this life with all its trials, difficulties and pain and just longs to go to heaven, putting all this behind them. And it has to be said there are a lot of Christians who would sympathize with that way of thinking: they are not happy with this life and long to move forward to the one that is promised. But that's not what Paul is saying.

In Philippians 3:8 Paul uses the word "gain" in a way that explains what he means. There he speaks about the day when Christ came into his life and how, as a consequence all that the world might think of as valuable "gain" (see 3:4–7), he now considered to be rubbish by comparison to having found Jesus (verse 9). This leads him to define his life as "gaining Christ" and his death as being the "ultimate gain". This presents Paul with a catch-22 situation. You could paraphrase him by saying, "As I serve Christ day by day and grow in my knowledge of Him, and He becomes more and more real to me, then life to me is Christ. But, as death will bring me closer to Christ, death to me is gain. So what do I do? Against the immediate gain of Christ death brings, I have to consider the increased fruit for Christ that continued life will bring. I just don't know. To die is gloriously to possess Christ, while to live is gloriously to bear fruit for Christ!"

So, as the context of the passage confirms in 1:12–14, Paul is not saying that he is discouraged because of his imprisonment, he's saying, "Don't worry about the circumstances that I am in, for my imprisonment has helped to advance the gospel in Rome as never before. I'm not discouraged; I'm rejoicing. Furthermore, the other Christians in Rome are stirred up and are preaching around the city."

If you study the context you can see what was happening. Nero, the emperor, had commanded that every six hours a soldier would be brought in and chained to the apostle Paul, which resulted in a picked band of men being formed who were being instructed in the Christian doctrine. Paul confirms this in 4:22 where he says, "All the saints send you greetings, especially those who belong to Caesar's household." Historians tell us that Nero was a prolific writer, but 2,000 years later no one bothers what he wrote about while Paul's letters are treasured, read and studied by hundreds of millions throughout the world. Truly the time has come when men call their dogs Nero and their sons Paul.

## The supreme example

In chapter 2 Paul focuses on Christian unity.

Your attitude should be the same as that of Christ Jesus: "Who, being in very nature God, did not consider equality with God something to be grasped" (Philippians 2:5–6).

Disunity is an ongoing problem in church life, and Philippi was no exception. Certain individuals were quarrelling and there were divisions within the body of the church. People get uptight over all kinds of things: the tone of someone's voice, the choice of music, what the church deems to be important etc. Then cliques with their "in-groups" tend to develop and bring division, which is always destructive to the life and vitality of a church. And in light of this Paul points to Christ as our example in settling difficulties and problems.

The phrase "to be grasped" in verse 6 means to be held onto at all costs. In other words, Jesus did not count the fact that He was equal with God the Father and God the Holy Spirit a thing to be held onto at all costs. But rather He,

> ... *made himself nothing,*
> *taking the very nature of a servant,*
> *being made in human likeness.*
> *And being found in appearance as a man,*
> *he humbled himself*
> *and became obedient to death –*
> *even death on a cross!*

PHILIPPIANS 2:7–8

Therefore, says Paul, just as Christ voluntarily laid aside His divine privileges out of love for His Father, you, in your disagreements with one another, should have this self-same attitude toward each other.

What was the result of Jesus' sacrifice of His privileges? It's given in verses 9–11:

> *Therefore God exalted him to the highest place*
> *and gave him the name that is above every name,*
> *that at the name of Jesus every knee should bow,*
> *in heaven and on earth and under the earth,*
> *and every tongue confess that Jesus Christ is Lord,*
> *to the glory of God the Father.*

When Jesus gave up His privileges, God the Father gave Him every privilege in the universe. He put His problem in God's hands and the Father vindicated Him. This is what Paul is saying to quarrelling Christians – give up your rights; don't insist on them. The opening words of chapter 2 are Paul's practical application of this truth. He says:

*If you have any encouragement from being united with Christ,*
*if any comfort from his love, if any fellowship with the Spirit, if*
*any tenderness and compassion, then make my joy complete by*
*being like-minded, having the same love, being one in spirit and*
*purpose. Do nothing out of selfish ambition or vain conceit, but*
*in humility consider others better than yourselves.*

PHILIPPIANS 2:1–3

If Christians could put that teaching into practice they would be different people. There would be no quarrelling within churches and no divisions among them.

## Profit and loss

In chapter 3 Paul presents Christ as the One who moves us to want earnestly what we ought to want and who makes us confident that it can be achieved.

A fashionable slogan today is "If you've got it, flaunt it!" But sometimes we go even further, flaunting "it" even if we haven't got "it"; for example, exaggerating our CV. However, in verse 10a Paul makes it clear he is working to another agenda: I want to know Christ and the power of his resurrection.

And by way of contrast, he mentions the things from his past that motivated him and gave him confidence, or rather a false sense of confidence, before he became a Christian. He tells those who think they have reason for confidence in the flesh to look over his CV, where they will find the following:

- His pedigree: He was "circumcised on the eighth day, of the people of Israel, of the tribe of Benjamin, a Hebrew of Hebrews" (verse 5a). "You can't beat that for ancestry," says Paul.
- His orthodoxy: "in regard to the law, a Pharisee" – the strictest sect of his religion (verse 5b).
- Enthusiasm for his work: "as for zeal, persecuting the church" (verse 6a).
- His morality: "as for legalistic righteousness, faultless" (verse 6b).

Paul had an impeccable CV.

But now, he says, "Whatever was to my profit I now consider loss for the sake of Christ" (verse 7). Paul's confessing, "All of it, my ancestry, my orthodoxy, my enthusiasm and morality – all the confidence I once got from those things – I have found to be of absolutely no value compared to that which Jesus Christ gives. I consider them rubbish, that I may gain Christ [verses 7–8].

He, Jesus Christ, is my confidence and in Him I will boast!"

Then, towards the end of chapter 3, Paul contrasts those who seek secondary values in the guise of religion. He says, "Their destiny is destruction, their god is their stomach, and their glory is in their shame. Their mind is on earthly things" (Philippians 3:19).

But then he goes on to say that those whose confidence is in Christ have an eternal life:

> *But our citizenship is in heaven. And we eagerly await a*
> *Saviour from there, the Lord Jesus Christ, who, by the power*
> *that enables him to bring everything under his control,*
> *will transform our lowly bodies so that they will be like his*
> *glorious body.*
>
> PHILIPPIANS 3:20–21

Paul is saying, you who know this and live this should stand fast in the Lord.

## Christian contentment

In chapter 4 Paul brings before us another picture: that of Christ as our strength.

Not only does God move us to want the right things but He makes it possible for us to do them by providing the dynamic that fulfils the desire. Paul explains this in verse 13: "I can do everything through him who gives me strength."

The practicality of these things is demonstrated in the context. First, there is the problem of getting along with others, as with the two ladies in the church at Philippi, Euodia and Syntyche (verse 2). There is an oft-repeated story of the man who couldn't quite pronounce these names but read them this way, "I plead with Odious and I plead with Soontouchy." Unfortunately, we still have in our churches odious people and soon-touchy people – those whose feelings get hurt very easily and those who delight in hurting others" feelings. But the apostle says, "I plead with you to agree with each other in the Lord." How can we do that? Answer: "I can do everything through him who gives me strength."

Then there is the matter of worry: "Do not be anxious about anything, but in everything, by prayer and petition, with thanksgiving, present your requests to God" (Philippians 4:6).

This is God's answer to anxiety. It's not switching off and it's not suppressing our worries; it's praying to God with thanksgiving, recognizing that His ways are not our ways. It may be in tears, and in some way or another all Christians have been there, but the Lord says pray to Him about it with thanksgiving and leave it with Him. Then the peace of God, which you will never be able to understand – where it comes from or how it gets there – will possess your heart and mind in Christ Jesus. Christ is our strength.

Finally, there is the matter of contentment. Paul says,

> *... I have learned to be content whatever the circumstances.*
> *I know what it is to be in need, and I know what it is to have*
> *plenty. I have learned the secret of being content in any and*
> *every situation, whether well fed or hungry, whether living in*
> *plenty or in want.*
>
> PHILIPPIANS 4:11B–12

And he passes the secret on to the Philippian Christians: "my God will meet all your needs according to his glorious riches in Christ Jesus" (Philippians 4:19).

Note: not greeds – needs! Christ is our sufficiency!

Paul's letter to the Philippians reveals the secret of a man who ran the full course, who fought the good fight and who kept the faith. It is his explanation of how he did it. We who live in this modern age with its particular frustrations, anxieties and pressures, need to discover and understand this because we have the same One indwelling us who indwelt the apostle Paul.

Christ is our life; Christ is our example; Christ is our confidence: Christ is our strength and Christ is our sufficiency.

# 51

## Colossians
## – Christ is All

Colossae was a small town situated 100 miles east of Ephesus in today's Turkey. It was from there that Epaphras, the founder of the Colossian church, visited Paul in Rome with the disturbing news that heretical teaching was threatening the well being of the church.

In *The Da Vinci Code*, Dan Brown makes much of the Gnostic gospels; a heresy which was to plague the Christian church until around the end of the second century. By that time the Gnostic threat had been largely overcome and the church emerged strengthened by the struggle with the Gnostics, though not without scars. In his letter to the church at Colossae, Paul is dealing with the symptoms of early Gnosticism, which was essentially a religious-philosophical attitude rather than a well-defined system. A contemporary example would be the way in which the majority of people in the Western world believe in the theory of evolution without understanding what exactly it means.

The term "Gnosticism", is related to the Greek *gnosis*, which means "knowledge". Gnostics taught that salvation is obtained not through faith but through knowledge known only to Gnostics. However, the reality was that it was an occult knowledge pervaded by superstitions of astrology and magic. Moreover, it was a mysterious knowledge, open only to those who had been initiated into the mysteries of the Gnostic system.

Gnosticism lent itself to an air of exclusiveness, cultivating an "enlightened" elite for whom alone salvation was possible. As the Gnostics believed all matter was evil and that God did not create the world, they refused to accept the

Christian belief in the incarnation of Christ. In their view, Jesus was only one of many intermediaries between God and the world and the advent of Christ was a piece of play-acting where God wore a mask of humanity on the stage of human history to give the appearance of being a man while remaining God in disguise.

The Gnostic belief that matter was evil led to a distorted view of the Christian life. Some turned to asceticism, hoping to free themselves from the influence of matter (the body) by inflicting punishment on their flesh. Others assumed an attitude of indifference to things physical and material and turned to self-gratifying license in the belief that only the soul is important and therefore the body may do what it pleases.

By combining oriental myths and Greek philosophy, Gnosticism sought to absorb the various religions with which it came into contact. The term we use today is "syncretism" – the taking on board of thinking and practices not found in the Bible. So, although Gnosticism wore the mask of Christianity in that it did not deny Christ, it did dethrone Him. It gave Christ a place, but not the supreme place. Christ was not the triumphant Redeemer to whom all authority in heaven and on earth had been committed; at best He was only one of many spirit beings who bridged the space between God and man. This downgrading of the person of Jesus Christ was the most dangerous aspect of the Colossian heresy and the early church was on the verge of losing its understanding of the real power by which the Christian life is lived. In response, Paul wrote this letter, the theme of which can be expressed by the words that form part of his introductory prayer: "May you be strengthened with all power according to his glorious might" (see 1:11).

## Paul affirms the deity of Jesus

Beginning on that note, and in one of the strongest and most glorious proclamations concerning Christ's deity, Paul sets forth Jesus Christ Himself as the source of all power in the Christian life (1:15–20): 'He is the image of the invisible God" (verse 15).

As an image is an exact expression, Paul is declaring that in the man Jesus we have the exact expression of all that God is. He is "the firstborn over all creation" (verse15).

Cults like the Jehovah's Witnesses use this passage to "prove" their point that Jesus Christ is not God, but that He was the first person ever created. There is, of course, a sense in which this word "firstborn" does have that meaning. When we refer to our children, we say that the eldest one is the firstborn because he or she appeared first on the scene. And to the unwary the Jehovah's Witnesses' explanation seems to be logical and scriptural. But this error is to give the term "firstborn" a modern meaning that is quite different from its usage in the New Testament. Here, the expression does not refer to the chronology of Jesus, which anyway would be out of context, but to His role or position. In other words, Jesus was not the first one of a line of creation, but the heir of all creation – the owner of it. And this fits with what the apostle goes on to say in verse 16:

> For by him all things were created: things in heaven and on
> earth, visible and invisible, whether thrones or powers or rulers
> or authorities; all things were created by him and for him.

In order to substantiate their misinformation about Jesus Christ, Jehovah's Witness literature has inserted the word "other" in these phrases so that it reads: "All other things were created by him. In him all other things were created." However there is absolutely no warrant whatsoever in the Greek text for the insertion of the word "other".

In verse 18 ("[He is] the firstborn from among the dead"), Scripture proves Scripture – there were quite a few other people raised from the dead before the resurrection of Jesus (Lazarus for one). So, just as "firstborn from among the dead" does not mean that in chronological terms Jesus was the first to die and come back to life, but that He is pre-eminent among those who came back from the dead, so too, "firstborn over all creation" does not mean Jesus was the first person ever to be born but that He is pre-eminent over all creation. Why? Because, as Paul declares, the Lord Jesus is the Creator! The One who flung the stars into space, who was present with God and who was God when the great words went out, "Let there be light"; "Let the land produce…", and all the other great declarations of creation that are recorded in Genesis, was Jesus Christ Himself. In fact, as Colossians 1:17 says, "He is before all things, and in him all things hold together." 'He is the head of the body, the church; he is the beginning, the firstborn from among the dead" (verse 18).

Paul then goes further with the declaration in verse 18. Twice, Paul uses this term, "the firstborn": He is the firstborn of the old creation and He is the firstborn of the new creation – the resurrection. That is, He is the firstborn from the dead. As we have seen, this does not mean that He was the first one ever to be raised from the dead, because Scripture records others who preceded Him; it means that Jesus is the head of the new creation. Christians are part of a new body, the new, born-again race of beings that God is forming through the centuries and who, after death will inherit the new heavens and the new earth. The head of that body is Jesus Christ. From Him, then, flows all power: the resurrection power that was demonstrated by raising Christ from the dead and against which no human power can resist. The power that has the ability to change hearts, lives and attitudes, making all things new from within, is resurrection power. It flows to us from the head of the new creation, the risen Christ, the source of all power.

## Christ, the source of all power

In verses 21–22 Paul tells us who are the intended recipients of this power: "Once you were alienated from God and were enemies in your minds because of your evil behaviour" (Colossians 1:21).

Before their conversion and acceptance of Jesus Christ as Lord of their lives all Christians had their minds closed against Jesus because they wanted to do their own thing, which was selfish and wicked. Incredibly though, they are the very ones through whom this power is now to operate: "But now he has reconciled you by Christ's physical body through death to present you holy in his sight, without blemish and free from accusation" (Colossians 1:22).

Paul then gives us the demonstration of this power in his own life by telling us that God called him and set him up in the ministry to proclaim a mystery. He tells us what it is in verses 25–26a:

> I have become its servant by the commission God gave me to
> present to you the word of God in its fullness – the mystery
> that has been kept hidden for ages and generations....

We do not find it explained in the Old Testament: it was experienced there, but it was never explained as verses 26b–27a tell us: "but is now disclosed to the saints. To them God has chosen to make known among the Gentiles the glorious riches of this mystery".

What is it? "Christ in you, the hope of glory" (Colossians 1:27b).

This is the supreme declaration of the Christian church: not only are our sins forgiven when we come to Christ, but that He, Himself, will live within us and will thus empower us to do everything expected of us. He died for us, so that He might live in us. This is the full glory of the Christian gospel.

Paul tells us how he himself experienced this. He says, "We proclaim him, admonishing and teaching everyone with all wisdom, so that we may present everyone perfect in Christ. To this end I labour" (Colossians 1:28–29a).

Where does the energy come from? This amazing apostle, with his unfaltering journeying night and day, through shipwreck and hardship of every kind, labouring, travelling the length and breadth of the Roman empire is ceaseless in his endeavours. Where does he get the energy? He tells us in verse 29b: "struggling with all his energy which so powerfully works in me". It is Christ in him, the hope of glory!

If Christian men and women could fully appreciate what it is that God has made available to them, they would never be the same again. They would not pursue the trivial, placing the church somewhere amongst all the other priorities in their lives. Paul says that here is a source of energy that is constant and consistent, and which flows through him created by the Spirit of God indwelling him. The result was that as he saw the task before him, he moved to meet it with the energy God gave. That is resurrection power, and it is available to Christians today, transforming their lives!

While the Gnostic heresy would later seriously concern the church, what Paul was dealing with in these early stages of Gnosticism was not so much a movement but a mood. It was this mood – hugely influential in its day – that was drawing Christian leaders not to a greater spirituality as they imagined, but actually away from Christ. They, of course, didn't see it that way, but Paul with his God-given wisdom recognized the danger and in chapter 2 he tells us how to recognize it.

First is the idea that power comes from human knowledge:

> See to it that no one takes you captive through hollow and
> deceptive philosophy, which depends on human tradition and
> the basic principles of this world rather than on Christ.
>
> COLOSSIANS 2:8

This can sound as though the gospel is anti-intellectual; however, the Bible is not against knowledge per se, but only against that knowledge which is not regulated by the Word of God. There is much that is right and true in what humankind has discovered through the ages, but Paul points out that the source is suspect when it comes from tradition, and we would add misapplied science and false worldviews. Tradition is accumulated knowledge built up through the centuries and passed along from one generation tos another. As secular knowledge is comprised of truth mingled with error, this means that if it is accepted uncritically it leads to mistaken concepts, untrue beliefs and harmful ideas.

Second, says Paul, human knowledge depends on the basic principles of this world. Ultimately this means occult powers govern the mind of men and women, darken their intellect and limit their understanding. So, human knowledge is essentially underdeveloped. That is, it stays on the borders of truth, never getting to the real heart of things. This explains why you can have a university community saturated with the highest exponents of human knowledge, and yet be filled with vileness, corruption, unrest, distress and suicide. Human knowledge does not go to the heart of things as the Word of God does. The two complement each other, but they are not equal – human knowledge must be critically evaluated against God's Word, and it must always be subject to the wisdom of God.

Paul's final objection is that as human wisdom is inferior to Christ's, it lacks the ability to insert the great positives into life – it is essentially negative. It does not produce the qualities of love, truth, joy, peace and power that come only from Jesus Christ. Paul's conclusion is that the answer to the lure of human wisdom is the judgment of the cross. The cross has delivered us and cuts us off from trust and admiration for human wisdom, bringing us to the place where we can judge these things and see their moral values properly in the light of the Word of God.

Paul then goes on to indicate another false source of power, which also leads many people astray:

> *Therefore do not let anyone judge you by what you eat or drink,*
> *or with regard to a religious festival, a New Moon celebration*
> *or a Sabbath day. These are a shadow of the things that were to*
> *come; the reality, however, is found in Christ.*
>
> COLOSSIANS 2:16–17

In that same vein, he continues,

> *Since you died with Christ to the basic principles of this world,*
> *why, as though you still belonged to it, do you submit to its*
> *rules: "Do not handle! Do not taste! Do not touch!*
>
> COLOSSIANS 2:20–21

The false source of power Paul is referring to is the spiritual power that supposedly comes from a dedicated zeal for God that shows itself in legalism and asceticism. These things can appear very impressive and powerful, and sometimes we cannot help but admire the zealous individuals whose spirituality seems to be so much more than ours. "But," says the apostle, "they are deceiving themselves." They do not discover real power:

> *Such regulations indeed have an appearance of wisdom, with*
> *their self-imposed worship, their false humility and their harsh*
> *treatment of the body. But, they lack any value in restraining*
> *sensual indulgence.*
>
> COLOSSIANS 2:23

Paul is saying that the most pious person can wear a hair shirt, yet still be filled with lust. They can beat their body black and blue and still be guilty all the time of thinking lascivious thoughts. These things provide no check to the indulgence of the flesh and do not provide the power needed to live the Christ-like life.

Paul continues with the third source of false power:

> *Do not let anyone who delights in false humility and the*
> *worship of angels disqualify you for the prize. Such a*
> *person goes into great detail about what he has seen, and his*
> *unspiritual mind puffs him up with idle notions.*
>
> COLOSSIANS 2:18

Here Paul puts the sword of truth through the "puffed-up" counterfeit who claims to possess superior spiritual power and deflates him. Christian men and women must always be on their guard for the plausible "would-be" leader who, with their dramatic personal experiences attempt to draw them towards themselves and away from the truth of Christ. Paul says their claim is unfounded because, "He has lost connection with the Head, from whom the whole body, supported and held together by its ligaments and sinews, grows as God causes it to grow" Colossians 2:19.

Paul can speak with great authority here, and sets an exemplary example when he refused to capitalize on his own "out of this world supernatural experience" (2 Corinthians 12:5).

In Colossians 3:1–2 Paul exhorts his readers to put into practice what he has been teaching:

> *Since, then, you have been raised with Christ, set your hearts*
> *on things above, where Christ is seated at the right hand of*
> *God. Set your minds on things above, not on earthly things.*

That doesn't mean we should be constantly thinking about heaven: there's nothing super-pious about this. He's simply saying, "Don't let your desires and your attitudes be governed by desires for earthly fame or power. Instead, let your desires be shaped by the Word of God." Paul gives us the formula for doing this: "Put to death, therefore, whatever belongs to your earthly nature" (3:5). God has already sentenced our earthy nature to death on the cross, so when it shows itself in you, treat it like that – as under the sentence of death from God. In the same verse, he goes on to list these earthly things: "sexual immorality, impurity, lust, evil desires and greed, which is idolatry" as the outworking of our earthly nature.

## Christian behaviour in church

Then Paul moves into the area of the Christian in the church:

> But now you must rid yourselves of all such things as these:
> anger, rage, malice, slander, and filthy language from your lips.
> Do not lie to each other, since you have taken off your old self
> with its practices.
>
> COLOSSIANS 3:8–9

Putting these away is the first step. The second step is in Colossians 3:12–14:

> Therefore, as God's chosen people, holy and dearly loved, clothe
> yourselves with compassion, kindness, humility, gentleness and
> patience. Bear with each other and forgive whatever grievances
> you may have against one another. Forgive as the Lord forgave
> you. And over all these virtues put on love, which binds them
> all together in perfect unity.

Paul is saying that as Christ dwells within us, we are to let the characteristics of His life be shown in our lives. And by way of example, Paul lists certain areas in which these are to be seen:

> Wives, submit to your husbands... Husbands, love your
> wives... Children, obey your parents... Fathers, do not embitter
> your children... Slaves, obey your earthly masters... Masters,
> provide your slaves with what is right and fair.
>
> COLOSSIANS 3:18–22; 4:1

In chapter 4 Paul brings his letter to an end with some practical advice:

> *Devote yourselves to prayer, being watchful and thankful.*
> *And pray for us, too… Be wise in the way you act toward*
> *outsiders… Let your conversation be always full of grace,*
> *seasoned with salt… .*
>
> COLOSSIANS 4:2–3, 5, 6

He follows this by sending some personal greetings from men who are with him, who are also demonstrations of the power of an indwelling Christ at work. Finally, as was his custom, he took the pen in his own hand and wrote:

> *I, Paul, write this greeting with my own hand. Remember my*
> *chains. Grace be with you.*
>
> COLOSSIANS 4:18

# 52

# 1 Thessalonians
## – Hope for a Hopeless World

The city of Thessalonica, located on the Egnatian Way, the main highway from Rome to the east, was the capital of the Roman province of Macedonia.

Acts 17 records how Thessalonica came to be evangelized. It explains how during Paul's second missionary journey in the company of Silas, Timothy and Luke around AD 50, they crossed the Aegean Sea into Europe. Then, following a remarkably successful mission in Philippi, they moved on to Thessalonica where Paul preached on three successive sabbaths in the local synagogue. Some of the Jews were persuaded and joined Paul and Silas, as did a large number of God-fearing Greeks and not a few prominent women. But it was not long before opposition arose and the Jews stirred up a riot under the pretext of accusing Paul of preaching a king other than Caesar. This resulted in Paul and Silas being smuggled out of town under cover of darkness and travelling south to Berea for a short evangelistic mission. However, the Jews followed them so Paul continued further south to Athens where he waited for Silas and Timothy. As he had only been in Thessalonica three weeks before he was forced to flee the city, Paul was anxious about leaving behind the immature Christians in Thessalonica with no trained ministers to lead and support them. So, Paul sent Timothy on a fact-finding mission to Thessalonica to report on the situation with regard to the local church. However, by the time Timothy was ready to return with his news, Paul had moved on to Corinth. It was in Corinth that they were reunited, and it was from there that Paul, prompted by Timothy's account of his visit, wrote this first letter to the Thessalonians.

# Problems concerning Thessalonians

Timothy's report raised a number of subjects for Paul to deal with.

Firstly, there was the ongoing problem of opposition to Paul from Jews spreading the false rumour that because he was not one of the original twelve he was not a genuine apostle. This was not only a problem for Paul but also for the Thessalonians. Furthermore, the pagans of Thessalonica were severely persecuting the Christians by threatening them and taking away their property. So, these early Christians, perhaps only three or four weeks old in the Lord, were called upon to endure hard things for the cause of Christ.

Secondly, in Thessalonica as in all Greek society, sexual promiscuity was common – even regarded as a religious norm. To live a life of chastity was to be regarded as freakish. Therefore, as is the case today, there was great pressure upon these new Christians to fall into line with the common sexual practices of their day.

Thirdly, a major problem affecting the church in Thessalonica was that the second coming of Jesus Christ was greatly misunderstood. Paul had evidently told them something, but they were confused about his teaching, and some of them, in the expectation that Christ's return was imminent, had actually stopped working and were waiting for Him to arrive. Since they weren't earning a living they were dependent on the rest of the congregation for support.

Fourthly, tensions were developing between the congregation and church leaders, and, finally, there were those who were somewhat indifferent to both the Holy Spirit's work amongst them and to the truth of God as it was being proclaimed in the Scriptures.

# The aims of the epistle

Thus, in response to Timothy's report, Paul had three chief aims in writing the epistle:

1. To express satisfaction and thanks to God for the healthy spiritual condition of the church (1:2–10).

2. To make a strong case against the false insinuations against himself and his associates (2:1 – 3:13).

3. To address issues of Christian behaviour relating to sexual morality, earning their own living, preparing for the second coming of Jesus and tensions within the fellowship (4:1 – 5:24).

## The good news is welcomed and spreads

Chapter 1 develops two important points regarding the church: "our gospel came to you and you welcomed it" (see verses 5–6), and it "rang out from you" (verse 8).

The lesson is that the men, women and children who are the body of Christ are to be like telecommunications satellites that first receive the message then transmit it onwards. This is the method by which God intends to evangelize the world: his people telling their own story of Jesus and having Bibles, tracts, Scripture portions, testimony books and booklets produced in hundreds of languages by thousands of sources in countries all over the world.

There is another important point in chapter 1 concerning the church: not only did the Word go forth in verbal evangelism but the news of their conversion went forth in conversational evangelism: "You became a model... your faith in God has become known everywhere... They tell how you turned to God from idols" (1 Thessalonians 1:7, 8, 9).

The word was out; everyone was talking about this new community which had been established in Thessalonica: their bold rejection of idolatry; their joy in the midst of opposition; their transformed values; their faith and love. And we can appreciate that people would want to come and see for themselves the remarkable transformation that was taking place in their midst, and would be convinced not just by what they heard, but by what they saw. For in truth, no church can spread the gospel with any degree of integrity, let alone credibility, unless it has been visibly changed by the gospel it preaches. It's not enough to receive the gospel and pass it on; Christians must embody it in their everyday lives of faith: love, joy, peace, righteousness and hope.

## Paul defends his character and motive

In chapter 2 Paul deals with the smear campaign that aimed to undermine his apostolic credibility and unsettle the new Christians.

Paul's response gives Christians a template for dealing with criticism. His critics alleged that his visit was a failure (verse 1), that he got his facts wrong, thus rendering the church's beliefs erroneous, and that Paul was like any pagan teacher peddling a form of cult prostitution, which is what "impure motives" implies (verse 3). They also condemned his methods as trickery, alleging that Paul was just out for personal profit (verses 3–4).

Paul denied the charges by appealing to the evidence of his visit that his readers could still remember. He said that his endurance of opposition was enough to show them he was genuine, for no trickster would put his life on the line (verse 2). He also made the point that his preaching had been straight and neither flattering nor profit-seeking. In fact, he and his colleagues had taken jobs in order to earn a living during their stay with them (verses 6–9). As for their sexual conduct, there had been no question of any indiscretion, let alone an affair (verses 10–12). Keep in mind, said Paul, that persecution is a hazard of being a Christian and preachers and church members were all in the same boat (verses 13–16). Finally, he reminded his readers that Christian leaders are to be respected (verses 10–12).

Paul's teaching here is twofold:
- Leaders should walk in the light; they should keep everything above board, doing nothing that can be misconstrued.
- Church members should check a critic's accusations against the facts.

## Against sexual promiscuity

In chapter 4 Paul turns his attention to the permissive and promiscuous lifestyle that pervaded Greek society.

Wives could be changed regularly and mistresses were common. Against this background Paul told the men in the Thessalonian church that they had to give up their prostitutes and mistresses and shun the promiscuous attitudes that prevailed. They were to honour their marriages by keeping the marriage bed pure. A wife was not to be treated like a prostitute or a mistress.

## The importance of work

Addressing those who wouldn't work (not those who couldn't work), Paul told them to earn their own living, making it their ambition to be dependent on no one. Able-bodied Christians should not live on the charity of other people but should earn their own living so as to support their families and give help to those in genuine need.

## Correction of ideas about the second coming

To address the confusion concerning Christ's return, Paul makes six points. It is important to note that this is not an exhaustive treatise of the last times but rather Paul answering questions put to him and covering matters being debated in the church at Thessalonica:

Has Jesus returned?

*Answer*: No! (2 Thessalonians 2:1–3).

Have those who have already died missed the celebration?

*Answer*: No! (1 Thessalonians 4:13–18).

How should the bereaved who mourn respond?

*Answer*: They can look forward in hope to sharing in the kingdom with their loved ones (1 Thessalonians 4:17).

When will Jesus come back?

*Answer*: Don't know! (1 Thessalonians 5:1–3).

What will happen to those who are persecuting us?

*Answer*: They will get their just deserts (2 Thessalonians 1:5–10).

Faced with the uncertain timing of Jesus' return, how should we live?

*Answer*: Christians are to be holy people for all time (1 Thessalonians 4:3–11).

It is important that we understand that Paul's teaching here is not primarily for the mind but for the heart. Though this life is often nasty, brutish and short, God wants His people to demonstrate hope where there is despair, faithfulness where there is deceit and goodness where there is evil. Our secular Western society sees little, if any, hope after death, with the result all the hopes, dreams, expectations and ambitions are focused on this life with their fulfilment being seen in terms of measurable wealth and wellbeing, status and success. The danger is that Christians can be seduced into this way of thinking and thus lose sight of God's greater eternal purposes. To keep the thought of heaven to the forefront of our thinking is to relegate the material and physical demands of an acquisitive world and keep it in its place.

# Disharmony within the church

In chapter 5 Paul offers practical teaching concerning the relationship between church members and leaders, and in verse 12 he uses three expressions.

## 1. Christian leaders are those who "work hard among you"

Though very different, working in full-time Christian ministry requires the same commitment and dedication as secular employment. Whether sermon preparation, studying, visiting the sick and bereaved, counselling the troubled, leading discipleship classes, instructing people for baptism, encouraging members to take up ministries and move on in the Lord, prayer and intercession, guarding doctrine and making sure the "flock" do not veer to the left or right and all that's involved in leading a church in the modern society demands hard work, especially emotional and spiritual.

## 2. Christian leaders are those "who are over you in the Lord"

In spite of the servant role, authentic leadership carries elements of authority. The city of Thessalonica operated with a democratic form of government. This had many positives but also a negative, in that church members treated their spiritual leaders the same way as they did their political leaders. And Paul tells the Thessalonians to respect their church leaders, noting that they cannot lead if they are not respected. The church is not a democracy, it's a theocracy. We serve King Jesus and His church is ruled by the Holy Spirit. He determines how His church is to be governed and He says it is to be by elders and deacons.

## 3. Christian leaders are those "who admonish you"

The Greek verb used here means "to reprove and discipline". It should not be hard and harsh; its primary purpose is to caution bad behaviour and warn of its consequences with a view to correction and restoration. Where repentance and restoration is not evident church discipline will be imposed by the leaders.

So, the local congregation is not to despise its leaders as though they were dispensable, nor flatter them as if they were popes, but rather respect them and "hold them in the highest regard in love because of their work". This combination of appreciation and affection will enable church leaders and the flock they lead to live in peace with each other (verses 12–13), and when churches enjoy unity there is blessing.

Paul's final prayer sums up the theme of the book:

*May God himself, the God of peace, sanctify you through*
*and through. May your whole spirit, soul and body be kept*
*blameless at the coming of our Lord Jesus Christ.*

1 THESSALONIANS 5:23

That is the Christian hope – that one day we will stand blameless before God because of what Jesus Christ has done for us on Calvary's cross.

# 53

# 2 Thessalonians
## – Lawlessness Restrained

Before he left earth, Jesus promised that at the end of the age He would return for His church (Matthew 24:30–31). However, He also said that just before His return would be a time of great distress, "unequalled from the beginning of the world… and never to be equalled again" (Matthew 24:21). As the Christians in Thessalonica were going through a time of persecution, many thought that they were experiencing that time of foretold tribulation and so were reacting in different ways. Some questioned the rationale for Christian suffering and were asking, "Why?"; others wanted to know what God would do to their persecutors. To add to their confusion, false teachers were circulating a forged letter, supposedly to have come from Paul, to the effect that the "day of the Lord" had already come. Also, those who stopped work in the belief that the second coming was imminent, and to whom Paul had addressed his first letter, were ignoring his teaching and causing concern for the Thessalonian church. In response to these issues, Paul writes a second letter to the Thessalonians, which breaks down as follows:

- Paul's encouragement to the church suffering persecution (1:5–10);

- Correcting false teachers by explaining "the Day of the Lord", especially in relation to the Antichrist (2:4–12);

- Emphasizing the responsibility of Christians to live holy lives (3:6–15).

# Paul encourages the persecuted church

In chapter 1 Paul says that suffering, glory, tribulation and the kingdom belong inseparably to one another.

However, Christians need to remember that God is on their side, sustaining, sanctifying and using their persecutions as a means through which He is developing their faith, love and perseverance – in contrast to the prejudice, anger and bitterness of their persecutors (verses 3–5). And, because God is just, one day He will vindicate His people publicly by reversing the fortunes of both groups: the persecutors will be persecuted when Christ returns:

> *He will pay back trouble to those who trouble you and give*
> *relief to you who are troubled… He will punish those who do*
> *not know God and do not obey the gospel of our Lord Jesus.*
>
> 2 THESSALONIANS 1:6–7, 8

However, when faced with apparent injustice or unfairness, such as the suffering of the innocent, it takes spiritual discernment to see evidence of the just judgment of God, for our fallen nature focuses upon surface appearance and leads us to make superficial comments. We see the suffering of the people of God who are opposed, ridiculed, boycotted, harassed, imprisoned, tortured and killed. We see pain, bewilderment and personal battering. In other words, what we see is injustice – the wicked flourishing and the righteous suffering, with the Christian going through what seems to be needless and unfair distress. And we are tempted to inveigh against God and against the apparent injustice of it all and complain, "Why? It seems so unfair. Why doesn't God do something?" The answer according to Paul is that God is doing something and will go on doing it: He is allowing His people to suffer in order to refine them for His heavenly kingdom. He is allowing the wicked to triumph temporarily but His just judgment will fall upon them in the end: "They will be punished with everlasting destruction and shut out from the presence of the Lord and from the majesty of his power" (1:9).

Hell is often pictured as a fiery furnace where people are being continually burned. The Bible uses symbolic language that reflects the suggestion of dreadful pain because non-believing men and women do not understand the very real pain that they will experience by being excluded from the presence of Jesus. He is the source of everything that is good – beauty, truth, life, love, joy, peace, grace, strength and forgiveness. All those things come only from God, and if a man or woman won't have them, then God finally says to them: "I've been trying my best to get you to take these, but if you won't have them, then you must have your own way", and they are shut out from the presence of the Lord. And if they're shut away from the source of all goodness, then what's left? The opposite – darkness and pain. That is what they had been dishing out and that is what they will finally obtain. God will let them have their own way, and when they get it, it will be the last thing they want. C. S. Lewis said that in the final analysis there are only two kinds of people, those who say to God, "Thy will be done" and those to whom God says, "Thy will be done." Thus, Paul sees evidence that God's judgment is right in the very situation that others might see nothing but injustice.

## The Antichrist

In chapter 2 it becomes apparent that it was not only the persecutors outside the church who were threatening the peace of the Thessalonian Christians.

False teachers inside were causing trouble in the area of the second coming of Jesus and of Christians being gathered to him on the last day.

The previous problem that Paul dealt with in 1 Thessalonians concerned believers who were troubled that the second coming had not come quickly enough, as some of their loved ones had died before it had taken place. Now their problem was that it had come too quickly, for the false teachers were saying, "that the day of the Lord has already come" (verse 2), which would have meant they had been left behind.

The modern example of this false belief was the Jehovah Witnesses' founder Charles T. Russell's teaching that the world would end in 1874, which he subsequently revised to 1914. When that year also passed with nothing happening, his successor, Judge J. F. Rutherford, announced that Christ did in fact come in October 1914, but that He came invisibly. Rutherford argued that on that day Christ exchanged His seat at the Father's right hand for the throne of His kingdom – so no second coming was to be expected as it had already taken place.

It was in response to some similarly bizarre notion that Paul tells the Thessalonian Christians, "not to become easily unsettled or alarmed by some prophecy, report or letter supposed to have come from us, saying that the day of the Lord has already come" (verse 2). In fact even more importantly, he says, "Don't let anyone deceive you in any way" (verse 3). Then, to put their minds at ease, he clarifies the order of future events and says that the day of the Lord will not come until two things have happened: a certain event must take place and a certain person must appear. The event Paul calls the "rebellion", and the person, "the man of lawlessness" – the Antichrist. This tells us that this person will be defiant of both moral and civil law, as Jesus Himself predicted: 'Because of the increase of wickedness, the love of most will grow cold" (Matthew 24:12)

Paul also tells us that this person will "oppose and will exalt himself over everything that is called God or is worshiped, so that he sets himself up in God's temple, proclaiming himself to be God" (2 Thessalonians 2:4). Many commentators do not take this to be a literal temple but an expression of ultimate opposition to God, which points to the principal targets of the Antichrist: God and law, religion and ethics – the forces which have been the glue that has bound society together, and to oppose them is to undermine the foundations of society.

This begs the question: Just who is the Antichrist?

There are two reasons for treading carefully here. First, verses 5 and 6 of chapter 2 make it clear that Paul taught the Thessalonians by word of mouth: "when I was with you I used to tell you these things" and "you know". This means there was background knowledge they had that we don't share. Second, church history is littered with self-confident but mistaken attempts to name the man of lawlessness.

While it is likely that Paul is referring to a single historical person, fulfilment of all details of the prophecy must await the future period of this man's prominence. "The man of lawlessness" (verse 3) will be a new figure whom Satan will energize to do his will in the world. Paul does not say what form the rebellion against God and law will take, but he says it will not occur until the chief rebel appears and, says Paul,

> *... you know what is holding him back, so that he may be revealed at the proper time. For the secret power of lawlessness is already at work; but the one who now holds it back will continue to do so until he is taken out of the way.*
>
> 2 THESSALONIANS 2:6–7

Two forces are at work in our world today. On the one hand, the secret power of lawlessness is at work surreptitiously and subversively, while on the other hand, the restraining influence of God is also at work preventing the secret rebellion from breaking out into open revolt. Only when this control is lifted will first the revolt and the second coming take place. It is evident that the restrainer, to accomplish his mission, must have supernatural power to hold back a supernatural enemy (verse 9). God and the outworking of His providence is the natural answer.

This is exactly what we see in the Western world today. Hand in hand with the move away from Christianity comes the godlessness and lawlessness the Antichrist embodies. His anti-social, anti-law, anti-God movement is to a great extent still underground. We detect its subversive influence all around us today in the militant atheistic hostility of secular humanism; in the totalitarian influences of extreme ideologies; in the materialism of the consumer society which puts things in the place of God; in the so-called theologies which proclaim the death of God and the end of moral absolutes; and in the social permissiveness which cheapens the sanctity of human life, sex, marriage and family, all of which God created or instituted. Were it not for God's remaining restraint, which preserves a measure of justice, freedom, order and decency, these evils would break out more virulently. And one day they will, for when the restraint is removed, the secret subversion will become open rebellion under the unscrupulous leadership of the lawless one (verse 8). We can expect a short period of political, social and moral chaos in which God and law are impudently flouted. The lawless one will be revealed, whom, suddenly, "the Lord Jesus will overthrow with the breath of his mouth and destroy by the splendour of his coming" (verse 8).

Just as the ministry of Jesus was accredited by miracles, signs and wonders (Acts 2:22), so the ministry of the Antichrist will be accompanied by counterfeit miracles. Probably not in the sense that they will be fakes but in the sense that they will deceive rather than enlighten (2 Thessalonians 2:9). Thus the comings of both Christ and Antichrist will be personal, visible and powerful. Tragically, the coming of the Antichrist will be such a clever parody of the coming of Christ that many will be taken in by the satanic deception.

The reason for their susceptibility to deception is that "they refused to love the truth and so be saved" (verse 10). Behind the great deception lies the great refusal. The whole deadly process is grimly logical: men and women deliberately refuse to believe in biblical truth and deliberately choose to live sinful lives. By rejecting Christ they become wide open to Satan's influence and he deceives them, resulting in God removing His restraining hand from them and giving them over to the lie they have chosen. As a result they are condemned and perish. Our country today shows every sign of the Lord's hand being loosened upon the restraint holding evil in check.

Paul's assurance regarding God's purpose for His people and advice for them is "So then, brothers, stand firm" (verse 15). He seems to picture a gale in which they are in danger of being swept off their feet and wrenched from their moorings. In the face of this hurricane he urges them to stand their ground, plant their feet firmly on terra firma and cling on to something solid and secure, clutching hold of it for dear life.

It's here that we see the ultimate secret of Christian stability: the love of God. Paul alludes to it three times. First, he describes the Thessalonians as "brothers loved by the Lord" (2:13). Second, he describes the Father and the Son as the "God who loved us" (2:16). Thirdly, he prays that the Lord will "direct your hearts into God's love" (3:5). Behind God's election and call lies God's love: that God is love and that He has set His love upon us and His love will never let us go. This love is the foundation not only of Christian confidence and stability: our strength is not only impossible but actually inconceivable apart from the steadfastness of the love of God. As Psalm 136:1 reminds us: "Give thanks to the Lord, for he is good. His love endures forever."

## Live disciplined lives

In chapter 3 Paul again speaks on the subject of Christians who gave up their employment because they thought the second coming was near.

This time the word "command" gives his words apostolic power. Verses 14 and 15 lay down five practical guidelines on when, why and how church discipline should be exercised.

First, the need for discipline does not arise from some trivial offence that can be dealt with discreetly in private but from a public, persistent disobedience to plain scriptural instructions. In this particular instance Paul had repeatedly communicated the apostles' teaching and the culprits were showing a spirit of defiance. It was those who refused to obey who must now be disciplined.

Second, the nature of the discipline which Paul demanded was a measure of social ostracism. Because those who refused to work had already received a general reprimand (1 Thessalonians 5:14) and disregarded it, the loyal church members were to keep apart from them. If anyone continued in disobedience the church was to "take special note of him" (3:14), which implies some form of public censure.

Third, the responsibility for administering discipline to a persistent offender belongs to the church leaders, but the entire church membership should be informed and involved.

Fourth, the spirit in which discipline is to be administered is to be friendly and not hostile: "do not regard him as an enemy" (verse 15). That would be excommunication.

Fifth, the purpose of discipline should be positive and constructive, aimed to restore the offender not humiliate him/her. It is rather to shame them into repentance for their past misdemeanours, encouraging them to a fresh start for their future and so be reinstated within the church community (14b).

A key reason for upholding church discipline is that the Lord's name will not be dishonoured; the community inside and outside of the church will see that disobedience to Scripture will not be swept under the carpet and a signal goes out to church members that a line is drawn which they cross at their peril.

Paul concludes his letter with a threefold blessing which takes the form of half-prayer and half-wish, and we cannot read these words without earnestly desiring for our church today what Paul desired for the Thessalonian church, namely, the peace, presence and the grace of the Lord: "Now may the Lord of peace himself give you peace at all times and in every way. The Lord be with all of you" (2 Thessalonians 3:16).

Finally, in an effort to avoid similar problems occurring in the future, Paul takes the pen from his scribe and writes in his own handwriting so that they may be able to check the authenticity of his letters:

> *I, Paul, write this greeting in my own hand, which is the distinguishing mark in all my letters. This is how I write. The grace of our Lord Jesus Christ be with you all.*
>
> 2 THESSALONIANS 3:17–18

# 54

# 1 Timothy
# – God's Leadership Manual for Church Organization

Timothy, the son of a Christian Jewess, Eunice, and a Greek father whose name is unknown, came from Lystra (Acts 16), and was raised to hear the faith by his mother and grandmother, Lois. After circumcising him as expedient for working with Jews, Paul adopted Timothy as his fellow-worker and took him to Asia Minor and Philippi. He was with Paul during his time in Ephesus and when Paul wrote his epistles to the Romans and Corinthians. Time passed, and Paul, getting on in years, aware that young Pastor Timothy was facing the heavy burden of responsibility in the church at Ephesus, wrote his first letter to Timothy from Macedonia in AD 62 or 63.

Reading the book of Acts we could mistakenly think that the early church was one big happy family with the occasional racial problem between Jew and Gentile. Their material possessions were shared, prayers were gloriously answered, there were miracles of healing and deliverance, and people were being saved everywhere the gospel was preached. But that was not the norm. Acts focuses on the big picture and not the humdrum affairs of normal church life. Certainly, the fever pitch of excitement and the miraculous did not continue forever. You only have to read Paul's letters to realize that the New Testament church was made up of human beings with all their failings and problems.

In writing to Pastor Timothy, Paul was aware of the magnitude of the task Timothy faced: false doctrine must be fought against, public worship safeguarded, mature leadership developed, and in addition to the conduct of the church, Paul talked pointedly about the conduct of the minister. Timothy must be on his guard lest his youthfulness becomes a liability rather than an asset to the gospel. He must be careful to avoid false teachers and greedy motives, pursuing instead righteousness, godliness, faith, love, perseverance and the gentleness that befits a man of God.

The call to Timothy, indeed the call to the pastorate, reminds us of Martin Luther when he was about to be ushered in to the presence of the papal assembly to defend himself against the charge of heresy. The much decorated knight, George Freundsberg, who commanded the guard, touched him on the shoulder and said kindly, "My poor monk, my poor monk, you have a march and a struggle to go through, such as neither I nor many other captains have seen the like of in our worst campaigns. But if your cause is just, and you are sure of it, go forward, in God's name, and fear nothing. He will not forsake you."

The church that Timothy pastored in Ephesus had been planted by Paul (Acts 19), and the riot that followed marked it out as frontline in the battle between the forces of good and evil. In Paul's time Ephesus was the provincial capital and religious centre of the province of Asia, and in spite of the silting of the harbour causing decline in commerce it still remained a key church in Paul's missionary strategy, hence his concern to root out error. Sadly, Paul's emotional farewell and tragic prophecy concerning the Ephesian church was being fulfilled. He said,

> *I know that after I leave, savage wolves will come in among you and will not spare the flock. Even from your own number men will arise and distort the truth in order to draw away disciples after them.*

ACTS 20:29–30

## Opposing false doctrine

There were a number of false doctrines that Timothy faced in the church at Ephesus:
- Devoting themselves to myths (1:4) – this is an excessive interest in legends about biblical or other "saints".
- Being fascinated by obscure genealogies (1:4) – either for theological reasons, such as, in today's world, the Mormons, or for personal status, such as the Jews tracing their descent from Abraham.

- Being argumentative (1:4; 6:4) – delighting in the argument rather than from a desire to grow in the faith.
- An unhealthy interest in the occult (4:1–2).
- Insisting on a legalistic lifestyle – regarding it as "super-spiritual" (4:3).

The net result was envy, strife, malicious talk, evil suspicions and constant friction, all of which destroyed fellowship (6:4–5). So, Timothy's first task was to counter false teaching and remain loyal to the apostolic faith.

# The priority of public worship

In chapter 2 Paul exhorted Timothy to give priority to public worship.

His reason was that the church is essentially a worshipping, praying community. Some think evangelism is the prime importance of the church, others think it is teaching and again others think music and praise. But that's not the biblical way. They are all important, but none of them is the sole reason for attending church. Worship needs to be balanced. Importantly, here in 1 Timothy 2, Paul placed a significant emphasis on prayer, for a praying church will be a healthy church.

Paul's teaching in verses 9–15 has proved to be controversial. The modest dress prescribed here is probably to prevent the church from becoming a dating agency. We meet to worship, not attract a mate. If relationships happen, that is a byproduct of faith, not a purpose of it. Motives have to be pure if worship is to be blessed, which leads into the potential problem of male attention being drawn to females whose dress is inappropriate.

# Paul's word to the women

The question is often asked: What does Paul mean in verses 11–15 when he commands women are not to teach or have authority over men?

The New Testament makes it plain that Christian women, like men, have been given spiritual gifts which are to be used to minister to the body of Christ, and their ministries are invaluable to the life and growth of the church. The expression "full submission" (verse 11) needs to be treated wisely. It's not a surrender of mind and conscience or the abandonment of private judgment. The phrase is a warning against wrongly assuming authority, as in verse 12, where Paul specifically says, "I do not permit a woman to teach or to have authority over a man." Some have said that the apostle's prohibition excludes women from teaching Sunday school classes, but Paul is talking about the public assembly of the church and speaks appreciatively of the fact that Timothy himself had been taught the right way by his godly mother and grandmother (2 Timothy 1:5; 3:15). The apostle also told Titus that the older women are to train the younger (Titus 2:3–4). Women have always carried the major responsibility for teaching small children in both home and Sunday school. Praise God for them. And further, in many evangelical churches major ministries are headed up by women. In 1 Timothy 2:12 the word "silent" translates in Greek to "in quietness" – a listening posture, the opposite of disturbance. Quietness is an important Christian virtue. Paul was especially opposed to confusion in the public services of the church (1 Corinthians 14:33).

In 1 Timothy 2:13–14 Paul adds that the wife's role of submission to her husband is inherent in creation. Adam was created first, and then Eve. The story is told in Genesis 2:21–23 how the Lord God made Eve from a rib taken from Adam. Matthew Henry, the Puritan commentator, pointed out beautifully the implication of this description: "The woman was not made out of his head to rule over him, nor out of his feet to be trampled upon by him, but out of his side to be equal with him, and near his heart to be beloved." This expresses perfectly the ideal of a happy married life. The husband who has this concept will usually find his wife eager to please him.

Paul makes one further point. It was the woman who was deceived by Satan and who disobeyed God by assuming the leadership role in her dialogue with Satan (Genesis 3:1–6). Since she was so easily tempted to assume authority over her husband she should not be trusted as a teacher. We must not make the mistake of writing this off; Paul refers to it several times in the New Testament and it is bound up in the mechanics of the fall, for example Genesis 3:6: "She also gave some to her husband, who was with her, and he ate it." Adam's sin was his not acting in his authoritative role and so protecting his wife from Satan's temptation. Eve's sin was assuming the authority that was not given to her by God; she argued with Satan and so ended up in trouble.

Think of this: Paul wrote this first letter to Timothy to remind him "how people ought to conduct themselves in God's household, which is the church of the living God" (1 Timothy 3:15). And we know that Paul had to send this reminder because the church at Ephesus was plagued with false teaching. While it is not explicitly stated in the text, it's pretty safe to assume that some of the false teaching was encouraging women to discard what might be called traditional female roles in favour of a more egalitarian approach to relationships between men and women. We have proof of this in the following verses.

Firstly, 4:3 tells us that the false teachers were encouraging women to abstain from marriage, which, in line with Paul's other remarks, suggests that there was a movement against long-established female roles.

Secondly, the counsel of 5:14 to young widows is "to marry, to have children, to manage their homes"; in other words, to engage in time-honoured female roles. Paul's command is issued because some have "already turned away to follow Satan" (5:15), and Paul has called the false teaching "demonic" (4:1). It is, therefore, probable that this turning away to follow Satan meant following the false teachers who were teaching the opposite of what Paul commands in 5:14, that younger widows marry, have children, manage their homes and give the enemy no opportunity for slander.

Thirdly, the false teaching that was besetting the church at Ephesus sounds very similar to the general problem experienced by the Corinthians, and of course that led, among other things, to wrong attitudes towards marriage and sex. What Paul was doing in his letters to the Corinthians and Timothy was seeking to right the balance, by reasserting the importance of the created order and the ongoing significance of those role distinctions between men and women that he saw rooted in creation.

If you view Paul's teaching this way, then, in context, the notoriously difficult verse in 2:15 makes absolute simple sense: "Women will be saved through childbearing – if they continue in faith, love and holiness with propriety."

Paul is simply saying that the circumstances in which Christian women will work out their salvation is by maintaining as priorities those key roles of being faithful, helping wives, raising children to love and reverence God and managing the household; not by assuming church leadership roles not assigned to them by God (1 Timothy 5:14; Titus 2:3–5). This is not to say, of course, that women cannot be saved unless they bear children. But the women whom Paul is addressing almost certainly were married, so that he can mention one central role – bearing and raising children – as a way of indicating appropriate female roles in general.

## Church leadership

From the importance of apostolic doctrine in chapter 1 and the conduct of public worship chapter 2, Paul turns to the pastoral oversight of the church in chapter 3.

The qualifications of church leaders fall into two major categories – elders and deacons.

In verses 2–7, speaking about elders, Paul teaches that the elder must be above reproach, the husband of but one wife, temperate, self-controlled, respectable, hospitable, able to teach, not given to drunkenness, not violent but gentle, not quarrelsome, not a lover of money. He must manage his own family well and see that his children obey him with proper respect. (If anyone does not know how to manage his own family, how can he take care of God's church?) He must not be a recent convert or he may become conceited and fall under the same judgment as the devil. He must also have a good reputation with outsiders, so that he will not fall into disgrace and into the devil's trap.

It must be remembered that all authority in the local church resides in the Lord Jesus Christ, and all Christians have access to His authority. Nevertheless, the New Testament does provide for strong leadership on the part of the elders (1 Thessalonians 5:12; 1 Timothy 5:17; Hebrews 13:17). Elders, therefore, must lead, but do so in a spirit of submission and service. Taken as a whole, the qualifications describe men who are mature Christians of good repute, with the ability to teach, being able to defend the faith and exercise a pastoral ministry.

The spiritual requirements for deacons are just as high as those for elders, and they are to be treated similarly with one exception – they are first to be tested; they are to be given work to do on a trial basis (3:10). If they perform it well, they are recognized as those who can be trusted with responsibility in the work of the church. From this group, deacons are appointed to serve in the practical areas of the church that support the spiritual ministry of the church. The effectiveness of their service will be determined by the measure of their commitment and faithfulness. This simply means that erratic church attendance would disqualify a person as a deacon. They are to be hands-on, committed, to take responsibility and show leadership – deacons are expected to serve the church by example, by their character as well as by their deeds.

## Combating false teaching

In chapter 4 Paul turns to the subject of the false teachers and their lies – apostasy.

An apostate is clearly one who has abandoned his or her held belief and some would consider the teaching in Hebrews 6 to be focused on this subject.

Paul tells us in verse 1 that apostate attitudes arise not merely from twisted ideas of men but from listening to deliberately deceitful ideas of wicked spirits who attempt to lead people astray.

Timothy is to communicate the truth, for ultimately the most important aspect of a church's life is good, consistent, systematic Bible teaching. Churches that are not receiving constant systematic teaching of God's Word become vulnerable to all kinds of mischief – but constant confrontation with the Word of God – communicating the truth of the gospel – will enable spiritual growth in the lives of those being taught.

Paul also instructed Timothy to confront the troublemakers, face them with what they were doing, deal with it quickly, get them out of the way and replace them with good elders. A church can stand anything from outside, but when it's attacked from inside, that's when it's in danger. Here, then, is the guarantee against apostasy – informing the congregation of the dangers, setting the example, and expounding the Scriptures.

In chapter 5 specific church issues are discussed.

Verses 1–16 cover the treatment of younger and older people within the church and include advice to women on various practical matters.

Then Paul takes up the problem of how to handle charges against the elders. Notice verse 19: "Do not entertain an accusation against an elder unless it is brought by two or three witnesses."

Adherence to this biblical principle would have silenced many a malicious talebearer and saved many pastors from unjust criticism and unnecessary suffering. Then Paul mentions certain personal problems that Timothy himself would encounter and offers advice for his chronic stomach problems.

## Social concerns

Chapter 6 goes into the matter of social problems.

First, a word concerning the downtrodden and degraded – the slaves. This most instructive passage helps us to answer some of the questions that are flung at us from every side about how to counsel those who are degraded, and deprived of certain human rights. And while we would wish that it hadn't taken so long for the Christian world to abolish slavery, Paul was offering practical wisdom that gave usable Christian advice to real people in real situations, rather than formulating abstract principles which would make the politically correct feel good but which would be no use to the people concerned.

Having begun with the poor, Paul closes by assigning Christian responsibilities to the rich and learned. They are rich, he says, because they have been blessed of God so that they could be a blessing to others, not to satisfy their own desires. They have a responsibility, he says, to be rich in good deeds and generosity, laying a foundation for the future so that they can take hold of the truly abundant life right now – not abundant in material possession but abundant in the things of God (verse 8–19).

The example of Gollum in J. R. R. Tolkien's *The Lord of the Rings* and his obsession with the ring that he called "my precious" is an illustration of money's unique power to enslave. The issue is not how much a person earns. Big industry and big salaries are a fact of our times – and they are not necessarily evil. The evil is in being deceived into thinking that a large income must be accompanied by a lavish lifestyle. God has made us to be conduits of His grace. The danger is thinking that the conduit must be lined with gold – it shouldn't, copper will do! It's food for thought that the Ten Commandments begin and end with virtually the same commandment: "You shall have no other gods before me" and "you shall not covet". Coveting means desiring anything other than God in a way that betrays a loss of contentment and satisfaction in Him. Covetousness is a heart divided between two gods. So Paul calls it idolatry.

In closing, Paul entrusts to Timothy a word of warning to those who trust in human knowledge:

> *Timothy, guard what has been entrusted to your care. Turn away from godless chatter and the opposing ideas of what is falsely called knowledge, which some have professed and in so doing have wandered from the faith. Grace be with you.*
>
> 1 TIMOTHY 6:20–21

Truly, Paul's letter to Timothy is a letter for our times and our own churches. It provides an objective standard against which to measure our modes of worship, church leaders, beliefs, doctrines and cultural attitudes. In short, it is a set of clear, profound instructions from God in how to build a church. May God grant that we will understand it and live by it.

# 55

## 2 Timothy
## – Stand Fast in the Ministry

Paul often used Timothy, who was not as timid as is sometimes made out, as a troubleshooter (1 Corinthians 4:17; Philippians 2:19–22; 1 Thessalonians 3:2, 6). It's possible that on his first missionary journey, building upon the foundation laid by Timothy's grandmother, Lois, and his mother, Eunice, (2 Timothy 1:5), Paul led Timothy into the Christian faith. We do not know this for certain, but what we do know is that Paul took a responsibility for Timothy and treated him as he would a son.

In July AD 64 much of Rome was destroyed by fire. Accusations of arson were directed towards the cruel and unbalanced Emperor Nero, and to divert suspicion from himself he pointed to the Christians, blaming them as the culprits. This resulted in Christianity being declared an illegal religion and persecution of those who professed Christ became severe. Upon Paul's return from Spain to Asia in AD 66, (Romans 15:24) his enemies used the official Roman hostility against Christianity to their advantage. The result was that, fearing for their lives, the Asian believers failed to support Paul after his arrest and no one supported him at his first defence before the imperial court (2 Timothy 1:15; 4:16). Apparently abandoned by everyone, the apostle found himself in very different circumstances from those of his first Roman imprisonment (Acts 28:30). Then, it was house arrest during which he could receive visitors and there was good hope of his release. Now he was in a cold Roman cell, regarded as a criminal with no hope of an acquittal (2:9; 4:6–8; 4:13). So, in AD 67, Paul wrote expressing the hope that Timothy would be able to visit him before the approaching winter (4:21) and while it was a very personal letter to his young friend, Timothy, it was also, consciously, his last will and testament to the church.

Paul's impending death would place a heavy burden on Timothy's shoulders, and Scripture suggests that he was not the obvious candidate for such a position of great responsibility. For one thing, while we do not know his precise age, he was comparatively young (1 Timothy 4:12; 2 Timothy 2:22). He also suffered ill health; Paul mentions his frequent illness (1 Timothy 5:23) and several times in his second letter Paul exhorts Timothy to take his share of suffering and not to be afraid or ashamed since God has not given us a spirit of cowardice (2 Timothy 1:7–8; 2:1, 3; 3:12; 4:5). This, then, was Timothy: young in years, frail in physique and retiring in disposition, who nevertheless was called to a demanding leadership role in the New Testament church. Like Moses, Joshua, Jeremiah and a host of others before and after him, Timothy was hesitant about accepting his role. This second letter from Paul has much to say to those who sense God calling them to leadership roles but are hesitating because they are afraid that they do not have the ability, gifting or temperament for the task to which they are being called.

Paul's main concern was what would happen to the gospel when he was gone. For thirty years or so he had faithfully preached the word, planted churches, defended the truth and consolidated the work. Truly, he had "fought the good fight... finished the race... kept the faith" (2 Timothy 4:7). Now nothing awaited him but the victor's crown of righteousness. A prisoner now, he would be a martyr soon. But what would happen to the gospel when he was dead and gone? Nero, misunderstanding the nature of the Christian church, was determined to destroy it, and heretics appeared to be preaching their false gospels everywhere. There had been almost total Asian apostasy, and humanly speaking the church showed every sign of trembling on the verge of extinction. Who, then, would battle for the truth when Paul laid down his life? This was the question that vexed his mind as he lay in chains, and in this letter he reminds Timothy that the precious gospel was now committed to him. It was his turn to assume responsibility to preach it, teach it and defend it against attack from within and without. That this was Paul's concern is seen in the way that his letter may be summarized in terms of a fourfold charge:

1. guard the gospel (1:14);

2. endure hardship for the gospel (2:3);

3. do not be led astray (3:13–14);

4. preach the Word (4:1–5).

# 1. Guard the gospel

Paul's first charge to Timothy is to guard the gospel (1:14).

God has committed to Timothy what Paul calls a "good deposit" which he is to guard, and Paul suggests certain ways to carry out this commission. This word of advice is needed by every Christian, because each one has been given the same deposit of truth: the fundamental revelation of Scripture concerning the nature of what the world is like, what God is like, what people are like and what we are personally like. What makes the world operate the way it does? Why does it fall apart all the time? Why it is that nothing good seems to prosper and everything evil seems to reign unchallenged? The explanation is found in the deposit of truth that has been given to us through Jesus Christ, and it is this that we are to guard.

Paul suggests three specific ways to do this.

## By exercising the spiritual gift that God has given to us

> For this reason I remind you to fan into flame the gift of God,
> which is in you through the laying on of my hands. For God did
> not give us a spirit of timidity, but a spirit of power, of love and
> of self-discipline.
>
> 2 TIMOTHY 1:6–7

To be more specific: it is not God that gives us a spirit of timidity, He gives a spirit of power and love and a sound mind.

Today we may ask: What is going to happen in the Middle East? What will be the result of the war on terror? No one knows. But this we do know, God does not give His people a spirit of timidity. If they are worried and troubled it's not from God. The Spirit of God is a Spirit of power and of love and of a sound mind. A Spirit of power in order to do, a Spirit of love in order to react properly, and a sound mind in order to be intelligently purposeful about what they do. That means becoming involved in church life. Christians can do something for God. Each Christian has an ability given to them by the Holy Spirit who dwells within them, and in the judgment of the Holy Spirit it is vitally important that they exercise their God-given gift, for when they do so they discover that He is right with them to back it up. That was the first word to Timothy on how to guard the gospel, how to keep the faith.

## By suffering patiently

> *So do not be ashamed to testify about our Lord, or ashamed of*
> *me his prisoner. But join with me in suffering for the gospel, by*
> *the power of God.* . . .
>
> 1 TIMOTHY 1:8

The suffering that is involved here is not only physical, it is also mental. It is the kind of suffering Christians endure when someone pokes fun at them for going to a prayer meeting, or laughs at the Bible, or excludes them from an invitation list or promotion because they profess to be a Christian. Believers are to take this patiently, says the apostle. And as they react, not with anger, disgust or vengeance, but quietly and patiently, as our Lord did, they guard the truth. One of the reasons the gospel is not widely accepted today is that Christians have been impatient in suffering and have refused to patiently endure the attitude of the world. Instead, they have taken offence and been hurt when people have treated them poorly, or they have given up and gone along with the crowd, refusing to take suffering for the Lord's sake. They have to learn that they cannot challenge the world in its wrongness without causing offence, and although they must challenge it in the least offensive way possible, the Scriptures make clear that there is constantly a place for Christians' suffering. It is one of the ways in which they guard the truth.

## By keeping the pattern of sound teaching

> *What you heard from me, keep as the pattern of sound teaching,*
> *with faith and love in Christ Jesus.*
>
> 1 TIMOTHY 1:13

That is, to read and trust the Scriptures. The main reason so many in our society are suffering today is that they listen to secular, humanist or occult teachers who are blind to the truth of God as revealed in His Word.

So, Timothy – so, Christian! – guard the gospel, and do so by exercising your gift. Suffer patiently, keep the pattern of sound teaching and God will see you right through. Why? How do you know this is true? "Because I know whom I have believed, and am convinced that he is able to guard what I have entrusted to him for that day" (2 Timothy 1:12).

## 2. Endure hardship

Paul's second charge to Timothy is to endure hardship for the gospel (2:3). He gives three illustrations:

### Being strong as a soldier

> *You then, my son, be strong in the grace that is in Christ Jesus.*
>
> 2 TIMOTHY 2:1

The thought here is dedication to the task. Christians are to give themselves to whatever they do so that they might please Him who has called them to be a soldier. How can you follow Christ if you have several conflicting aims in your life? If you want to be strong, be as dedicated as a soldier is to the task set before him.

### Being strong as an athlete

> *Similarly, if anyone competes as an athlete, he does not receive the victor's crown unless he competes according to the rules.*
>
> 2 TIMOTHY 2:5

That means discipline with no shortcuts, no cutting corners or breaking the rules. Just as an athlete is not crowned unless he observes the rules, so, if you are going to be a Christian, do not take any moral shortcuts.

### Being hardworking like a farmer

> *The hardworking farmer should be the first to receive a share of the crops.*
>
> 2 TIMOTHY 2:6

That means attentiveness. Any farmer knows that if he expects a crop in the summer or autumn he has to spend some time working and planting in the spring. And it ought to be that simple with the Christian. The Christian life is not one in which we simply relax while it rolls along in its own way. No, it calls for diligence, discipline, reading, praying and giving yourself to the task of knowing the Scriptures, and deliberately applying the great principles of truth that you learn. And if you do these things, Paul says you will be able to be strong, strong in the Lord.

# 3. Do not be led astray

Paul's third charge to Timothy is not to be led astray (3:13–14).

Here Paul is telling us to avoid the traps and pitfalls along the way, and he outlines three of these for us:

## Trap 1: Arguments over words

Examples of this are the way Christians get upset over secondary issues like end-time eschatology, the mode of baptism and so on.

You may have heard the story:

> *I was walking across a bridge recently. I saw this man who looked like he was ready to jump off.*
> *"Don't jump!" I said.*
> *"Why not?" he said. "Nobody loves me."*
> *"God loves you," I said. "You believe in God, don't you?"*
> *"Yes, I believe in God," he said.*
> *"Good," I said. "What religion?"*
> *"Christian," he said.*
> *"Me too!" I said. "What denomination?"*
> *"Baptist," he said.*
> *"Me too!" I said. "Independent Baptist or Southern Baptist?"*
> *"Independent Baptist," he said.*
> *"Me too!" I said. "Moderate Independent Baptist or Conservative Independent Baptist?"*
> *"Conservative Independent Baptist," he said.*
> *"Me too!" I said. "Calvinistic Conservative Independent Baptist or Armenian Conservative Independent Baptist?"*
> *"Calvinistic Conservative Independent Baptist," he said.*
> *"Me too!" I said. "Dispensational Calvinistic Conservative Independent Baptist or Historical Calvinistic Conservative Independent Baptist?"*

*"Dispensational Calvinistic Conservative Independent Baptist," he said.*

*"Dispensational?" I said, and shouted "Die, heretic!" as I pushed him over the side!*

While some of the subjects in the above illustration are important there are areas in the Scriptures in which earnest scholars will find differences of opinion and we do well to avoid getting into controversies in those areas and not make final decisions and divisions over that kind of thing.

## Trap 2: Being used for ignoble purposes

This is outlined in 2:20–26 and Paul gives the following illustration:

*In a large house there are articles not only of gold and silver, but also of wood and clay; some are for noble purposes and some for ignoble.*

2 TIMOTHY 2:20

The house is the church and the vessels are the two types of teachers: the ignoble are divisive and argumentative and do not have the good of the church at the forefront of their thinking. Conversely, the noble are gathering and building, uniting, healing, and harmonizing, and each of us is going to be used of God in one way or another. Now, says Paul, if you want to be used for a noble purpose rather than for an ignoble purpose then separate yourself from the things that destroy your Christian walk. Verse 22's call to "flee the evil desires of youth" is not to be purely understood as referring exclusively to sexual lust, but to self-assertion as well as self-indulgence, selfish ambition, headstrong obstinacy and arrogance. Positively, Timothy is to aim for the four essential marks of a Christian: "righteousness, faith, love and peace."

## Trap 3: A rebellious attitude

*But mark this: There will be terrible times in the last days.*

2 TIMOTHY 3:1

The term the "last days" does not refer to the final end-time of the church on earth but rather encompasses the period of time between the first and the second comings of Christ. So, Paul is speaking about the present time. These are days when peace has forsaken the world and men and women are fearful, when there are strange, demonic forces at work in society creating immense problems. Through these times of distress we will see certain characteristics at play and Paul lists them:

> *People will be lovers of themselves, lovers of money, boastful,*
> *proud, abusive, disobedient to their parents, ungrateful, unholy,*
> *without love, unforgiving, slanderous, without self-control,*
> *brutal, not lovers of the good, treacherous, rash, conceited,*
> *lovers of pleasure rather than lovers of God – having a form of*
> *godliness but denying its power.*
>
> 2 TIMOTHY 3:2–5

Paul tells us how to respond to such people: "Have nothing to do with them" (3:5). And take heart, this kind of rebellion always ends in tears. This is what happened to Jannes and Jambres, the two magicians who withstood Moses before the court of Pharaoh (Exodus 7:11). And people with the same attitude today will not get very far either – their folly will be plain to all as was that of those two magicians. That is a comforting word in this hour of lawlessness when we wonder how far today's lawless forces are going to go. Well, says Paul, they won't go too far because their folly will soon become obvious to all.

In the closing part of the chapter (verses 10–17), the apostle tells Timothy the twofold way ahead: patience in suffering and persistence in truth. "Remember the way I behaved," he says to Timothy. "You watched me; you've seen how I've endured all the trials that came my way. Remember that if you are quietly patient in suffering and continue in the truth holding to the Scriptures and what God has said, you will find your way safely through all the involvements and the perils and the pitfalls of the world in which you live." And then comes his final charge:

> *In the presence of God and of Christ Jesus, who will judge*
> *the living and the dead, and in view of his appearing and his*
> *kingdom, I give you this charge: Preach the Word... .*
>
> 2 TIMOTHY 4:1–2A

In short, proclaim the gospel! Don't merely believe it, speak it, tell it to others: "be prepared in season and out of season; correct, rebuke and encourage" (4:2b).

These three things – correct, rebuke and encourage – counteract the characteristics of a decaying age. Timothy is to be motivated in this by two things. First, he is to do it in view of the fact that he lives in the presence of God. The whole universe is watching us; our faithfulness is under observation all the time. The Father is watching, Christ is watching and in His presence we are to live.

Second, he is to do it in view of the peril of the times:

> For the time will come when men will not put up with sound doctrine. Instead, to suit their own desires, they will gather around them a great number of teachers to say what their itching ears want to hear.
>
> 2 TIMOTHY 4:3

Do not give way to this, Paul says, but speak the truth, proclaim the word!

## 4. Preach the word

Paul then closes with a marvellous word of testimony of his own experience:

> For I am already being poured out like a drink offering, and the time has come for my departure. I have fought the good fight, I have finished the race, I have kept the faith. Now there is in store for me the crown of righteousness, which the Lord, the righteous Judge, will award to me on that day – and not only to me, but also to all who have longed for his appearing.
>
> 2 TIMOTHY 4:6–8

That's magnificent, especially when we remember its setting. Here is the apostle in this tiny cell, cramped and cold, in semi-darkness writing by the light of a spluttering lamp. He knows that his fate is sealed. He has already appeared once before Nero, that monstrous wretch of an emperor, and now he must appear before him once more knowing what the result will be this time. He will be taken outside the city wall and with a flash of the sword his head will roll in the dust, and that will be the end. But Paul is looking beyond all that. He is seeing the day when he appears before the Lord Himself, when he is suddenly ushered into His presence in which he has always been by faith, and discovers himself with the Lord on that great day. However, mixed with this is a very human emotion as he addresses himself to Timothy:

*Only Luke is with me. Get Mark and bring him with you,*
*because he is helpful to me in my ministry… When you come,*
*bring the cloak that I left with Carpus at Troas, and my scrolls,*
*especially the parchments.*

2 TIMOTHY 4:11, 13

He is bored in mind, lonely in spirit and cold in body. Though he could look beyond to all the greatness of the glory of God to come, see how human he is.

There is nothing wrong with this. When we get cold or lonely or bored, we can just admit it freely; there is nothing sinful about that. But we must also look beyond these circumstances and add that dimension of faith that sees the reality of an unseen world that changes the whole complexion of the circumstances in which we live.

Speaking of his first appearance before Nero, Paul says, "the Lord stood at my side and gave me strength, so that through me the message might be fully proclaimed" (4:17).

Isn't that challenging? Paul stood before that wretch, Nero, and proclaimed the word fully, that "all the Gentiles might hear it. And I was delivered from the lion's mouth". That was his first appearance, but he knows it will be different this time, and history records that the day when Paul did stand before the emperor the second time. The name of Nero was a name honoured among men and known throughout the empire, but who had heard of this little Jew from Tarsus with his bald head, bowed legs, bad eyesight and poor speech? Yet today, 2,000 years later, we name our sons Paul, and our dogs Nero!

Then Paul concludes with some personal words to his friends. It is interesting to note that the final words of Paul are to preach the Word, and the final words of Jesus are to preach and teach the Word (Matthew 28:19 and Luke 24:46–47).

What a wonderful letter this is. What a challenge it must have been to young Timothy's heart and what an encouragement it is to us today to stand firm, to hold fast to the pattern of sound words, to take our share of suffering for the gospel's sake with joy and equanimity of spirit – not returning evil for evil, but good for evil, all the while remembering that He is able to keep that which He has deposited with us.

# 56

## Titus
## – Doctrine and Duty for Home, Church and World

There was a period in world history from approximately 2600 to 1450 BC when the Minoan civilization on the island of Crete was the major power in the Mediterranean. The Minoans, also known as the Cretans, were great traders, and though inhabiting a small island they wielded great influence. However, by the end of the Old Testament era Crete was divided into a community of city states who were at each others' throats until the Romans imposed their law and order in 67 BC. Paul's assessment of the Cretan church in Titus 1:12–13 reflects how the Cretans were viewed by the rest of the world. He quoted Epimenides, one of their own reputed poets, who said that "Cretans are always liars" (1:12). As a people they were disliked and the phrase "to the play the Cretan" was an expression meaning "to play the liar". These then were the people Paul left Titus to deal with. His job description is in 1:5: "The reason I left you in Crete was that you might straighten out what was left unfinished and appoint elders in every town, as I directed you."

### The selection of elders

Paul was aware of the vital importance of good leadership and Titus was to appoint elders in every church. The evangelical church has made a terrible mistake in the past when it adopted the custom of having the pastor as the elder and then running the church with deacons. Nowhere in the New Testament is this practised; it is always "elders", plural, unless referring to a certain individual and within fifteen years of the resurrection there was already a plurality of elders in the Jerusalem church (Acts 11:30).

The model of selection of elders was to be a corporate responsibility. Although Paul told Titus to appoint elders and lay down the conditions of their eligibility, his emphasis on their need to have a blameless reputation (1:6) indicates that the members will, in some way, have a say in the selection process.

In Titus nothing is said about the gifts or calling of an elder; we look to other parts of the New Testament for that, but the attribute of blameless is key (see 1:6–7). This does not mean to be perfect, otherwise no one could qualify. The Greek word means "unblemished" and points towards someone who is "not accused". In other words, they should have a good reputation and not be marred by disgrace that could give rise to personal criticism.

Verse 6b says the elder must be "the husband of but one wife, a man whose children believe and are not open to the charge of being wild and disobedient." The point is that if a man cannot manage his home and family he will be unable to manage the church. Dr Martyn Lloyd-Jones used the helpful analogy of a married couple going overseas on missionary business asking themselves if they would leave their child with the family of the potential elder! Obviously there is a cut-off point in terms of the age at which adults are no longer primarily responsible for their children's spirituality. Paul is referring to youngsters who are still in their minority (which of course varies in different cultures) and are therefore still regarded as being under their parents' control.

> *[An elder] must be blameless – not overbearing, not quick-tempered, not given to drunkenness, not violent, not pursuing dishonest gain. Rather he must be hospitable, one who loves what is good, who is self-controlled, upright, holy and disciplined.*
>
> TITUS 1:7–8

In other words, candidates for the eldership must give visible evidence in their behaviour that they have been regenerated by the Holy Spirit, that their new birth has led to new life, that their fallen passions are under control and that the ninefold fruit of the Spirit has appeared and is shown to be ripening in their lives.

Paul then lists five negatives that relate to the areas of strong temptation: pride, temper, drink, power and money. They are an occupational hazard for Christian leadership, and all five challenge self-mastery. Paul's point is simply that they cannot be in charge of the church if they can't be in charge of themselves.

After five negatives come six positives in verse 8, which are largely self-explanatory: an elder must be hospitable, welcoming members and non-members into his home; must love what is good, being a supporter of good causes; be self-controlled, having a sensible and sober lifestyle; be upright in his dealings with people; be holy or devout in his attitude to God; and finally he must be disciplined.

Paul then moves on in regard to qualifications for the eldership from his home, family, character and conduct, to his necessary grasp of the truth: "[An elder] must hold firmly to the trustworthy message as it has been taught" (Titus 1:9).

Why? Because he will need it in his teaching ministry: "so that he can encourage others by sound doctrine and refute those who oppose it" (Titus 1:9).

The word "for" in verse 10 leads us into the reason a teaching ministry is so necessary, as Paul now alerts Titus to the nature of the false teachers:

- They follow the teachings of men rather than God (verse 14b).
- They have a false understanding of purity (verse 15).
- They do not live up to their profession (verse 16a).
- They are disobedient, insubordinate and rebellious (verse 16b).

In chapter 2 Paul turns to Titus's responsibilities as a true teacher: "You must teach what is in accord with sound doctrine" (Titus 2:1).

## Christian family living

Paul here stresses the importance of building up the inner life of believers as the best antidote against error because sound doctrine will lead to ethical conduct in the lives of all the groups in the congregations. In other words, being taught the Bible changes people! This evident truth is a key reason for men and women to attend evangelistic courses that are designed to introduce them to the Christian faith and present them with an opportunity to accept Christ as Saviour and Lord. For when a family become "Christians" the benefits in their new family life-style are noticed by non-Christians who can appreciate the change for good and recognize how it could change their own home and family too. Aware of this, Paul's emphasis is directed towards family groups, as it was there that the false teachers had apparently done their greatest damage (verse 11).

First, in verse 2, recognizing that the senior male members would comprise the leadership of the church, four qualifications are insisted on. They must be:

**Temperate** – an adjective basically meaning "abstaining from wine", but having a wider meaning of being "clear-headed", and showing self-possession under all circumstances.

**Worthy of respect** – that is, having a personal dignity and seriousness of purpose that invite honour and respect.

**Self-controlled** – for example, having self-mastery in thought and judgment.

**Sound in faith, in love and in endurance** – meaning they must be mature in their exercise of genuine love, must not be bitter or vindictive and must demonstrate that steadfast persistence that bravely bears the trials and afflictions of life.

The use of "likewise" introducing verse 3 indicates that the same kind of demeanour is expected of the "older women", although the demands on them are related to their own station in life. The basic demand is that they "be reverent in the way they live". The Greek conveys the image of a good priestess carrying out the duties of her office, which basically means the conduct of the older women must reveal that they regard life as sacred in all of its aspects. There is an implied link here between a loose tongue and intoxicating drink – so they will "not be slanderers or addicted to much wine". The older women must fulfil a positive role: by personal word and example, they must teach what is morally good, noble and wholesome. The reference is not to public instruction but to their teaching function in the home. In verse 4 the training of the younger women is given as a duty, not of Titus, but of the older women who are qualified to do so by position and character. "Train" means "to school in the lessons of sobriety and self-control".

In verses 4 and 5a Paul lists seven characteristics that must be commended:

- love their husbands;
- love their children;
- be self-controlled;
- be pure;
- be busy at home;
- be kind;
- be subject to their husbands.

The domestic affection they are to show for their husbands and children stands at the very heart of any Christian home.

The requirement for the young men is brief but wide-ranging: "Similarly, encourage the young men to be self-controlled" (verse 6). As a young man, Titus must convey his instructions for the young women indirectly but his age was an advantage in dealing directly with the young men. In the Greek, "encourage" is stronger than "teach" and may be rendered "urge" and is an appeal to their sense of personal moral responsibility. Since young men are inclined to be impetuous and unrestrained in conduct, their basic need is to be "self-controlled", cultivating balance and self-restraint in daily practice. It was a quality of which Paul found it necessary to remind the Cretan believers. In verses 7 and 8 he tells Titus to set the example. It's not just "do as I say" but also "do as I do". Teaching and example, the verbal and the visual, always form a powerful combination and his teaching was to have three characteristics:

1. integrity,

2. seriousness,

3. soundness of speech that cannot be condemned.

Titus was to combine his honesty of character, his pure motive and his serious and sound manner so that, "those who oppose you may be ashamed because they have nothing bad to say about us" (verse 8).

## Guidance for slaves

In verse 9 Paul's ethical instructions are addressed to a distinct social group that overlaps age and sex. Slaves formed a significant element in the apostolic churches, and the welfare of the faith demanded that they too accept their spiritual responsibility as believers. Paul here makes no distinction between slaves who had Christian masters and those who did not. Their fundamental duty is "to be subject to their masters in everything", voluntarily accepting subjection to their masters as a matter of principle. But Paul's other teachings were careful to point out the necessary limitation on this demand, for a Christian slave could not submit when his pagan master demanded things contrary to Christian conscience. In serving their masters slaves were "to try to please them". Instead of having a sullen disposition, let them aim to give full satisfaction to their masters. They are "not to talk back to them", not to dispute their commands or by deliberate resistance, seek to thwart their will.

Further, as petty theft was common among slaves in Roman households, in verse 10, Paul tells Titus to teach slaves "not to steal from [their masters]" to "show that they can be fully trusted". Paul again undergirds his ethical conduct with a profound spiritual motive, "so that in every way they will make the teaching about God our Saviour attractive". For a Christian there can be no higher motive.

# Right Christian behaviour

In chapter 3, having given Titus directions about doctrine and duty in the church and home, Paul now develops the same theme in regard to the world.

Christians are to be conscientious citizens, and as long as their Christian conscience permits, not just law-abiding but public-spirited as well, not reluctant to do good (verse 1). Then, from the Christian responsibility towards their leaders of society, Paul turns to their relationship with everyone in the community and in verse 2 selects four attitudes which for the Christian are to be the norm. They are to:

- slander no one;
- be peaceable;
- be considerate;
- show true humility towards all men.

The "all" means that irrespective of race or religion Christian men and women are to be conciliatory, courteous and gentle.

In verses 3–8 Paul spells out the theological reason why Christians should have a social conscience and behave responsibly in public life. In verse 3 he states that the remembrance of their own past should be a powerful motive for gentleness and consideration toward the unsaved. We were "foolish", meaning lacking discernment of spiritual realities because of the darkening effect of sin on the intellect. As evidence of our alienated condition we were also "disobedient", meaning wilfully disregarding authority, refusing obedience to God's law and fretting under human authority. The word "deceived" (verse 3) pictures us actively straying from the true path by following false guides and allowing our conduct to be dictated by a variety of personal "passions and pleasures", the inevitable result of which was our enslavement to them. Never finding true personal satisfaction in their pursuit, we lived our lives in the grip of the antisocial forces of what Paul calls "malice and envy" which is an attitude of ill will toward others while enviously begrudging them their good fortune. "Being hated and hating one another" means that the hostility which we experienced in our relationships was reciprocal.

The word, "but" introducing verse 4 leads into the contrast between what Christians were before conversion and what they have become afterwards. This answers the question, "How is it possible to change inwardly to get out of one mindset and lifestyle into another and so exchange slavery for freedom?" Verse 5 simply says, "he saved us". This is in direct opposition to modern thinking and false religions that teach that all the answers, even salvation itself, lie within ourselves. They say look within to find salvation. Christianity, though, says that we are incapable of saving ourselves. Paul spells it out beginning in the rest of verse 5: "he saved us, not because of righteous things we had done", that is, our salvation is not based on our merit, our good works, or anything like that, "but because of his mercy" we have been "justified by his grace" (verse 7). These verses teach that salvation originated in the heart of God. It's because of His kindness, love, mercy and grace that He intervened on our behalf. He took the initiative, He came after us, and He rescued us from a hopeless predicament. Note the Trinity in verses 5b, 6: "the Holy Spirit… he [the Father]… Jesus Christ". Each member of the divine Trinity has His own special function in the work of human redemption.

So far in Titus 3, Paul has done two things. First, he has told Titus to remind the Christians in his care to be conscientious citizens and to live consistent lives of peace, courtesy and gentleness. Second, he has explained the doctrine of salvation and so given Titus grounds for confidence that the people to whom he ministers can be changed so as to live the new life to which they have been called. Now Paul brings his letter to a close with a cluster of miscellaneous messages which all instruct Titus to do something.

## Paul's instructions for Titus

He is to "avoid foolish controversies and genealogies and arguments and quarrels about the law, because these are unprofitable and useless" (verse 9). They produce no spiritual benefits and lead to no constructive results. He is to discipline contentious people (verse 10). The term "divisive" used here is an opinion or belief without true scriptural basis used by a dissident to stir up divisions in the church. Such a person Titus must "warn" by faithfully and lovingly pointing out his error. If a second effort to deal with them proves ineffective, let Titus "have nothing to do with them", refusing further to bother with them. Further efforts would not be a good stewardship of his time and energies and would give the offender an undeserved sense of importance.

Finally, in verse 12, as the apostle closes with some personal words of admonition and advice, we have a glimpse into his own circumstances. He says, "As soon as I send Artemas or Tychicus to you, do your best to come to me at Nicopolis, because I have decided to winter there". Nicopolis was on the western shore of Greece, just across the Adriatic Sea from the heel of the Italian boot. The apostle was apparently writing this letter from Corinth and was sending two young men down to replace Titus in Crete so that he could rejoin Paul. Later we read that Titus went on up to Dalmatia, on the northern coast, sending Zenas, the lawyer, and Apollos on their way, perhaps to Alexandria which was Apollos" home, and the apostle admonishes Titus to see that they lack nothing.

Paul then closes the letter as he opened it: "Our people must learn to devote themselves to doing what is good" (Titus 3:14).

How did he open the letter? "Paul, a servant of God and an apostle of Jesus Christ for the faith of God's elect and the knowledge of the truth that leads to godliness" (Titus 1:1).

There is the theme of this letter: truth that matches up with godliness; sound doctrine and good deeds going hand in hand. And the basis of it, as we have already seen, rests "on the hope of eternal life, which God, who does not lie, promised before the beginning of time" (1:2).

# 57

# Philemon
# – Isn't Grace Wonderful?

The fact that this is the only private letter written by Paul that we possess gives his letter to Philemon a unique interest and significance.

There are two interpretations of the events to which this letter refers. The ordinary view is quite straightforward; the other, connected with the name of E. J. Goodspeed (whose book *The Key to Ephesians* was published by the University of Chicago Press in 1937 and then reproduced by William Barclay in his commentary *Letters to Timothy, Titus and Philemon*) is rather more complicated, and is certainly more romantic and dramatic. Let us take the simple view first.

Onesimus was a runaway slave who had robbed or in some other way wronged his master: "If he has done you any wrong", Paul writes, "or owes you anything, charge it to me... I will pay it back" (1:18–19). Somehow, the runaway Onesimus found his way to Rome, lost himself among the masses in the imperial city, and come into contact with Paul. Then, Onesimus had become a Christian: "who became my son while I [Paul] was in chains" (verse 10). And although Onesimus had become a real asset to Paul, both knew that, as a Christian, Onesimus had a responsibility to return to Philemon.

Paul would have liked to keep Onesimus with him: "I would have liked to keep him with me so that he could take your place in helping me while I am in chains for the gospel" (verse 13). But Paul will do nothing without the consent of Onesimus' master, Philemon. So Paul sends Onesimus back, and knowing that it would be safer to return Onesimus with a companion, Paul sent Tychicus along with him as the bearer of the letter (Colossians 4:7).

Now, no one knew better than Paul how great a risk he was taking. Remember, a slave was not a person; he was a living tool. The master had absolute power over his slaves. He could punish them or condemn them to hard labour, making them, for instance, work in chains upon his land. He could punish them with blows of the rod, the lash or the knot and if they were thieves or runaways he could brand them on the forehead, and if they proved irreclaimable, he could crucify them.

The Roman senator, Pliny, tells of a young slave being thrown into a pond of flesh-eating fish because he dropped a crystal goblet and broke it. The poet, Juvenal, known for coining the phrase "bread and circuses" to describe the primary pursuits of the Roman populace, writes of the mistress who will beat her maidservant at her whim and the master who "delights in the sound of a cruel flogging, deeming it sweeter than any siren's song", and who is never happy "until he has summoned a torturer to brand someone with a hot iron for stealing a couple of towels." The slave was always at the mercy of the whim of a master or a mistress.

The Romans were very aware that less than a century before this letter was written Spartacus led an uprising of some 90,000 slaves. Although the rebellion was put down and thousands of slaves crucified, given that there were 60,000,000 slaves in the Roman empire they inevitably formed a potential threat, so rebellious slaves were promptly eliminated. If a slave ran away, at best he would be branded with a red-hot iron on the forehead with the letter F (standing for *fugitivus*, which meant "runaway"), and at worst he would be crucified, dying a torturing death. Paul well knew all this and that slavery was so ingrained into the ancient world that even to send Onesimus back to the Christian Philemon was a considerable risk.

So Paul gave Onesimus this letter, and he puns on Onesimus' name. In Greek, Onesimus literally means "profitable or useful", so in verse 11: "Formerly he was useless to you, but now he has become useful both to you and to me."

Now, he is not only Onesimus by name, he is also Onesimus by nature. And Paul says in verse 15: "Perhaps the reason he was separated from you for a little while was that you might have him back for good."

Philemon must take him back, not just as a slave, but as a Christian brother (verse 16). He is now Paul's son in the faith and Philemon must receive him as he would receive Paul himself. Such, then, was Paul's appeal.

The question is often raised why Paul says nothing in this letter about the whole matter of slavery. He doesn't condemn it nor does he tell Philemon to set Onesimus free; it is still as a slave that he would have him taken back. But there are certain reasons for Paul's silence on this difficult subject.

Slavery was an integral part of the ancient world; the whole of society was built on it. Aristotle held that it was in the nature of things that certain men should be slaves, hewers of wood and drawers of water, to serve the higher classes of men. Further, if Christianity had, in fact, given the slaves encouragement to revolt or leave their masters, nothing but tragedy and disaster could have followed. Any such revolt would have been savagely crushed; any slave who took his freedom would have been mercilessly punished, and Christianity would itself have been branded as a revolutionary and subversive treason. Given the Christian faith, emancipation was bound to come. However, the time was not ripe, and to have encouraged slaves to hope for it and to seize it would have done infinitely more harm than good. There are some things which cannot be achieved suddenly and for which the world must wait until time and distance allow for radical social change.

What Paul did do was to include the practice of slave trading as sinful in his letter to Timothy (1 Timothy 1:10) and begin the break-up of slavery from the inside, starting within the church. For Christianity introduced a new relationship between man and man. A relationship in which all external differences were abolished because all Christians are one body in Christ whether they are Jews or Gentiles, slaves or free men (1 Corinthians 12:13). As Galatians 3:28 puts it: "There is neither Jew nor Greek, slave nor free, male nor female, for you are all one in Christ Jesus", and Colossians 3:11: "Here there is no Greek nor Jew, circumcised or uncircumcised, barbarian, Scythian, slave or free, but Christ is all, and is in all."

It was as a slave that Onesimus ran away, and it was as a slave that he was coming back, but now he was not only a slave, he was a beloved brother in the Lord. When a relationship like that enters into life, social grades and castes cease to matter – the very titles "master" and "slave" become irrelevant. If the master treats the slave as Christ would have treated him, and if the slave serves the master as he would serve Christ, then it does not matter if you call the one "master" and the other "slave"; their relationship does not depend on any human classification for they are both in Christ. That's why Christianity in the early days did not openly attack slavery and never urged the emancipation of the slaves. To have done so would have been worse than useless; it would have been disastrous. But Christianity introduced a new relationship in which the human grades of society ceased to matter.

However, the new relationship never gave the slave the right to be idle or lazy. It did not give him the right to take advantage of this new relationship; it made him a better slave and a more efficient servant, for now he must do things in such a way that he could offer them to Christ. It did not mean that the master must be soft and easy-going, willing to accept bad workmanship and inferior service; but it did mean that he no longer treated any servant as a thing, but as a person and a brother in Christ.

There are two passages in which Paul sets out the duties of slaves and masters: Ephesians 6:5–9 and Colossians 3:22 – 4:1. Both these passages were written when Paul was in prison in Rome and most likely when Onesimus was with him. So it is difficult not to think that they owe much to long talks that Paul had with this runaway slave who had become a Christian. Taking this view, Philemon is a private letter sent by Paul to Philemon when he sent back Onesimus, Philemon's runaway slave. And it was written to urge Philemon to receive back Onesimus, not as a pagan master would but as a Christian receives a brother and forgives him.

Now let's look at the other view of what lies behind this letter.

We may begin our study of this view with a consideration of the place of Archippus. Archippus appears in both Colossians and Philemon. In Paul's letter to Philemon greetings are sent to Archippus, "our fellow-soldier" (verse 2); and such a description might well mean that Archippus is the minister of the Christian community in question. Archippus is also mentioned in Colossians 4:17: "See to it that you complete the work you have received in the Lord."

Now, that injunction comes after a whole series of very definite references, not to Colossae, but to the church at Laodicea (Colossians 4:13, 15–16). This means that Archippus in all probability was at Laodicea, otherwise why should he get this personal message? If he was at Colossae he would hear the letter to Colossians read as everyone else would. Why has this personal, verbal order to be sent to him? It is surely possible that the answer is that he is not in Colossae at all, but in Laodicea.

If that is so, it means that Philemon's house is in Laodicea, and it means that Onesimus was a runaway Laodicean slave. This must mean that the letter to Philemon was in fact written to Laodicea. And, if that is so, the missing letter to Laodicea, mentioned in Colossians 4:16, is none other than the letter to Philemon. This indeed solves problems.

Now, remember that in ancient society, with its view of slavery and its treatment of slaves, Paul took a very considerable risk in sending Onesimus back at all. So, it can be argued that Philemon is not really only a personal letter but was written to Philemon and to the church that meets in his house. And further it has also to be read at Colossae. What, then, was Paul doing? Knowing the risk that he took in sending Onesimus back, he was mobilizing church opinion both in Laodicea and in Colossae in his favour. Onesimus' reception is not to be left to the personal inclination of Philemon; it is one in which the church is to be in agreement, and Christian opinion is to be lined up, so that the Christian thing may be done. In other words, the decision about Onesimus is not to be left to Philemon; it is to be the decision of the whole Christian community.

It so happens that there is one little, but important linguistic point, which is very much in favour of this view. In verse 12 Paul says that he is "sending back" Onesimus to Philemon. The verb is commonly used for officially referring a case to someone for decision. And verse 12 should most probably be translated: "I am referring his case to you", that is, not only to Philemon, but also the church in his house.

This raises a difficulty about Goodspeed's theory. In Colossians 4:9 Onesimus is referred to as "one of you", which certainly looks as if he was a Colossian. But Goodspeed, who states this view with such scholarship and persuasiveness, argues that Hierapolis, Laodicea and Colossae were so close together and so much a single church that they could well be regarded as one community. Therefore, "one of you" need not mean that Onesimus came from Colossae but simply that he came from that closely connected group. If we are prepared to accept this, then the last obstacle to his theory is removed.

The commentator Goodspeed does not stop there. He goes on to reconstruct the history of Onesimus in a most moving way.

In verses 13 and 14 Paul makes it quite clear that he would have liked to have kept Onesimus with him:

> I would have liked to keep him with me so that he could take
> your place in helping me while I am in chains for the gospel.
> But I did not want to do anything without your consent, so
> that any favour you do will be spontaneous and not forced.

In verse 19 he reminds Philemon that he owes Paul his very soul and with charming wit in verse 20 says, "I do wish, brother, that I may have some benefit from you in the Lord; refresh my heart in Christ."

He goes on to say in verse 21: "Confident of your obedience, I write to you, knowing that you will do even more than I ask."

Now, reader, do you think for a moment Philemon could have resisted Paul's appeal? In the face of language like that could he do anything else than send Onesimus back to Paul with his blessing? So it is argued that Paul got Onesimus back and that Onesimus became Paul's helper and ally in the work of the gospel.

But now let us move on about fifty years. Ignatius, one of the great

Christian martyrs, is being taken from his church in Antioch to be executed in Rome. As he goes, he writes letters (which still survive) to the churches of Asia Minor. He stops at Smyrna, and he writes to the church at Ephesus, and in the first chapter of that letter he has much to say about their wonderful bishop. And what is the bishop's name? It is Onesimus; and Ignatius makes exactly the same pun as Paul made – that he is Onesimus by name and Onesimus by nature, the profitable one to Christ. This all leads to the suggestion that it may well be that Onesimus, the runaway slave, had with the passing years become none other than Onesimus, the great bishop of Ephesus.

And, if all this is so, it would give us the explanation of how this little letter, this single papyrus sheet, half-personal, half-official, survived and found its way into the collection of the Pauline letters. It deals with no great doctrine, it attacks no great heresy; it is the only one of Paul's undoubted letters written to an individual person.

It is almost certain that the first collection of Paul's letters was made at Ephesus. There, maybe, about the turn of the century, these letters were collected, edited and published. It was just at that time that Onesimus was bishop of Ephesus. And it may well be that it was Onesimus who insisted that this letter must be included in the collection, little, short and personal as it was, in order that all men might know what the grace of God had done for him. Through it the great bishop tells the world that once he was a runaway slave and thief, and that he owed his life to Paul and to Jesus Christ. Through it the great bishop insists on telling of his own shame so that his very shame might rebound to the glory of God.

Did Onesimus come back to Paul with Philemon's blessing? Did he become the great bishop of Ephesus, he who had been the thievish runaway slave? Did he insist that this little letter must be included in the Pauline collection to tell what Christ, through Paul, had done for him? We can never tell for certain; but if that is so, then here is one of the great romances of grace of the early church.

The lesson from this book comes out in verse 18: "If he has done you any wrong or owes you anything, charge it to me."

Isn't that wonderful? That's grace. Here, wonderfully portrayed in this little letter, you have the doctrines of acceptance, substitution, justification and, as Onesimus goes on to be a profitable person, sanctification. God receives us in the person of another; we were like Onesimus we are the slave who ran away from God. We were no use to God. We merit nothing. We have done things that are wrong. We stand before a God who is righteous and holy and yet the Lord Jesus says, "If he has done anything wrong or owes you anything, charge that to my account. I will pay it." That's grace and that is what Paul says here:

*I, Paul, am writing this with my own hand. I will pay it back*
*– not to mention that you owe me your very self. I do wish,*
*brother, that I may have some benefit from you in the Lord;*
*refresh my heart in Christ.*

PHILEMON 19–20

Paul was simply doing for the slave, Onesimus, what Jesus Christ had done for him. He was saying to Onesimus, "Jesus paid for you and rescued you and recycled you and sent you back to serve the Father. Now go and do that to others."

It's more than likely that Philemon's heart was moved by this wonderful word of grace from the apostle, as he thought of that dear man sitting in the loneliness of his prison cell writing this letter. He had nothing of himself. He had no money, nothing with which to repay and yet he wrote, "If he owes you anything, don't worry about it. I'll pay it myself when I come." That probably was the crowning touch. Philemon's heart just broke, he welcomed Onesimus and they forgave one another. As they wept on one another's shoulders, the fellowship of the family was restored once again.

Then see what Paul writes at the end: "Confident of your obedience, I write to you, knowing that you will do even more than I ask" (verse 21).

Do you see the extent to which grace will go?

If Paul had been writing this on a legal basis he would have said: "Philemon, as the Holy Apostle of the Holy Church, I command you to receive back this young man and to give him back his job!"

That's as far as law could go. And Philemon would probably have had to obey it or else get into trouble with the church. But grace goes much farther. It has not only restored Onesimus to his place in the household, but it has restored him to his place in the family as well. It breaks down all the barriers, smoothes out all the friction that has developed, and creates a better situation than ever existed before.

Isn't grace wonderful!

# 58

# Hebrews
## – It's All About Jesus

The original recipients of this letter were the Jews, and of course with their Hebrew background they knew it was always dangerous to come too near to God. After all, hadn't God warned Moses that "no one may see me and live" (Exodus 33:20). The extent to which this was believed is seen in Jacob's astonished exclamation at Peniel, "I saw God face to face, and yet my life was spared" (Genesis 32:30). That this belief was long established is confirmed in the time of the New Testament. The greatest day of Jewish worship was the Day of Atonement, when in the temple at Jerusalem the High Priest entered the Holy of Holies into the very presence of God. No man ever entered except the high priest, and he only on that day – it was dangerous to enter the presence of God, and if a man lingered too long he might be struck dead.

The Jews held the view of being in a covenant relationship with God. That meant God, in His grace and in a way that was quite unmerited, approached the nation of Israel and offered them a special relationship with Himself. But this unique access to God was conditional on the observance by the people of the Law that He gave to them. To break the law was sin, and sin put a barrier between man and God. which prevented approach into His presence. It was to remove this sin barrier that the system of the Levitical priesthood and sacrifices was constructed.

The Law was given but man sinned, so the barrier went up: the sacrifice was then made and man was forgiven. However, man sinned again and so it went on – step forward, step backwards, year after year with a growing realization based on divine revelation through the prophets and confirmed by life's experiences that there had to be a better way. What was needed was a perfect priest and a perfect sacrifice, someone who could bring to God a sacrifice which once and for all would open the way of access to Him. And that, said the writer to the Hebrews, is exactly what Jesus Christ did. He is the perfect priest because He is perfect God and man. In His sinless manhood He can take man to God and in His Godhead He can bring God to man, and constitutes a sacrifice so perfect that no other shall ever be required again.

To the Jews the writer to the Hebrews is saying, "All your lives you've been looking for the perfect priest who can bring the perfect sacrifice which will open the way to God that your sins have closed. You have Him in the Messiah, Jesus Christ, and in Him alone." To the Greeks the writer is saying, "You are looking for the way from shadow to reality: you will find it in Jesus Christ who came from heaven to open the way up for us after death."

The letter to the Hebrews is a substantial book but it breaks down to seven comparisons and five warnings.

In the first ten chapters Jesus Christ is compared to leaders, systems and religious values that people once felt were of supreme importance but which ultimately proved to be insufficient.

## Comparison 1: The prophets of the Old Testament

*In the past God spoke to our forefathers through the prophets at many times and in various ways....*

HEBREWS 1:1

These remarkable writers of the Old Testament – Isaiah, Jeremiah, Ezekiel, Daniel, Hosea, Habakkuk and the others – who meant so much to Hebrew thinking, were way ahead of all the philosophies and philosophers the world had ever known. These prophets were great men, and God spoke to them and through them in the past: "but in these last days he has spoken to us by his Son" (Hebrews 1:2a).

Therefore, says the writer, great as the prophets were, the logical conclusion is, they are not equal to Jesus Christ. They were just spokesmen, but He is the God enthroned as king of the universe, forming the boundaries of history and upholding everything by the power of His Word. How can a prophet compare with someone like that? He is incomparably superior to them and therefore, the writer argues, anybody who trusted in prophets ought to be interested in listening to Jesus Christ.

## Comparison 2: The angels

In the Greek world in which the New Testament church found itself, angels were regarded as very important beings. Of course, people knew they were not divine but they were regarded as a kind of divinity junior-grade, and were treated as such. But here the writer poses the question, "Who is greater, the angels or the Son?" and points out the logic that says the Son, the Lord Jesus, is superior to any angel: "For to which of the angels did God ever say, 'You are my Son?'" (Hebrews 1:5a).

The answer is He never said that to any angel. In fact the angels themselves worshipped Jesus, thus freely admitting that He is superior, and they obey Him. In chapters 2 and 3 the writer argues that as the last Adam, Jesus was the perfect man who came to fulfil the destiny for humankind that the first Adam lost. God made man ultimately to be higher than the angels. He said of man, "Let us make man in our image" (Genesis 1:26). He did not say that about any angel, only of man. Our destiny to be rulers and kings in the universe is reflected in Psalm 8:

> *When I consider your heavens,*
> *the work of your fingers,*
> *the moon and the stars,*
> *which you have set in place,*
> *what is man that you are mindful of him,*
> *the son of man that you care for him?*
> *You made him a little lower than the heavenly beings*
> *and crowned him with glory and honour.*
>
> *You made him ruler over the works of your hands.*
>
> VERSES 3–6A

That is God's destiny for men and women, yet it is a destiny impossible to obtain in our fallen state. But, says the writer to the Hebrews, although we do not yet see man fulfilling his destiny, we see Jesus sitting at the right hand of God and sitting there as the true man, man as God intended him to be and ultimately how Christians will be when they join Him and are made like Him.

In the midst of this argument about the angels, the writer of Hebrews gives the first of five warnings.

## Warning 1

> *We must pay more careful attention, therefore, to what we have heard, so that we do not drift away.*
>
> HEBREWS 2:1

The Greek term here is nautical and can be used for a ship that has been carelessly allowed to slip past a harbour entrance because the captain neglected to allow for the wind, current or tide. The verse could be vividly translated as "Christian men and women must pay attention to the anchoring of their lives to the things we have been taught, lest the ship of life drifts past the harbour and is wrecked." The remedy is summed up in the exhortation "fix your thoughts on Jesus" (3:1).

## Comparisons 3 and 4: Moses and Joshua

The Hebrews almost idolized Moses (chapter 3) and Joshua (chapter 4) as the supreme examples of men mightily used of God, and the writer's point is that whereas Moses was a servant in the house of God, Jesus is the Son to whom the house belongs and for whom it is built, so He obviously has superiority. Likewise, Joshua, for all his leadership abilities, found life in Canaan was one long battle, and he was never able to lead the Israelites into anything like the peace that Jesus offers.

## Warning 2

> *Today, if you hear his voice,*
> *do not harden your hearts.*
>
> HEBREWS 3:7–8A

The writer is quoting from Psalm 95:7b–11, which tells of a rebellious incident in the wilderness after the exodus from Egypt. He is saying, "Take care that you do not show the same disobedience and distrust of God that your forefathers showed, and that you do not for that reason lose the blessings you might have had, just as they lost theirs. Don't harden your hearts and resist God's lead. Don't say "I'm all right the way I am. What do I need with anything further?" You may be satisfied with the way you are now but it will not last very long. Sooner or later you will find that what you have got now is not enough: therefore, do not harden your hearts but let God lead you into His rest or you will be in serious trouble."

That rest is defined for us: "For anyone who enters God's rest also rests from his own work, just as God did from his" (Hebrews 4:10).

For the Israelites in the time of Moses and Joshua this rest was the earthly rest to be found in the Promised Land. For the Christian it is peace with God now and eternal rest in a new life later. Joshua could not lead the Israelites into that rest, says the writer. He took them into the symbol of rest, the land, but he did not take them into real rest. But Jesus can. Therefore, he says, "Let us, therefore, make every effort to enter that rest" (4:11a).

## Warning 3

In connection with this, there is a third warning found in chapter 6, and it comes from Hebrews 5:11–14:

> We have much to say about this, but it is hard to explain because you are slow to learn. In fact, though by this time you ought to be teachers, you need someone to teach you the elementary truths of God's word all over again. You need milk, not solid food! Anyone who lives on milk, being still an infant, is not acquainted with the teaching about righteousness. But solid food is for the mature, who by constant use have trained themselves to distinguish good from evil.

Here the writer rebukes the Jews who have made a commitment to Christianity but have failed to grow and mature as Christians. He likens them to "babes in Christ". By contrast spiritually mature men and women are always hungering and thirsting after biblical truth. That's how they find soul satisfaction and, in turn, are able to help others. Healthy Christians are growing Christians, and verse 12 shows the contrast. The "babes in Christ" should have been teachers but instead need to be taught – worse, not just taught, but taught again. Their lack of spiritual understanding is to their shame, they are like children who, unable to write, have to return to the basics and start all over again with their ABCs. Christians must experience spiritual growth, and in 5:14 – 6:1 the writer explains this because he wishes his readers to aim for it. That means leaving the elementary teachings and growing into maturity. By elementary teachings the writer is saying there are fundamental doctrines that are essential to the Christian faith, and he goes on to mention them. We need to have a good grasp of their importance and what they teach. But we need to move beyond (but not away from) the elementary teachings to a more complete understanding of the faith.

So far in his letter to the Hebrews the writer has been largely negative. In other words, God's Word has been presented as a two-edged sword: all-seeing in its judgmental role, able to prize apart the spiritual from the carnal, and if you do not believe in Jesus who is superior to the angels, Moses and Joshua, you will be doomed to spend eternity in a state of condemnation removed from the love of God.

Now we come to the more positive aspect.

## Comparison 5: The earthly priesthood

Here the writer moves us closer to the overriding feature of his letter: the high-priestly ministry of Jesus. This he presents positively and compellingly, encouraging his readers to come to Jesus because of His character, His ability and His achievement. The writer's emphasis is now on what Christians have: those who thought they were losing out by leaving Judaism were in fact better off now because in Jesus they have a "great high priest" (4:14). The priests' task is spoken of in Hebrews 5:1: "Every high priest is selected from among men and is appointed to represent them in matters related to God, to offer gifts and sacrifices for sins."

But now the writer proceeds to prove that Jesus Christ has a higher priesthood. He does this by referring to the time of Abraham in Genesis 14. There we read how a man named Melchizedek suddenly appeared out of nowhere and received homage from Abraham.

The Hebrew meaning of "Melchizedek" is "king of righteousness", and we are told he was the "king of Salem", and as *salem* means "peace", he was the "king of righteousness and peace". This helps us to recognize that we have here a type, foreshadowing the king who alone is righteousness and peace – the Lord Jesus Christ. Further proof of this is given when we are told distinctly that Melchizedek is a king and a priest of the God most high.

It's quite fascinating. Here is the greatest man of the times, a man before whom Abraham, the father of Israel, the honoured of all nations, bowed and paid tithes. Yet this royal priest without predecessor or successor, honoured to stand and minister between Abraham and God, commissioned to bless the man in whom rests the promised blessing for all humankind, appears and passes away like a vision in the night. He's forgotten for one thousand years till David, speaking of the future Messiah Jesus Christ in Psalm 110, says, "You are a priest for ever, in the order of Melchizedek" (verse 4). Mention of Melchizedek then disappears for another thousand years till brought forth in the letter to the Hebrews.

In other words, the Jewish readers of this letter were being told, "Moses informed you that Abraham worshipped a priest, Melchizedek, before the founding of the Jewish nation, and David told you the Messiah would be a priest like Melchizedek, outside the Jewish system, a priest older and more distinguished than one from the Levitical Law – and Jesus Christ is that Priest." In no other part of the New Testament does the word "priest" apply to Jesus; it is only here in Hebrews that He receives His official title of "great high priest" (4:14).

The reason this was so important was that Israel's kings were descendants from the tribe of Judah and the house of David, and the priests descended from the tribe of Levi and the house of Aaron. When the Jews returned from Babylonian captivity those priests who could not prove their family ancestry were removed. So, to call Jesus a priest when He was not of the house of Aaron was unacceptable until the writer to the Hebrews proves from Holy Scripture how Christ could be a priest even though not possessing the legal qualifications for the Levitical priesthood. The writer does so on the basis that Melchizedek's priesthood was recognized by Abraham before the Levitical system came into being. Abraham's submission to Melchizedek in accepting his blessing, and his act of offering a tenth of the spoils of war to Melchizedek, confirms his recognition of this "priest-king's" great personal religious worth – for he who blesses is greater than he whom he blesses (Hebrews 7:7). Therefore, as Melchizedek on God's behalf blessed the head of the Israelite nation, his priesthood is superior to that of the Levites. Just as Abraham stands above his descendants, so the one who blesses him is above Abraham: therefore Melchizedek is above the Levites. When Abraham knelt beneath Melchizedek's royal and priestly hand, he did so as head of the Jewish race, and his descendants were identified with him in his action.

Now in a persuasive argument the writer to the Hebrews builds on what he has said.

# Comparisons 6 and 7: The earthly ministry and the old covenant

The sixth comparison is with Christ's eternal ministry in heaven and the seventh is with the new covenant instigated by Jesus.

Hebrews 8:1–6 explains that there is a better covenant in Christ, based upon its better promises. The better ministry that Christ renders as High Priest in heaven is based on His position of being seated at the right hand of God. This being the case, we can see how Jesus is truly "our glorious High Priest". The ministry He now offers is as intercessor, not as sacrificer. His sacrificial work was "once for all" in history. His present work is to pray for us and that He does, with compassionate understanding.

The writer's line of reasoning is that being seated at the right hand of God, Jesus is a minister of the sanctuary and true tabernacle pitched by God and not man, whereas the priests of Aaron's line only ministered on earth and in the typical sanctuary and tabernacle (8:1–2). This means that as the ministry of Christ in the true sanctuary (heaven) is much superior to the ministry of the priests in the shadowy one (on earth), Jesus is the mediator of a better covenant (8:6). The writer also reasons that the original covenant was flawed and succeeded by another, which he proves from a passage in Jeremiah 31:31–34. In these verses mention is made of a new covenant distinct from that made with the Jewish fathers and broken by them. The writer's conclusion in Hebrews 8:7–13 is that the promises of God's new covenant were foretold by the prophet Jeremiah, and are now fulfilled through the coming of Jesus and His death on the cross. As a result, the new covenant is blessed with "better promises" because of the better sanctuary and the better sacrifice.

## Warning 4

In his fourth warning, the writer exhorts believers not only to hold fast to the hope they have in Christ and persevere in face of difficulties, but to witness to their faith in the midst of them (see chapter 10).

It would appear that some who professed belief in Christ were drifting away from the truth (2:1). This was not simply the everyday problems that are the lot of the believer, but a deliberate rejection of God's truth (10:26–28). In light of this, the writer warns that such people have rejected the sacrifice of Christ, and, as he has already argued, since there is no other sacrifice if they revert to the Jewish sacrificial system, they go back to sacrifices that their knowledge of Christianity teaches them cannot put away sin (10:4). That being the case, only a fearful expectation of judgment awaits such apostates.

With angels, prophets, Moses, Joshua, priests, tabernacle and law eliminated, there is nothing left to compare with to Jesus Christ. All that remains is to answer the question, "How do we obtain all that God has for us?" And the last section says the answer is by faith. In God's "Hall of Fame" in chapter 11 we learn what faith is, how it acts, how it looks and how to recognize it as we consider the accounts of the people mentioned there.

As we read through this wonderful chapter we find that faith anticipates the future, acts in the present, evaluates the past, dares to move out and persists to the end. That is what faith is and in the last two chapters the writer tells us how it is produced in our lives and how God goes about making us strong in the faith.

Firstly, we are made strong by looking to Jesus. We cannot read about the Lord Jesus or live with Him and think of what God has revealed about Him and believe these great declarations of His power, His availability and His life without finding our faith strengthened. We can look at all these other men of faith – Abraham, David, Moses, Barak, Samson and a whole host of more recent saints such as Luther, Wesley, Whitefield and Spurgeon – and they will inspire us but they cannot enable us. But when we look at Jesus, He will not only inspire us but He will empower us. That is why we are exhorted to look away from these others unto Jesus, the author and perfecter of our faith, who will make us strong in the time of weakness (12:2).

Secondly, our faith is increased by the problems and difficulties we incur through our normal lives, which the writer calls God's discipline (12:7–13). If we did not have any problems, how could we exercise faith? If we did not have any difficulties, how could we ever learn to depend on God?

And finally, we exercise faith as we learn about the resources God has given us. It is explained in the majestic passages:

> *You have not come to a mountain that can be touched and that*
> *is burning with fire; to darkness, gloom and storm; to a trumpet*
> *blast or to such a voice speaking words that those who heard it*
> *begged that no further word be spoken to them....*
>
> HEBREWS 12:18–19

That was the law given on Mount Sinai. You have not come to that:

*But you have come to Mount Zion, to the heavenly Jerusalem, the city of the living God. You have come to thousands upon thousands of angels in joyful assembly, to the church of the firstborn whose names are written in heaven. You have come to God, the judge of all men, to the spirits of righteous men made perfect, to Jesus the mediator of a new covenant, and to the sprinkled blood that speaks a better word than the blood of Abel.*

HEBREWS 12:22–24

Isn't that wonderful? Doesn't that encourage your faith?

## Warning 5

In connection with this we have the fifth and final warning:

*See to it that you do not refuse him who speaks. If they did not escape when they refused him who warned them on earth, how much less will we, if we turn away from him who warns us from heaven? At that time his voice shook the earth, but now he has promised, "Once more I will shake not only the earth but also the heavens." The words "once more" indicate the removing of what can be shaken – that is, created things – so that what cannot be shaken may remain.*

HEBREWS 12:25–27

We're back to the scene described earlier of God's proclamation from Sinai, but there is a second shaking in 12:26b, and with this we are propelled to the end of the world.

The demise is set forth in catastrophic terms: the entire created order will be involved in a cosmic shake-out unparalleled since the beginning of time. The old will pass away, giving room for the new. All that is imperfect and insecure will be removed. Everything that is hostile to God will be purged and eradicated from the universe. Eden will be restored, paradise regained and the final purpose for which Christ came into the world, bled, died and was raised again to new life will be realized. This last shaking is none other than the second coming of Jesus Christ when the universe will be transformed and changed to a condition of stability that cannot be shaken. Gloriously, Calvary has cosmic consequence for the whole new order which is yet to be and which has as its foundation the one perfect sacrifice of Jesus Christ – and it will stand for ever.

How can we respond to such overwhelming prospects? Hebrews 12:28 tells us:

> *Therefore, since we are receiving a kingdom that cannot be shaken, let us be thankful, and so worship God acceptably with reverence and awe.*

Let us persevere to the glorious, sublime end!

# 59

# James
# – Faith in Action

The book of James uncompromisingly challenges Christian men and women to examine their faith and determine if it is real, for if faith is unaccompanied by action it is dead (2:17). Throughout his book James promotes the characteristics of faith and uses examples to assist us to evaluate the quality of our relationship to Jesus Christ. He also lays down a test as to whether we have true saving faith or not.

## Growing in faith

In chapter 1 we are told that the two mechanisms that make faith grow are trials and God's Word.

With regard to trials we are to:

> *Consider it pure joy, my brothers, whenever you face trials of many kinds, because you know that the testing of your faith develops perseverance. Perseverance must finish its work so that you may be mature and complete, not lacking anything.*
>
> JAMES 1:2–4

These are reassuring verses when we go through the trials and difficulties of life, for they remind us that not only are trials part and parcel of normal life but, more, we actually need trials in order to develop our faith. This being the case, says James, we are to accept trials as from God, and if you lack wisdom about this ask God to explain what's going on (1:5). But, you have to ask in faith and not doubt, because the person who doubts will not receive anything from the Lord (1:6–7). Though it may not seem like it at the time, trials are a source of blessing:

> *Blessed is the man who perseveres under trial, because when he has stood the test, he will receive the crown of life that God has promised to those who love him.*

JAMES 1:12

It reminds us of Paul's experience described in 2 Corinthians 11:24–25b: on five occasions he was bound at a stake and the Jews took their leather whips and beat him thirty-nine times across his back. Three times he was beaten with rods and once he was even stoned. How did he respond to all that? Well, the wonderful thing about these early Christians is that when they went through trials they rejoiced and counted themselves fortunate to be considered worthy to suffer for the name of the Lord (Hebrews 10:34). Today we need to appreciate more the scriptural perspective that God sends trials because we need them. They teach us lessons that we could never otherwise learn, and if we did not have them we would be weak, incomplete Christians. Trials, of course, are not something to which we look forward. The thought of counting it joy when instead we want to cry seems ridiculous. But Scripture is perfectly clear, and it's our thinking that must change. Korean Christians liken believers to nails – the harder you hit them the deeper you drive them.

James goes on to say that perseverance produces the character that is evidence of us being tested and approved. It works like this. When under pressure, as Christians abide in Christ a sense of His approval begins to appear in our lives. And when we recognize this, our attitude towards the pressure changes dramatically – we know that God is allowing it and we know He has our best interests at heart. Meanwhile, the Holy Spirit is shedding the love of God into our hearts saying, "I love you so much that I want you to have a little more pressure in order that I can drive you deeper into Christ so that you can grow up and reflect His glory." This is how Christians can eventually say, "All right, Lord, I accept my trial. You know that I don't fully understand it and I don't really appreciate it but I will rejoice in You through it, because I trust You and what You are going to accomplish through it."

The second mechanism that makes Christians grow in faith is God's Word:

*Do not merely listen to the word, and so deceive yourselves. Do*
*what it says. Anyone who listens to the word but does not do*
*what it says is like a man who looks at his face in a mirror and,*
*after looking at himself, goes away and immediately forgets*
*what he looks like. But the man who looks intently into the*
*perfect law that gives freedom, and continues to do this, not*
*forgetting what he has heard, but doing it – he will be blessed in*
*what he does.*

JAMES 1:22–25

Notice the "continue to do this" and "not forgetting". The thought behind these
verses is not reading the Bible to find out about God, but rather to find out what
God expects from us in terms of holiness, given His definition of our sins. One
thinks of someone looking into a mirror and finding blemishes on their face. So,
says James, our faith will grow by coming to terms with trials, accepting them
for what they are, and by understanding and being obedient to what we learn
about ourselves in relation to God from His Word.

# Recognizing faith

In chapters 2 and 3 James tells us how faith can be recognized and he highlights
three indicators that show the presence of faith.

## 1. There must be no favouritism or prejudice

In 2:1–13, James tells how, if a man is prejudiced against another because of, for
example, the colour of his skin or the state of his bank account, and he treats
him as though he were unimportant, then obviously he has no faith. Faith
destroys prejudice.

## 2. Faith is seen in acts of compassion

James uses the analogy of someone who shows up at your door and says, "I
don't have anything to eat – we're starving over at our house." If you say,
"Well, brother, I feel for you, let's say a prayer together", then pray for him
and say, "Now go your way, the Lord will work everything out", that, says
James, is hypocritical. For "faith by itself, if it is not accompanied by action,
is dead" (2:17, 26).

James emphasizes this important truth by comparing the faith of Abraham and demons. They both have faith that God exists but without works it is a dead faith, not a saving faith. As an example James says that if our faith does not lead us to share with our destitute brother, there is something desperately wrong with it. In fact, it shows that we don't have faith at all because faith in Jesus Christ means that we actually have the life of the Lord Jesus permeating us. That's why we are called His ambassadors. This being the case, then, just as the Lord Jesus would not treat someone who had a need in that way, Christians should be unable to shut their hearts to the needs of those around them. So, if we want our faith to be seen and recognized, it must manifest itself in actual deeds. This is why the Lord Jesus said that in the Judgment He will say, "I was hungry, thirsty, imprisoned, destitute and in need, and you did nothing about it" (see Matthew 25:41–46).

### 3. Faith is seen in a controlled tongue

In chapter 3 James uses a series of vivid images to make his point. He says we can tame every beast, bird and reptile but no man by himself can control his tongue. Then in a most revealing statement James says that the tongue is the member of our body most closely linked to our real nature. It shows what is motivating us, and therefore what we say reveals what we are! So, if we claim to be a Christian and to have faith in Jesus Christ, something will be happening to our tongue. Faith will be reducing its sharpness and stopping its caustic bitterness by turning it off when appropriate, keeping it from lashing out in sharp reproof and criticism. Not that there is no place for reproof among Christians, but not in a caustic, uncensored way.

In chapter 4 James explains the cause of fights and quarrels amongst Christians.

He does so by continuing his theme from the end of chapter 3, where he has been writing about bitter envy, selfish ambition, disorder and evil practice, and asks, "What causes fights and quarrels among you?" (4:1a). He answers with a rhetorical question: "Don't they come from your desires that battle within you?" (4:1b). James uses the vocabulary of war to express the effect of controversies, quarrels and bad feeling among Christians because it perfectly describes the horror of it. The problem lies in our self-willed determination, summed up in the phrase "desires that battle within you" (4:1). Because we are fallen creatures our desires are often motivated by self-love thah will attempt to protect us by any means, including attacking anyone who threaten us. The solution is prayer, but in practice prayer goes unanswered because of the hindrance of our desires, which in verse 3 James calls "wrong motives". Instead of asking God to give us a sweeter tongue that will give a soft answer when we are hurt and insulted, and for His help to be more patient and forgiving in times of trial, we harbour grudges and adopt wrong attitudes. The inevitable price is damage to our human relationships and a break in our spiritual relationship with God. An added danger here is that the love of the world, which is never far from a believer's heart, will gain entry; hence James' warning in verse 4: "You adulterous people, don't you know that friendship with the world is hatred towards God? Anyone who chooses to be a friend of the world becomes an enemy of God."

James therefore challenges us in this verse with the contrasting words "friendship" and "hatred". We must be under no illusion: that's the reality of the two irreconcilables – friendship or hatred. In other words, we must not deceive ourselves into thinking that we can live in intimate fellowship with Jesus when the desire of our hearts is towards the world. The proof of this is seen in the way that it is often the apparently minor incidents at the early stages that end in deep pain. We need to learn that from unimpressive and unsuspected sources, great rivers of consequences can flow.

When we stop believing what the Scriptures say and move away from the company of Jesus we will find ourselves being drawn to the lies and illusions of the world around us. We will then start living to the world's agenda, and our time, finances and thoughts will be invested in the material and personal things that the world says are important. The danger then is that we drift into a state of concern for the things of this life only and end up living perfectly conformed to the pattern of this world. That is a direct result of a lack of faith.

Another result of lack of faith is the sin of presumption: "Now listen, you who say, 'Today or tomorrow we will go to this or that city, spend a year there, carry on business and make money.'" (James 4:13).

Here, James is speaking of the dangerous presumption that our lives are ours to do with as we wish, that we will live as long as we want and can choose what we will do on the assumption that we will be successful in that to which we put our minds. Again, the danger lies in the naturalness of this way of thinking, and therein lies the peril of acting as if our choices and resources were the only deciding factor. James, of course, is not stopping us from planning, but only that sort of self-sufficient, self-important planning that keeps God for Sunday but out of Monday to Saturday, which remain our exclusive domain.

# Warnings about wealth

In chapter 5 James introduces another high-risk topic: the use and abuse of wealth.

He starts by condemning the hoarding of wealth, which reminds us of Jesus' teaching about the rich fool who thought all was well because he had stored away enough wealth to see him through the years ahead, little suspecting that his soul would be demanded of him that night.

Then in verse 4, James raises the sin of fraudulence. As in the charge of sinful hoarding he immediately takes us straight from the earthly to the heavenly significance. He could have talked about the pain and suffering caused by the rich withholding their giving to others but, more importantly, he points to the fact that the Lord is aware of what happened and the injustice has not escaped His attention so the rich oppressor will be called to account.

The two words "luxury" and "self-indulgence" used by James in verse 5 spotlight the sin of indulgence. Used together, luxury and self-indulgence suggest the breaking down of divine restraints – not necessarily corrupt in every way – but offering no resistance to sin where there is promise of comfort and enjoyment. His phrase "you have fattened yourselves in the day of slaughter" (5:5) reminds us that the well-fed beast has no thought of the impending abattoir and butcher. In a similar manner, James sees the unthinking wealthy as blind to both heaven and hell, living for this life and forgetting the day of slaughter to come. To sum up, there is no sin in being rich. Where sin exists among the rich it arises from the way wealth is acquired, the spirit that it tends to cultivate in the heart and the way in which it is used.

In the final section of chapter 5 there is a wonderful picture of early Christian fellowship.

It involved four things:

## 1. Integrity

> *Above all, my brothers, do not swear – not by heaven or by*
> *earth or by anything else. Let your "Yes" be yes, and your*
> *"No", no, or you will be condemned.*
>
> JAMES 5:12

Christian men and women are to be dependable and trustworthy. One of the characteristics that makes for fellowship among people is that they can count on you.

## 2. Fellowship

In James 5:13–16, Christians are encouraged to talk to one another about their problems. Pray for one another, confess faults to one another, bear one another's burdens, open up hearts, take down façades and fences, come out from behind masks, stop pretending to be something you are not and be what you are. And immediately, the grace of the God of truth, who loves truth, will begin to flow through your life and friends, which will develop a fellowship that will make the world eager to join.

## 3. Prayer

The effectiveness of prayer is recorded in 5:16b–18. James reminds us:

> *Elijah was a man just like us. He prayed earnestly that it would not rain, and it did not rain on the land for three and a half years. Again he prayed, and the heavens gave rain, and the earth produced its crops.*
>
> JAMES 5:17–18

It's rather obvious that many Christians have little or no idea of the power that is committed to them in the ministry of prayer; power to control the effects of their daily lives and to quieten dissension and fears within their hearts so that, as Paul put it, "we may live peaceful and quiet lives in all godliness and holiness" (1 Timothy 2:2b).

## 4. Love, expressed as genuine concern for each other

> *My brothers, if one of you should wander from the truth and someone should bring him back, remember this: Whoever turns a sinner from the error of his way will save him from death and cover over a multitude of sins.*
>
> JAMES 5:19–20

And so James finishes with a wonderful glimpse of the life of the early church and the church as it should be today. No wonder these Christians turned the city of Jerusalem upside down. Under the leadership of this man James, the church grew (Acts 12:17; 15:13; 21:18) until there was a vast multitude of believers who lived by mutual confession, prayer, honest fellowship and love.

This is what the world needs to see, and in seeing Christian faith in action they cannot help but be impressed by the character of Jesus Christ as displayed by His ambassadors.

# 60

# 1 Peter
# – Through Persecution to Glory

Historians tells us that in July AD 64, the emperor Nero set fire to the city of Rome, destroying hundreds of public buildings and thousands of homes in order that he might create space to erect palaces and monuments that would establish his name in history. Understandably, the population of Rome were infuriated, and talked of rebellion and removing the emperor. So, seeking to divert blame from himself, Nero looked for a scapegoat he could hold responsible for the fire and the Christians fitted the bill. They were a people already under deep suspicion for following a man named Jesus Christ about whom extraordinary things were said, and it was even rumoured that they were cannibals because they talked about drinking someone's blood and eating His body. So, the emperor started the rumour around Rome that the Christians had burned down the city.

However, a lot of people refused to believe it, and in order to enforce his accusation Nero began a series of persecutions against the Christian faith. It was during this time that Christians were dipped in tar and burned as torches to light the gardens of Nero when he held an outdoor party. They were tied to chariots and dragged through the streets of Rome, thrown to the lions in the Colosseum, and in a hundred other horrible ways Nero sought to impress upon them the folly of being Christians while using them for his own political ends. It was shortly before this time of severe persecution that the apostle Peter wrote his letter. While Peter says he is writing from Babylon, it is unlikely he was in the uninhabited ruined city of that name. Rather, he was using the term as it is used in Revelation as a codeword for Rome, for all the evil and idolatry of Babylon had now been transferred to the capital of the Roman empire. Peter's purpose is to help believers see their temporary sufferings in the light of the coming eternal glory and to assure them that in the midst of all their discouragements the Sovereign God will keep them and enable them by faith to have joy. Jesus Christ by His patient suffering and glorious future destiny has given them the pattern to follow and is their living hope.

## The joy of salvation

Peter begins his letter by commenting upon the joy of salvation.

He says in the day men and women were born again they were given a new hope in this life and a new home in the next, and that hope is certain because the home is certain (1:3–4). When we use the word "hope" in our everyday conversation we automatically include the possibility of disappointment. For example, when we say, "I hope to be with you at 7 o'clock," we mean that is my intention, but the traffic may delay me, the car may break down, or a hundred and one other things may make me late. But Christian hope in the Bible looks forward with certainty without any implied reservations that it might not work out. This is expressed in the following lines from a well-known song:

> We have a hope that is steadfast and certain,
> Gone through the curtain and touching the throne.
>
> EXTRACT TAKEN FROM THE SONG "JESUS IS KING" BY WENDY CHURCHILL.
> COPYRIGHT © 1982 AUTHENTIC PUBLISHING.

Our hope is anchored in the past: Jesus rose! Our hope remains in the present: Jesus lives! Our hope is completed in the future: Jesus is coming!

This magnificent truth, says Peter, gives the Christian great joy (1:6). However, some would raise the obvious objection that they are going through a difficult time, and ask how can they be expected to rejoice when it feels as though God has deserted them? The answer is: while our natural reaction to trouble often is to view it as harmful, we learned from James that we are to consider it pure joy whenever we face trials because that is just what they are – trials of our faith (James 1:2). And when we are subject to pressure and heartache, not only does a lot of the dross, that is, our self-importance, self-reliance and self-satisfaction, get burned up, it also proves that we are not fair-weather Christians. We are encouraged that on the day Jesus is seen by everyone, our proven faith will result in much praise to Him and honour to us (1:7).

Just in case Christians are tempted to take their salvation for granted, Peter reminds them of two groups, both great servants of God, who would just love to change places with them and stand in their shoes: the prophets and the angels. Verses 10–12 tell us that although the Holy Spirit made certain truths very plain, the prophets still racked their brains putting the clues together, but now we have a much fuller picture. An amazing seemingly throw-away verse (1:12c) tells us that the angels, those majestic, powerful ministers of God, would love to know more about God's great salvation and what it's like to be saved. This picture of them straining for a better view inspired the lines from Charles Wesley's great hymn, "And Can It Be":

> *In vain the first-born seraph tries*
> *To sound the depths of grace divine.*
>
> CHARLES WESLEY (1707–88)

In verse 13, the "therefore" connects the description of the glorious salvation God has provided with the exhortation to live in the light of that salvation, which means Christians are to be holy. This involves a purifying departure from conformity to the world's godless agenda to biblical godliness in behaviour and love. This does not mean Christians are to live to a legalistic list of dos and don'ts – holy living cannot be reduced to a number of "saintly" actions. To live a holy life is to imitate the love of grace that saved us, and live the Christian life with respect and reverence for God (verse 17). This means that holy living should flow from the heart, and the key is love: to love the Lord our God with heart, soul, strength and mind, and to love our neighbour as ourselves (see Matthew 22:37–39).

## Peter's temple theology

In 1 Peter 2:4–12 Peter sets out the substance of what we might call "temple theology".

The astounding truth Peter states here is that the temple of God and the people of God are the same thing, and through the work of Jesus Christ on the cross every Christian is part of a new priestly order. This great truth, known as the "priesthood of all believers" was rediscovered and re-emphasized during the Reformation. It means that every Christian has immediate access to God, serves God personally, ministers to others and has something to contribute to the building of God's kingdom. It does not mean that each Christian has public gifts of preaching or teaching. In this verse Peter is stressing the reassuring fact that through Christ the believer is able to worship and serve God in a manner pleasing to Him.

The disobedient men and women who reject Jesus in 2:7–8 are contrasted by the "but you" in verses 9–10:

> But you are a chosen people, a royal priesthood, a holy nation,
> a people belonging to God, that you may declare the praises of
> him who called you out of darkness into his wonderful light.
> Once you were not a people, but now you are the people of God;
> once you had not received mercy, but now you have received
> mercy.

Calling the church a "chosen people" stresses God's loving initiative in bringing the church to Himself. A "royal priesthood" emphasizes the dignity of the church because of its union with Christ and its corporate role in worship, intercession and ministry. "Holy nation" shows that God has set apart the church for His use. The title a "people belonging to God" stresses ownership of a people who are His very own. "That you may declare the praises of him who called you out of darkness into his wonderful light", means that God wants us to praise and worship Him, and in doing so we will tell what He has done for us and what He means to us. When we do that, we offer a sacrifice unto God that is like a sweet-smelling offering and aroma of worship unto Him.

## Acceptable conduct

From verse 11 of chapter 2 Peter deals with the more practical aspects of life and shows his readers what is acceptable Christian conduct in a variety of circumstances.

Firstly he discusses behaviour in the realm of politics (verses 13–17). Jesus did not align Himself with the Jewish nationalist party of His day – they were known as the Zealots. He was prepared to pay the council tax and went on record that one should render to Caesar what is due to Caesar. Peter's teaching shadows that of his Master and promotes obedience to the rule of the politicians, except of course when the law of the state is opposed to the law of God (Acts 4:19). At other times the believer will be submissive and if he has a political creed it is summed up in verse 17: "Show proper respect to everyone: Love the brotherhood of believers, fear God, honour the king."

Secondly, Peter turns to the realm of labour (verses 18–25). Here he teaches the nature of conduct expected of servants and slaves to their masters whether they are fair or harsh, and says in verse 18, "submit yourselves". The standard expected of Christians is high, and in verse 21 Peter points us towards the Lord Jesus as the example: "To this you were called, because Christ suffered for you, leaving you an example, that you should follow in his steps."

Christ taught His disciples three things about suffering:

1. He must suffer because He was the Christ;

2. His suffering was for others, to provide for many a ransom and remission of sins;

3. all who followed Him must similarly be prepared to suffer.

When Christian men and women go through times of personal difficulties, even suffering unfairly, and they are tempted to retort in anger and bitterness, they should note how Peter brings in the thought of God-consciousness in verse 19, reminding them of how often suffering is the pathway to a deeper experience of the Lord. Remember, it was Jesus who dared to talk about the blessedness of suffering for righteousness' sake. But He not only talked about it, He illustrated it, as Peter goes on to show in some of the most wonderful verses describing the patience and courage of the Lord (verses 23–25).

In chapter 3 Peter moves into the third realm of marriage and home (3:1–7).

Ladies are the focus of the first six verses, and the words "in the same way" (verse 1), are the link with what has gone before. Submission neither means subservience nor inferiority. Just as there are difficult masters, so there are difficult husbands. That "they may be won over without words" means that the inner beauty of the wife's character will have a drawing and wooing effect. Fashions come and go, and sadly bodies grow old, but "the unfading beauty of a gentle and quiet spirit" merits God's approval and makes an eloquent statement, the worth of which has been demonstrated biblically and historically (verse 6). It has been said, "just as Abraham is called the father of the faithful so his wife Sarah may be described as the mother of the obedient". In other words, the lofty aim of a Christian wife is to be the daughter of Sarah.

Verse 7 has a briefer word for husbands: they are to recognize that in marriage the wife is the weaker partner (despite the fact that she bears children, lives longer and more often than not works harder). This obviously does not mean weaker morally, spiritually or intellectually; it simply means that women have less physical strength, and their husbands are to recognize this difference and take it into account. Together, husbands and wives are heirs of the "gracious gift of life". As they have been given to one another they should enjoy one another both sexually and spiritually, remembering that selfishness and egotism in the marriage relationship will mar their relationship with God.

Then we have the notoriously difficult passage in verses 19–20:

> *through whom also he [Jesus] went and preached to the spirits*
> *in prison who disobeyed long ago when God waited patiently in*
> *the days of Noah while the ark was being built. In it only a few*
> *people, eight in all, were saved through water.....*

As Peter expounds the great truth of verse 19, he is reminded of the way the gospel has been preached as far back in time as Noah's day when the Spirit of Christ, speaking through Noah, preached to the people in order that He might bring them to God. But they refused, and so the ark becomes a picture of the Lord Jesus Christ as the means of safety (salvation) through the flood of judgment to life beyond death. Then in verses 21–22, Peter uses the ark as the vehicle to take us into the subject of baptism. However, after illustrating the method of passing through water he immediately follows up with a note of clarification in case anyone thinks they are saved because they have received "external washing". Water baptism does not save us – it is, as Peter says in verse 21, a symbol and a sign of acceptance and obedience to the Lord Jesus, identifying with him in his death and resurrection. The baptism that saves is the inner cleansing which is obtained only through being born again and receiving a new heart.

## Peter on spiritual gifts

In chapter 4 Peter gives advice regarding spiritual gifts.

> *Each one should use whatever gift he has received to serve*
> *others, faithfully administering God's grace in its various*
> *forms. If anyone speaks, he should do it as one speaking the*
> *very words of God. If anyone serves, he should do it with the*
> *strength God provides, so that in all things God may be praised*
> *through Jesus Christ. To him be the glory and the power for*
> *ever and ever. Amen.*
>
> 1 PETER 4:10–11

First, note that gifts are not for a few but for all, and every believer has abilities that the Holy Spirit has given.

Second, American pastor John Piper is helpful here: he says the picture we have in verse 10 is of a house with variously talented stewards who are given the owner's funds to administer. The house is the church, the stewards are all of you, the various talents are all our varied gifts, the funds are God's grace and the administration is the exercise of our gifts. So now we have another definition of spiritual gifts: they are abilities by which we receive the grace of God and give out that grace to others.

The third observation from 1 Peter 4:11 is that grace can be given through gifts that are word-oriented or deed-oriented: "If anyone speaks... If anyone serves". So then grace can be given to other people either by gifts of word or gifts of deed, if we speak with the words and act with the strength that God supplies. And bear in mind, says Peter, the aim of all spiritual gifts is "that in all things God may be praised through Jesus Christ" (verse 11). This means that God's aim in giving Christians gifts, and in giving them the faith to exercise them, is that His glory might be displayed.

Anticipating that growing hostility towards Christianity will require many of his readers to defend their faith and conduct, Peter encourages them to be ready to do so in an intelligent and gracious way (verses 13–16). Three times he says that if they must suffer, it should be for righteousness' sake and not as a result of sinful behaviour (4:15–16; see also 2:20 and 3:17).

## Suffering for the cross

In 1 Peter 4:12–19 as if to emphasize our ability to read and forget, Peter returns to the theme of suffering for the cross and tells believers how to respond to it.

> *Rejoice that you participate in the sufferings of Christ, so that you may be overjoyed when his glory is revealed. If you are insulted because of the name of Christ, you are blessed, for the Spirit of glory and of God rests on you.*
>
> 1 PETER 4:13–14

Remember, however, it is not the suffering that makes us rejoice but the cause for which we are suffering; namely the cause of Christ. It is the duty of those in authority to uphold the law, and Christians are not to get themselves into positions where they are being punished for crimes they have committed, that's not suffering for the sake of Christ. In fact, it does Christianity a great disservice when ungodly men and women rightly sentence Christians for crimes of which they are guilty. Non-believers will all too readily hold up a fallen Christian to ridicule and contempt.

In 1 Peter 4:16, Peter reminds us that there is no easy gospel: "However, if you suffer as a Christian, do not be ashamed, but praise God that you bear that name." The road ahead will not be smooth and it will be difficult to reach our destination, but reached it will be, exactly as promised. We are not promised a smooth journey but we are promised a safe arrival. Therefore, the Lord's people should be very aware of the value of their souls and commit them (the Greek, "deposit") as if in trust for their protection (verse 19). Ancient Israel had no banking system. If someone was undergoing a long journey they would deposit ("commit") their life savings to a neighbour or friend for safekeeping. In doing this it would be natural to be concerned about the friend's integrity, and so it is with us. But we have the assurance that we know whom we have believed, and are convinced that He is able to guard what we have entrusted to Him for that day (2 Timothy 1:12).

Notice how Peter expresses himself in chapter 5.

Whatever the claims made for him, he never used papal terms. He tells us three things in verse 1:

1. he is a fellow elder;

2. he was a witness at the death of the Saviour;

3. he will share in the coming glory.

## A word to elders, young men and the tempted

First, he has a word for elders (verses 2–4). Since the position of elder carries much responsibility, and as elders will have to give an account of their work, no one should be forced into this position. Willingness and not compulsion should be the driving force for those exercising this noble office. Other essential attributes include a spirit of service and, as power can corrupt, Peter warns against the danger of having a dictatorial attitude.

Second, a word to young men (verse 5–7). Youth is not always wrong: look at the intelligence of the young man in Job 32 as the example of a sensible young man. But young men can be dangerously impetuous. Think of Peter's attempt to walk on water (Matthew 14:29), or the rebuke he delivered to the

Lord Jesus (Mark 8:32) and the hot-headed response of James and John when the Samaritan villagers were inhospitable (Luke 9:54). However, there is a sense that you are as young as you feel, and the impetuousness of youth flows on into later years. So Peter's antidote of humility must be offered to the total body of Christ.

Third, a word to the tempted (verses 8–9). Peter, of course, knew what he was talking about: he gave the account of his fall to Mark and the rest of the Gospel writers. Temptations came thick and fast to the big fisherman, but thank God they weren't edited out of Scripture but remain as a source of encouragement to us in times of failure. Humility (verse 6) and self-control (verse 8) are related, for the humble man will always recognize his need for fine-tuning in personal discipline and, of course, as we saw in 1:6–7, God has His ways of doing this.

Peter's depiction of the devil as a lion is uniquely appropriate. The king of the jungle prowls with might and stealth, and though as prince of this world the devil has great power, God has limited both his power and abilities. The Christian response is not to panic or to flee, but to offer firm resistance in the faith. Peter is also a good psychologist and he urges us to remember that support in the struggle also comes from the realization that other Christians are going through their hard times. Think about them. Others too are facing the test. Hold on (verse 9).

Peter brings his letter to a close with a word to the failed (verses 10–11).

Here Peter is even more helpful. Though Scripture does not excuse failure, it teaches that failure need not be the end. Discipleship does not stop when you warm your hands by the high priest's fire in a courtyard where you should never have even been and utter curses from your mouth that you should never have thought, let alone spoken. All this Peter knows painfully too well from his own experience (Mark 14). But God's grace can and will restore the lapsed Christian. It's shown in verse 10:

> *And the God of all grace, who called you to his eternal glory in*
> *Christ, after you have suffered a little while, will himself restore*
> *you and make you strong, firm and steadfast.*

This must not be confused with the unwarranted idea of purgatory or as implying penance. Peter is talking here of a corrective learning process by which restoration is effected in our lives and circumstances. Joseph is an example of someone who went through this process. It toughened him up. He experienced it at the hands of his brothers, through the injustice of Potiphar and the amnesia of the Pharaoh's butler. But it was this suffering that put iron into his soul, strengthening and equipping him for the awesome responsibility of becoming the first and only Jewish prime minister of Egypt. No wonder Peter finishes this section with an acknowledgment to this source of power:

> *To him be the power for ever and ever. Amen.*
>
> 1 PETER 5:11

# 61

## 2 Peter
## – Stand Fast Against Falsehood

The main purpose of Peter's second letter, like that of his first, is to strengthen believers in their faith. But where his first dealt with opposition from without in the form of external persecution, his second letter deals with the dangers threatening the spiritual life of the believer from within, specifically false teachers, who, in the words of 2:1 "will secretly introduce destructive heresies". So, Peter's purpose in his second letter is twofold:

1. to expose the false guides for what they are,

2. more importantly, to set before the churches the conditions of survival and true spiritual growth when doctrinal and moral perversions attempt to infiltrate their fellowships.

Peter's greeting in verses 1–2 introduces the theme of chapter 1, which is that the best antidote against error is knowledge of the truth. He starts by defining the person of Jesus Christ, and says that He is Saviour, God, the Christ and Lord. This fourfold description of Jesus puts Him at the focal point of human history. As God, He guarantees that His words and His works cannot be replaced or revoked; as Christ, He fulfils all the Old Testament prophecies; as Saviour, He died on the cross for our past, present and future; and as Lord, He claims our individual love and obedience. Peter's purpose here is to lay down unchanging foundational beliefs for Christians, unlike the false teachers who pick and choose what they believe. So, insists Peter, the titles go together: it is only because Jesus is the Lord that He can be Saviour, and since He is the Saviour He owns those He has saved. Therefore, He has the right to be their Lord.

Then, as today, false teachers were claiming to be the spiritual elite. They insisted that their superior experience elevated them onto a higher spiritual plane giving them a deeper understanding of the things of Christ. But Peter's statement, "To those who through the righteousness of our God and Saviour Jesus Christ have received a faith as precious as ours" (verse 1), means that the apostles never thought of themselves as being above ordinary believers in their grasp of knowledge and truth. They regarded themselves as no more than everyday normal Christians with the same equality of opportunity in faith as any other believer enjoyed. In other words, even the weakest believer holds in his hands all that the mightiest saint ever possessed, and that's the theme of Peter's opening chapter: "His divine power has given us everything we need for life and godliness" (2 Peter 1:3a).

It is, therefore, vitally important that Christian men and women understand that as believers in Christ they have all they will ever need to meet any trial or difficulty they may encounter in this life. Other than Jesus there is no mysterious transcendental secret, no ecstatic experience, no super-spiritual wisdom that takes them up onto some higher plane of spiritual life. Because many professing Christians find that hard to accept, they think that they need something more – some new experience, some further revelation without which they can never be the kind of Christian they ought to be. But Peter flatly denies that way of thinking. He says that if you come to Christ and accept Him as Lord and Saviour you have Him. And if you have Him, you have in the fullest sense all that God is ever going to give you. This does not mean Christian men and women will not have wonderful personal experiences of Christ – they may or may not. But, it does mean that none of these experiences, marvellous as they may be, are any substitute for a personal deepening relationship with Jesus. This means if we have everything in Christ, we only need to know more of Him and we will have all that it takes to solve the problems and difficulties that confront us.

Of course, the reality is that when we come into the Christian life, although we have all that we will ever need, there is much that we do not yet know. But as we grow in our biblical knowledge of Christ, and as our subsequent relationship with Him deepens, we increasingly gain an insight and an understanding of how to handle the difficulties, heartaches and problems we face, and most importantly we start to understand ourselves.

There are two ways by which insight and understanding come.

# 1. Through God's promises

*... he has given us his very great and precious promises...*

2 PETER 1:4A

These are the sure and certain guarantees that God has given us in the pages of Scripture that He will honour with all that He has. His very nature and magnificence is at stake in these words; they refer to promises that are sure and certain. Therefore, it is vital that Christian men and women learn what God has promised, which means learning from the Bible. That is why it is impossible to find fulfilment in life and really discover the kind of person God wants us to be unless we understand the Word of God. Secular counselling only gives the accumulation of man's knowledge with its mixture of truth and error and no ability to distinguish one from the other. This explains why highly educated men and women make the most appalling blunders and wrong decisions. It's only when people begin to understand God's great and mighty promises that they understand what life is all about.

Notice the effect of relying on these promises from God: "you may participate in the divine nature and escape the corruption in the world caused by evil desires" (2 Peter 1:4b).

In this fallen world we are surrounded by evil and corruption. Our media in its many forms, our social arenas and even our workplaces are polluted by the evil of this world. We see sexual corruption, greed, materialism, ambition, pride and selfishness. All of these are the outworking of sin that is wrecking the lives of men and women all over the earth, and those are the sins from which the truth of God particularly delivers us as we understand and obey it.

# 2. Through Christian living

The second way to discover all that is available to Christians is found in verses 5-7:

> *For this very reason, make every effort to add to your faith goodness; and to goodness, knowledge; and to knowledge, self-control; and to self-control, perseverance; and to perseverance, godliness; and to godliness, brotherly kindness; and to brotherly kindness, love.*

All this we have in Christ but we need to work at putting it into practice which means applying it in our daily lives with the people with whom we live and work. Verse 8 tells us the result of doing this: "For if you possess these qualities in increasing measure, they will keep you from being ineffective and unproductive in your knowledge of our Lord Jesus Christ."

Here we have the recipe for success as a Christian – to know God and to become like Him – it's faith and obedience. The knowledge of the promises of God and the application of the promises in life's circumstances will keep us from being unfruitful and ineffective. That being the case, the apostle says,

> ... *be all the more eager to make your calling and election sure. For if you do these things, you will never fall, and you will receive a rich welcome into the eternal kingdom of our Lord and Saviour Jesus Christ.*
>
> 2 PETER 1:10–11

By practising Christian living, when it comes time for us to go home we will receive the final accolade, "Well done, my good and faithful servant!"

Peter then reveals two guarantees that undergird his teaching

## 1. The eyewitness account of the apostle himself

He says in verse 16a, "We did not follow cleverly invented stories when we told you about the power and coming of our Lord Jesus Christ." And then in verses 16b–18 he recites his experience of being present at the transfiguration of Christ recorded in Matthew 17, telling us, "we were eyewitnesses of his majesty". And that's where Christian faith rests – on the eyewitness accounts of men and women who were there, and who simply reported what they saw and heard and what Jesus did.

## 2. Fulfilment of prophetic words from the Old Testament

In verses 19–21 Peter goes further, saying that the truth of the Christian faith is confirmed also by the prophets of the Old Testament. We have here the clearest biblical description of the divine–human process of inspiration. These men wrote not by their own inspiration – they did not write their own opinion – but wrote what they were given by the Spirit of God, and accurately predicted events that were to follow centuries afterwards. If that is not confirmation of the truth, what could be? So two things – eyewitnesses and prophetic words – underlie our faith.

In chapter 2, having reminded the New Testament church of the great truths on which they stand, Peter now warns them of false prophets in the churches.

> *But there were also false prophets among the people, just as*
> *there will be false teachers among you. They will secretly*
> *introduce destructive heresies, even denying the sovereign Lord*
> *who bought them....*
>
> 2 PETER 2:1

This tells us that these false teachers are not mere hostile atheists – we've always had them – but they are people who claim to be Christians, who profess to love and follow the Lord Jesus, yet the things that they teach will deny everything that Jesus stood for. Their teaching "will bring the way of truth into disrepute" (verse 2). Today, this is the teaching of liberal men and women who sneer at Christians who believe the Bible is the inerrant Word of God, calling them deluded, trapped in the past with no understanding of the great cultural issues of the day. But, warns Peter, "Their condemnation has long been hanging over them, and their destruction has not been sleeping" (verse 3). Speaking of the certainty of the judgment on these people, Peter recounts three instances from the past which prove that God knows how to handle people like this:

- He did not spare the angels when they sinned; He judged them.
- He did not spare Sodom and Gomorrah when they sinned; He judged them.
- He did not spare the ancient world; He judged it in the flood.

Yet through all of these judgments He preserved a remnant of integrity (verses 4–6). Therefore, Peter's conclusion is:

> *if this is so, then the Lord knows how to rescue godly men from*
> *trials and to hold the unrighteous for the day of judgment,*
> *while continuing their punishment.*
>
> 2 PETER 2:9

Peter follows this incredible promise and assurance with an extended description of the false teachers in verses 10–22, which gives rise to some of the most colourful and shocking language in the New Testament.

## 1. They will be presumptuous and ignorant

They will speak eloquently and confidently about things having to do with life, death, salvation and other great themes but they do not know what they are talking about. "They are like brute beasts, creatures of instinct, born only to be caught and destroyed, and like beasts, they too will perish" (verse 12).

## 2. They will be shameless

They will encourage licentiousness and sexual misconduct, openly urging people to indulge their lusts freely and shamelessly (verse 13).

## 3. They will be greedy

For the sake of money, they will teach almost anything they think people want to hear (verse 14b).

## 4. They will be pretentious

> *For they mouth empty, boastful words and, by appealing to the lustful desires of sinful human nature, they entice people who are just escaping from those who live in error.*
>
> 2 PETER 2:18

## 5. They will promise freedom

This portrayal is so appropriate for our day: "they promise... freedom, while they themselves are slaves of depravity" (verse 19). This is the truth about the "feel good" factor that drives alcohol misuse, materialism and selfishness, and that encourages abortion, sodomy and godlessness. They all promise freedom but with it comes an increasing bondage that destroys.

So in verses 20–21, Peter concludes with some of the most sobering words in Scripture:

> *If they have escaped the corruption of the world by knowing our Lord and Saviour Jesus Christ and are again entangled in*

*it and overcome, they are worse off at the end than they were at*
*the beginning. It would have been better for them not to have*
*known the way of righteousness, than to have known it and*
*then to turn their backs on the sacred command that was passed*
*on to them.*

Peter does not specify how they are worse off. The likelihood is he means their sin is more serious, their hearts more hardened, their minds more cynical and their slavery to self more intense. That is the condition of those who are put in what 2:4 calls "gloomy dungeons" to await the Judge.

## Assurance of Jesus' return

In chapter 3 Peter faces up to a key question that was being raised by the false teachers. Could it be that they have a point when they argue that the long delay they have experienced effectively invalidates the promise of Jesus" return? The point being: if Jesus is not going to return physically then the promise is false and there is no point in waiting for it so believers may as well join in the self-centred lifestyle of the people Peter is attacking. How can he argue that they are wrong and he is right? How can he justify the continuing embarrassing wait for Jesus?

Peter's reply is to sound a note of certainty. Do not be discouraged, he says, by the sneering scepticism that attacks the base of Christian thinking. Remember that One is coming who will settle the whole thing.

The term "last days" (verse 3) is not some future date when scoffers will appear; the "last days" are today, the church age, the gospel age, which will always be marked by the presence of scoffers. Peter says they will base their arguments against the second coming of Christ on the fact that all things have continued as they were since the beginning of creation (verse 4). They will say, "God does not intervene in world affairs, there can be no intrusion into this universe of a divine power that operates in any way differently than what you can observe around you." But, says Peter, they're wrong. They have been wrong in the past and they will be wrong in the future.

To clinch his argument he points to two past and one future divinely induced catastrophic events: the creation, the flood and the dissolution of the present heavens and earth. And, yes, it may look as if the promise of Christ's return will not be fulfilled but this is untrue for two reasons:

1. God's perspective on the passing of time is quite unlike that of men – a

day with the Lord is as a thousand years and a thousand years is as a day. Therefore, what seems to drag on endlessly for us is but a few moments for God;

2. His apparent delay in waiting to usher in the end of the age is due to His patience in waiting for more men and women to come to knowledge of Christ (verse 8–9). But God has spoken and the day of consummation will come when all the matter of this universe will evidently be transformed into a new heaven and a new earth (verses 10–13). We do need to keep in mind the wonder of this promise and remember, "No eye has seen, no ear has heard, no mind has conceived what God has prepared for those who love him" (1 Corinthians 2:9).

In verse 11 Peter asks the rhetorical question: "In light of all this what kind of people ought Christians to be right now in terms of holiness and godliness as they wait for the coming of the day of God?" He answers his question in verse 14: "So then, dear friends, since you are looking forward to this, make every effort to be found spotless, blameless and at peace with him."

In a final postscript, Peter says that Paul agrees with him, and says that those things that our beloved brother Paul has written, "ignorant and unstable people distort, as they do the other Scriptures, to their own destruction" (verses 15–16).

He then sums up his letter with two closing verses:

> *Therefore, dear friends, since you already know this, be on*
> *your guard so that you may not be carried away by the error of*
> *lawless men and fall from your secure position. But grow in the*
> *grace and knowledge of our Lord and Saviour Jesus Christ. To*
> *him be glory both now and for ever! Amen.*
>
> 2 PETER 3:17–18

These verses re-emphasize what he has already taught: that the way to stand fast, grow and be productive in the Christian life is to put faith and obedience into practice. That way leads to us knowing God and so becoming like Him.

It reminds us of the famous statement made by John Newton (1725–1807):

> *I am not what I ought to be. I am not what I want to be. I am*
> *not what I hope to be. But I can truly say I am not what I once*
> *was. By the grace of God I am what I am.*

That is the foundation for authentic Christian assurance. The question is not whether we are perfect or have arrived. We are not perfect and none of us have yet arrived. But, are we moving? Are we growing? Is our knowledge of God improving? Is our relationship with Jesus deepening? Are we walking closer and closer to Him? For if we are growing in the grace and knowledge of our Lord and Saviour, the glory will certainly be His, now and for ever.

# 62

# 1 John
## – Genuine Christianity

John states his purpose in writing this letter in 1 John 5:13.

He says, "I write these things to you who believe in the name of the Son of God so that you may know that you have eternal life."

Where John's Gospel focused on presenting the truth of Jesus and the way of salvation in order to lead people to faith, his first letter is directed towards those who have professed Christian belief. He encourages them to live out their belief in the face of increasing criticism and temptation to doubt the basic tenets of the Christian faith.

From the contents of the letter it is clear that a number of dissident members, including teachers, had left the church and started their own apostate fellowship. They were actively enticing Christians to leave the church and join their group (2:19, 26). John recognized that the break-away group were deficient in their foundations of the Christian faith. What may have been hypothetical questions in the context of a home-group discussion had become the tenets of a rival faith community that eventually developed into a widespread movement which has been given the name Gnosticism.

So, around AD 90, in the city of Ephesus, John was anxious to correct the false teaching and sinful behaviour that led to heresy and immorality. He did this by answering questions that would be troubling those who stayed in the church. Questions like: "Were the new teachers right?"; "Was the old teaching superseded by a new, higher spirituality?"; "Was their faith authentic and were they really saved?" In other words, how could someone know they were a genuine Christian? How could they know that they were born again?

It was in answer to questions like these John offers three tests by which an individual may understand if they are born again. They have been defined as:

1. the doctrinal test (the test of belief in the Lord Jesus Christ) (1:1–4); "That which was from the beginning, which we have heard, which we have seen with our eyes, which we have looked at and our hands have touched – this we proclaim concerning the Word of life. The life appeared; we have seen it and testify to it, and we proclaim to you the eternal life, which was with the Father and has appeared to us. We proclaim to you what we have seen and heard, so that you also may have fellowship with us. And our fellowship is with the Father and with his Son, Jesus Christ. We write this to make our joy complete."

2. the moral test (the test of righteousness or obedience) (2:28); "And now, dear children, continue in him, so that when he appears we may be confident and unashamed before him at his coming."

3. the social test (the test of love) (1 John 3:11); "This is the message you heard from the beginning: We should love one another."

## The doctrinal test

John begins his message with this first test (1:1–4).

This is the test of belief in the Lord Jesus Christ, and for this to be effective a relationship is necessary. John calls it fellowship with God – fellowship with the Lord Jesus as He dwells in us and we dwell in Him. According to John this is the bottom line, for without that relationship it is impossible to produce genuine Christianity.

Aware of the special relationship he had with the real, historical Jesus in the flesh, John starts his letter from this basis: "I saw Him, I heard Him, I touched Him. He was a real person – there was nothing false about Him."

Throughout his letter John emphasizes the fact that Jesus appeared in history as both God and man. He is both the eternal God, linked with all the great revelations of the Old Testament that mark out the being and character of God, and He is man, having come in the flesh. He lived among us as a man, suffered as a man, and died as a man. So, the basis for Christian faith and hope of salvation is not mystical and philosophical. It's down to earth and observable, in that at a geographical place at a specific time in history the real man Jesus lived with real men and women and was publicly executed by Pontius Pilate outside the gates of Jerusalem – fact! All this, so that we might have fellowship with Jesus and partake of His divine nature.

In effect John is arguing, "Don't be deceived by Gnostic heresy. Jesus is the God–Man, eternal Spirit bonded to a human body and anyone who denies this truth is a liar. Secure in the knowledge of this truth, you Christians have the assurance of your sins being forgiven and you can enjoy fellowship with God. Therefore it would be foolish for you to turn away from the teachings of the apostles to the inventions of the antichrists".

He amplifies this point with his warning in 1 John 2:15–17:

> *Do not love the world or anything in the world. If anyone loves the world, the love of the Father is not in him. For everything in the world – the cravings of sinful man, the lust of his eyes and the boasting of what he has and does – comes not from the Father but from the world. The world and its desires pass away, but the man who does the will of God lives forever.*

So, the first mark of genuine Christianity is understanding and holding fast to doctrinal truth and not being swayed by social pressure or popular forms of spirituality that are a distortion and corruption of genuine Christianity.

## The moral test

John now takes us into his second premise (2:28). This is the test of righteousness or obedience, which involves more than intellectual understanding. For, just as being in a relationship with Jesus is the essential foundation for genuine Christianity, so too new behaviour is the sign of genuine Christianity. He argues that regeneration must be seen in the practice of righteous living (2:7–10).

John explains that, because Christians are children of God through faith in Christ, they have a firm hope of being fully conformed to Him when they see Him, for they will be like Him. It then follows that their present likeness to Christ places them in a position of incompatibility with sin because sin is contrary to the work and person of Christ. It's not just agreeing with the doctrine, it's much more than that, important as that may be. It's also righteousness. For to profess knowledge of God and to be in a personal relationship with Jesus Christ without a holy life, without a clean break with sin and a deep love for other Christians, is as much of a delusion as to deny the incarnation of our Lord

Jesus. Belief and behaviour are inseparable; mind and heart belong together and true light leads to true love.

This means that behaviour changes lives. The emphasis of John, as with all the writers of the New Testament, is this: "Look," he says, "if you really have Jesus Christ living in you, you can't be the same person. You cannot go on living in sin, doing wrong things, lying and stealing, and living in sexual immorality. You cannot do it."

"Yes you can!" said the Gnostics. They said, "If spirit is good and matter is evil, and our bodies are matter, then the only thing that counts is the spirit. What you do with your body doesn't make any difference. So if you want to indulge in its lusts, go ahead, it won't affect your spiritual standing with God."

As a result they were turning the grace of God into what Jude called a "licence for immorality" (Jude 4). People were being taught, Christians were being taught, that they could practise all the immorality of their day and God would still treat them exactly the same; it would not change their relationship one whit. But, John says, this is very wrong, for no one who is born of God will deliberately choose to continue to sin precisely because he has been born of God (3:9) – the two are incompatible. You cannot have the Holy Spirit living in you and live an unholy life. If you live the unholy life and profess to be a Christian, you are a liar, says John. When dealing with the signs of a true, genuine faith, John is very blunt:

> *If we claim to have fellowship with him yet walk in the*
> *darkness, we lie and do not live by the truth.*
>
> 1 JOHN 1:6

> *This is how we know who the children of God are and who the*
> *children of the devil are....*
>
> 1 JOHN 3:10

> *Whoever hates his brother is in the darkness....*
>
> 1 JOHN 2:11

> *Anyone who hates his brother is a murderer....*
>
> 1 JOHN 3:15

John's strong language should awaken Christians to the standards God requires of those who profess to follow Him. There are too many "laid-back" Christians. John was very direct – it hurts.

547

# The social test

The third mark of a true Christian is the social test. This is the test of love. Regeneration is the radical inward change in thinking by which God brings an individual from a life of spiritual defeat and death to a renewed life of holiness and life.

Paul discusses the results of regeneration in a believer in Ephesians 4:17–32 where he says that each believer has put off the old way of life, become clothed with a new way of life and is in the process of having one's mind renewed in its thinking and reasoning.

However, as John makes clear, the experience of regeneration does not leave a believer content with their new position and inactive in their effort at Christian growth. With the old powers of evil broken, the possibility of victory in the constant struggle with sin becomes certain, so the believer strives to show the visible evidences of genuine Christianity by righteous living. Yet, while doctrinal truth and righteous living are difficult to master, these first two aspects of genuine Christianity are relatively easy compared with the third, which is love. In 1 John 3:10–23 John teaches that knowing the truth and being righteous is unmistakably revealed in love.

Sometimes we hear Christian testimony along the lines of, "I've given up my sins and worldly lifestyle. I used to drink, sleep around and gamble, but I don't do any of them any more because I now believe in the Lord I've stopped all these things." Now we must never ever minimize the wholesome changes in the life of a person who becomes truly committed to Jesus Christ, upholding His truth and forsaking sinful behaviour. Praise God! But if what we have stopped doing is the extent of our Christian testimonies, we will find that most unbelieving people are generally unimpressed by what we have stopped doing. There are, of course, several reasons for this response: many non-Christian people can stop doing these things if they have a good reason to do so – or at least they think they can – and, importantly, many of the things Christians no longer do are things people in this world love to do, don't want to give up and so view them as a lifestyle choice.

The bottom line is that people are not impressed by the negative things that Christians don't do; they are impressed by the positive things that Christians do. It is this positive action, expressed in love, that impresses the world and makes the gospel attractive to people outside the Christian faith. That's why John says the third mark of a genuine Christian is that he begins to love – not just those that love him, anybody can do that, says Jesus: "Even 'sinners' love those who love them" (Luke 6:32) – but also those who do not love us. We are called to treat kindly those who mistreat us; to return good for evil and to pray for those who spitefully use us; to welcome and treat kindly those who are against us and are trying to hurt us. That's the standard. No longer treating those in need with callous indifference but responding to them and not shutting them out.

The ultimate expression of love was demonstrated by our Lord on Calvary's cross when He forgave those who hammered the nails into His hands and feet, and the crowds who jeered Him in His dying moments. D. L. Moody, in one of his sermons, depicts the Lord Jesus after His resurrection giving directions to Peter: "Go, find the man," He says, "who thrust his spear into my side and tell him there's a much quicker way to My heart. Find the man who crowned M0e with thorns and tell him I should like to give him the crown of life."

It's a dramatic way of depicting the love of Christianity. Opposition, hatred and persecution are to be repaid positively with good. On no account is a Christian to seek revenge for injuries done to him. That's why John writes in 4:19, "We love because he first loved us." And then he gives a practical example in verse 20, paraphrased helpfully by Eugene Peterson in The Message:

> If anyone boasts, "I love God," and goes right on hating his brother or sister, thinking nothing of it, he is a liar. If he won't love the person he can see, how can he love the God he can't see?

The command we have from Christ is blunt: loving God includes loving people. We've got to love both. The way this works out in our lives is by fellowship with the Lord Jesus, opening our hearts to His Word, letting His light shine upon us and walking with Him day by day. As the power of Jesus changes us we will grow not only in truth and righteousness, but in love towards our Christian brothers and sisters, and in our love towards those who are outside the faith. This does not come naturally; it's something Christians have to work at. However, genuine Christianity does not stop at knowledge (truth) or righteousness (holy living), but is seen in the way Christians express their love for their fellow men.

From 5:18 John brings his letter to a close with words of assurance.

In three consecutive verses (18, 19 and 20) he begins with the confident phrase, "We know... .'

### "We know that anyone born of God does not continue to sin"

In saying this in 5:18a, John is not contradicting his earlier statement in chapter 1 that anyone who says he does not sin or has never sinned is either self-deceived or a liar. Rather, here in 5:18 the verbs are in the present tense in the Greek, indicating habitual or continuous action. So the statement is not that the Christian cannot fall into sin; indeed, they can and do. It is that while they may fall into sin, they cannot continue in it indefinitely. In other words, if the individual is truly born of God, the new birth will result in new action.

### "The one who was born of God keeps him safe, and the evil one cannot harm him"

Why does the Christian need to be kept safe (5:18b)? The answer is given by John in verse 19: "We know that we are children of God, and that the whole world is under the control of the evil one."

Scripture, church history and personal experience all testify to the fact that this world is motivated by the gods of idolatry, selfishness and sin, and born-again Christians are constantly being tempted to compromise their faith. But believers have the assurance from the Word of God that we belong to Him and can stand fast in this age of uncertainty and confusion.

### The most fundamental of John's affirmations

> We know also that the Son of God has come and has given us understanding, so that we may know him who is true. And we are in him who is true – even in his Son Jesus Christ. He is the true God and eternal life.
>
> 1 JOHN 5:20

This strikes at the very root of Gnostic theology for it is the affirmation that the Son of God, Jesus, has come into this world to give us both a knowledge of God and salvation. In other words, it is the assurance that He and nothing else is at the heart of Christianity. He and only He provides what all men and women desperately need, and that is not philosophical enlightenment, valuable as that may be in some areas, but to know God and have the assurance of salvation.

For Christians today the question can be asked: "Once we know Him what then?" In verse 18 John has written that the Son of God will keep Christians safe, but this does not relieve us from our own responsibility to persevere in God's service as verse 21 confirms: "Dear children, keep yourselves from idols." After the hard lesson of the Babylonian captivity Israel never had much of a problem with idol worship. But in the context of his letter, it's more likely that John's warning represents a final depiction of the "heresy" represented by the false teachers. For ultimately false teaching is not the worship of the true God made known in His Son Jesus, but a false god – an idol, invented by false teachers.

This sort of thing is heard today in the argument over moral issues: "My God wouldn't do that"; "The Jesus I follow would want this!" The lesson for Christians is to remember that the use of the name Jesus or God or Christian, does not authenticate the message or the religion of the one presenting it. On the contrary, the profession must be tested by the basic doctrines of apostolic Christianity: What does the person speaking really believe about Jesus? Is He God incarnate or just a teacher? Did He die a real, atoning, vicarious death for sinners? Or is His death merely a symbol? Did He physically rise from the dead? Is the teaching of Jesus true, complete and authoritative? Or is His teaching partial, thereby needing the teaching of others to bring us to a higher and indeed new form of "Christianity"? Then, Christians' lives must be open to scrutiny: Do they strive to be holy? Do they show forth Jesus in their lives? Are they ambassadors for Christ? And finally, do they show their faith by their love?

# 63

## 2 John
## – Despatches from the Front Line

While the Christian gospel of good news was spreading throughout the world and the apostle's writings were circulating and being read, the apostolic generation had all but died out. It seems likely that John was the only remaining member of the original group of twelve. Consequently, the watchful oversight of the church depicted in the Acts of the Apostles was no longer possible, though the need was never greater. For with an ever-increasing church there came an ever-increasing number of visiting speakers who claimed to have new insights into the Christian faith. They claimed the original gospel as given to the apostles was primitive and unsophisticated, and so taught a perverted gospel which became known as Gnosticism. They, of course, were prepared, for a price, to initiate others into the secret deeper truths, and the temptation to join these self-appointed spiritual elite must have been very strong. To counter this onslaught against the revealed Christian faith, some believers wanted to turn the clock back to the Old Testament law and circumcision and add them onto the Christian belief. The burden that exercised John's mind and troubled his spirit was how the young New Testament churches were to stand fast against compromise, be kept strong in the true faith, and how they were to respond to visiting missionaries.

# In love and in truth

First, John says that Christians must embrace and obey the truth, and at the same time love those who are brothers and sisters in Christ. These must be the key characteristics that distinguish Christians from others. Allied to that is the necessity for believers to defend the faith in love and truth against those who have left it to follow the Gnostic teaching and are preaching a new gospel.

John is not saying anything new; he himself recorded Jesus' teaching:

> *A new command I give you: Love one another. As I have loved you, so you must love one another.*
>
> JOHN 13:34

> *My command is this: Love each other as I have loved you…*
> *This is my command: Love each other.*
>
> JOHN 15:12, 17

The difficulty of balancing truth and love is well known to Christian men and women: truth without love produces domineering harshness, but love without truth produces undiscerning sentimentality. The constant temptation is to emphasize one at the expense of the other. Some may rightly emphasize truth and doctrine, insisting that the Scriptures be followed carefully, but do so at the expense of love. When they do this, they become cold and judgmental, sometimes even cruel in the way they say things. Even though what they say is correct they are trying to defend the truth of God at the expense of love. On the other hand, there are those who make the mistake of emphasizing love at the expense of truth. They feel that they should accept everyone and everything, being non-judgmental and tolerant in all circumstances.

The challenge is to keep truth and love in balance as was so beautifully demonstrated by the Lord Jesus. He could deal tenderly with the immoral sinner and outcast from society who came to Him yet, with a searing word, He could scorch a Pharisee until he turned red with shame as all the hypocrisy in that man's inner life was revealed. He spoke the truth, dealt in love and kept them in perfect balance. John says, "When you go to handle a problem of doctrinal error, emphasize both truth and love." A lot of people who read this letter miss these opening words thus overlooking the wisdom of balance that pervades the letter.

## How to recognize deception

In verses 7–11, with stunning precision, John moves from the truth and love that inspires celebration and joy, to the treachery and deception that is lurking just outside the door of the church. John no doubt has in mind the defectors who had split from the church in the recent past, and there were a lot of them as alluded to by "many deceivers" (verse 7). The word "deceivers" can also be translated "liars"; it's the word Jesus used in Matthew 24:4, 11 and 24 to warn against false prophets and messiahs who will lead people astray. Clearly, these people have not only left the traditional Christian teaching but they have "gone out" into the world in order to spread their own perverted philosophy.

There are two subjects John speaks of here that describe the two fundamental Christian perversions from which all Christian error and heresies grow.

## 1. Deception about the person of the Lord Jesus

This subject concerns those who are deceived about the person of the Lord Jesus: "Many deceivers, who do not acknowledge Jesus Christ as coming in the flesh, have gone out into the world. Any such person is the deceiver and the antichrist" (2 John 7).

At Christmas we celebrate that Christ the Redeemer, God Himself, came to earth as a man born of a virgin in Bethlehem. The term we use to describe this is "incarnation", and it refers to the affirmation that God the Son, without in any way ceasing to be the one true God, has revealed Himself to humanity for its salvation by becoming human. The man, Jesus from Nazareth, is the incarnate Word or Son of God. As the God–Man He mediates God to humans; as the Man–God He represents humans to God. The incarnation is an essential doctrine of the Christian faith and throughout the New Testament letters the apostles of our Lord set this incarnation at the centre of Christian theology: the Word becoming man. And, says John, if anyone does not affirm that, no matter what else they may say, they are deceivers. Now, of course, they may be deceived as well as being deceivers, but they are anti-christ. They are against the doctrine of Jesus. Therefore, they are to be recognized for what they are, people who are mistaken and trying to deceive others.

## 2. Belief that the Bible is insufficient

This subject, which spawns error and encourages heresy, focuses on a misunderstanding or false conception of the teaching of the Lord Jesus, which John warns about in verse 9: "Anyone who runs ahead and does not continue in the teaching of Christ does not have God; whoever continues in the teaching has both the Father and the Son."

Someone with such a wrong view may be very persuasive and sincere, and may be a great personality. But this is the test: if they do not believe the biblical doctrine of Christ is complete and trustworthy, then they are not of God. There are many people today who say the Bible is for a bygone age, that modern man can no longer accept these simplistic teachings and the contemporary mind must find satisfaction in a more scientific approach. Perhaps even more dangerously tempting for the true believer is the "liberal Christian" who says that the Bible must be viewed in the light of today's understanding, which means Scripture is at the mercy of prevailing social trends.

John explains in verse 8 what will happen if Christians fall in with this kind of thing: "Watch out that you do not lose what you have worked for, but that you may be rewarded fully."

We need to clarify that here John is not talking about salvation but the Christian's future reward in heaven. This subject is raised several times in the New Testament. For example, 1 Corinthians 3:11–15 warns:

> For no one can lay any foundation other than the one already laid, which is Jesus Christ. If any man builds on this foundation using gold, silver, costly stones, wood, hay or straw, his work will be shown for what it is, because the Day will bring it to light. It will be revealed with fire, and the fire will test the quality of each man's work. If what he has built survives, he will receive his reward. If it is burned up, he will suffer loss; he himself will be saved, but only as one escaping through the flames.

In Revelation 3:11, the apostle John says something similar: "Hold on to what you have, so that no one will take your crown."

The crown is the symbol of honour and authority that is given to those who have made themselves available to do the work of God and have given their bodies as living sacrifices for God to work through. If they get involved in something that is grounded upon false teaching, all their efforts are wasted.

They are building nothing but an imposing façade: it may be self-satisfying or look good, but at the end it will crumble and find no acceptance before God.

Truly born-again believers will not lose their salvation that rests upon the work of Christ for them. They are not going to lose their place in heaven, nor their redemption, nor their part in the body of Christ, but if they waste time and effort in fruitless unscriptural thinking they do lose a great deal, as John makes clear. They lose the value of their lives spent here; they waste their time. They throw away precious moments and years involved in that which is utterly worthless, and which will be displayed on the day of judgment as wood, hay and stubble to be consumed in the fire of God's searching gaze. And most importantly – they will lose their reward.

## How to relate to false teachers

So to the crux of John's teaching: What do you do about people like this?

> *If anyone comes to you and does not bring this teaching*
> *[authentic Christianity], do not take him into your house*
> *or welcome him. Anyone who welcomes him shares in his*
> *wicked work.*
>
> 2 JOHN 10–11

We have to be careful and understand this properly: there's a lot of potential pain here. My brother-in-law, Francis, was raised in the home of a sect known as the Taylorite Christian Brethren. Francis did not accept their teachings, and in their misunderstanding of verses like this, his family, convinced of the rightness of their doctrine, forced their son Francis to eat his meals in a shed constructed for him in the garden separated from the rest of the "believing" family. That is a perfect example of what John is teaching about the balance of truth and love.

It is so easy for those who are concerned about doctrinal matters of Scripture to forsake the courtesy and charity that is expected of every Christian and interpret a passage like this to mean that Christians are to slam the door in the face of anyone who offers them some of their heretical ideas or to order them out of their house the minute they bring up some kind of heretical teaching. If that were the case it would be impossible to have people of different faiths in our homes, and apart from being offensive we could never extend our friendship to those of another religion. We would be acting in defence of the truth but not manifesting anything of the grace of love. It's more likely that John is referring to a visiting teacher being welcomed into the church, rather than into an individual's home. It is unlikely that travelling teachers would be involved in door-to-door work, and much more likely that they would arrive at a church, which of course would be meeting in someone's home, and ask to speak in open worship. John's teaching is clear: Christians are not to receive false teachers in such a way as to imply that they are authenticating or accepting their teaching. In this situation they would not be welcomed and be refused permission to speak or enjoy fellowship with practising Christians.

An example of deviation from John's teaching was told by Patrick Sookhdeo, International Director of the Institute for the Study of Islam and Christianity, and International Director of the Barnabas Fund. He related the story of how the UK's BBC Radio 4 broadcast a worship service from Blackburn Cathedral. Midway through the service, the choir sang the Kyrie (that's a sung prayer). But mingled with the traditional Christian prayer, "Lord have mercy, Christ have mercy", were the words of the Islamic call to prayer, the Adhan. This combination of Christian and Muslim prayer, beginning with the Islamic proclamation "Allahu Akbar" (God is great), sung unblushingly in a British cathedral brings to mind the golden calf and the gods of other religions which the Israelites were so prone to add to the worship of the true God. For what does the Islamic Adhan say? It includes within it the Islamic creed: "I bear witness that there is no divinity but Allah. I bear witness the Muhammad is Allah's messenger." This is an Islamic apologetic that affirms the unity of God, as opposed to the Trinity. It affirms Muhammad as God's final revelation as opposed to Jesus Christ. Like the Christian creeds it was specifically designed to counteract what its originators saw as false beliefs and heresies of the time; in this case Christian beliefs at odds with Islam. Such is the state of Christianity in Britain that a cathedral choir can sing during Sunday worship simultaneously of Christ our Lord and words that were specifically designed to deny His divinity, Sonship and finality. That is an example of Christians in their effort to be tolerant and non-judgmental ignorantly giving authenticity to anti-Christian belief.

Notice how John underscores the importance of his teaching: "I have much to write to you, but I do not want to use paper and ink. Instead, I hope to visit you and talk with you face to face, so that our joy may be complete" (2 John 12).

It was difficult to write letters in those days. Mail was uncertain and I suppose the apostle John, like most of us, found it difficult to sit down and write. So, he said, "I'm not going to write more, but this matter is so important that I have taken the time to write it anyhow. There are a lot of other things I would like to discuss, but this could not wait."

Then he extends greetings from the Christian family with whom he is evidently staying, and underscores the need in the Christian life for both truth and love. Christians need to pray that God will give them the ability to learn doctrine and see the importance of it but also to pray for grace, so that when they speak and deal with others opposed to the Christian faith they will do so with the graciousness and gentleness of Christ. But their love must not be so tolerant that it excludes the great fact that Jesus Christ is the only way to God. No other Saviour has been sent; He alone is the answer to humanity's hopelessness

Make no mistake; Christians have to guard the message of the church. Voices in our culture without and within would have them dilute the exclusive, hence offensive, nature of the cross. For some, Jesus is one more problem that makes genuine union among the religions of the world impossible. For others, the incarnation and death of Jesus is one more embarrassment that harks back to an out-of-date barbaric age when crosses and sacrifice meant something. And for still others, Jesus Christ is one more offence that promotes a patriarchal system of abuse that we must purge from the gender-equal modern society.

Christians can still expect pressures like those faced by the early church to dilute the message of Christ. John's followers felt acute pressure from the sophisticated halls of Gnostic teaching – not to mention the popular voices of the marketplace – to reduce the person of Christ into something less than He was. John called his followers to stand firm, and he would have the Bible-believing church do the same. May God grant us courage and strength, balanced by truth and love, as we stand up for Jesus.

# 64

# 3 John
# – A Tale of Three Men

Imagine a house-church in the grip of the theological struggle described in 1 John and confronted by the false teaching in 2 John and you have the background to John's third letter. Where John's second letter teaches us how to handle false teachers, his third was written to instruct the church on how to take care of the visiting authentic teachers who were ministering the Word of God. There is thus both a contrast and a similarity in these last two letters from the pen of John.

John, the last of the original twelve disciples, wrote a letter that carried his apostolic authority to an influential man named Diotrephes who led the church.

However, John's letter and his authority were rejected (verses 9–10). In response, John sent envoys to the church but Diotrephes refused to welcome or acknowledge them. Even worse, he repudiated John, spreading rumours about his character and threatening to expel from the church anyone who showed sympathy to the visitors or tried to speak to them.

But the Christian missionaries found a courageous host in a man called Gaius who was well known to John (verse 1). It's clear that Gaius knew Diotrephes but did not feel threatened by his power, so much so that it was his habit to offer hospitality to travelling Christians, and to give them money to help finance their onward journeys (verses 5–6). This allowed the missionaries to return to John with their report about the rebellion of Diotrephes' church and Gaius' faithfulness (verse 3). John wanted to visit the church personally but could not presently do so (verse 14), yet he knew that he must encourage and strengthen the faithful Christians, like Gaius, who held on to the truth and who he called his friends (verse 5). So he wrote this letter in anticipation of his future visit. As the letter reveals something of the problem of personalities within the church, and revolves around the character of these three men, it helps to use them as the focal point of the message, for Gaius, Diotrephes and Demetrius are like three kinds of Christians found in the church in any age.

John evidently knew Gaius well and addressed the letter to him in a warm and friendly way saying three important things about him.

1. He was strong of soul and that warmed John's heart:

> *Dear friend, I pray that you may enjoy good health and that all may go well with you, even as your soul is getting along well.*
>
> 3 JOHN 2

2. Gaius lived up to his testimony.

What impressed John was not just that Gaius knew the truth, but that he lived up to his testimony and acted out the faith he believed:

> *It gave me great joy to have some brothers come and tell about your faithfulness to the truth and how you continue to walk in the truth.*
>
> 3 JOHN 3

3. Gaius was generous in his giving:

> *Dear friend, you are faithful in what you are doing for the brothers, even though they are strangers to you. They have told the church about your love. You will do well to send them on their way in a manner worthy of God.*
>
> 3 JOHN 5–6

One of the signs that a person has genuinely been touched by God is that their wallet loosens up. More than one pastor has noted that the wallet is often the last part of a man to be converted! But once that step is taken giving becomes generous, gracious and cheerful just as God loves. And being faithful in this matter meant that Gaius was regular and systematic in his giving. He does not just give when his emotions are moved, but plans his giving and he carries it through faithfully. So, regular systematic giving is good for the individual and good for the church. It is clear, too, that Gaius gave cheerfully, because John says he gave "in a manner worthy of God". God doesn't want us to give because we feel we have to or because somebody is taking a special offering and we feel that if we don't give we will be looked down upon by other Christians. Gaius gave because he delighted in giving.

When we look at the next man, Diotrephes, we can see the nature of his problem.

John records:

> I wrote to the church, but Diotrephes, who loves to be first, will have nothing to do with us. So if I come, I will call attention to what he is doing, gossiping maliciously about us. Not satisfied with that, he refuses to welcome the brothers. He also stops those who want to do so and puts them out of the church. Dear friend, do not imitate what is evil but what is good. Anyone who does what is good is from God. Anyone who does what is evil has not seen God.
>
> 3 JOHN 9–11

It raises the question why was Diotrephes so antagonistic towards John?

In the original Greek, the tense of "will have nothing to do" is present. This means that John is not referring to a single act but an ongoing attitude. Diotrephes was rejecting not just his obligation to be hospitable but in his rejection of the missionaries he was refusing to acknowledge John's apostolic authority. This is the first example in the New Testament church of someone who tries to run a church. The likelihood is that Diotrephes was a strong-willed member who took upon himself the leadership role, and if anyone protested, they were put out of membership. John objected to that and said Diotrephes was guilty of four particular wrong attitudes and actions:

**1. John says that Diotrephes was guilty of slandering the apostle:** "gossiping maliciously about us" (verse 10a). We know from other New Testament letters that the apostles had a unique role in the history of Christianity. They were to lay the foundations of the Christian faith and were given the authority to settle all questions within the church. It is this apostolic word that is passed along to us in the New Testament, which is why the New Testament is so authoritative to Christians. So here was a man who not only disregarded the authority of the apostle John but even said slanderous things against him.

**2. Diotrephes would not offer hospitality to travelling ministers (verse 10b).** John says that when travelling ministers who went from place to place speaking the truth of God came to his congregation, Diotrephes would have nothing to do with them. He turned them aside and refused to allow them to speak in the church.

**3. He put people out of the church who would have taken these men in (verse 10c).** Diotrephes indulges in what we would call today "secondary separation". He not only objected to the men who came but he objected to those who would have received them. This has been one of the curses of the church ever since. Because of this tendency to refuse fellowship to someone who favours an individual you do not like, a wide divisiveness comes into the church doing immense injury and harm.

**4. Diotrephes loved to be first (verse 9).** Of all the charges that John had against Diotrephes, this was the most severe. Diotrephes loved to be first, which was a dead giveaway that he was acting in the flesh. It is always the philosophy of the flesh – me first! In doing that, he was robbing the Lord Jesus of His prerogative. It is He who has the right to pre-eminence. Jesus rightly is first, but in Diotrephes we have a man who put himself first and sought his own glory. It's the sin of Satan, who was unwilling to be what God created him to be, and desired rather to be like the "Most High" (Isaiah 14:14).

It is the opposite to the nature of Christ:

> *Who, being in very nature God,*
> *did not consider equality with God*
> *something to be grasped,*
> *but made himself nothing,*
> *taking the very nature of a servant,*
> *being made in human likeness.*
> *And being found in appearance as a man,*
> *he humbled himself*
> *and became obedient to death*
> *– even death on a cross!*

PHILIPPIANS 2:6–8

Satan's attempt to exalt himself led him to be brought low. By contrast, for Jesus Christ's humility and obedience, "God exalted him to the highest place and gave him the name that is above every name" (Philippians 2:9).

Conflict is no stranger to the church. Strong-willed people like Diotrephes often become leaders and teachers. In fact, they are often invited and encouraged in those roles and quickly enjoy a following which can be well and good. But what happens when the views of people like this conflict with pastoral leadership? How does John handle it? Notice, he does not advise Gaius to organize a split away from the church. Rather, he says, "Dear friend, do not imitate what is evil but what is good. Anyone who does what is good is from God. Anyone who does what is evil has not seen God" (verse 11). In other words, John's first reaction is to advise Christian men and women not to follow the people who want the pre-eminence. If you see someone who is always positioning themselves up front, drawing attention to themselves and wanting to be in the public eye, do not follow them. They are following their own way and not that of God. In church life it often starts with cliques who gather around such a leader, and when the whispering starts, the criticisms directed towards other leaders are subtly encouraged and the false leader's position is enhanced. You are on the way to trouble.

We could be forgiven for expecting John to threaten Diotrephes with excommunication for his disgraceful conduct but, significantly, John doesn't say that, he says only that when he comes he will "call attention to what he is doing" (verse 10). That is, he will expose Diotrephes. It's most likely John intended to exercise some form of remedial discipline if it became necessary, in line with that outlined by Paul when he excommunicated an unrepentant man in 1 Corinthians 5. But John does not threaten this; nor does he indicate that a severe penalty, such as excommunication, would be desirable. Perhaps in his attitude he shows his true, legitimate authority and reveals the character of Christ, who desires not that sinners should be condemned, but that they come to repentance.

On the other hand, Diotrephes should not take comfort from John's restrained tone, for the time is coming when he will be faced with his arrogance and evil conduct and will have to give an account for them. So will all Christ's servants when the Lord Himself returns, as Paul warns us in Romans 14:12. We Christians are to build our lives according to God's biblical teaching so that we will stand approved on that day.

The temptation to avoid Diotrephes and stay silent must have occurred to John. It is one thing to write a letter or even send a messenger, but it is another matter altogether to go and personally confront your antagonist. But John is confident that he can face this confrontation successfully because he is prepared. He has stayed in communication with those in the church, he has counselled his couriers, he will talk deeply with Gaius when he gets there. He knows that God is with him and that God's desire is for the truth to win and for His people to walk in freedom and joy. God wants His church to grow in love and truth. If leaders and members alike fail to stand for the truth and do not act in sincere, courageous love, the strength and vigour of the church will be compromised.

Demetrius is the third person mentioned here.

He was most likely the bearer of this letter to Gaius and was probably one of those missionaries who travelled from place to place. Verses 7–8 describe the type of man he was: "It was for the sake of the Name that they went out, receiving no help from the pagans. We ought therefore to show hospitality to such men so that we may work together for the truth."

This tells us that as the travelling missionaries laboured as evangelists, reaching out into places where the church had not yet gone, they would enjoy hospitality and be supported and encouraged by these various churches.

The apostle John says of them that they have gone out having left things behind; they gave up their incomes and their work and went out to obey this high calling. Not everyone goes – that was as true in the early church as it is today. There were some, such as Gaius, who were to stay to help support these men. But there were others to whom the Holy Spirit said, "Come, I've called you to a special task." Their motive is given here, too: "for his sake." Literally, for the name's sake – the name of Jesus.

Back in Old Testament times, the Jews treated the name of God in a unique way. The name of God, Jehovah, which appears throughout the Old Testament, was called the Ineffable Tetragrammaton. "Tetragrammaton" means "four letters" and "ineffable" means "unspeakable" or "incommunicable". So whenever they came to these four Hebrew letters for God they did not dare speak them, so holy was the name. Even when the scribe wrote them he would change the pen after writing each letter throwing the pen away and continuing with another one. Scribes also changed their garments before they would write the sacred name, so reverently did they regard the name of God. In the famous passage of Deuteronomy, "Hear, O Israel: The Lord our God, the Lord is one" (Deuteronomy 6:4), the name occurs twice, which would have required two changes of clothes and eight pens to execute.

In the New Testament, then, the name is that of Jesus. The apostle Paul says in Philippians 2:9–11 that,

> *God exalted him to the highest place*
> *and gave him the name that is above every name,*
> *that at the name of Jesus every knee should bow,*

*in heaven and on earth and under the earth,*
*and every tongue confess that Jesus Christ is Lord,*
*to the glory of God the Father.*

Concern for His name was the underlying motive for missionary work in the first century and it ought to be the underlying motive for missionaries today. The major New Testament motivation is not concern for the lost but obedience to Jesus. We do not need to wait for a call to be involved in the work of making Christ known, since the Great Commission recorded in Matthew 28:19–20 to "Go and make disciples of all nations… teaching them to obey everything I have commanded you" remains and has not been rescinded; "to the very end of the age" is for all of us. It is obedience to the authority of King Jesus that justifies Christian mission and must ultimately motivate us, not merely a response to the needs of the world.

That being the case, the whole church is the serving body with different members variously gifted to fulfil diverse functions. While some will be "sent out" others will be required to support them. Christian workers are not to be vagrants, as this would bring dishonour to the name in which they go. 3 John 8 confirms this, but also contains an intriguing challenge and promise: "so that we may work together for the truth". Wouldn't it be wonderful if, after you got to glory, God wrote "FWT" after your name: "Fellow Worker in the Truth". What a degree to have!

The third man, Demetrius, was one who was sent out, and all we know of him is what John says in verse 12: "Demetrius is well spoken of by everyone – and even by the truth itself. We also speak well of him, and you know that our testimony is true."

John is speaking here as an apostle with the gift of discernment and is saying, "I want to emphasize what everyone thinks about Demetrius. Here's a man you can trust. He is a man of the truth. He has borne testimony from all that he is to be trusted."

In verse 11 we have what seems to be a general exhortation to do good and not evil. In the context of this letter the evil example is obviously Diotrephes, and the good is Demetrius and Gaius. This conveys a great lesson for us, since it teaches that men and women will always imitate other men and women, perhaps never more so than in our celebrity culture today. But Christian men and women must be very careful who it is they imitate, for even in Christian circles there will be a Diotrephes and a Demetrius and Gaius. So we must choose our examples carefully. And John gives the reason:

> *Dear friend, do not imitate what is evil but what is good.*
> *Anyone who does what is good is from God. Anyone who does*
> *what is evil has not seen God.*

3 JOHN 11

This intriguing letter reminds us that the early church had the same troubles that plague the church in our day. There are problems with man's sinful nature that will be with us until Christ returns – yet every one of them can be met by God's super-abundant grace. As we look at these three very different, and yet representative, church members around whom this letter revolves, we cannot fail to be challenged concerning our own discipleship. The ultimate proof of the truth we profess to believe and the love we profess to exercise will be seen neither in words nor in feelings but in the progressive transformation of our character, and therefore of our lifestyle, into a new image of Christ.

The challenge each Christian man and woman faces is how much he or she is prepared to let Jesus change them. Is it my will or His? Who is at the centre of our lives? Is it self, with its longing to be first, to be number one? Or is it Christ, enabling us to keep faithful and to continue to walk in the truth? This is the big issue with far-reaching implications for the church and the Christian.

# 65

# Jude
## – Contend for the Faith

It would appear from Jude's opening comments that his original intention was to write a letter containing insights of the Christian faith. However, that task was laid aside when he heard about the false and offensive teaching that was an increasing threat to the church, and instead he wrote a letter to rally Christians in defence of the faith.

His opening exhortation is very instructive: "I had to write and urge you to contend for the faith that was once for all entrusted to the saints" (Jude 3).

This authoritative declaration from the brother of James reminds us that the Christian faith is not a man-made philosophy but rather one body of facts given to us by God's divinely appointed messengers, the apostles. And more, says Jude, it was "once for all entrusted". This means that it was only given at one time in the history of the world and does not require any subtractions or additions; it is complete. This is the answer to the cults and philosophies that have plagued the Christian faith throughout history. For example, the Worldwide Church of God's *Plain Truth* magazine subtracts from the faith entrusted to the saints by teaching that Jesus was no more than a perfect human being while on earth, that the Holy Spirit is not a divine person but only a power and force, and that there is no Trinity.

On the other hand, the Mormons add to the faith entrusted to the saints by teaching that the revelation that God gave us did not stop with the New Testament but that we need the new revelations contained in The Book of Mormon and The Pearl of Great Price. Jude's authoritative declaration in verse 3 (quoted above) exposes such deceptions. It also answers the "liberals" in every age who want to redefine biblical Christian doctrine to make it more in keeping with the social and moral ideals of their time.

When Jude says, "I… urge you to contend for the faith", he means the Christian faith needs to be declared, and as a result when men and women ask genuine questions they should receive helpful and convincing answers. To enable Christians to do that effectively they must be prepared to spend time studying and learning doctrine and theology. Jude tells us the reason this was necessary in his day was that false teachers had infiltrated the church. He called them "godless men, who change the grace of our God into a licence for immorality and deny Jesus Christ our only Sovereign and Lord" (verse 4).

Jude's concern was this was an assault on the gospel from inside the church. The false teachers were not pagans outside the church, but people who professed to be Christians and wormed their way in to the church. Once "inside" and accepted, under the influence of what later would be known as Gnostic teaching, they taught that as it was only the spirit that counted, the body was essentially no good. That being the case, according to Gnostic thinking, it didn't make any difference what you did with your body as long as your spirit was right. This unbiblical thinking allowed them to pervert God's grace into a licence to live an immoral, sexually degraded life, by arguing that the grace of God is so broad that He will forgive anything we do. Worse, they taught that the more one sins the more grace God gives, so go to it.

The theological name for this way of thinking is antinomianism. It is practised today when people within the church teach that we are no longer under God's law and instead we have a new morality based on love. This being the case, nothing really matters so long as you do everything in love. It's an exact duplicate of this first-century heresy that called forth such condemnation from the apostle Jude.

Using three biblical examples Jude points out that God will not ignore this type of sin – judgment of this kind of person is certain.

# 1. The history of Israel recorded in the book of Numbers 13 and 14

In Jude 5, we are reminded of the miraculous exodus from Egypt when the mighty hand of God delivered the people from slavery, led them through the Red Sea and safely across the wilderness to the borders of the Promised Land. Nothing even remotely like this has been seen before or since. What greater act of deliverance could there be than that? Then, before entering the Promised Land, Moses sent twelve men ahead to spy out the land but, with the exception of Joshua and Caleb, they brought back a negative report. The people responded in an appalling act of disobedience and lack of faith by refusing to enter the land that God had promised to them. The result was that out of the entire multitude that left Egypt only Joshua and Caleb entered into the land promised by God. Their children entered in but the rest all perished in the wilderness. This was God's way of saying that He has a way of handling those who are guilty of disobedience and faithlessness.

## 2. The fallen angels

The fallen angels Jude is referring to in verse 6 lived in the very presence of God and ministered before Him, serving constantly at His bidding. Yet by following Satan in his rebellion they were expelled from heaven and reserved for judgment. Jude's point is that even the angels are not excluded from judgment when they rebel. And just as pride and lust characterized the people Jude was talking about in his day, it characterizes the people of our day. It is still true that pride leads men and women to think that they know better than God but the desire for the things forbidden by God is still the way to ruin in time and eternity.

## 3. The destruction of Sodom and Gomorrah

In a similar way, Sodom and Gomorrah and the surrounding towns gave themselves up to sexual immorality and perversion (verse 7). They serve as an example of those who suffer the punishment of eternal fire.

These two cities at the southern end of the Dead Sea had fallen into the practice of lust and unnatural vices. So blatant and widely accepted was the practice of sodomy that when the angels visited Lot the men of the city surrounded his house and ordered Lot to bring the visitors out so that they might have their way with them. For this, God judged and destroyed their city (Genesis 19). Jude is reminding his readers that God does not take sin lightly and that there is a judgment coming. It may be sudden, as in the case of Sodom and Gomorrah, or long-delayed, as in the case of the angels.

Reading further we see what was wrong with these people: "In the very same way, these dreamers pollute their own bodies, reject authority and slander celestial beings" (Jude 8).

This probably indicates people with no respect for Bible teaching regarding the authority of Jesus and His church, and in their pursuit of the flesh life have no regard for the spiritual forces both of good and evil. Taking them in reverse order in verses 9–13 Jude expands on these three accusations.

# 1. They slander the angels

Jude's first accusation is that they slander celestial beings – the angels. He refers to an incident that is not recorded in our Bible. It comes from a book called *The Assumption of Moses*, which was familiar to readers in the first century. Understandably, Jude, quoting from a book in the Apocrypha, troubles evangelical Christian people today because they know the apocryphal books are not part of the canon of Scripture, and are a mixture of truth and error. However, the New Testament writers do occasionally refer to accurate parts of these books. Further on in Jude's letter there is a quotation from the book of Enoch, another book from the Apocrypha that we do not find in our Bible. Jude is merely using these as illustrations citing traditional thinking, and is not giving any authority to these writings as divine truth. By quoting Enoch, Jude is simply stating that what Enoch said has turned out to be true in view of the ungodly conduct of the false teachers.

In relation to the archangel Michael, the important point Jude is making here is that if the greatest of the good angels refused to converse with or pass judgment on the greatest of the evil angels, even in circumstances like that, then surely no human being may converse with or pass judgment on any angel. It's something to think about when people today carelessly scoff at the very idea of demons or Satan, or when professing Christians act or speak inappropriately when considering these fallen angels.

# 2. They reject authority

Jude then turns to Israel's history to illustrate the consequences of rejecting authority. "Woe to them! They have taken the way of Cain; they have rushed for profit into Balaam's error; they have been destroyed in Korah's rebellion" (Jude 11).

Tracing the way that the sin of rebellion develops, Jude personifies it with three biblical examples:

## Cain, the murderer of his brother Abel

'The way of Cain" was essentially selfishness. Cain's insolent question to God, "Am I my brother's keeper?", forever marks him as the man who, thinking only of himself, had no concern or love for his brother (Genesis 4). A materialistic, cynical unbeliever, he looked out only for his own welfare, and Jude says selfishness is the first step on the way to ultimate rebellion.

## The error of Balaam

There are two stories about Balaam in the Old Testament. The first mention of him occurs in Numbers 22–24, where he is hired by the pagan king, Balak, to curse the nation of Israel and prevent them entering the Promised Land. As he was riding along on a donkey to do this, the donkey balked because he saw the angel of God blocking the way. Balaam could not see the angel and finally God enabled the donkey to speak with a human voice in order to rebuke the madness of the prophet (Numbers 22:21–35). The thing that leaps out at us in the story is Balaam's greed, which is confirmed by his action recorded in Numbers 25 where, in return for money, Balaam seduced the nation of Israel into the worship of Baal with all its evil and repulsive moral consequences. So, Balaam serves as an example of two things:

1. the covetous man who was prepared to sin in order to gain reward

2. the evil man who stooped so low as to teach others to sin.

## Korah's rebellion

The account of Korah's sin is found in Numbers 16 where it is recorded that he led a rebellion against the leadership of Moses. When the sons of Aaron and the tribe of Levi were made the priests of the nation, Korah was not willing to accept that decision. He wished to exercise a function which he had no right to exercise, so he openly and blatantly challenged the God-given authority of Moses and Aaron. He therefore represents the person who refuses to accept authority, and who reaches out for things he or she has no right to take and no right to have. Jude is charging his opponents with defying the legitimate authority of the church and therefore of preferring their own way to that of God. We need to remember that there are things that pride incites us to take but which are not for us, and if we take them, the consequences can be disastrous.

In verses 12–16 Jude's indignation is plainly evident as he ransacks sky, land and sea for illustrations of the character of these men.

Jude sees in their actions a clue to the type of people they are: "They are clouds without rain' – they promise much but deliver nothing. They are "blown along by the wind; autumn trees, without fruit and uprooted – twice dead' – they reject Christ. They are "wild waves of the sea, foaming up their shame; wandering stars, for whom blackest darkness has been reserved forever" (verses 12b–13). In that statement Jude is quoting from the book of Enoch and making the point that these people are exactly the kind of people that lived before the flood. He describes them as "grumblers and faultfinders; they follow their own evil desires; they boast about themselves and flatter others for their own advantage" (verse 16). Unfortunately, we know all too well that a person can be simultaneously pretentious towards those he wishes to impress and flattering to people he thinks are important but condescending to others. Jude's opponents are glorifiers of themselves and flatterers of others as they think the occasion demands – and their descendants are still around today.

## 3. They defile their bodies

Jude continues: "these dreamers pollute their own bodies" (verse 8); they are "blemishes at your love feasts" (verse 12). The "love feast" was similar to an informal church lunch, where members bring food to share with each other. These occasions are, of course, a wonderful opportunity for fellowship. However, some had begun to form cliques, keeping the quality food for themselves, and probably what was happening here was that the godless leaders were encouraging the others to use the feast as an excuse for a boisterous social gathering.

As Jude moves towards the end of his letter he makes the point in verse 17 that nothing has happened which they might not have expected: "But, dear friends, remember what the apostles of our Lord Jesus Christ foretold."

What did they foretell? Verse 18 supplies the answer: the apostles said that we live in the end times. That there will be scoffers who will follow their own ungodly desires, and in doing so will attempt to divide the church. And they do so because they do not have the Spirit of God within them (verse 19), which means that no matter what their religious persuasion and protestations of belief, they are not Christians.

The church's response to this onslaught against truth and purity is given in four pieces of pastoral wisdom (verses 20–23).

## 1. "Build yourselves up in your most holy faith"

Verse 20 states that this is learning what the truth is and putting it into action by being immersed in the Christian lifestyle. That means fellowship with the Lord and His people, continuing to study and learn from Scripture, worshipping regularly and remembering the Lord's Table.

## 2. "Pray in the Holy Spirit"

In the context of Jude's letter, to "pray in the Holy Spirit" (verse 20) means to pray according to His teaching and depending upon God in His power.

## 3. "Keep yourselves in God's love"

This is found in verse 21. Jesus taught in John 15 that the way His followers show their love towards Him is by being obedient to His teaching and living accordingly. Jude has made it very clear by using the example of the Israelites in the wilderness, the angels who sinned, Sodom and Gomorrah, Cain, Balaam and Korah, that a self-seeking rebellious attitude is the complete opposite of Christianity in action.

## 4. "Wait for the mercy of our Lord Jesus Christ to bring you to eternal life"

In verse 21b Jude is referring to the second coming and exhorting Christian men and women to keep alert to the times they live in, to keep their hope burning bright by remembering Christ's promised return.

Once men and women are firmly established as Christians, Jude wants them to become involved in the painful work of helping those who are coming under the influence of dangerous doctrine.

He mentions three things in verses 22–23:

## 1. "Be merciful to those who doubt"

We need to bear in mind that the Christian mission is not to condemn the world but, as Jesus said in John 3:17, to save it! We must not treat people who doubt or question the Christian faith as enemies of the faith, nor as hopeless sinners (verse 22). Christians are in the reclamation business and must do all in their power to reclaim men and women out of spiritual darkness into the light and love of the truth of Jesus Christ. To do this they must be able to defend the faith and be able to give a reason for the hope that is within them so they can commend their faith to others. They must know what they themselves believe so that they can meet error and heresy with truth. They have to be steadfast and firm and not water down Christian doctrine, nor insist on secondary matters that have nothing to do with salvation being given undue importance.

## 2. Rescue others from disaster

Jude's second bit of advice is for those dealing with people who have gone further than doubt and begun to play with fire: "snatch others from the fire and save them" (verse 23a). There are dangerous moments in some people's lives, when the Christian must move in fearlessly so as to try to bring them back from disaster.

## 3. Be careful

Jude's third principle is directed towards those who deal with people who have become fully involved in false doctrine: "to others show mercy, mixed with fear – hating even the clothing stained by corrupted flesh" (verse 23b). This is a cautionary note from a wise apostle: Be careful! Recognize that due to your inexperience there are some people you are unable to help. Even the wisest Christian has to handle people like this with great caution, being very careful not to contract the disease they are trying to cure. Those who would win this type of person for Christ must themselves be very sure of Christ. Those who would fight the disease of sin must have the strong antiseptic of a strong faith. Ignorance can never be met with ignorance nor with half-baked knowledge, no matter how good the intentions. It can only be met by the Christian who, like Paul, can say, "I know whom I have believed!" (2 Timothy 1:12).

At the end of Jude's letter we have a magnificent benediction:

*To him who is able to keep you from falling and to present you*
*before his glorious presence without fault and with great joy*
*– to the only God our Saviour be glory, majesty, power and*
*authority, through Jesus Christ our Lord, before all ages, now*
*and for evermore! Amen.*

This too falls into three divisions:

## 1. "To him who is able to keep you from falling"

Verse 24a implies the potential for difficulty in the Christian life. And having
seen what Jude has taught about the dangers that surround even the most
ordinary Christian, it is a wonderful reassurance to know that God is able to
keep us from falling: "He will not let your foot slip – he who watches over you
will not slumber" (Psalm 121:3). When we secure ourselves to God, we can
trust Him, He can keep us safe.

## 2. "To present you before his glorious presence without fault"

Christian, the meaning of verse 24b is wonderful! Don't miss this point: God
can make you stand blameless in the presence of His own glory. This is the
final aim of justification and sanctification. God has so completely dealt with us
through Christ that all our faults have been wiped off the record and He is able
to present us faultless before His glory. Praise God! And this will be done, says
Jude, "with great joy". Christ will rejoice (John 15:11), the angels will rejoice
(Hebrews 12:22) and we will rejoice (1 Peter 4:13). When we arrive in glory we
can say, "Hallelujah! Thank God, I've won!" As Paul says in 2 Timothy 4:7–8,
"I have finished the race, I have kept the faith. Now there is in store for me the
crown of righteousness."

## 3. The final recognition of the only God, our Saviour, the Lord Jesus Christ

This is it, Christian. This is the only beam of brightness that offers any flicker
of hope to those who live in a world with a grim present and an even grimmer

future under God's judgment: the only God is our Saviour (verse 25). When that great and terrible Day of the Lord finally comes, and we see who it is we were in rebellion against, when we see His absolute holiness and how ghastly our sin really is, when we see how seriously He meant all the Old Testament warnings of judgment on the grumbling Israelites, the mutinous angels and Sodom and Gomorrah, then shall we see with fear and wonder what a mighty work the cross of Jesus was, and is, and shall be for evermore.

> *To him… be glory, majesty, power and authority, through Jesus*
> *Christ our Lord, before all ages, now and for evermore!*

That summarizes everything, doesn't it? From the beginning, through the present to the eternal future, Jesus is the One around whom the universe itself revolves.

# 66

# Revelation
# – The Lamb in All His Glory

As one reads through the Bible, great themes are introduced and developed; themes such as heaven and earth, sin and its curse, man and his salvation, Satan and his fall, Israel and her election, blessing and discipline, the nations, the kingdom of Babylon and all it represents, and the kingdom of God. But, ultimately, all these subjects find their fulfilment and resolution in the book of Revelation. The Gospels and epistles draw them together, but it is not until we come to Revelation that they all converge into one great consummation.

It is important to bear in mind that the book of Revelation has to make sense not only to us, but also to all Christians throughout church history and to the people to whom it was originally written. Thus, the various figures in Revelation symbolize powerful moral and spiritual forces over which the forces of God are ultimately triumphant, which makes it relevant to all the saints from John's day onwards. While the book makes no specific reference to Rome, Islam, or any significant event, it does, in dealing with Satan and the powers of darkness, reveal the principles of victory through righteousness and truth and the ultimate failure of evil and falsehood. This means that some of the prophecies are still to be fulfilled. For example, although John saw the Roman empire as the great beast that threatened the extinction of the church in the last days (that is, from the time of Christ's ascension), another beast will arise that will have the same type of relationship with the church in the end times.

Jesus laid down the principle of the imperceptible transition from present to future when He spoke with the disciples on Mount Olivet in Matthew 24.

There He clearly answered their questions regarding the Temple by telling them about its coming destruction, and then slipped smoothly into explaining how the coming fall of Jerusalem would be finally fulfilled as a sign of the end of the age. This principle operates for us today in the book of Revelation. We see that the events in the book were written to encourage the faithful to stand fast and resist evil even unto death, and we, like the early church, take heart in the fact that the final showdown between God and the forces of darkness is imminent and that we are sealed against any spiritual harm. We will be vindicated when Christ returns, the wicked will be destroyed, and God's people will then enter an eternity of glory and blessedness in the company of the Lamb.

The term "revelation" means "a revealing of something hidden", and John is writing to hard-pressed Christians using language and terms familiar to them; a symbolic code, understandable to people who know the Bible. For example, Jesus is referred to as the Lamb and Satan as the Dragon, while the holy city, Jerusalem, is the church and the great city, Babylon, is the world. It is also important to remember that, as the Old Testament is the only common source of literature read by all Christians down through the centuries, much of the symbolism and imagery in Revelation comes from there and can thus be readily understood by the church in every age.

The purpose of the book is to reveal the full identity of Jesus Christ and to give warning and hope to believers. It is also important for us to note that the Revelation comes from Jesus – this is not the revelation of John.

Jesus has been here! Christmas celebrations remind us of the wonderful truth of the Son of Glory entering this world, yet the world was so blind to who He was that it offered Him a cattle shed for His birth and a cross for His death. One day, however, He is coming back in majesty and power accompanied by the hosts of heaven. Then His deity, seen now only through the eye of faith, will blaze forth like flaming lightning. In the book of Revelation the Person of Christ is unveiled, and we are given view after view of this glorious God–Man, this Wonderful Being who fills all heaven with His praise!

Without question, seven is the outstanding number in this book.

It occurs scores of times in the Old Testament, often in symbolic significance, but it is in the book of Revelation that it stands out most prominently, occurring twenty times more here than in all other books of the New Testament combined. From its repeated use in Scripture we can see that seven stands as the numerical symbol of the complete or perfect. If it is correct that three is the symbolic divine number (for example, God's attributes are three – omniscience, omnipresence and omnipotence; the Trinity is three), and four is the symbolic world or creation number (for example, four is the number of the great elements – earth, air, fire, and water; there are four regions of the earth – north, south, east, and west), then a proper combination of these would be perfection, completeness and fullness. It should, therefore, come as no surprise to find that there are seven sections in the book of Revelation.

## 1. Christ among the lampstands

The essential theme of the first three chapters of Revelation is Christ in the midst of seven golden lamp stands that represent the seven churches to which John is instructed to write. As the number seven is recognized as symbolic of completeness, each church is, as it were, a type, which means that it does not represent just one specific geographical location or one particular period of history, but describes conditions which are constantly repeating in the life of the worldwide church. So, the seven churches of Revelation represent all the churches from Christ's first coming to save His people (1:5) to His second coming to judge all nations (1:7).

## 2. The vision of the throne room of God and the seals

This is the theme of chapters 4–7. Chapter 4 introduces the One who sits upon the throne of heaven. Here is the centre of our universe – not London, New York or Rome. Contrary to popular opinion God is not dead; He sits on His throne directing the affairs of His universe, both the seen and the unseen. This is the ultimate point of the vision: that the real mind directing and controlling the universe, while at the same time allowing us responsibility and freedom as individuals, is the mind and will of the almighty God. The throne comes first in this vision to show us in striking symbolism that all things are governed by God from His throne. This is a source of true comfort in our trials and tribulations.

Around the throne were twenty-four elders. Think of the twelve tribes of Israel from the old covenant and the twelve apostles from the new, and you see how the twenty-four elders represent the church. They are dressed in white symbolizing the righteousness and purity Christ gives to repentant, pardoned sinners through the shedding of His own blood (Revelation 7:13–14). Upon their heads were golden crowns of victory, the crowns of righteousness, which, Paul says, "the Lord, the righteous Judge, will award to me on that day – and not only to me, but also to all who have longed for his appearing" (2 Timothy 4:7).

As John watches in breathless amazement, God issues a challenge: "Who is worthy to break the seals and open the scroll?" (Revelation 5:2).

The challenge goes out, and the ranks of those in heaven, on earth and under the earth are combed for a worthy king, but there is no volunteer, no one steps forward. The requirement is not for physical strength but moral competence. Who is worthy? No one above the earth is worthy – no angel or archangel; no one on the earth is worthy – no politician, industrialist, philosopher, pope, archbishop, revolutionary hero; and no one under the earth is worthy – no fallen angels or spirits or even the prince of darkness himself. This is a verse that puts creation in its place.

The moment the scroll is opened and the seals broken, the universe is governed in the interests of the church. Then, God's glorious redemptive purpose will be realized. As His plan is carried out, the contents of the scroll shall come to pass in the history of the universe. But if that scroll could not be opened it would mean no protection for God's children in their hour of bitter trial, no judgment upon a persecuting world, no ultimate triumph for believers, no new heaven, no new earth and no future inheritance.

As John stood choking in his tears because there seemed no one worthy to open the scroll, one of the elders stepped down from his throne, walked over to him and gently wiped away the tears from his eyes: "Do not weep! See, the Lion of the tribe of Judah, the Root of David, has triumphed. He is able to open the scroll and its seven seals" (Revelation 5:5).

Who is it? Who can it be? It is the Lord Jesus Christ, for He alone is worthy.

From chapter 6 the Lord Jesus begins to open the seals which are symbolic of the times of trouble and persecution which cover the entire dispensation from the first to the second coming of Christ. We do well to remember the church is not exempt from suffering. Assaults from without and within will test to the limit those who are prepared to stake everything, even their lives, on the Word and witness of God. But for how long will this go on? Will there never be a respite for God's suffering people? Again the answer is "No", not in this world: only with the end of the world and the completion of the total number who are to witness and suffer for Christ will there come a day of reckoning for their persecutors. In other words, rampant evil will be abroad, bringing suffering to the world in general, and to the church in particular, through the entire period from the time of John's vision to the time of Jesus' return. Seals 1–5 portray different aspects of the whole of history from the church's perspective, and seal 6 describes the day it will end. Now we can see why the scene for those dramatic events was set in such detail.

In chapter 6 John is shown a succession of woes that sweep across church history and often cause the believer to wonder whether the forces of evil are out of control. The events of chapters 4 and 5, coming beforehand, are meant to impress on us the only source of true power, while chapter 7 warns us that true believers may, indeed will, have to go through temporary suffering. However, our eternal safety is never in doubt as we see in 7:16–17, which pictures the entire church triumphant, gathered out of all the nations and thus, in its entirety, standing before the throne and before the Lamb at the end of the great consummation.

## 3. The seven trumpets

And so to chapters 8–11. We must keep in mind that the book is a revelation of the fortunes of the church in the world and of the destiny of the world as it opposes the church, and that the climax of history is judgment.

The interlude that was described in chapter 7 is finished; the seventh seal is opened and for a symbolic period there is a breathless silence as all await the judgments of the scroll now unsealed. This is the silence of expectancy for it is the last seal. It is also a silence of foreboding that precedes the onslaught of judgments.

The trumpets of judgments indicate a series of happenings, that is, calamities that will occur again and again through the entire dispensation. They do not symbolize single and separate events, but refer to woes that may be seen any day of the year and in any part of the globe. Yet, even by means of these judgments, God is constantly calling the ungodly to repentance. So, while these woes are not the final judgment they are serious warnings, hence they symbolically affect only a third part – not the whole of the earth, sea, waters, sun, moon and stars. But at the close of this section there is a very clear reference to the final judgment (11:15–18). And having reached the end of the dispensation the vision fades.

## 4. The persecuting dragon

The persecuting dragon features in chapters 12–14. Chapter 12 opens with a new scene but the theme remains the same – the victory of Christ and His church over the dragon, Satan, and his helpers. Whereas the previous panorama showed the outward struggle between the church and the world, this new backdrop takes us, as it were, behind the scenes and reveals the same war from the perspective of the battle between Christ and Satan. This war is being waged in time and history and has a cosmic dimension. It is this Paul speaks of when he insists that our struggle is not against flesh and blood but against the authorities and powers of the spiritual forces of evil in the heavenly realms (Ephesians 6). Revelation chapters 12 and 13 are the account of this battle: the woman is the true church of God throughout all history, Old Testament and New; the great red dragon with seven heads is the ancient serpent called the devil or Satan; and the son is Jesus, against whom the dragon's hatred is primarily directed.

As Christ ascends to His throne, Satan turns his attention to persecuting the church, and as his helpers, he employs the two beasts of chapter 13. The first is Satan's hardware and the second his software. The first represents the persecuting power of Satan operating in and through the nations of this world and their governments. The second symbolizes the false religions and philosophies of this world. Both these beasts oppose the church throughout this dispensation. In 14:8 a third agent is mentioned, namely Babylon the harlot. So, in all, three agents are employed by Satan in his attack: antichristian persecution, antichristian religion and antichristian seduction.

Again this section, though presented by John in terms of his time, nonetheless covers the entire dispensation, and once again it ends with a stirring description of Christ's second coming in judgment (14:14–16).

## 5. The seven bowls

Where the trumpets affect only one third of society as they warn the earth and draw the Lord's people to Himself, the bowls of chapters 15–16 bring final wrath and judgment. If proclaiming the good news of redemption does not cause men and women to fear God, and if partial judgments do not turn them from humanism and materialism to repentance, then such an unregenerate society forfeits its right to continue. Destruction by judgment is inevitable and just, and this is what the seven bowls foretell.

## 6. The fall of Babylon

Babylon and the mindset of a Babylonian-type lifestyle symbolize our God-hating civilization; also called "the mother of prostitutes" (verse 5). It's the anti-Christ system that stands for everything opposed to the bridegroom, Jesus

Christ, and His radiant bride, the Christian church. Its form and substance may change but its essence remains the same: Babylon stands for any world system in opposition to God. That's been the way of it since Adam and Eve sinned in Eden. The bride of Christ, the church, has always stood in contrast against Satan's system, the whore, and waged relentless war. But the whore's day is coming.

It is written:

> Therefore in one day her plagues will overtake her:
> death, mourning and famine.
> She will be consumed in fire,
> for mighty is the Lord God who judges her.

REVELATION 18:8

One day sitting as a proud arrogant and boastful queen, encouraging the world to live in any way other than God's way – and the next day down in the dirt, fallen and ruined, never to rise again. And they'll weep! All those who trusted the system and put their faith in a Babylonian-type lifestyle. They may think that they gained the whole world, but in the process they have lost their souls. In following the "Mother of Prostitutes" men and women got everything they thought they wanted – and now it's gone they are bereft of everything they were promised. Their religion of self-indulgence is now gone, salvation by chequebook is gone, God on demand is gone, religion based on feeling is gone, as is the notion of "self as God"; it's all gone!

The men and women who rejected Jesus are left with nothing, and so everyone who lived by Babylon's philosophy will weep. And through it all there is a double-edge of bitterness, for the plain teaching of the Bible is that while the world's system will one day fall, men and women will live on after death. Those who do not spend their eternity with Christ amidst the delights of glory must spend their eternity among the agonies of hell.

This is the thrust of chapters 17–19: if men and women believe the world, the flesh and the devil, they will ignore Jesus Christ and place their trust in the doctrine of John Lennon's "Imagine" and Frank Sinatra's "My Way". As they identify with Babylon so they will fall with Babylon. The harlot offers them all they could ever want in this life, so they will spend eternity with her in the next.

# 7. The great consummation

Revelation 20 clearly introduces a new section and a new subject: the devil's doom, the last judgment, and the new heaven and earth are all themes of chapters 20–22.

One by one we have witnessed the destruction of the enemies of God: the beasts, which we saw as the world's political and financial system and the world's false religious organizations; adulterous Babylon, the devil's appeal to self-satisfaction and pleasure; and finally Satan himself. And it's in the steady and relentless progression towards the end of the world that we see the theme of this book unfold: Jesus Christ, and not the devil, will be triumphant. God's plan and purpose will triumph, and with the second coming of the Lord Jesus and the day of judgment behind them, believers will rejoice and celebrate at the wedding supper of Christ, the bridegroom, and His church, the bride.

In these closing chapters of the Revelation we are given a vision of heaven in symbolic language based on the Old Testament, especially the book of Genesis: The Garden of Eden was man's first inheritance, and it is an example of his last inheritance, heaven. The paradise the first Adam lost for us, the last Adam, Jesus Christ, will regain. This is the new world Jesus tells us about in Matthew 19:28, literally "the New Genesis". The first chapter of the Bible explains how God made the world, the last chapter how He will remake it. Creation as it was and as it will be – an immense organism, alive with the energy and life of God. What was lost in Eden will be fully restored; God's purpose achieved, we need to fix our eyes and hearts on heaven for that's where Christians are heading. That's where they belong.

That brings us to the final invitation.

The closing verses of Revelation bring the gospel of the church to its conclusion. They remind us of a composer gathering up the themes of his symphony in a closing burst of glorious music, and poised on the verge of the crescendo we see all the revealed truth of God crystallized in two verses. The first is 22:16b: "I [Jesus] am the Root and the Offspring of David, and the bright Morning Star."

David was Israel's greatest king and he represents the glory that is Israel – but Jesus is much more. Not only is He David's greater Son, Lord and King of the new Israel, the church, He is also David's Lord. He is Isaiah's everlasting Father who was and is before all things. He is the Alpha and the Omega, the First and the Last, the Beginning and the End. Christians, this is He to whom we belong. He is the Lover of the church, the Lord of all the earth, the light of all creation and we belong to Him. O Hallelujah!

Just as the "bright morning star" shines alone in the new morning sky, Jesus heralds the dawn of eternity, telling us that this life is only a prelude to the real life to come, which leads us to the second verse (22:17):

> *The Spirit and the bride say, "Come!" And let him who hears*
> *say, "Come!" Whoever is thirsty, let him come; and whoever*
> *wishes, let him take the free gift of the water of life.*

As the revelation of John's vision fades from our view and the last words echo in our souls, now that we, with John, have advanced from glory to glory in this drama of spiritual history, conflict and victory, many of us will feel we are more than excited spectators in a divine theatre. We are part of the drama, for we continue to share with those early Christians the pressures of political power and intrigue, the subtlety of false religious appeal through human wisdom, philosophy and tradition, and the seduction of the world of lust. But we also share with them the strength, power and help of the Spirit that comes from our heavenly Father through faith in the blood of Jesus, and we share with them the eternal reward of victory and inheritance in God's celestial city as the bride of the Lamb. And so, with the voice of all creation, let us join in song as they sing:

> *To him who sits on the throne and to the Lamb*
> *be praise and honour and glory and power,*
> *for ever and ever!... .*
> *Amen.*

REVELATION 5:13–14

It's fitting that Scripture should close with a reference to the Holy Spirit for He is the author of the book, the One who has inspired every chapter, verse, and line. He is the omniscient genius behind this miracle in words, the Bible, who inspired prophets and apostles. He was present as the third member of the Trinity at the creation, He brought forth Jesus from the womb of Mary, He raised Him from the dead and He now calls out the final invitation that has resounded in the hearts and minds of fallen sinful men and women down the long weary centuries, "Come!..."

It's the sweetest sound in the gospel. It first rang out in the days of Noah when God was about to pour His wrath against the world. The ark was finished and salvation was provided when God figuratively stepped into the ark and said to Noah, "Come!" Again and again the blessed word rings out, and time and again through the centuries men and women recognizing sin in their hearts

585

have responded to the irresistible call of God and made their way to the cross of Jesus. And now, before closing the book forever, the Holy Spirit sounds it again, "Come!" Come to Christ and be saved! It's the last welcome, and those who refuse to heed it will one day, in its place, hear the dreaded word, "Depart!"

Reader – do you hear the message? Do you hear the invitation? Have you responded? Will you come? Are you thirsty for such a blessing? Do you recognize you live in a world that is barren and bare to your soul? Can you look around you and see men and women dying from spiritual thirst? Can you explain the madness that holds them back from throwing themselves on their faces before God and drinking deep of the water of life? Do you understand something of this? You do? Praise God. Then come and partake of "the free gift of the water of life". What was forbidden to the first man, Adam, is now available to you. If only you will come. Will you not come to Jesus?

# About the Author

When he retired from full-time pastoral ministry, Hugh Hill was employed by the FIEC and with his wife, Joyce, administered the Bible school PfS North. Hugh currently travels throughout the UK helping churches to focus on the spiritual priorities of gospel ministry, mission and growth.

Hugh's first book, *I Did It His Way*, continues to be in popular demand in evangelical circles.

Hugh can be contacted at:

H & J Publishing Ltd
8 Albion Crescent
Lincoln
LN1 1EB

Email: hugh@hughhill.co.uk
www.hjpublishing.co.uk